91634

STUDIES IN RENAISSANCE AND BAROQUE MUSIC

Studies in Renaissance
and Baroque Music
in Honor of
Arthur Mendel

Edited by
Robert L. Marshall

BÄRENREITER KASSEL · BASEL · TOURS · LONDON
JOSEPH BOONIN, INC. HACKENSACK, NEW JERSEY
1974

Portrait of Arthur Mendel: Ulli Steltzer (Princeton, New Jersey)
All Rights Reserved. Printed in Germany
© Bärenreiter-Verlag Kassel 1974
Exclusive Distributor in the U. S. and Canada:
Joseph Boonin, Inc. Hackensack, New Jersey
Entire Production by Bärenreiter Kassel
ISBN 3-7618-0412-1 (Bärenreiter)
ISBN 0-913574-26-0 (Boonin)

CONTENTS

Foreword 7
Arthur Mendel: A Portrait in Outline 9

I: RENAISSANCE RESEARCHES: HISTORIOGRAPHY, ANALYSIS, AND DOCUMENTARY BIOGRAPHY

Lewis Lockwood: *"Messer Gossino" and Josquin Desprez* 15
Walter Gerstenberg: *Das Alleluia in Senfls Propriumskompositionen* 25
Harold S. Powers: *The Modality of "Vestiva i colli"* 31
Anthony Newcomb: *Alfonso Fontanelli and the Ancestry of the Seconda Pratica Madrigal* 47

II: PROBLEMS OF RHYTHM, METER, AND TEMPO: c. 1500—1750

Philip Gossett: *The Mensural System and the "Choralis Constantinus"* 71
Heinrich Husmann: *Johann Faulhaber (1580—1635): Mathematiker und mensuraler Meistersinger* 108
Carl Dahlhaus: *Zur Geschichte des Taktschlagens im frühen 17. Jahrhundert* . . . 117
Ulrich Siegele: *„La Cadence est une qualité de la bonne Musique"* 124

III: JOHANN SEBASTIAN BACH: APPROACHES TO ANALYSIS AND INTERPRETATION

Walter Blankenburg: *Die Bedeutung der solistischen Alt-Partien im Weihnachts-Oratorium, BWV 248* 139
Edward T. Cone: *Bach's Unfinished Fugue in C Minor* 149
Walter Emery: *Cadence and Chronology* 156
Robert L. Marshall: *The Genesis of an Aria Ritornello: Observations on the Autograph Score of "Wie zittern und wanken", BWV 105/3* 165
Frederick Neumann: *The Question of Rhythm in the Two Versions of Bach's French Overture, BWV 831* 183
Norman Rubin: *"Fugue" as a Delimiting Concept in Bach's Choruses: A Gloss on Werner Neumann's "J. S. Bachs Chorfuge"* 195
William H. Scheide: *Some Miscellaneous Chorale Forms in J. S. Bach's Vocal Works* . 209

IV: JOHANN SEBASTIAN BACH: STUDIES OF THE SOURCES

Paul Brainard: *Cantata 21 Revisited* 231
Alfred Dürr: *De vita cum imperfectis* 243
Gerhard Herz: *JSBach 1733: A "new" Bach Signature* 254
Ernest May: *J. G. Walther and the Lost Weimar Autographs of Bach's Organ Works* 264
Christoph Wolff: *Johann Sebastian Bachs „Sterbechoral": Kritische Fragen zu einem Mythos* 283

V: HANDEL AND THE OPERA SERIA

Robert Freeman: *Farinello and his Repertory* 301
J. Merrill Knapp: *The Autograph of Handel's "Riccardo Primo"* 331
Alfred Mann: *Bass Problems in "Messiah"* 359
Pierluigi Petrobelli: *Un cantante fischiato e le appoggiature di mezza battuta: Cronaca teatrale e prassi esecutiva alla metà del '700* 363

VI: BIBLIOGRAPHY OF THE WRITINGS OF ARTHUR MENDEL

. . . . 377

INDEX OF NAMES AND SUBJECTS

. . . . 387

FOREWORD

It is a pleasant obligation to recall some of the principal stations in the history of this volume. The prime movers in the enterprise — J. Merrill Knapp, Kenneth J. Levy, Lewis Lockwood, Harold S. Powers, and William H. Scheide — conceived the idea of presenting a volume of *Bach Studies* to Arthur Mendel in the course of several conversations early in 1970. Professor Levy, then Chairman of the Department of Music at Princeton University, thereupon guided the first steps towards its realization. And the undersigned, after receiving assurance of the continued advice and assistance of the initiators, was honored to serve as the editor for the project. Eventually, the scope of the volume was expanded to include topics in Renaissance and Baroque music — thus reflecting Professor Mendel's own interests more accurately — but retaining a concentration of studies on J. S. Bach.

From the beginning it was clear that the volume was to be international in representation, since that seemed to be the most fitting recognition of Arthur Mendel's international stature. The multi-lingual format (to our knowledge it is the first multi-lingual tribute to an American musicologist) easily suggested that the Bärenreiter-Verlag was "destined" to publish the collection. But it is obviously most appropriate that the volume ultimately appears under international aegis: a co-publication of Bärenreiter-Verlag and Joseph Boonin, Inc.

Scholarly enterprises as ambitious as this are normally plagued by innumerable crises and delays. But thanks to the enthusiastic interest of Dr. Wolfgang Rehm of Bärenreiter-Verlag and Mr. Joseph M. Boonin, to the financial support of the Department of Music, Princeton University, and a number of most generous friends (notably Professor Samuel Pogue, but also Messrs. Nathaniel Burt, Paul Fromm, Frazier McCann, Frank Taplin, and William Scheide), and in particular, to the initiative, resourcefulness and inexhaustible energies of Professor Lewis Lockwood, the successful and remarkably expeditious completion of this project was assured.

Robert L. Marshall

Arthur Mendel: A Portrait in Outline

Arthur Mendel's international eminence, to which this volume attests, rests not only on his definitive researches into the history of pitch, on his perceptive analyses of the rhythmic structure of Renaissance and Baroque music, his resourcefulness as an editor, or on the achievements that have made him America's foremost Bach scholar. Mendel's unique contribution to musicology rather transcends any of his individual accomplishments, although it is manifested in all of them. In contemplating his publications as a critic-reviewer, translator, editor, and researcher one most values not so much the demonstrated reliability and pertinence of the information or the conclusions they afford but rather the more general lessons — explicit or implicit — which they impart along the way: lessons in scholarly responsibility, in judgment, and in method. Arthur Mendel's most significant publications can be regarded in fact (and may even have been partly conceived) as models to be emulated by others when engaged in any of the several areas of intellectual endeavor musical scholars are called upon to perform. Simply put, Arthur Mendel's major work is exemplary in the most literal sense.

Nowhere can one find, for example, a more brilliantly executed musical documentary biography than *The Bach Reader*, compiled by Mendel together with the late Hans T. David. The volume succeeds as perhaps no other in being at once comprehensive and informative yet compact and highly readable — a testimony to the unerring discrimination of the editors in the selection of the most pertinent documents and to the skill with which the often convoluted and obscure language of Bach and his contemporaries has been faithfully but intelligibly rendered into 20th-century English.

Mendel's editions of works by Heinrich Schütz and J. S. Bach almost seem to have been deliberately chosen to survey in systematic fashion the varieties of problems facing the 20th-century editor and to explore the editorial possibilities open to him. Thus Mendel's contributions here include vocal scores and full scores, practical as well as critical editions. His practical edition of Schütz's *The Christmas Story (Historia von der Geburt Jesu Christi)* provides a lesson in preparing a convincing musical text from incomplete sources, while the critical edition of Bach's *St. John Passion* confronts the problem of extracting an authentic and integral text from a superabundance of original sources interwoven into a complex tangle of readings and versions. Mendel's highly original and imaginative edition of Schütz's *A German Requiem (Musicalische Exequien)*, similarly, can be understood as an attempt to deal effectively with an inevitable ambiguity of older sources by devising a practicable transcription method that (in Mendel's words) would "clarify the composer's rhythmic intentions" for the modern musician.

Altogether as illuminating and valuable as the editions themselves are Mendel's introductions and commentaries to them with their eminently sensible suggestions for achieving historically accurate and musically convincing performances of the works — suggestions based to a large extent on his own practical experience as the founder and conductor of The Cantata Singers, one of the first groups in the United States devoted to the authentic

rendition of Baroque music. But these essays offer much more than suggestions for performance. The introduction to the vocal score of the *St. John Passion* remains, for all its concise-
ness, the most complete and valid single description available of J. S. Bach's performance
practice. And the analysis of the hierarchical organization of rhythm in the music of Schütz,
presented during the discourse on "Rhythm in Notation and Performance" in the foreword
to the *Musicalische Exequien*, constitutes a milestone in our understanding of a significant
aspect of rhythmic structure in 17th-century music. Finally, the critical reports
accompanying Mendel's editions for the *Neue Bach-Ausgabe* of Cantata 174 *(Ich liebe
den Höchsten von ganzem Gemüte)* and the *St. John Passion* combine the most painstaking
attention to detail with *tours de force* of evidential reasoning which in both cases succeed
not only in clarifying the exceptionally complicated source histories of the works but
ultimately in uncovering in Bach's Weimar period "Traces of the Pre-History of Bach's
St. John and St. Matthew Passions" and, quite unexpectedly, of the Third Brandenburg
Concerto as well.

The sheer range of topics to which Mendel has addressed himself in his scholarly
articles reveals his remarkable ability to train a fine and powerful intellect with equal
effectiveness on music-historical matters as specific and narrow in their focus as the
"Wasserzeichen in den Originalstimmen der Johannes-Passion Johann Sebastian Bachs"
or on those as broad in scope as his efforts to reconstruct an accurate history of pitch
or to expose "Some Ambiguities of the Mensural System."

On more than one occasion Mendel has examined the goals and tasks of higher musical
education and of musicology itself, considering the "Services of Musicology to the
Practical Musician" or the question of "The Doctorate in Composition." And from the
outset of his career as a (self-taught) scholar over 40 years ago when he investigated
"Spengler's Quarrel with the Methods of Music History" to his seminal keynote
address on "Evidence and Explanation" to the Eighth Congress of the International
Musicological Society in 1961 on the occasion of its first meeting ever held in the western
hemisphere, Arthur Mendel has challenged his colleagues and himself to reflect critically
on the most fundamental assumptions and methods of their discipline. This same concern
for soundness of method and for responsible scholarly procedure has prompted Mendel
to become one of the pioneers in exploring the possible applications of computer tech-
nology to musicological problems.

Throughout this scholarly *œuvre* one encounters the unparalleled discipline and clarity
of thought, the uncompromising intellectual integrity that have earned for Arthur Mendel
the admiration of his profession as a veritable symbol of musicological enlightenment.

But yet one cannot say whether it is intellectual integrity or simple personal candor
that makes it impossible for Mendel to conceal his indignation in the face of what he
recognizes as unprofessional behavior or frivolous scholarship (perhaps the willful
suppression of disconcerting evidence). Nor can one determine whether it is a highly
trained sense of scholarly responsibility or an inborn humility that urges him to counsel all
of us to be skeptical of sensational discoveries or interpretations (particularly our own),
and to resist the temptation to claim more than our evidence will bear. It is most clearly

genuine personal humility, along with an uncommon openness and candor, that prompts him to acknowledge on every appropriate occasion, publicly and with obvious pleasure, his indebtedness to students or colleagues and to express his enthusiasm for those accomplishments or ideas of others that have caught his interest — more often than not having forgotten that he may have suggested the ideas or encouraged and guided the accomplishments in the first place. Indeed, few teachers or colleagues have invested so much time, interest and effort in the projects of others as has Arthur Mendel.

No one who knows Mendel at all can fail to have been touched by his warmth and unaffected cordiality, nor to have been delighted time and again by the sparkling and spontaneous wit that has animated so many conversations, classroom seminars and public symposia. One realizes quite soon indeed that the intellectual and personal virtues — in almost a classic fulfillment of the humanistic ideal — are thoroughly fused in Arthur Mendel. And while the awesome achievement and the rigorous method have compelled admiration, it is Arthur Mendel's truly refreshing and inspiring manner that has captured the unrestrained affection of his colleagues, students, and friends. This collection of essays is offered as a token of this admiration and heartfelt affection.

I

RENAISSANCE RESEARCHES: HISTORIOGRAPHY, ANALYSIS,
AND DOCUMENTARY BIOGRAPHY

LEWIS LOCKWOOD

"Messer Gossino" and Josquin Desprez

As I have recently had occasion to reconstruct the documentary basis of Josquin's relationship to the court of Ferrara and to supplement what had previously been brought to light by Edmond Vander Straeten and Helmut Osthoff, my purpose in this brief note is to show that a pair of documents that have long been taken to refer to Josquin actually do not and cannot refer to him, and that this small point has a bearing on certain larger aspects of our knowledge of his life and our interpretation of his work[1]. I hope this contribution may form a small sample of the problem of historical evidence and explanation set forth some years ago by Professor Mendel in his address to the International Musicological Society at its New York Congress in 1961[2].

The two documents in question were first made known by Vander Straeten, who turned them up in the Archivio di Stato in Modena, and published them for the first time in Volume VI of his *La Musique aux Pays-Bas* (1882)[3]. They consist of two undated memoranda concerning singers heard in Flanders, Picardy and Brabant by an emissary of the court of Ferrara, presumably during the reign of Duke Ercole I d'Este, who ruled from 1471 to 1505. Actually it is obvious from the texts alone, as Vander Straeten noted, that one of these memoranda is a variant version of the other, but although they have been quoted and cited fairly often since his first mention of them, they have not been re-examined closely until now. One good reason for this is that they were difficult to find. In 1968, I came across them, more or less by chance, at the end of a folder in the Archivio di Stato in Modena entitled *Musica e Musicisti, Busta* 2[4].

The texts, very slightly emended from Vander Straeten's readings, are as follows:

---

[1] The most far-reaching collective survey of current knowledge about any composer before the 18th century was recently accomplished for Josquin Desprez by the International Josquin Festival-Conference held in New York, June 21—25, 1971. My own contribution, a paper entitled "Josquin at Ferrara: New Documents and Letters" will appear in the proceedings of the conference, and forms part of a larger documentary study of music and musicians at the court of Ferrara in the late 15th and early 16th century. This paper will be referred to hereafter as "Josquin at Ferrara ...".

[2] "Evidence and Explanation", *Report of the Eighth Congress of the International Musicological Society, New York 1961*, Volume II (Kassel, 1962), 3—18.

[3] Pp. 73—74.

[4] This group of documents is maintained in a total of four *Buste* plus an *Appendice*. They include a large group of documents by and about music and musicians, culled during the 19th century from other *fondi* in the Archive and assembled more or less at random. Many of these documents remain unstudied and unused, even though they represent the most visible fraction of the archive's documentary material bearing on the history of music. Busta 4 contains not only some inventories of earlier holdings but some musical manuscripts and prints, including an undated print by Ottaviano Scotto entitled *Del Secondo Libro de Madrigali di Verdelotto, B.,* Bassus part only.

See Plate 1
[Document A]

In anversa, uno tenorista cioe taglia, il suo nome Willechin, / uno altro misser Piero Pannethin. Uno altro misser Rogier, tuto tre quisti sono boni tenoristi cioe taglie. /

In quilla medesima terra, el ge doi contra alti, l'uno se chiama / misser cornelio svaghere, altro misser guillelmo inglese / el quale è cappellano de la nacion et marchadanti inglesi. /

In questa medesima terra, el ge uno nobile contrabasso / el quale a nome messer gossino. /

In una terra chiamata teruana, in Picardia, el ge dui / bellissimi sovrani tuti doi puti; uno se chiama Johannes / laltro è suo compagno.

In Antwerp, a *tenorista*, that is, *taglia*, whose name is Willechin; another named misser Piero Pannethin; another named misser Rogier, all three are good *tenoristi*, that is, *taglie*[5].

In the same place there are two contra alti; one is named misser Cornelio Svaghere[6], the other misser Guillelmo Inglese, who is chaplain of the English colony and merchants[7].

In the same place, there is an excellent contrabass singer, whose name is messer Gossino.

In a place called Therouanne, in Picardy, there are two very fine sopranos, both boys, one is called Johannes, the other is his companion[8].

See Plate 2
[Document B]

Quisti sono li nomi de li cantori quale ha olduto Bartholomio / de fiandra, cantore nostro, vz: / Prim in Anversa ne la ecclesia cathedrale, tenori alti tri / li nomi soi sono: Messer Rugiero, Messer Piero pannechin, Villichin / quale Vil-

These are the names of the singers heard by our singer Bartolomeo de Fiandra:

First, in Antwerp, in the cathedral, three tenor altos, whose names are Messer Rugiero, Messer Piero Pannechin,

---

[5] The term *taglia* is of course the Italian form of the French *taille*, an early term for tenor or middle voice or instrument. The singers Willechin, Piero Pannethin, and misser Rogier are not presently known from any other source, and are not mentioned by L. de Burbure, "La Musique à Anvers", *Annales de l'Académie royale d'archéologie de Belgique*, LVIII (1906), 159—256.

[6] Cornelio Svaghere is not to be confused with the Ferrarese singer named Cornelius or Cornelio, often called Cornelio de Fiandra, who was a ducal singer at Ferrara in 1470—71, then again from 1477 without interruption until 1511.

[7] Guillelmo Inglese, chaplain of the English company of Merchants at Antwerp, is unknown to music historians by this name and role.

[8] According to Vander Straeten, the town of Therouanne in Picardy was entirely destroyed in 1553 by the siege of Charles V; see *La Musique aux Pays-Bas*, VI (1882), 73, note 1. In a recent article on the Strozzi chansonnier, Howard Brown called attention to a little-known composer named Henricus Morinensis whom he equates with "Henri de Therouanne"; see his article "The Music of the Strozzi Chansonnier," *Acta Musicologica* XL (1968), 115—129 and especially 117, note 11 and 126.

Modena. Archivio di Stato, *Musica e Musicisti, Busta 2.* "Document A".

Questi Sono li Nomi de li Cantori quali ha adduto Bartholomio
de fiandra Cantore mio vz.

Primo Jn Anuersa ne la ecclesia cathedrale tenori altri tri
li nomi soi sono. Mr Rogieri. Mr piero pannechin, villichin,
quale villichin secondo il judicio de dicto Bartholomio è il
migliore.

Jn questa modesima terra e ecclesia cathedrale sopradicta
sono dui contra alti, il nome suo è d'uno Mr Cornelio
L'altro Mr Guilielmo Jngelese, il quale è capellano de la
natione e mercadanti Jngelesi.

Et ne la predicta certa gie è uno nobile contrabasso il quale
ha nome Mr Gossino prete, di statura longa e homo bello.

Jn unaltra terra nominata Terruana ch è Jn picardia sono
dui soprani boni ne la certa cathedrale L'uno si chiama
Jannes et è prete Laltro non sua il nome ma è suo compagno.

A brugis ne la certa de la nostra dona gie è uno contraalto
molto bono ma bisogna B loro dimandino il nome suo
al mo di pun il quale ha nome Alamus et canta ne le
pun tenori.

Modena. Archivio di Stato, *Musica e Musicisti*, Busta 2. "Document B".

lichin, secondo il judicio de dicto Bartholomio, e il megliore. /

In questa medesima terra et ecclesia cathedrale sopradicta / sono dui contra alti, il nome suo e de uno Messer Cornelio / laltro Messer Gulielmo Ingelese il quale e capellano de la / natione et mercadanti ingelesi. /

Item, ne la predicta ecclesia, gie e uno nobile contrabasso, il quale / ha nome Messer Gossino prete, de statura longa et homo bello. /

In un altra terra nominata Terruana che e in Picardia, sono / dui sovrani boni, ne la ecclesia cathedrale; l'uno se chiama / Jannes et e prete, laltro non scia il nome ma es suo compagno. /

A Bruges ne la ecclesia de la nostra donna, gie e uno contra alto / molto bono, ma bisogna che loro domandino il nome suo / al maestro di puti, il quale ha nome Aliamus, et canta cum li / puti tenore. /

and Villichin; this Villichin, according to the judgment of Bartolomeo, is the best of them.

In this same place and cathedral there are two contra altos, of whom one is named Messer Cornelio, the other Messer Gulielmo Inglese, who is chaplain of the English colony and merchants there.

Also, in the same church, there is an excellent contrabass singer named Messer Gossino, who is a priest, of tall stature and a handsome man.

In another place called Therouanne, which is in Picardy, there are two good sopranos, in the cathedral; one is called Jannes, and is a priest; the other's name is not known, but he is his companion.

At Bruges, in the church of Our Lady, there is a contra alto who is very good, but it is necessary that they ask his name of the master of the boys, whose own name is Alianus, and who sings tenor with the boys [9].

Although Vander Straeten takes Document A to be an abridgment of Document B, it seems to me much more likely that A is the antecedent and B an expanded version of it. From a close look at the originals it is obvious that A is a crudely and rapidly written note, while B is a formal document: it is written in the careful hand of a court scribe, it adds information not found in the shorter version, and it implies the practical use of the information it gives on the location of the singers. The point at issue is that Vander Straeten and later biographers have taken the allusion to "messer Gossino" to refer to Josquin himself, and it thus stands as the only contemporary testimony we have on Josquin's personal appearance, voice, and status as "prete". I believe it can be convincingly shown that, whoever the "messer Gossino" mentioned here may be, he is not Josquin Desprez.

I should mention that I am not the first to doubt the attribution. While it was accepted by some scholars who followed Vander Straeten, including Blume and Osthoff, it was rejected by Suzanne Clercx on the grounds that the major church of Antwerp is named

---

[9] On musicians at Bruges in the Church of Our Lady see Charles van den Borren's excellent article "Brügge" in *MGG*, Band 2, col. 385, in which he notes that as a center for musicians this church ranked below the local church of Saint Donatian, whose musicians included at various times Cornelius Heyns, Obrecht, Jerome de Clibano, Jean Cordier, Antonius Divitis, and Lupus Hellinck.

in the document as "ecclesia cathedrale"[10]. Madame Clercx cites evidence to show that since this church became a cathedral only in 1559, the memoranda themselves date from the last 40 years of the 16th century and therefore have nothing to do with Josquin Desprez, who died in 1521. Besides, Josquin is not known on any other evidence to have been in service at Antwerp. But as Madame Clercx admits, she herself had not actually seen the original documents when she wrote, and a close examination of them in the light of other sources permits a definite dating in the years 1503—1504, that is, from the very period of Josquin's personal association with the court of Ferrara. Perversely, it is precisely because these documents do come from a datable period of Josquin's lifetime that they cannot refer to him.

A first clue to the date and meaning of the documents is the name Bartolomeo de Fiandra, called "cantore nostro" in Document B; he is the emissary whose report on singers is embodied in the remainder of both texts. Bartolomeo de Fiandra (not known by any other name) is listed in court registers as having been a paid court singer at Ferrara from late in 1499 until 1505[11]. From the payment registers for these years we can see that he entered the service of Duke Ercole I d'Este on November 26, 1499, as one of six new singers, all of whom were added as a group to an already large musical staff[12]. Throughout most of 1499 there were no fewer than 29 regular singers at the court of Ferrara, and the group brought in consisted of these *cantori*: don Nicola Fiorentino, messer Roberto Inglese, messer Bartolomeo de Fiandra, messer Tommaso de Parixe, messer Gillet Picardo, and messer Piero Picardo. Conceivably this substantial influx of singers in 1499 reflects the interim state of the chapel's leadership during this period. Two years before, in 1497, the chapel had lost its leader, Johannes Martini, who had been Duke Ercole's principal singer for over 25 years[13]. No singer-composer of comparable status had yet been found to replace him in 1499, though the Duke tried in that year to secure Gaspar Weerbecke in Milan[14]. Still, in size and continuity of tradition the *cappella musicale* of the court ranked as one of the most important in Italy, indeed in Europe.

The records mentioning Bartolomeo de Fiandra from 1499 to 1502 give the impression that the group with whom he arrived at Ferrara were musicians of some stature, for they were at once installed at a uniform salary that was higher than that of any other court singers. In the summer of 1502, Bartolomeo turns up conspicuously in several documents other than payment records, some of which have been made known in an

---

[10] Suzanne Clercx, "Introduction à l'Histoire de la musique en Belgique," *Revue Belge de Musicologie* V (1951), pp. 119—120; see also Gustave Reese, *Music in the Renaissance* (New York, 1954), p. 229, note 252.

[11] See my paper "Josquin at Ferrara ..." for the documentation.

[12] Archivio di Stato di Modena, Archivio Segreto Estense, Camera, Memoriale del Soldo, 1499 (Register No. 4903/97), fol. 45r, under the date "Marti adì xxvi de nouimbre".

[13] For a survey of the development of music at Ferrara under Ercole I (from 1471 to 1505) see my paper "Music at Ferrara in the Period of Ercole I d'Este," *Studi Musicali* Vol. I, No. 1 (1972), 101—132.

[14] For the documentation see the article mentioned in note 13.

earlier study. In a letter of August 13, 1502, addressed to Duke Ercole, Bartolomeo himself requests the Duke to give him a leave of absence of three months so that he can go to his home to take care of some important affairs[15]. As Bartolomeo adds, he had asked permission for this journey at an earlier date, but the Duke had then refused on the grounds that "the chapel was in a poor state and principally in need of contralti." Now, however, says Bartolomeo, since "the chapel is better furnished than ever before and especially with contralti" he asks the Duke's leave once more.

Bartolomeo's request receives direct and immediate support from an important figure in the musical, political, and social affairs of the court — Girolamo da Sestola, nicknamed "il Coglia." In a letter written the next day (August 14, 1502) Coglia tells the Duke that he should indeed permit Bartolomeo to go to Flanders because he has not been home for a long time, has a great deal to do there, and "wants to bring a brother of his back to stay in Ferrara." Coglia was himself one of Ercole's principal agents for the procuring of singers and music, especially from the Low Countries, and he was also a major proponent of the plan to bring Josquin Desprez into Ercole's service. Indeed, in the spring of 1503, it is Coglia himself who accompanies Josquin from France to Ferrara[16].

But despite Bartolomeo's request and Coglia's support, it appears that he did not actually depart for Flanders before early June of 1503, some ten months after his letter to the Duke. We can infer these dates from further documents, heretofore unpublished, which enable us to chart some phases of his journey.

The payment records for the court singers in 1503 show that Bartolomeo was paid his regular monthly salary on February 23, March 14, April 12, and May 2[17]. On May 17 a notice records that the Duke "has lent Bartolomeo de Fiandra 25 gold ducats" (that is, L. 78.15.0), an amount equal to more than four months regular salary[18]. On June 8, 1503 a special payment of L. 12.15.0 is made to him (though apparently in his absence and collected for him by someone else, to judge from evidence to be seen shortly)[19]. From June through part of October he is not included in the monthly lists of singers paid by the court bureaucracy, and thus the salary records suggest an absence of about four months from Ferrara, from about June 1 to the end of October, 1503. This corresponds in all particulars to a series of diplomatic dispatches from Lyons, in which the Ferrarese ambassador to the French court, Bartolomeo de' Cavalieri, refers to music given to him there by Bartolomeo de Fiandra.

These references (of which the texts are given in the Appendix) can be interpreted as follows. The first dispatch is one in which the Duke reminds Cavalieri to obtain a Mass

---

[15] For the original text and translation of the letter see my paper "Josquin at Ferrara ...," Document 13.

[16] For full texts of the documents and evidence regarding Coglia and the ducal chapel in 1502—1503 see my "Josquin at Ferrara ..." Documents 6, 10, 11, 14, 15, 19, 20, 21.

[17] ASM, Memoriale del Soldo, 1503 (Reg. No. 4908/97), fols. 16r, 26r, 49v, 58v.

[18] *Ibid.*, fol. 66v: "Bartolamio de fiandra Cantore de dare adi xvii de marzo ducati vinti cinque d'oro ... a conto delo suo pago segondo che gia ochorerano per tanti che sua Signoria li aprestado ... L.78.15.0."

[19] *Ibid.*, fol. 78r.

for him from the French court:

1. *May 23, 1503* (Dispatch from Duke Ercole I d'Este to Bartolomeo de'
   Cavalieri):
   "... and when you are in a place in which you can try to obtain that Mass from
   His Most Christian Majesty, we will be very pleased to have you send it to us"[20].

On June 6 Cavalieri replies from Lyons that he is sending "the Mass that his Most
Christian Majesty promised to Your Excellency at Pavia" but in a postscript to the same
letter he explains that he is not sending it after all "since I could not fold it so that it
would fit properly into the wallet; I will send it by the first trustworthy messenger"[21].
On June 8 he reports he is sending it by the hand of Alberto da Canossa. On June 10 the
name of Bartolomeo de Fiandra appears in the correspondence.

2. *June 10, 1503* (Bartolomeo de'Cavalieri to Duke Ercole I d'Este):
   "... yesterday a singer in the Archduke's service was with me and brought with
   him Bartolomeo your singer, who is on his way to Flanders. He told me that he
   wants to give me a certain good composition to send to Your Excellency; as
   soon as I have it I will send it to you."

The same day Cavalieri reports again:

3. *June 10, 1503* (Bartolomeo de'Cavalieri to Duke Ercole I d'Este):
   "I send herewith enclosed the Credo given to me by your singer Bartolomeo.
   I beg Your Lordship to be kind enough to acknowledge receipt of it as soon as
   possible."

A few days later, following accepted practices in diplomatic correspondence, Cavalieri
reaffirms his earlier message and adds more information[22]:

4. *June 13, 1503* (Bartolomeo de' Cavalieri to Duke Ercole I d'Este):
   "I have sent to Your Lordship by means of Cordetta the Mass that his Most
   Christian Majesty promised to Your Worship from Blois, and a Credo that was
   given to me by Bartholomeo Fiamengo your singer, who is leaving tomorrow
   morning to travel on his way to Flanders. Here enclosed is a motet that he is
   sending to Don Alfonso . . ."

[20] ASM, Archivio Segreto Estense, Cancelleria, Estero, Ambasciatori, Francia, B. 3, Filza 35—IX
(Minute di Lettere a Bartolomeo de' Cavalieri), Minute of 23 May 1503.
[21] *Ibid.*, Filza 35—V, Dispatch of 6 June 1503 from Lyon: "Non mando la messa a vostra Excellentia per non la potere plicare che vadi bene nella bolzetta, per il primo fidato laman-
darò . . ." In a dispatch of May 23 Cavalieri had reported being told by the King that the Mass
wanted by the Duke was at Blois.
[22] On the customs and practices governing Italian diplomatic dispatches of this period see Garrett
Mattingly, *Renaissance Diplomacy* (Penguin Books, 1964), p. 97.

On June 17 Cavalieri again reports that he has sent the Mass and Credo, in a dispatch that adds nothing new and need not be quoted here. And again on June 27 he repeats the message once more and adds that he has also sent the Duke a copy of a diplomatic document concerning the Archduke Philip the Fair (heir to the throne of Spain) as well as a ring on which was carved an image, appropriate for the Duke, of Hercules with Anteus[23]. At last on July 7, 1503 the Duke sends word of his receipt of the music:

> 5. *July 7, 1503* (Duke Ercole I d'Este to Bartolomeo de' Cavalieri):
> "By the route of Milano, and thus by means of Cordetta, and of Mantua, at various times we have received several of your letters: that of the 8th, 10th, 18th, 23rd, 27th, and 30th of last month. And in this letter we will reply to all the points that require answers.
> We have received the Mass that you have sent to us and which was promised to us by his Most Christian Majesty last year when we were at Pavia. And since this Mass pleases us, we give you great praise for your diligence in sending it to us. Thus also we commend you for the Credo that you have sent us, which was given to you by Bartholomeo our singer.
> . . . .
> If that singer of the Most Illustrious Archduke gives you some good composition to send to me, as he told me he would, send it to me safely"[24].

From these letters we see that Bartolomeo de' Fiandra was in Lyons on at least the dates June 10—13, 1503, and that he was expected to leave for Flanders on June 14 (see Document 4). If he returned to Ferrara only in October, as the records seem to indicate, then his notes on the musicians heard at Antwerp and Picardy must have been compiled between mid-June and October of 1503. This then is the meaning of Document A, which probably is Bartolomeo's own hand-written memorandum, or a rough copy of what he reported, naming exceptionally competent musicians heard during this journey.

That "Gossin" cannot be Josquin emerges from corroborating evidence which enables us to place Josquin squarely in Ferrara during the entire period of Bartolomeo's journey. Letters and payment records have made it possible to determine Josquin's precise period of service at Ferrara; it falls between late April of 1503 and April of 1504, during which he was the leader of the ducal musical forces and was regularly paid for each

---

[23] ASM ... Amb., Francia, Busta 3, Filza 35—V, dispatch of 27 June 1503 (from Lyons): "Io ho mandata la messa con uno Credo a vostra Reverentia et la copia del mandato fecero li serenissimi Re di Spagna il Illustrissimo Arciduca, et uno anello dove è una coemola ligata in oro dove e sculpito hercule che ha uno anteo ..."

[24] "That singer of the Archduke's" refers to an as yet unidentified member of the musical company in service of Duke Philip the Fair, who was entertained by King Louis XII of France at Lyons in April of 1503, having returned from his first trip to Spain. His musicians included Pierre de la Rue and Alexander Agricola, either of whom could be the singer intended by Ercole. See G. van Doorslaer, "La Chapelle musicale de Philippe le Beau," *Revue Belge d'Archéologie et d'Histoire de l'art* IV (1934), 21 ff., 139 ff.

month of his service at the court[25]. It is possible that he may have made brief trips to nearby Italian centers during this time — for example to Venice, Mantua, Florence — though no such trips are now documented. But he clearly cannot be identified with a singer who was at this same time a member of the regular musical forces of the Cathedral at Antwerp.

That Josquin was definitely in Ferrara up through April of 1504 enables us also to clarify the exact meaning and use of Document B. A Ducal minute of May 17, 1504 issued by Duke Ercole to his son and heir Alfonso D'Este, gives the answer. In May of this year Alfonso set off on a journey to France, "sent by his father," as a chronicler tells us, "to visit His Majesty the King of France." Alfonso returned only on August 8, 1504, having travelled not only to France but to England. Ercole's preliminary instructions to Alfonso, as recorded in the memorandum, include the following:

> *Ducal Minute of May 17, 1504* (Duke Ercole I d'Este to Don Alfonso d'Este):
> "In addition, since we still have need of singers for our chapel, we would gladly obtain a good Tenorista alto, two good contraltos, a good contrabasso, and two good soprani. And we understand that there are such singers in the places that are indicated in the enclosed document, in which their names are also indicated. And it seems to me that you should use all diligence to see if these singers are good and able and to our purpose — and those whom you find who are really excellent, you should bring here. But we do not want singers who are not really perfect. And this note which we send to you was given to us by Bartholomeo de Fiandra our singer ... Thus you will use all possible diligence in this matter.
>   Ferrara, 17 May 1504[26]

A glance back at Document "B" discloses that it fits hand in glove with the note mentioned as being enclosed with the Ducal minute, and either *is* that document itself or is a copy of what the Duke sent to Alfonso. If we compare the Minute with the memorandum, furthermore, with regard to the number of singers and their voice-ranges, we see that they correspond almost exactly:

Singers heard by Bartolomeo (Documents A and B)	*Singers requested by Duke Ercole* (Minute of May 17, 1504)
Antwerp: 3 *tenoriste*	1 *Tenorista alto*
2 *Contra alti*	2 *Contra alti*
1 *Contrabasso*	1 *Contrabasso*
Therouanne: 2 boy soprani	2 soprani

---

[25] ASM, Memoriale del Soldo, 1503 and 1504 (Regs. 4908/97 and 4910/97); see my paper "Josquin at Ferrara ..." for details.

[26] For the original text of this document see my "Josquin at Ferrara," Document 25.

Presumably Duke Ercole tailored his request of 1504 to the voice-ranges and singers he knew to be available, at least on the basis of Bartolomeo's report. What is equally certain is that this attempt to procure more singers coincides almost exactly with the departure of Josquin Desprez from Ferrarese service, apparently at the end of April or even in early May of 1504 (he is paid in the registers of 1504 for "four months" of service, which may have included all of April); for what destination we do not know. As for the identity of the "messer Gossin" heard in Antwerp, he might possibly be the singer "Gosswin de Catulle" mentioned by Burbure as being at the cathedral sometime after 1450[27]. A tendency in Ferrarese orthography at this time is to transform an initial "C" into "G", so that the name of the famous painter Cosimo Tura is often found in the registers as „messer Gosme." Another possibility is that "Gossin" may be a Ferrarese version of a name such as "Cossin", and perhaps the family of musicians named "Caussin" may be represented here. Could he be an older relative of that Ernoul Caussin who was later (around 1520) found as a boy singer at the Cathedral of Cambrai and subsequently went to Italy[28]? The name, at least, is plausible.

The net effect of this exercise in the interpretation of documents is to deprive us of the only morsel of contemporary evidence that gave us any supposed clue to Josquin's voice-range und physical appearance, as a contemporary might have heard and seen him. While subtracting this information from the biographical documentation is scarcely of more than passing importance in itself, it may be suggestive for certain aspects of interpretation of Josquin as musician and composer. It can now no longer be assumed that Josquin was himself a *contrabasso*, and that anything in his approach to composition would have been conditioned by his experience as a bass in vocal ensemble performance in his time; and it can no longer be assumed that his priestly status was more than that of a cleric who had taken minor vows — though this point is still uncertain. A Milanese document of 1479 refers to him as "cantore et cappellano nostro"[29]. "Cappellano" here may mean nothing more than "member of the ducal cappella" and while it is true that *cappella* in the stricter sense had meant a place of religious worship, often even a travelling shrine belonging to a nobleman and his entourage, it is clear that in the last quarter of the 15th century it came increasingly to refer to the members of a "chapel" who had a consistently musical as well as a religious role. The present biographical evidence provides little basis on which to judge Josquin's outlook as a composer with regard to his depth and sincerity of religious outlook (above all in an age conspicuous for the secularization of much religious life). But we can at least dispense at present with the only document in which the term "priest" is specifically used about him, and to that extent we can regard more critically the strongly "religious" interpretation of this work that has recently

[27] L. de Burbure, "La Musique à Anvers," *op. cit.* (see note 5), p. 255.
[28] See N. Pelicelli, "Musicisti in Parma nei secoli XVI-XVII," *Note d'Archivio* VIII (1931), p. 141 f.
[29] See *MGG* VII, cols. 193—194, Abb. 2 for a facsimile of the document, which refers to "Joschin picardo" as "cantore et cappellano;" it is a safe-conduct issued for him at Milan on April 12, 1479.

been advanced[30]. The whole matter also demonstrates once again how little is really known about Josquin's entire career and, consequently, about the real chronology of his development as a composer, and how much painstaking research will have to be done before a truly comprehensive portrait begins finally to emerge.

APPENDIX

Texts of Documents given in translation

No. 1. Dispatch from Duke Ercole I d'Este to Bartolomeo de' Cavalieri, May 23, 1503:
"E quando seriti in loco che potiate operare de hauere de la Maestà Christianissima quella Messa, haueremo caro che ce la mandiati".

No. 2. B. de' Cavalieri to Duke Ercole I d'Este, 10 June 1503:
"heri era con mi uno cantore de monsignore larciducha Il quale meno con luy Bartholomeo vostro cantadore Il quale va in fiandra, ma dicto volermi dare una certa bona cosa da mandare avostra Excellentia como lhabi subito la manderò . . ."

No. 3: B. de' Cavalieri to Duke Ercole I d'Este, 10 June 1503: (separate note on same day as No. 2; following is the entire text of this note):
"Illustrissimo et Reverendissimo Signore Mio: Mando qui incluso il Credo che miha dato messer Bartholomeo vostro cantore prego la Signoria Vostra che se digni subito aduisarmi dela recevuta et a sua bona gratia continue me recommando scritte a Lion adj 10 zugno 1503".

No. 4. B. de' Cavalieri to Duke Ercole I d'Este, 13 June 1503:
"ho mandato a vostra Reverentia per lauia del Cordetta la Messa che la Maestà Christianissima promesse a vostra Reverentia a Bles et uno credo che mi ha dato messer Bartholomeo Fiamengo cantore il quale se parte domatina per aduiarse alsuo camino verso fiandra / e qui aligato serà uno motet chel manda al signore don Alfonso . . ."

No. 5: Duke Ercole I d'Este to B. de' Cavalieri, 7 July 1503:
"Per la via de Milano, et cussi, per la via del Cordetta, et de Mantua, in piu volte havemo havuto piu vostre lettere de VIII, X, XVIII, XXIII, XXVII et ultimo del passato. Et per questo responderemo de tute le parte, che ricerchano risposta: Havemo havuto la Messa, che ce hauiti mandato, la quale ne promise la Maestà Christianissima quando lo ano passato eravamo a Pavia. Et si come dicta messa ne piace cussi ve comendemo assai de la diligentia che hauiti usato in mandarcela./ Cussi anche vi comandemo del Credo che ne haviti mandato quale vi è stato dato per Bartholomeo nostro Cantore . . . . . . Se quello Cantore de lo Illustrissimo Archiduca ve darà qualche bona cosa da mandarmi, come il me dixe, ce la mandariti salvamente".

---

[30] See Helmuth Osthoff, *Josquin Desprez*, Vol. I, p. 86 f.

WALTER GERSTENBERG

Das Alleluja in Senfls Propriumskompositionen

Die Bezeichnung „Choralbearbeitung" hat sich seit langem als fruchtbar und erhellend erwiesen, denn dieser Doppelbegriff nennt zwei Grundkräfte der Musikgeschichte und schließt sie zusammen, die auf dem langen historischen Wege vom Mittelalter zum Barock ein essentiell tragendes Fundament der Musik gewesen sind. Nur wenn man das Gemeinsame bedenkt, wird man dem tiefgreifenden Wandel gerecht werden, den dabei beide, der Choral ebenso wie die Art seiner Bearbeitung, erfahren haben. Von dieser Einsicht aus wird es möglich, einen weiten Kreis zu ziehen, der die deutsche Musik der Reformationszeit, aber auch die Johann Sebastian Bachs einschließt. Die geistliche Kantate Bachs ist eine späte Frucht jener an den Rhythmus des Kirchenjahres gebundenen Propriums-Musiken, die im Zeitalter Kaiser Maximilians unter den Hofkapellmeistern Heinrich Isaac und Ludwig Senfl eine erste Blüte erlebt haben. Aus dem lateinischen gregorianischen Choral ist inzwischen das deutschsprachige Kirchenlied geworden, doch leben im protestantischen Gottesdienst Traditionen weiter und verbürgen eine geschichtliche Kontinuität; kaum weniger tief eingreifend haben sich gleichzeitig Modelle und Typen verändert, die Cantus firmi der alten und der neuen Kirche kunstvoll polyphon auszusetzen. Obgleich das instrumentengetragene Concerto neue Klangregionen öffnet, bleibt der vierstimmige Satz für die getrennten Epochen gemeinsame Grundlage. Glareans bekanntes Wort: *Ex ... quatuor vocibus, tanquam ex quatuor elementis, corpus mixtum fit pulcherrimo naturae munere* (Dodekachordon, 1547, S. 240) weist weit über seine Zeit hinaus. Die Anerkennung dieses naturgegebenen Gesetzes ist, allen stilistischen Wandel überformend, für die Kantate Bachs wie für die Propriumsmusik Senfls gleichermaßen verbindlich. Von diesem Regulativ aus werden Wachsen und Abnehmen der Stimmenzahl überhaupt erst sinn- und bedeutungsvoll, verlieren sie alles Beiläufige und Zufällige. Ähnlich haben neuere Untersuchungen für das Zeitalter Bachs die Existenz eines Grundgefühls für musikalische Bewegungscharaktere wahrscheinlich und anschaulich gemacht, das auf Traditionen der klassischen Mensuralmusik zurückweist.

Nicht leicht wird man in der deutschen Musikgeschichte auf eine ähnlich enge Verbundenheit stoßen, wie sie zwischen Isaac, dem Lehrer, und Senfl bestanden hat. Leben und Werk haben hieran übereinstimmend Anteil. Bekanntlich ist das umfangreiche Corpus ihrer zyklischen Propriumskompositionen vor allem in zwei großen Sammlungen überliefert, deren eine, der dreibändige *Choralis Constantinus*, posthum, Jahrzehnte nach dem Tode Isaacs, gedruckt worden ist (Band I 1550, II und III 1555); die andere dagegen, das *Opus Musicum*, ist einzig in vier Codices der Bayerischen Staatsbibliothek München handschriftlich überliefert (Signatur: *Mus. ms. 35—38*). Während sich Senfls Mitarbeit am *Choralis Constantinus* zur Hauptsache darin abzeichnet, daß er Johann Ott, der anfänglich als Verleger des Werkes in Aussicht genommen war und die Druckvorlagen in Besitz gehabt hatte, beraten und bei der Zusammenstellung der Propriums-Zyklen zur Seite gestanden hat, liegen die Verhältnisse beim *Opus Musicum* anders. Nur zum kleineren Teil ist es Isaacs Werk, vielmehr erfahren wir aus dem Titelblatt, daß es Senfl nach

Isaacs Tod vollendet und, wie wir ergänzen können, den weitaus größeren Teil der Sätze dafür geliefert hat. In den Bänden VIII—X der Senfl-Gesamtausgabe sind nunmehr auch diese Sätze zugänglich[1], während der *Choralis Constantinus* bereits seit längerem in freilich uneinheitlicher Neuausgabe vorliegt[2]. Beide Sammlungen berühren und überschneiden sich in einigen Partien ihres Repertoires, ein überlieferungsgeschichtlich komplizierter Vorgang, an dessen Klärung neuerdings vor allem zwei Tübinger Dissertationen Hand angelegt haben[3]. Der Weg für eine innermusikalische Erschließung dieser Musik ist damit freigelegt.

Glareans zuvor erwähnter Vergleich beruht auf der Vorstellung, daß die vier Stimmen des musikalischen Satzes bei aller Verschiedenheit gleichen Rang bei der Bildung des Klangkörpers haben, keine der anderen voransteht. Diese Meinung könnte in einer Zeit, welche das deutsche Tenorlied ausdrücklich in den Vordergrund der weltlichen Musik rückt und satztechnisch die Prädominanz der überlieferten Cantus-Tenor-Struktur weithin bewahrt hat, überraschen. Gerade das *Opus Musicum* hat in dieser Beziehung eine, soviel wir sehen, bemerkenswerte Bresche geschlagen, indem der Titel ausdrücklich eine einzige Stimme, die *Gravis vox,* den Part des Basses, als cantusführend bezeichnet. Während für Tinctoris der Tenor das *Fundamentum relationis* ist, wobei sein *Diffinitorium* (circa 1473/74) die obere und untere Contrastimme kurz erwähnt, kann, knapp zwei Generationen später, der Baß diese Aufgabe übernehmen. Zarlino (*Istitutioni harmoniche* III, 1573, p. 282) sieht diese Aufgabe eher in der Regelung der Harmonie und der Zusammenklänge: *quando'l Basso mancasse, tutta la cantilena si empirebbe di confusione e di dissonanza; e ogni cosa andarebbe in ruina.* Glareans *Dodekachordon* legt den Akzent auf das „Moralische", die Würde der Musik, die ihm die Anwesenheit des Basses repräsentiert:

> *Inde etiam videmus quam nihil efficiant voces superiores absque inferiorum vocum Basi . . . Neque vero iucundior alius cantus est, quam in quo firma sonabit infima vox, etiamsi suprema suavius auditum permulcet, sed omnino in garritum veniunt omnes superiores voces, si robore infimae vocis destituantur. (p. 84) . . . Ubi enim in concentu ea vox minus firma fuerit, ibi reliquae voces omnes evanidae apparent . . . nec maiestatem ullam habere possunt. (p. 240)*

Daß sich hiermit der gesamte Klangraum, der nunmehr von der Tiefe her gesehen wird, umformt, jede Stimme zu jeder in eine neue Relation tritt, sind kompositionstechnische

---

[1] Ludwig Senfl, *Sämtliche Werke.* Band VIII, Motetten, II. Teil: *Kompositionen des Proprium Missae I,* ed. Walter Gerstenberg, 1964; Band IX, Motetten, III. Teil: *Kompositionen des Proprium Missae II,* ed. Walter Gerstenberg, 1971; Band X, Motetten, IV. Teil: *Kompositionen des Proprium Missae III,* ed. Walter Gerstenberg, 1972.

[2] Band I, edd. Emil Bezecny und Walter Rabl, *Denkmäler der Tonkunst in Oesterreich (DTÖ)* V/1 (Wien 1898); Band II, ed. Anton von Webern *DTÖ* XVI/1, 1909; Band III, ed. Louise Cuyler (Ann Arbor 1950).

[3] Gerhard-Rudolf Pätzig, *Liturgische Grundlagen und handschriftliche Überlieferung von Heinrich Isaacs „Choralis Constantinus".* Phil. Diss. (Tübingen 1956), maschinenschriftlich; Martin Bente, *Neue Wege der Quellenkritik und die Biographie Ludwig Senfls.* Phil. Diss. (Tübingen 1966, gedruckt Wiesbaden 1968).

Konsequenzen, denen sich die Autoren des *Opus Musicum* konfrontiert sehen. Dabei bleibt offen, auf wen die aufschlußreiche Formulierung des Titels zurückgeht, auf die Auftraggeber oder auf die Musiker, die das Werk ausführen: jedenfalls spricht unüberhörbar der Geist der Zeit daraus.

II

Betrachtet man die der Regel nach aus einer Folge von Introitus — Alleluia — (Sequenz —) Communio bestehenden Formulare der Propriumsmusiken insgesamt, über die Grenzen des *Opus Musicum* hinaus, so fällt auf, daß die intonierende Stimme, also der gregorianisch einstimmige Beginn von Introitus und Communio, entweder dem Diskant oder dem Baß zugehört, wenn nicht, eine dritte Möglichkeit, überhaupt auf solchen Beginn verzichtet wird. Jedenfalls der Tenor hat diese Führungsfunktion verloren. Natürlich markiert die Lage der Intonation bis zu einem bestimmten Grade, welche Stimmen im weiteren Verlauf den Cantus vorzugsweise übernehmen. Um so mehr überrascht und befremdet es, daß eine keineswegs periphere Handschrift der Zeit, der Berliner Codex 40 024, eine etwa 1537 entstandene Handschrift des Sophonias Päminger, diese Verbindung ignoriert und vielfach die Intonation der darin verzeichneten Sätze irregulär in den Cantus verlegt [4].

In den Propriumssätzen ist die polyphone Rezeption des Chorals von der Art, daß man wurzelhafte Verbindung ein Prinzip dieser Musik nennen kann; in gleicher Tendenz wechseln in den oft ausgedehnten Sequenzen gregorianisch-einstimmiger und polyphoner Vortrag von Vers zu Vers ab oder ist für die den Introitus beendende Doxologie ein gregorianischer Vortrag anzunehmen. Um von einer dominierenden Stimme aus das Satzganze an den Cantus firmus zu binden, gibt sich die Imitation locker und leicht; im Bereich des Kanons waltet eine Freiheit, daß man sich versucht fühlt, im Anschluß an ein bekanntes Wort des Tinctoris, geradezu von einer *Varietas canonica* zu sprechen.

III

Damit imitatorische Polyphonie in alle vier Stimmen des Satzes einströmen kann, wird der Komponist die gregorianische Weise von Abschnitt zu Abschnitt motettisch befestigen; dabei hat er sie in doppelter Hinsicht zu befragen, melodisch, sofort aber auch rhythmisch. Diese doppelte Umformung des Cantus planus ist Basis alles Folgenden. Ein drittes Ferment ist die Sprache der meist biblischen Texte, die Forderung, daß die korrespondierenden kontrapunktierenden Satzabschnitte und Figuren die gleichen Textworte deklamieren. Die Notatoren der Münchner Chorbücher, unter denen man vielleicht auch Senfl selbst vermuten kann, verhalten sich dieser Forderung gegenüber merkwürdig unbestimmt und schwankend: auf weite Strecken genügen sie ihr, scheinen sie dagegen auf anderen Blättern der Codices aus den Augen zu verlieren. Dem so skizzierten Rahmen fügt sich der syllabische Duktus der Sequenzmelodien ohne Schwierigkeit, ungezwungen, ein. Die Ansprüche an den Komponisten wachsen, wenn er in anderen Teilen des Pro-

---

[4] Gerhard Pätzig, *Das Chorbuch Mus. ms. 40 024 der Deutschen Staatsbibliothek Berlin.* In: Festschrift Walter Gerstenberg (Wolfenbüttel 1964), S. 122—142.

priums für den Choral so charakteristische, weit ausholende und ausschwingende Melismen antrifft; sie widerstreben der Aufnahme in einen polyphonen Satz, welcher auf Korrespondenz der musikalischen und sprachlichen Phrase beruht. Beobachtet man, wie der Komponist Senfl sich mit melismatischen Partien auseinandersetzt, die den Fluß einer sonst konzis deklamierenden gregorianischen Melodie unterbrechen, so erkennt man, daß Kürzung und Kontraktion der Melismen, die sich bis zu ihrer Eliminierung steigern können, ein Gesetz für den Polyphonisten ist. Kritisch aber wird seine Situation dann, wenn in ebensolchen wortentlasteten Vokalisen Sinn und Idee eines Propriumsstückes beschlossen sind. Beim Tractus hat sich der zeitgenössische Notator so beholfen, daß er weite Partien der in die Polyphonie rezipierten Melismen untextiert gelassen hat [5], anders aber stellt sich das Problem bei der Komposition des Alleluia: — und anders hat es hier der Komponist gelöst.

IV

Zur Analyse und zum Verständnis des mehrstimmig komponierten responsorialen Alleluia ist es notwendig, kurz an einige Vorschriften zu erinnern, die das Zeremoniell seines einstimmigen Vortrags im Gottesdienst regeln. Seit alters erfolgt er so, wie es das *Missale Romanum* mit einfachen, klaren Worten beschreibt: ... *post Graduale dicuntur duo Alleluia, deinde Versus, et post Versum unum Alleluia.* Angesichts der Tatsache, daß die Auswahl des dem doppelten Alleluiaruf folgenden Versus wenig befestigt ist, die Choralhandschriften daher zahlreiche regionale und örtliche Varianten aufweisen, ist die konservative Kodifizierung der Vortragsweise des Alleluia, die über das Tridentium hinweg ins Mittelalter zurückweist, bemerkenswert. Das *Graduale Romanum*, das Gesangbuch der Messe, differenziert die Ausführungsvorschrift und nennt dabei die einzelnen Glieder, aus denen sich das Alleluia zusammensetzt: ein Solist stimmt es bis zum Asteriscus an, der Chor wiederholt diese Partie; auf dem letzten Vokal des Wortes Alleluia mündet sie in ein Schlußmelisma, das traditionell Jubilus heißt. Alsdann beginnt der Solist mit dem Vortrag des Versus bis zu einem Punkt, der in den neueren liturgischen Büchern wiederum durch einen Asteriscus bezeichnet ist; der folgende Chorabschluß stimmt in einer jüngeren Schicht der Alleluia-Gesänge zumindest partiell mit dem Jubilus überein; endlich intoniert der Solist das Alleluia ein zweitesmal, und der Chor schließt mit der Wiederholung des Jubilus.

Kehrt man von dem so umrissenen Schema zu Senfls Aussetzungen zurück, so ergeben sich auf den ersten Blick Fragen und Zweifel. Nirgends läßt die originale Notierung der Chorbücher erkennen, kein Hinweis darauf findet sich, daß der Alleluia-Ruf nach dem Vers zu repetieren ist, der tatsächliche Abschluß des Satzes also in der Mitte seiner Niederschrift liegt — wofern man jedenfalls die Überzeugung gewonnen hat, daß Senfls Komposition sich dem überlieferten Rahmen der Liturgie einfügen will. Weiter: wie verhält sich der polyphone Satz zu der Forderung, der Alleluia-Ruf habe vor dem Versus zwiefach zu erklingen, danach jedoch nur einmal? Zuletzt aber fragen wir: was widerfährt dem Jubilus, in welchem die Kirche von alters her den innersten Ausdruck des Alleluia erkannt hat?

---

[5] Siehe Band X, Nr. XIX.

Der Komplex dieser Fragen betrifft die Praxis eines responsorialen Alternatim-Musizierens, das im Alleluia gleichsam prästabiliert ist: wie, in welcher Art wirken in der Polyphonie Solist und Chor zusammen? Daß es dabei weniger um einen Musizierbrauch, um allein klangliche Abwechslung oder Differenzierung geht, vielmehr die Struktur des Alleluia berührt und ergriffen wird, ergibt eine nähere Betrachtung. Wenn es das Ziel auch dieser Musik ist, mit ihren Mitteln den Gottesdienst festlich zu schmücken — *pro servitio divino multiplicando* —, dann mutet es unwahrscheinlich an, daß Senfl gerade denjenigen Komplex des Propriums, welcher der Musik am nächsten steht, stark redigiert haben sollte. Dem Bearbeiter des liturgischen Cantus firmus steht ja eine Fülle konträrer Möglichkeiten zu Gebote: Einerseits kann er, wie wir wissen, die Linien der Melodie kürzen, widerstrebende Melismen kontrahieren oder eliminieren, wie er umgekehrt Melodien durch Zwischennoten oder Wiederholungen erweitert, sie rhythmisiert und so Figuren prägt, die sich im Satz für eine Strecke imitatorisch ausbreiten und befestigen.

Man darf es als eine Huldigung an den musikalischen Genius des Alleluia ansehen, daß der Symphonet Senfl, vielleicht angeregt von Isaac, bestrebt scheint, dies einzige Wort polyphon hervorzuheben, und zwar durch die Technik einer imitatorischen Verdoppelung der Cantus-firmus-Töne[6]; mag Ähnliches hier und da in anderen Formen des Propriums begegnen, so doch stets im Zuge der allgemeinen Tendenz auf eine Varietas des Satzes. Das Alleluia aber sieht darin ein Kompositionsprinzip, das vom Ausgangspunkt des Kanons her andere, freie Formen der Duplizierung entdeckt. Daß ein Part eines solchen Stimmpaares dem Baß zugehört, ist im *Opus Musicum* vorgegeben; die bestimmende Rolle der *Gravis vox* zeigt sich darin, daß sie in vielen Sätzen diejenige Stimme ist, in der das Wort Alleluia, der liturgischen Vorschrift entsprechend, ein einziges Mal erklingt[7]. Diese Tendenz ist kaum anders als mit einer vorausgehenden gregorianischen Wiedergabe dieses Rufes zu erklären, auch wenn die Quelle darüber schweigt. Deutlich dem Vorbild Isaacs verpflichtet ist eine zweite Art, das Alleluia auszusetzen. Sie steht im Zeichen der Durchimitation einer melodisch-rhythmischen Figur, die weniger unmittelbarer Bestandteil des Cantus firmus ist, als daß sie ihm abgewonnen zu sein scheint[8]. Da der Baß auf diese Weise eine Stimme neben anderen wird, er seine Führung jedenfalls aufgibt, ist dieser ältere Typus bei Senfl den Propriumskompositionen außerhalb des *Opus Musicum* vorbehalten.

Auf das Bestreben des Komponisten, das Wort Alleluia — auch über Pausen hinweg — in einer Hauptstimme dominieren zu lassen, fällt neues Licht durch die Tatsache, daß die Aussetzung nahezu regelmäßig beim Zeichen des Asteriscus ihr Ende findet[9]. Mit anderen Worten: Der Komponist übergeht den Jubilus, jenes innerste Substrat des Alleluia, allenfalls findet er sich umrißhaft angedeutet[10]. Erinnert man sich, daß die neuere Schicht des

---

[6] Siehe Band IX, Nr. IV.
[7] Man vergleiche die verschiedene Behandlungsweise in den folgenden Sätzen: Band VIII, Nr. IV und Nr. XI; Band IX, Nr. XV; Band X, Nr. III.
[8] Siehe Band IX, Nr. VIII.
[9] Siehe Band X, Nr. III.
[10] Siehe Band X, Nr. XIX.

Alleluia und damit ihr weitaus größerer Bestand mit der Wiederaufnahme des am Ende des Versus in der Regel textierten Jubilus zu enden pflegt, und bemerkt man, daß Senfl auch diesen Abschnitt, falls er ihn überhaupt aufnimmt, entschieden zu kontrahieren pflegt, so wird die formale Proportion der beiden Satzabschnitte, des Alleluia und des Versus, stark angegriffen. Wiederum nämlich fällt ein Chorteil aus, der getrennte Partien von der Musik her zusammenführt und zusammenschließt. Denn anzunehmen, auch hier, am Versende, könne ein Solosänger die vier Stimmen in einer einzigen gregorianischen Weise fortführen, widerspräche die oft enge formale Verknüpfung der Verstexte mit dem Jubilus.

Von dieser Norm weicht Senfl im Alleluia des Fronleichnamsfestes bedeutsam ab; denn hier ist, von aller Regel abweichend, die Wiederholung des Jubilus am Versende vollständig rezipiert, er an dieser Stelle also auskomponiert[11]; durch Wiederholung der heilsgeschichtlich inhaltsschweren Worte *in eo* wird die gregorianische Vokalise in der Münchner Handschrift gleichsam rationalisiert. Ohne Zweifel ist es der Festgedanke, der die polyphone Rezeption des Jubilus bewirkt hat und seine musikalische Substanz in den ganzen Stimmverband einströmen läßt.

Auch in anderer, prononzierter Weise schlägt die kontrapunktierende Musik eine Brücke vom Alleluia zum Versus und vertieft so den Hintergrund[12]. Am Schluß des (ersten) Verses erklingt im Stimmverband (51 ff.) wiederholt eine überaus charakteristisch geprägte Figur: In spiritueller Polyphonie verknüpft sie die Textworte *et sedebat super eum* mit dem Initium des Alleluia.

Endlich ist aufschlußreich zu beobachten, wie Senfl die Tonalität in den typisch verkürzten Alleluia-Kompositionen regelt. Im allgemeinen endet das Initium, wie später der Jubilus, auf der Finalis. Im Oster-Alleluia *Pascha nostrum* springt jedoch die Linie vom Rezitationston eine Quinte abwärts in die transponierte Finalis c[13]. Im ersten Himmelfahrts-Alleluia verknüpft Senfl die beiden Teile durch eine harmonisch plagale Wendung[14]. Die melodische Linie des *Gaudete justi* wendet er dagegen zum Schlußton B, einigermaßen künstlich statt zur regulären Finalis A[15].

So führt eine jede Betrachtung der Senflschen Alleluia-Sätze, die von der originalen Notierung ausgeht, von verschiedenen Seiten her zu der Frage, wie sich in der Praxis des Gottesdienstes das Zusammenwirken der alternierenden Klangkörper tatsächlich abgespielt haben möge. Während sich die anderen Teile des Propriums in der Polyphonie dem Zeremoniell ohne Schwierigkeit, widerspruchslos, einfügen, kann es für das Alleluia eine allseits befriedigende Antwort offenbar nicht geben. Aber ist nicht auch dies Aufgabe der Historie: Zu erkennen, wo sie an ihre Grenzen stößt? Denn die künstlerische Wirklichkeit geschichtlichen Lebens ist zuletzt reicher, als es jede wissenschaftliche Phantasie sich vorzustellen vermag.

[11] Siehe Band IX, Nr. V.
[12] Siehe Band VIII, Nr. XIV.
[13] Siehe Band VIII, Nr. XIII.
[14] Siehe Band VIII, Nr. XVI.
[15] Siehe Band X, Nr. XIX.

HAROLD S. POWERS

The Modality of "Vestiva i colli"

Presupposed to any analysis of such a piece as, let us say, the second movement of Beethoven's Opus 10 #3 is the two-fold designation of its tonality, "d" and "minor", with all that is implicit therein about a normative background of expectable musical relationships. No analogous presupposition can be made for such a piece as Palestrina's "Vestiva i colli" by assigning it to some particular mode in a closed modal system, be it of 11th-century, 15th-17th century, or 20th-century provenance. Modality is not a necessary precompositional assumption for Medieval and Renaissance polyphony in the way in which tonality is precompositional for 18th-19th-century art music. The compositional techniques of Palestrina's time are essentially those of elaborating what Zarlino defines as a "soggetto" in Part III, Chapter 26 of his Le Istitutioni harmoniche (Venice, 1558): working out parts to a tenor, elaborating or paraphrasing pre-existing monophonic or polyphonic materials, or carrying out points of imitation with original (or borrowed) thematic material. None of these processes entails any prior systematic assumptions beyond: 1) the aggregate content of the diatonic system as organized in the deductions of the hexachord, with chromatic adjuncts; 2) the inferrable rules of intervallic counterpoint, including the rules for interval progression (especially at cadences).

The importance of modality seems to vary greatly in different kinds of repertoires, and with different genres and works within the output of one master. Even within a piece demonstrably conceived modally there can be deviations from "the" mode — modal mixture, cadences to degrees normally non-cadential for that mode, chromatic replacement of diatonic degrees — as well as departures from "modality" altogether in circle-of-fifths or chromatic-chord sequences. All this has been discussed by various scholars, especially Bernhard Meier, most recently and particularly in the Foreword to Volume IV of his edition of the Rore works[1]. I merely mean to point out here that if a passage can exist without having *any* modality, so can a piece — which is not at all to say that a piece or passage not modal must therefore necessarily be tonal.

The distribution of scale-degrees of melodic and cadential emphasis within the *ambitus* of the several parts is of great structural significance in polyphonic compositions of the Renaissance, and these relationships are generally held to be in some sense modal. Siegfried Hermelink[2] has convincingly shown how these relationships in the music of Palestrina are necessarily correlated with the precompositional selection (precompositional in the sense that selection of a tonality is precompositional) of one of the four possible combinations from the antinomies "chiavette/normal cleffing" and "no signature/ b-flat signature". Morley calls them "high key" versus "low key" and "properties . . .

---

[1] Cipriano de Rore, Opera omnia, ed. Bernhard Meier, Corpus mensurabilis musicae, XIV, Vol. 4: Madrigalia 3—8 vocum (Rome, 1969), pp. v—ix.
[2] Siegfried Hermelink, Dispositiones modorum (Tutzing, 1960).

in pricked song . . . either sharp or flat"[3]. I shall simply call them "high clefs" versus "low clefs" and "cantus durus" versus "cantus mollis".

Hermelink further supposes, thus making explicit and formal what many take for granted, that there is one single degree which functions as a principal degree, a *Grundton*, in each composition. Here he seems to go too far, particularly when we see that in his modal analyses the *Grundton* alway turns out to be the root of the final triad. There is a double assumption here, both terms of which are doubtful. First, it is assumed that a mode is ultimately grounded in a tonic which overrides all other structural considerations. Second, it is assumed that "tonic" (*Grundton*) and *finalis* are always synonymous.

Hermelink's observations about cantus durus/cantus mollis and high clefs/low clefs, combined with his supposition about the relationship of a *Grundton* with the ambitus signalized by the cantus-clef combination, allow him to construct a system of twenty modalities, to one or another of which every composition in the Haberl edition is unequivocally assigned. "Vestiva i colli" turns out to be high-clef cantus-durus, which may be observed, and Aeolian, because its *Grundton* (sc. final triad) is the degree A. (Hermelink calls this mode "Fis-Aeolisch", which raises other questions here irrelevant.) In a sense "Vestiva i colli" is his prototype for this mode, for Hermelink used the Agnus from Palestrina's *Missa Vestiva i colli* as the demonstration piece for Fis-Aeolisch in his book. Yet there is no reason beyond the assumed tonic — for which concept there is no explicit practical or theoretical 16th-century warrant — for calling this piece Aeolian. Hermelink himself points out the close connection of his Fis-Aeolisch with his H-Dorisch (cantus-durus/high-clefs, *Grundton* degree D). Example 1 shows Hermelink's diagram of the constituent tones of the two modes as they appear first, and then the illustration of their close relationship, to which he comments:

> As we already saw in the general remarks on the Aeolian, there exists a relationship between the Fis-Aeolisch and the Cis-Phrygisch. Yet in our tonality, as mentioned, the turn towards the Phrygian does not turn up so frequently; a stronger connection is operative, that to the H-Dorisch. It results from the placement of the fourth in the domain auxiliary (Nebenbereich) to the constituent tones (p. 140).

Ex. 1

One can see that it is only the placement of the square note-head signalizing the Grundton that makes any basic distinction between these two modes, Fis-Aeolisch and H-Dorisch. Examination of Palestrina's music, in particular his madrigals, shows that there is indeed a large group of cantus-durus high-clef pieces, some of which end with an A triad

---

[3] See Thomas Morley, *A Plain and Easy Introduction to Practical Music,* ed. R. Alec Harman (London, 1952), pp. 274 and 114 respectively.

and some of which end with a D triad, but which are otherwise of the same harmonic-melodic type.

In Chapter 1 of his *Trattato . . di tutti gli tuoni di canto figurato* (Venice, 1525), Pietro Aaron observes, that "the cognition of the end (*fine*) is not cognition *per se* and therefore not always necessary". He had prepared this statement with the classic example of man as both rational and mortal, thus alluding to "formal" and "final" causes[4]. He then goes on to show that even if a proper modal final is present, a composition may still not be modal:

> and this is demonstrated by certain compositions which, having the ordinary and regular final [that is, ending with D sol re, E la mi, F fa ut, or G sol re ut], but lacking the ascent and descent of some of its species, are not said to be of any tone but (as was shown in Chapter 30 of the first book of another work of mine, *De institutione harmonica*) are merely called *Canti euphoniaci*[5].

With regard specifically to pieces ending with the degree A, Aaron had written earlier in the *Trattato,*

> if a composition (I speak always of masses, motets, canzoni, strambotti, madrigali, sonetti, and capitoli) ends in the position called A la mi re and there is no flat in the signature, the final will be common to the first and second tones with respect to confinality (*confinalità*) and also to the third with respect to difference (*differenza*), provided — as you will understand from what follows — that the procedure (*processo*) in the composition be suited to confinality or difference (Strunk, p. 208).

In Zarlino's argument for the propriety of sometimes understanding the conclusion of a composition ^o be something other than the "regular" *finalis* of its mode the justification is similarly made by an appeal to Aristotelian formal versus final causation. In Part IV, Chapter 30 of his *Istitutioni harmoniche* (2nd. ed., Venice, 1573) we read:

> . . . if we put these two species together, that is the diatessaron E and a and the diapente a and e, putting the latter above and the former below, there is no doubt that we have the form (*forma*) of the twelfth [Hypoaeolian] mode, contained within the third species of the octave arithmetically divided, so that that composition (*compositione*) that we judge to be of the fifth mode [Phrygian] turns out to have nothing of that Mode except the end, because it finishes on the degree E.

> But then even if the final degree of the mode is that from which (as from the end and not before) we ought to judge the composition (*cantilena*) — as some wish, inasmuch as everything is correctly judged from the end (*fine*) — we must not,

---

[4] Latin *species* and *finis* are translations of Aristotle's εἶδος and τέλος.
[5] Translations from Oliver Strunk, *Source Readings in Music History* (New York, 1950), p. 209.

however, understand that simply from that [final] degree can we come to a cognizance of the Mode on which the composition is based; for it is not to be thought that from that [in itself] should the judgment be made, but [rather] that we should wait until the composition has been brought to the end, and there judge correctly, since then the composition is complete (*perfetta*) and has its true Form, whence is taken the opportunity for making such a judgment. But [therefore] it is to be noted that from two things one can get the same opportunity: first from the form (*forma*) of the whole composition; then from its end (*fine*), that is, its final degree (*chorda finale*). Being that it is the Form that gives the essence to a thing, I would judge that it were reasonable that one have to make such a judgment not simply from the final degree, as some have wished, but from the form contained [as a] whole in the composition.

Hence I say that, having to judge any composition (*cantilena*) from such a form, that is, from its procedure (*procedere*), it is not improper that the principal [authentic] Mode be able to finish on the medial degree (*chorda mezana*) of its octave harmonically divided, and so [also] the collateral [plagal] Mode on the extremes of its octave arithmetically divided, leaving aside the final degree (*lasciando ad un canto la Chorda finale*).

Hermelink interprets this last sentence to mean that

Zarlino does not reckon it [the Finalis] among the secure critical characteristics because, as he says, the tenor closes sometimes also in the fifth and abandons the *Grundton* to another voice (*Dispositiones modorum*, p. 56).

Leaving aside any possible misunderstanding of Zarlino's final expression, there is every reason simply to take this passage at its face value: Zarlino provides an explanation for the commonplace E-major triad conclusion on pieces which, from their emphasis of the degrees E and A (as well as from other aspects of *procedere* and *ambitus*), he has to assign to his Hypoaeolian tonality, whose *finalis* is the degree A. It is Aaron's traditional eight-mode argument presented in Zarlino's rational twelve-mode terms.

Zarlino's discussions and examples of conflicts of species and final may be made to reveal much that is of crucial importance in establishing the background for analysis of 16th-century music. But from a follower of Zarlino we get something specific to "Vestiva i colli". Lodovico Zacconi's twelve modes include the degree A as an Aeolian *finalis*; yet on pp. 41-42 of his *Prattica di musica Seconda parte* (Venice, 1622) appears the following:

To compose the second Tone *per natura*, one has not only to make and use for the tenor the F-clef on the second line from the top, but also to put the same F-clef on the top line for the bass, and on the middle line for the contralto; and because the said Tone is much brighter (*molto più allegro*) than the first [Tone], what do the composers do? If they want to compose a tearful and sad song, they compose it in its natural place, using the aforesaid positions and clefs. But then when they want to compose for the same Tone something bright, that produces a cheerful effect, they compose it as is seen here, making use of the octave [transposition]:

Ex. 2

Secondo Tuono   disposto per natura delle proprie corde.

Il medemo trasportato all'ottava.

"Vestiva i colli", along with many other things, is in this tone thus transposed, which sufficing myself with having demonstrated and made apparent, I shall now get down to other things I have to say.

Zacconi's younger contemporary Adriano Banchieri had alluded to "Vestiva i colli' in the discussion of the second mode/second tone in his *Duo spartiti al contrapunto* (3rd impression, Venice, 1613), which forms part of his *Cartella musicale*. Unlike Zacconi, however, Banchieri evidently felt that the transposition so far upwards of the traditionally low-lying second tone forced a change from plagal to authentic:

This second Mode is like the second Tone, only it has the transposition for low instruments more; and similarly, transposing this last example [see Example 3 below] an octave higher works charmingly for high instruments, changing from Plagal to Authentic, as Palestrina has well shown in his sonnet "Vestiva i colli" (*Cartella musicale*, 115).

Ex. 3

Duo del secondo modo Plagale & secondo Tuono

Alto [sc. Tenore]

Per voci humane   [etc]   Per stromenti gravi

Basso   Trasportato una quarta sotto

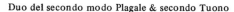

...chorde...   [...chorde...]   ...trasportato una quarta sotto

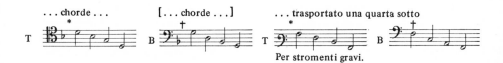

T   B   T   B

Per stromenti gravi.

[... questo ultimo esempio un'ottava sopra ...]

fughe,   chorde,   cadenze,   e finali.

Example 3 is copied and reconstructed after the *Cartella musicale*. Banchieri first gives the second mode "for human voices", in cantus mollis with normal clefs, illustrating it with a duo for bass and tenor. As can be seen from the "points of imitation, principal degrees, cadences, and conclusions" later on, the upper voice label "alto" is incorrect. Banchieri's transposition "down a fourth for low instruments" corresponds to Zacconi's second mode "per natura delle proprie chorde". The designations of the "points of imitation, principal degrees, cadences, and conclusions" for each of the four voice ranges follows Zarlino's doctrine slavishly. Example 3 shows the designations for the tenor and bass voices only, transposed (by me) up an octave from those given "for low instruments" in accordance with Banchieri's instruction. The example concludes with the tenor only of the illustrative duo, similarly transposed. This last corresponds with Zacconi's octave transposition of the second mode tenor.

Both Zacconi's outline and Banchieri's more complete exemplification derive from Zarlino's construction of the Hypodorian mode. Though they cite "Vestiva i colli" as an instance, be it of second mode an octave higher or of second transformed into first mode by the high tessitura, Palestrina's melodic-cum-modal procedure is considerably more complex, as a look at Example 4, showing the two tenor parts of the madrigal, will reveal. The example shows the settings for the first four lines of the *ottava*, which is repeated for lines 5 through 8. The ambitus of the parts is *a* to *aa*, which would suit the traditional second mode (an octave higher), as well as the Glarean-Zarlino Aeolian to which Hermelink assigned the madriagal. But where Zacconi and Banchieri divide the octave at *d* (illustrating the first-species fourth plus first-species fifth called for by rudimentary modal theory), Palestrina works in the lower part of the *a—aa* octave largely with the first-species fifth plus half-step above, a configuration common to Aeolian and Dorian. The first species fourth comes out strongly only in the opening fourth skip. Yet he normally does not complete the *a—aa* octave (with the first-species fifth *a—e* at the bottom) using the second species fourth *e—aa* at the top, which would form the Aeolian mode. Rather, he works chiefly with the other first-species fifth of the cantus durus, *d—aa*, plus the tone below.

Ex. 4

Example 5 is an outline sketch of Palestrina's registral shaping of the two tenor parts (and the cantus), showing at a glance the characteristic overlapping disposition and melodic separation of the two cantus-durus first-species fifths *a—e(f)* and *(c)d—aa*. The third species fourth *c—f* is a locus of melodic activity linking the two main registers: sometimes *c—e* is central, sometimes *d—f*. (Compare Hermelink's generalized disposition of Fis-Aeolisch and H-Dorisch cantus in Example 1 above.)

The cantus part is registered like the tenor but is prevented by the boundaries of the cantus-durus system from reaching the upper end of the hypodorian octave beginning from *aa*. Theorists around 1600 still followed the tradition of regarding the tenor part as the part from which the mode should be judged. But to include the cantus part and even to use it as the first part from which to begin analyzing the mode of a polyphonic

Ex. 5

[Tenor, Quinto „Vestiva i colli"]

[Soprano „Vestiva i colli"]

composition, as Hermelink does, seems to me quite proper, given the well recognized parallelism at the octave of ambitus in tenor and cantus parts. On pp. 11—12 of his *Musica poetica* (Rostock, 1606), Joachim Burmeister provides a useful term for the discantus-tenor (or altus-bassus) relationship, saying that

> voices which have one and the same degree (*sonus*) at the juncture of their modes, or, which have their [common] limit placed at the mean [between them], and thus are made similarly, are conterminous (*voces . . . coterminae*) (pp. 11—12).

The distribution of cadences in "Vestiva i colli" (of which about half are cantus-tenor cadences and half involve other pairings) is as follows: *ten* (or eleven) of all the cadences are with *aa*, normally with its lower octave or unison [6], *five* cadences are with *dd* and/or *d*, including the conclusion of the *ottava* (i.e., the *Prima Parte*); there is *one* cadence *each* to *f/f*, to *cc/c*, and to *ee/e* with *a* beneath. This distribution confirms the "Dorian" character of the piece, helping us to hear the *a-e* first-species fifth as paralleling the *d-aa* first-species fifth rather than being completed by the second-species fourth *e-aa*.

Given that "Vestiva i colli", despite its final A triad, is not "Aeolian", we may then wish to follow Zacconi and think of it as a high-register second-mode composition. We may even lean towards Banchieri's novel suggestion that it be regarded as having been forced into the authentic, first mode by virtue of its high tessitura. But we cannot directly prove that Palestrina himself in mid-century would consciously have regarded a composition like "Vestiva i colli" in modal terms at all. It is only late in his life, with the publication of his two books of spiritual madrigals, that there is direct evidence for intentional modalism in any compositions of Palestrina's to Italian texts. But Hermelink's analysis of the whole output by cantus-clef groups, whether those constitute modes or not, does group "Vestiva i colli" with other cantus-durus high-clef pieces ending with the degree A, which one can consider in conjunction with the similarly made pieces ending with the degree D. To those he lists should be added the fourteen "Pace non trovo" madrigals published in 1557. All are high-clef cantus-durus, eight of them ending with A, and six (including the last) with D [7].

In forming the conclusions of some of the madrigals of the "Pace non trovo" set, Palestrina sometimes had to go to considerable trouble to provide a finish with A or D

---

[6] There is one such cadence where the cantus goes up to *cc* rather than down to the unison. One *aa/a* cadence has *F* beneath, and one *aa/a* cadence has *D* beneath.

[7] The possible conflict between Aeolian and Phrygian tonalities for pieces ending with the degree A, which is discussed by both Glarean and Zarlino at some length, simply does not arise in Palestrina's work. See Example 1 and Hermelink's comment above.

to the phrase given by his model[8]. Yet this unified set of pieces confirms the impression one gets from the seven separate madrigals of this type in Palestrina's first book for four voices of 1555: in cantus-durus high-clef madrigals ending with degrees D or A, no distinctions in *ambitus, procedere,* or distribution of cadences can clearly be correlated with the different concluding sonorities, nor with the final cadences (which of course often precede the end and are not infrequently on the degree other than the root of the final triad). Carl Dahlhaus describes the general situation, with reference to a different pair of degrees, in his wide-ranging *Untersuchungen über die Entstehung der harmonischen Tonalität* (Kassel, 1967):

> The A-degree is related to the E-degree, but the connection comprises no dependence of the one degree upon the other. The fifth-relationship is nothing but a bilateral relation, which is perceived as such, without E being referred to A as dominant, or A to E as subdominant. ... If the fifth-(and analogously the third-) relationship is understood as bilateral, then the sense of a phenomenon which can negatively (and insufficiently) be described as "modal indecisiveness" is demonstrated. The notion of bilateral relation signifies that the fifth-relationship establishes a connection between the degrees E and A which is independent of the alternatives whether E is supposed to be *finalis* and A *repercussa* or conversely, A is supposed to be *finalis* and E *repercussa*. But if the sense of the relation between E and A has no reference to the indeterminacy of the *finalis*, then the decision between E and A can be left open, without comprehensibility being endangered. The bilateral relation is the primary element, the determination of a *finalis* the secondary element (pp. 201—202).

This "modal indecisiveness" can as well be attributed to the pieces here in question, including "Vestiva i colli", with respect to the degrees D and A. In fact Dahlhaus proceeds next to cite the first four motets of Palestrina's *Offertoria* of 1593, which are also of this type, as a case in point:

> ... the mode of settings 1—4 is intended as d-Dorian. The effective mode, however, is a Dorian-Aeolian "Modus commixtus" ... the essence of a Dorian-Aeolian "Modus commixtus" is not the alternation, the "modulation" between Dorian and Aeolian, but the "bipolar" relation, as a constant condition (p. 202).

With the second book of spiritual madrigals of 1594, the last publication of Palestrina's lifetime, there appears a substantial cycle of Italian madrigals arranged in cyclical order of the modes with a number of pieces in each mode. Furthermore, I would argue that the distinction of authentic from plagal is not only intended but realized[9]. Unfortunately, Palestrina's treatment of the clearly distinguished protus tonalities in the

---

[8] See James Haar, "Pace non trovo: a study in literary and musical parody". In: *Musica Disciplina* XX (1966), 95—149, especially pp. 130 ff.

[9] The use of only low cleffing in the deuterus tonality reflects the much greater practical closeness of the authentic and plagal forms of this tonality. In Glarean's Dodecachordon II. 18 and II. 23, on Hypophrygian and Phrygian respectively, the two modes are said in practice both to have their lower effective limit at C.

1594 collection gives no help with the modal analysis of "Vestiva i colli"; for he uses the cantus mollis for both plagal and authentic Dorian, as he had done for the set of ten authentic Dorian madrigals in the first book of spiritual madrigals of 1581 (nos. 9—18). But from the numbers 1 to 8 of the 1581 collection we can get some notion about what Palestrina might have thought about the modality of "Vestiva i colli", if not securely at and prior to the time of its composition, at least a decade and a half later.

"Vergine bella", the first of Palestrina's eight madrigals on Petrarch's famous poems, is extraordinarily like "Vestiva i colli". The scope and configuration of resemblances goes beyond style and seems to go even beyond the putatively modal similarities of cleffing, cantus, ambitus of parts, general motivic contours, and cadential preferences for D and A with E as a secondary degree of rest near the beginnings. All these features are common to a large group of compositions. But these two pieces are enough alike to raise a question whether Palestrina might even have intended to open his "Vergine" set — which had to compete with Cipriano's among others — with an evocation (without resorting to parody) of his by then very popular "Vestiva i colli".

"Vestiva i colli" is conventionally laid out to match its sonnet text: the two quatrains of the *ottava* have the same music, the fourth strain being repeated with line 8 to conclude the *Prima Parte* with the degree D; the *sestina* is through-composed, making up a *Seconda Parte* ending with the degree A. This same AAB design is followed, as a continuous one-part arrangement, in four of the "Vergine" madrigals, including "Vergine bella", where the music for lines 1—3 and lines 4—6 in the *fronte* is the same, while the rest is through-composed (sometimes with short immediate repetitions).

It may be that the resemblances in the subjects are, like the similarities in plan, reflections of general type rather than specific to the pieces: the "canzona" rhythms and any one of the motivic and sub-motivic *minutiae* considered separately are commonplace. Nonetheless, the resemblances in Gestalt are strikingly apparent, and if they are not thematic they must certainly be considered modal. The resemblance of opening subject shows most succinctly in the first entrances in the tenor registers proper, in answer to the upper-voice *exordium* (arrows and scale-degree letters in the examples indicate cadences):

Ex. 6

The parallel rhythmic and metric layout of the points of imitation (as well as subject contours) is also more simply to be seen with the entries of the pair of lower voices:

Ex. 7

The repeated music for the *ottava* of "Vestiva i colli" and the *fronte* of "Vergine bella" show the larger-scale modal Gestalt clearly, since the music's repeatability demarcates it as a large formal unit. In Example 8 the two cantus parts are aligned in such a way as best to illustrate the general shape of the music; what seem to be modally characteristic motives are marked with braces. The half-*fronte* of "Vergine bella" has one line less than the half-*ottava* of "Vestiva i colli", so the third strain in "Vestiva i colli" has no musical counterpart in "Vergina bella".

Ex. 8

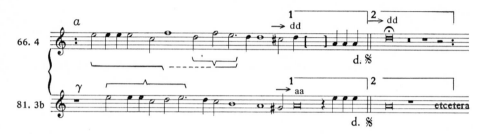

The eight "Vergine" madrigals as a set are clearly intended to represent the modes in cyclical order. The signatures, clefs, and endings are shown in the table below. The rubric for the ending shows 1) the voices forming the last two-voice cadence above whatever is the bass at that moment, 3) the "root" of the final (major) triad, and 2) the number of *tactus* between them.

Table I

1. Vergine bella	[♮]	G₂ C₂ C₃ C₃ C₄	$\frac{aa/a}{a}$	—4—	A
2. Vergine saggia	[♮]	G₂ C₂ C₃ C₃ C₄	$\frac{dd/f\#}{D}$	—0—	D
3. Vergine pura	[♮]	C₁ C₃ C₄ C₄ F₃	$\frac{aa/a}{A}$	—1—	E
4. Vergine santa	[♮]	C₂ C₃ C₄ C₄ F₄	$\frac{e/E}{C}$	—6—	E
5. Vergine sola [10]	♭	G₂ C₂ C₃ C₃ F₃	$\frac{f/F}{FF}$	—0—	F
6. Vergine chiara [10]	♭	C₁ C₃ C₄ C₄ F₄	$\frac{f/a}{FF}$	—0—	F
7. Vergine quante lagrime	[♮]	G₂ C₂ C₃ C₃ C₄	$\frac{g/G}{G}$	—0—	G
8. Vergine tale è terra	[♮]	C₁ C₃ C₄ C₄ F₄	$\frac{g/G}{Γ}$	—0—	G

[10] The flat signature does not signify transposition in the context of a composition intended to be in a tritus tonality.

Authentic-plagal pairs for the tritus and tetrardus tonalities are clearly distinguished by their motivic emphases, cadential preferences, and regular finals both in cadence and sonority. Distinctions in the *ambitus* of the conterminous pairs of voices are signalized and limited by systematic choice of high clefs for the authentics and low clefs for the plagals. The deuterus modes also show some contrast in cleffing, but only in the outer voices; this reflects that same rather close ambitus of the two deuterus tonalities referred to in Glarean's *Dodecachordon* II.18 and II.23, cited in note 9. Only in the first pair is there ambiguity: instead of being in two contrasted sets of still lower clefs (cf. Zacconi above), they are both in the same high-clef cantus-durus disposition, so that the ambitus of all voices is the same (including the high and narrow tessitura of the cantus parts). "Vergine saggia", however, both cadences and ends with D rather than A, and it has no counterpart to a strong cadential emphasis on *f* heard in lines 7—9 of "Vergine bella" (though there is an exceptional cadence with *g* for line 5 of "Vergine saggia"). The modal distinction is still far from clear, however, and even so astute a modern modal theorist as Bernhard Meier mentions in passing of this set that "Palestrina uses modes two to seven"[11]. I have to assume that "seven" is a mistake for "eight", incidentally, since the tetrardus tonalities are clearly distinguishable by *ambitus* and *procedere*. In the protus tonality, however, Meier seems quite reasonably to be seeing both "Vergine bella" and "Vergine saggia" as second mode up an octave, just as Zacconi had interpreted "Vestiva i colli".

The question arises as to whether Palestrina meant to distinguish the protus tonalities since he so carefully distinguished the others. There is good indirect evidence that he might so have intended in the *Offertoria* of 1593. Every indication of cleffing (hence ambitus in general) and melodic shaping is that Palestrina meant the first thirty-two motets, from Advent through Trinity Sunday, to represent a modal cycle in traditional numerical order. Carl Dahlhaus argues in his *Untersuchungen* (pp. 184-185, 189-190) that even if a distinction was intended it is not there in the music. But Dahlhaus's normally brilliant style of analysis is uncharacteristically superficial here, perhaps because he is using the pieces to refute Bernhard Meier rather than for themselves. He borrows three rigid modal criteria proposed by Meier, claims that they must needs be correlated to be useful, and applies them mechanically and inflexibly, claiming then that the resulting inconsistencies show that whether or not Palestrina *intended* to make plagal-authentic distinctions, he succeeded only in making distinctions of *maneria*. But it is Meier's criteria so applied that fail, not Palestrina's intentions. Dahlhaus seems to fall into the erroneous assumption that a great part of his study is aimed at extirpating, namely, that there must be a sort of universal background "modalism" at the very base of the 16th-century musical language, a system of "modalities" analogous to and contrasting strongly with the "tonality" of later eras. In this case Palestrina's intention is clear from the pattern of cleffing, and this in itself ensures that the *ambitus* of the various

---

[11] See footnote 10 in the Foreword to Volume 3 of his Rore edition. Cipriano de Rore, *Opera omnia* ... Vol. 3: *Madrigalia 5 vocum* (Rome, 1961), p. i.

voices will contrast, as can be seen in the cleffing of the eight deuterus motets below (nos. 9—16).

TABLE II

1. [♮] G₂ C₂ C₃ C₃ C₄ $\frac{aa/a}{a}$ —3— A	9. [♮] G₂ C₂ C₃ C₄ F₃ $\frac{ee/e}{a}$ —3— E	
2. [♮] G₂ C₂ C₂ C₃ C₄ $\frac{aa/a}{a}$ —0— A	10. [♮] G₂ C₂ C₃ C₃ C₄ $\frac{ee/e}{a}$ —1— E	
3. [♮] G₂ C₂ C₃ C₃ C₄ $\frac{aa/a}{a}$ —0— A	11. [♮] G₂ C₂ C₃ C₃ C₄ $\frac{cc/e}{a}$ —2— E	
4. [♮] G₂ C₂ C₃ C₃ C₄ $\frac{aa/a}{a}$ —0— A	12. ♭! G₂ C₂ C₃ C₃ C₄ $\frac{aa/a}{D}$ —1— A	
5. [♮] G₂ C₂ C₃ C₃ C₄ $\frac{dd/d}{D}$ —0— D	13. [♮] C₁ C₃ C₄ C₄ F₄ $\frac{e/E}{A}$ —2— E	
6. [♮] G₂ C₂ C₃ C₃ C₄ $\frac{dd/d}{D}$ —2— D	14. [♮] C₁ C₃ C₄ C₄ F₄ $\frac{e/c}{A}$ —1— E	
7. [♮] G₂ C₂ C₃ C₃ C₄ $\frac{dd/d}{D}$ —0— D	15. [♮] C₁ C₃ C₄ C₄ F₄ $\frac{e}{E}$ —3— E	
8. [♮] G₂ C₂ C₃ C₃ C₄ $\frac{dd/d}{D}$ —0— D	16. [♮] C₁ C₃ C₄ C₄ F₄ $\frac{e}{E}$ —4— E	

With complete inconsistency, the twelfth motet, uniquely in the set of thirty-two, is transposed. Though the ambitus of the tenors is set squarely in the *a-aa* octave, extended a degree or two downward, the exterior limitation on the upper reach of the cantus part helps to give its patterns a plagal effect, even though on the whole the piece seems more like third than fourth mode. Be that as it may, the cleffings of other seven deuterus pieces are in clear contrast, of 9—11 versus 13—16, reflecting the contrast in ambitus; and the subjects and *tessiture* in the cantus and its conterminous lower voice or voices absolutely support the intended distinction of authentic and plagal.

In the protus tonality the disposition of the first eight *Offertoria* is exactly parallel with that of the first two "Vergine" madrigals: all are in high-clef cantus-durus, but 1—4 have the final cadence and sonority on the degree A, while 5—8 have the final cadence and sonority on the degree D. Furthermore, there are enough pieces to justify interpreting the distribution of internal cadences. In both groups of four the majority of cadences are on the degrees A and D, with some on E. In the first set of four — those ending with A — there are also some cadences on the degree F, and occasionally a cadence on degrees G or C; in the second set of four, however, there are no cadences at all on degrees F, G, or C. The consistency of internal cadence pattern, correlated with the consistency in choice of final cadence and sonority, coupled with the cyclic modal ordering of the rest of the first thirty-two motets allow one to infer that Palestrina intended the first four *Offertoria* to *represent* (whether or not they actually *embody* it) specifically the first mode. By the same token, then, given the congruence of the first two "Vergine" madrigals of 1581 with this pattern in the *Offertoria*, I think one may assert quite confidently that Palestrina intended "Vergine bella" to *represent* the first mode in the cycle of Petrarch settings.

Earlier I cited Dahlhaus's characterization of the apparent modal ambiguity of the first four *Offertoria* as an instance of a "bipolar Modus commixtus" of Dorian-Aeolian, used to represent the general protus tonality. In the foregoing I have proposed that Palestrina intended those *Offertoria* and also "Vergine bella" to represent the authentic protus, distinguished with some consistency from other pieces used to represent the plagal protus. I can only offer some suppositions as to why he arranged them as he did. First, for whatever reason, in the "Vergine" and Offertory cycles — in contrast to the second book of spiritual madrigals — Palestrina labored to keep the modes in their proper and regular keys. Normally he much preferred high-clef and low-clef cantus-mollis for the protus modes; for the low-clef cantus-durus d-mode Hermelink's list shows only one madrigal, no motets, and very little else. Given Palestrina's decision, however, not to use cantus mollis for the protus tonalities, one can see why he might have chosen to make the dispositions this way. The registers for the voices in the untransposed second mode are very low, as Zacconi pointed out, and a tranposition up an octave is almost unavoidable if the second mode is to be used in the cantus durus. But in a modally ordered cycle, the authentic dorian could hardly be set at pitch-levels a half-octave *lower* than its own plagal! So if the representation of the *second* mode is in high clefs, so also must be the representative of the *first* mode, and some way other than ambitus must be found to distinguish them.

I don't think the first four *Offertoria* and "Vergine bella", as Palestrina both intended and composed them in their particular contexts of an ordered eight-mode cycle, show Dahlhaus's "modal indecisiveness", but I do think the term aptly characterizes the type on which they are modeled. "Vestiva i colli", the "Pace non trovo" madrigals, and other madrigals of the cantus-durus high-clef type ending with the degrees A or D are certainly modally indecisive, in the sense that they cannot be assigned unequivocally to a single mode in any closed system, be it of eight or twelve modes, on the basis of their musical structure; nor is there any direct evidence that there was *intention* (realized or not) that they be so regarded. What Palestrina did, then, when he needed to distinguish the two modes of the protus tonality *without using the cantus mollis transposition*, was to take an old, well-worked "bipolar" type and refine its distinctions. Most obviously, he assigned the A ending to represent the first mode, as its *confinalis*, and the D ending to represent the second, as its *finalis*; he seems further to have restricted — in our sample, to have eliminated — the F cadence and others from the second mode representations.

"Vestiva i colli", then, should not be considered originally to represent any particular mode at all, and certainly not one in a closed modal system either contemporaneous or contemporary. But in later years, when Palestrina needed something to stand for a cantus-durus first mode to be contrasted with a second mode having its proper degrees up an octave — most notably for the first madrigal of the "Vergine" cycle — it was to the type most prominently represented by "Vestiva i colli" that he turned. But if "Vestiva i colli" itself is to be given a modal designation, it can be neither Aeolian nor undifferentiated protus, probably not even "Dorian-Aeolian modus commixtus", at least as far as Palestrina's intention is concerned. Maybe we could call it "first mode retroactive", however. That has a nice grammarian's tone to it, in a nonetheless authentically musical mode.

ANTHONY NEWCOMB

Alfonso Fontanelli and the Ancestry of the Seconda Pratica Madrigal

What do we mean when we use the phrase "*seconda pratica*"? Even in the first decade of the 17th century, the phrase had two appreciably different meanings. In his *Dichiaratione* of 1607 [1], Claudio Monteverdi's brother Giulio Cesare stated as its defining characteristic that *l'oratione sia padrone del armonia è non serva* — an important general principle that all the composers listed by Giulio as composers in the *seconda pratica* could subscribe to. In terms of specific musical style, however, the group of men listed by Giulio turns out to be a rather heterogeneous lot. The broad and general nature of Giulio's use of the term may have been conditioned by the political and propagandistic purpose of his *Dichiaratione*. His list seems to have been structured not primarily according to musical but according to social and chronological criteria.

In the controversy between Claudio Monteverdi and the theorist Artusi (the stimulus for Giulio's *Dichiaratione*), the phrase *seconda pratica* is connected to a much more specific element of musical style: the handling of dissonance — in this case the handling of dissonance in the polyphonic madrigal. Giulio himself mentions that Claudio (in his always forthcoming but never produced book) will assert the treatment of consonance and dissonance as the basis of the new style. In addition, Claudio's letter of 1605, in which the phrase was first published, was attached to and referred to a set of polyphonic madrigals, and Artusi's attack was directed against dissonance treatment in certain polyphonic madrigals [2].

I should like here to use the phrase in this second, more restrictive meaning. If, then, the crux of the matter was, at least initially, the treatment of dissonance in the traditional and well-defined context of the voices of a polyphonic madrigal, where might we look for the ancestry of adventurous behavior such as Monteverdi's in the madrigals of Books Four, Five, and Six? In terms of specific musical techniques, this should be the immediate ancestry of the *seconda practica* as conceived by Monteverdi.

This crucial stage in the evolution of the new style can, I believe, be located in Ferrara in the middle of the 1590's. Various hints in the Monteverdi-Artusi controversy itself point in this direction. First, it was in Ferrara that Artusi was given the first letter written by Monteverdi's defender, *l'Ottuso Accademico* in 1599. Second, it was in a Ferrarese academy — where the *maestro di cappella* of the Ferarrese court, Luzzaschi, was present — that Artusi heard the then unpublished madrigals of Monteverdi to which he objected.

---

[1] The complete *Dichiaratione* is published in facsimile in *Tutte le opere di Claudio Monteverdi*, G. F. Malipiero, ed., Vol. X (Bologna, 1929), pp. 69—72; it is translated in Oliver Strunk, *Source Readings in Music History* (New York, 1950), pp. 405—412.

[2] The entire question of the concepts of dissonance treatment associated with the *seconda pratica* has been admirably treated by Prof. Claude Palisca in recent years. The best review of the problem is to be found in the "The Artusi-Monteverdi Controversy", in *The Monteverdi Companion*, Denis Arnold and Nigel Fortune, eds. (New York, 1968).

Finally, the musical ancestry of the *seconda pratica*, as sketched in the second part of the list of composers given by Giulio[3], leads to Ferrara. Both parts of the list agree in stressing Rore as the father of the new style, and our own historical perspective reinforces this view. In Rore's madrigals we find the abrupt contrasts both of rate of motion and of texture, the extension of the harmonic realm, the direct chromaticism, the strange intervallic vocabulary, the unusual spacings, the striking juxtapositions of style, and the extreme stylistic self-consciousness that characterize many *seconda pratica* madrigals. Yet Rore was only the beginning; we do not find in his works the anomalies of dissonance treatment cultivated by Monteverdi and certain of his predecessors. Rore did, however, leave behind him a school of composers that was to maintain his conception of the madrigal as a serious piece, almost expressionistic in its reflection of the emotional content of the text. The principal composers in this school were Luzzaschi and Wert, both of whom were probably pupils of Rore[4]. In opposition to the mindless hedonism of many madrigals of the 1570's and 1580's, Luzzaschi and Wert continued to develop the musical techniques for expressing vividly the emotional content of the text[5]. They were joined in the 1580's by an occasional outsider, most notably Marenzio[6]. These composers, together with Monteverdi's teacher Ingegneri, comprise the first section of the second part of Giulio's list — the professionals who foreshadowed the *seconda pratica* polyphonic madrigal in their works of the late 1570's and 1580's. They push to greater lengths the techniques developed by Rore, but they do not yet indulge in explicit violations of the traditional style of dissonance treatment.

As far as I know, such explicit violations first appear in a group of madrigals that is — at least as we see it reflected in published books — chronologically and geographically extremely concentrated. This group of madrigals comes from a homogeneous group of composers and a tiny period of time that falls between the modern, mostly Florentine noblemen of the first part of Giulio's list and the older Ferrarese and Mantuan professionals of the second part. I refer to the remarkable flowering of highly unusual madrigals to be found in the prints emanating from the court printer at Ferrara in 1594—97. The composers directly involved were Luzzaschi, Gesualdo, and Fontanelli; all were,

---

[3] The first part of the list is to be found at the end of the fifth paragraph of Giulio's *Dichiaratione*, the second part in the middle of the sixth. These parts of the *Dichiaratione* are also published in Emil Vogel, *Bibliothek der gedruckten weltlichen Vocalmusik Italiens ... mit Nachträgen von Prof. Alfred Einstein* (Hildesheim, 1962), Vol. I, p. 516.

[4] See Luzzasco Luzzaschi, *Madrigali per cantare e sonare a uno, due e tre soprani*, Adriano Cavicchi, ed. (Brescia and Kassel, 1965), pp. 7—8 and Carol MacClintock, "New Light on Giaches de Wert", in *Aspects of Medieval and Renaissance Music* (New York, 1966), pp. 598—601.

[5] For a more thorough consideration of the Ferrarese environment in the early and middle 1580's, see my forthcoming study on secular vocal music at Ferrara during the years 1579—97.

[6] See, for example, Marenzio's *Dolorosi martir* from his first book of 1580 (printed in *Publikationen älterer Musik*, Jahrgang IV, Vol. I, pp. 16—18) and G. M. Nanino's reaction to it in his third book of 1586 (to be published in my above-mentioned study).

at the time, in Ferrara. To them we should add Monteverdi, who by his own admission[7] spent a great deal of time in this musical environment and composed for it many of the madrigals of his Books Four and Five.

Why, then, did Giulio not stress this important group of composers in listing the ancestors of the *seconda practica*? I propose that he did not do so because the group belonged neither to the present, before which he was defending his brother, nor to the grand tradition of the past, to which he appealed for authority. It had been a fleeting occurrence in time, however important stylistically. Its members were neither all noblemen (as were the composers in the first part of Giulio's list) nor all professionals (as were the composers in the second). The court that had supported the group had vanished with the annexation of Ferrara by the Papal States in 1598. Giulio's list therefore does not reflect the Ferrarese school of the middle 1590's. He puts its three most important members — Gesualdo, Fontanelli, and Luzzaschi — into two separate parts of the list, because they belonged to two separate generations and two separate social layers.

In writing the history of the evolution of the *seconda pratica* as a musical style, however, we must assign a large place to the Ferrarese happenings of the middle and late 1590's. Once we recognize the importance of this moment in the history of the madrigal, we must also recognize how little we know about what led up to it. The numerous collections of madrigals dedicated to the new Ferrarese *concerto di donne* in the early 1580's contain as their most modern and representative pieces a kind of madrigal quite different from the *seconda pratica* madrigal of the 1590's: these earlier pieces tend to be bright, sonorous, frothy, canzonetta-influenced pieces — pieces exploring the possibilities of written-out diminution, pieces wherein scarcely a serious moment is allowed to interfere with the pastoral dancing, singing, swooning, and dying. Even the temperamentally serious Luzzaschi keeps his colors as bright as possible (see his Third Book of 1582 and his contributions to *Il Lauro Secco* of 1582 and *Il Lauro Verde* of 1583). The most important exceptions to this general trend away from the serious madrigal are to be found in Wert's Seventh and Eighth Books of 1581 and 1586 respectively[8], where he begins to explore the possibilities of using diminution for expressive purposes (see his setting of the line, *al fin sgorgando un lagrimoso rivo* from *Giunto a la tomba* in the Seventh Book) and of responding to textual extremes with textual or melodic extremes (see the beginnings of *Solo e pensoso* in the Seventh Book and *Forsennata gridava* in the Eighth). After 1586, perhaps when young Vincenzo Gonzaga became Duke in 1587, Wert seems to have turned his attentions back to Mantua and to a less sophisticated audience and group of performers, for his later books no longer show this degree of experimentation.

---

[7] See the dedication to his Fourth Book of 1603 (printed in Vogel, *Bibliothek*, Vol. I, pp. 504—05). It is likely that Monteverdi became a frequent visitor to the Ferrarese court only after 1594 (see Valeriano Cattaneo's letter of December 1594, quoted on p. 60 below).

[8] Giaches Wert, *Opera Omnia*; American Institute of Musicology (Corpus Mensurabilis Musicae, XXIV), ed. Carol MacClintock, Vols. 7 (1967) and 8 (1968).

During the years 1586—93 the number of musical documents — even the number of archival documents concerning music — coming from the Ferrarese court fell off sharply. Marenzio, especially after the death of his patron, Cardinal Luigi d'Este in December of 1586, turned away from the Este; Luzzaschi published no madrigal books between 1582 and 1594. How, then, are we to form some idea of the circumstances under which the new style of the mid-1590's took root and matured?

Happily two previously unknown bodies of material can help to answer this question. Both concern the composer and courtier Alfonso Fontanelli. Since one led me to the other, I shall introduce them in the order in which I encountered them.

There are in the Biblioteca Estense in Modena two volumes of autograph letters written by Fontanelli to his good friend Ridolfo Arlotti[9]. Each volume contains about 235 letters; the letters cover three decades, beginning in 1585 and ending with Arlotti's death in 1613.

Arlotti, like Fontanelli, came from a prominent family of Reggio, a city in the Duchy of Ferrara. He was born in the middle 1540's. In the late 1580's he became tutor, advisor, and private secretary to Duke Alfonso's nephew, Cardinal Alessandro d'Este. Arlotti, a friend of Tasso, Guarini, and other poets of the day, was himself a poet of considerable fame in Ferrarese circles. (Since Fontanelli was himself an amateur poet of some pretensions, we find him often sending madrigals to Arlotti for advice and asking for madrigals and pastorals from Arlotti in return). Of the very few poems by Arlotti that I have managed to trace, three appear among the texts set by Fontanelli, Gesualdo, and Monteverdi[10]. It seems likely that Arlotti supplied a good many texts for this group of composers.

In letter #145 of the first volume, I was intrigued to read the following passage:
Passage #1 From Letter #145, Volume I   From Ferrara, 10 July 1590

> Penso di voler for dar al Sr Duca una copia scritta a penna di Madregali in musica composti in varie volte da me in

> I intend to give to the Duke a manuscript collection of madrigals, set to music on various occasions by me in my

---

[9] The letters appear to have been brought together into two volumes just as they fell into the binder's hands; their ordering suggests no rational principle. The literary scholar Venceslao Santi clearly had seen these letters, for he printed most of Passages #6 and #7 below (the latter incorrectly dated 5 April 1591) in the appendix to his study "La Storia nella *Secchia Rapita*" (*Memorie della Reale Accademia di Scienze, Lettere ed Arti in Modena*, Serie III, Volume IX, Modena, 1910, pp. 439—440), without indicating his source. Girolamo Tiraboschi, in his *Biblioteca Modenese* (Vol. II, Modena, 1782, p. 328) refers to two volumes of manuscript letters said to be in the possession of Fontanelli's heirs. In the appendix volume of the same work (Vol. VI), he mentions (p. 118) that two volumes of Fontanelli's letters have recently come to the Estense library from the library of the Padri Teatini, to which they had been given by Cardinal Alessandro d'Este, Arlotti's patron. At the end of his life Fontanelli himself had joined the Teatini. It is impossible to tell if these are the same two volumes of letters as those referred to in Tiraboschi's Vol. II.

[10] Indeed, every one of Arlotti's poems that I have found that is not a sonnet is to be found set in one of the Ferrarese madrigal prints of the 1590's. (Sonnets were not often set by this group of composers.)

quest'otio, ma perche voglio farlo con qualche decoro hó pensato di mandar una polizza al Gianluca del tenor alligato. V. S. la veda et me n'avvisi il parer suo postillando ancu la polliza et acconciandola ove le par diffettiva con scrivermene le ragioni che la muoveranno. Potrà parer à V. S. vanità, ma io son in obbligo da un canto di gir confermando l'inclinat.^{ne} che S. A. mi mostra, et dall'altro di mostrar che così fatto studio e più tosto per compiacere et servir l'Alt.ª sua che per ch'io non desideri di passar più inanzi. In somma vorrei far capire ch'io sono svisceratiss.º al serv.º et modesto assai ma non debile ne di poca levatura. bacio le mani a V. S. . . .

V. S. avertisca ch'io voglio usar arte perche il Gianluca nel dar i madregali a S. A. le mostri anco la pollice.

inactivity, but, because I want to do so with some decorum, I thought I would send an accompanying letter to Gianluca [*Maestro della Guardarobba* to Duke Alfonso], a draft of which I have enclosed. Would Your Lordship look it over and give me your opinion on it, both annotating the letter itself and appending to it a note as to whether it appears defective, specifying your reasons. It may seem vanity to Your Lordship, but I am obliged, on the one hand, to reinforce the favor that the Duke shows me, and, on the other, to show that such efforts are rather to please and serve his Highness than because I desire to pursue them further. In short, I would like to make it understood that I am a most devoted servant and modest enough, but neither weak nor of little spirit.

Your Lordship should observe that I want to do all I can to insure that Gianluca, in giving the madrigals to the Duke, also shows him the letter.

My reaction was naturally to wonder if this collection of madrigals still existed. Of the few manuscript anthologies still in the Biblioteca Estense, one anonymous collection seemed, from its general description and aspect, to offer the possibility of being the collection referred to by Fontanelli. Upon closer inspection, one of the madrigals in this collection turned out to be identical with the madrigal ascribed to Fontanelli (his first published madrigal) in the printed anthology *La Gloria Musicale* of 1592[11].

The manuscript in question, Biblioteca Estense Mus. F 1525[12] is a set of five part books, bound in parchment. All are written in the same hand, with elaborate capital letters for the first word of each text. The anthology contains fifteen complete madrigals, three of which have two sections and the last of which, a canzona, has six sections.

I believe that this is the collection referred to by Fontanelli in his letter of July 1590. The evidence for this conclusion is as follows: The collection contains one madrigal that

---

[11] Vogel, *Bibliothek*, Sammlung 1592[5].

[12] See *Catalogo delle opere musicali . . . Città di Modena, R. Biblioteca Estense* (Parma, without date), (*Bollettino dell'associazione dei musicologi italiani, Serie VIII*), p. 299, col. I, where a list of textual incipits is given.

we know to have been composed by Fontanelli before February 1592. All the other madrigals in the collection share with the madrigal that we can identify some rather uncommon stylistic traits, which are similar to traits displayed in Fontanelli's later printed books of madrigals: a considerable use of the general pause, of harsh accented passing-tone dissonances in minims and in two or three voices at once, of imitative lines doubled in thirds or sixths, of abrupt contrasts of tempo and style, of cadences where all but one or two voices drop out before reaching the tonal goal, and of intricate imitative sections in short rhythmic values. Finally, the long canzone, a setting of which closes the anthology, is by Fontanelli's close friend Arlotti [13].

Let me now turn to biographical matters. I shall be concerned here mainly with the 1580's and early 1590's, when Fontanelli was connected with the Este court at Ferrara. The Arlotti letters, together with a few other spotty sources, can give us a fairly complete idea of his movements at this time. More interesting, they can give us some idea both of his impressions of the court during those crucial years and of his efforts to search out his own place there.

Fontanelli was born in 1557, the first son of a minor nobleman, lord of a territory ceded by the Dukes of Este. We may perhaps infer from the dedication of Gherardini's First Book of madrigals and from Fontanelli's continuing association with Horatio Vecchi throughout his career [14] that Fontanelli was, like Vecchi, a student of Salvatore Essenga in Reggio, probably in the middle 1570's. We know nothing else about the years of his youth.

In the winter of 1584—85, he was still in Reggio, where he helped to supervise the festivities for the visit of the Duke and Duchess of Ferrara [15]. At this time he appears to have drawn to himself the attention of the Ferrarase court, for he went into the service of Duke Alfonso's uncle, Don Alfonso d'Este, Marchese di Montecchio, at sometime between late 1584 and April 1586 [16]. That Gherardini dedicated his first book of madrigals (printed by the Ferrarese court printer Baldini) to Fontanelli in May of 1585 seems to suggest that Fontanelli was already known in the Ferrarese court at that time. In any case, he did not stay with Don Alfonso long, for from 1 April 1586 he appears as a gentleman of the court on the salary rolls of Don Alfonso's son, Don Cesare d'Este (the future Duke of Modena). From this position he began rapidly to penetrate into the inner circles of the Ferrarese court. From the letter below, written during his first months as a gentleman of Don Cesare, we can gather that Fontanelli had already determined to use his musical ability as a means of drawing himself closer to the music-mad Duke

---

[13] The canzone, attributed to Arlotti, is printed in *Rime degli illustrissimi Sig. Accademici Eterei,* Ferrara (Baldini), 1588. This collection was first printed in Padua in 1567 (Tiraboschi, *Biblioteca Modenese,* Vol. I, p. 110), and the dedicatory letter to the 1588 volume suggests that the later volume was a simple reprint. I have not been able to ascertain, however, whether Arlotti's canzona is indeed in the first edition of 1567.

[14] See the letter of 3 July 1589 (Passage # 4 below) and Vecchi's dedication to the reprint of Fontanelli's first book of five-voiced madrigals (Vogel, *Bibliothek,* Vol. I, p. 244).

[15] Tiraboschi, *Biblioteca Modenese,* Vol. II, p. 323.

[16] Tiraboschi, *Biblioteca Modenese,* Vol. II, p. 323—324.

Alfonso. As we shall see, this technique was to meet with considerable success in the next five to six years and was to place Fontanelli in a highly ambiguous position, not unlike that of the famous bass Count Giulio Cesare Brancaccio ten years before[17]. Both men were minor noblemen who used their fine musical abilities to gain them distinguished and well-rewarded positions in an important court. Once there, however, both had to resist as socially demeaning any implication that their position in court smacked in the slightest of the professional musician's. Fontanelli, at least, was slightly luckier than Brancaccio in that he was younger, more flexible, and not primarily a performer.

Passage # 2   From Letter # 190, Volume II   From Ferrara, 25 August 1586

Il mio madregale doveva andare al cospetto di queste Altezze per mezzo del Luzzasco, ma doppo l'havermi detto egli un paio di volte che la pᵃ volta che si canti a l'impᵃ lo metter[ebbe] [18] inanzi, non hó più inteso altro. Quel dí ch'io ci fui non si fece tal sorte di musica, molti altri giorni anco di novo pur così, onde non ci e l'occasione o pur il sudº Luzzasco non se ne vuol servire. Talche concludo ch'il poverello si morrà di quella morte che fece già la b.m. [beata memoria] del Dialogo delle tre Ninfe. una sola cosa mi conforta che questo o [non?] sara sentito, o sara cantato come si déé, la dove quel disgr[atiato] [18] fù trattato di maniera, che mai più ardirìa di comparire, benche forse (per fattura di mio novizzo) non ne fosse affatto indegno.

My madrigal was supposed to go before their Highness through the agency of Luzzasco, but, after his having told me a couple of times that, the first time one read new music, he would put it forward, I have heard nothing further. The day I was there, they did not do that kind of singing. And so on for many days, whence [I gather that] either the occasion has not arisen or else the above-mentioned Luzzasco does not want to take advantage of it. Thus I conclude that the poor little thing will die the same death as the late lamented Dialog of the Three Nymphs. One thing alone consoles me: [the new piece] will be heard and sung as it should be, whereas that poor [dialog] was treated in such a manner that it would never again dare to show its face—although perhaps, as a product of my apprentice years, it was not unworthy of such treatment.

The court of Ferrara became particularly famous in the 1580's for its concerts of madrigals, presented almost daily to Duke Alfonso and his wife in their private apartments. The singers, one to a part and including from two or four ladies, were highly

---

[17] See Angelo Solerti, "Ferrara e la corte estense nella seconda metà del secolo XVI" in *I Discorsi di Annibale Romei*, Città di Castello, 1891, pp. LXI—LXII, or my own forthcoming study (cf. footnote five).

[18] The edge of the paper has crumbled away here. Did Fontanelli omit *non* in the passage immediately preceding the second instance of this crumbling? Did he mean to say "... either [the new piece] will *not* be heard, or it will be sung as it should be ..."?

skilled musicians and rehearsed extensively together; in their concerts they either sang
by memory richly ornamented, pre-rehearsed pieces or read from part books the new
music coming into the court. This is the group that Fontanelli in the above letter mentioned having heard. He had written of the occasion more extensively in a letter of the
previous day:

Passage # 3   From Letter # 32, Volume I   From Ferrara, 24 August 1586

Hieri fui alla musica. mi disse il s^r
Duca che poi che l'altro di non ci fui,
voleva ch'io me la godessi da mia posta
con maggior commodità. et così ordinò
che si facessero tutti i concerti che
s'erano fatti il giorno istesso che ci fu il
Card^{le 19} onde per spatio di due hore io
hebbi buoniss° tempo. Io mi vò confermando nel dubio quella musica camini
verso l'Occidente, non tanto per la decli-
natione del Principe, quanto per la de-
bilitatione della voce delle Dame, che
fornite di pancia, et d'altre cond.ⁿⁱ così
fatte, pare a me c'habbiano raucedine
più del solito. Pure sono Angeli. Io non
ci tornarò perche non fui invitato. et
essendosi usata diligenza perch'io sen-
tissi ogni cosa in un giorno, ho interpre-
tato, che non sia bene ch'io mi dome-
stichi, come già solevo quando m'era
data l'udito.

Yesterday I was at the concert. The
Duke said to me that, since I had not
been there the other day, he wanted me
to enjoy it from my seat in complete
comfort. Thus he ordered that all the
pieces that had been done on the occasion of Cardinal [Vincenzo Gonzaga]'s¹⁹
visit be done for me, with the result that
for two hours I had a great good time.
My suspicions are becoming confirmed
that those concerts are going downhill,
not so much through lack of enthusiasm
on the part of the Duke as through the
falling off of the voices of the ladies,
who are accumulating bellies and other
such accessories, and seem to me somewhat hoarser than usual. And yet they
are heavenly. I shall not return because
I was not invited. From the fact that
one was careful that I should hear
everything in a single day, I inferred
that I would not do well to make myself at home there, as I was beginning
to do when I was accorded the privilege
of hearing them.

Fontanelli's amusing impression of the Duke's *concerto di donne* at this point on its
rapid trajectory across the Italian musical horizon agrees with the interpretation that I
have advanced elsewhere (see fn. 5): that the Duke's *musica secreta* had, by 1586, reached
the peak of its excellence and vitality, had thrown off several important satellites, and
had begun its slow decline.

¹⁹ Letter # 130 of Vol. II makes clear that this was Cardinal Gonzaga. It must have been Cardi-
nal Vincenzo Gonzaga, since Scipione Gonzaga did not receive the purple until the following
year.

In early 1587, Fontanelli was harnessed with the task of protecting Don Cesare's interests in the estate of Cardinal Luigi d'Este, who had recently died. This task kept him in Rome from February through September. Although no letter from this period deals specifically with music, Fontanelli almost certainly took part in the world of Roman secular music during his stay. His two long sojourns in Rome in 1586 and 1587 clearly influenced both his choice of texts and his musical style in the anthology of 1590.

Shortly after returning to Ferrara from Rome, Fontanelli was given the advancement towards which all in his position aspired: he was accepted as a gentleman of the Duke's court (with over twice his previous salary). Unfortunately, he was drawn away from Ferrara by personal matters almost immediately after his promotion and was more often in Reggio or Parma than in Ferrara for the next year. Not until June 1589 could he settle down in Ferrara to enjoy the delights of life as a gentleman of the Duke. From that time onward, however, Fontanelli was with the court and privy to all its intrigues, conversations, and concerts. Much of his excitement at his new surroundings he passes on to his friend Arlotti in newsy letters that give a vivid picture of court life in the late 16th century. One letter of July 1589 is particularly interesting to us, for it tells us how Fontanelli set about making his presence felt as a musician in this surrounding.

Passage # 4   From Letter # 179, Volume I   From Ferrara, 3 July 1589

Il mio mestiero é stato di far cantar certe villanelle d'Horatio Vecchi a un cotal mio modo ch'a S. Alt.ª há grattato l'orecchie assai, di leggere del Boccaccio tré o quattro novelle per giorno, giuocar' al pallone, dir facetie di quelle ch'in effetto hanno dell'insipido, ma perche mi si parton dal cuore hanno una certa gratiazza [?], et in somma far del conversevole à più non posso facendo dello sprezzator del sussiego in tutto et per tutto.

In somma (notate) ognuno doppo le spalle dice bene di me più del quel ch'io merito, ma non mi trattano però infatti com'io merito, se ben poi anco a dir il vero non hó di che dolermi.

My occupation has been to sing certain villanelle by Orazio Vecchi in a particular way of mine, which rather tickled the ears of His Highness, to read three or four tales of Boccaccio per day, to play ball, to make jokes of the sort that are, in truth, rather insipid, but— because I tell them naturally and sincerely—have a certain charm, and, in short, to be as sociable as can be, opposing stuffiness wherever I find it.

In short (notice) [perhaps a reference to his use of the phrase directly above] everyone privately speaks well of me, more than I deserve; but they do not treat me as I deserve, even if, to tell the truth, I have nothing to complain about.

One postscript to a letter of early 1590 is of more than passing interest, for it enables us to identify the author of a text set by both Gesualdo (in his Fourth Book of 1596) and Monteverdi (in his Fourth Book of 1603, dedicated to the memory, as it were, of the Ferrarese court).

Passage # 5   From Letter # 52, Vol. II   From Ferrara, 19 Feb. 1590

Questa sera alla musica cantandosi il Madregale Luci serene e chiare, et lodando il s^r Gio: Bardi[20] le parole S. A. há detto che sono dell'Arlotti, huomo solito a far di buone cose in questo genere ma ch'al presente fá prof[essi]-one d'attender a cose più gravi, et ch'egli è quel ch'è col s^r Don Aless^ro d'Este à Pad^a et molte altre cose che è solita di dire quando si vuol far honore di una persona.

During this evening's concert the madrigal *Luci serene e chiare* was sung, and Sig. Giovanni Bardi[20] praised the text. His Highness then said that it was by Arlotti, who was wont to do good things of this sort but who at present was attending to more serious matters with Don Alessandro d'Este at Padua — and many other things of the sort that one says when one wants to do honor to a person.

Since neither Gesualdo nor Monteverdi were yet connected even indirectly with the Ferrarese court and since their settings of this text seem to have been composed later in the decade, we must be dealing with another setting here. I do not know of another setting of this text by a composer in the Ferrarese circle; it is probable that the setting heard in 1590 either never was published or has been lost.

The next letter of interest to us is the one of 10 July 1590, from which I have quoted in Passage # 1 above. We can now understand somewhat better the dilemma to which Fontanelli refers at the end of this letter. Fontanelli wants to make himself more valuable to the Duke by playing on the Duke's love of music and pride in his chamber concerts. On the other hand, he wants to dissociate himself from the posture of the common musician seeking patronage. This, of course, is the reason for the coy veneer of anonymity surrounding his first printed madrigal collection of 1595[21]; this may well also explain the similar anonymity of the manscript anthology. The very anonymity of the manuscript can thus be seen as another link (admittedly a tenuous one) connecting the anthology with Fontanelli.

I shall present together a group of letters, written over a two-year period, that seems to reflect a single trend of thought on Fontanelli's part. It helps us to form a bridge from the canzonetta days of his first activities at Ferrara to the eruption of the new style in the middle 1590's. Of the three composers directly involved in this stylistic movement, the leader and source of inspiration seems to have been Luzzaschi[22]. One might almost say that he played for the two younger men a role somewhat similar to that played by

---

[20] Bardi, together with Jacopo Corsi and Ottavio Rinuccini, visited the court for three weeks in February 1590. They were showered with favors by the Duke, who "held them every evening till 11:00 P.M. to hear the *concerto delle Dame*, which is always different". See Florence, *Archivio di Stato, Archivio Mediceo*, f. 2906, dispatch of 5 February 1590, or my forthcoming study (cf. footnote 5).

[21] See Vogel, *Bibliothek*, Vol. I, pp. 243—244.

[22] For evidence that Gesualdo also looked up to Luzzaschi as his mentor, see Anthony Newcomb, "Carlo Gesualdo and a Musical Correspondence of 1594" in *The Musical Quarterly*, Vol. LIV (1968), pp. 429—431.

C. P. E. Bach for Haydn, in that he seems to have held out for seriousness of emotional expression during a period dominated by frivolity, hedonism, and unrestrained sensuousness, by polyphonic simplicity, and by the canzonetta and the pastoral madrigal. In the following letters we can, I think, see Fontanelli yielding to the general taste for lighter pieces with an explicit reluctance that contrasts clearly with his attitude of 1589 (cf. Passage # 4 above). We can also see his attitude toward Luzzaschi changing from the diffidence and mild distrust of 1586 to a posture of great admiration and affection.

Passage # 6　From Letter # 140, Vol. I　From Mesola, 5 Dec. 1590

Alla Mesola et nelli altri luoghi fuori ho manco tempo d'attender a componimenti di musica che in Ferrara[,] con tutto ciò V. S. havrà di quà da Natale il suo Madrigaletto composto a guisa d'aria con intentione che solo il soprano habbia a farsi sentir con la voce, et l'altre parti nel clavichordo o in altro strumento. Di questa sorte di canti io non ne fó volontieri [sic], perche se non ci metto studio mi par di gettar l'opera, et se vel metto mi par di gettar il tempo. Se'l Madregal ch'ella scrive non mi dèe obligar a termine alc° io la riceverò volentieri per metterlo poi in musica a mia sodis.ne quando verrà la vena. ma se V. S. ha altra intent.ne io non me n'affaticarò volentieri, se non quanto non potrei far di manco s'ella me'l comandasse. non me'l commandi però di gratia se non se ne cura più che mediocremente. Ma se può darmelo con la condit.ne detta di sop.a me ne favorisca.

At Mesola and at the other places outside of the city I have less time to compose than in Ferrara. Nonetheless Your Lordship will have his madrigal by Christmas, set as a solo song, with the intention that only the soprano should be sung, while the other parts should be played by the clavichord or other instrument. I do not willingly write this kind of music, since, on the one hand, if I put no effort into it, I produce a worthless piece, yet on the other, if I put effort into such a piece, I waste my time. If the madrigal that you are writing does not carry with it any deadline, I shall receive it gladly and set it to my satisfaction when the spirit moves me. But if Your Lordship has other intentions, I shall not labor over it happily — although I would not be able to do any less than you ask of me. Please do not ask it of me, however, if it does not mean a great deal to you. If, on the other hand, you can give it to me under the above conditions, send it on.

Passage # 7　From Letter # 23, Vol. I　From Ferrara, 2 Feb. 1591

Ho caro che V. S. sia risanata. le rimetto la copia della lettera del Cav. Guarino. et le mando l'aria sop.a le parole ult.e che mi commandò. Questa é una sorte di composit.ne ch'io non fo volentieri. faccia conto V. S. d'esser ricer-

I am glad to hear that Your Lordship's health is restored. I am returning to you the copy of the letter of Cav. Guarino. I am also sending you the setting of the latest text, as you asked of me. This is a kind of composition that

cata a far parole d'una villanella quando sono io ricercato di cosa simile. Se costesti musici la sentono se ne rideranno se non sanno l'uso a che deve esser impiegata. Sappia e voglia dirlo V. S. e sop.ª tutto che alc° non si meravigli se le parti fossero alle volte sconcie, per che il soprano solo ha da esser cantato. ci ho messo que' ritornelli non perch'io sia ben risoluto che vi stiano bene ma perche chi vuol servirsene sia in sua libertà. In tutti i casi a servirsene o non[,] non bisogna che si fermino più della tenuta delle note, et o ricominciando o seguendo non si dèe far posata alcuna.

V. S. si raccordi però ch'io non voglio a modo alcuno passer per professor di musica. La 7ⁿ⁰ passata habbiamo havuto qui Don Cesare d'Avalos al quale habbiamo fatto miracoli di musiche oltre gli altri favori ... 23 La Sigª Lavª suprale da leggere a canto il fuoco con la plica V. S. a favorirla della sua Pasto-Sʳª Clelia, et promette che non sarà vista da alcuno altro ne potrà esesrne tratta copia.

I do not do willingly. (Your Lordship may rely on being asked to write words for a villanella, when I am asked for such a thing.) When the musicians over there hear it, they will laugh at it, if they do not know the purpose that it is to serve. Please be aware of this and tell others; especially let no one be surprised if the parts are sometimes defective, since the soprano alone is meant to be sung. I have included repeat signs not because I am determined that they must go there, but in order that whoever wants to use them is at liberty to do so. In any case, whether one uses them or not, it is not necessary to wait longer than the value of the notes, and one should not make a pause, either in repeating or going on.

Your Lordship should remember, however, that I in no way want to pass as a professor of music. Last week we had here Don Cesare d'Avalos, for whom we produced musical miracles, in addition to other kindnesses ... 23

Signora Lavinia begs Your Lordship to send her your pastoral play to read beside the fire with Signora Clelia; she promises that it will be seen by no else, nor will she allow it to be copied.

Passage # 8   From letter # 181, Vol. II   From Ferrara, 6 May 1591

Rido vedendo che V.S. loda un Madregale del Giardino de' musici ferraresi 24 credendo che sia mio. Voglio dir una parole arrogante, non ci é madre-

I am amused to see Your Lordship praise a madrigal from *Il giardino de' musici ferarresi* 24, believing it to be mine. I am going to say something arro-

---

23 See Anthony Newcomb, "Carlo Gesualdo" in *The Musical Quarterly*, Vol. LIV, p. 429. In September 1591 Scipione Dentice sent to Duke Alfonso a book of madrigals — probably his first book for five voices, dedicated in August 1591 to Duke Alfonso — together with a letter, which mentions how impressed the Neapolitan d'Avalos had been by Alfonso's music.

24 A printed anthology of madrigals, dedicated on 1 April 1591 to Duke Alfonso. See Vogel, *Bibliothek, Sammlung* 1591⁵.

gale su quella copia ch'io mi compiacessi d'haverlo fatto salvo uno del Luzzasco alla cui firma io però non potrei attingere. hor andate s^r mio et fondate che credito possiate haver con me quallhor mi celebrate alc^a mia simil compositione. In istampa però V. S. é sicura di non dover veder alc^a cosa mia.

gant: there is not a madrigal in that collection that I would be pleased to have composed, save one by Luzzasco, to whose signature, however, I could not aspire. You had better set about reenforcing whatever prestige you still have with me after complimenting me for such a composition. Your Lordship, however, can be certain of seeing nothing of mine in print.

Passage # 9 From Letter # 121, Vol. II From Ferrara, 29 Aug. 1592

Scrissi anco a di passati a favor d'un certo giovine Ferrarese che trovandosi fuori vorrìa trattenimento h^{esto} [honesto?] et ciò feci a instanza di Luzzasco del quale non ho cinque huomini al mondo ch'io ami più.

I also wrote a few days ago on behalf of a young Ferrarese who, having ventured out into the world, would like a respectable position. I did so at the request of Luzzasco, whom I hold among my most beloved friends [lit.: than whom there are not five men in the world that I love more].

Passage # 10 From Letter # 156, Vol. II From Ferrara, 2 Jan. 1593

La sig^{ra} Duchessa d'urbino ha auta l'aria musichale sopra le parole della canzonetta di V. S. che comintia, quando lietta ti mostri in Ciel sereno, et è venuta in gran desiderio d'haver l'altre parole smarrite tutte de ma dal primo quartetto in poi.

The Duchess of Urbino received the setting of Your Lordship's canzonetta text that begins, *quando lieta ti mostri in ciel sereno*, and wants greatly to have the rest of the words, all of which after the first four lines I have forgotten.

We can draw a few important points from these passages. First, Fontanelli was still, as in passage # 4 of 1589, dealing with canzonettas — this time with composing not with singing them. In 1590—91, however, he took great pains to make clear how unhappy he was about this state of affairs, as we can see from passages # 6 and # 7 above. Passages # 6, # 7, and # 10 make clear that this kind of music continued in demand in the circles in which Fontanelli worked. This impression is reinforced by a note to the Duchess of Ferrara from Valeriano Cattaneo, an official of the Mantuan court. Cattaneo wrote as follows from Mantua on 19 December 1594 [25]:

[25] Modena, *Archivio di Stato*; *Particolari,* Cattaneo. The Duchess of Ferrara, Margherita Gonzaga, was the sister of Duke Vincenzo of Mantua.

Mando à V. A. quattro canz.te di ms Claudio Monteverde, musico quì del Sr Duca, conforme a quanto Lei mi commandò, Le quali sono simili à quelle che già mandò Don Bassano per quanto si raccorda, però per maggior sodisfattione della Sig.ra Duchessa d'urbino [26], se S. A. manderà paruole, et anco avvisi del stile che sarebbe di suo gusto, sarà servita in quanto si può.

In conformity with the orders of Your Highness, I am sending four canzonettas by Mr. Claudio Monteverde, a musician here of the Duke. The pieces are similar to those already sent by Don Bassano, as far as one can remember. However, in order to provide for the greater satisfaction of the Duchess of Urbino [26], if Your Highness will send texts, and also some indications of the style that would be to her taste, she will be served to the limits of our abilities.

The Don Bassano mentioned here is almost certainly Don Bassano Cassola, a musician at the Mantuan court since at least 1587 [27]. Perhaps his were the canzonettas received in late 1592 (see passage ♯ 10 above). The identification attached here to Monteverdi's name *(musico quì del Sr Duca)* suggests that Monteverdi was not yet well known in Ferrara. Perhaps these canzonettas gained him entry there, and his close contact with the world of Ferrarese music took place during the last five years of the century.

Passage ♯ 8 makes it clear that Fontanelli resisted and held in contempt not only the canzonetta, but also the light canzonetta-madrigal: what one can gather about the style of the music in *Il giardino de' musici ferraresi* (only the Alto, Tenor, and Bass part books are known to survive) indicates that the madrigals therein were mostly in that style.

Finally, passages ♯ 8 and ♯ 9 make it clear that Fontanelli had by this time come to regard Luzzaschi as a very fine composer and close personal friend, an attitude also suggested by the passages from Fontanelli's letters of 1594—95 in my above-mentioned article in *The Musical Quarterly,* Vol. LIV.

All of this taken together would seem to suggest that, during the years 1589—92 Fontanelli's attitude toward secular vocal music had moved, perhaps under the influence of Luzzaschi, from the lighter to the more serious side of the stylistic spectrum. The patrons around him, however, were not quite ready to accept this view of music; they continued to ask for canzonettas.

This tension between what the inner development of the musicians involved was leading them to want to express and what their patrons demanded of them represents, I believe, the typical state of the nascent *seconda pratica* style in Ferrara during the decade preceding 1594. At the root of the movement was Luzzaschi, who bent with the new wave of sensuousness yet held out, perhaps unconsciously and by the very nature

---

[26] The Duchess of Urbino was Lucrezia d'Este, the sister of Duke Alfonso. She had long been estranged from her husband and living at the Ferrarese court.

[27] See Carol MacClintock, *Giaches de Wert (1535—1596). Musicological Studies and Documents,* No. 17 (Rome, 1966), p. 48.

of his personality and compositional style, for a more serious orientation. One can see, for example, in his contributions to the Ferrarese anthologies *Il Lauro Secco* of 1582, *Il Lauro Verde* of 1583, *I Lieti Amanti* of 1586, and *La Gloria Musicale* of 1592 [28] that, although he had adapted himself as much as possible to the current climate, he remained dedicated to emotional expressivity and that his style remained serious and, in the context of the 1580's, even somewhat difficult. Towards the end of the decade Wert was no longer beside him as a powerful ally, but Fontanelli was gradually taking a position there [29]. With Fontanelli the emerging style had found a politically powerful proponent, for, by the early 1590's, both his charm as a courtier and his skill as a statesman had made him a valued member of the Duke's immediate entourage [30]. Fontanelli's influence with Duke Alfonso may have been a primary factor in preparing the way musically for the arrival of Gesualdo in 1594 and the launching of the new style in court-sponsored publications during the ensuing three years.

The tension between the style of the 1580's and the new style that some were beginning to develop can be seen in manuscript F 1525, which contains pieces written by Fontanelli probably between 1587—88 and the middle of 1590. Parts of the collection, while showing various stylistic characteristics associated with the followers of Rore—unusual intervallic vocabulary, abrupt contrasts of motion and style—are simple and diatonic in harmonic vocabulary and lapse often into the dance-like homophony of the canzonetta, even sometimes into triple meter. Other madrigals, however, are of a different cast. They use the grating cross-relations, the passing chords in long values, the re-attacked suspension dissonances (often in more than one voice simultaneously), the collisions of ornamental formulas, even the unprepared attacked sevenths that were to be characteristic of the *seconda pratica* madrigal of the late 1590's and early 1600's.

I do not intend to list elements of variety and of consistency in the style of the madrigals in this anthology. Instead I have selected for discussion a single piece, in order that the reader may discover how Fontanelli handles an entire madrigal at this stage of his development [31]. It is, of course, too much to ask of a single madrigal that it

[28] Vogel, *Bibliothek, Sammlungen* 1582 [1], 1583 [3], 1586 [6], and 1592 [5] respectively.

[29] For a reflection of this situation around 1585, see Tasso's dialog *La Cavaletta, o vero della poesia toscana*, where *il Forestiero Napolitano* (Tasso) calls upon *"lo Striggio e Iacches* [Wert] *e'l Lucciasco e alcuno altro maestro di musica eccelente"* to bring the madrigal back to the seriousness [*gravità*] that it had abandoned in recent years. For further information on this concern of Tasso's see Nino Pirrotta's forthcoming study, *"Note su Marenzio e il Tasso"*.

[30] For example, he accompanied Duke Alfonso on the crucial trip to Rome in the summer of 1591 to press the question of the Ferrarese succession with Pope Gregory XIV. These negotiations — the last hope for the Este dominion in Ferrara — seemed on the point of coming to a successful conclusion, when Pope Gregory died in October. Cf. Ludwig, Freiherr v. Pastor, *History of the Popes*, transl. R. F. Kerr (London, 1932), Vol. XXII, pp. 379—80 and Tiraboschi, *Biblioteca Modenese*, Vol. VI, p. 115.

[31] The madrigal is printed at the end of this study. One other madrigal by Fontanelli (*Io mi son giovinetta* from his Second Book of 1604) has been published (see *Monatshefte für Musikgeschichte* VIII, pp. 165—176, edition by G. Becker). The text of this later madrigal, incidentally, is not by Boccaccio. It is the same text used by Luzzaschi and Monteverdi in settings published in 1601 and 1603 respectively; its author is unknown.

exemplify all of the stylistic traits that I listed above. This single piece does, however, exemplify many of them, and it seems to be one of the most advanced and one of the best pieces of the collection: it is the madrigal that Fontanelli (or the compiler of *La Gloria Musicale*) selected for inclusion in that anthology of 1592. The text of the madrigal is as follows:

Com' esser può mia vita	How can it be, my life,
Che giamai non vi doglia	That you do not grieve
Del martir ch'io sostengo	At my bitter and intense
acerbo e forte [?]	suffering?
Ahi, che vostr'empia voglia [,]	Ah, that your pitiless will,
Che del mio mal non cura [,]	Which cares not for my
	misfortunes,
Tosto darà mi morte [;]	Will soon move to kill me;
Ch'intensa doglia gran tempo	For intense pain does not
non dura.	last for long.

Com' esser puo mia vita
Alfonso Fontanelli, in *La Gloria Musicale* (Venice, 1592), p. 9 [32]

[32] This transcription is based on *La Gloria Musicale* rather than MS F 1525 for reasons of appearance: because the beginning of each line is capitalized, the structure of the text is clearer in the printed anthology. There are three small differences between the musical texts of the two versions. In MS F 1525 the *Canto* and *Quinto* parts are exchanged, the last note in m. 3 of the *Canto* part (in my transcription) is prefexed by a sharp, and the second note in m. 35 of the *Altus* part is g'.

Fontanelli seizes upon the light, emotionally neutral tone of the first line of text as a pretext for exhibiting the kind of stylistic contrast and self-consciousness that is characteristic of so many madrigals (and, indeed, of some lighter forms) at the end of the century. He begins the piece in the transparent four-voiced homophony of the lighter forms, even employing the stereotyped dance rhythm found in *frottole* of 1500 through *scherzi musicali* of 1600. A bit of imitation for the beginning of the second line of text suggests a more complicated style. Then, at the words *del martir,* a broad cadential extension (mm. 5—7) takes us not only to the relative major, but also into the world of the serious madrigal. The third line of text is then given a fairly extensive and complex treatment involving the simultaneous imitative exposition of two contrasting motives. Especially noteworthy here are the strong dissonant clashes provoked by the rise of a second in the setting of the word *sostengo* against sustained notes above (see the bass in m. 14).

The most striking use of dissonance — and one that is a clear example of the unprepared dissonances of the *seconda pratica* — is reserved for the exclamation *Ahi* at the beginning of the fourth line of the madrigal. Here the middle part (I take this part, written in the alto clef, to be designed for a high tenor voice) sustains an f', the third of the preceding d-minor cadence, as the other supporting voices drop out below. Then, with the f' still sounding, the two sopranos enter above with the resonantly placed fifth e"—a'. Both tenor and first soprano abandon their notes right away, as if they had touched something hot. The pungent and brightly scored attacked dissonance has made its effect, however, especially after the previous somber cadence on d.

One should note that the strong cadences, the forceful and harmonic bass line, and the clear tonal design of this madrigal are not characteristic of the Ferrarese madrigal style of 1594—97, and hence do not appear often in Fontanelli's later madrigals. In this context, we may regard them as carried over from the clearly tonal style of the lighter forms.

After a rather neutral treatment of line five of the text, Fontanelli illustrates the desire for rapid death, indicated in the line six of the text, by hurtling through the line with one of the fugitive, rapidly vanishing swirls of close imitation that were to become so characteristic of the *seconda pratica* Ferrarese style after 1594.

For the last line of the text Fontanelli permits himself a broad and leisurely exposition of two similar scalar motives, related by free inversion. This kind of lush and sonorous music, which one would not be surprised to find in a Roman madrigal of the 1580's, represents yet another style in this single short piece. Like the strongly tonal bass lines in long note values, this is a kind of writing that will largely disappear from Fontanelli's madrigals published after 1594.

In *Com'esser può* three or four styles are juxtaposed, each of them in a fairly pure form, and each skillfully handled. One might suggest that it was the work of a talented young man searching for his own style. Indeed, Fontanelli does seem to have "purified" his own style of some of these traits in the first book of published madrigals in 1595. Most important for our concern here, however, is that, especially in his setting of lines three and four of the text, Fontanelli was willing to employ a harmonic palette considerably more unusual than that of any published madrigal that I know of before 1594.

One small question remains concerning the influence of Fontanelli in the early development of the *seconda pratica,* and this question leads us directly back to the Artusi-Monteverdi controversy of the beginning of the 17th century. In his article in the *Monteverdi Companion* to which I have referred above, Prof. Palisca raises the possibility that Fontanelli may have been the *Accademico Ottuso* who defended the new style in letters written to Artusi between 1599 and 1603 [33].

I believe that we should cross Fontanelli's name off the list of possible candidates, for the following reasons: First, Ottuso's letter, as printed in Artusi's *Seconda parte dell'Artusi overo Delle imperfettioni della moderna musica* (Venice, 1603), pp. 13—21, seems too

---

[33] See Palisca, "The Artusi-Monteverdi Controversy", pp. 142—145.

hysterical, too learned (the reader will recall Fontanelli's *"non voglio a modo alcuno passer per professor di musica"*), and too witless to be connected with the urbane, mildly cynical style of Fontanelli. Second, and most important, Fontanelli was an important nobleman at the Este court; he would never have let himself get embroiled in such an acrimonious public dispute with a mere music-theoretician, nor would the theoretician have been in a position to attack him is violently as Artusi did Ottuso.

The above conclusions are drawn from the non-musical evidence surrounding the dispute. When we turn to the musical evidence — the „*minime particelle*" from Ottuso's madrigals — which Artusi prints on pp. 50—51 of his *Seconda parte* of 1603, these conclusions are reinforced. I have been unable to locate the examples quoted by Artusi in any of Fontanelli's published or manuscript madrigals. This is, of course, not conclusive, since other madrigals by Fontanelli were doubtless circulating in manuscript in Fontanelli's time. The general style of the examples given by Artusi, however, makes it unlikely that they could, as an entire group, be by Fontanelli. It is true that some of the examples seem quite comprehensible in terms of the style of Fontanelli and Gesualdo in the late 1590's — provided one supplies the proper textual and musical context. Others are rendered incomprehensible by obvious printer's or copyist's errors — for example, an insufficient number of beats to fill the measure in one voice part. Two of the examples, however, seem musically comprehensible yet not typical of Fontanelli: one (bar two in Artusi's examples) has parallel octaves; a second (bar thirteen in Artusi's examples) has parallel fifths. Artusi singles out the parallel octaves in bar two for special comment and maintains that Ottuso had defended this practice to him in conversation. Fontanelli does not indulge in parallel perfect intervals in any madrigal that I have seen. His care in avoiding them makes it unlikely that he would have defended them in conversation. Admittedly, it is vaguely possible that Fontanelli would excuse the practice in the accompanimental parts of an *"aria"* such as he wrote for Arlotti in 1591 (cf. passage ♯ 7 above), that Artusi has drawn his example from such a piece, and that Fontanelli had indeed defended parallel perfect intervals under these particular circumstances.

The musical evidence, then, while leaning heavily against Fontanelli, is not absolutely conclusive either way. The considerations concerning the relative social positions of Fontanelli and Artusi seem to me to be much more so.

We should, then, almost certainly deny to Fontanelli the position of the (rather inept) defender of Monteverdi in Artusi's treatise of 1603. We should, on the other hand, assign to him a greater role in the formation of the new Ferrarese style of the 1590's, just as we should assign to the Ferrarese style a greater role in the development of Monteverdi's style during the last years of the 16th century. At the beginning of this short period of intense stylistic evolution stands a large void, representing our knowledge of Ferrarese practice and thought at the end of the 1580's and the beginning of the 1590's. The early madrigals and letters of Fontanelli can begin to fill that void.

II
PROBLEMS OF RHYTHM, METER, AND TEMPO: c. 1550—1750

PHILIP GOSSETT

The Mensural System and the "Choralis Constantinus"

Nowhere in the practical sources of the Renaissance are the complexities of the mensural system more fully exemplified than in the music of Heinrich Isaac. Since the sixteenth century, theorists and historians have invoked his compositions to illustrate notational problems arising from unusual combinations of mensural signatures and frequent changes from one signature to another[1]. Yet there has been no serious attempt to study systematically Isaac's mensural practice. Indeed most efforts to examine or edit his music have met with frustration. Forty years ago Herbert Birtner projected an edition of the Masses in *Denkmäler der Tonkunst in Österreich (DTÖ)*, but only now has this edition begun to appear[2]. The first two volumes of the *Choralis Constantinus* (henceforth *CC*), after the Formschneider prints of 1550 and 1555, were published in 1898 and 1909, but the third volume of 1555 waited until 1950 and 1956 for publication[3]. Of these editions only that of Book I utilizes any manuscript sources, despite the significant variants found in them[4]. The American Institute of Musicology has recently announced its intention to publish a complete edition of Isaac's music edited by Edward Lerner. The achievement of this project would fill a major lacuna in our knowledge of Renaissance music.

The careful treatment of mensural problems will be essential to the success of this new edition. As both Arthur Mendel and Clement Miller have emphasized, theoretical sour-

---

[1] Sebald Heyden, in his *De Arte Canendi* (Nürnberg, 1540), offers compositions by Isaac as the *ne plus ultra* of intricate proportions. See particularly pp. 107—109 and 114—118. The latter, the infamous "De radice Jesse" from the sequence for the Conception of the BVM in Book II of the *Choralis Constantinus*, is given both in its original notation and in a "resolutio" utilizing only the signatures ¢ and $\frac{3}{1}$. For a discussion of this treatise see Clement A. Miller, "Sebald Heyden's *De Arte Canendi*: Background and Contents", *Musica Disciplina*, XXIV (1970), 79—99. "De radice Jesse" is also offered with a resolution in the *Dodecachordon* of Heinrich Glarean (Basel, [1547]). Glarean too objects to the "obscure" and "nearly enigmatic" arrangement of the original. In the edition by Clement A. Miller, *Heinrich Glarean: Dodecachordon* (American Institute of Musicology, 1965), 2 vols., Vol. 2, pp. 278—281, facsimiles of the original notation and resolution are given. Some interesting variants between these two resolutions are discussed below. Among the moderns, Willi Apel depends on Isaac for several examples of proportions in *The Notation of Polyphonic Music 900—1600*, 5th edition (Cambridge, Massachusetts, 1953), pp. 168—174.

[2] See the introduction to the first volume of Martin Staehelin's edition, *Heinrich Isaac: Messen* in the series *Musikalische Denkmäler*, Vol. VII (Mainz, 1968?).

[3] Vol. I, edited by Emil Bezecny and Walter Rabl, appeared as *DTÖ*, Vol. V, 1 (Vienna, 1898); Vol. II, edited by Anton von Webern, as *DTÖ*, Vol. XVI, 1 (Vienna, 1909). The propers and ordinaries, respectively, from Vol. III were edited by Louise Cuyler as *Heinrich Isaac's Choralis Constantinus Book III* (Ann Arbor, 1950) and *Five Polyphonic Masses by Heinrich Isaac* (Ann Arbor, 1956).

[4] An extensive, but incomplete, listing of sources and variants is given by Gerhard-Rudolf Pätzig in his unpublished dissertation, *Liturgische Grundlagen und handschriftliche Überlieferung von Heinrich Isaacs 'Choralis Constantinus'* (Tübingen, 1956), Vol. II.

ces of the period, while important, often give confusing and contradictory testimony[5]. Examination of the musical sources themselves may not eliminate all problems, but it can remove the phantom barriers that speculative theoretical views erect. These issues affect the editing and performance of the music of Isaac in a profound fashion, as a glance at existing editions reveals.

Martin Staehelin takes a straightforward approach to mensural problems. All note values are reduced by half and only the original mensural signatures are given. When differing simultaneous signatures demand that at least one voice be in a reduction ratio other than 2:1, Staehelin follows the transcriptions of Birtner in deciding which voices remain in a 2:1 reduction[6]. He does not explain the criteria used, though they are easily determined. Of the ten cases of simultaneous signatures in this volume, five pit ¢ against ¢3 or 3[7]. Where the relationship is unequivocal (pp. 7, 37, and 79), ¢3 produces a sesquialtera relation to ¢, with the perfect breve in ¢3 equal to the imperfect breve in ¢. The remaining five involve proportions in which differing reduction ratios are necessary[8]. The relations among these signatures are summarized in Example 1.

Example 1   Simultaneous Signatures from Staehelin.

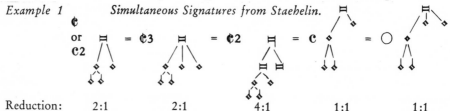

Reduction: 2:1   2:1   4:1   1:1   1:1

In each case, ¢ or ¢3 acts as an *integer valor* in the transcriptions, a standard against which other signatures are measured. Thus, values under ¢2 are reduced 4:1, while those under c or ◯ are not reduced[9].

When a single signature appears simultaneously in all voices, however, Staehelin uses the standard reduction of 2:1. He suggests no temporal relation between sections. Perhaps he believes that no proportional relations are intended, with any tempo appropriate for any section depending only on the musical instinct of the performer. In alternatim Masses, such as these, where separate sections are not performed contiguously, this theory could be attractive. But why, then, in the *Missa De beata virgine, V vocum* (I) did Isaac notate the beginning of the second Kyrie in ¢3 and its end in ◉ (see pp.

[5] Arthur Mendel, "Some Ambiguities of the Mensural System", in *Studies in Music History: Essays for Oliver Strunk* (Princeton, 1968), pp. 137—160; Miller, "Sebald Heyden's . . .", p. 99.

[6] Staehelin, see particularly p. X. This edition is based on Birtner's papers, though Staehelin has made some alterations: consulting sources unknown to Birtner, modernizing clefs, reducing note values by half, etc.

[7] See pp. 7, 37 (notes under ¢ are entirely in coloration here), 57 and 69 (in both cases vocal parts in ¢3 hold a final long while other voices change to ¢), and 79.

[8] See pp. 5 (c—¢ 3), 5 (◯—¢), 7 (¢—[¢]2), 18 (c 2—¢—¢ 2), and 61 (¢—¢ 2).

[9] Notice that c 2 and ¢ seem to mean essentially the same thing, though c 2 might indicate a musically significant imperfect division of the long. Furthermore, ¢ 3 and ¢ 2 differ substantially in meaning. The former stands for sesquialtera, rather than proportio tripla, while the latter is a true proportio dupla.

19—20)? It is striking that in 23 measures of ¢3 there are only four measures in which any eighth-notes appear in the transcription (a total of five), while under ⊕, eighth-notes occur in seven of eight measures before the final long (a total of 47). Staehelin does not assert that no proportional relation is intended. He says nothing. The first Kyrie of the *Missa De beata virgine, IV vocum* (I) is notated in ○, while the Christe is in ¢ and the second Kyrie in ¢3. What should be the relative tempos be? In particular, if ○ is read without reduction when it appears simultaneously with ¢ in the "Adoramus te" section of the Gloria of this Mass, is it intuitively obvious that it should be read in a 2:1 reduction in the first Kyrie? And how should we treat sequences of signatures such as ○, ○2, ¢ and ⊕ in the Kyrie of the *Missa De beata virgine, V vocum* (II)? The practice of indicating original mensuration signatures throughout a composition is sound and should be followed in all musicological publications, but it is no substitute for interpreting what the symbols mean.

Fabio Fano is more explicit in his edition of the four settings of the Ordinary by Isaac in the Gaffurius codices of the Duomo of Milan[10]. In an earlier volume of this series he describes his method for treating mensural signatures, particularly the four most common signs: c, ¢, ○, and ⊕[11]. Though he is consistent and, consequently, the relationship between the transcription and original can be deduced, Fano's procedures are confusing.

In the three Petrucci Masses (the fourth Mass is in ¢ throughout), there are no simultaneous occurrences of different signatures. All relations are therefore postulated for successive signatures. Fano proceeds as follows:

A) c and ¢.

1) c. All degrees are imperfect. All values are reduced in the ratio 2:1, and a single measure equals a breve. Hence the transcription is in 4/4 with the semibreve equal to a half-note. There are two tactus per measure, each represented by a semibreve.

2) ¢. All degrees are imperfect. Values are still reduced in the ratio 2:1, but a single measure equals a long. Hence the transcription is in 8/4 with the semibreve equal to a half-note. There are two tactus per measure, each represented by a breve. Fano does not specifically assert the equivalence of the tactus in c and ¢, but he speaks of ¢ as the "misura proporzionale detta 'dupla'," presumably intending: c ♄ = ¢ ♄[12].

---

[10] Fabio Fano, ed., *Heinrich Isaac: Messe*, in the series *Archivium Musices Metropolitanum Mediolanense*, Vol. X (Milan, 1962). The three Masses found in Librone 2 (Codex 2268), *La Bassadanza* (= *La Spagna*), *Quant j'ay*, and *Charge de deul*, have concordances with the Petrucci print of 1506, *Misse henrici Jzac*. Following Ambrosian usage, the Milanese manuscript contains only the Gloria, Credo, and Sanctus of the first two Masses; it also includes Agnus I of the *Missa Charge de deul*. The Petrucci print gives the complete compositions. According to Fano (p. XXV), the fourth Mass, found in Librone 3 (Codex 2267) without title, is related to two six-voice Masses of Isaac on the tune "Wohlauf Gesell von hinnen" found in Munich, Mus. ms. 3154. Edward Lerner, however, in a private communication, informs me that the two Masses in the Munich manuscript are essentially the same composition.

[11] Fabio Fano, ed., *Franchino Gaffurio: Magnificat*, in the series *Archivium...*, Vol. IV (Milan, 1959).

[12] *Ibid.*, p. II.

B) ◯ and ⦶.

1) ◯. The breve is perfect and the semibreve imperfect. All values are reduced by 2:1 and one measure equals a breve. Hence the transcription is in 3/2 with the semibreve equal to a half-note. There are three tactus per measure, each represented by a semibreve.

2) ⦶. The long is imperfect, the breve perfect, and the semibreve imperfect. ⦶ is in "proporzione dupla" to ◯, just as ¢ was to c. Each measure equals a long, as in ¢, but all values are now reduced in the ratio of 4:1. Hence a semibreve equals a quarter note. The transcription is in 6/4, with two tactus per measure, each represented by a breve. Fano specifically asserts that one measure of 6/4 "abbia a equivalere circa alla durata di una misura ternaria normale", or ◯ ╞ = ⦶ ╞ [13].

He does not specify the relation of ◯ and c. If the tactus remained constant, the semibreve would be equal under both signs. But the tactus cannot be uniformly constant since, for Fano, three tactus in ◯ equal two tactus in ⦶. Discussing the relation between ◯ and ⦶, Fano says: "Si noti, per altro, che questo non sarebbe l'esatto significato del segno [⦶], ma un travisamento di esso abbastanza diffuso", but he does not describe its "exact significance" [14]. His method is summarized in Example 2.

Example 2   *Relationships among* c, ◯, ¢, *and* ⦶ *from Fano.*

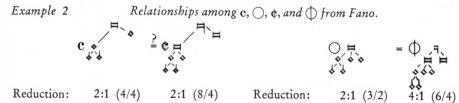

Reduction: 2:1 (4/4)   2:1 (8/4)   Reduction: 2:1 (3/2)   4:1 (6/4)

The internal relationships are largely obscured by the notation. If Fano really intends that ¢ have the same relation to c as ⦶ to ◯, the differences in reduction ratios are confusing. Values under ¢ are predominately quarters and eighths, while those under ⦶ are largely eighths and sixteenths. He offers no evidence for the assertion that ◯ ╞ = ⦶ ╞. Since values under ◯ are essentially the same as those under ⦶ in the original notation, sections in ⦶ go approximately twice as fast as those in ◯. The same would be true for ¢ and c, if he intends c ╞ = ¢ ╞, although in the transcription note values are the same under these signatures.

The few other signs appearing in this volume only compound the problem. ¢3 occurs three times, while 3 follows ¢ twice [15]. Fano claims that the imperfect breve of ¢ equals the perfect breve of ¢3, but he uses a 4:1 reduction in ¢3, unlike the 2:1 reduction in ¢, "ad evitare come di solito la misura inusitata di $\frac{6}{2}$ " [16]. In transcription, then, the dotted half note of ¢3 equals a whole note in ¢. ¢3 is thus transcribed similarly to ⦶ (4:1), while ¢ follows c and ◯ (2:1). The symbol ₵ occurs once

[13] *Loc. cit.*
[14] *Loc. cit.*
[15] See Fano, *Heinrich Isaac: Messe . . .*, pp. 48 (¢ 3), 59 (¢ . . . 3), 85 (¢ . . . 3), 86 (¢ 3), and 97 (¢ 3), together with the commentary. In each case the Petrucci print reads $\frac{0}{8}$.
[16] *Ibid.*, p. XVI.

(p. 41), and Fano asserts that its perfect semibreve equals the imperfect semibreve of ¢. Using the reduction 2:1, with each measure equal to a long, his transcription is in 12/4 (hardly more common than the 6/2 he avoids for ¢ 3)[17]. Finally, the sign c 2 occurs once in the manuscript (see p. 92), though Petrucci has ¢. Fano believes the symbols interchangeable and transcribes c 2 accordingly[18].

In Fano's edition of Masses by Isaac from the Gaffurius codices, then, we are left with uncertainties about many temporal relations among sections; we are told that proportional relations exist whose effect is to make one section of a piece twice as fast as another; and we are given capricious reduction ratios in which values meant to be equivalent look quite different on the page. Even among pieces whose mensural signatures are relatively simple, then, significant problems arise.

The *Choralis Constantinus*, on the other hand, is a labyrinth of mensural intricacies. This monumental series of Mass Propers, printed more than thirty years after Isaac's death, appeared in modern editions before scholars began considering with care its origin, contents, and manuscript sources[19]. Only recently has the nature of this work been scrutinized, particularly by Gerhard Pätzig and Martin Bente[20]. Though questions remain unanswered, particularly concerning the problematic manuscript Weimar A, we can now study the mensural signatures with knowledge of both the manuscript sources and the printed editions[21].

Mensural signatures interact in two ways: simultaneously and successively[22]. When two or more signatures occur simultaneously, we can establish unequivocally their relationship. If these relationships remain consistent whenever the signatures appear

[17] This symbol occurs once simultaneously with $\bigcirc$ in CC II, p. 106, the introit verse for the Proper of Maria Magdalena. There ¢ ♩ = $\bigcirc$ ♦ (= ¢ ♦ in *CC* — see below). Fano's posited relation, then, is at least debatable.

[18] He differentiates them, however, in his edition of anonymous Magnificat from the Gaffurius codices, Vol. VII of the *Archivium* ... (Milan, 1965), p. 45.

[19] The Ordinary cycles of CC III will not be included in the general discussion here. They are mentioned briefly, however, near the end of this paper.

[20] Pätzig, *op. cit.*; Martin Bente, *Neue Wege der Quellenkritik und die Biographie Ludwig Senfls* (Wiesbaden, 1968). I have examined microfilms of the following manuscripts:

Augsburg, Staats-, Kreis-, und Stadtbibliothek, Mss. Tonk. Schl. 7, olim 31 and Tonk. Schl. 23, olim 29.

Berlin, Deutsche Staatsbibliothek, Ms. 40024, olim Z. 24.

Leipzig, Universitätsbibliothek, Ms. Thomaskirche 49.

Munich, Bayerische Staatsbibliothek, Mss. Mus. 26, 29, 35, 36, 37, and 38.

Regensburg, Proskesche Bibliothek, Ms. C. 96.

Stuttgart, Landesbibliothek, Mss. Mus. I, 32, 40, and 42.

Vienna, Oesterreichische Nationalbibliothek Cod. 18745.

Weimar, Stadtkirche, Chorbuch A (located in Jena, Universitätsbibliothek).

I would like to thank the Princeton University Library for the permission to use several microfilms in their collection. I would also like to thank Professor Herbert Kellman of the University of Illinois for making available to me several films from the archive of Renaissance manuscripts being assembled there. The Oesterreichische Nationalbibliothek was kind enough to supply a film directly to me. For information about other sources, all of secondary importance, I have depended on the work of Pätzig.

simultaneously, we can assign them definite "meanings." If they do not remain consistent, we can identify *where* ambiguities arise. These are matters of fact. When signatures occur successively, greater caution is needed. It is not at all obvious that results obtained from a study of simultaneous signatures can be used to establish relationships among successive signatures. Indeed the problem is quite different, for here artistic questions rather than explicit facts are involved. Performers rightly object to the notion that all tempi are inexorably fixed. With many sequences in CC having six or seven successive sections written in ¢, to insist that the tempo should undergo no change from section to section seems overly severe[23]. Modifications for expression and variety are essential. Still, if there exist correct proportional relationships between successive signatures and if we can establish them and incorporate them in modern editions, performers will have a clear framework for making artistic decisions. It is one thing to admit that in performance a certain artistic flexibility must exist; it is quite another for musicologists to produce editions in which basic relative tempi are incorrectly or incompletely indicated. We shall begin by considering simultaneous signatures in CC and then examine the uncertain, but artistically more important cases in which different signatures occur successively.

SIMULTANEOUS SIGNATURES

Simultaneous relationships among signatures demanding imperfect subdivision at all levels are unambiguous in CC. They are summarized in Example 3. All instances of these relationships are specified in Appendix I[24].

Example 3
Relationships among Imperfect, Simultaneous Signatures in "CC"

$$c \downarrow = ¢ \diamond = c2 \diamond = ¢2 \sqcap = ¢ɔ\sqcap = \flat\sqcap = 4\sqcap$$

[21] Among the peculiarities of Weimar A (see the description in Karl Erich Roediger, *Die geistlichen Musikhandschriften der Universitäts-Bibliothek Jena* [Jena, 1935], 2 vols.), there are several compositions from CC preserved with the discant identical to the printed edition and the other voices different. These versions are intriguing because the lower voices are often based on cantus firmus tunes, some sacred, some secular. I suspect these versions to be earlier than the printed compositions. One of them is mentioned neither by Roediger nor Pätzig. The Introit for Palm Sunday (CC I, pp. 225—226) is found in Weimar A, ff. 167'—169, with the same discant but different lower voices. Here the latter are largely constructed throughout from the melodic material of the opening phrase in the discant, "Ne longe facias". The Introit verse in Weimar A is identical to the printed edition.

[22] Arthur Mendel has given a lucid tabular presentation of problems surrounding the mensural system in his article, "Some Ambiguities ..", cited above.

[23] Since alternate stanzas of sequences are normally set by Isaac, these sections would not be performed contiguously in the liturgy.

[24] To identify compositions, symbols such as II.24.ix are used. This stands for CC, Book II, the 24th composition in the book (composition meaning an introit with its verse, an alleluia with its verse, all the sections of a sequence or tract, etc.), section ix (if the piece is sectional). Though modern editions are not so numbered, this is the simplest way to identify compositions. To facilitate reference, page numbers in the modern editions are also given. Only one reference needs explanation. In the Alleluia: *Tu es Petrus* for the Feast of Saints Peter and Paul, III.111 (p. 371), a second alleluia verse, "Beatus es Simon Petre", is set polyphonically. The latter will be identified as III.112 (p. 372). Important references in the body of the text will include titles.

These relationships are consistent with only one apparent exception: that between c and ¢. Cuyler says (p. 26), "c and ¢ ... seem to be used interchangeably among the several voice parts of the same composition, as well as among the various movements", but offers no evidence. In the Formschneider edition (henceforth Form), ¢ is found together with c in the proper proportional relationship six times; on seven other occasions no proportional difference exists. Were the latter intentional? Could c and ¢ really mean the same thing? Or are these instances attributable to carelessness on the part of composer, compiler, or editor? Since the successive relationship of c and ¢ is a crucial matter, this question is important.

There are manuscript concordances for five of the seven irregularities in Form, and in each case the problem evaporates. In II.28.i (p. 52) and III.95.iii (p. 325), manuscript concordances use only ¢[25]. Three examples, II.36.iv (p. 69), III.48.i (p. 177), and III.76 (p. 252), have mixed signatures in Form but not in manuscript concordances. Instead the manuscripts show different successive signatures, with all voices changing together from c to ¢[26]. No concordances exist for II.76.xi (p. 148) or II.80.i (p. 154). Stanza x of the former, the sequence for the Dedication of a Church, is in three voices: —, c, c, c. Stanza xi has the signatures: ¢, ¢,[c], ¢. The absence of a signature in the tenor, with the consequent persistence of c, is surely without significance, and the tenor too should read "¢". The second case, for Feasts of the Sacred Cross, is more troublesome. In the first stanza the signatures are: ¢, c, c, ¢; in the second the tenor reads ¢, but no other signatures are present. The alto c is never cancelled by ¢. Of the two main possibilities, that all voices should read ¢ from the start or that the first stanza should be in c and the second, etc., in ¢, I believe the latter is correct[27].

When c and ¢ are used simultaneously, then, proportional meaning is indeed intended. Carelessness in Form, and more rarely in manuscripts, can result in c and ¢ being used

---

[25] The signatures for II.28.i, which opens the sequence for Ascension, read c, c, c, ¢ in Form. When signatures are unchanged from section to section of a multi-sectional composition, they are often omitted in the sources, particularly in Form. I shall use brackets to indicate that a signature persists from an earlier section. As a result of these omissions, further conflicts arise in II.28. The signatures of II.28.v, for example, are ¢, ¢, [c], [¢]. Both concordances, however, Augsburg 23 and Regensburg C96, use only ¢ from the beginning. The signatures of Form might imply that at some point all voices were meant to begin in c and change to ¢, probably in section ii, but the conflicting signatures are surely a mistake. In III.95.iii, where discant, alto, and bass move from ¢ ... 3 or ¢3 to ¢, the Form tenor changes to c without proportional significance. Berlin has the correct reading, ¢. (The symbol "¢ ... 3" means that "3" alone follows a passage in ¢.)

[26] The signatures of the Alleluia, III.76, from the Common of Virgins, are ¢, ¢, c, c in Form, while those of its verse *Omnis gloria eius* are [¢], [¢], ¢, ¢. In Berlin all voices have c for the Alleluia and ¢ for its verse. For II.36, all voices in Augsburg 7 and Stuttgart 40 show c for stanza ii and ¢ for stanzas iii and iv. All voices in Berlin read c for stanza i of III.48 and ¢ for stanza ii, though in Vienna the tenor in stanza i (c in both Form and Berlin) has an incorrect ¢.

[27] This piece is discussed further under successive signatures.

simultaneously without proportional meaning, but in every case where a concordance exists, the offending reading of Form is superseded. It does not necessarily follow, however, that when c is succeeded by ¢ in all voices a proportional degree of difference exists. That must be investigated separately.

Simultaneous relationships among signatures with some level of perfect subdivision are equally consistent. They are summarized in Example 4, apart from some problematic signatures to be discussed separately. All instances of these relationships are specified in Appendix II.

Example 4

Relationships among Simultaneous Signatures in CC
with Some Level of Perfect Subdivision. *

a)

$$\phi\,\text{H} \quad \begin{array}{l} = \quad 4\,\text{HH} \\ = \quad \phi 2\,\text{H} \quad = \quad \text{①}\;\text{H} \\ = \quad \phi 3\,\text{H} \quad = \quad \text{◯}2\,\text{H} \quad = \quad \text{c}2\,\text{H} \\ = \quad \text{c}\;\diamond \quad = \quad \text{◯}\;\diamond \quad = \quad \text{◗}\;\diamond \\ = \quad \text{c}\;\text{◆} \quad = \quad \text{◯}\;\text{◆} \end{array}$$

b)

$$\phi\,\diamond \quad \begin{array}{l} = \quad \text{①}\;\text{H} \\ = \quad \text{①}\;\diamond \\ = \quad \text{◯}\,\text{◆} \quad = \quad \text{c}\;\text{◆} \quad = \quad \text{Ȼ}\;\text{◆} \end{array}$$

* Significance of signatures with some level of perfect subdivision:

¢3	L imp; B per; SB imp.	Rarely: L imp; B imp; SB per.
◯	L imp; B per; SB imp.	
①	L imp; B per; SB imp.	
◯2	L per; B imp; SB imp.	
C	B imp; SB per.	
Ȼ	B imp; SB per.	
◖	B imp; SB per.	
☉	B per; SB per.	

There are very few errors of signature in Form or the manuscripts, and the relationships of Example 4 are unequivocal. The most common is between ¢ and ¢ 3. In every instance where his meaning can be known, Isaac uses ¢3 to indicate sesquialtera (three semibreves in the place of two), never proportio tripla (three in the place of one). This relationship obtains whether the signature is ¢3, ¢ . . . 3, or even c2 . . . 3. In this light, a comparison of the versions of "De radice Jesse" given by Glareanus and Heyden (see fn. 1) is instructive. Glareanus consistently uses the signature ⅜ instead of ¢3 or 3, while Heyden uses ⅜. Both writers intend sesquialtera with respect to ¢, as is clear from their texts and the resolutions they offer to simplify the original notation. One may join with Leeman Perkins in wondering whether proportio tripla had much practical importance during this period[28].

A few notational peculiarities and the problem of fractional signatures require brief discussion.

1) ⊕ 2. (III. 10. v; p. 88) As Pätzig indicated, section iv of this sequence for the Common of Apostles was composed in four voices, two of which are missing in Form and consequently in Cuyler[29]. The other voices, present in both Berlin and Vienna, are certainly authentic, for the bass carries the liturgical melody. Section v uses the same melody in the bass, now set forth in equal values. A simple cantus firmus of this kind is often singled out for special mensural treatment. In section v, the three upper voices are notated in ⊕, the bass in ⊕ 2. The bass includes only breves and a final long, with ⊕ 2 ⊨⊨ = ⊕ ⊨ . No further layers of organization under ⊕ 2 can be inferred from the music. The relation between ⊕ 2 and ⊕ should be logically parallel to that between ◯2 and ◯, but this is in fact not the case. In simultaneous appearances, ◯2 ⊨ = ◯◇ , which implies ◯ 2 ⊨⊨ = ◯ ◇◇ . But the breve is perfect under ◯, so that ◯2 ⊨ ⊨≠◯⊨. This should serve as a warning that the use of mensural signatures by an individual composer may not have a consistent theoretical basis. We must examine how composers actually use signatures, not what they abstractly "should" mean.

2) ⊕ 3. (III. 66. iv; p. 225). The sequence *Ad laudes salvatoris* from the Common of Confessors offers numerous mensural problems, further complicated by manuscript sources which preserve signatures largely different from Form. These variants (see

---

[28] See his review of Edward E. Lowinsky, ed., *The Medici Codex of 1518*, Vols. III, IV, and V of *Monuments of Renaissance Music* (Chicago, 1968), in *The Musical Quarterly*, LV (1969), 255—269, particularly pp. 258—259. One sympathizes with Lowinsky's desire to have different symbols mean different things (see Vol. III, pp. 88—89). In fact, Isaac's practice is not as capricious as it might appear. ¢3 and ¢ . . . 3 are discussed under successive signatures.

Glareanus' presentation of "De radice Jesse" is peculiar in several ways. He uses the text of the first stanza of the sequence *Conceptio Mariae Virginis*, instead of the second stanza set by Isaac. (The complete text, in its form for the Nativity of the BVM, is given in Cl. Blume and H. M. Bannister, eds., *Analecta Hymnica Medii Aevi* (henceforth *AH*), 54 [Leipzig, 1915], # 188, p. 288.) Glareanus also changes the pitches at the end of the bass part and notates it in "$\frac{5}{2}$", a signature whose meaning is obscure. Three longs under his $\frac{5}{2}$ equal two longs under 4, an effect achieved in the alto of the original through coloration alone. Glareanus finally omits a necessary $\frac{2}{1}$ in the alto of his resolution, just before the final black breves. Heyden avoids these problems, using in his resolution only ¢ and $\frac{3}{1}$, the latter meaning proportio tripla with respect to c but sesquialtera with respect to ¢. Miller, "Sebald Heyden's . . .", also discusses this passage.

[29] See Pätzig, Vol. II, p. 95. The melody for the entire sequence, *Clare sanctorum* (Clemens Blume and Henry Bannister, eds., *AH*, 53 [Leipzig, 1911], # 228, p. 367) is given by N. de Goede, ed. *The Utrecht Prosarium*, Vol. VI of the *Monumenta Musica Neerlandica* (Amsterdam, 1965), Sequence # 69, pp. 120—121. Berlin is surely accurate in assigning the sixth stanza of *AH* 53, # 228 to section iv and the seventh to section v; Form and Vienna incorrectly use the sixth stanza for both sections.

Example 6 below) establish the same set of simultaneous relations as Examples 3 and 4. Form alone uses the signature ⊕ 3 at the beginning of the tenor in section iv, "Et gaudium Angelis". It seems to imply here perfect division of the long and breve, imperfect division of the semibreve, with ⊕ 3 ⊟ = ¢ ⊟. If this is correct, then ⊕ 3 is distinguished from ¢ 3 only at the level of the long, there being three breves to the long in ⊕ 3 and only two in ¢ 3. In III. 66. iv, however, there is no meaningful musical organization at that level in the tenor. Considering the rarity of the signature, we may well wonder whether it was not meant to be ¢ 3 [30].

  3) Fractional signatures used simultaneously.

  a) $\frac{0}{3}$. (II. 36. x; p. 73) The signatures of section x, "In figuris praesignatur", of the sequence for Corpus Christi are:

Discant, alto, bass: ¢   3   ¢
Tenor: ¢ $\frac{0}{3}$ ¢

¢ ... $\frac{0}{3}$ has precisely the same meaning as ¢ ... 3. The signature $\frac{0}{3}$ was common early in the century, and Petrucci often uses it where manuscript sources read ¢ ... 3 [31]. In both manuscript concordances for II. 36. x, Augsburg 7 and Stuttgart 40, $\frac{0}{3}$ is replaced by 3.

  b) $\frac{2}{3}$. (III. 48. iv; p. 181) The signatures of section iv, "Caeci claudi", of the sequence for a single Martyr are: Discant, alto, tenor: ¢3

Bass: ¢3 $\frac{2}{3}$

Under $\frac{2}{3}$ the long is perfect, the breve and semibreve imperfect, with ¢3 ... $\frac{2}{3}$ ⊟ = ¢3 ⊟. The bass part in Berlin is written in the same time values, but the signature reads: $\frac{2}{1}$. The difference between Berlin and Form (with which Vienna agrees) is caused by a different way of understanding the relationship between successive numerical signatures. The $\frac{2}{1}$ of Berlin signals two semibreves where there was one before. Thus there are six semibreves under $\frac{2}{1}$ in place of three in ¢3. In Form and Vienna, $\frac{2}{3}$ relates back to ¢, not to ¢3. Instead of ¢3 the basic mensuration becomes ¢2, with ¢3 ⊟ = ¢2 ⊟, while the denominator 3 signifies the perfect division of the long [32].

---

[30] ⊕3 appears only once again in Form, in III. 48. v (pp. 181—182). All voices in this section from the first sequence of the Common of a single Martyr begin in ⊕ and change to "3". Under ⊕ ... 3 the breve and semibreve are both perfect, presumably with ⊕ ◇ = ⊕ ... 3 ◇. This is a more intuitively reasonable use of the signature than that of III.66.iv, for there really is no other way to indicate this organization. ⊙, a possible candidate, always implies augmentation and hence is not acceptable.

  The signature ⊕3 does appear several times, however, in manuscript concordances. In Augsburg 23 it replaces ¢3 as the opening signature of II.24.x (p. 47), II.25 (p. 49), and II.28.vii (p. 54). In Munich 37 it replaces ⊕ as the signature of III.101.ii (p. 336). Augsburg 23 is a late manuscript (dated 1575) and its readings here, which make no particular sense, can be discounted. Munich 37, on the other hand, is part of the Ludwig Senfl collection "Opus Musicum" (see Bente), an important source. The meaning of ⊕3 here is not clear to me, but perhaps a comprehensive study of the Munich choirbooks would clarify this question.

[31] See, for example, fn. 15.

[32] There is a similar instance in II.100.i (p. 194), where the succession of signatures ¢ ... 3 ... 2 means ¢, ¢3, ¢2, *not* ¢, ¢3, ¢6.

c) $\frac{c}{3}$. (III.118.vi; p. 393) In this example the mensural signatures have a symbolic meaning totally lost in modern transcription. The text of section vi of the sequence *Coeli enarrant* for the feast *In Divisione Apostolorum* is[33]:

> Hinc Petrus Romam,
> apostolorum
> princeps, adiit,
> Paulus Graeciam,
> ubique
> docens gratiam;
> ter quattuor alii
> proceres in plagis terrae
> quattuor evangelizantes
> trinum et unum.

The three voices begin together in ¢, and change at the words "trinum et unum"[34]. The alto goes into coloration; the tenor receives the signature 3; the bass $\frac{c}{3}$. Under $\frac{c}{3}$ the semibreve is perfect, with $\frac{c}{3}$ ◊ = ¢ . . . 3 ⊟ .

Why did Isaac notate this simple sesquialtera relation in three different ways[35]? The answer lies in the text. The apostles split up and roamed throughout the world in order to teach the lesson of the three and the one; that is, that Father, Son, and Holy Ghost are one. Isaac sets the stanza for three voices and uses three different notational devices to express "one" triple time simultaneously.

d) $\frac{0}{3}$, $\frac{0\ 2}{3}$ ¢$\frac{2}{3}$. (III.66.v; pp. 226—227) Section v of *Ad laudes salvatoris* (see ◯• 3 above) is particularly confusing in Form. The signatures are:

Discant: ◯ $\frac{0}{3}$

Alto: ◯ 3

Tenor: [¢]

Bass: ◯• $\frac{0\ 2}{3}$ ¢ $\frac{2}{3}$

Now, ¢ ⊟ = $\frac{0}{3}$ ⊟ = ◯ . . . 3 ⊟ = $\frac{0\ 2}{3}$ ⊟. In each case, except ¢, the breve is perfect. $\frac{0}{3}$ means ¢3 here, as in paragraph (a) above, even though it follows ◯. Likewise "3" following ◯ still means ¢3, though it could be argued that just as ◯ ◊ = ◯2 ⊟ = ◊ ◊, so ◯ ◊ = ◯ . . . 3⊟ = ◊ ◊ ◊, or ◯3⊟ = ¢⊟. In all simultaneous occurences in CC, ◯2 ⊟ = ¢ ⊟. The addition of the "3" makes the breve perfect. Under ¢ $\frac{2}{3}$, as in paragraph (b) above, ¢$\frac{2}{3}$⊟= ¢⊟, but here the long is, by implication,· imperfect and the breve perfect. Shortly after the change to triple time in discant, alto, and bass, the tenor also moves into triple time, produced notationally by coloration.

[33] I give the text after Guido Maria Dreves, ed., *AH*, 50 (Leipzig, 1907), #267, pp. 344—346. The minor variants in the Isaac sources do not affect the crucial final line.

[34] The text underlay is incorrect in Cuyler. The alto should not have the text "hi proceres in plagis" at all, so that the text "terrae quatuor evangelizantes" can be moved back three measures. All voices thus sing "trinum et unum" together and no splitting of ligatures is necessary. Manuscript sources, which are more fully texted than Form, agree unanimously.

[35] The successive sesquialtera is unequivocal, since coloration under ¢ is unambiguous.

Again the text may offer an explanation for this confusion [36]:

Qui cuique suam
tritici dat mensuram,
Ad fidei caulas
congregans oviculas
lupi praevidit insidias;

A possible paraphrase would be: "This man who gives his measure of wheat to each man; who, by herding the little sheep into the folds of faith has forestalled the ambush of the wolf". Herding sheep together could be expressed musically by accommodating these four different notations in a single fold, while the change to $\mathvarphi$ $\frac{2}{3}$ falls precisely on the text "lupi praevidit insidias". Through its essential sameness to the other parts, its having been "herded together" with them, the bass can escape the ambush this mensural wolf lays for the unsuspecting singer. I suggest this interpretation with some reservations, but I believe the entire issue of mensural symbolism must be considered more closely.

These fractional signatures are summarized in Example 5.

Example 5

Relationships among Simultaneous Fractional Signatures in CC.

$$\mathsf{C}\mathbb{H} \quad = \quad \mathsf{C}3\,\mathbb{H} \quad =\,{}^{0}_{3}\mathbb{H} \quad =\,{}^{02}_{3}\mathbb{H} = \bigcirc \ldots 3\,\mathbb{H}$$

$\frac{0}{3}$ and $\bigcirc \ldots 3$ appear to be ways of writing a simple sesquialtera proportion. For all other fractional signatures, the numerator, including the mensural sign and sometimes a number, indicates the basic mensuration in which the section is to be read. The denominator, consistently a "3", specifies triple organization at some level, though that level has to be determined from the context. Thus in III. 48.iv (p. 181) the long under $\mathsf{C}3 \ldots \frac{2}{3}$ is perfect, while in III.66.v (pp. 226—227) the breve under C $\frac{2}{3}$ is perfect.

SUCCESSIVE SIGNATURES

The relationships among simultaneous signatures summarized in Examples 3 through 5 are used consistently by Isaac in *CC*. Relationships among successive signatures, on the other hand, are not subject to the same degree of verification. Still, some principles can be applied. Though questionable places will undoubtedly remain, more problems are essentially soluble than are generally thought to be. I put forth four principles that I believe to be true for the *Choralis Constantinus* and to have wider application among composers contemporary to Isaac.

---

[36] *AH*, 54, #88, stanza 8, pp. 126—128. I wish to thank Prof. Nicholas Rudall and Miss M. E. C. Bartlet of the University of Chicago for their assistance with the Latin texts.

Principle I: Single-voice continuity. If the mensural signature of a voice in a polyphonic complex remains unchanged, either within a section or between sections, the tempo and organization of that voice should not be altered. A single singer, in short, will not shift his mensural gears unless explicitly directed.

This principle has not always been followed. The original signatures of II.52.i (p. 98), section i of the sequence for the Visitation of the BVM, "Piae vocis laudes canta", are:

Sections:	a	b	c	d
Discant, alto, tenor:	¢	Ċ	¢	3
Bass:	Ċ	[Ċ]	¢	3

Webern transcribes both Ċ and 3 as "3" and changes ¢ to ¢ (though elsewhere, e. g., II. 68, i [p. 130], he introduces "¢" where Form reads ¢); thus:

Sections:	a	b	c	d
Discant, alto, tenor:	¢	3	¢	3
Bass:	3	[3]	¢	3

The bass in section *a*, under Ċ, contains two breve rests, while section *b*, with all voices under Ċ, is one breve long. Thus, following Principle I, section *a* should be twice as long as section *b*. In Webern, however, there are six measures in section *a*, each equal to a breve under ¢ or two minims under Ċ, and two measures in section *b*, each equal to a semibreve in Ċ. His transcription implies that a measure in his ¢ is equal to a measure in his 3. Therefore, for Webern, section *a* is three times as long as section *b*. This is simply wrong[37]. In the correct solution, the simultaneous relationship, ¢ ◇ = Ċ ♦, continues to hold successively.

The signatures for III.77.ii (p. 255), the section "Quarum Christe" from the sequence for the Common of Virgins, are:

Discant, alto, tenor:	¢	Ɔ	¢
Bass:	¢		

The successive relation between ¢ and Ɔ is defined unequivocally by the bass continuity, but Cuyler's modern edition ignores this. In mm. 1—4 of her version, with all voices in ¢, Cuyler transcribes ¢ ⊨ as a whole note, using the standard 2:1 reduction. In mm. 5—9, with the upper voices in Ɔ and the bass remaining in ¢, she transcribes ¢ ⊨ as a half note, using a 4:1 reduction and doubling the tempo. When the upper voices return to ¢, in mm. 10—11, she returns to the 2:1 reduction. It is implausible that a singer would do this without notice. Surely mm. 5—9 should be half as fast as indicated in the transcription[38].

---

[37] Apel, *The Notation . . .*, gives this section as facsimile 36 (see pp. 170—171). He correctly identifies the proportional relationship, though his suggestion that section *a* should be transcribed as four measures in 3/4 seems arbitrary. Six measures in duple meter are preferable, but the relationship between a measure in section *a* and one in section *b* must be explicitly indicated.

[38] Ɔ is an unusual signature, and it occurs here with all notes in coloration. But simple coloration under ¢ would have had the same effect. Perhaps Cuyler doubled the tempo in an effort to ascribe a "meaning" to Ɔ. An analysis of the signature, however, precludes this interpretation. In simultaneous use here, ¢ ⊨ = Ɔ ◖ ♦ . The normal organization of Ɔ is apparently an imperfect breve and perfect semibreve, as in Ċ. Coloration reverses this, creating a perfect breve

Principle II: Cross-voice continuity. If the mensural sign in one voice of a polyphonic complex reappears successively in another voice, either within a section or between sections, the tempo and organization under that sign should not be altered. This principle is valid only if signatures are not cumulative. But if signatures were cumulative, no consistency could be hoped for among simultaneous signatures. The complete consistency of the latter in *CC* assures us that signatures are not generally cumulative and that Principle II holds. The only exceptions would involve single numerals. In the following hypothetical situation:

$$\phi \qquad\qquad 3$$
$$c \qquad 3 \qquad \oplus,$$

the two "3's" are *not* really continuous, since one modifies c and the other ¢.

An example occurs in II.56.x (p. 111), the verse "Qualis sit tu scis" from the sequence for Maria Magdalena. The signatures read[39]:

and imperfect semibreve. Thus, c ♯ = ꓭ ♯ or c ◊ = ꓭ ◊. Extrapolating the relation C ♭ = c ◊ from our knowledge of simultaneous signatures (see also the discussion of II.52.i [p. 98] above), we find that Ꮯ ♭ = ꓭ ◊. Though we might not have been able to predict this precise relationship, the reversal of the signature surely must indicate a diminution, cancelling the augmenting effect of the dot.

Compare III.77.iv (p. 257). Here the signatures read:

Discant: — — —   Tenor: ○   ꓭ
Alto: ○   Bass: ○

All parts are in coloration at the change, alto and bass under ○, tenor under ꓭ. Note values are the same with ꓭ ◆ ◆ = ○ ◊. It is easy to show that this is consistent with our prior results:

$$\text{ꓭ} \quad ◆ \quad ◆ \quad ◆ \quad = ○ \quad ◊$$
$$\text{ꓭ} \quad ◆◆◆◆◆◆ = ○ \quad ◊◊$$
$$\text{ꓭ} ♯ \qquad\qquad = C \quad ♯$$

Thus, the sign ꓭ is used consistently in these two sections. That it is rather anomalous, since the same results are obtainable with simple coloration, should not compel us to create false meanings for it. (Indeed, Cuyler is inconsistent, since in III.77.iv she introduces no doubling of the tempo.) If we must explain Isaac's practice, we had best search in the direction of symbolism or perhaps the fondness for notational puzzles he shared with much of his generation.

[39] The two concordances for this section, Leipzig 49 and Heyden (1540), pp. 108—109, both differ in signatures from Form. In Leipzig 49, a late and unreliable set of partbooks containing several compositions from *CC*, the signatures are:

Alto: 3   ₵   4
Tenor: 3 $\frac{c}{2}$ ꓭ
Bass: 3   ꓭ   c

Note values are identical to Form. In Heyden, the signatures are:

Alto: ¢$\frac{3}{2}$ ¢2   ↑
Tenor: ¢$\frac{3}{2}$ c2   ꓭ
Bass: $\frac{3}{2}$¢   ꓭ   c

For the theorist, the signature ꓭ is cumulative, but this is not true for Isaac, as we have seen above. Perhaps through Heyden, though, Leipzig 49 uses ꓭ, but its substitution of ₵ for ¢2 and $\frac{c}{2}$ for c 2 is strange. Leipzig 49 also offers a puzzling resolution of this section into "simpler" notation which will be discussed later.

Alto: ¢3 ¢2 4
Tenor: ¢3 c2 𝄒
Bass: ¢3 𝄒 c

Assuming cross-voice continuity for 𝄒, the temporal relation between the last two parts is determined. The resulting successive relationships agree, as they must, with the normal simultaneous relationships among these signatures.

Principle III: Persistence of relationship. If within a single composition or part of a composition the successive relation between two signatures can be demonstrated once, this relationship can be presumed to persist in any voice throughout that composition or section. A demonstrable relationship, in short, should not change locally[40].

The signatures of II.100.i (p. 194), the famous "De radice Jesse" already referred to, from the sequence for the Conception of the BVM, are[41]:

Discant:	⊙		Ꞓ	○	○2	C	C2	3
Alto:	○2		C	¢	3	¢2	4	
Tenor:	Ꞓ	○		○2	C	¢	3	2
Bass:	○		○2	C	C2	3	¢Ɔ	4

The same succession of signatures, ⊙ Ꞓ ○ ○2 c or 3 or 4 governs all
                                          c2   ¢2
                                          ¢   ¢Ɔ

voices, with the discant beginning with ⊙, the tenor with Ꞓ, the bass with ○, and the alto with ○2. The successive relation between Ꞓ and ○ is defined by the early appearance of ○ in the tenor. This in turn establishes the successive relations of ⊙ and Ꞓ, ○ and ○2, and ○2 and c, following Principle I. These relationships persist throughout the section, according to Principle III, new ones are consequently established, and the process defines temporal relations throughout II.100.i. The resulting successive relationships are identical to the simultaneous relationships given in Examples 3 and 4.

A simple example involving more than one section of a composition is the tract I.117, *Qui confidunt,* for Laetare Sunday. In I. 117. ii (p. 215), the discant has the series of signatures ¢ 3 ¢, while the other voices remain in ¢. Here ¢ ⊟ = ¢...3 ⊟. In I.117.i (p. 214), all voices change near the end from ¢ to 3. Surely ¢ ... 3 cannot mean two different things for the discant in sections i and ii. The relation demonstrable for I.117.ii must also apply to I.117.i.

Principle IV: Commutative law. The successive relationship of signatures is independent of their order. Again, single numerals modifying different basic signatures must be ex-

---

[40] The precise meaning of "locally" is problematic and may have to be defined for each context. Here I take it to mean a single piece, such as a Communion, or a single section, such as a verse of a sequence. I believe, as will be seen, that this principle can be applied more generally throughout a multi-sectional work in CC.

[41] Webern's table of signatures (p. 199) has several errors. For the second signature in the tenor he gives Ꞓ instead of ○ and fails to indicate the overlap. For the next to last signature in the bass he gives ¢3 instead of ¢ Ɔ. Apel offers a facsimile and transcription of this passage (facsimile 38, p. 173).

cepted. In the sequence for the feast *In Divisione Apostolorum*, III. 118. v—vii (pp. 391—395), the following series of signatures occurs:

Sections:	*v*			*vi*			*vii*		
Discant:	[¢]	3		—			¢	3	¢
Alto:	[¢]	3	¢	coloration		[¢]	3	¢	
Tenor:	[¢]	3	¢	3		¢	3	¢	
Bass:	¢	3	[¢]	$\frac{c}{3}$		[¢]	3	¢	

The continuity of ¢ in the alto of section vi establishes the successive relation between ¢ and 3 in the tenor. By Principle IV this relation remains the same for ¢ ... 3 and ¢, a fact further verified by the continuity of ¢ in the alto between sections vi and vii. These relationships, still following Principle IV, hold in sections v and vii, so that throughout this passage ¢ ... 3 ⊟ = ¢ ⊟ [42].

Other principles could be established. A deductive law would hold that if within a composition the successive relationship of signatures A and B and signatures B and C can be established, then the successive relationship of signatures A and C is determined. Using our four principles, however, we can unravel one of the more complex pieces in *CC*, III.66 (pp. 222—231), the sequence *Ad laudes salvatoris* from the Common of Confessors. There are three sources for this composition, Form, Berlin, and Vienna. The signatures in the two manuscripts differ significantly from those in Form. Both sets are given in Example 6:

Example 6
Signatures for III.66 (pp. 222—231) in Form, Berlin, and Vienna.

Section:	i	ii	iii	iv		v				
FORM:	○	○2	¢	¢	3 ¢ ○		$\frac{9}{3}$			
	○	○2	[¢]	○2	○		3			
	○	○2	¢	⊕3	¢	[¢]				
	○	○2	¢	¢		⊕	○2 3	¢ $\frac{2}{3}$		
BERLIN	○	○2	⊕	¢	3 ¢ ○		○2 3	$c\binom{2}{3}$		$¢\binom{2}{3}$
and:										
VIENNA	○	○2	¢	○2		c	¢3	c3	or	[¢3]
	○	○2	c	c3	¢ 2 ¢			c		[¢]
	⊙	☾	○	c		⊕	○2 3	$c\binom{2}{3}$		$¢\binom{2}{3}$

                                         Berlin   Vienna

[42] In the motet by Boyleau, "In principio erat uerbum", ♯2 in *The Medici Codex*, Vol. IV, pp. 5—19, the sequence of signatures in all voices ¢ ⊕ $\frac{3}{2}$ ¢ occurs in both the first and second parts. Lowinsky defines the temporal relationships each time as: ¢ ◇ = ⊕ $\frac{3}{2}$⊟ = ¢⊟. But whatever relationship between ¢ and ⊕ $\frac{3}{2}$ is correct, it must hold surely hold in both directions.

Section:	vi	vii	viii			ix						
FORM:	○2	¢	¢			¢	*		*		*	
	○2	[¢]	¢			¢	3	¢	3	¢	3	¢
	○2	¢	[¢]			¢3		¢	3	¢	3	¢
	○2	¢	[¢]			¢	*		*		*	
BERLIN	○2	¢	4									
and:	○2	¢	c	¢	2							
VIENNA	○2	¢	○	c ¢	2	4	Equal to FORM.					
	○2	¢	¢2									

* Sesquialtera produced through coloration.

The bass signatures in Berlin and Vienna show a progression similar to II. 100. i (p. 194), moving from "augmenting signatures" with smaller note values, through uncut and cut signatures, to "diminishing signatures" with larger note values[43]. The clarity of this plan and its similarity to mensural procedures in other Isaac compositions lead me to believe that the manuscript version is authentic.

Our principles can be applied to either version. For Berlin — Vienna the relationship between sections iii and iv is determined by cross-voice continuity. The commutative law establishes the relation between sections ii and iii (○2 ... ¢ ... ○2), while the persistence of the relation ○ ... ○2, defined between sections iii and iv, sets the relation of sections i and ii. Single-voice continuity covers section iv internally; the relation between sections iv and v is governed by cross-voice continuity; and single-voice continuity again covers section v internally (using the Vienna version). The other relations follow similarly. The same principles applied to the Form version, in different combinations, fully determine the relative tempi there. The successive relationships thus established produce the same relative tempi in both versions. Without exception these successive relationships are identical to the simultaneous relationships used throughout CC[44].

[43] The progression is interrupted in II. 100. i by the insertion of O2 between O and c instead of after c. In III. 66 the progression is steady if we accept the Berlin reading at the close of section v. If we prefer Vienna (which has the same musical result as Form), there is an interruption. This variant is significant, for the section goes half as fast in Berlin as in Vienna and Form. Because of the peculiar organization of notes under "c 3" in Berlin (see the discussion of this signature below), I shall take the Vienna-Form version to be correct.

[44] It could be objected that the identity of simultaneous and successive signatures follows necessarily from these four principles. This may be true in part, but it is built into the

Cuyler's reading of this piece founders on her apparent belief that successively ¢ ◇ = ○2 ᕬ. As a result, she halves the proper speed of section iii, upsetting the relation between sections ii and iii and sections iii and iv. In the latter instance she effectively states that ¢ ◇ (section iii) = ¢ ᕬ (section iv) in both the discant and bass of Form, creating a single-voice discontinuity without apparent justification. Section vii is half as fast as it should be with respect to section vi; sections viii and ix, although correct with respect to section vii, are also half as fast as they should be relative to section vi [45].

Successive signatures, then, are not totally independent in meaning from simultaneous ones. To what extent, though, can the results obtained thus far be expanded to cover all successive relationships in *CC*? There are two major categories of successive relationships: those on the same mensural level and those involving cross-levels (e.g., cut and uncut signatures). With regard to the former, the evidence of *CC* is consistent and extensive enough to establish the following proposition:

> Signatures on the same mensural level in simultaneous occurrences (e.g., ¢, ¢3, ◐, and ○2, or c and ○, or C and ⊙, etc.) preserve these simultaneous meanings when they are found successively.

I know no instance in *CC* where this proposition seems invalid. Two of these relationships, ¢ — ¢3 and ¢ — ◐, deserve closer examination.

There are some 80 instances in *CC* where a section for all voices in ¢ is followed by a section in "3" or "¢3". These signatures always define a sesquialtera relation, and there is no evidence they can *ever* be interpreted as proportio tripla within *CC*. If our musical instinct rebels, our instinct needs correction, though in fact sesquialtera always produces

mensural system. Thus, in II.3.iv (p. 9), where the signatures in Form read:
Discant, alto, tenor: [¢]
Bass: ○   c   ¢ $\frac{2}{1}$ $\frac{4}{1}$
the successive relationships of ○—c, c—¢, ¢—$\frac{2}{1}$, $\frac{2}{1}$—$\frac{4}{1}$ are unambiguously defined, unless we deny single-voice continuity. *Within* a section, however, this principle seems to me inviolable throughout the fifteenth and sixteenth centuries, not merely in Isaac. In short, we are not defining the equivalence of simultaneous and successive signatures in the large; we are presenting reasonable principles by which this equivalence must result in the small. The application of these results to larger contexts is not a *logical* necessity.

[45] It would be better to transcribe section i without reduction and sections ii—ix in a 2:1 reduction with respect to ¢. Cuyler gives this peculiar interpretation of ○2 elsewhere. In III.30, the second sequence for the Common of Martyrs, sections i through vi are in ¢. Section vii (p. 139) has ○2 in discant, alto, and tenor, and C in the bass, with ○2 ᕬ = C♭ simultaneously, in agreement with Example 4. Cuyler transcribes ¢ in a 2:1 reduction and ○2 in a 4:1 reduction, so that ¢ ◇ = ○2 ᕬ and ¢ ◇ = C ♭ . She offers no explanation, though both relations differ from the evidence of Example 4 and of other successive situations to which our principles apply. Likewise, the signatures of III.126.i—iv (pp. 422—424), the beginning of the sequence for the Feast of the Assumption of the BVM, are: ○2 ◐ ○ ¢. Cuyler indicates the following successive relationships: ○2 ᕬ = ◐ ◇◇   =○ ◇= ¢ ◇ . The relations between sections i, ii, and iii follow Example 4, but that between sections iii and iv is never found among simultaneous signatures. We shall return to the question of cut and uncut signatures below.

a musically sensible reading[46]. There has been speculation that ¢3 differs in meaning from ¢ . . . 3[47]. In Appendix III (a) all places in *CC* in which all voices proceed together from ¢ to either "3" or "¢3" are catalogued. The evidence of these instances is overwhelming: ¢ is followed by "3" within a composition or section of a composition; ¢ is followed by "¢3" between sections of a composition, with "¢3" signalling the start of an entire composition, an introit verse, alleluia verse, or section of a sequence or tract. The few anomalous cases, listed in Appendix III(b), do not significantly challenge this statement. Nor does Isaac's use of "3" or "¢3" simultaneously with other signatures alter this perspective. The difference between ¢3 and ¢ . . . 3 in *CC* is a matter not of proportional difference but rather of the place within a composition where the signature occurs.

There are fewer instances in which all voices in ¢ are followed by ⊘; these are recorded in Appendix IV. As we would expect, there is a significant musical difference between sections in 3 or ¢3 following ¢ and sections in ⊘ following ¢. Under 3 or ¢3 the smallest value at which there is significant motion, as opposed to ornamental turns, is normally the minim, while under ⊘ (and ¢) the smallest value is normally the semiminim. In no case under 3 or ¢3 is there significant motion at the semiminim level. Under 3 or ¢3 significant motion is sometimes restricted to the semibreve level, just as under ¢ or ⊘ significant motion is sometimes restricted to the minim level. This distinction between 3 or ¢3 and ⊘ agrees with our understanding of their relative meaning with respect to ¢.

---

[46] The breve in ¢3 is always equal to the breve in ¢. With few exceptions the breve in ¢3 is perfect and the semibreve imperfect. In Books I and II, ¢ . . . 3 is occasionally used for a short passage with the rhythm: | ♪ · ♦ ♦ ♦ · ♦ ♦ | (e.g., I. 96. iv—p. 153, last system; I. 102. ii—p. 165; I. 108. viii—p. 186; I. 120. ii—p. 220; II. 61—p. 120), often as a concluding figure against a long in another part. These examples are indeterminate for the division of the breve and semibreve. On other occasions, only imperfect semibreves are present, though the musical sense implies an imperfected perfect semibreve, with the rhythm: | ◊ ♦ ◊ ♦ | predominating (e. g., II. 84. v—p. 165). Since the rhythmic activity in ¢3 normally involves breves and semibreves, with figures such as: | ⊨ ◊ | ⊨ ◊ |, an example like II. 84. v might well be considered an explicit proportio tripla. In two short passages in II. 14 (p. 25) and II. 33 (p. 64), the rhythm is essentially | ♪ · ♦ ♦ ♦ · ♦ ♦ |, but the alternate rhythm | ◊ ◊ ◊ | is also present. In II. 14 coloration is used, though inconsistently, to achieve this rhythm, implying a perfect semibreve. (The effect of three imperfect breves replacing two perfect breves, the usual motivation for coloration in ¢3, is not in question here.) In II. 33 coloration is used consistently, implying that the breve is in fact imperfect and the semibreve perfect. In only one instance, III. 126. v (p. 425) is a passage in ¢ . . . 3 entirely organized with an imperfect breve and perfect semibreve. These exceptions, only two of which are perhaps significant, among over 120 examples of ¢3 or ¢ . . . 3 in *CC*, do not alter the essential meaning of these symbols.
c 3 and c . . . 3, on the contrary, signify an imperfect breve and perfect semibreve, with c 3 ◊ = c ◊ . See, for example, II. 52. i (p. 98), III. 66. iv (Berlin—Vienna version; p. 225), and III. 89. v (p. 305). The Berlin version of III. 66. v (see fn. 43) has the signature c 3 to indicate a perfect breve and imperfect semibreve. This irregularity causes me to prefer the reading of Vienna.

[47] Particularly by Lowinsky, see fn. 28 above.

These relations are seen most directly when the signatures ⊙ ¢3 ¢ occur successively in all voices, as they do several times in CC. I cite two peculiarities in editorial practice:

a) In I.120.iv (p. 222), the stanza "Prolongaverunt iniquitatem sibi" from the tract *Saepe expugnaverunt* for Judica Sunday, the three signatures occur successively in all parts. The editors treat ⊙ and ¢3 as if they were identical in meaning and transcribe the entire opening duet (⊙) and the section in four voices (¢3) under the ubiquitous signature "3". That the movement under ⊙ is largely in minims and semiminims, with occasional fusae, while the movement under ¢3 is in semibreves and minims causes them no concern [48].

b) In III.106.v — vi (pp. 358—359), the stanza "Tu qui praeparas" from the sequence *Sancti Baptistae Christi* for the Nativity of St. John the Baptist, the same signatures occur:

Section:	*v*		*vi*
All voices:	⊙	¢3	¢

Here, after transcribing ⊙ in "3/2" with the normal 2:1 reduction, Cuyler transcribes ¢3 in "¢" with a 4:1 reduction and triplet figures, with ⊙ ◊ = ¢3 ⊟ . On the other end she presumably wants ¢3 ⊟ = ¢ ◊ , which is equally wrong. There is no justification for this, nor indeed is there any musical difference between this situation and III.92.iii (pp. 313—314), where the same sequence of signatures is handled correctly.

A relatively simple example, such as II.19.vi (p. 38), the verse "Ideoque" from the tract *Ave Maria* for the Feast of the Annunciation of the BVM, has plagued both Webern and Willi Apel. The first five sections are in ¢, though the signature is not always explicit in Form, the only source. Section vi begins without signature, but ¢ is unmistakeably continued from earlier sections. The discant is silent here and remains so as the lower voices change to triple time through coloration. The perfect breve in coloration is thus equal to the imperfect breve in ¢. Now all voices change signatures:

Discant:	[¢]		⊙
Alto:	[¢]	coloration	𝄇
Tenor:	[¢]	coloration	c
Bass:	[¢]	coloration	◯

Webern provides no new signature for the bass, implying that it continues as under coloration. One of his measures under ◯, however, is ◊ + ♪ of the original notation; thus, for Webern, ¢ ⊟ = ◯ ◊ + ♪ . This further implies that in the discant ¢ ⊟ = ⊙ ⊟ , which is incorrect. He transcribes both c and 𝄇 in ¢ 3, by which he seems to mean that the long is divided into three breves under these signatures, with his ¢3 ⊟ = ⊙ ⊟ ⊟ (the latter transcribed as "3"). The interpretation is wrong, and the signatures used peculiar.

---

[48] Form actually has the signatures ¢3—¢3—3—3. Munich 26 has ¢3 in all voices!

But Apel does no better. This is his first example from *CC*, and he transcribes part of it [49]. Unfortunately he treats the first section as if it were in his "integer valor", that is, in c, though the prevailing signature is in fact ¢. His final section thus goes twice as fast as it should with respect to the opening. The extreme discrepancy in note values should have signalled this, as should the appearance of the signature c in the tenor, which would have been superfluous had the earlier signature been c. The correct proportional relationship between the sections is evident in the discant, where the change from ¢ to ⊘ demands a constant semibreve.

Cross-level successive relations (such as between c and ¢ or Ȼ and c) are more diffi- cult to handle. Their strictly proportional meaning in simultaneous occurrences in *CC* has been established. Their successive relations, however, have elicited solutions ranging from strict proportion to complete disregard. Modern editions are unreliable, for in numerous places they give the wrong signature, even when supplying an incipit [50]. The scholarly attitude that spawns these practices is stated by Cuyler in her edition of the Masses from *CC*, Book III [51]:

> Time signatures are, variously, c, ¢, ○, ⊘, and proportions of all of these. Isaac worked in that intermediate period when the meaning of *alla breve*, in particular, appears to have been inconsistent, ambiguous, or both. In the present transcrip- tions, therefore, ¢ and ⊘ are transcribed according to context, sometimes as a doubling of the tempo (diminution), often as merely indication of an *accelerando*, with no change of unit value.

Though Cuyler does indicate her procedure in each instance, no justification is offerred apart from the vague "context".

The alleged inconsistency and ambiguity disappear when we examine these Masses. The two signatures on the "uncut" level, ○ and c, appear *only* at the start of a movement, and never after a signature on the "cut" level, except simultaneously with cut signatures in a strictly proportional relationship. Occasional errors crop up, such as the ⊘ in the tenor of the first Kyrie in the *Missa Pascale*. This should surely read ○, as in the other parts. ○ is used as the first signature eleven times in 25 movements; c opens another four; while c follows directly on ○ three times. Nor are these results limited to the

---

[49] Apel, *The Notation ...*, facsimile 35, p. 169 and transcription No. 23.

[50] See, for example, I. 135 verse (p. 250) — the modern edition has c instead of ¢; II. 50 verse (p. 96) — ¢ instead of c; II.52.i. (p. 98) — ¢ instead of c; II.67 verse (p. 129) — c instead of ¢; II.68.i (p. 130) — c instead of ¢; II.72.ii (p. 137) — c instead of ¢; II.76.x (p. 148) — ¢ instead of c; II. 82 (p. 161) — c instead of ¢; II. 84.i (p. 163) — c instead of ¢; II. 88. ix (p. 173) — c instead of ¢; III.12 (p. 93) — ¢ instead of c; III.89.iv (p. 304) — ¢ instead of c; III.99 (p. 331) — c in the incipit instead of ¢; III.119.i (p. 401) — c in the incipit and first section instead of ¢; III. 127 (p. 429) — c in the incipit and alleluia instead of ¢.

[51] Cuyler, *Five Polyphonic Masses ...*, p. 6. Part of the problem is self-spawned. The following signatures, indicated in the commentary, are incorrect. In the *Missa Solemne* Gloria, "Quoniam", the signature is ¢ not ¢3. In the Credo under "Ex Maria" at the text "Et homo factus est" the music is in ¢ and ⊘, not in c and ○. The Agnus 2 begins in ¢3, not in ¢. In the *Missa De Confessoribus*, the signature of the Pleni is ¢ not c, while that of the Agnus discant is also ¢ not c. Only the Formschneider readings are in question here.

Masses in *CC*. Of the fifteen movements in the three Petrucci-Gaffurius Masses edited by Fano, thirteen begin with ○, and c follows ○ once. These uncut signatures are not used as primary signatures elsewhere. In the Masses edited by Staehelin, ○ opens five movements and is never used internally as the main signature. c here occurs once for an internal movement.

However we interpret these uncut signatures, then, the notion that they are used ambiguously in Isaac, at least, is fallacious. The consistency of Isaac's mensural practice throughout *CC*, indeed, would seem to call for a consistent handling of cross-level signatures too, but problems arise. The kinds of note values found under successive cut and uncut signatures, for example, are essentially identical. A proportional interpretation of successive cut and uncut signatures would therefore make most passages governed by uncut signatures half as fast as those under cut signatures. Is such an interpretation viable? III.66 is crucial here (see Example 6, etc.). In Form, the first two sections have the signatures ○ and ○2, respectively, in all voices. This is a classic case of uncut and cut levels found successively. Adopting a scrictly proportional relationship, with ○ ◊ = ○2 ◫ means that the general motion under ○2 is approximately twice as fast as under ○. Yet there are compelling reasons to accept this. Throughout this sequence, the bass carries the liturgical melody[52]. In the first four sections, at least, if the correct proportional relations are observed, the melody is declaimed in the bass at the same tempo. This is apparent in Cuyler's version, except for section iii, which should be in the relation: ○2 ◫ = ¢ ◫ = ¢ ◫ with its neighbors, instead of ○2 ◫ = ¢ ◊ = ¢◫. In addition to this musical continuity, the signatures in Berlin and Vienna present, in the bass, an instance of successive signatures on the same mensural level, ⊙ and ⊙. The validity of this relationship is much more certain, following our proposition stated above. In short, for III.66 at least, the strictly proportional relation of sections i and ii, that is of an uncut and cut signature, is almost certain.

All the instances of cross-level successive relationships in *CC* are listed in Appendix V. Also listed are places where a signature on a mensural level other than ¢ occurs alone, without a simultaneous signature on the "cut" level. In all of *CC* there are at most 23 compositions in which such sections occur. Signatures at the uncut or dotted (i.e., augmenting) levels are so rare that they emerge as rather special, reserved for particular contexts and perhaps demanding unusual modes of performance. Might they not be truly proportional, producing sections which function as "Largos" with respect to the normal tempo? There are many places in the history of music where we accept such successive relations between musical sections. One need only think of the typical *sonata da chiesa* of the 17th century or many of the slow movements of classical sonatas. Could there have been a convention whereby the opening section of many Mass movements in the 16th century was a true "Largo"? And could not such a convention carry over into multi-sectional works such as those found in *CC*?

---

[52] See the version given in *The Utrecht Prosarium*, Sequence ♯58, pp. 99—100. In the first few sections of III.66 the melody is given unadorned; towards the end of the setting it becomes more ornamented.

Many sections in *CC* under uncut signatures are further related by their text. In the two sequences, II.52 and II.76, for example, the passages set to uncut signatures are quite similar. The first section of II.52 (p. 98), the sequence for the Visitation of the BVM discussed above, has the text[53]:

> Piae vocis laudes canta,
> Quia maior omni sancta
> Chorisque angelicis.

This call for pious voices to sing praises to the Virgin is followed by a descriptive stanza telling how Maria was filled with the word of the father. The musical references in the first section set it off from the rest and make a proportional slow performance plausible.

The sequence for the Dedication of a Church, II.76, uses an uncut signature for section x (p. 148). Section ix speaks of the congregation beholding the Lord forever in his eternal city; section xi details how those who are thirsty draw on God, those who are hungry are nourished by him. Section x, however, has the following text[54]:

> Sed frequenter sollemnizat
> Iucundatur, symphonizat
> Ac tibi laudes hymnizat
> Tota caeli curia.

The senate of Heaven makes music, sings hymns of praise to God. Once again a specifically musical context brings forth a "Largo" movement.

Isaac composed two settings of the sequence for Feasts of the Sacred Cross, *Laudes crucis attollamus* by Adam de St. Victore, II.80 and III.101. He selected different stanzas in part each time. In II.80, Isaac omits the opening strophe of the poem and sets the following stanzas as his sections i and ii (pp. 154—155)[55]:

> i. Dulce melos pulset coelos
>   Dulce lignum dulci dignum
>   Psallamus melodia.
> ii. Servi crucis crucem laudent
>   Qui per crucem sibi gaudent
>   Vitae dari munera;
>   Dicant omnes et dicant singuli:
>   Ave, salus totius saeculi,
>   Arbor salutifera.

---

[53] *AH*, 54, ♯196, p. 305.
[54] Clemens Blume, ed., *AH*, 55 (Leipzig, 1922), ♯36, pp. 43—44.
[55] The text is given after *AH*, 54, ♯120, p. 188, with emendations from Form.

The first section speaks of the sweet strains that reach up to heaven, and calls for the singing of psalms in praise of the sweet tree, that is the cross. In the next section servants of the cross are told that they may praise the cross, that it will give them eternal life. In the stanza "Dulce melos pulset coelos", with its musical imagery, Isaac uses an uncut signature, although Form is inconsistent in its presentation.

In his second setting of this text, III. 101 (p. 336), Isaac begins with the opening stanza of the poem:

> Laudes crucis attollamus
> Nos, qui crucis exsultamus
>   Speciali gloria,

and then continues with the two strophes set in II. 80, now sections ii and iii. Section i speaks of raising praises to the cross, exalting it with special glory. The first three sections have the signatures: ○ ⊘ ¢, respectively. ⊘, in short, is used for "Dulce melos," the "musical" passage for which an uncut signature was used before. Cuyler treats this example of cut and uncut signatures in a peculiar manner, but gives the unsuspecting reader no warning. Marking the first verse ♩ = ♩, she transcribes ○ in a reduction of 2:1, ⊘ in 4:1, and ¢ in 2:1, implying successively, ○ ◊ = ⊘ ◊◊ = ¢ ◊. This plays havoc with the relation between ⊘ and ¢, though it shows the proportional relation of sections i and ii. Even with the first section in ○ proportional to the second in ⊘, the latter moves quite slowly for a cut signature. This is clear with respect to section iii in ¢. In section ii (⊘) there are only two ornamental semiminims, for instance, and relatively few minims, while in ¢ (and in ○ of section i) there are many minims and semiminims. While section ii is about the same tempo as section i, then, despite the difference in signatures, both sections are significantly slower than section iii if the relationship ⊘ ◊ = ¢ ◊ is honored. But the section in ⊘ is precisely to the text "Dulce melos tangat coelos". With so few examples of the manipulation of successive cut and uncut signatures in CC, is it merely accidental that two of them affect the same text?

Despite this evidence, there are passages in uncut or dotted signatures which might seem too slow if performed in a proportional relationship to the surrounding cut signatures. Furthermore, there are instances in which musical relationships would be upset by a strictly proportional reading[56]. In other instances, however, these are brought out by a correct proportional reading. The case of III.66 has already been discussed. Another good example is the sequence for the Assumption of the BVM, III.126 (pp. 422 —428). Cuyler reads sections i (○2) and ii (⊘) in a 4:1 reduction, section iii (○) in 2:1, and sections iv—ix (essentially ¢) in 2:1. This implies: ○2 𝄴 = ⊘ ◊◊ = ○ ◊ = ¢ ◊. If instead of ○ ◊ = ¢ ◊ we read ○ ◊ = ¢𝄴, which is proportionately correct, one

---

[56] See II.50 (pp. 95—96), where the introit is in ¢ and its verse in c. The cadential measure at the end of the two sections, however, is essentially identical. Similarly, in II.100 (pp. 194—195), the opening figure of section ii is much the same as the opening figure of section iv, but the former is in c and the latter in ¢.

advantage musically is apparent in the final section, "Ut sibi auxilio". The melody of "Congaudent" from section i in the alto reappears again and again throughout the last section, while the melody of "gloriosae" in the tenor of section i reappears at "esse" in the discant of the last section. With the proper proportions observed, these melodic references have the same tempo.

While I am not prepared, then, to assert that cross-level signatures must always receive proportional treatment, I consider it a strong possibility. Only for sections not on the normal, "cut" level in *CC* must the editor's discretion be relied upon. In III.126, for example, it may be justifiable to deny a strict proportional relation between ○ and its surrounding signatures, but to read ⊕ in a false proportional relationship to ¢ is indefensible.

Throughout *CC*, then, it is almost always possible to know the correct proportional relationship between successive signatures. Even if we do not read successive cross-level signatures in a strictly proportional manner, uncut signatures clearly demand a significant slowing down of the tempo. To indicate this, they might be transcribed at a lesser reduction ratio than the norm. In no case do I believe the performer to be obligated to follow a strictly proportional reading from section to section of a composition, though within a section I think it imperative. But a modern edition must offer him the correct range in which to make his decisions, and this range should be immediately apparent in the notation. An edition of *CC* embracing these features would go a long way towards making intelligent performance of this music feasible.

To what extent can the results of this analysis be applied to other composers, or indeed even to the entire œuvre of Isaac? At this stage it is impossible to say. The need for similar analyses of other composers of the Renaissance is clear. Regional variations in practice may exist and a study of manuscript groups or individual printers may provide further insights. We must always remember that the meaning of proportions was a contested issue in the 16th century as well, not only in theoretical literature but in practical sources. That this affected the music of Isaac may be seen in one final example. The section "Qualis sit tu scis" from the sequence for Maria Magdalena, II.56. x (p. 111), is provided with a resolution in the manuscript Leipzig 49 (see fn 39). It is written in ¢ throughout, eliminating the complex (and in the Leipzig version peculiar) signatures of the original. But in the resolution, ¢3 ◇ is made equivalent to the resolving ¢ ◇ , while in the next section c2 ◇ is correctly made equal to the resolving ¢◇. Thus, in the resolution, ¢ 3 ◇ = c 2 ◇ , a successive relation between these signatures that is unquestionably wrong for Isaac. Yet in the midst of the 16th century, at least one scribe believed it to be correct[57].

To understand the music of Isaac one must study his mensural system. The implications of mensural practice for the correct performance of the music have been amply demonstrated. It should be apparent too that mensural symbolism was not unknown to Isaac.

---

[57] Professor Winfried Kirsch in a private communication has assured me that Leipzig 49 is a very unreliable manuscript. Nonetheless, it does attest to the confusion about proportional relations that existed even at approximately the time of publication of *CC*.

The *Choralis Constantinus* in particular probably represents the most extensive and unified single source we have for information about the practical workings of the mensural system. The lessons we learn from it should help dispel the myths that have arisen around the problem of mensural practice and ultimately lead us to unravel the overlapping strands of theory and practice that dominated this most central feature of the "Künste" of the Netherlanders.

APPENDIX I

Data for Example 3: Relationships among Imperfect, Simultaneous Signatures in "CC".

Signatures Compared	Simultaneous Occurrences
¢ ◇ = c ◇ ¢ / c	II.3.iv (p. 9) (Rhau, RISM 1545⁵, resolves c to ¢; Augsburg 23 does not change from ○ to c, but this has no practical effect); II.48.iv (p. 92); II.94 — verse (p. 183); II.100.i (p. 194) (twice); III.48.iii (p. 180).
¢ ◇ = c ◇ ¢ / c	See pp. 77—78 above. II.28.i, etc. (p. 52); II.36.iv (p. 69); II.76.xi, etc. (p. 148); II.80.i, etc. (p. 154); III.48.i, etc. (p. 177); III.76 (p. 252); III.95.iii (p. 325).
¢ ◇ = c2 ◇ ¢ / c2	III.89.vi (p. 306) (Form has c2 in alto; Berlin, Munich 38, and Vienna also have c2 in bass).
¢ ◇ = ¢2 II (a) ¢ / ¢2	I.75 (p. 121); I.76 (p. 122); II.40.vi (p. 80); II.94 (p. 182); II.100.i (p. 194); III.57 — verse (p. 201) (only in Berlin).
(b) ¢ / ¢ ... 2	I.123.iv (p. 230) (Munich 26 remains in ¢); II.99 (p. 192); III.48.iii (p. 180).
(c) ¢ / ²⁄₁	II.3.iv (p. 9) (Rhau, RISM 1545⁵, resolves ²⁄₁ to ¢).
¢ ◇ = 4 II ¢ (a) ¢ / ¢ ... 2 ... 4	II.99 (p. 192); III.48.iii (p. 180).
(b) ¢ / ²⁄₁ ... ⁴⁄₁	II.3.iv (p. 9) (Rhau, RISM 1545⁵, resolves ⁴⁄₁ to ¢).
¢2 or II = c2 ◇ (a) ¢2 / c2	II.56.x (p. 111).*
(b) ¢ / c2 (C)	II.100.i (p. 194).
¢2 II = Ͻ II ¢2 / Ͻ	II.56.x (p. 111).*
¢2 or II = 4 II ¢2 ... 4 ◇Ͻ ... 3 ... 2 CϹ ... 4	II.100.i (p. 194).

Signatures Compared	Simultaneous Occurrences
4 𝄵 = ⊖ ◇	¢2 … 4 ⟜	II.56.x (p. 111).*
c ◇ = c2 𝄵	(a) c / c2	II.100.i (p. 194). •
	(b) c / c … 2	III.71—verse (p. 243) (Berlin erroneously has $\phi \ldots {}^{2}_{1}$).
c ◇ = ¢2 𝄵	c / ¢2	II.100.i (p. 194).
c ◇ = ⊘ 𝄵	⊘ c	II.19.vi (p. 38); II.56.x (p. 111).*
c ◇ = 4 𝄵	c / ¢2 … 4	II.56.x (p. 111).*
c2 ◇ = ⊘ 𝄵	¢2 / ⟜	II.56.x (p. 111).*
c2 ◇ = 4 𝄵	c2 / ¢2 … 4	II.100.i (p. 194).

♀ Notice that "4" is not cumulative; that is, here it means ¢4, not ¢2 x 4 or ¢8.

* See fn. 39 for a discussion of the variant concordances for II.56.x (p. 111).

APPENDIX II

Data for Example 4: Relationships among Simultaneous Signatures in CC with Some Level of Perfect Subdivision.

Signatures Compared		Simultaneous Occurrences
¢ II = ¢3 or II 3	(a) ¢ ¢...3	I. 96.iii (p. 153); I.96.iv (p. 153); I.102.ii (p. 165); I.108.x (p. 188); I.117.ii (p. 215); II.9—verse (p. 18) (triple meter in discant produced through coloration under ¢); II.14—verse (p. 25); II.17.ii (p. 32); II.22 (p. 42); II.24.iii (p. 45); II.76.xii (p. 150); III.66.iv (pp. 225—226); III. 66.ix (pp. 229—231) (triple meter in discant and bass produced through coloration under ¢); III.112 (pp. 373—374); III.118.vi (p. 393); III.126.v (p. 425).
	(b) ¢ ¢...3	In the following, "3" appears against a final long, so that the proportion is not unambiguous. I.108.viii (p. 186); I.120.ii (p. 220); II.61 (p. 120); II.80.ix (p. 158) ("3" merely annotates coloration here).
	(c) ¢ ¢3	II.3.v (p. 9) (Augsburg 23 has "3" instead of "¢"; only breve rests are involved); II.7.iii (p. 14) (Form: [¢], ¢, 3, ¢3; Augsburg 23: 3, 3, 3, 3; only breve rests in discant and alto); II.31 — verse (p. 57) (Form: c3, [¢], ¢, ¢3; Augsburg 7 and Regensburg C96: ¢3, ¢3, ¢3; c3 in Form is an error; only breve rests in alto and tenor); II.80.x (p. 159); III.66.ix (p. 229); III.95.iii (p. 324) (Form: all ¢; Munich 36: ¢, ¢, ¢3, ¢3; only breve rests in tenor and bass); III.126.v (p. 424).
	(d) ¢3...¢ ¢3	II.32.x (p. 62); III.192.iii (pp. 313—314) (Munich 38, Berlin, all voices return to ¢; only breves involved).
	(e) ¢...3...¢ ¢...3	The concluding "¢" appears against a final long, so that the proportion is not unambiguous. II.7.vi (p. 16); III.4.ix (p. 75).
	(f) c2...3	II.100.i (p. 194) (NB: "3" continues to mean ¢3, even when it follows c2).
¢ II = ⊙·♭ ¢ II = ⊙○◊		III.48.iii (p. 179). II.3.iv (p. 9) (Rhau, RISM 1545⁵, resolves ○ to ¢); II.100.i (p. 194); III.48.iii (p. 180); III.66.v (p. 226).
¢ II = ⊙♭ ¢ II = ⊙2 II ¢ ◊ = ⊕◊◊		III.48.iii (p. 179). II.100.i (p. 194); III.66.iv (p. 225). II.11.vii (p. 23) (Augsburg 23 also gives a resolution in ¢ throughout); III.66.v (p. 226).

Signatures Compared		Simultaneous Occurrences
¢3 𝄵 = ¢2 𝄵	¢...3 ¢2	II.100.i (p. 194) (twice).
¢3 𝄵 = ¢2 (etc.) or 𝄵 / ¢C	c...c2...3 ¢2....4.... ¢....3....2 c2..3.....¢C..4	II.100.i (p. 194) (three times).
¢3 𝄵 = O2 𝄵	(a) ¢...3 O2	II.100.i (p. 194).
	(b) ¢...3 O2	III.66.iv (p. 226).
¢3 𝄵 = 4 𝄵𝄵	c2...3 ¢2....4..... ¢....3....2 ¢C....4	II.100.i (p. 194) (twice).
⊖ ◇ = O ◇		II.19.vi (p. 38); III.66.v (p. 226). (In III.49.v [p. 185], Form has O against ⊖ without proportional meaning. In Berlin the tenor is correctly notated in ⊖.)
⊖ ◇ = c ♭		II.19.vi (p. 38).
⊖ ◇ = ⊕ ◇		II.54—verse (p. 106).
⊖ ◇ = ⊖ 𝄵		II.19.vi (p. 38).
c ◇ = ⊙ ♭		II.52.i (p. 98); II.100.i (p. 194).
c 𝄵 = ⊙ 𝄵		III.77.ii (p. 255).
c ◇ = O ◇		II.19.vi (p. 38); II.100.i (p. 194) (twice); III.71 — verse (p. 243) (Berlin has c, O, and ¢ together; the latter is incorrect and should read c).

Signatures Compared | Simultaneous Occurrences

Signatures Compared	Simultaneous Occurrences
¢ ◊ = ○2 𝍇	II.100.i (p. 194) (three times).
¢ ◊ = ¢3 𝍇 (a) ¢...3 ¢ (b) ¢2...3 ¢	II.100.i (p. 194).
⊙ ◊ = ⊙ ◊	II.100.i (p. 194).
¢· ◊ = ○2 𝍇	II.100.i (p. 194) (twice); III.30.vii (p. 139).
¢2 ◊ = ○2 ◊	II.100.i (p. 194).
○ ◊ = Ɖ 𝍇	II.19. vi (p. 38).
○ 𝍇 = ¢· ◊	II.96.i (p. 184); II.100.i (p. 194) (twice).
○ ◊ = ·⊃ ◊	III.77.iv (p. 257).
○ 𝍇 = ⊙ ◊	II.36.i (p. 68); II.100.i (p. 194).
○ ◊ = ¢2 𝍇 ¢...2 ○	III.71—verse (p. 243) (Berlin has ¢ incorrectly).
○ ◊ = ○2 𝍇	II.100.i (p. 194) three times); III.65.v (p. 221) (○ ...2).
⊙ ◊ = ○2 𝍇	II.100.i (p. 194).

APPENDIX III

(a). *Successive Appearance of ¢ and "3" or of ¢ and "¢3."*

¢ followed by "3" in all voices

I.1 (pp. 7—9) (twice); I.17 (p. 37); I.24 (p. 49); I.55 (p. 93); I.61 (p. 102); I.108.xiii (p. 192); I.109 (p. 193) (Form erroneously has "2" in the discant; Munich 26 has the correct "3"); I.112 (p. 200); I.115 (p. 210); I.116 (p. 212); I.117.i (p. 214); I.118 (p. 216); I.123.i (p. 227); I.135 (p. 249); II.7.vi (p. 16); II.11.vi (p.23); II.17.iii (p. 33); II.25 (p. 49) (twice); II.26 (p. 50); II.27—verse (p. 52); II.33 (p. 64); II.36.vi (p. 70); II.36.xi (p. 73); II.41 (p. 81); II.44.vii (p. 87); II.49 (p. 94); II.57 (p. 112); II.60.iv (p. 117); II.76.ix (p. 148); II.78 (p. 152); II.84.v (p. 165); II.96.ix (p. 189); III.3 (p. 66); III. 4.ix (p. 75); III.26 (p. 125); III.37 (p. 152); III.50 (p. 189); III.68 (p. 236); III.84.ii (p. 282); III.86.iv (p. 296); III.93 (p. 318); III.95.iii (p. 324) (Munich 36 and Vienna begin tenor and bass with ¢3 instead of ¢ as in Form; only breve rests are involved); III.118.v (p. 392); III.118.vii (p. 394); III.130 (p. 439).

¢ followed by "¢3" in all voices

I.4.vii—viii (p. 16); II.11.ii—iii (p. 21); II.28.vi—vii (p. 54) (Augsburg 23 has Ⓞ3; Regensburg C96 agrees with Form); II.38 (p. 76); II.46 (p. 90) (the discant in the verse reads "¢3" in Form, not "3" as in Webern); II.48.ii—iii (pp. 91—92); II.52.iv—v (p. 100); II.56.ix—x (pp. 110—111); II.64.vii—viii (p. 125); II.68. viii—ix (p. 132); II.70 (p. 135); II.88.viii—ix (pp. 172—173); III.10.vi—vii (pp. 89—90); III.29.vi—vii (p. 134); III.48.iii—iv (p. 180); III.49.vi—vii (p. 187); III.77.viii—ix (p. 260); III.92.v—vi (p. 315); III.101. iv—v (p. 339); III.101.xi—xii (pp. 344—345); III.110 (p. 370); III.119.ix—x (pp. 405—406); III.126.vii— viii (p. 426); III.128.iv—v (p. 434); III.131.ix—x (p. 446); III.133.vi—vii (p. 453).

(b). *Places with Inconsistencies.*

I.70 (p. 115).

	Discant, alto, tenor:	¢	3	¢		Augsburg 7: All voices:	¢	3	¢.
	Bass:	¢3		¢.					

The same piece is preserved in CC as II.57 (p. 112), where the bass in Form is ¢   3   ¢. The confusion in Form may have arisen because the bass changes to "¢3" at the start of a new staff.

I.96.iv (p. 154).

					Munich 26: All voices change to ¢3 at the end.
Discant:	[¢]			¢3	
Alto:	¢	3	¢	¢3	
Tenor, bass:	¢	3	¢	3	

When all voices change to triple time, the piece changes from a two-part to a four-part texture (tenor and bass had only rests until this point). "¢3" may make sense in that context.

II.7.iii (p. 14).

Form: Discant: [¢]   3
        Alto: ¢   3
        Tenor: 3   ¢   ¢3
        Bass: ¢3   ¢   ¢   3

II.24.ix—x (pp. 47—48).

Neither source is consistent. The discant and alto have only breve rests until the tenor and bass switch to ¢.

Form: Section: i—ix   x
        Discant: ¢   3
        Alto, tenor, bass: ¢   ¢3

Augsburg 23:   All voices: ⊕3   ¢

Surely ¢3 is intended for the discant in Form. For the use of ⊕3 in Augsburg 23, see fn. 30.

II.32.iv. (p. 59).

Form: Section: iii   iv   v
        Discant, alto, tenor: ○2   ¢3   ¢
        Bass: ○2   3   ¢

Augsburg 23:
   Discant: 3   ¢   3
   Alto: 3   ¢   3
   Tenor: 3   ¢   ¢3
   Bass: 3   ¢   3

Augsburg 7:   Section: iii   iv   v
Regensburg C96:   All voices: ○2   ¢3   ¢

The manuscript reading is correct.

II.36.vi (p. 70).

Form: Section: v   vi
        Tenor: ⊖   ¢3   3
        Bass: ⊖   3   3

Augsburg 7:   Section: v   vi
Stuttgart 40:   All voices: ⊖   ¢3   ¢

Again the manuscript reading is correct.

III.119.xii (p. 407).

Form   Discant, tenor, bass: 3   ¢
and: Alto: ¢3   ¢
Berlin

Munich 35:   All voices: ¢   3   ¢

The reading of Munich 35 is correct.

APPENDIX IV

Successive Appearance of ¢ and ⊙ in All Voices.

I.4.ix—x (p. 17); I.114.iv—v (pp. 207—208); I.120.iii—iv (p. 222); I.136 (p. 251); II.11.iv—v (p. 22); II.28.viii—ix (pp. 54—55); II.32.i—ii (p. 59) (Regensburg C96 has ◯ in alto instead of ⊘; it is without proportional meaning and presumably is an error); II.32. viii—ix (p. 61); II.36.iv—v (p. 70) (for the problem of ¢ and ¢ in Form, see p. 77 above); II.84.vi—vii (p. 165); II.92.x—xi (pp. 180—181); III.10.iv—v (p. 88); III.10.vii—viii (p. 91); III.49.iv—v (p. 185) (◯ in the tenor in Form is incorrect; Berlin and Vienna both have ⊘); III.89.ii—iii (p. 303); III.92.ii—iii (p. 313); III.106.iv—v (p. 358); III.117.iii—iv (p. 386); III.124.vii—viii (p. 419).

APPENDIX V

Cross-level Successive Signatures in CC.

Composition	Signatures	Comments
II.11.vi—vii (p. 23)	*vi* *vii* — ₵ 3 ⊙ — ⊕ — ₵ (bass)	Augsburg 23, a late manuscript, offers a resolution of section vii in ₵ throughout in which ₵ ♭ = ₵ ◇ . This posits a single level of difference between the signatures, whereas a proportional reading would demand a double level. In the Augsburg reading, section vii is at the same tempo throughout; in a proportional reading, the first part would be significantly slower.
II.28.i—ii (p. 52)	*i* *ii* — ₵ ₵	This is a possible interpretation. Manuscript evidence is discussed on pp. 77—78.
II.36.i—ii—iii (pp. 68—69)	*i* *ii* *iii* — ○ (tenor) C ₵ — ⊙	This is the probable order. Manuscript evidence is discussed on pp. 77—78.
II.50 (pp. 95—96)	Introit verse — ₵ c	No concordances exist.
II.52.i—ii (p. 98)	*i* *ii* — c C 3 — ₵ c 3 — Bass:	No concordances exist.
II.76.ix—xi (p. 148)	*ix* *x* *xi* — ₵ 3	₵ — c ₵	No concordances exist.
II.80.i—ii (pp. 154—155)	*i* *ii* — o ₵	This is a possible interpretation. No concordances exist. See the discussion on pp. 77—78 and on pp. 93—94.
II.96.i—ii (pp. 184—185)	*i* *ii* — ○ (tenor) ₵ — C —	No concordances exist.

Composition	Signatures	Comments
II.98 (pp. 191—192)	*Introit verse* ○ ○2	No concordances exist.
II.100.i—ii—iii (pp. 194—195)	*i* *ii* *iii* [c2] 3 | ¢ [¢2] 4 c [¢] [¢3] 2 | ¢ [¢ ¢] 4 c ¢	There are concordances only for section i.
III.12 (p. 93)	c *Communion*	Form and Berlin have c alone; Augsburg 23 has ¢.
III.48.i—ii (pp. 177—178)	*i* *ii* c ¢	This is the probable order. Manuscript evidence is discussed on pp. 77—78.
III.60 (p. 206)	*Alleluia* *verse* ¢ c	Cuyler incorrectly shows "¢" for the verse. Both Form and Berlin have "c".
III.65.iv—v—vi (pp. 220—222)	*iv* *v* *vi* [¢] ○○ c 6 c ○○ 2 (discant)	Berlin has $\frac{6}{2}$ instead of simply "6." Cuyler reads six semibreves under "6" in the place of two under c. This interpretation seems reasonable, particularly in the light of the signature in Berlin. It is not clear, however, why all notes under "6" are given in coloration.
III.66.i—ii (pp. 222—223)	*i* *ii* ○ ○2	See the discussion of this piece on pp. 86—87 and 92 above.
III.71 (p. 243)	*Introit* *verse* ¢ c ¢ ○○ ¢ c 2	Berlin incorrectly has a ¢ at the beginning of the discant in the verse.

Composition	Signatures	Comments
III.76 (pp. 252—253)	*Alleluia verse* i ii iii iv v c ¢ ¢ ○ v	This is the probable order. Manuscript evidence is discussed on pp. 77—78.
III.77.i—x (pp. 254—261)	i ii iii iv v vi ⊕ c ¢ ○ ○2 c2 vii viii ix x ¢ ¢ ¢3 ¢₃⊂ ⊙	The meaning of ⊃ internally in sections ii and iv is discussed above (p. 83 and fn. 38). The meaning of the signatures in section x is not entirely clear. ⌇ is used in III.118.vi (p. 393) with the semibreve perfect. Here, however, the breve is perfect under ⌇ and the semibreve imperfect. Nonetheless, it seems possible that the successive relation used by Cuyler: ¢ ⊟ = ³⌇⊟ = ⊃ ⊟ , which treats ⌇ as if it meant the same as ¢3, should be revised, with ³⌇= ¢ ⊟ , as in III.118.vi. This is the only time Isaac uses ⊃ in CC. It is presumably identical in meaning to ¢.
III.79 (p. 265)	*Communion* ¢ ⊂3 ¢ iii iv v vi ¢ ¢ c3 ¢3	Berlin has "c3" instead of ⊂3. This passage is problematical and the meaning of the signature obscure.
III.89.iii—vi (pp. 303—305)		Form has "c" for section iv, but Berlin, Vienna, and Munich 38 all have "¢".
III.90 (pp. 307—309)	*Introit verse* c ¢ ¢ ¢	Berlin and Munich 38 agree.
III.101.i—iii (pp. 336—337)	i ii iii ○ ⊕ ¢	Form and Berlin agree that the signature of section ii is ⊕. Munich 37 has ⊕3, which makes no sense in this context.
III.126.i—iv (pp. 422—424)	i ii iii iv ○2 ⊕ ○ ¢	Munich 36 agrees.

HEINRICH HUSMANN

Johann Faulhaber (1580–1635):
Mathematiker und mensuraler Meistersinger

Seit über siebzig Jahren ist der Ulmer Meistergesang der Musikwissenschaft bekannt[1]. Robert Staiger hat ihn in seiner Berliner Dissertation über Benedict von Watt (1908) berücksichtigt[2] und erst jüngst erscheint er auch in einer Göttinger Dissertation von Eva Schumann[3]. Hier soll etwas näher auf die Ulmer Meistersinger, insbesondere den bedeutendsten von ihnen, Johann Faulhaber, eingegangen werden, als es in den beiden anderen Publikationen geschieht.

Vom Ulmer Meistergesang sind uns im ganzen 17 Melodien erhalten, die von Dichtern zweier Generationen stammen: Fünf Melodien kommen von Johann Faulhaber und sind alle 1604 komponiert, vier Melodien schuf Augustin Löschenbrand 1607, während Mattheus Rembold 1642 eine Melodie beisteuerte, Johannes Baur zwei Melodien 1661 und Michael Scheifele fünf Weisen, 1663, 1663, 1664, 1665 und 1665. Die Berufe dieser Sänger sind nur zum Teil bürgerlich: Johann Baur ist Weber, Mich. Scheifele Kürschner, der Beruf des sonst nicht erwähnten Augustin Löschenbrand ist unbekannt; dagegen war Mattheus Rembold ein hoch angesehener Kupferstecher, der die Stiche zu Joseph Furtenbachs *Architectura privata* (Augsburg 1641) schuf, und Johann Faulhaber vollends gehört zu den besten Mathematikern seines Zeitalters.

Johann Faulhaber war in Ulm am 5. 5. 1580 als Sohn des Webers Samuel Faulhaber geboren, — seine Biographie findet man in Albrecht Weyermanns *Nachrichten von Gelehrten, Künstlern und anderen merkwürdigen Personen aus Ulm* (Ulm 1798, S. 206 bis 215), eine neuere Darstellung von Höchstetter in der *Allgemeinen Deutschen Biographie* 6 (1877, S. 581—583). In den vollständig erhaltenen Rathsprotokollen (im Stadtarchiv Ulm) kann man weitere Einzelheiten, in seinem Nachlaß auch einige weitere Gedichte u. ä. finden. Faulhaber ist ein interessanter Mann, Mathematiker, Astronom, Astrologe, Alchimist, Angehöriger der Rosenkranzfraternität, Meistersinger und endlich einer der berühmtesten Festungsbaumeister seiner Zeit, der für Fürsten und Könige baute. Er starb an der Pest in Ulm 1635. Zwei markante Ereignisse haben immer wieder besonderen Eindruck erweckt, seine Vorhersage eines Kometen für 1618, der auch tatsächlich pünktlich erschien, und der Besuch, den ihm Descartes um 1620 machte und den Daniel Lipstorp in seinen *Specimina Philosophiae Cartesianae* (Leyden 1653, S. 78 ff.) so farbig beschrieben hat.

[1] Siehe Georg Richard Kruse, *Die Ulmer Meistersinger*. In: Neue Musikzeitung, Jg. 22, Heft 4, Stuttgart—Leipzig 1901, S. 44—45.

[2] Robert Staiger, *Benedict von Watt. Ein Beitrag zur Kenntnis des bürgerlichen Meistergesangs um die Wende des XVI. Jahrhunderts* (= *Publikationen der Internationalen Musikgesellschaft*. Beihefte. 2. Folge, XIII), Leipzig 1914.

[3] Eva Schumann, *Stilwandel und Gestaltveränderung im Meistersang*. Phil. Diss. Göttingen 1970 (erschienen als Band 3 der *Göttinger Musikwissenschaftlichen Arbeiten*, 1972).

Daß es sich bei dem Meistersinger auch wirklich um den berühmten Mathematiker handelt, geht einwandfrei aus den Ulmer Musikheften hervor, in denen er „Rechenmeister Ulmensis, jetziger Zeit bestellter Ingenieur daselbsten anno 1627" genannt wird, — er war in der Tat Leiter einer Rechenschule, also „Rechenmeister", und Festungsbauingenieur. Freilich sind seine Weisen Erzeugnisse seiner Jugend, — 1604 war er 24 Jahre alt. Was den Melodien Faulhabers und der ihm folgenden späteren Ulmer Meistersinger ihre besondere Charakteristik gibt, ist ihre mensurale Messung. Darin ist ihnen auch Johann Christoph Wagenseil in seinem *Buch von der Meistersinger Holdseligen Kunst* (in dessen *De sacri Romani imperii libera civitate Noribergensi*, Altdorf 1697, S. 433 bis 576) bei der Aufzeichnung der vier gekrönten Töne (a.a.O., hinter S. 554) gefolgt, während die Nürnberger Meistersinger auch des 17. Jhs. (s. unten) an einer mensurlosen Rhythmik festhielten, die nur etwa bei Ambr. Metzger Zerlegungen in Fusae (Achtel) aufnimmt. Wagenseil benutzt im letzten, vierten Ton sogar Taktstriche, was nicht einmal die Ulmer Meistersinger in Betracht zogen.

Ich teile als erstes Beispiel die dritte Weise Faulhabers, die „Gedichtklingende Reimweise" mit. Durch kleine Striche über den Notenlinien deute ich Semibreven an, — zwei weiße Minimae füllen bei Wagenseil einen Takt, wobei Wagenseils Vorzeichnung c ist. Da Faulhabers Melodien ¢ (alla breve) vorgezeichnet haben (was nur gerade bei Nr. 3 versehentlich fehlt), zeige ich nur jede zweite Semibrevis durch Striche an, damit man kontrollieren kann, inwieweit sich jeweils zwei Semibreven zu einem Brevistakt zusammenschließen[4]:

Ex. 1

Joh. Faulhaber, Gedichtklingende Reimweise, 1604

---

[4] Zur Schreibung von c und ¢ in dieser Zeit vergleiche man Praetorius' *Syntagma musicum* III (1619, S. 48 ff.), und hierzu die Kontroverse Carl Dahlhaus, *Zur Entstehung des modernen Taktsystems im 17. Jahrhundert.* In: Archiv für Musikwissenschaft XVIII, 1961, S. 223—240; Hans Otto Hiekel, *Der Madrigal- und Motettentypus in der Mensurallehre des Michael Praetorius.* Ebenda, XIX/XX, 1962/63, S. 40—55; Carl Dahlhaus, *Zur Taktlehre des Michael Praetorius.* In: Musikforschung XVII, 1964, S. 162—169; und Paul Brainard, *Zur Deutung der Diminution in der Tactuslehre des Michael Praetorius.* Ebenda, S. 169—174.

recht___ tut _____ lie - ben der wird die ru - ten an ihm___ ü - ben

Abgesang

gibt es ein _____ gros - se freud___ von ___ her - zen

dann wo schon _____ sein va - - - ter mit _____ schmer - zen

In der zweiten und vierten Zeile geht der Notentext auch nicht in Semibreven auf, — durch Voransetzung einer halben Pause nach dem Vorbild der Zeile 3 kann man diesen Schaden beheben. Dann aber gehen alle Zeilen des Stollens sogar auch in Breven auf. Dem setzt sich aber der Anfang des Abgesangs entgegen, — hier steht, wenn man Brevistakte durchführt und zwar so, daß wie in allen übrigen Versen auch hier an das Ende des 1. Abgesangverses ein voller Takt tritt, eine Semibrevis als Auftakt.

Sieht man sich die Textdeklamation an, so stellt man fest, daß auf sie nicht die geringste Rücksicht genommen wird. Die Taktgliederung ist also nur eine rein geometrische Koordinate, auf der die Melodie abrollt. Dagegen spiegelt sich die Verteilung der Hebungen und Senkungen des Textes in Längen und Kürzen der Melodie wider: Der weibliche Schluß der Verse ist stets als Ganze — Halbe gestaltet. Auch im Innern der Verse trifft man oft Fälle, in denen betonte Silben als Längen ausgebildet sind; aber dem stehen andere Stellen — z. B. *in dem dreißigsten* oder *also heben* — gegenüber, die gerade umgekehrt verfahren. Unbetonte Silben können beliebige Längen haben, — Melismen auf leichten Silben begegnen ja in allen europäischen einstimmigen Musikstilen von der Gregorianik an. Es sind also nur die Versenden reguliert, — und dies auch nur als lang—kurz, nicht als betont—unbetont, da ihre taktische Einfügung der Taktgliederung widerspricht.

Rob. Staiger hat die mensurierte Schreibung überhaupt als Andeutung betrachtet und eine taktlose „Übertragung" in gleichen Notenwerten (mit Ausnahme der Koloraturen) hinzugefügt[5]. Selbst in den Koloraturen hat er die Notenwerte nach eigenem Ermessen ohne irgendein ersichtliches Prinzip ganz willkürlich verändert. Das alles ist unnötig; denn bei Faulhabers Gebrauch sogar von Semifusae (Sechzehntel, — so in der „Absterbenden Versmelodie") hat man ein sehr langsames Vortragstempo zu wählen, damit die Melismen klar herauskommen. Dann tritt der Unterschied zwischen betonten und unbetonten Taktteilen aber ganz zurück und es entsteht eine Folge von ziemlich gleich schweren Minimae. Die dann durchaus sympathische Melodiegestalt zeigt aber damit wieder den gregorianischen Charakter, den man dem Meistergesang öfter vindiziert hat.

Diesem Musikbeispiel, das die besondere Behandlung der weiblichen Versenden klar zeigt, obwohl im Versinnern keine Charakterisierung betonter oder unbetonter Silben

[5] Siehe Anmerkung 2; S. 27 des originalen Teildrucks.

eintritt, stelle ich ein zweites Musikbeispiel entgegen, das die Behandlung der männlichen Versenden demonstriert. Es handelt sich um Joh. Faulhabers 4. Weise, den „Vierzehnbündigen Carmenton".

Ex. 2

Joh. Faulhaber, Vierzehnbündiger Carmenton, 1604

Die Textunterlegung ist in diesem Beispiel so ungenau, daß sich für das Innere der Verse keine exakten Feststellungen machen lassen. Am Versende aber fällt die Schlußsilbe immer auf den Anfang des Brevistaktes. Die Schlußsilbe kann, wie im 1. Vers, sogar ein Melisma von drei Brevistakten Länge umfassen; aber andererseits, wenn sie kein Melisma trägt, ist nur eine Semibrevis notiert und man darf annehmen, daß sie auf die Länge einer vollen Brevis zu dehnen ist. Auch bei männlichen Versen tritt also eine charakteristische Behandlung der Schlußsilbe ein.

Drei der Ulmer Meistersinger haben auch den Weg in das Repertoire der Nürnberger Meistersinger gefunden, die beiden hier (eben deshalb) als Beispiele veröffentlichten Töne Faulhabers und die Goldfarbene Jungfrauweise Löschenbrands. Die drei Stücke stehen in der Handschrift Will III 793 der Stadtbibliothek Nürnberg als Nummern 29, 30 und 52 (f. 11, f. 11 und f. 22 respective). Es ist sehr interessant zu sehen, wie die mensurlosen Nürnberger Meistersinger die mensurierten Ulmer Melodien aufgefaßt haben. Als Beispiel gebe ich in Notenbeispiel 3 die in Notenbeispiel 2 in der Ulmer Fassung gebrachte „Vierzehnbündige Carmenweise" Faulhabers in der Form der Handschrift Will III 793.

Ex. 3

Joh. Faulhaber, Vierzehnbündiger Carmenton 1604 in der Fassung der Handschrift Nürnberg, Stadtbibliothek, Will III 793

Die Weisen dieser späten Nürnberger Meistersingerhandschriften sind, wie auch das wiedergegebene Beispiel, zumeist ohne Text aufgezeichnet. Dieser ist ja in der Tat überflüssig, da man nur die Melodie benutzt, um einen neuen, zu ihr passenden Text zu dichten. Für die nicht abbrechende Kontroverse instrumental—vokal liegt hier ein beachtenswerter Fall quasi instrumentaler Aufzeichnung einer vokalen Melodie vor, der in keiner Weise instrumentalen Vortrag bedeutet.

In der Nürnberger Fassung von Faulhabers Weise ist die Nürnberger Notationspraxis konsequent durchgeführt: alle Einzelnoten und alle Anfangsnoten eines Melismas sind als Semibreven geschrieben, alle zweiten und folgenden Noten einer Koloratur erscheinen als Semiminimae, auch die letzte einer Verszeile des Stollens oder des ganzen Stückes, die dann öfter deswegen eine Corona zeigt. Den weißen Semibreven dieser Handschriften sind später oft Hälse angefügt worden, so daß nunmehr die Einzelnoten und die Anfangsnoten der Melismen doppelt so lang sind wie die inneren Noten der Melismen; denn diese Anfügung der Minimahälse ist als Mensurierung zu verstehen, — so sieht etwa auch Wagenseils Schreibung der vier gekrönten Töne aus. Deshalb ist eben die vorliegende ursprüngliche Fassung als nicht mensuriert anzusehen, d. h. die Semiminimae der Melismen sind nicht etwa als Viertelnoten, die Semibreven als ganze Noten aufzufassen, sondern das Verhältnis zwischen ihnen wird — der späteren mensurierten Notierung entsprechend — als 2:1 anzunehmen sein. Eine ähnliche Notierung, die das Wertverhältnis 2:1 durch ein Notenverhältnis 4:1 darstellt, findet man schon im 15. Jh., wo, wie etwa im Utrechter Liederbuch, Longen (statt Breven) und Semibreven als Grundwerte benutzt werden. Mit der einheitlichen Schreibung von Semibreven und Semiminimen ist die komplizierte Rhythmik der Faulhaberschen Melodie restlos zerstört worden. Aus der äqualen Nürnberger Fassung ist sie auch in keiner Weise wieder rekonstruierbar. Sollten die Nürnberger Meistersinger trotz der äqualen Schreibung der Melodien diese in improvisierter komplizierter Rhythmik ausgeführt haben, was nicht unbedingt von der Hand zu weisen ist, so hätten sie jedenfalls die Originalform der Faulhaberschen Melodie nicht durch reine Intuition aus dieser äqualen Fassung finden können. Es läßt sich auch denken, daß eine kompliziert erfundene Melodie einfach notiert wurde, aber in der mündlichen Tradition ihre rhythmisch komplizierte Form unverändert beibehielt. Dies wird aber durch den Handschriftenbefund widerlegt, der eindeutig beweist, daß nicht nur die älteren Minnesängermelodien, sondern auch die eigenen Meistersingerweisen in der Meistersingertradition erheblichen Veränderungen unterlagen. Als Beleg dafür gebe ich in Notenbeispiel 4 den Anfang des Überlangen Tons von Hans Sachs nach dem Zwickauer Autograph (die Melodie nicht autograph, aber wohl nach Sachs' Diktat), nach der in Notenbeispiel 3 schon herangezogenen Nürnberger Handschrift Will III 793, nach der Handschrift Fenitzer 5, 182, 4° des Nürnberger Landeskirchenarchivs, endlich nach Puschmanns Singebuch [6].

Die weitausschwingende Melodie, die gleich in der ersten Melodiezeile zweimal auf das hohe f heraufgeht, haben die drei späteren Quellen auf den Umfang einer Sext zu-

---

[6] *Das Singebuch des Adam Puschmann nebst den Originalmelodien des M. Behaim und Hans Sachs,* hrsg. v. Georg Münzer, Leipzig 1906.

Ex. 4

Hans Sachs, Überlanger Ton 1529

Zwickau, 3. Meistergesangbuch, f. 323

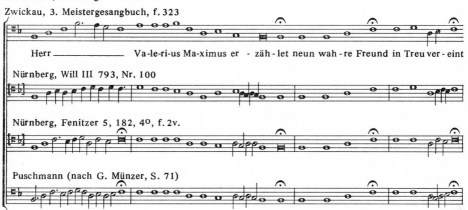

Herr _____ Va-le-ri-us Ma-ximus er - zäh - let neun wah - re Freund in Treu ver - eint

Nürnberg, Will III 793, Nr. 100

Nürnberg, Fenitzer 5, 182, 4º, f. 2v.

Puschmann (nach G. Münzer, S. 71)

sammengedrängt. In der letzten Kurzzeile des Beispiels zeigt sich deutlich, wie die Handschrift Will III 793 die originale Fassung am treuesten bewahrt hat. Die Zwickauer Form zeigt dabei mensurale Einschläge — gleich im Anfangsmelisma ein Nebeneinander von Semibrevis, Minima und Semibrevis —, und andere Melodien sind (bis auf wenige Notationsfehler wie in Beispiel 4, wo im Anfangsmelisma die Halbe d wohl in eine Ganze und im Schlußmelisma die Viertel a und b wohl in Halbe zu korrigieren sind) voll durchmensuriert (wie auch die Weise von Notenbeispiel 4, wenn man den Mut hat, die eben angegebenen Änderungen auch dort in allen, freilich sehr häufigen Fällen von „fehlerhafter Schreibung" durchzuführen). Die originale Mensurierung der Hans-Sachsschen Melodien ist in den nächsten zwei Handschriften des 17. Jhs. und in Puschmanns (noch aus dem Ende des 16. Jhs. stammender) Aufzeichnung dann ebenso verschwunden wie die Mensurierung der Ulmer Melodien in Notenbeispiel 3.

Zum Vergleich mit den Weisen Faulhabers sei in Notenbeispiel 5 die 1. Zeile von Löschenbrands Goldfarbener Jungfrauweise mitgeteilt, die wieder auch in der Nürnberger Fassung vorliegt.

Ex. 5

Augustin Löschenbrand, Goldfarbene Jungfrauweise, 1607

Ulm, Stadtarchiv

Wie _____ die stadt _____ war Tro-ia _____ so - - gar _____

Nürnberg, Will III 793, Nr. 52

Die Weise zeigt in der rhythmischen Faktur große Ähnlichkeit mit Faulhabers Tönen. Demgegenüber besitzen die Kompositionen der nächsten Ulmer Meistersingergeneration

einen viel abgeklärteren, liedhaften Stil. Dafür bringt Notenbeispiel 6 einen Beleg, die
1. Zeile der 2. Weise von Joh. Baur.

Ex. 6

Johannes Baur, Verlassne Schafweise, 1661

Ich dan - ke Dir_____   o _ Du _ mein_____ Gott

Wie Johann Faulhaber auf die Idee gekommen sein mag, die Weisen des Meistergesangs zu mensurieren, ist schwer zu sagen. Hans Sachs' Töne waren mensuriert. Die Jenaer
Meistersingerhandschrift, 1558 von dem Magdeburger Valentin Voigt geschrieben, hatte
alle ihre Töne mensuriert, selbst die alten Töne der Minnesinger. So war in der 2. Hälfte
des 16. Jhs. die Tendenz zur Mensurierung durch ganz Deutschland hindurch lebendig
und es mag gut sein, daß ein Nürnberger, Augsburger oder Münchener Meistersinger sie
auch nach Ulm gebracht hatte. Um auch den Vergleich mit Valentin Voigts Meisterliedern
zu ermöglichen, teile ich in Notenbeispiel 7 aus dieser Handschrift die ersten Zeilen eines
Liedes eines etwa 1535/40 vielleicht in Nürnberg lebenden Meistersingers Balthasar Fridel
mit. Seinem Namen entsprechend nennt er seine einzige Weise die Fridtweise [7].

E. 7

Balthasar Fridel, Fridtweise, Voigts Handschrift Musikteil f. 28v.

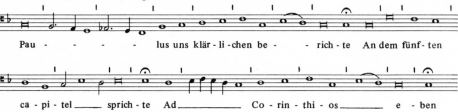

Pau - - - lus uns klär - li -chen be - - rich - te An dem fünf- ten

ca - pi - tel_____ sprich - te Ad_____ Co - rin - thi - os_____ e - ben

Fridels Fridtweise unterscheidet sich in der Voigtschen Redaktion in nichts von einer
Melodie des Hans Sachs, wie sie in Notenbeispiel 4 aus Hans Sachs' 3. Meistergesangbuch
mitgeteilt wurde. Aber andere Melodien zeigen größere Koloraturen mit komplizierterer

Ex. 8

Hans Sachs, Gesangweise 1518

Zwickau, 2. Meisterliederbuch, 1528

Sieh Her - re sie ha - ben Dein Volk   er - - schla - gen

Jena, Valentin-Voigt-Handschrift, 1558, Musikteil f. 18v.

und dem Baum des Le - bens mit - ten im _____ Gar - ten

---

[7] Sehr gern bezeichnen die Meistersinger zumindest ihre erste Melodie nach ihrem Namen oder
   ihrem Beruf; der Rechenmeister Faulhaber nannte seinen ersten Ton daher die „Junge-Schul-
   knaben-Weise", Löschenbrand seine erste Weise die „Feurige Brandweise".

Rhythmik. Ja, obwohl Hans Sachs' Töne selbst schon oft rhythmisch recht kunstvoll sind, hat Voigt gerade ihre Melismen noch komplizierter gemacht. Das soll eine Zeile aus der Gesangsweise von Hans Sachs (s. Notenbeispiel 8) belegen.

In der Zwickauer Fassung liegt gegen Ende ein Fehler vor, wie die Jenaer Version zeigt: es ist offenbar die ganze Note a auf *er-(schlagen)* auf eine Halbe zu kürzen. Aber auch die kompliziertere Form bei Voigt kommt immer noch volltaktig auf der weiblichen Endung aus. Dies ist bei einer letzten Gruppe von Melodien aber auch nicht mehr der Fall, wie das folgende Beispiel 9 aus dem Schwarzen Ton Hans Vogels, eines Nürnberger Meistersingers um 1540/1550, zeigt.

Ex. 9

Hans Vogel, Schwarzer Ton
Voigtsche Handschrift Musikteil fol. 38

der ein fah-ren-der Schü-ler wa - re und ein Schwarz-kunst-ner of - fen - - - ba - re

Hier gerät die weibliche Endung im zweiten Vers auf die leichte Taktzeit, da die vorhergehende leichte Silbe ein Melisma von Brevislänge trägt. Damit aber ist die Taktmessung ebenso zu einer reinen Zeitachse geworden, wie sie es bei Faulhaber war. Solche Beispiele auf leichten Taktteilen stehender weiblicher Enden gibt es zahlreiche in der Voigtschen Fassung, und sie zeigen, wie diese Eigentümlichkeit der Faulhaberschen Lieder schon ein halbes Jahrhundert vorher existierte. Freilich besteht immer noch ein bedeutsamer Unterschied zu der Faulhaberschen Rhythmik: die erste Silbe der weiblichen Endung ist bei Valentin Voigt stets kurz, wenn sie auf einem leichten Taktteil steht, so daß die zweite Silbe den nächsten Takt beginnt, während die lange erste Silbe bei Faulhaber eine Synkope bildet. Auch Voigt hat lange, oft melismatische erste Silben von weiblichen Endungen; aber sie stehen stets auf dem schweren Taktteil. Wie bedeutungslos die Brevisrhythmik bei Valentin Voigt geworden ist, mag ein Beispiel aus dem Schatzton Hans Vogels zeigen, wo (siehe Notenbeispiel 10) dasselbe Schlußmelisma einmal auf schwerem, das andere Mal auf leichtem Taktteil erscheint, wenn man eine Einteilung in Breven durchführt.

Ex. 10

Hans Vogel, Schatzton, Voigtsche Handschrift, fol. 41v. / 42v.
Schlußzeile der Stollen

noch   ih - rem   Wil - len   thä - te

Schlußzeile der Strophe

hub   an   zu   seuf - zen   e - - - - - - re

Die rhythmische Faktur dieses Beispiels ist kaum von den Faulhaberschen Kompositionen verschieden, — man vergleiche etwa oben Notenbeispiel 1. Es ist daher nicht anzunehmen, daß Faulhaber der erste Ulmer Meistersinger war, der die mensurale Rhythmik in Ulm einführte, — Augustin Löschenbrands Meisterlieder sind mit den seinen ja auch fast gleichzeitig. So wird man eher annehmen, daß schon die vorangehenden Ulmer Meistersingergenerationen, von denen uns nur Namen erhalten sind — Staiger, Engelhardt —, in ihren Liedern mensurale Wertmessung benutzten und daß uns nur aus Zufall erst Kompositionen des 17. Jhs. vorliegen. Daß aber ein so bedeutender Mathematiker wie Faulhaber sich auch mit der Komposition von Meistertönen beschäftigte, ist ein gutes Zeichen für die Atmosphäre des Ulmer Meistergesangs, — der Meistergesang des nahen Augsburg zeigt ja sogar eine ausgesprochen akademische Note.

Zur Geschichte des Taktschlagens im frühen 17. Jahrhundert

I

Der erste Theoretiker, von dem der vierteilige Taktschlag, die Aufspaltung des traditionellen zweiteiligen Tactus, erwähnt wird, ist nach den Untersuchungen Georg Schünemanns[1] Lorenzo Penna. „Ha la Battuta quattro parti, la prima è battere, e la seconda è fermare in giù, la terza è alzare, e la quarta è fermare in sù. Nelle Note nere spiccano benissimo queste quattro parti di Battuta, perche la prima è nel percuotere, la seconda è nel levare un poco ondeggiando la mano, la terza è nell' alzata, e la quarta è nel fermare in sù"[2]. Penna beschreibt den vierteiligen Takt zweifach: zunächst als Niederschlag, Innehalten unten, Aufschlag und Innehalten oben, dann als Niederschlag, Zurückfedern der Hand („levare un poco ondeggiando la mano"), Aufschlag und Innehalten oben. Vom ⁴/₄-Takt, dem Takt mit „schwarzen Noten" als Zählzeiten, heißt es, daß in ihm der vierteilige Schlag am deutlichsten hervortrete, und zwar als ein Schlag, für den statt des Innehaltens unten ein Zurückfedern der Hand charakteristisch ist. Das Zurückfedern ist weniger eine eigene Taktierbewegung[3] als vielmehr eine Modifikation des Innehaltens, die sich unwillkürlich aus einem nachdrücklicheren Schlag ergibt. Der vierteilige Schlag ist also nach Penna primär ein ⁴/₄-Schlag, eine Unterteilung des Tactus alla Semibreve, ohne daß der ⁴/₂-Schlag, die Unterteilung des Tactus alla Breve, ausgeschlossen wäre. Außerdem unterscheidet Penna einen ruhigeren Schlag mit Innehalten unten von einem prononcierteren mit Zurückfedern der Hand. (Die Differenzierung leuchtet musikalisch ein, wenn man an den pointierten ⁴/₄-Takt der Kanzonette denkt.)

Pennas Beschreibung ist allerdings nicht das erste Zeugnis für den vierteiligen Taktschlag. Bereits ein halbes Jahrhundert früher, 1627, ist in den wenig beachteten „Misure harmoniche regolate" des Francesco Piovesana aus Salice von vier Zeiten des Taktes die Rede. „La Compositione di poi della battuta è di due parti, la prima delle quali è il battere, e la seconda l'elevar della mano: di più in cadauna di queste parti sono duoi Tempi, di modo che in tutto sono quattro: et questi si distribuiscono in questo modo: cioè, nell' istesso tempo dell' abbassat' uno, e nel fermar la mano à basso, un' altro vien distribuito: nell' elevar poi similmente si applica il terzo, e nel fermar la mano in alto, il quarto: il qual modo di distribuir questi tempi è il vero, e reale"[4]. (Der Takt besteht aus

---

[1] G. Schünemann, *Geschichte des Dirigierens*, Leipzig 1913 (Nachdruck Hildesheim 1965), S. 122 f.

[2] L. Penna, *Li primi albori musicali*, Bologna 1679 (erste Auflage 1672), S. 32.

[3] Schünemann spricht mißverständlich von einem „mäßigen Heben der Hand, die man ein wenig wiegen läßt" (S. 122). Der Terminus „ondeggiando" wurde vermutlich aus der Tanztheorie übernommen, in der er ein leichtes Federn auf den Fußspitzen bedeutete.

[4] Francesco Piovesana Sacilese, *Misure harmoniche regolate*, Venedig 1627, S. 60. Von Piovesana

zwei Teilen, deren erster der Niederschlag und deren zweiter der Aufschlag der Hand ist. Ferner umfaßt jeder dieser Teile zwei Zeiten, so daß es im Ganzen vier sind, die sich folgendermaßen verteilen: Die erste Zeit entspricht dem Niederschlag der Hand, die zweite dem Innehalten unten, die dritte dann analog dem Aufschlag und die vierte dem Innehalten oben. Dies ist die wahre und wirkliche Art, die Zeiten zu verteilen.)

Der Unterschied zwischen dem Schlag, den Piovesana beschreibt, und dem zweiteiligen, aus positio und elevatio zusammengesetzten Tactus des 16. Jahrhunderts ist scheinbar gering. Daß Piovesana das „fermare in giù" und „in sù" als eigene Zeiten zählt, modifiziert, so könnte man meinen, nicht die Schlagtechnik, sondern besagt lediglich, daß man im frühen 17. Jahrhundert den Takt als vierteilig empfand, obwohl er zweiteilig geschlagen wurde.

Die Auffassung, daß sich zwar das Bewußtsein vom Takt, aber nicht dessen äußere Darstellung änderte, ist jedoch zu grob, um triftig zu sein. Die Theoretiker des späten 15. und des 16. Jahrhunderts beschreiben den Tactus, das Auf und Ab der Hand, als ruhige, stetige Bewegung, als „continua motio", die nirgends stockt oder innehält: Gleichmaß und Gelassenheit sind die Grundzüge eines Tactus, der weniger Akzente oder Schwerpunkte setzt als vielmehr bloße Zeitstrecken mißt. Dagegen beschreiben Piovesana und Penna, wenn sie von einem „fermare in giù" und „in sù" sprechen, einen diskontinuierlichen statt eines kontinuierlichen Schlages, und die Differenz ist keineswegs geringfügig oder bedeutungslos. Erstens kann das Innehalten, der Gegensatz zur Bewegung, durchaus als eigenes Zeichen, also als sichtbare Darstellung einer Zählzeit, aufgefaßt werden: Die Vierteiligkeit ist nicht nur empfunden, sondern durch den diskontinuierlichen Schlag auch sinnfällig gemacht worden. Und zweitens erscheint die Art des Schlages als Ausdruck der Funktion, die er erfüllt. Der Übergang vom stetigen zum unterbrochenen Taktschlag verrät einen Funktionswechsel, eine Umdeutung des Schlages vom zeitmessenden, orientierenden Zeichen zu einer Markierung von Akzenten oder Schwerpunkten.

Ob Piovesana primär an einen 4/4- oder an einen 4/2-Takt denkt, läßt er offen. Penna beschreibt den 4/4-Takt als besonders prononciert (mit Zurückfedern der Hand), so daß es naheliegt, den ruhigeren Schlag (mit Innehalten unten), den er außerdem erwähnt, mit dem 4/2-Takt zu verbinden. Die Unterscheidung gilt jedoch nicht für Piovesana: Mit dem Schlag, den er schildert und zur Norm erklärt, kann sowohl der 4/4- als auch der 4/2-Takt gemeint sein. (Der eine ist durch Unterteilung des Tactus alla Semibreve, der andere durch Aufspaltung des Tactus alla Breve entstanden.)

Zu unterscheiden wären demnach drei Schlagarten, die verschiedene Entwicklungsstufen des Rhythmus repräsentieren, obwohl sie schlagtechnisch nichts anderes als unscheinbare Varianten des einfachen Auf und Ab der Hand sind: Der stetige Tactus alle Breve oder alla Semibreve (2/1 oder 2/2), der diskontinuierliche Schlag, bei dem das Innehalten unten und oben als eigene Zählzeit empfunden werden soll (4/2 und 4/4 als Unterteilungen von 2/1 und 2/2), und schließlich der von Penna beschriebene Schlag mit Zurückfedern der Hand, der als Pointierung des diskontinuierlichen Schlags entstanden ist (4/4).

ist nichts anderes bekannt, als daß er aus Sacile bei Udine stammte und die Dedikation seines Traktats in Venedig zeichnete.

II

Die Unterschiede der Schlagarten, wie sie von Piovesana und Penna beschrieben wurden, sind als sinnfällige Darstellung von Differenzen in der Akzentuierung und Tongebung zu verstehen; und es liegt darum nahe, die Schlagarten auf bestimmte Gattungen zu beziehen, deren rhythmischem Charakter sie angemessen sind.

Daß der stetige, unscheinbare Tactus des 16. Jahrhunderts, die „continua motio" als Ausdruck eines nahezu akzentlosen Rhythmus, im 17. Jahrhundert in Messen und Motetten, die sich an die Tradition der Prima prattica anschlossen, bewahrt wurde, scheint fast selbstverständlich zu sein, ist jedoch eher unwahrscheinlich. Denn gerade der Rhythmus, die Art der Akzentuierung, läßt sich kaum unverändert aus einer Epoche in eine andere übertragen[5]. Er ist es vielmehr, der in archaisierenden Werken deren Entstehungszeit verrät, mag auch sonst die Stilnachahmung oder -restauration makellos geglückt sein. (Man könnte einwenden, daß die äußere Darstellung durch eine Schlagart nicht immer dem Wesen eines Rhythmus zu entsprechen brauche, daß also die Tradition des kontinuierlichen Tactus zu überdauern vermochte, obwohl sie ausgehöhlt war. Doch ist erstens anzunehmen, daß sich die Schlagart unwillkürlich und beinahe reflexionslos dem Rhythmus anpaßt, den sie darstellen soll. Und zweitens darf von einer Technik, die ein provinzieller Theoretiker wie Piovesana beschreibt, vermutet werden, daß sie in den Zentren der musikalischen Entwicklung längst verbreitet war.)

Monteverdis „Messa a 4 da Capella" aus der „Selva morale e spirituale" von 1641[6] ist zweifellos, trotz einiger Lizenzen in der Dissonanzbehandlung, als Werk im Stile antico gemeint. Der rhythmische Charakter ist jedoch von dem einer Gombert- oder einer Palestrina-Messe grundverschieden. Die Minimen, die Zählzeiten des Tactus alla Semibreve, schließen sich nicht zu einer ununterbrochenen, fließenden Bewegung zusammen, sondern stehen — um es drastisch auszudrücken — wie Punkte nebeneinander; der Rhythmus hat eher nachdrücklich schreitenden als schwebenden Charakter. Die von Piovesana beschriebene Schlagart, bei der durch ein „fermare in giù" und „in sù", ein Innehalten unten und oben, der Nieder- und der Aufschlag des Tactus alla Semibreve deutlich voneinander abgehoben werden, wäre also dem Werk nicht inadäquat, obwohl andererseits von einer Verselbständigung der Semiminimen zu Zählzeiten, wie sie Piovesana voraussetzt, nicht die Rede sein kann; die Semiminimen sind bloße Spaltwerte der Minimen, die als Silbenträger und Zählzeiten fungieren.

Der vierteilige Schlag, den Piovesana und Penna beschreiben, macht eine Gewichtsabstufung der Zählzeiten sinnfällig, für die Heinrich Besseler den Terminus „Akzentstufentakt" geprägt hat[7]. Die erste und dritte Zählzeit sind schwerer oder betonter als die zweite und vierte, und die erste, durch den Taktstrich als Hauptakzent gekennzeichnet,

---

[5] G. Becking, *Der musikalische Rhythmus als Erkenntnisquelle*, Augsburg 1928.
[6] C. Monteverdi, *Opere*, 2. Auflage Wien 1967, Band XV/1, S. 59.
[7] H. Besseler, *Das musikalische Hören der Neuzeit*, Berichte über die Verhandlungen der sächsischen Akademie der Wissenschaften zu Leipzig, Philologisch-historische Klasse, Band 104, Heft 6, Berlin 1959, S. 29.

ist wiederum gewichtiger als die dritte. Muster des „Akzentstufentakts" sind nach Besseler die „Balletti di cantare, sonare e ballare" (1591) von Giovanni Giacomo Gastoldi.

Eine geringe Abstufung der Zeiten muß allerdings auch beim Tactus des 16. Jahrhunderts, trotz der Tendenz zu einem schwebenden Rhythmus, empfunden worden sein. Ohne daß die Gewichtigkeit durch einen Druckakzent unterstrichen wurde, war dennoch der Niederschlag, die Thesis, schwerer als der Aufschlag, die Arsis. Sonst wäre es kaum zu erklären, warum beim Tactus alla Semibreve zwar die zweite Minima und deren erste Semiminima, aber nicht die erste Minima oder deren Anfangs-Semiminima dissonieren durften. Setzt man aber eine Gewichtsabstufung von Thesis und Arsis voraus, so erscheint der vierteilige, aus Niederschlag, Innehalten unten, Aufschlag und Innehalten oben zusammengesetzte Schlag, der aus der Aufspaltung des Tactus alla Semibreve resultierte, als genaues Abbild des „Akzentstufentakts".

In der Theorie des Rhythmus ist der „Akzentstufentakt" offenbar weder im 17. Jahrhundert[8] noch im 18. adäquat beschrieben worden. Noch 1787 erklärte Heinrich Christoph Koch, zweifellos einer der repräsentativen Theoretiker der Zeit um 1800, den $^4/_4$-Takt als „zusammengesetzte" Taktart, als Ergebnis der Schreibgewohnheit, „zwei Tacte in der äußerlichen Gestalt eines einzigen, vermittelst Auslassung eines Tactstriches vorzustellen"[9]. Daß die erste Zählzeit schwerer ist als die dritte, wird von Koch nirgends erwähnt.

Man braucht sich jedoch durch die Verspätung der Theorie nicht in der Interpretation des vierteiligen Taktschlags, wie ihn Piovesana und Penna schildern, beirren zu lassen. Denn erstens war die Theorie durch Befangenheit in einer antikisierenden Terminologie gehemmt, einer Terminologie, die den Sachverhalt, den sie ausdrücken soll, halb verdeckt: Man bezeichnete einen Schwerpunkt oder Akzent als „innere Länge" (quantitas intrinseca) und kannte, nach dem Muster der Metrik, nur zwei Werte, die Länge und die Kürze (die akzentuierte und die nicht akzentuierte Zeit), konnte also eine differenziertere Abstufung nicht beschreiben. Zweitens erscheint der Taktschlag als unmittelbarer, unwillkürlicher Ausdruck eines rhythmischen Charakters, als Ausdruck, der des Umwegs über die Reflexion nicht bedarf; und es ist darum kaum erstaunlich, wenn die Schlagart einen rhythmischen Sachverhalt früher sinnfällig macht, als ihn die Theorie in Begriffe zu fassen vermag.

Um 1600 war der „Akzentstufentakt", wie erwähnt, am deutlichsten in der Kanzonette und im Balletto ausgeprägt. Deren Tempo bestimmte Franz-Jochen Machatius[10] als ♩ = 120. Die Vermutung, daß ein Tactus alla Minima (mit Semiminimen als Thesis und Arsis) geschlagen wurde, ist jedoch fragwürdig. Einerseits war die Gewöhnung an den Tactus alla Semibreve fest eingewurzelt; und andererseits wurde die Modifikation

---

[8] H. Heckmann, *Der Takt in der Musiklehre des siebzehnten Jahrhunderts*, Archiv für Musikwissenschaft X, 1953, S. 128.

[9] H. Chr. Koch, *Versuch einer Anleitung zur Composition*, Band II, Leipzig 1787 (Nachdruck Hildesheim 1969), S. 286 f.

[10] Fr.-J. Machatius, *Über mensurale und spielmännische Reduktion*, Die Musikforschung VIII, 1955, S. 146.

des Tactus alla Semibreve, die Piovesana beschreibt, dem rhythmischen Charakter der Kanzonette und des Balletto eher gerecht als der hypothetische Umschlag in einen Tactus alla Minima, der die Differenz zwischen dem ersten und dem dritten Viertel nicht ausdrückt. Die nachdrücklichere Akzentuierung — der „aggressiv klopfende Kanzonettenpuls", um mit Machatius zu sprechen[11] — fordert eine Pointierung des Tactus alla Semibreve heraus, und aus der Verschärfung des Schlages resultiert die Aufspaltung in Bewegung und Innehalten, also die Unterteilung des $^2/_2$-Tactus in einen $^4/_4$-Takt. Der von Penna beschriebene Schlag mit Zurückfedern der Hand — einem Zurückfedern, das sich aus der spitzen Nachdrücklichkeit des Niederschlags ergibt — ist dem Kanzonettenrhythmus noch adäquater als der einfache Wechsel zwischen Bewegung und Innehalten. Doch wird das entscheidende Moment des „Akzentstufentakts", die dreifache Differenzierung des Gewichts der Zählzeiten, auch durch die von Piovesana geschilderte Schlagart sinnfällig gemacht.

Das Verfahren, bei $^4/_4$-Rhythmen am gewohnten Tactus alla Semibreve festzuhalten, statt ihn mit einem Tactus alla Minima zu vertauschen, ist auch insofern musikalisch legitim, als es einem Phänomen gerecht wird, das man als rhythmischen „Systemwechsel" bezeichnen kann. In dem Chor „Nulla impresa" aus Monteverdis „Orfeo"[12] ist zu Anfang und am Schluß die Minima, in der Mitte dagegen die Semiminima oder Viertelnote primärer Silbenträger und Zählzeit. Dennoch braucht sich nicht der Bezugswert des Tactus, sondern lediglich der Charakter des Schlages zu ändern: Um den rhythmischen „Systemwechsel" schlagtechnisch darzustellen, genügt es, von der „continua motio" des traditionellen Tactus zu der von Piovesana beschriebenen Variante überzugehen.

III

Das Ritornell zu der Arie „Vi ricorda o boschi ombrosi" aus Monteverdis „Orfeo"[13] ist in einer Notation überliefert, die nicht grundlos zum Gegenstand divergierender Interpretationen geworden ist[14].

[11] Machatius, S. 146.
[12] C. Monteverdi, *Opere*, Band XI, S. 107.
[13] C. Monteverdi, *Opere*, Band XI, S. 48.
[14] Facsimile bei W. Apel, *Anent a Ritornello in Monteverdis Orfeo*, Musica Disciplina V, 1951, S. 214.

Daß ein ⁶/₈-Takt mit einem ³/₄-Takt abwechselt, dürfte trotz der abweichenden Deu-
tungen, die immer wieder versucht worden sind[15], kaum bezweifelbar sein.

Rätselhaft aber sind die in den Notentext eingestreuten Ziffern, durch die sich Robert
Eitner, Vincent d'Indy, Hugo Leichtentritt, Carl Orff und Willi Apel zu manierierten
Übertragungen herausgefordert fühlten. Die Ziffer 3 wurde entweder als Zeichen einer
Triole oder einer Proportio tripla aufgefaßt. Beide Interpretationen führen jedoch
zu Verzerrungen des von Monteverdi intendierten rhythmischen Schemas, eines Schemas,
das um 1600 Modellcharakter hatte und das in der Arie, zu der das Ritornell gehört,
unmißverständlich notiert ist. (Außerdem gerieten die Interpreten, die aus den Ziffern
eine den Rhythmus verändernde Bedeutung herauslasen, in die philologische Verlegen-
heit, einen Teil der Ziffern für überflüssig oder falsch plaziert erklären zu müssen.)

Man kann dem Dilemma, entweder die Ziffern als bedeutungslos abtun zu müssen
oder die Übertragung zu gefährden, jedoch entgehen, wenn man die Ziffern als auf-
führungspraktische Hinweise auffaßt: Sie greifen nicht in den Rhythmus ein, sondern
deuten eine Modifikation des Taktschlags an.

Daß durch die Ziffer 3 Gruppen von vier Achtelnoten voneinander abgegrenzt werden,
ist scheinbar widersinnig. Die Ziffern stehen jedoch, anders ausgedrückt, regelmäßig vor
der dritten Zeit einer ³/₈- oder einer ³/₄-Gruppe (einzig im zweiten „Takt" fehlt eine
Ziffer analog zum ersten), und zwar immer dann, wenn der ⁶/₈- in den ³/₄-Rhythmus
oder der ³/₄- in den ⁶/₈-Rhythmus umgeschlagen ist (also nicht bei der Ergänzung einer
ersten ³/₈-Gruppe durch eine zweite). Bezeichnet werden nicht die ³/₈- und ³/₄-Gruppen
selbst (wären sie gemeint, so müßten die Ziffern zwei Achtel oder zwei Viertel früher
stehen), sondern deren dritte Zählzeiten[16].

Zusatzzeichen drücken Abweichungen von einer Norm oder Konvention aus. Und
das Ungewohnte, Unerwartete, das durch die Ziffern angedeutet werden soll, besteht
in einer Modifikation des zweizeitigen Tactus, den das Mensurzeichen c vorschreibt
oder impliziert.

Das Ritornell kann kaum anders als im Tactus alla Minima (mit Viertelnoten als
Thesis und Arsis) geschlagen worden sein. Der zweizeitige Tactus durchkreuzt jedoch die
rhythmische Struktur des Satzes; er steht gleichsam quer zu dem Wechsel zwischen ⁶/₈ und
³/₄. Und der Widerspruch zwischen Tactus und Rhythmus, der im 16. Jahrhundert von
geringer Bedeutung war, da der Tactus unauffällig blieb und eher eine bloß zeitmessende

---

[15] Die verschiedenen Lösungsversuche werden von W. Apel, S. 215 ff., abgedruckt und kommentiert.
[16] Daß im ersten „Takt" in einer Mittelstimme die Ziffer 3 vor einer ³/₈- statt einer ⁴/₈-Gruppe
steht, braucht nicht zu beirren; die Plazierung vor einer ⁴/₈-Gruppe ist zweifellos die lectio
difficilior.

als eine akzentuierende Funktion erfüllte, muß im 17. Jahrhundert, nachdem der Taktschlag zum Schwerpunktzeichen geworden war, als kaum erträglich empfunden worden
sein. Die scheinbar irrelevanten oder sogar störenden Ziffern erhalten also, wenn man
sie als Mittel versteht, um den Konflikt zwischen Tactus und Rhythmus zu vermeiden,
einen einleuchtenden Sinn: Sie sind ein — allerdings kaum geglückter — Versuch, ein
drängendes Problem zu lösen. Und zwar fordert die Ziffer 3, als Bezeichnung einer
zusätzlichen dritten Zeit, eine Dehnung des Schlages: Im $^6/_8$-Rhythmus werden die
einzelnen Nieder- und Aufschläge des Tactus alla Minima verlängert (♩. statt ♩), im
$^3/_4$-Rhytmus der ganze Tactus (♩. statt ♩). Man mag also die Notation des Ritornells
als mißlungen empfinden: Sinnlos ist sie nicht[17].

---

[17] Machatius (S. 143) vermutet zwar, daß die Ziffern ein „Hilfsmittel (etwa beim Taktschlagen)
    sein sollen, ein Nota bene beim Umspringen des Taktes an unübersichtlicher Stelle", hält aber
    (S. 144) die Ziffern vor der dritten Zeit der $^3/_4$-Takte für „geradezu störend".

ULRICH SIEGELE

„La Cadence est une qualité de la bonne Musique"

„... que le tout, avec la
commodité d'un Diction-
naire, eût l'avantage d'un
Traité suivi" (Préface).

Jean-Jacques Rousseau schreibt in seinem *Dictionnaire de Musique* (ich benütze die zweibändige Ausgabe Paris 1775) unter dem Stichwort „Mouvement", „Taktbewegung" (I, 485): „Grad der Schnelligkeit oder der Langsamkeit, der dem Taktmaß den Charakter des Stückes gibt, das man ausführt. Jede Taktart hat eine Taktbewegung, die ihr die eigentümlichste ist, und die man auf Italienisch mit diesen Wörtern bezeichnet, *Tempo giusto*." Der Artikel „Battre la Mesure", „Taktschlagen" präzisiert, wovon diese eigentümlichste Taktbewegung jeder Taktart, ihr „rechtes Zeitmaß", abhängt (I, 80): „Der Grad der Langsamkeit oder der Schnelligkeit, den man dem Taktmaß gibt, hängt von mehreren Dingen ab: 1. Vom Wert der Noten, die das Taktmaß bilden. Man sieht leicht, daß ein Taktmaß, das eine Ganze enthält, gesetzter *geschlagen* werden und länger dauern muß als das, das nur ein Viertel enthält."

Dieser Artikel fährt fort: „2. Von der Taktbewegung, angezeigt mit einem französischen oder italienischen Wort, das man gewöhnlich am Kopf des Air findet; *Gai, Vîte, Lent* usw. Alle diese Wörter zeigen ebensoviel Änderungen in der Taktbewegung derselben Taktart an." Hierin ist der Artikel „Mouvement" genauer; er fährt fort: „Aber außerdem gibt es fünf hauptsächliche Änderungen der Taktbewegung, die, in der Ordnung von langsam nach schnell, ausgedrückt werden mit den Wörtern *Largo, Adagio, Andante, Allegro, Presto;* und diese Wörter werden auf Französisch wiedergegeben mit den folgenden, *Lent, Modéré, Gracieux, Gai, Vîte*." Und tatsächlich nennen die Artikel „Adagio" (I, 40), „Andante" (I, 48), „Allegro" (I, 46), ähnlich auch „Presto" (II, 111) die Stellung innerhalb der „fünf hauptsächlichen Grade der Taktbewegung, die in der italienischen Musik unterschieden werden"; nur der Artikel „Largo" (I, 419f.) begnügt sich mit der allgemeinen Formulierung: „Eine Taktbewegung, langsamer als *Adagio*, und die letzte von allen hinsichtlich der Langsamkeit."

Für das Verhältnis des „Tempo giusto" und dieser fünfstufigen Skala gibt es zwei Möglichkeiten. Entweder, die fünfstufige Skala dient dazu, Änderungen des „Tempo giusto" jeder Taktart anzuzeigen. Da jede der fünf Stufen eine Änderung des „Tempo giusto" anzeigt, könnte das „Tempo giusto" nie mit einer der fünf Stufen identifiziert werden; es müßte stets zwischen zweien der fünf Stufen (oder außerhalb ihrer Grenzen) liegen. Die fünfstufige Skala wäre also relativ, auf jedes „Tempo giusto" bezogen. Die andere Möglichkeit (und sie wird von der Rede der „fünf hauptsächlichen Grade der Taktbewegung" gestützt) denkt die fünfstufige Skala absolut. Jedes „Tempo giusto" wäre dann mit einer der fünf Stufen zu identifizieren; die anderen vier Bezeichnungen forderten Änderungen dieser Stufe.

Der Artikel „Mouvement" bemerkt weiter (I, 486): „Jeder dieser Grade unterteilt sich und ändert sich noch in andere, bei denen man unterscheiden muß die, die nur einen Grad der Schnelligkeit oder der Langsamkeit anzeigen, wie *Larghetto, Andantino, Allegretto, Prestissimo,* und die, die überdies den Charakter und den Ausdruck des Air kennzeichnen, wie *Agitato, Vivace, Gustoso, Conbrio* usw." Die Bezeichnungen der ersten Art sind unter ihren Stammwörtern erklärt. „Prestissimo" bezeichnet eine Steigerung, „Allegretto" eine Mäßigung. „Das Diminutiv *Andantino* zeigt ein bißchen weniger Heiterkeit im Taktmaß an: was wohl zu beachten ist, indem das Diminutiv *Larghetto* ganz das Gegenteil bezeichnet." „Das Diminutiv *Larghetto* kündigt eine Taktbewegung an etwas weniger langsam als *Largo,* langsamer als *Andante,* und sehr ähnlich dem *Andantino.*" Diese Ähnlichkeit von „Larghetto" und „Andantino" scheint eine benachbarte Stellung von „Largo" und „Andante" vorauszusetzen. „Affettuoso" (I, 41) indessen zeigt, übereinstimmend mit der Anordnung der fünfstufigen Skala, „eine mittlere Taktbewegung zwischen *Andante* und *Adagio*" an.

Merklichere Unstimmigkeiten ergeben sich bei der Gleichsetzung der italienischen und der französischen Bezeichnungen. „Largo" wird im Artikel „Mouvement" wiedergegeben, in seinem Artikel umschrieben mit „Lent"; entsprechend verweist der Artikel „Lentement" (I, 420) auf „Largo". „Presto" wird in seinem und im Artikel „Mouvement" wiedergegeben mit „Vîte"; entsprechend verweist der Artikel „Vîte" (II, 350) auf „Presto". „Allegro" wird in seinem und im Artikel „Mouvement" mit „Gai" wiedergegeben; entsprechend verweist der Artikel „Gai" (I, 359) auf „Allegro". Gleichzeitig aber zeigt „Gai" „eine mittlere Taktbewegung zwischen vîte und modéré" an. „Modéré" entspricht, nach dem Artikel „Mouvement", der italienischen Bezeichnung „Adagio". „Allegro" also eine mittlere Taktbewegung zwischen „Adagio" und „Presto"? Wo bleibt „Andante"? Der Artikel „Adagio" übersetzt keineswegs, wie der Artikel „Mouvement", „Modéré", sondern *„à l'aise, posément".* Unter diesen Wörtern ist kein Eintrag zu finden. Dem Artikel „Modéré" (I, 472) zufolge zeigt dieses Wort „eine mittlere Taktbewegung zwischen lent und gai" an; „es entspricht dem italienischen *Andante*". „Andante" wird im Artikel „Mouvement" mit „Gracieux" wiedergegeben; nach seinem Artikel „entspricht es ungefähr dem, was man auf Französisch mit dem Wort *Gracieusement* bezeichnet". Unter diesen Wörtern ist kein Eintrag zu finden.

Die Artikel der französischen Bezeichnungen sind in sich ebenso ohne Widerspruch wie die der italienischen. „Vîte" und „Lent" als Grenzwerte; „Gai" als mittlerer Wert zwischen „Vîte" und „Modéré", „Modéré" als mittlerer Wert zwischen „Lent" und „Gai". Der fünfstufigen italienischen Skala steht also eine vierstufige französische Skala gegenüber:

Presto	Vîte
•	•
•	•
Allegro	Gai
•	•
Andante	•

. Adagio . . Largo	Modéré . . . Lent

Rousseau stand vor der Aufgabe, die fünfstufige italienische und die vierstufige französische Skala zueinander in Beziehung zu setzen. Zwei Versuche sind bezeugt. Der Artikel „Mouvement" zeigt ein Verfahren. Er setzt, wie es die Nachbarschaft der Anordnung nahelegt, „Gai" und „Allegro", „Modéré" und „Adagio" in Beziehung und wählt für den mittleren Wert, „Andante", der in der vierstufigen Skala fehlen mußte, als ungefähres Äquivalent „Gracieux". Dieses Wort, „anmutig", und „gai", „heiter" (das „auch verstanden werden kann vom Charakter einer Musik, unabhängig von der Taktbewegung"), entstammen ähnlichen Vorstellungsbereichen. Rousseau mäßigt „gai" zu „gracieux", um den mittleren Wert bezeichnen zu können, läßt den Vorstellungsbereich „modéré" unberührt. Umgekehrt verfährt er in den Artikeln „Modéré" und „Adagio". Er läßt den Vorstellungsbereich „gai" unberührt, ordnet „modéré" dem mittleren Wert „Andante" zu und mäßigt „modéré", „mäßig", zu „à l'aise, posément", „bequem, gesetzt", um das nun auf „Adagio" beziehen zu können.

Presto		Vîte	
Allegro	Gai		Gai
Andante	Gracieux		Modéré
Adagio	Modéré		à l'aise, posément
Largo		Lent	

Übrigens hatte Rousseau gute Gründe, sowohl „gracieux" wie „modéré" für die Bezeichnung des mittleren Werts in Betracht zu ziehen. Bei „modéré" liegt das auf der Hand. „Gracieux", das meint: unberührt von den großen, den extremen Leidenschaften (Artikel „Expression" gegen Ende; I, 342). Es ist eine Sache des „Goût" (gegen Ende des Artikels; I, 374). „Gens de Goût", „Menschen mit Geschmack", aber sind „bien organisés", „ausgeglichen" (ebenda I, 372 f.). Der Geschmack ist dem „ordre des beautés naturelles", der „Ordnung der natürlichen Schönheiten", verbunden wie „gracieux" einem Gesang, der als „natürlich" bezeichnet wird (Artikel „Naturel"; II, 1). Was keinem Extrem zuneigt, was ausgeglichen, was natürlich ist, scheint ebenso wie „mäßig", wie „gemäßigt" zur Bezeichnung eines mittleren Werts geeignet.

„Légèrement", „leicht", ist als Zwischenstufe der vierstufigen französischen Skala bestimmt (I, 420): „Dieses Wort zeigt eine Taktbewegung an, noch lebhafter als Gai, eine mittlere Taktbewegung zwischen gai und vîte. Es entspricht ungefähr dem italienischen *Vivace.*" Mit „Vivace" gleichgesetzt wird „Vif, vivement", „lebhaft" (II, 348): „Dieses Wort kennzeichnet eine heitere, flinke, belebte Taktbewegung, eine Ausführung, kühn und voll Feuer." „Tendrement", „zärtlich" (II, 309), dem italienischen „Amoroso" verwandt, und „Grave ou Gravement", „schwer" (I, 374), sind zwei ver-

schieden charakterisierte langsame Taktbewegungen. „Très-Vîte" und „très-Lentement"
überschreiten die Grenzen der Skala nach beiden Seiten wie „Presto assai" (oder „Prestissimo") und „Largo assai", die der Artikel „Assai« (I, 55) mit „fort vîte" und „fort lent"
umschreibt.

Bei der Zuordnung der fünfstufigen italienischen und der vierstufigen französischen
Skala läßt Rousseau die fünfstufige italienische Skala unberührt. Er wollte diese fremde
Skala seinen französischen Lesern erläutern und suchte deshalb, wie man das bei Über-
setzungen zu tun pflegt, nach Näherungswerten in der Sache und Sprache seines eigenen
Landes. Doch könnte das auch darauf hindeuten, daß die italienische Skala mehr ver-
festigt ist, musikalisch und terminologisch ein fixiertes System darstellt. Die französische
Skala, musikalisch und terminologisch weniger gebunden, wäre diesem System gegenüber
beweglich.

Der Artikel „Mouvement" sagt: „Es ist indessen nötig zu beachten, daß, da die *Taktbewegung* stets viel weniger Genauigkeit hat in der französischen Musik, die Wörter,
die sie bezeichnen, dort einen sehr viel unbestimmteren Sinn haben als in der italienischen
Musik." Rousseau hat zuvor für die italienischen Bezeichnungen der fünf hauptsächlichen
Grade der Taktbewegung französische Übersetzungen gegeben. Die französischen Wörter
aber treffen die italienischen Wörter nicht genau; denn die französische Sache trifft die
italienische Sache nicht genau. Genauigkeit der Taktbewegung ist die Genauigkeit, mit
der eine Musik hier die fünf hauptsächlichen Grade, allgemein eine bestimmte Taktbewegung trifft. Diese genaue Intention einer bestimmten Taktbewegung fehlt der französischen Musik.

Indessen fehlt der französischen Musik die Intention einer Taktbewegung überhaupt.
Der Artikel „Pathétique" (II, 82 f.) sagt das. Ich übersetze das Stichwort nach dem Vorgang von Heinrich Christoph Koch (*Musikalisches Lexikon*, Frankfurt am Main 1802,
1143) mit „Erhaben" und verweise zur Stütze auf den Artikel „Opéra" (II, 50), wo Rousseau einer „Musique passionée et pathétique" die „Théatres des Foires" entgegen-, ein
„Spectacle touchant et majestueux" parallel setzt. Das Stichwort meint „Gattung der
dramatischen und theatralischen Musik, die danach strebt zu malen und zu erregen die
großen Leidenschaften, und ganz besonders den Schmerz und die Trauer". Hier heißt es:

> „Der ganze Ausdruck der französischen Musik in der *erhabenen* Gattung besteht in
> gezogenen, verstärkten, kreischenden Tönen und in einer solchen Langsamkeit
> der Taktbewegung, daß jede Empfindung des Taktmaßes verwischt ist. Daher
> kommt es, daß die Franzosen glauben, alles, was langsam ist, ist *erhaben*, und alles,
> was *erhaben* ist, muß langsam sein. Sie haben sogar Lieder, die heiter und scherzend
> oder zärtlich und erhaben werden, je nachdem, ob man sie schnell oder langsam
> singt . . . Das ist der Vorteil der französischen Melodie; sie dient zu allem, was
> man will."

Der Satz, daß die Franzosen glauben, alles, was langsam ist, ist erhaben, und alles,
was erhaben ist, muß langsam sein, kann ergänzt werden mit dem Satz, daß die Franzosen
glauben, alles, was laut ist, ist erhaben, und alles, was erhaben ist, muß laut sein. Der

„bruit", das Geräusch, oder besser: der Lärm der französischen Musik wird durch das Buch hin gegeißelt. Während man in Italien zuerst Treffsicherheit und Geschmeidigkeit der Stimme sucht, fordert man in Frankreich vor allem eine gute Stärke (Artikel „Corps-de-Voix"; I, 215). In der französischen Musik „ist das erste Verdienst, gut zu schreien" (Artikel „Son"; II, 206), sie „will geschrien sein; denn darin besteht ihr größter Ausdruck" (Artikel „Crier"; I, 218). So „ähnelt in der französischen Oper der leidenschaftliche Ton den Schreien der Kolik" (Artikel „Expression"; I, 336). Und den Superlativ „Fortissimo", den die Italiener haben, „braucht man in der französischen Musik selten; denn man singt dort gewöhnlich *sehr laut*" (Artikel „Fort"; I, 352).

Der Ausdruck der französischen Musik besteht allein in der Taktbewegung. Eine Taktbewegung ist von der Musik, genauer: von der Melodie selbst nicht intendiert. Deshalb kann die Taktbewegung und mit der Taktbewegung der Ausdruck der Melodie geändert werden. So unterscheidet sich die französische Musik von der italienischen Musik. In dem folgenden Zitat ist von dem „Erhabenen in Akzent und Melodie" die Rede. Der Artikel „Accent" (I, 1 f.) sagt: „Man nennt so, nach der allgemeinsten Bedeutung, jede Änderung der Sprechstimme in der Dauer oder in der Tonhöhe der Silben oder der Worte, aus denen die Rede gebildet ist; das zeigt ein sehr genaues Verhältnis zwischen den zwei Anwendungen der *Akzente* und den zwei Teilen der Melodie, nämlich Rhythmus und Intonation." Wiewohl also Akzent und Melodie Dauern- und Tonhöhenverhältnisse unter sich begreifen, kann ein terminologisch lässiger Sprachgebrauch Akzent im Sinn von Rhythmus, Melodie im Sinn von Intonation gebrauchen, eine Lässigkeit freilich ohne System (Artikel „Quantité" II, 123). Der Artikel „Pathétique" fährt fort:

> „Aber die italienische Musik hat nicht denselben Vorteil: jeder Gesang, jede Melodie hat ihren derart eigentümlichen Charakter, daß es unmöglich ist, ihn davon abzuziehen. Ihr *Erhabenes* in Akzent und Melodie läßt sich empfinden in jeder Taktart und selbst in den schnellsten Taktbewegungen. Die französischen Airs ändern den Charakter, je nachdem man die Taktbewegung drängt oder verlangsamt: jeder italienische Air hat seine derart bestimmte Taktbewegung, daß man sie nicht verändern kann, ohne die Melodie zu vernichten. Der so entstellte Air wechselt nicht seinen Charakter, er verliert ihn; das ist nicht mehr Gesang, das ist nichts."

Auch der Ausdruck der italienischen Melodie besteht in der Taktbewegung. Diese Taktbewegung aber ist vom Charakter der Melodie intendiert. Ist der Charakter der Melodie bestimmt, ist auch die Taktbewegung bestimmt. Der Artikel „Battre la Mesure" nennt als drittes Kriterium den „Charakter des Air selbst, der, wenn er gut gemacht ist, davon die wahre Taktbewegung notwendig empfinden lassen wird". Wird die bestimmte Taktbewegung verfehlt, wird auch der bestimmte Charakter der Melodie, und damit die Melodie überhaupt verfehlt. Charakter der Melodie und Taktbewegung sind aufeinander angewiesen. Dieses Verhältnis fordert Genauigkeit.

Die französische Melodie intendiert keine genaue, intendiert überhaupt keine Taktbewegung. Sie intendiert auch keine gleichmäßige Taktbewegung. Der Artikel „Chrono-

metre" (I, 156—159) resümiert die in der Praxis erfolglosen Versuche, die Dauer eines
Taktes mechanisch zu bestimmen. Die anschließende Argumentation, die diese Erfolg-
losigkeit in der Sache zu begründen sucht, konfrontiert verschiedene Positionen. Die
Befürworter beziehen sich auf die italienische Musik; das verrät die Wendung „die
wahre Taktbewegung der Airs, ohne die sie ihren Charakter verlieren":

> „Mehrere behaupten indessen, es wäre sehr zu wünschen, daß man ein solches
> Instrument hätte, um mit Genauigkeit die Zeit eines jeden Taktes in einem Musik-
> stück festzulegen: man bewahrte mit diesem Mittel leichter die wahre Taktbewe-
> gung der Airs, ohne die sie ihren Charakter verlieren, und den man nicht kennen
> kann, nach dem Tod der Verfasser, außer durch eine Art von Tradition, die sehr
> unterworfen ist sich auszulöschen oder sich zu verändern. Man beklagt sich schon,
> daß wir die Taktbewegungen einer großen Zahl von Airs vergessen haben, und
> es ist zu glauben, daß man sie alle verlangsamt hat. Wenn man die Vorsorge
> getroffen hätte, von der ich spreche, und gegen die man nichts hat, dann hätte man
> heute das Vergnügen, eben diese Airs so zu hören, wie der Verfasser sie auf-
> führen ließ."

Die Einwände beziehen sich auf die französische Musik. Die Argumentation stützt sich
auf den Begriff der Harmonie und zuvor auf den „Goût"; das ist der Geschmack allgemein, hier besonders der „Goût-du-Chant" (I, 374; dazu Artikel „Proprement" II, 119 f.):
„So nennt man in Frankreich die Kunst, die Noten zu singen oder zu spielen mit den
Verzierungen, die ihnen zukommen." Der Artikel „Chronometre" fährt fort:

> „Hierauf bleiben die Kenner von Musik nicht ohne Antwort. Sie werden ein-
> wenden, sagt Herr Diderot . . ., gegen jedes *Chronometer* überhaupt, daß es in
> einem Air vielleicht nicht zwei Takte gibt, die genau dieselbe Dauer haben; indem
> zwei Dinge notwendig dazu beitragen, die einen zu verlangsamen, die anderen
> zu überstürzen, der goût und die Harmonie in den Stücken für mehrere Stimmen,
> der goût und die Ahnung der Harmonie in den Soli. Ein Musiker, der seine
> Kunst versteht, hat keine vier Takte eines Air gespielt, ohne daß er dessen Cha-
> rakter begreift und sich ihm überläßt; er hat nur das Vergnügen der Harmonie,
> das ihn in Spannung hält. Er will, daß die Akkorde hier zuschlagen, dort sich
> entziehen; das heißt, daß er mehr oder weniger langsam singt oder spielt vom einen
> Takt zum andern, oder sogar von einer Taktzeit und vom Viertel einer Taktzeit
> zum folgenden."

Der französischen Musik fehlt die Genauigkeit der Taktbewegung. Deshalb könnte
eine mechanische Bestimmung ihrer Taktbewegung wünschenswert scheinen. Diese mechanische Bestimmung ihrer Taktbewegung ist aber unmöglich, weil ihr auch die Gleichmäßigkeit der Taktbewegung fehlt. Der italienischen Musik eignet die Gleichmäßigkeit der
Taktbewegung. Insofern wäre die mechanische Bestimmung ihrer Taktbewegung möglich.
Diese mechanische Bestimmung ihrer Taktbewegung — und das verkennen die Befürworter — ist aber überflüssig, weil ihr auch die Genauigkeit der Taktbewegung eignet.

Es genügt, sich auf die Chronometer „des wahren Charakters und der wahren Taktbewegung" zu beziehen. So kommentiert der Artikel den Einwand:

> „Allerdings hätte dieser Einwand, der großes Gewicht hat für die französische Musik, keines für die italienische, die dem genauesten Takt unerbittlich unterworfen ist: nichts sogar zeigt besser den vollendeten Gegensatz dieser zwei Musiken; da doch das, was in der einen Schönheit ist, in der anderen der größte Fehler wäre. Wo die italienische Musik ihre Kraft aus der Unterwerfung unter die Strenge des Taktes zieht, sucht die französische die ihre darin, zu meistern nach ihrem Belieben eben diesen Takt, ihn zu drängen, ihn zu verlangsamen, je nachdem, wie es der Goût-du-Chant oder der Grad der Geschmeidigkeit der Organe des Sängers fordert."

Der folgende Absatz aus dem Artikel „Battre la Mesure" (I, 81 f.) faßt diesen Sachverhalt in eine Pointe zusammen. Er schließt an an die Unterscheidung der italienischen und der französischen Schlagfiguren. Über den Stock, von dem die Rede ist, steht etwas mehr in dem Artikel „Bâton de Mesure" (I, 76); „der kleine Prophet" meint Friedrich Melchior Baron von Grimms Schrift *Le Petit Prophète de Boemisch Broda* von 1753.

> „Indessen hätte die französische Musik einen gut markierten Takt sehr viel nötiger als die italienische; denn sie trägt ihre Cadence überhaupt nicht in sich selbst; ihre Taktbewegungen haben keine natürliche Genauigkeit: man drängt, man verlangsamt den Takt nach dem Belieben des Sängers. Wieviel Ohren sind nicht in der Oper von Paris beleidigt worden von dem abscheulichen und ununterbrochenen Lärm, den mit seinem Stock der macht, der *den Takt schlägt*, und den der kleine Prophet im Scherz vergleicht mit einem Holzfäller, der Holz hackt! Aber das ist ein unvermeidliches Übel; ohne diesen Lärm könnte man den Takt nicht empfinden; die Musik aus sich selbst markiert ihn nicht: auch die Fremden nehmen die Taktbewegung unserer Airs gar nicht wahr. Wenn man seine Aufmerksamkeit hierauf wendet, wird man finden, daß darin einer der spezifischen Unterschiede der französischen Musik zur italienischen besteht. In Italien ist der Takt die Seele der Musik; es ist der wohl empfundene Takt, der ihr diesen Akzent gibt, der sie so reizvoll macht; es ist auch der Takt, der den Musiker bei der Ausführung führt. In Frankreich dagegen ist es der Musiker, der den Takt führt; er macht ihn nervös und entstellt ihn bedenkenlos. Was sage ich? Der gute Geschmack selbst besteht darin, ihn nicht empfinden zu lassen; eine Vorkehrung, die er zudem nicht sehr nötig hat. Die Oper von Paris ist das einzige Theater Europas, wo man *den Takt schlägt*, ohne ihm zu folgen; überall sonst folgt man ihm, ohne ihn zu *schlagen*."

Entscheidend ist der Anfang des Absatzes: die französische Musik „trägt ihre Cadence überhaupt nicht in sich selbst; ihre Taktbewegungen haben keine natürliche Genauigkeit", das meint: keine Genauigkeit, die in der Natur der Sache liegt. Schlüsselbegriff ist „la Cadence" (I, 108). Sie „ist eine Eigenschaft der guten Musik, die denen, die sie ausführen oder hören, eine lebhafte Empfindung des Taktes gibt, derart, daß sie ihn markieren und ihn fallen empfinden im rechten Augenblick, und ohne daß sie daran denken und wie aus Instinkt".

Eine weitere Bestimmung des Begriffs der Cadence gibt der Artikel „Marche" (I, 434 f.): „Militärische Weise, die gespielt wird von Kriegsinstrumenten und die das Metrum und die Cadence der Trommeln markiert, welche im engeren Sinn der *Marsch* ist." Später heißt es statt „le Mètre et la cadence des Tambours" „le Mètre et la batterie des Tambours". Die Cadence, das ist der Schlag der Trommeln, der mit dem Schritt und Tritt des Marsches in eins gesetzt wird. Die Cadence, das ist die nach gleichmäßigen Abständen unterteilte Zeit. Die Cadence, das ist der Taktschlag.

Die Musik selbst soll eine lebhafte Empfindung dieses Taktschlags geben. Der Artikel „Tems" bemerkt (II, 308): „Von den verschiedenen *Zeiten* eines Taktes gibt es empfindbarere, markiertere als andere, obwohl die Werte gleich sind. Die Zeit, die stärker markiert, wird *starke Zeit* genannt; die, die weniger markiert, wird *schwache Zeit* genannt."

Der Nachdruck, der Stärkeakzent, das, was wir als Akzent zu bezeichnen pflegen, fehlt in der Definition des Artikels „Accent"; das Starke und das Schwache tritt nur unter dem Stichwort „Forte-Piano" (I, 353) im Sinne des Clair-obscur als Schattierung auf. Wenn aber die Musik eine lebhafte Empfindung des Taktschlags geben soll, dann muß sie auch die verschieden empfindbaren Grade des Nachdrucks empfindbar machen. Die Cadence ist also der gleichmäßige, im Nachdruck gestufte Schlag des Akzenttakts.

Wie die lebhafte Empfindung dieses Schlags entsteht, sagt der Artikel „Cadencé" (I, 109):

> „Eine Musik gut, bien *cadencée* ist die, wo die Cadence empfindbar ist, wo der Rhythmus und die Harmonie so vollkommen wie möglich zusammenwirken, um die Taktbewegung empfindbar zu machen. Denn die Wahl der Akkorde ist nicht gleichgültig, um die Zeiten des Takts zu markieren, und man darf nicht unterschiedslos dieselbe Harmonie auf den Niederschlag und auf den Aufschlag setzen. Desgleichen genügt es nicht, die Takte in gleichmäßige Werte zu teilen, um ihre gleichmäßige Wiederkehr empfindbar zu machen; vielmehr hängt der Rhythmus nicht weniger vom Akzent (das meint hier: von den Tonhöhen) ab, die man der Melodie gibt, als von den Werten, die man den Noten gibt; denn man kann Taktzeiten haben in den Werten sehr gleichmäßig, und dennoch sehr schlecht *cadencés*; es ist nicht genug, daß die Gleichmäßigkeit da ist, es ist außerdem nötig, daß man sie empfindet."

Die Cadence ist also der gleichmäßige, im Nachdruck gestufte Schlag des Akzenttakts, den die Musik satztechnisch allseitig bestimmt und damit empfindbar macht.

Im Artikel „Cadence" ist von einer „lebhaften Empfindung des Taktes" die Rede; der Artikel „Cadencé" nennt als Ziel, „die Taktbewegung empfindbar zu machen". Takt, das meint: Taktmaß, und Taktbewegung scheinen identisch. Die Mensuraltheorie hatte hier eine in sich ruhende proportionale Zahlenordnung, die am Maßstab des tactus dort in eine sinnlich wahrnehmbare Bewegungsordnung übersetzt wurde. Es ist das Modell von Urbild und Abbild. Dieses Modell verwandelt sich in der französischen Musik in das Modell von Körper und Seele. Die Taktbewegung belebt das reglose Taktmaß, haucht ihm Odem ein, Rousseau würde sagen, nach dem Belieben des Sängers, François Couperin würde sagen, nach der Empfindung oder den besonderen Vorstellungen, die jedes Stück solistischer französischer Instrumentalmusik bezeichnet und ausdrücken zu wollen scheint. Auch wenn sich bei ihm, wie der Zusammenhang (*L'Art de toucher le Clavecin*, Paris 1717, 38—42; *Oeuvres Complètes* I, Paris 1933, 41) lehrt, Cadence auf die Inégalité bezieht und das je spezifische Verhältnis der ungleichmäßigen Ausführung gleichmäßig notierter stufenweise aufeinanderfolgender Achtel meint. Rousseau aber kontert: „In Italien ist der Takt die Seele der Musik." Das sagt: Körper und Seele, Taktmaß und Taktbewegung sind identisch. Das Abbild ist die Sache selbst. Takt ist keine in sich ruhende Zahlenordnung, kein regloser Körper, Takt ist selbst Bewegung, und zwar bestimmte, kompositorisch bestimmte Bewegung. So wird „Mesure", „Taktmaß", nicht als Ordnung von Zahlen, sondern als Gliederung von Zeit definiert (I, 445): „Teilung der Dauer oder der Zeit in mehrere gleichmäßige Teile, hinreichend lang, daß das Ohr ihre Größe auffassen und unterteilen kann, und hinreichend kurz, daß die Vorstellung des einen sich nicht verwischt vor der Wiederkehr des anderen, und daß man ihre Gleichmäßigkeit empfindet. Jeder dieser gleichmäßigen Teile wird ebenfalls Mesure genannt; sie werden unterteilt in andere Aliquoten, die man Taktzeiten nennt, und die markiert werden mit gleichmäßigen Bewegungen der Hand oder des Fußes." Und „Tems" bedeutet Bewegungseinheit (II, 307): „Es gibt so viel verschiedene Werte der Taktzeiten, wie es Taktarten und Änderungen der Taktbewegung gibt."

Die Bewegungsstruktur ist Konstituens des Satzes und damit Konstituens der Aufführung. In Frankreich reguliert der Sänger das Orchester, in Italien das Orchester den Sänger. In Frankreich führen die Oberstimmen den Baß, in Italien der Baß die Oberstimmen. In Frankreich betont der Baß die Acht-Fuß-Lage, ist mit wenig Kontrabässen und viel Violoncelli besetzt; in Italien ist eine ausgeglichene Zahl von Kontrabässen und Violoncelli um die beiden Cembali (das des Kapellmeisters und das des Accompagnateurs) und durchs ganze Orchester verteilt. In Frankreich ist der Dirigent auf der Vorbühne, die Sänger im Auge, das Orchester im Rücken, und bedient sich seines Stocks; in Italien ist der Komponist am Cembalo inmitten des Orchesters, und so wichtig eine gute erste Violine für die Verständigung im Ensemble ist: die Singstimme folgt dem Baß und dem Takt (kann also auch nur ein gebundenes Rubato ausführen), die erste Violine folgt der Singstimme, das Ensemble der ersten Violine, alle zusammen endlich folgen dem Cembalo des Komponisten. Auch das Accompagnement wird in Frankreich und in Italien verschieden ausgeführt, desgleichen die Notenwerte, die in Frankreich der Inégalité unterworfen sind (Artikel „Orchestre" II, 60 ff.; „Ensemble" I, 317 ff., dazu „Maistre de Musique" I, 433 f.; „Accompagnement" I, 9 ff. und „Accompagnateur" I, 8 f.; „Pointer" II, 104 f.).

Die Vorstellung des Taktes als eines von Anfang an bestimmt bewegten, das ist unsere Vorstellung des Taktes. Wir sind nur auf Grund von Überlegungen imstande, ihn anders zu denken. Rousseau benennt die Distanz der Bewegungsstrukturen der italienischen und der französischen Musik und gibt uns damit eine Grundlage für solche Überlegungen. Die Distanz wird uns weniger an einer konkreten Vorstellung von der Bewegungsstruktur der französischen Musik bewußt als an der Schwierigkeit, uns diese Bewegungsstruktur konkret vorzustellen, eine Schwierigkeit, der anscheinend schon Rousseaus Zeitgenossen unterlagen (Artikel „Musique" I, 503). Die Bewegungsstruktur der Mensuralmusik allerdings ist noch weiter von unserer Vorstellung der Bewegungsstruktur der Musik, von unserer Vorstellung des Taktes entfernt.

Im Laufe des achtzehnten Jahrhunderts hat die Vorstellung der italienischen Musik diese Vorstellung der französischen Musik auch in Frankreich überformt. Die klassisch-romantische Musikkultur, das „Zeitalter der Sonate", basiert auf der italienischen Musikkultur. So ist unter dem Gesichtspunkt der historischen Wirksamkeit die Beschäftigung mit Vorstellungen der französischen Musik kaum zu rechtfertigen. Wohl aber zeigt uns die Distanz, der „vollendete Gegensatz" der zwei Musiken, wie wenig selbstverständlich manche unserer grundlegenden Vorstellungen von Musik sind. Und damit erweitert sich unser Begriff von Musik.

Der Vorzug, den Rousseau der italienischen Musik vor der französischen gibt, ist keine Willkür, will sich auch nicht auf das späte Urteil der Geschichte berufen; er folgt aus einer Reduktion auf die Prinzipien der Natur.

Damit die Musik nicht nur ein „physisches", sondern auch ein „moralisches Vergnügen" gewährt, damit die Musik eine der „schönen Künste" wird, muß sie eine „nachahmende Kunst", aus einer „natürlichen" eine „nachahmende Musik" werden (Artikel „Expression" I, 336 und 342; „Mélodie" I, 438 f.; „Musique" I, 493 f.; „Opéra" II, 36 f. und öfter). Die Musik ahmt Gegenstände nach, malt „Bilder" oder „Gemälde". Sie ahmt die „Empfindungen" dessen, der diese Gegenstände betrachtet, nach und die großen, die erhabenen „Leidenschaften" (etwa Artikel „Imitation" I, 400 ff.; „Opéra" II, 54 f.). „Vor allem muß man wohl beachten, daß der Reiz der Musik nicht bloß in der Nachahmung, sondern in einer angenehmen Nachahmung besteht" (Artikel „Expression" I,

Die „Empfindungen" drücken sich aus im „Akzent", und zwar im „erhabenen oder rednerischen Akzent" der Sprache. Die Nachahmung der Empfindungen ist also zuvor Nachahmung dieses Akzents. Da die Musik eine Kunst ist, die sich primär an die Sinne, an einen bestimmten Sinn wendet und nicht an den Verstand, ist ihr dieser Akzent adäquater Gegenstand der Nachahmung.

Die Möglichkeiten der Nachahmung dieses Akzents sind an die Möglichkeiten des Gegenstands dieser Nachahmung, an die Möglichkeiten der Sprache gebunden. Je reicher die Akzente einer Sprache sind, desto „musikalischer" ist sie, desto leichter lassen sich ihre Akzente in der Musik nachahmen, desto inniger kann die Verschmelzung von Akzenten der Sprache und Akzenten der Musik geraten. Der Reichtum der Akzente einer Sprache, ihr „akzentisches Idiom" hängt von „Einbildungskraft" und „Empfindung" ab. Einbildungskraft und Empfindung aber hängen von dem Klima (wir würden sagen: von der Geschichte — oder von der Gesellschaft) ab, worunter die Menschen geboren sind (Artikel „Accent" I, 2 ff.; „Mélodie" I, 439; „Opéra" II, 39 und 49 f.; „Voix" II, 364 f.).

Wenn Nachahmung in der Musik zuvor Nachahmung des rednerischen Akzents ist, dann müssen in einer Musik, die den Rang einer nachahmenden Kunst behauptet, Gesang und Melodie an erster Stelle stehen; gegenüber einer sich verselbständigenden Instrumentalmusik ist Zurückhaltung am Platz (Artikel „Chant" I, 132 ff.; „Mélodie" I, 438 ff., und „Rhythme" II, 163 f.; „Sonate" II, 217 ff.).

Von der Melodie aus wird ein Einheitsprinzip entwickelt, das der notwendigen Einheit der Wahrnehmung entspricht: „Einheit der Melodie", Einheit, die die Melodie stiftet (Artikel „Unité de Mélodie" II, 354 ff., dazu „Basse-Fondamentale" I, 73 f.). „Einfall", „Thema", „Anlage" sind die Stufen, in denen sich zunächst dieses Einheitsprinzip realisiert (Artikel „Motif" I, 483 f.; „Sujet" II, 224 f.; „Dessein" I, 226 ff.). Die Anlage hat „Einheit" und „Mannigfaltigkeit" zu verbinden; Einheit ohne Mannigfaltigkeit wäre Eintönigkeit, Mannigfaltigkeit ohne Einheit, der bloße Kontrast (Artikel „Contraste" I, 192 f.), wäre Monstrosität. So scheint hier das Prinzip des klassischen Ausgleichs auf.

Die Einheit, die die Melodie stiftet, bestimmt insbesondere die Verhältnisse des mehrstimmigen Satzes. Die Harmonie im weiten Sinn besteht ohne den Akzent der Dauer; deshalb kann sie aus sich selbst nichts nachahmen, ist nur sinnliches Vergnügen (Artikel „Harmonie" I, 377 ff.). Mehrere Melodien zugleich sind theoretisch auszuschließen, praktisch unter bestimmten Vorkehrungen möglich. Das regelt das Urteil über „Duo", „Trio", „Quatuor", „Quinque", „Fugue" und „Imitation" als satztechnische Erscheinung. Mehrfach klingt der Gedanke der „entwickelnden Variation" an, wie denn auch der Begriff des „harmonischen Bandes" erläutert wird (Artikel „Liaison" I, 421). Melodie ist definiert als Hauptstimme, die von realer zu realer Stimme wandern, ja nur in aufeinanderfolgenden Anschlägen verschiedener realer Stimmen bestehen kann. Auf diese Hauptstimme sind die Begleitstimmen zu beziehen. Sonst sind sie bloßes Füllsel. Es wird hier ein Repertoire von Einheitsbegriffen unter dem Titel des musikalischen Sinns, des Zusammenhangs entwickelt, das für den obligaten Stil bis hin zu Schönberg gültig ist. Am höchsten verwirklicht sich dieses Konzept im Air der Oper: er kann ein „chef-d'œuvre de la Musique" sein (Artikel „Air" I, 44; dazu „Récitatif" II, 132 ff.).

Die Nachahmung des rednerischen Akzents, in dem Empfindungen und erhabene Leidenschaften ihren Ausdruck finden, und damit die Nachahmung von Empfindungen und Leidenschaften kann, wie die Realisation des Einheitsprinzips, nur dem Genie gelingen; denn es gibt dafür keine Kunstregeln. Das Genie trifft die Nachahmung, die Einheit, die vereinigte Wirkung von Macht und Einfachheit, von „edler Einfalt und stiller Größe"; sein höchstes Vermögen wird offenbar in einem „Air *di Prima intenzione*" (Artikel „Génie" I, 364 f.; „Accent" I, 6; „Compositeur" I, 172 f.; „Effet" I, 306 f., dazu „Exécuter" I, 331; „Monologue" I, 482 f.; „Pathétique" II, 83; „Préluder" II, 108 f.; „Prima Intenzione" II, 111 ff., dazu „Canon" I, 112; „Scene" II, 174 f.).

Die Voraussetzung für die Nachahmung und damit für die Verwirklichung des Einheitsprinzips ist die Musikalität der Sprache. Daraus resultiert die Überlegenheit der italienischen Musik (II, 358): „Es ist dieses Prinzip der *Einheit der Melodie*, das die Italiener empfunden und befolgt haben, ohne es zu wissen, das aber die Franzosen weder gewußt noch befolgt haben; es ist, sage ich, dieses große Prinzip, in dem der wesentliche Unterschied der zwei Musiken besteht."

In der Tat scheint die Ausbildung des obligaten Stils nur auf dem Grund der Bewegungsstruktur der italienischen Musik möglich. Insofern verweist Rousseau mit Recht nachdrücklich auf Pergolesi (etwa Artikel „Dessein" I, 227).

Die Vorstellung des Genies impliziert die Vorstellung der Autonomie des Künstlers und seines Werks. Die Musik ist Sprache, Sprache der Empfindung, gegründet auf die Natur, „empfindbar allen Menschen, wissenden und unwissenden" (Artikel „Harmonie" I, 387). Aber hier sind nicht nur die Kategorien für zweihundert Jahre Musikgeschichte entworfen; Rousseau greift weiter und definiert das musikalische Material nach seinen Parametern (Artikel „Musique" I, 490):

> „Musiktheorie ist, wenn man so sagen kann, die Kenntnis des musikalischen Materials; das heißt, der verschiedenen Verhältnisse des Tiefen zum Hohen, des Schnellen zum Langsamen, des Sauren zum Süßen, des Starken zum Schwachen, deren die Töne empfänglich sind; Verhältnisse, die, indem sie alle möglichen Kombinationen der Musik und der Töne umfassen, auch alle Ursachen der Eindrücke zu umfassen scheinen, die ihre Aufeinanderfolge auf das Ohr und auf die Seele machen kann."

Und der Artikel „Copiste" (I, 197—210) gibt eine Theorie der Editionstechnik. Doch ich halte ein.

Was Rousseau im Artikel „Style" (II, 224) über die nationalen Musikstile sagt, ist nach seinem Konzept nicht Willkür, sondern Stimme der Natur, auf die sich Menschen mit Geschmack sollten einigen können, worauf sie sich, was den Vorzug zwischen der französischen Musik und der italienischen betrifft, in der Mehrzahl geeinigt haben (Artikel „Goût" I, 373). „Der Stil der deutschen Kompositionen ist sprunghaft, zerschnitten, aber harmonisch"; sie haben keine Einheit, keinen Zusammenhang, bloße Sinnlichkeit. „Der Stil der französischen Kompositionen ist fade, flach oder hart, schlecht ,kadenziert', eintönig." „Fade", das meint ohne Reiz und Kraft der Akzente. „Flach oder hart" bezieht sich auf eine Eigenschaft der französischen Musik, die der Artikel „Roulade" (II, 170) beschreibt: „Die Franzosen, verpflichtet, beinahe ihre ganze Musik syllabisch zu komponieren wegen der wenig günstigen Vokale, sind gezwungen, den Noten einen langsamen und gesetzten Gang zu geben, oder die Konsonanten aufeinanderstoßen zu lassen, indem sie die Silben laufen machen; was den Gesang notwendig matt (das steht hier für flach) oder hart macht. Ich sehe nicht, wie die französische Musik jemals diesen Mißstand übersteigen könnte." Auf entsprechende Verhältnisse im Bereich der Ausführung läßt der Artikel „Débiter" (I, 222 f.) schließen. „Schlecht kadenziert" meint ohne genauen, ohne kompositorisch bestimmten Taktschlag, „eintönig" ohne Mannigfaltigkeit. Der Stil „der italienischen Kompositionen ist blühend, prickelnd, voll Kraft"; er hat Mannigfaltigkeit, unterhält das Interesse, was nur bei erkennbarer Einheit möglich ist, hat Größe und Erhabenheit in der Nachahmung der Empfindungen und der Leidenschaften. Die Möglichkeit der Nachahmung, die Musik zur schönen Kunst macht, ist nur der italienischen Musik gegeben, und das zumal auf Grund ihrer Bewegungsstruktur: „Der Taktschlag ist eine Eigenschaft der guten Musik."

JOHANN SEBASTIAN BACH:
APPROACHES TO ANALYSIS AND INTERPRETATION

WALTER BLANKENBURG

Die Bedeutung der solistischen Alt-Partien
im Weihnachts-Oratorium, BWV 248

Es ist bis jetzt noch wenig darüber nachgeforscht worden, unter welchen Gesichtspunkten Bach im Weihnachts-Oratorium (WO) die einzelnen solistischen Vokal-Partien den verschiedenen menschlichen Stimmlagen zugewiesen hat. Selbstverständlich werden gemäß der Tradition der älteren Weihnachtshistorien die Evangelistenworte durchgehend von einem Tenor sowie die Worte der Verkündigung des „Angelus" im zweiten Teil von einem Sopran und die des Herodes im sechsten von einem Baß gesungen [1]. Die Worte der Hohenpriester und Schriftgelehrten (Matthäus Kapitel 2, 5—6) jedoch bringt Bach entgegen dem herkömmlichen Brauch nicht als Turba-Chor, sondern läßt sie vom Evangelisten mit übernehmen, wohl ein Zeichen, daß die ältere Gepflogenheit zu seiner Zeit nur noch bedingt nachgewirkt hat. Wie steht es aber nun mit den Zuweisungen der Accompagnato-Rezitative und Arien? Sind darin gewisse Prinzipien zu erkennen? Es liegt zunächst die Annahme nahe, daß Bachs Entscheidungen sich aus der Anwendung des Parodieverfahrens, von dem er im WO bekanntlich besonders reichlichen Gebrauch gemacht hat, ergaben [2]. Das trifft jedoch nur teilweise zu. Die Teile I—III und (für sich gesondert) der Teil IV sind nach einem strengen Tonartenplan, der der Herstellung einer symmetrischen Anlage dient, aufgebaut, was verschiedentlich Transpositionen der parodierten Vorlagen erforderlich machte [3]. Auch im Teil V weicht Bach bei der Baß-Arie „Erleucht auch meine finstre Sinnen" von der Vorlage BWV 215 Satz 7 ab. Mit den Transpositionen der Vorlagen aber ergaben sich zwangsläufig andere Stimmlagen für die Gesangspartien wie natürlich auch teilweise die Verwendung anderer obligater Instrumente. So handelt es sich bei BWV 215 Satz 7 um eine Sopran-Arie gegenüber der Baß-Arie „Erleucht auch meine finstre Sinnen".

Diese fügt sich zwar ebenfalls in eine sinnvolle Tonartenordnung ein; jedoch ist damit noch nicht deren Zuweisung der Baß-Stimme und nicht, wie es vom Gesamtplan her ebenfalls möglich gewesen wäre, dem Alt erklärt. Auf diesen bemerkenswerten Sachverhalt müssen wir später zurückkommen.

[1] Ich setze mich nachdrücklich dafür ein, beim WO von sechs „Teilen" zu sprechen, wie es Bach getan hat, und nicht von Kantaten, wie es heute weithin, häufig sogar in der Fachliteratur, geschieht; denn eine Kantate ist textlich und demzufolge musikalisch anders gegliedert als ein Oratorium.

[2] Vgl. den Kritischen Bericht zur Neuausgabe des WO in der Neuen Bach-Ausgabe (NBA) von Walter Blankenburg und Alfred Dürr, Kassel 1962, Seite 167—172, ferner Walter Blankenburg „Das Parodieverfahren im WO J. S. Bachs" in „Musik und Kirche" 32. Jahrgang, 1962, Seite 245—254 (Wiederabdruck in „Johann Sebastian Bach", herausgegeben von Walter Blankenburg in „Wege der Forschung", Darmstadt 1970, Wissenschaftliche Buchgesellschaft, Seite 493—506) und Alfred Dürr „Johann Sebastian Bach — Weihnachts-Oratorium BWV 248" (Meisterwerke der Musik" Heft 8), München 1967.

[3] Vgl. die Tabelle auf Seite 248 des genannten Aufsatzes in „Musik und Kirche" bzw. auf Seite 499 des Wiederabdrucks.

Im Teil VI freilich, in dem eine verlorengegangene Kantate (BWV 248a) weitgehend parodiert worden ist, hat Bach offenbar die Tonarten der Vorlage beibehalten; denn es fällt hier der ungewöhnliche Tatbestand auf, daß in dem Evangelisten-Rezitativ „Und Gott befahl ihnen im Traum" (Satz 3), dem Accompagnato-Rezitativ „So geht! Genug, mein Schatz geht nicht von hier" (Satz 4) und der Arie „Nun mögt ihr stolzen Feinde schrecken" (Satz 5) drei Tenor-Partien unmittelbar aufeinanderfolgen. Zu Satz 4 vermerkt Alfred Dürr: „Auch die Frage der Vokalstimmlage (der Vorlage) muß offenbleiben, doch dürfen wir mit großer Wahrscheinlichkeit annehmen, daß der Singpart auch schon in der älteren Fassung dem Tenor zugewiesen war; denn was hätte Bach veranlassen sollen, für dieses Rezitativ ausgerechnet die Stimmlage des Evangelisten zu wählen, wenn er sich nicht durch die Vorlage gebunden gefühlt hätte?" Und zur folgenden Arie sagt Dürr: „Für die Frage der Besetzung der älteren Fassung mit Oboen (Flöten? Soloviolinen?) gilt das oben Gesagte, desgleichen für die Zuweisung der Gesangspartie an den Tenor: Bach hätte schwerlich Alt und Baß mit derart kleinen Solopartien abgespeist und den Tenor derart belastet, hätte er nicht die Bevorzugung von Sopran und Tenor in der älteren Fassung vorgefunden" [4]. Dürrs Vermutung, daß im Teil VI des WO die Tonarten der Vorlage beibehalten worden sind, ist sicherlich richtig. Aber sollte Bach sich tatsächlich an diese gebunden gefühlt haben, weil er „schwerlich Alt und Baß mit derart kleinen Solopartien abgespeist hätte"? Diese Annahme ist doch wohl nicht überzeugend; bleibt doch unter den gegebenen Umständen für Alt und Baß dann überhaupt nur noch die Mitwirkung bei dem Rezitativo à 4 „Wo bleibt der Höllen Schrecken nun?" vor dem Schlußchoral, also eine weit geringere „Abspeisung", übrig. Konnte es für Bach eine derartige Überlegung überhaupt geben, wo die Solisten zugleich Mitglieder des Chores waren? Gebunden fühlte sich Bach an die Tonarten der parodierten Vorlagen grundsätzlich überhaupt nicht. Wenn er sie beibehielt, dann hatte dies — das meint Dürr wohl auch selbst — einen bestimmten Grund. Dieser aber scheint bei Teil VI des WO kein anderer als der der Arbeitserleichterung gewesen zu sein, weil vermutlich die Zeit zur schnellen Fertigstellung des Werks drängte [5]; denn die Stimmenzuweisung vom Accompagnato-Rezitativ „So geht! Genug, mein Schatz geht nicht von hier" und der anschließenden Arie „Nun mögt ihr stolzen Feinde schrecken" an den Tenor ist, wie weiter unten noch darzulegen sein wird, im Rahmen des Gesamtwerks offensichtlich inkonsequent. Dafür aber gibt es sicherlich keine andere Erklärung als die besagte der Arbeitsökonomie.

Haben wir somit bisher zweierlei Gründe für die Stimmenzuweisungen bei den Accompagnato-Rezitativen und Arien im WO, nämlich entweder die Herstellung einer symmetrischen Tonarten-Ordnung (diese vor allem in den Teilen I—III und IV) oder

---

[4] Vgl. den Kritischen Bericht zum WO a. a. O., Seite 218! Die dort und an anderen Stellen mitgeteilten Forschungsergebnisse über die Entstehung des Sechsten Teils vom WO gehen spziell auf Alfred Dürr zurück.

[5] Vgl. im Kritischen Bericht a. a. O. Seite 209—210 den Abschnitt „Die Entstehung der Komposition". Dort u. a. die Feststellung: „In Wahrheit dürfte sich Bach der Arbeit am WO vorzugsweise in den an Kirchenmusik armen Wochen zwischen 1. Advent und Weihnachten 1734 gewidmet haben."

die Anlehnung an die Tonarten der Parodievorlagen, festgestellt, so ist im ersteren Fall
damit aber noch nicht erklärt, warum Bach sich im Einzelfall für den Alt und nicht — was
ja ebenfalls musikalisch möglich gewesen wäre — für den Baß und warum er sich an bestimmten Stellen für den Sopran und nicht den Tenor beziehungsweise hier wie dort nicht
umgekehrt entschieden hat.

Bei der Untersuchung dieser Frage stoßen wir auf die Nachwirkungen des liturgischen
Weihnachtsspiels, die im WO noch spürbar sind. Bereits Philipp Spitta stellte für das WO
fest: „Wo es nur anging, ist auch im poetischen Teile auf die Anschauungen der weih-
nachtlichen Volks-Schauspiele und -Lieder und die mit ihnen zusammenhängenden Cere-
monien Rücksicht genommen. Die Sitte des Kindleinwiegens wird durch das Schlummer-
lied des zweiten Teils, ‚Schlafe, mein Liebster‘ zurückgespiegelt . . .“[6]. Neuerdings hat zwar
Renate Steiger unter Bezugnahme auf diese Äußerung Spittas die „Fragestellung nach
dem Brauchtum" als „in der Romantik verwurzelt", die „allenfalls sekundäre Momente
erkläre", bezeichnet[7]; jedoch schon kurz vorher hatte Ludwig Prautzsch unübersehbare
Zusammenhänge des WO mit Elementen, die aus dem Bereich der „volkstümlichen Weih-
nachtsfeiern" herrühren, aufgedeckt und vor allem auf die Verkündigung des Engels
(Nr. 13, 16, 17), den Lobgesang der Himmlischen Heerscharen (Nr. 21) und das „Kind-
leinwiegen" (Nr. 18, 19) — sämtliche Stücke stehen in Teil II des Werks — hingewiesen[8]. Entscheidend bei alledem ist freilich, daß die Verwendung solcher Elemente
keinen Selbstzweck hat, sondern daß diese zur theologischen Durchdringung und Ver-
tiefung der musikalischen Aussagen im WO beizutragen haben. Dabei aber geht es nicht
zuletzt um mehr oder weniger offen zutage tretende Personifizierungen der bei den
Accompagnato-Rezitativen und Arien wirkenden Einzelstimmen. In diesem Zusammen-
hange hat Prautzsch bereits eine ganze Anzahl Hinweise gegeben. Daß die Tenor- und
vor allem die Baß-Partien im zweiten und dritten Teil des WO Stimmen der einzelnen
Hirten meinen und daß sicherlich auch das Duett „Herr, dein Mitleid, dein Erbarmen"
(Teil III) in diesen Vorstellungsbereich (Beteiligung eines Hirtenknaben) gehört, wird
man kaum bezweifeln können. Im fünften Teil ist die Arie „Erleucht auch meine finstre
Sinnen" offenkundig auf die Gestalt des Herodes bezogen. Aber gerade an dieser Stelle
wird, wie es auch sonst im WO allenthalben der Fall ist, der Unterschied zwischen geist-
lichem Spiel und Oratorium besonders deutlich. Dieser besteht ja nicht nur in der fehlen-
den dramatischen Handlung beim Oratorium, sondern in der hier gleichzeitig mit Hilfe
der poetischen Betrachtungen ständig vollzogenen theologischen Durchdringung und
existentiellen Aneignung der biblischen Verkündigung, wie es in den Accompagnato-
Rezitativen und Arien geschieht. Die Worte „Erleucht auch meine finstre Sinnen" knüp-
fen zwar an die düstere Gestalt des Herodes an, meinen aber zugleich den Menschen
schlechthin, für den Herodes nur Prototyp ist.

[6] Vgl. Philipp Spitta, *Johann Sebastian Bach* (Leipzig 1880), II, Seite 408.
[7] Vgl. deren sehr aufschlußreichen Aufsatz „Die Welt ist euch ein Himmelreich. Zu J. S. Bachs
Deutung des Pastoralen" (Schluß) in „Musik und Kirche" 41. Jahrgang, 1971. Seite 71.
[8] Vgl. den Aufsatz „Die Echo-Arie und andere symbolische und volkstümliche Züge in Bachs
Weihnachtsoratorium", ebenda Jahrgang 1971, Seite 221—229. Ich bin vor allem durch diese
Abhandlung zu meinen vorliegenden Ausführungen angeregt worden.

Wenn die Stimmenzuweisungen der solistischen Partien im WO im Hinblick auf bestimmte Personen der Weihnachtsgeschichte erfolgt sind, so schließt dies nicht aus, daß im Verlauf des Werks ein und dieselbe Stimmlage verschiedene Personifizierungen meinen kann. Wir haben dies z. B. für die Baß-Partien, die sich in Teil II auf einen der Hirten und in Teil V auf Herodes beziehen, festgestellt. Das wird noch deutlicher, wenn wir die Arie „Großer Herr und starker König (Teil I) hinzunehmen. Hier ist jedoch schwerlich die Stimme des Joseph gemeint, wie Prautzsch annimmt [9]; vielmehr deutet die Baßlage in Verbindung mit dem Attribut der Majestät, nämlich der Trompete, auf Gott selbst, d. h. auf seine Menschwerdung in dem Kind von Bethlehem.

Umsomehr besagt es nun, daß eine einzige Stimmlage in ihrer Bedeutung durch das gesamte WO nicht wechselt, nämlich der Alt. Folgerichtig hätten ihm im sechsten Teil nur auch noch das Accompagnato-Rezitativ „So geht! Genug, mein Schatz geht nicht von hier" und die Arie „Nun mögt ihr stolzen Feinde schrecken" (wie erwähnt, beides Tenor-Partien) zugewiesen werden müssen. Wie dargetan, hat Bach aber hier offenbar aus Zeitbedrängnis auf ein größeres Maß an Umgestaltung der Vorlage, die sich sonst ergeben hätte, verzichten müssen.

Bei folgenden Stücken ist die Altlage im WO verwendet:

Teil I

Accompagnato-Rezitativ„ Nun wird mein liebster Bräutigam" (Nr. 3)
Arie „Bereite dich, Zion" (Nr. 4)

Teil II

Arie „Schlafe, mein Liebster, genieße der Ruh" (Nr. 19)

Teil III

Arie „Schließe, mein Herze, dies selige Wunder" (Nr. 31)
Accompagnato-Rezitativ „Ja, mein Herz soll es bewahren" (Nr. 32)

Teil IV

(Dieser Teil ist insgesamt ohne personalen Bezug und stellt eine Meditation über den Jesus-Namen dar.)

Teil V

Accompagnato-Rezitative „Sucht ihn in meiner Brust" und „Wohl euch, die ihr das Licht gesehen" (im Turba-Satz Nr. 45)
Accompagnato-Rezitativ „Warum wollt ihr erschrecken" (Nr. 49)
Terzett-Arie „Ach, wenn wird die Zeit erscheinen?" (Nr. 51)

Teil VI

Rezitativo à 4 „Was will der Höllen Schrecken nun?" (Nr. 63)

Die Bedeutung der Alt-Stimme im WO erhellt aus ihrer Verwendung im zweiten und dritten Teil des Werks; sie stellt die Mutter Maria dar. Die Arie „Schlafe, mein Liebster,

---

[9] A. a. O. S. 227.

genieße der Ruh" ist das Wiegenlied, das sie im Stall zu Bethlehem singt. Dabei deuten die charakteristischen Baßfiguren im Takt 1—8, die von Takt 97—104 noch einmal wiederkehren und auch sonst im Verlauf des Stückes in mannigfacher Abwandlung erscheinen, auf die alte kirchliche Sitte des „Kindelwiegens".

Man vergleiche damit die zwar andersartige und doch verwandte Baßfigur in den Intermedien 1 und 7 der Weihnachtshistorie von Heinrich Schütz, bei denen sich der ausdrückliche Hinweis findet: „Worunter bisweilen des Christkindleins Wiege mit eingeführet wird."

Nicht weniger deutlich ist der Sachverhalt im Teil III. Die Arie „Schließe, mein Herze, dies selige Wunder" folgt hier unmittelbar auf die Evangelistenworte „Maria aber behielt alle diese Worte und bewegte sie in ihrem Herzen"; darauf gibt der Text der Arie die Deutung, daß die Bewegung des Herzens sich nur in einem starken persönlichen Glauben erfüllen kann. Aus diesem Zuspruch der Maria zu sich selbst ergeben sich Gelöbnis und Bekenntnis in den Worten „Ja, ja, mein Herz soll es bewahren", die in dem Choral „Ich will dich mit Fleiß bewahren" aufgegriffen werden.

Hier nun wird bereits wieder die Besonderheit des Oratoriums gegenüber dem Krippenspiel offenkundig: Die der Maria angedichteten Verse meinen nicht sie allein als die Mutter des Christuskindes, sondern verstehen sie deutend zugleich als „des Herrn Magd" (Lukas Kapitel 1, 38), als den Inbegriff der Demut und Hingabe und somit als das Urbild des Glaubens und der Kirche. Als dieses Urbild hat es seit den Tagen Luthers ein eigentümliches protestantisches Marien-Verständnis gegeben. So ist es zu begreifen, daß auch alle Texte, die von Christus als dem Bräutigam sprechen, der Alt-Stimme zugewiesen werden; denn der Bräutigam holt seine Braut heim, d. h. die glaubende Kirche, die im Sprachgebrauch des WO mit dem Wort „Zion", das gleichbedeutend mit „Gottesvolk" und „Christenheit" ist, bezeichnet wird. Das sind vor allem die betreffenden Stellen im ersten Teil, die Ankündigung der Kirche „Nun wird mein liebster Bräutigam ... zum Trost, zum Heil der Erden einmal geboren werden", worauf die Mahnung an sich selbst, an die Christenheit, in der Arie „Bereite dich, Zion" folgt.

Von besonderer Anschaulichkeit sind die Alt-Partien im fünften Teil des Werks, der den Anfang der Perikope von den Drei Weisen aus dem Morgenlande behandelt. Hier schiebt sich der Solo-Alt in den Turba-Chor der drei Weisen „Wo ist der neugeborene

König der Juden" mit den Worten „Sucht ihn in meiner Brust, hier wohnt er, mir und
ihm zur Lust" ein und beschließt nach den Worten „... und sind gekommen, ihn anzu-
beten" (Matthäus Kapitel 2, 2) diesen Satz mit dem Ausruf „Wohl euch, die ihr das Licht
gesehen ...". Wieder bleibt es in der Schwebe, wer hier redet, die Mutter Maria, bis zu
der die Drei Weisen eben noch gar nicht gelangt sind, oder die Kirche. Und auch die Fort-
setzung des Evangeliums nach der erwähnten Baß-Arie „Erleucht auch meine finstre
Sinnen" wird nach dem Bericht „Da das der König Herodes hörte, erschrak er und mit ihm
das ganze Jerusalem" von dem Alt mit den Worten „Warum wollt ihr erschrecken? Kann
meines Jesu Gegenwart euch solche Furcht erwecken? ..." unterbrochen. Unüberhörbar,
daß hier die gleiche innere Stimme redet! Und schließlich folgt nach dem Ende des ersten
Teils der Perikope (Vers 6), dem alttestamentlichen Zitat Micha Kapitel 5, 1, das Aria-
Terzetto, das in einzigartiger Weise den alten und neuen Bund, alttestamentliches Hoffen durch Sopran und Baß als die Stimmen der forschenden Hohenpriester und Schriftgelehrten (Matthäus Kapitel 2, 4) zum Ausdruck gebracht, und neutestamentliche Erfüllung durch den Alt wiedergegeben, einander gegenübergestellt. Folgendermaßen wird
die Da-capo-Form der Arie durchgeführt: Im Teil a singt der Sopran unentwegt die
Frage „Ach, wenn wird die Zeit erscheinen?" und der Tenor die andere „Ach, wenn kömmt
der Trost der Seinen?". Dazu kommt erst von Takt 34 ab der Alt mit dem vielfachen Ruf
„Schweigt, er ist schon wirklich hier!". Im Teil b, in dem der Alt pausiert, singen Sopran
und Tenor ausschließlich die vierte, auf „Schweigt, er ist schon wirklich hier" sich reimende
Textzeile der Arie: „Jesu, komm, ach komm zu mir!". Im Da-capo-Teil a' erscheint Teil a
variiert, indem jetzt der Tenor die erste und der Sopran die zweite Frage bringt, während
der Alt wiederum ausschließlich die Worte „Schweigt, er ist schon wirklich hier!" singt.
Selbstverständlich wird dieser Dialog des Alt mit den beiden anderen solistischen Stimmen
noch in manchen musikalischen Einzelheiten verdeutlicht. Vor allem kennzeichnet das
charakteristische Motiv der sehnsuchtsvollen Erwartung, das im Bereich der musikalischen
Figurenlehre wohl als Emphasis anzusprechen ist,

allein die Stimmführung von Sopran und Tenor sowie die der mit diesen beiden Stimmen
engverbundenen obligaten Violine. Dem Alt liegt demgegenüber der völlig andersartige
Affekt freudiger Gewißheit in folgender Figur zugrunde:

Dieser wird auch eindrucksvoll hörbar in dem „gehorsamen", dem Gebote des Schweigens folgenden, plötzlichen Verstummen der beiden fragenden Stimmen am Ende von a und a', während der Alt über dem kadenzierenden Continuo danach noch einmal die Worte „Er ist schon wirklich hier" nachdrücklich als eine unumstößliche, nun auch bildhaft „außer Frage" stehende Wirklichkeit bezeugt. Dabei möchte man in der abschließenden Wendung von Teil a' die Figur der Katabasis als Zeichen der Deszendenz Gottes erkennen [10].

er   ist schon wirk - lich hier

Man vermag sich die tiefsinnige Anlage dieses Terzetts schwer als Parodie, wie es im Kritischen Bericht (S. 205) angenommen wird, vorzustellen. Sollte dafür tatsächlich einmal eine Vorlage ermittelt werden, dann wird diese gewiß besonders wichtige Aufschlüsse über Bachs Parodieverfahren vermitteln können.

An das Terzett schließt sich als Übergang zum Schlußchoral vom fünften Teil noch das Accompagnato-Rezitativ

„Mein Liebster herrschet schon.
Ein Herz, das seine Herrschaft liebet
und sich ihm ganz zu eigen gibet,
ist meines Jesu Thron."

Dieser Text ist eine unmittelbare Fortführung der Worte des Alt vom vorangegangenen Stück, wie er daher auch nur als Zuweisung zu dieser Stimme, gleichsam als Rede der Maria, die von fern her an das Ohr des Hörers dringt, verständlich erscheint. Unverkennbar begegnet uns somit in den Alt-Partien von Teil V das Zeugnis des Glaubens und der Kirche mit besonderer Eindringlichkeit. Die Gestalt der Maria bildet dabei nur noch den geschichtlichen Hintergrund; hervorgetreten ist jetzt mehr die Urgestalt der glaubensvollen Hingabe und der bekennenden Demut.

Nur im sechsten Teil des Werks stellen wir, worauf bereits hingewiesen wurde, eine Inkonsequenz in der Stimmenzuweisung fest. Dem Inhalt der Dichtung nach hätten das Accompagnato-Rezitativ „So geht! Genug, mein Schatz geht nicht von hier" und die anschließende Arie „Nun mögt ihr stolzen Feinde schrecken, / was könnt ihr mir für Furcht erwecken?" unbedingt zur Sinnbildlichkeit der Alt-Stimme im WO gehört. Liegt doch hier zudem eine besondere Nähe zur zweiten, abschließenden Hälfte der Perikope von den Drei Weisen aus dem Morgenlande (Matthäus Kapitel 2, 7—12) vor;

---

[10] Diese musikalische Figur zeigt übrigens eine überraschende Verwandtschaft mit dem ständig sich wiederholenden absteigenden h-moll-Dreiklang im Satz „Et incarnatus est" der h-moll-Messe, über dessen Sinnbildlichkeit ich in dem Aufsatz „Der Titel und das Titelbild von Johann Heinrich Buttstedts Schrift ‚ut, mi, sol, re, fa, la — tota Musica et Harmonia aeterna oder Neueröffnetes altes, wahres, einziges und ewiges Fundamentum musices' (1717)" Näheres ausgeführt habe; vgl. „Die Musikforschung" 3. Jahrgang, 1950, Seite 64—66.

denn die Worte beider Stücke sind der Mutter Maria gleichsam in den Mund gelegt. Vom mutmaßlichen Grund der Abweichung war vorher die Rede [11]. Nun aber tritt in diesem letzten Teil des Werks doch auch der Alt noch einmal in seiner Besonderheit hervor, nämlich im Recitativo à 4 vor dem Schlußchoral, das Ludwig Prautzsch mit dem Solistenensemble im Finale einer Oper verglichen hat [12]. Während darin Sopran, Tenor und Baß den vollständigen Dreizeiler

> „Was will der Hölle Schrecken nun?
> Was will uns Welt und Sünde tun,
> da wir in Jesu Händen ruhn?"

singen, bringt der Alt dreimal lediglich die Worte „da wir in Jesu Händen ruhn". Die Mutter Maria bedarf der Frage nicht, sie weiß sich in dem Christuskind geborgen. Jetzt aber finden sich alle Gestalten der Weihnachtsgeschichte zusammen, um den letzten Schritt zum Glauben zu vollziehen und sich mit dessen Urgestalt in einem quasi Unisono-Abschluß, dessen Symbolik besonders tiefsinnig ist, auf die Worte „da wir in Jesu Händen ruhen" zu vereinen.

Oft wird dieses Stück, um seine Ausdruckskraft zu erhöhen, von den Dirigenten chorisch wiedergegeben. Daß dies der inneren Intention Bachs widerspricht, steht außer Frage, wenn es auch sehr schwer ist, hierbei vier eigengeprägte solistische Stimmen zu einem wirklich homogenen Klang, der um seiner Sinnbildlichkeit willen unerläßlich ist, zu verschmelzen. Auch bei diesem Recitativo à 4 vermag man sich ein Urbild schwer vorzustellen (Kritischer Bericht, S. 215); es würde im Falle seiner Entdeckung seinerseits für Bachs Parodieverfahren sehr aufschlußreich sein.

Recitativo à 4

---

[11] Vgl. S. 140.
[12] A. a. O. Seite 227.

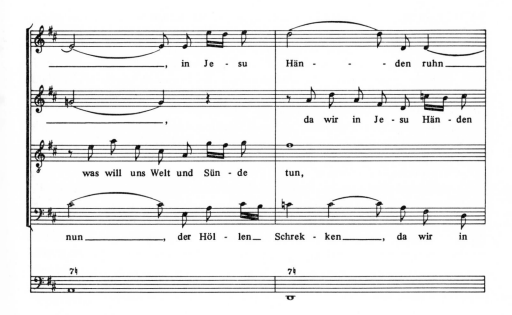

Was lehren uns die in unserer Untersuchung gemachten Beobachtungen? Die solistischen Alt-Partien im WO werfen in einer ganz bestimmten Richtung ein Licht auf Bachs Kompositionsweise, nämlich auf eine sinnbildliche Durchdringung der musikalischen Formgebung aufgrund theologischer Gedankenarbeit. Dieser Schaffensvorgang ist zwar bereits durch das höchst wahrscheinlich auf Christian Friedrich Henrici zurückgehende Textbuch, bei dem Bach allerdings sicherlich selbst mitgewirkt hat [13], vorgezeichnet. Die der explicatio und applicatio des zugrundeliegenden Bibeltextes, d. h. deren gedanklichen Entfaltung und persönlichen Aneignung, dienende Oratoriendichtung wird jedoch im Bereich der Musik zusätzlich und eigentümlich veranschaulicht und vertieft. Bach vermag mit seiner Kompositionsweise mehr zu sagen, als das formulierte Wort des Textbuches et tut. Er verändert dabei dessen Aussagen nicht, sondern schöpft nur dessen verborgene Inhalte und Verstehensmöglichkeiten vollends aus. Sicherlich ist Bachs Schaffensweise im Hinblick auf derartig interpretierende Behandlung der jeweiligen textlichen Vorlage noch keineswegs hinreichend untersucht. Unsere kurzen Ausführungen, die einem Manne gewidmet sind, dem die Bachforschung unserer Zeit besonders viel verdankt, möchten einen kleinen Beitrag dazu liefern.

---

[13] Dafür sprechen auch die Beobachtungen in der vorliegenden Abhandlung. Vgl. den Kritischen Bericht a. a. O. Seite 190.

EDWARD T. CONE

Bach's Unfinished Fugue in C Minor

The unfinished fugue that accompanies Bach's clavier Fantasy in C minor (BWV 906) is not universally accepted as being by the master. Forkel, after insisting that the connection of the fugue with the fantasy is adventitious, continues: "But it cannot be doubted that at least the first thirty measures are by Sebastian Bach, for they contain an extremely daring experiment in the use of diminished and augmented intervals together with their inversions in three-part harmony. No one but Bach has ever dared such a thing. What follows the first thirty measures appears to be added by another hand, for it bears no trace of Sebastian's style"[1]. Forkel was probably writing on the basis of early copies; according to Bischoff, the original manuscript (Dresden, Sächsische Landesbibliothek, Mus. 2405 T 52 Aut. 3) was discovered in Dresden in 1876[2]. It is an apparently authentic holograph that bears no obvious trace of "another hand".

Both Spitta and Schweitzer, on the other hand, accept the entire fugue, and they further agree in deploring its incomplete state. Lovers of funny coincidences may be amused by comparing their remarks on the subject[3].

Despite the evidence of the autograph, Schreyer repudiates the entire fugue, on grounds not only of its contrapuntal technique, which he finds faulty, but also of the strict da-capo form that he believes it to display. In typically categorical fashion he states that this "three-part song-form", as he calls it, "is by no means admissible in fugal composition, whose essence it contradicts". After rejecting for this reason two fugues for lute — those found in the Prelude, Fugue, and Allegro in Eb (BWV 998) and in the Partita in C minor (BWV 997) — he then claims that "not only both these fugues, but also the 'Unfinished C-Minor Fugue' ... are built on the same pattern, a pattern that not a single authentic fugue of Bach displays"[4].

The quotation marks around "Unfinished C-Minor Fugue" indicate Schreyer's conviction that the piece in question is not in fact unfinished, even though the autograph breaks off after the first quarter of m. 48. According to his theory, the fugue is in da-capo form; the last two complete measures of the manuscript, which bring in the subject at the original pitch-level, are the first two measures of the reprise, which then proceeds verbatim until the cadence at m. 33.

Even the most superficial analysis shows why this reconstruction is unacceptable. The fugue begins with a long expository section coming to a tonic cadence at m. 33. Its first 24 measures present a strictly fugal aspect, for even after the exposition (in three voices, with a strictly retained counter-subject) there is not a single measure that fails

[1] J. N. Forkel, *Über Johann Sebastian Bachs Leben, Kunst, und Kunstwerke* (Leipzig, 1802), p. 56.

[2] Hans Bischoff, ed., *Joh. Seb. Bach's Klavierwerke* (Leipzig, n. d.), VII, 152.

[3] Philipp Spitta, *Johann Sebastian Bach* (Leipzig, 1873—80), II, 662; Albert Schweitzer, *J. S. Bach* (Leipzig, 1908), p. 316.

[4] Johannes Schreyer, *Beiträge zur Bach-Kritik* (Leipzig, 1911—13), II, 34—36.

to refer to the subject, either by complete statement (including an entire counter-exposition at mm. 17—22) or by motivic sequences [5]. The following nine measures are free, consisting largely of conventional scale-figures leading to a full and conclusive cadence in the tonic. At this point both texture and theme change: the number of voices is reduced to two, and they state a combination of two new ideas — a theme with accompaniment, so to speak — later to be inverted in free double counterpoint. What is remarkable here is the way the "theme" turns each time into an unusual variation of the fugue-subject — a kind of single-voiced hocket (mm. 36—37 and 42—43) [6]. But by the time the first subject returns at m. 46, the new combination has been stated only twice: once in the tonic and once, with the voices freely exchanged, in the dominant. It is highly unlikely that any composer would go to the trouble of introducing such elaborately contrived new material only to relinquish it almost immediately. Furthermore, the proportions of Schreyer's reconstruction are unsatisfactory and improbable: his *ABA* would be 33—12—33 measures, or roughly 8—3—8. After such a brief contrast one would hardly be ready for a complete recapitulation of a fairly lengthy first section, one containing a good deal of internal repetition to boot!

This opinion is supported by a look at other compositions in the same form. These include not only the two lute fugues already cited but also the final Allegro of the Brandenburg Concerto No. 5 and the second of the Four Duets (the one in F major) from the *Clavierübung III*. (So whether or not Schreyer is right in refusing to accept the lute examples, his insistence that da capo fugues are foreign to Bach's style is certainly wrong. Or perhaps the two last examples are not "authentic" fugues because they are not so named.) In every case, the digression is longer than the original statement — sometimes even twice as long. Here are the proportions:

Brandenburg Finale: 78—154—78 (ca. 1—2—1)
Second Duet: 37—75—37 (ca. 1—2—1)
Lute Fugue in C minor: 48—60—48 (4—5—4)

Lute Fugue in E♭: 28—46—28 (because of an overlap, the middle section could also be taken as 48, in which case 7—12—7).

I conclude that the "Unfinished Fugue" is indeed an unfinished fugue.

At this point the reader may wonder why I have discussed at such length a position I find untenable. The reason is that, in spite of my conviction that the fugue is incomplete, I do accept Schreyer's hypothesis that it was intended to be in da-capo form, for it is hard to imagine the passage from m. 34 on as functioning in any other way than as the commencement of the middle section of an *ABA*.

---

[5] These include Forkel's "daring experiment", first broached in mm. 7—8. The flats in the soprano on the third beat of each measure here, as well as the corresponding ones in mm. 11—16, are not found in all early copies, and hence not in all printed editions, but they are clearly present in the autograph. Certainly, without them Forkel's experiment seems hardly daring.

[6] For the suggestion of the term "hocket" I am indebted to Professor Arthur Mendel. He has been most helpful in many other respects, too, in the preparation of this paper — although I hope completely unaware of the use to which it was to be put!

Again a comparison of the complete examples will be helpful. In each of these an opening section is brought to a definitive tonic close. Then a lengthy central section begins with a "second subject"—material apparently new, but actually incorporating elements of the original subject in more or less disguised form. Such elements are clearly discernible in the two lute fugues; less so in the Concerto, whose new theme is a marvelously free augmentation of the old; least of all in the Duet, which creates a second subject from the first by an elaborate transformation involving a striking change of mode into the harmonic minor, the addition of passing notes and neighbors, and the use of octave displacement. In each case, however close to or far from the first subject the second may be, it is soon succeeded by one or more overt statements of the first, and the section proceeds by alternation or free combination of the two ideas. But these are not true double fugues, for their contrasting subjects are never presented in strict contrapuntal simultaneity; such a possibility is at most only suggested. On the other hand, the middle section is sometimes the scene of freshly ingenious treatment of the first subject, e. g., inversion in the Lute Fugue in C minor and stretto in the Duet. The close of this section and the return to the opening are variously treated. Two extremes are exhibited by the Concerto, which comes to a full submediant cadence followed by a half-measure rest, and the Lute Fugue in E♭, which allows an overlap of two measures. In all examples, once the reprise is underway it continues literally to the end.

Turning now to the Unfinished Fugue, we find many indications that it was intended to be of this type: the formal tonic close of the first section; the new material, not designed as a future counter-subject but incorporating a new variation of the first subject (the hocket); the overt return to that theme in its original form; the (incomplete) stretto in Bach's last measures. From these hints I have attempted a reconstruction of the entire fugue.

Using the Duet in F major as a free model, I have developed the middle section by a strict alternation of the new material with the old, although at one point (mm. 55—56) I have briefly allowed their simultaneous statement. I have followed through on Bach's own suggestion by working out several stretti, not only continuing his incomplete one (mm. 46—54) but also introducing some complete ones of my own, first at the distance of a half-note (mm. 61—65), then of a quarter (mm. 65—70).

My proportions are 33-49-33, or roughly 2-3-2. Bach's first section proceeds in groups of eight measures, as marked off by the return of the subject in m. 9, the beginning of a complete counter-exposition in m. 17, and the introduction of free material in m. 25. The central portion, however, begins with six-measure phrases, defined by the length of the new theme. This grouping I have of course retained, but I have alternated it with nine-measure stretto passages. The entire middle section is symmetrically constructed: 6-6-9-6-9-6-6, thematically *bbababb*. And just as Bach allowed himself an extra measure of cadence at the end of his first section, I have allowed myself one to expand the return to the tonic at the end of the second.

Whether the fugue, as it stands in the autograph, is wholly, or partly, or not at all by the master, I find it hard to say. The "daring experiment" bespeaks his hand, but its persistent reiteration does not. Similarly, the hocketed variation is a strikingly original idea; not so the two measures that each time precede it. Even the evidence of the autograph can never be final: after all, Bach *could* have copied another's work, just as another could have copied his. To tell the truth, I prefer not to know. If I had been sure of Bach's authorship of the fugue, I should never have had the temerity to attempt its completion; if I had been convinced that it was spurious, I should probably never have made the effort.

Dresden. Sächsische Landesbibliothek, *Mus. 2405 T 52, Aut. 3*, p. 3. J. S. Bach autograph: BWV 906, end of Fantasy, beginning of Fugue, mm. 1 — 12.

Dresden. *Mus. 2405 T 52, Aut. 3*, p. 4. BWV 906, Fugue, mm. 13 — 38.

Dresden. *Mus. 2405 T 52, Aut. 3,* p. 5. BWV 906, Fugue, mm. 39 — 48.

* The autograph breaks off here.

D. S. al Fine

WALTER EMERY

Cadence and Chronology

Several years ago, in an article on the development of Bach's organ style[1], I remarked that one of Bach's dotted cadential formulae (Type C in Ex. 1, below) might be of some use to chronologists as a sign of early date. Further study has now convinced me that this is unlikely, but it has also directed my attention to another abnormal cadential pattern. Although this latter formula (Type D in Ex. 1) also seems to be of dubious chronological value, it is of interest because it is just rare enough to be in danger of being dismissed as a corruption. I have not had time to make a complete study of it and shall present here such information as I have been able to collect, in the hope that someone may find it suggestive.

Example 1 presents four of Bach's cadential formulae, as they would appear in C major[2] (Ex. 1).

Types A and B seem to have been used at all periods of Bach's life. They often carry shakes, and perhaps ought always to do so. Such shakes normally, perhaps invariably, begin with the upper note. Type C is less familiar in Bach's music, but it occurs in the works of Böhm, Bruhns, Brunckhorst, Buxtehude, Kneller, Kuhnau, Leyding, Lübeck, Pachelbel, Reinken, Weckmann, Zachow (the cantata, *Herr, wenn ich*), Corelli, Albinoni, Rameau, and Purcell. It is not very common in the music of J. G. Walther. It sometimes carries a shake, and an upper-note shake quite often makes consecutives (Ex. 2).

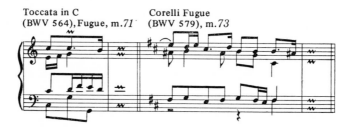

Toccata in C
(BWV 564), Fugue, m.71

Corelli Fugue
(BWV 579), m.73

In Bach's music the Type C formula occurs in Cantatas 131, 106, 71, 196, 4, 150, and 199, and in the following organ works: BWV 532, 535a, 551, 552, 564, 569, 570, 579, 588, 690, and 699. It seems to be less common in the two-hand works but does appear in BWV 895 and 993 (though not in 992) as well as in the doubtful Overture in F, BWV 820.

---

[1] Walter Emery, "Some Speculations on the Development of Bach's Organ Style", *The Musical Times*, CVII (1966), 602.

[2] In some of the examples referred to below, the note-values may be twice or even four times as long, and the formula may be in a lower part.

This cadence type may well have been a European commonplace that Bach picked up — as its presence in BWV 535a shows — before 1707 and then used fairly often until the time of Cantata 150 (at latest, the beginning of 1710). Thereafter it becomes unusual, but it does occur in BWV 199 (1714), in BWV 552 (published in 1739), and also in BWV 996. There seems no particular reason why all the above organ works (except BWV 552) should not have been written by the beginning of 1710; but that is not news.

I have found the following examples of Type D in compositions of Bach:
Ex. 3: BWV 535a, an early version of the Prelude and Fugue in G minor (surviving autograph, before 1707)[3],

BWV 535a, m.63

Ex. 4: Cantata 131 (surviving autograph — in private possession — 1707),

Ex. 5: BWV 574, Fugue in C minor on a Theme by Legrenzi (no surviving autograph)[4],

---

[3] Autograph score: Berlin Staatsbibliothek, *mus. ms. 40644;* facsimile in NBA IV/6, pp. viii—x. For some unexplained reason the printed text of the NBA (p. 113) has even quavers. For the date see Georg von Dadelsen, *Beiträge zur Chronologie der Werke Johann Sebastian Bachs* (Trossingen, 1958), p. 74. Henceforth, MSS belonging to the Bach collection of the Berlin State Library, bearing the call number *mus. ms. Bach P . . .,* will be cited simply as *P . . .*

[4] NBA IV/6 prints three texts: BWV 574, 574a (a variant), and BWV 574b (early version of BWV 574). BWV 574a omits m. 80 of the other texts, has no final flourishes, and no Type D figuration in the measures quoted.

Ex. 6: BWV 579, Fugue in B minor on a Theme by Corelli (no autograph; see also m. 73 in Ex. 2).

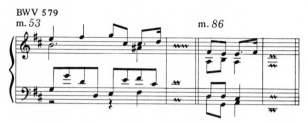

Two versions exist of Bach's Fugue in B minor on a Theme by Albinoni: BWV 951, and an earlier, shorter version, BWV 951a. There is no autograph of either. Each version contains Type D cadences that the other does not (Ex. 7):

But this seems to be due to revision in general — not to any change in Bach's attitude towards Type D — except perhaps in m. 59. Even there, the Type B cadence of BWV 951 (m. 61) may be a corruption. At m. 62 (64), the two versions differ, but only in the alto part. Albinoni's original trio (Op. 1, no. 8) is quoted by Spitta [5]; it uses Type C, but not Type D.

I have also found the Type D cadence in the following works:
Ex. 8: BWV 588, Canzona in D minor (no autograph),

[5] Philipp Spitta, *Johann Sebastian Bach* (Leipzig, 1873—80), II, Beilage 2.

Ex. 9: BWV 543, Prelude and Fugue in A minor (no autograph),

Ex. 10: BWV 533, The "Little" Fugue in E minor (no autograph)[6],

Ex. 11: BWV 720, Chorale Prelude on *Ein feste Burg* (no autograph).

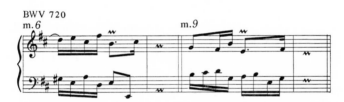

The Type D cadence in m. 6 found in all the manuscripts of this work; in m. 9, however, it is found only in the manuscript ascribed to J. T. Krebs (P 802). Here the other manuscripts have presumably been corrupted in order to avoid the clash with the left-hand g

Ex. 12: BWV 582, Passacaglia in C minor (the established text is derived from a reputed autograph, now lost),

[6] Type D occurs in the "Schubring" MS (see BG 15, p. 102) and in P 804.

Ex. 13: BWV 653, Chorale Prelude on *An Wasserflüssen Babylon.*

This composition, too, exists in more than one version. BWV 653b is the original version, in five parts with double pedal; BWV 653a is a four-part reduction. Both these versions require high pedal notes that were not available at Arnstadt or Mühlhausen, and were probably written for the Weimar organ[7]. Neither version exists in autograph; but the Type D cadences of BWV 653a reappear in BWV 653, a revision, for which the autograph (P 271), dateable c. 1744, does survive.

Ex. 14: BWV 562, Fantasia in C minor:

See m. 65, alto. The autograph (P 490) is post-Weimar; but as it is a fair copy, the date of composition is unknown. The skip from the mediant in the bass of m. 56 (not quoted here) is not a specimen of Type D; Bach omitted an appoggiatura.

[7] See Walter Emery, "The Compass of Bach's Organs as Evidence of the Date of his Works", *The Organ,* XXXII (October, 1952), 94.

Ex. 15: BWV 61/1   *Nun komm, der Heiden Heiland.*
      BWV 62/6

BWV 61 is dateable to 2 December, 1714. The surviving score (P 45/6) is mainly non-autograph; but the text of Ex. 15 is established. BWV 62 (autograph: P 877) is a Leipzig cantata (3 December, 1724) based on the same chorale. Compare its harmonization with that of BWV 61; the other Leipzig settings are essentially the same.

Like Type C, the Type D cadence seems to be less common in two-hand works. The specimens in the "Allemande" from the *Sarabande con Partite*, BWV 990, are not likely to be authentic.

Of the cantatas ascribed to the years 1707—14: BWV 131, 106, 71, 196, 4 (Mühlhausen); 150, 18, 21, 63, 208 (Weimar, through 1713); BWV 182, 12, 172, 54, 199, 61, 152 (Weimar, 1714), only BWV 131 (1707) and BWV 61 (December, 1714) contain genuine examples of the Type D cadential pattern. Cadences skipping from the mediant occur in other cantatas of this period (e.g., BWV 71, 150, 63, 208, 182); but they do not use the dotted formula. In the music of other composers, Type D occurs in Bruhns' Prelude and Fugue in E minor; in several chorale preludes of Buxtehude (e. g., *Ich ruf, Te Deum, Ein feste Burg, Es ist, Gott der Vater, Herr Christ* II, *Komm heiliger Geist* I), in the music of Vincent Lübeck, and in Franz Tunder's cantatas *Ein feste Burg* and *Hosianna*, as well as in an organ Prelude in G minor. Tunder often used Types C and D simultaneously, as Bach did in BWV 131, m. 53 (Ex. 4, above). I have found Type D only once in the works of J. G. Walther (*Nun komm*, Verse 3), not at all in the music of Kuhnau and Pachelbel[8]. It therefore seems that Type D was a Northern mannerism. In any case, as mentioned before, its appearance in BWV 535a reveals that Bach had picked it up before 1707.

The Bach examples quoted above seem to fall into two groups. In most of them, he may be said to have used Type D for its own sake; in the others, because he was in some sense forced to.

---

[8] Modern editions of the works cited can be found in the following publications: Nikolaus Bruhns, *3 Praeludien und Fugen*, ed. Max Seiffert, *Organum*, IV/8 (Leipzig, [1925]), pp. 10—11; Dietrich Buxtehude, *Sämtliche Orgelwerke*, ed. Josef Hedar (Kopenhagen, 1952), Vols. III and IV; Vincent Lübeck, *Orgelwerke*, ed. Hermann Keller (Leipzig, 1941), pp. 13, 40, 43, 45; Franz Tunder, *Ein' feste Burg ist unser Gott*, ed. Max Seiffert, *Organum*, I/15 (Leipzig, [1929]), pp. 14, 16, 23; Franz Tunder, *Hosianna*, ed. W. Hinnenthal and H. Kaminski (Bielefeld, 1931), p. 13, mm. 80—83; Franz Tunder, *4 Praeludien für Orgel*, ed. Max Seiffert, *Organum*, IV/6 (Leipzig, [1925]), p. 11; Johann Gottfried Walther, *Gesammelte Werke für Orgel*, ed. Max Seiffert, *Denkmäler deutscher Tonkunst*, I/26—27 (Leipzig, 1906), p. 183.

In Exx. 3—11 and 12 (m. 47), Bach apparently used Type D as a deliberate change from Type B. Note the gratuitous clashes of mediant and supertonic in Ex. 6 (m. 53), Ex. 7 (m. 58), and Ex. 12 (m. 47). And compare Ex. 11 (m. 9), and the oddity in Ex. 5 (m. 68). Type B would sometimes have sounded harmonically smoother as well as melodically more normal; and in the manuscript P 274, the cadence of Ex. 12 (m. 47) is in fact of Type B. Presumably this is a copyist's corruption.

On the other hand, consider Ex. 12 (m. 63) and Ex. 13 (mm. 11, 23). Here Type B would have made consecutive fifths with the other parts, and Type D was the easiest way of avoiding them. The compulsion in Ex. 14 was of a different kind. In m. 65 Bach wished to refer to his main subject; he preserved its rhythm but was forced to distort its melody by introducing a skip (instead of conjunct motion) after its second note. M. 64 shows an even more drastic distortion.

In Ex. 15 the chorale tune itself skips down a third, in even notes. The abnormal harmony of the Leipzig settings shows that Bach found this a problem, although in 1714 he had solved it by dotting the "supertonic" and by using Type D.

Whether m. 71 of Ex. 13 was forced on Bach by the upper pedal part, I cannot say. As for Ex. 8, at first sight it seems that Bach was avoiding consecutives; but they could have been avoided so easily in other ways that I think he here used Type D for its own sake. Perhaps he wished m. 166 to carry on the falling thirds in the previous three bars (Ex. 16):

BWV 588
m. *163*

My first group includes two works (Exx. 3 and 4) composed before the end of 1707; my second group includes Exx. 13—15, which for various reasons must have been composed after Bach had gone to Weimar in the summer of 1708. It seems possible that Exx. 5—11 were composed before the end of 1707, and that Ex. 12, which belongs to both groups, marks a point of transition at about the end of 1707, when, as the cantatas suggest, Bach lost interest in Type D.

As chronological evidence, cadences of Type D are not very satisfactory. To interpret them, one has to speculate too much about the workings of Bach's mind. But so little is known of these early years that even speculation may be helpful, so long as it does not pretend to be anything else. And before the implications of Type D are rejected on principle, it may be as well to ask exactly what they are.

Unlike most critics, Hermann Keller regarded BWV 533 (Ex. 10) as a pre-Weimar work[9]. The appearance of the Type D cadence may suggest that he was right. The accepted date of BWV 720 (Ex. 11) is not well founded. According to two manuscripts, both now lost, this prelude should begin on *Fagotto* and *Sesquialtera*[10]. Bach mentioned these desirable effects in his specification for rebuilding the Mühlhausen organ; and at

[9] Hermann Keller, *Die Orgelwerke Bachs* (Leipzig, 1948), pp. 60 f.
[10] See NBA IV/3, *Kritischer Bericht*, pp. 45 f.

first sight it seems obvious that he must have composed the piece specifically to show off the new effects, and have played it, probably in 1709, at a re-opening ceremony. Unfortunately, there is no evidence of any such ceremony. Moreover, according to Jakob Adlung, the *Fagotto* was of such short compass that not even the first notes of the piece could have been played on it[11]. But Adlung may have been mistaken, and I am willing to believe that BWV 720 was indeed played at Mühlhausen in that year. I doubt, though, whether it was composed for the occasion. I suggest that Bach took a piece that he had already written and used it to warm himself up before he improvised. He certainly did this sort of thing in later years.

Exx. 5—8 may be taken together, for they are all based on themes borrowed, or supposedly borrowed, from Italian composers. Such works are usually ascribed to the Weimar years; for there exists a rather confused impression — fostered no doubt by the facts that Bach studied Italian *concertos* (NB) at Weimar and that he acquired a copy of Frescobaldi's *Fiori musicali* in 1714 — that previously he had known little of Italian music. This seems doubtful. He was a string player; he had frequented the court of Celle; and he had worked for a few months at the minor court of Weimar. The Duke of Celle had French sympathies, and his players were mostly French. But they did sometimes put on Italian operas; and the music of Corelli, Albinoni, and Legrenzi can hardly have been unknown either there or at Weimar in 1703. The dates of the originals present no difficulty; for that of the Corelli fugue was published in 1689, and that of the Albinoni in 1694. The original of the Legrenzi fugue has never been traced, but presumably it circulated in manuscript — even if it was not published — before its composer's death in 1690. I suggest that Bach may have borrowed these chamber music themes before 1708; and surely by that time he would have made the Legrenzi fugue end convincingly in fugal style without tacking on an irrelevant toccata-like coda.

One point must be made clear: the Type D cadences in the Corelli and Albinoni fugues were not borrowed from the Italian originals; they were invented by Bach.

The *Canzona in D minor*, BWV 588 (Ex. 8) is another story; for the alleged original was not chamber music. Furthermore, the real question is not whether Bach could have known Frescobaldi's little piece before he acquired that manuscript in 1714, but whether he borrowed at all. To anyone who has seen the Frescobaldi piece itself[12] — as distinct from the quotations in the usual textbooks — it must seem strange that Bach should have been so fascinated by this theme that he took the trouble to improve and extend it, and then made it his main subject. For to Frescobaldi it was a countersubject, referred to only obscurely, if at all, in his second section. In any case, there seems no reason why Bach should have written an exercise in this outdated form as late as 1714. Is there, in fact, any solid evidence that these four works — BWV 574, 579, 951, and 588 — were not written before 1708?

---

[11] Jakob Adlung, *Musica Mechanica Organoedi* (Berlin, 1768), p. 261. Facsimile edition, Christhard Mahrenholz, ed. (Kassel, 1931).
[12] *Canzona dopo l'Epistola* from the *Fiori musicali*, 1635. Modern edition, Girolamo Frescobaldi, *Orgel- und Klavierwerke*, ed. Pierre Pidoux (Kassel, 1953), Band V, p. 53.

As for Exx. 9 and 12, the "Great" A minor and the Passacaglia have sometimes been regarded as Weimar or even post-Weimar works; but the fact that they are over-whelmingly effective in performance ought not to blind us to their early features — to the possibility that they were a young man's lucky shots. Dietrich Kilian has indeed already put forward the very attractive suggestion that the Passacaglia was composed at Arnstadt, soon after Bach's return from Lübeck[13]; and I see no stylistic reason why the A minor should not be of about the same date. All the same, both these works require E flat (D sharp), a note that was lacking on the Arnstadt organ. It was, however, available at Mühlhausen; and, as I have already remarked, the Type D cadences of Ex. 12 do tentatively suggest that the Passacaglia was written there, about the end of 1707.

So much for chronology. For the rest, it is clear that Bach used Type D on occasion; and this affects the authenticity of Ex. 10. The Type D cadence occurs in only one of the four manuscripts known to Wilhelm Rust, the editor of the Bach-Gesellschaft edition. Although it occurs in P 804 as well, I used to regard it as a copyist's corruption, and I am probably not alone in having done so. The boot now seems to be on the other leg: copyists would tend not to liven up the normal Type B cadence, but to conventionalize Type D. They might do so accidentally — by reading the tonic instead of the mediant; misreading by a third is a common error. But they might also do this deliberately, to normalize the melody and (sometimes) to smooth out the harmony. Even editors have taken a hand in this latter game[14].

It seems possible that Bach wrote more cadences of Type D than his copyists and editors have presented to us; and certain that when other examples are found, as they probably will be, they ought to be taken seriously. They will not necessarily be authentic; but they must not be dismissed automatically as corruptions.

---

[13] Dietrich Kilian, "Studie über Bachs Fantasie und Fuge c-moll (BWV 562)", *Hans Albrecht in Memoriam* (Kassel, 1962), pp. 134 f.

[14] See Ernst Naumann's remarks in BG 36 on the final version of the Albinoni Fugue (BWV 951). Of the MSS known to Naumann, all but one had Type D at m. 58 (quoted in Ex. 7, above); but the Peters and Steingräber (Hans Bischoff) editions printed Type B. In BG 36, m. 58 is on p. 181, brace 2, first whole measure; Naumann's comment is on p. lxxix.

ROBERT L. MARSHALL

The Genesis of an Aria Ritornello:
Observations on the Autograph Score of "Wie zittern und wanken"
BWV 105/3

In his address to the International Musicological Society in 1961, Arthur Mendel offered at one point a paraphrase of a suggestion by Benedetto Croce in these terms: "Do you wish to understand the true history of the *Missa Pange lingua*? Try, if you can, to become Josquin Desprez composing the *Missa Pange lingua*". He went on to caution against the perils of such a project and wondered aloud "to what extent, then, can we imaginatively 'become Josquin Desprez composing the Mass' and to what extent is it necessary that we should? Can we do so by analysis of the work"[1]?

The following is an attempt to "become" Johann Sebastian Bach "composing" the aria — more specifically, the ritornello of the aria — "Wie zittern und wanken" from the cantata *Herr, gehe nicht ins Gericht*, BWV 105. Guidance will be provided by the composer in the form of the earliest notation of the ritornello preserved on f. 5r of the autograph composing score of the complete cantata: Berlin Staatsbibliothek, *mus. ms. autogr. Bach, P 99*. For it seems clear that if we are to try to "become" Bach, or any other composer, "composing" a work, we should first try to witness him in the act of composition; and the evidence for this should be preserved, if at all, in the original autograph score of the work.

The specific wording of the Croce-Mendel exhortation deserves close attention. The aim of the attempt is to "understand" the "true" history of the composition. This suggests that our aim, or "wish", is not particularly to narrate the chronicle of what may be called its "external" history, for example, the order in which its constituent sections or lines were entered, or even to establish, say, what aspects of the work proved more difficult to compose than others, or whether the composer made extensive or minimal use of preliminary sketches and drafts, or whether he tended to elaborate or simplify his initial ideas. For such information is ultimately biographical in nature — concerned with the composer and how he went about putting the particular work together. "Understanding the true history" of the work rather implies empathetically recreating its "internal" history — reconstructing from moment to moment the compositional motivations that guided and justified the determination of each specific reading. This "internal" history is indeed to some extent recorded in the autograph score, but only when the autograph contains a correction; for only corrections (along perhaps with other anomalies visible in an *Urschrift* but nowhere else) provide evidence of the internal dialog — the weighing of choices — entailed in the compositional act. For the rest we witness little more than the composer copying — writing out music.

---

[1] Arthur Mendel, "Evidence and Explanation", in *Report of the Eighth Congress of the International Musicological Society. New York 1961. Volume II — Reports*, ed. Jan LaRue (Kassel, 1962), p. 15.

To the extent that we can reconstruct the musical logic that led first to a rejected reading, then uncover the perceived consequences of that reading which led to its rejection, and thereupon do the same with regard to the final reading and its acceptance, we are, it would seem, to the same extent, "imaginatively becoming" the composer composing and hence deriving an "understanding of the true history" of the work. We should therefore be willing to consider every such clue that the composer has left, that is, to discuss and interpret every observable correction and anomaly, no matter how unimportant its significance may appear at first (or may even turn out to be in the end) in terms of its compositional rationale.

In choosing a Bach composition we are perhaps in a relatively favorable position to pursue an experiment of this kind. A similar approach to a composition by Beethoven, for example, — the attempt to uncover the compositional meaning of every detail in a Beethoven autograph — would surely prove to be an enterprise of infinite tedium and perhaps ultimate futility. The problems of decipherment posed by a Beethoven autograph or sketch and the sheer number of details demanding individual explication would make the project forbidding if not impossible. Furthermore, the investigator of a Beethoven autograph can rarely be certain that he has assembled all the material, scattered quasi-chaotically over numerous volumes and sheets, that may be related to the work under consideration, or that he has successfully determined the chronological order of this material — a step that must precede any meaningful analytical scrutiny.

The student of Bach's autographs is not so plagued. Since Bach was a "clean" worker, the absolute number of corrections in any particular composition is rarely overwhelming, and legibility is not usually problematic. Moreover, after Bach settled in Leipzig, he apparently always composed (vocal works at least) directly in score and made no use of independent sketchbooks or sheets. The analyst, therefore, can be reasonably certain that the autograph score of P 99, for example, contains all, or almost all[2], the autograph material that ever existed in connection with the structural origin of Cantata 105. Finally, since all compositional corrections were entered into an integral score of the work, questions of chronology are simplified considerably; for one may proceed on the initial assumption that corrections were entered into the score approximately in the order in which they appear[3]. The reduced volume of data, then, the more limited number of known, unknown, and complicating factors, encourage an attempt in Bach's case to "become the composer composing".

This attempt will be limited to the opening ritornello of "Wie zittern und wanken", since a discussion of all the corrections visible in the entire aria autograph — although relatively few in number — would require a full-length study. But the present limitation

---

[2] While proofreading the original performing parts (which were normally prepared by apprentice copyists from the autograph score), Bach occasionally introduced corrections of a structural nature along with dynamics, slurs, continuo figures, and other performance indications.

[3] The possibility cannot be eliminated, however, that a particular correction may have been "delayed", i. e., introduced after — perhaps in response to — corrections affecting later details of the work.

should not prevent a meaningful conduct and evaluation of the experiment; for it is in the ritornello that the operating forces of the composition are set in motion, and the ritornello, designed to function as both the beginning and end of the aria, is, to some extent, an autonomous, if miniature, composition.

The approach chosen here will often expose a basic article of faith surrounding autograph evidence that should be confessed at once. It is the assumption — or prejudice — throughout that in every instance — unless the contrary is blatantly obvious — the final reading is superior to the rejected reading. On the other hand, it should be emphasized that when, in speculating about the meaning of the autograph corrections of Bach — or of any creative artist, for that matter — we attribute to the artist certain reasons for writing this or changing that, we only seem to be guilty of some form of the "intentional fallacy". It is more than obvious that we can never know what in fact went on in Bach's mind at the moment he wrote down or corrected any symbol. Such phrases as "Bach changed x to y because . . ." or "the a'♭ was rejected for the following reasons . . ." are expressions of convenience which really mean: "the observable effects or consequences of this reading or that correction are the following . . ." The composer may well have been totally unaware in any verbally conscious sense of these "reasons" — as they are perceived by a later observer. The very fact that we can never know what the composer himself really meant should encourage us, not inhibit us, to speculate about the meaning of autograph revisions[4].

For convenience, the autograph of the aria ritornello is reproduced here in facsimile and in transcription (Ex. 1).

As an aid to legibility, the original readings of corrections have been placed on interlinear staves above the final readings. A number of idiosyncrasies of the autograph — the duplication of accidentals in key signatures and within measures, as well as beaming and the placement of autograph slurs — have been retained in the transcription. Any non-autograph entries in the manuscript — occasional slurs (see below), the quarter-rests in the oboe part of m. 17, and the presumably non-autograph entry of the aria text below the score — have been omitted[5].

The first observable correction in the autograph: the extension of the score bracket before the first system from four to five staves, seems to confront us at once with an "external historical" problem of the kind just described. It also makes us aware of several peculiarities in the opening score system which do not entail any visible corrections. The first of these is the designation "Soprano" above the fourth stave — a totally superfluous entry, for the clef on the stave sufficiently identifies the vocal part. The entry is particularly puzzling since there is no (necessary) verbal identification for

---

[4] It is my personal conviction — unverifiable, of course — that Bach expended practically no conscious verbal effort at all about why he chose or rejected a reading. The internal verbal dialog probably consisted rarely of expressions more eloquent than, "this is not good", or "this is better".

[5] I am indebted to Arthur Mendel and Alfred Dürr for their convincing demonstrations of the probably non-autograph nature of this text entry.

Ex. 1:

Berlin. Deutsche Staatsbibliothek, *Mus. ms. autogr. Bach P 99*, f. 5r. J. S. Bach
autograph: BWV 105/3, „Wie zittern und wanken", mm. 1 — 21a.

any of the instrumental parts[6]. A further anomaly is the appearance of the calligraphic
form of the c-clefs in this system; the remaining systems of the movement (and of the
entire cantata) make exclusive use of the "hook" form c-clefs which are the norm in

[6] That the instrumentation is not self-evident is revealed by an early 19th-century copy of the
cantata, P 838, prepared from the autograph (directly or indirectly) by one Fr. Knuth. The
instrumental indications are given as follows: Stave 1: *Violino 1*, Stave 2: *Violino 2*,
Stave 3: *Viola*, Stave 5: *Violon* (changed from *Violonc*). Wilhelm Rust, who edited the cantata
for the Bach-Gesellschaft (BG), conscientiously reproduced the word *Soprano* in the manner
of the autograph and refrained from adding indications for the accompanying instruments.
He identified the obbligato instrument, within editorial parentheses, as an oboe. See BG 23,
p. 131 and p. xxxvi of the foreword.

Leipzig composing scores. The ornate form is typical of the earliest Bach autographs and is found in fair copies throughout Bach's career, but it rarely appears in composing scores of the post-Mühlhausen period. In the early sources they were sometimes restricted in use — to vocal staves as a means of visually differentiating them from instrumental staves [7]. The presence of the calligraphic form in both the vocal and instrumental staves of the first score system here cannot be explained by the rationale of Bach's pre-Leipzig practice. The following hypothesis, admittedly elaborate and tentative, does manage to account for the constellation of anomalies.

The clean appearance of the opening measures of the aria reveals that the composer had a precise conception from the beginning of the musical means to be employed in creating a vivid "pictorial" representation of the text: broken, "shaking", four-note motives in the melody were to be projected upon a chordal accompaniment of repeated sixteenth-notes "trembling" above ominously thumping eighths, the latter constituting the sole "bass" support in the symbolic absence of a "fundamental" basso continuo. It is evident from the score as well that a five-part texture and — since Bach did not normally enter more than one real part on a single stave — its necessary disposition on a five-stave system had already been determined. In order to economize on space and paper, however, Bach decided at first — here, as elsewhere [8] — to omit the stave of the resting vocal part and drew the initial four-stave bracket. But while so many specifics had been established from the first, there is reason to believe that Bach may not have known, or was perhaps reluctant to indicate, the precise instrumentation for the aria, indeed for much of the cantata, until the entire autograph had been written down [9]. Bach may have intended, for example, to convey the sensation of "groundlessness" not only by dispensing with a continuo but with a lower register (bass and tenor) altogether. It is possible that he planned at first to prevent the "bassetto" from descending below the

---

[7] See Georg von Dadelsen, *Beiträge zur Chronologie der Werke Johann Sebastian Bachs* (Trossingen, 1958), p. 86, fn. 56, and the facsimile edition of the autograph score of *Gott ist mein König*, BWV 71 (Volume 9 in the *Faksimile-Reihe Bachscher Werke und Schriftstücke* [Leipzig, 1970]). The differentiated use of c-clef forms is observable throughout the autograph score of the Mühlhausen cantata, BWV 131 (score in private possession), and sporadically in several later autographs, e.g., the scores for BWV 199 (Royal Danish Library, Copenhagen) and BWV 12 (P 44/6 an, Berlin-Dahlem), both written in 1714; fairly consistently in the secular Cöthen cantata, BWV 173a (P 42/1 an); and in several movements of the Leipzig cantata, BWV 24 (P 44/3 an), composed in 1723.

[8] Reduced systems without staves for resting parts are frequently found in the Bach autographs. See Robert L. Marshall, *The Compositional Process of J. S. Bach* (Princeton, 1972), I, p. 47—58, and the facsimle editions of the *Messe in H-moll*, ed. Alfred Dürr (Kassel, 1965), p. 20, and of the aria "Heute noch", from the *Kaffeekantate*, Universal-Edition (Vienna, 1923), f. 6v.

[9] In addition to the soprano aria, instrumental indications are missing in the two recitatives (where they are hardly necessary) and the final chorale (where they can barely be reconstructed). The indications *Corno. è Hautb. all unisoni* and *Hautb 2. all unison*, entered in the first system of the opening movement above the first two staves respectively, as well as the words *col Corno in unison* added after the heading *Aria* for the fifth movement, are written in a darker ink than the rest of the headings. These designations were presumably added when Bach learned that two oboes and a horn would be available for the performance.

open g-string of the violin [10] and therefore chose to notate the part in the soprano clef, a practice he occasionally adopted when writing for string parts in this tessitura [11]. In order, now, to call attention to the rather unusual employment of the soprano clef for an instrumental part, Bach introduced the equally unusual calligraphic form of the clef. This recalls the differentiation of vocal and instrumental c-clefs encountered in Weimar autographs but with the specific identifications reversed. Before entering a single note on this stave, however, Bach, according to our hypothesis, realized that in the course of a movement in E-flat major (the key had also been already determined) the bassetto would inevitably descend at least to f — the dominant of the dominant. He therefore added a fifth stave to the system with an alto clef — again in the calligraphic form. This time the calligraphic form was a cautionary signal indicating that the stave with an alto clef below the soprano stave was intended not for an alto voice but for an instrumental part. Finally, Bach extended the score bracket to five staves and added the word "Soprano" over the fourth stave, perhaps as a reminder to himself not to enter the bassetto on that line as he had originally planned.

With the possible exception, then, of the specific scoring [12], the absence of any visible correction in the first two measures of the autograph discloses that every musical detail related to the rhetorical conception of the aria — the portrayal, with the means described above, of the *zittern und wanken* (trembling and shaking) afflicting the tormented thoughts of sinners — was clear in Bach's mind before he set these measures to paper [13].

The structural conception of the opening measures was also, despite the presence of corrections as early as m. 3, evidently secure from the first. This was the presentation, after an introductory measure, of a symmetrical four-measure phrase constructed upon

[10] The lowest pitch in the aria, f (see below), appears for the first time in m. 37 where it is introduced as a correction. (See the facsimile of P 99, f. 5v, printed in BG 44, Bl. 38, the second full measure of the third system.) Friedrich Erhardt Niedt's description of the bassetto (or *Bassetgen*) printed in the second edition of his *Musicalische Handleitung zur Variation des Generalbasses* (Hamburg, 1721) is quoted in J. S. Bach, *The Passion According to St. John*, vocal score, ed. Arthur Mendel (New York, 1951), p. vii.

[11] The violin-viola unison parts in BWV 115/1, for example, are notated in this fashion in the autograph score (Fitzwilliam Museum, Cambridge). (See the transcription of the first system in Marshall, *The Compositional Process*, II, Sketch No. 84, Final Version.) In BG 24 the part is reproduced in the treble clef.

[12] Although Bach never entered instrumental indications for this aria into the autograph as he did ultimately for the first and fifth movements, there is still hardly any doubt what the scoring of the movement should be. A mid-18th-century score (P 48), in the hand of S. Hering, a copyist for C. P. E. Bach, which was clearly prepared from the lost original performing parts, identifies the obbligato instrument as an oboe and the supporting parts as *Violino 1*, *Violino 2*, and *Viola*. The parts will be referred to thus in the course of this discussion. The evidence demonstrating the derivation of P 48 from the lost parts will be included in the critical report for the cantata in NBA I/19.

[13] The symbolism of the aria has been commented upon in similar terms by several generations of interpreters. See, for example, Arnold Schering's foreword to the Eulenburg edition of BWV 105, (No. 1040), p. ii, Friedrich Smend, *Joh. Seb. Bach. Kirchen-Kantaten*, Heft 3 (Berlin, 1950), p. 25, and the standard biographies of Ph. Spitta and Albert Schweitzer.

the primary harmonies: I—IV, V—I of the tonal cadence, here elaborated to I $\frac{5}{3}$ — ♭7 —
IV, V⁷—I and grouped into two two-measure pairs of antecedent-consequent subphrases.
The melody to be borne by this basic cadential pattern, however, was not to be so
straightforward, but rather, in illustration of the tortured conscience, would skip about the
constituent tones of the supporting harmonies, suppressing, or, with the aid of sudden
shifts to the lower or higher octave, disguising a melodic gesture in essence as basic as the
cadential pattern from which it emerges: the direct scalar ascent from the tonic to the
mediant, e"♭—f"—g" (Ex. 2).

Ex. 2:
m.   1   2 3   4   5

The "foreground" of the theme is characterized on the one hand by a direct
"rhetorical" leap of a minor seventh [14] to the unexpected pitch d"♭, a chromatic alteration
that introduces a degree of ambiguity ("wanken") concerning the tonal orientation of the
movement—an ambiguity often attending the early introduction of the I♭7 sonority.
The almost inevitable resolution of the melodic seventh, e'♭—d"♭, to the sixth, e'♭—c",
in the context of an A-flat chord hardly reinforces the impression of E-flat as the true
tonic, which had of course been assumed on the basis of the atmospheric E-flat triad in the
introductory measure. Just as characteristic of the theme as the initial leap is the slow,
mordent-like decoration of the downbeats in these opening measures, a device suggestive
of the sense of dizziness again conveyed by the word "wanken".

   Each of the details of this foreground, which together constitute the realization of a
common underlying harmonic and linear groundplan as a unique, indeed particularly
complex, "theme", carries its own implications for continuation. By the third measure of
the composition these have become numerous enough to make the specific readings of
even the second half of the phrase — in principle only a symmetrical complement of the
first half — anything but self-evident.

   The change of pitch in the Violin 2 part on the first beat of m. 3 is the first correction
of musical substance to appear in the autograph. Although, as will be shown presently, it
could not have been the first correction entered, it is advisable to consider it first. The
change has more than one effect. The friction of the simultaneous and repeated minor
seconds g'—a'♭ in the violins may be interpreted as an expressive nuance in the service of
the general Affect, perhaps related to (and thus "implied" by) the melodic minor and

---

[14] This "exclamatio" figure is used also at the beginning of the tenor aria, where it was introduced as an afterthought and serves rather to define than to obscure the principal tonality. See
   my "Musical Sketches in J. S. Bach's Cantata Autographs", in *Studies in Music History. Essays
   for Oliver Strunk*, ed. Harold S. Powers (Princeton, 1968), pp. 410—411.

major seconds in the mordent figures of the theme [15]. But the correction also has structural significance. The four-measure design of the opening phrase with its harmonic plan I(♭7)—IV, V⁷—I was surely intended as a cogent, yet spacious expression of the basic tonality of the aria. But the "inevitable" resolution of the antecedent (and dissonant) E♭ dominant seventh to the consequent (and consonant) A-flat major triad this early in the movement and at the relatively slow tempo at which the aria should doubtless be performed creates a sense of closure strong enough to jeopardize the larger four-measure phrase. The insertion of g' into the A-flat triad insures the cohesion of the four-measure unit. There is now, despite the fragmented character of the theme and the 7—6 intervallic succession embodied in the first subphrase, no interruption in the continuity of the phrase until the kinetic series of sevenths, I♭⁷—IV⁷—V⁷, is resolved with the arrival of the E-flat major triad in the middle of m. 5.

The layout of the autograph makes clear that throughout the ritornello the oboe part was as a rule written down first in any measure. (After the barlines were then drawn to accommodate this part, the inner parts — Violins 1 and 2 — were entered, which with their greater number of notes were necessarily crowded into the space thus marked off and often extended over the barline.) It is almost certain therefore, that the upbeat to m. 4 was entered, and, as the readings make clear, corrected (more than once) before the inner parts were entered at all. Here, too, as with the later change of the Violin 2 part on the first beat of m. 3, considerations of continuity seem to have motivated the corrections.

The first reading of the upbeat seems to have been f'. Assuming that the e"♭ downbeat of m. 4 was entered together with this reading, then the f'—e"♭ leap would disclose an early intention to relate the second antecedent-consequent pair of subphrases to the first by repeating in transposition the opening melodic interval. This parallelism may have been sensed as overarticulating the subdivision of the four-measure phrase and, accordingly, was smudged away. Another rejected reading for the upbeat is probably covered by the heavy penstrokes before the final reading. They may cover a ♮-sign applying to the a'. An a'♮-e"♭ configuration here would testify to an intermediate attempt by Bach to retain more than a suggestion of a caesura at midphrase but one with less interruptive force. The diminished fifth, as a controlling interval of the dominant seventh harmony, could, like the minor seventh, form the core of an antecedent subphrase. In the present context, moreover, it would not create a parallelism with the first pair nor would it merely contrast with it, but would rather issue from the first pair; for the tritone would be heard as part of a series of contracting intervallic leaps: minor seventh, major sixth, and now the tritone, within the succession of upbeat patterns. The

---

[15] The clash was evidently too strong for the taste of Adolf Bernhard Marx, the first editor of the cantata, who in his editions of the full and vocal scores of the aria published by Simrock (Bonn, 1830) removed the g' from the chord. Günther Raphael, who arranged the vocal score of BWV 105 for the Breitkopf edition (Nr. 6372, Leipzig, 1931), did the same. Both editors may have justified their emendation by noting that there is no similar dissonance in m. 19. Here, however, the continuity of phrase which the addition of g' effects (see below) is provided by the canonic dialog between the soprano and oboe.

inappropriateness, however, of the particular tritone, a'♮-e"♭ (or for that matter, but to a lesser extent, the minor seventh f'-e"♭), with its suggestion of the applied dominant of the dominant, is evident [16]. The necessity of some form of B-flat resolution for the interval would either have provoked an expansion of the second half of the phrase, thereby destroying its 2X2-mm. symmetry, or it would have disturbed the regular one-measure harmonic rhythm underlying the phrase. In either event the fine balance with the first half would have been sacrificed, and, more critical, the momentary tonicizing of the dominant would have anticipated the cadence on B-flat undoubtedly already planned for m. 9 at the midpoint of the ritornello. In the final reading the perfect fifth, a'♭-e"♭ retains the idea of a progression of contracting upbeat intervals discovered with the a'♮ experiment, while the need for an unstable "antecedent" sonority is fulfilled by treating the e"♭ downbeat as a dissonant appoggiatura to d". In this particular context, then, the perfect melodic fifth, a'♭-e"♭, is less stable, i.e., more dissonant, than the tritone a'♭-d" to which it "resolves". The formulation: "dissonant appoggiatura resolving to a weaker dissonance" is in addition an harmonic intensification — hence in yet another respect an organic outgrowth — of the dissonance-consonance pattern of the first subphrase.

The new reading, finally, calls attention to and at the same time re-interprets the motivic role of the descending half-step in the melody. The melodic minor second was first introduced within the expressive mordent d"♭-c"-d"♭ on the downbeat of m. 2, the c" functioning as a decorative lower neighbor to the d"♭. In the following measure, the d"♭, now regarded as the upper member of a minor seventh, is resolved, by half-step motion, to the same c". The half-step has thereupon been elevated from decorative to structural significance. In m. 4, the half-step progression, now associated as „appoggiatura-plus-resolution", takes place from one beat to the next rather than from measure to measure; and this rhythmic acceleration impresses the melodic half-step as a thematic motive while providing a "drive" to the cadence. In the cadential measure itself Bach apparently was tempted to suggest a further acceleration of the half-step by anticipating the resolution tone, g', of the appoggiatura resolution pattern, a'♭-g', on the second eighth-note of the measure. But this would have released the accumulated tension of the entire four-measure construction anti-climactically on the weakest metrical position of the measure: the second half of the downbeat. The final reading, f', removes this infelicity, and, by repeating the double appoggiatura pattern introduced in m. 4, creates a further source of unity within the second subphrase contrasting with the simple mordent figure of the first subphrase. The changing significance of the half-step in the opening phrase can be summarized with an analytical diagram (Ex. 3).

Ex. 3:
m.

[16] It is important to remember that the inner parts were almost certainly not entered in m. 3 until the final upbeat reading was determined. Therefore there is no need to speculate as to whether the f' and a'♮ readings were rejected in order to avoid the unthinkable tone clusters e'♭—f'—g'—a'♭, or e'♭—g'—a'♭—a'♮ on the third beat of the measure.

Multi-level consequences attending seemingly modest corrections of detail are not only present in the opening phrase, where crucial inter-relationships and governing patterns are normally first established, but are encountered throughout the ritornello. The correction of the viola in m. 6 — at the beginning of the second phrase — from e'♭ to e'♮ replaces a redundant repetition of the E♭ dominant seventh chord which occupies the same position in the first phrase with a coloristic chromatic alteration. The resulting sonority, though, the VII⁷ of F, reveals at once the formal significance of the second phrase to be the gradual but inevitable motion away from the tonic and hints as well at the specific goal: a full cadence on the dominant, B-flat. In the Violin 2 part of m. 7 Bach changed the original reading (repeated f' on beat 1 followed by repeated e'♭ on beat 2) by crossing out the second group and inserting a group of four b'♭s on the barline between m. 6 and 7. The substitution of b'♭ for f' on the first beat results in a complete triad; the rationale for the correction of the second beat is not found in local considerations. The F-dominant seventh chord created by the presence of e'♭ on the second beat (and presumably to have been maintained through the third beat as well) would either have forced a premature arrival of the B-flat cadence in m. 8 or have obliged the composer to invent some kind of time-marking and tension-dissipating filler material for the remainder of that measure. As it happened, the problem posed by m. 8 was to cost the composer further pains.

As in m. 4, the challenge here was to generate an accumulation of tension before its release at the cadence while insuring that the means employed would be perceived as a logical, organic consequence of preceding events. In contrast to its treatment throughout the first phrase as a static pedal unaffected by the harmonic motion of the other parts, the bassetto is activated in the second phrase (an event also signalled by the correction in m. 6), and, through mm. 6, 7, and the beginning of m. 8, ascends one step per measure. The sense of the original reading, f', in the viola on the second beat of m. 8 seems to have been to take up the ♩ ♩ harmonic rhythm introduced in the upper strings in the preceding measure and to extend it to all the voices of the accompaniment. But before completing this initial conception, Bach evidently felt the need for an accompaniment that would provide more active rhythmic reinforcement for the melodic climax on b"♭ and for the release of rhythmic motion issuing from it. The new reading of the viola part, e'♮, introduces together with the motion of the upper accompanimental parts a quarter-note harmonic rhythm that forms the climax of a paced accelerando in harmonic rhythm that, one realizes in retrospect, was initiated in m. 6:

m.   6   7   8   (9)
| ♩. | ♩ ♩ | ♩ ♩ ♩ | (♩.) |

The e'♮, in addition, is the bass of the same e-diminished seventh chord added as an afterthought in m. 6; and here again it proceeds to an F-major triad. The last two beats of m. 8 accordingly recapitulate in diminution the harmonic content of mm. 6 and 7, this time including (as a passing tone in the oboe) the seventh, e"♭, which had been removed from the harmony of m. 7. In moving on — this time at the proper formal moment — to the B-flat cadence, the new formulation brings to fulfillment the harmonic scheme which at the beginning of the phrase could only be suggested[17].

There is also a correction in the oboe part in the same measure: a descending hook added to the accidental before the second a" reveals that it has been changed from ♭ to ♮. From the beginning of the second phrase in m. 6, the presence of d♭ has created doubt about the modal character of the imminent B-flat cadence. The harmonic context of these measures, in fact, is hardly ambiguous at all but quite definitely belongs to B-flat minor[18]. Within such a context the melodic line would normally descend from the b"♭ through the lowered seventh, a"♭; and this is what Bach wrote down at first. The a"♭ was then rejected for the following reasons. An a"♭ in the melody on the second beat of the measure would have created a cross-relation with the a'♮ of the F-dominant seventh harmony on the third beat and would have weakened the effect of the more dramatic cross-relation impending between the d"♭ in the oboe melody at the end of the measure and the now not-quite-unexpected but still stunning appearance of d'♮ in the long-awaited B-flat major cadence in m. 9[19]. In addition, the appearance of a"♭ here would have been undesirable with respect to the larger structural design of the ritornello. As indicated in the accompanying diagram, the basic linear motion of the complete ritornello describes an almost perfectly symmetrical arc which in the first half rises by step from e"♭ to b"♭ and in the second half returns, again by step, to e"♭ (Ex. 4).

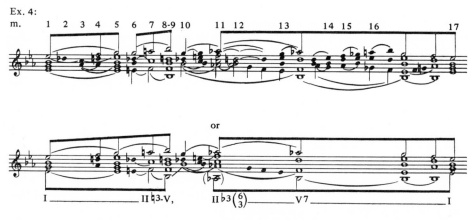

Ex. 4:

[17] One could speculate as well as to whether the configuration g'♭ — e'♮ — f', in the final reading of the viola is an intentional reference, in augmentation and with more structural weight, to the e"♭ — c" — d", and a'♭ — f' — g' appoggiatura figures in the oboe part of mm. 4—5 which play such a conspicuous role in forming the cadence of the first phrase.

[18] This mode-obscuring d♭ should perhaps be heard in connection with the d"♭ which appeared as the second note of the melody (m. 2) and served there to cast momentary doubt on the tonality.

[19] The veritably brutal force of this modal shift, along with the less spectacular but equally marked change of modal color from E-flat major in phrase 1 to the B-flat minor context of phrase 2 and then to the B-flat major cadence, paint yet another aural representation of "wanken".

It is part of the tonal logic of this scheme that the approach to b"♭ be reinforced harmonically with an applied dominant sonority and melodically with its leading tone, a"♮, and that the return from b"♭ to e"♭ be underlined by the cancellation of that a"♮, or, what is the same thing, by the definitive reinstatement of a"♭, now as part of the "natural" dominant seventh, B♭⁷. In short, the essential tonal drama of this design centers on the changing inflection of the fourth degree in ascent and descent within the basic arc[20]. It will therefore be the first substantial piece of business of the second half of the ritornello to introduce the a"♭ in the appropriate harmonic context (this occurs in m. 11). An a"♭ in m. 8 would have been, in the truest sense of the word, "profoundly" premature.

The corrections encountered in the opening nine measures of the aria, then, are few in number; but each of them has turned out to be of crucial importance in establishing the structural framework, the stylistic idiom, and the expressive means for the entire aria. With the resolution of these fundamental concerns the composition of the second half of the ritornello was, as the autograph confirms, relatively unproblematic. There are fewer corrections, and they belong to a lower order of significance. No further correction in fact is clearly visible until the pitch change in m. 12 (Violin 2)[21]. It is possible, however, that the first beat of the oboe in m. 11 at first read ♫ ♩, f"—g"—a"♭, and was later changed to ♫♩ f"—g"—a"♭—a"♭ [22]. The present reading can be understood, in any event, as a motivic derivation from, and thus a justification in the large for the dactylic ♫♫ rhythm which was introduced in m. 8, along with the syncopation on the first beat, as a necessary but local effect providing the climactic concentration and release of tension at the approach to the medial cadence.

The introduction of the dactylic rhythm in m. 11 (whether as an afterthought or not) thus creates a perceptible link between the end of the first half of the ritornello and the beginning of the second. It also prepares for the intensified treatment of this rhythm throughout the second half, that will culminate in its ultimate dissolution at the final cadence of measures 16—17. In this regard it is worth noting as well that there is a parallelism between the two interior phrases of the ritornello which serves both to unify

[20] The play upon d"♭—d"♮ within the space of a third: e"♭—d"♭—c"—d"♮—e"♭ which fills the first phrase of the aria is perhaps (along with whatever other significance may have been attributed to it in these pages) a reflection in miniature, and as it were in reverse, of the larger arc.

[21] The slur over the last five notes of the melody in m. 8 has been corrected — but apparently not by Bach — from ♫♫. The change is barely apparent in the facsimile; but it is clear in the original that the lower "u"-shaped slur that connects the two autograph overhand slurs was added with the same thin quill and blacker ink found again on this folio in the oboe, mm. 15, 18—21a, and in the viola, mm. 11—12, as well as elsewhere in the movement. These non-autograph slurs have not been reproduced in Ex. 1.

[22] There is some visual evidence for this, although it is not unambiguous. First the leger line through the a"♭ is unusually long and may have been drawn with the emphatic gesture often characteristic of Bach's corrections. (See, for example, the hook of the corrected ♮-sign in m. 8.) Second, the stem of the g" does not reach the lower beam of the three-note group, an indication, perhaps, that the note was inserted after what was originally the second note was changed — with the addition of the leger line — from g" to a"♭.

its two halves further and to underline the crucial transformation of the fourth degree that takes place within these phrases. The initial oboe motif in both phrases is identical (Ex. 5), and part of the accompanimental sonority (the d"♭ and b'♭ in the inner voices

Ex. 5:

m. {5   6
m. {9   10

supporting the mordent figure, mm. 6 and 10) has been retained. In the following measure of phrase 2 (m. 7), the oboe motif ends on the critical a'♮ — a pitch emphasized at first by skip (the first skip to appear in this position within the four-note motivic cell) and later, as the original parts reveal, by a trill[23]. The corresponding measure of the third phrase (m. 11) reinstates a"♭ which, too, is emphasized by special means, this time, by the ♩♫ rhythm. The treatment of a'♮ in m. 7 as part of the pivotal F-major applied dominant harmony is balanced here by the incorporation of a"♭ within an F-minor triad in ⁶₃ position. This harmony is experienced as the supertonic of E-flat owing to the linear conduct of the bassetto following an authentic B-flat major cadence, that is, with the return of a'♭ just after the b'♭ and precipitating the stepwise progression in m. 12 (a'♭, g', f') to e'♭ in m. 13.

Disregarding the questionable existence of a change in the oboe part of m. 11, the first unambiguous correction in the second half of the ritornello appears on the second beat of the Violin 2 part in m. 12. The original reading of the measure — repeated f', g', a'♭ — would have been the first obviously melodic gesture to appear in an inner part and would have formed a contrary motion relationship between the Violin 2 and the viola. It would thus in two ways have articulated the strategic moment of the scalar descent of the bassetto from the by-now famous a'♭ in m. 11 to the original e'♭ tonic[24]. This basically contrapuntal conception, however, created an incomplete and awkwardly spaced sonority on the second beat (Oboe: b"♭, Violin 1: b'♭, Violin 2, Viola: g') and was

[23] See the BG edition. The trill is found in P 48 and therefore was presumably added, by Bach, in the lost oboe part. Since the trill serves more than a merely ornamental function, its later introduction into the parts should be considered a compositional, if delayed, correction. Evidence that Bach did occasionally enter "ornamental" notes in a composing score is provided in this same phrase by the grace-note in m. 9. The grace-note not only adds a piquant dissonance to the cadence but completes the scalar descent through the octave from b"♭. It also results in the rhythmically subdivided downbeat pattern characteristic of the theme throughout and thus reserves for the final cadence of the ritornello the conclusiveness of a masculine ending. Perhaps as preparation for this truly "wesentliche Manier" Bach added the trill in m. 7, the upper auxiliary of which by nature fills the skip, c"—a'♮, and provides an accented dissonance on the strong half of the beat, analogous to that in m. 9 and, again, serving to emphasize the appearance of a'♮.

[24] The pitch is conspicuously represented in three voices and further emphasized by means of a quasi-*Stimmtausch* interplay between the oboe and viola.

modified by adding the root, e'♭, in the Violin 2 part while retaining the original viola reading. Precisely Bach's concern for the linear integrity of the bassetto, incidentally, reveals that the viola part throughout this passage is conceived — and indeed perceived — as the true bass, even though the e'♭ in the new reading of the Violin 2 crosses below the viola. (The same is evident in mm. 8—9 where the f'—b♭ progression in the viola, presented in the differentiated portamento eighth-note rhythm reserved for this part, functions as the harmonic bass of an authentic V⁷—I cadence, although the second violin here, too, crosses below the viola[25].

The concentration of corrections in the approach to the final cadence is restricted to the inner parts, particularly to the Violin 2 in mm. 15—16. These particular corrections pose an insoluble problem of transcription. It is not certain, first of all, whether m. 15, first quarter, originally read 4 X c", 4 X b'♭, or 2 X c" plus 2 X b'♭. Furthermore, it is

[25] The continuo figures for the first movement, preserved in P 48, suggest that the instrumental bass was regarded as the harmonic bass even when the vocal bass crossed below it. (Ex. 6):

Ex. 6:

A passage such as mm. 73—93, moreover, in which the continuo sometimes doubles the vocal bass at the unison, sometimes at the lower octave (descending to contra C), sometimes crosses above it, and sometimes continues into the bassetto register (mm. 109—112 are notated in P 99 in the tenor clef), makes it unlikely that Bach assumed or even desired contrabass doubling when he determined the continuo-vocal bass relationship or when he entered the figures in the continuo part. (F. E. Niedt, in the passage referred to in fn. 10, above, restricts the use of 16' doubling of continuo parts to heavily orchestrated compositions with trumpets and timpani.)

not clear whether the corrections on the first and third beats of m. 15 and on the first and second beats of m. 16 were made in one gesture, and accordingly the original readings of these four beats together with the second beat of m. 15 were conceived as one integral version, thus (Ex. 7):

Ex. 7:

or whether each of the beats was drafted and corrected independently of the others (as suggested by the broken interlinear stave in Ex. 1), or, finally, whether some of the original readings were rejected in one gesture and the others in one — or more — further gestures.

The most satisfactory reconstruction seems to be the following. After having initially harmonized the first beat of m. 15 as a sequential repetition of the same beat in the preceding measure, Bach changed the harmonic color from that of the dominant triad to the more kinetic dominant seventh sonority that had been associated with the dominant pedal point since its inception in m. 13 [26]. This change also inspired the idea of leading the first and second violins in parallel motion to the cadence, and accordingly suggested the reading c" for the third beat of the measure. But this reading resulted, once again, in the omission of the seventh, a'♭, from the dominant sonority. The re-introduction of a'♭ at this point proved particularly fortunate. It allowed for an unobtrusive shift from parallel fourths between the violin parts to the more sonorous and usable sixths, and not only maintained the conjunct motion of the second violin part, but insinuated into this part yet another exposition of the scalar descent from the fourth degree to the tonic (Violin 2: m. 15, third beat, through m. 16, second beat). The same a'♭ also results in a cross-relation with the a"♮ of the oboe in the following measure which dovetails with the g'♭—g"♮ clash taking place between the Violin 2 and oboe on the first and second beats of m. 16 — the latter cross-relation recalling in transposition and transformation the powerful d♭—d♮ succession of the medial cadence (mm. 8—9).

The absence of a correction in the Violin 1 part on the first beat of m. 16 suggests that the correction in the Violin 2 part on this beat can be dismissed as a slip of the pen; for there is reason to believe that Bach composed the inner parts within a homophonic texture from "the top down" [27]. The unchanged reading in the Violin 1 part therefore reveals that the accelerated rate of pitch change in the inner parts from the quarter to the eighth at the approach to the final cadence was determined from the first. The correction in the Violin 2 part on the second beat, however, is not trivial. It was probably related to — and entered after — the correction of the Violin 1 part on beat 3.

[26] Both the dominant pedal and the dominant-seventh sonority pervading the last phrase of the ritornello serve to raise the harmonic tension during the approach to the final cadence to a level above that attained at the medial cadence where the (applied) dominant-seventh chord sounded only momentarily on the last half-beat of m. 8. The dominant pedal point corresponds, of course, to the tonic pedal of the opening measures.

[27] See my *The Compositional Process*, Vol. I, p. 138, and the discussion below.

The original conception — partially carried out — evidently was to lead the Violin 1 to the cadence in the smoothest manner with the Violin 2 following in its train (Ex. 8)[28].

Ex. 8:

This reading would not have been altogether satisfactory, though, since the mediant was not represented on the second half of beat 2[29], the fifth, f', was missing from the first part of beat 3, and, finally, the pattern of pitch change in the accompaniment every half-beat which had just been established on the first beat of m. 16 was already abandoned on the second beat.

But it is altogether possible that this last observable correction in the ritornello was not primarily concerned with local details of chord-tone disposition and voice leading but rather with matters of larger design. The new disposition of the cadential V⁷—I harmonies projects just those pitches, f" and e"♭, necessary — and expected — for the completion of the structural arc illustrated in Ex. 4 into the highest voice of the texture, and exposes them in the same register in which the earlier tones of the arc appeared. Bach may well have been consciously aware of the artistic necessity of this[30] and understood that only by thus redistributing the accompanying harmonies would the oboe part be freed to fulfill a further imperative residing in the symmetrical design of the ritornello. For the climactic, but seemingly rhapsodic, cadenza is in fact a retrospective review of the entire compass gradually spanned by the ritornello melody in its first nine

[28] The original reading of the first two notes in Violin 1 is clear; there seems to be visual evidence for the third note as well in the thickening between the two sixteenth-beams at the base of the stem.

[29] The g', however, could and may have been introduced into the Violin 2 part within the context of this first reading and led by skip to d'.

[30] We can infer that Bach recognized the structural ramifications of chord-tone disposition from the fact that the cadence in mm. 24—25, while corresponding to and essentially identical with that in mm. 16—17, has a different configuration of the chord-tones, and that this was brought about in an autograph correction. (See the facsimile in BG 44, Bl. 38.) In mm. 24—25 the necessity was not to complete the structural line but to leave it open. In the final reading of m. 25 the highest pitch of the cadential complex, g', refers back to the g' of the soprano in m. 21 and carries over to the same pitch in mm. 29—30, now transposed into the "structural register" established in the ritornello in preparation for the ensuing tonal development. In the course of the first vocal section of the aria (mm. 25—45) the g" of mm. 29—30 moves on to f" in m. 35 ("prolonged" through mm. 38, 41, 43), and in mm. 43—45 finally descends e"♭ — d"(♭) — c" — b'♭.

measures, now compressed into a single measure and returning the melody from the high b"♭ at midpoint to its point of origin, e'♭.

Would it be hubris to assert that in the course of this discussion we have — to some extent — imaginatively become Johann Sebastian Bach composing the ritornello of "Wie zittern und wanken"? Perhaps; but by consulting — or confronting — the composer's own record of its genesis we have surely adopted the approach most likely to have any degree of success. Moreover, the exercise has led to some understanding of the work, particularly in regard to the logical relationship between immediate detail and larger design, that is perhaps not so readily discovered in an analytical study devoted exclusively to the finished, frozen, product. And the discovery of this logic has perhaps given us some idea at least of what it must have felt like to be Bach composing. The definition of "internal history" offered at the beginning of this essay suggests the notion of an active, "guiding" intelligence "determining" and "justifying" every detail of the work. The composer may not have experienced the creative act quite that way. He may rather have felt aware of an inherent and perhaps inexorable logic governing the evolution of the work "from within". And, in attempting to recreate the "internal history" of the work here, we seem indeed, upon reflection, to have been tracing the composer's responses to the ramifications of his own ideas, as these ramifications became ever clearer to him in the course of composition. For once the "operating forces" are set in motion, the creative process is not so much the active exercise of arbitrary jovian will as it is a process of discovery and response. This brings to mind a remark that Albert Einstein is said to have made to an assistant apropos his search for the basic laws at work in the universe:

"What really interests me is whether God had any choice in the creation of the world"[31].

---

[31] Quoted by Gerald Holton in his review of Ronald W. Clark, *Einstein. The Life and Times*, in *The New York Times Book Review* for September 5, 1971.

FREDERICK NEUMANN

The Question of Rhythm in the Two Versions
of Bach's French Overture, BWV 831

Bach's French Overture-Suite for harpsichord exists in two versions: an earlier one in C minor, a later in B minor. The principal source of the C-minor version is a manuscript by Anna Magdalena Bach at the *Deutsche Staatsbibliothek* in Berlin (*Mus. ms. Bach, P 226*, hereafter referred to as P 226). Its title page is written by Bach himself whose hand can also be seen, according to Walter Emery, in a few editorial additions and emendations[1]. The exact date of this manuscript cannot be established, but Emery, on the basis of the watermark and the character of Anna Magdalena's handwriting considers a date prior to July 1733 as most likely. A second source is a manuscript by Johann Gottlieb Preller, written probably in the 1730s, and contained in the extensive "Mempell-Preller" collection of Bach manuscripts in the Leipzig *Musikbibliothek* (Ms 8)[2]. As Emery convincingly shows, this second source is not derived from P 226, but from a third source, presumably Bach's autograph sketch. Very little is known about Preller except that he was an organist born around 1700 and that his Bach manuscripts date from the 1730's and 40's.

The second version of the Overture in B minor is the one which Bach published in 1735 together with the Italian Concerto as the Second Part of his *Clavier Übung*[3].

Ex. 1
a) P 226

b) Original Print

---

[1] I am greatly indebted to Walter Emery, who has prepared the edition and the *Critical Commentary* of this work for the *Neue Bach-Ausgabe*, for sending me Xerox copies of those pages of his manuscript that are pertinent to this paper. All further references to Mr. Emery will be to this still unpublished manuscript.
[2] I am very grateful to Mr. Ernest D. May for lending me his photocopy of the Preller MS.
[3] It was engraved twice because the first edition contained too many mistakes.

Apart from the altered key the main differences between the two versions concern the first movement, the Overture proper, in which the rhythm is strikingly changed by being sharpened throughout in the manner shown in Ex. 1 for the opening measures.

Both change of key and change of rhythm for this Overture have given rise to much speculation.

Concerning the reason for the changed key, the first explanation that comes to mind — that the transposition may have resulted in a better adjustment to the compass of the instrument — does not answer the question. As was already pointed out by Hans Bischoff in his Steingräber edition of the 1880's and confirmed in more detail by Emery, the transposition to B minor not only offers no advantages in the upper register but in fact is a liability in the bass where two cadences had to be modified.

Bischoff (relating a private communication by Spitta), Hans David in his Schott edition of 1935 (presenting the C-minor version), Erwin Bodky, and recently Rudolf Eller, attempted explanations for the change of key that would integrate the First and the Second Parts of the *Clavier Übung* into a unified scheme of key relationships[4]. Each explanation is different (which in itself arouses skepticism), and none is convincing. This is not surprising, since it is unlikely that Bach would have linked into a single key scheme two publications of totally different inner organization. The first Part is homogeneous with its six Partitas; the second Part is heterogeneous: its very point is to contrast the two leading national styles, the Italian and the French, in the form of their most typical representatives: the Concerto and the Overture-Suite. This purpose lends support to Hermann Keller's suggestion that Bach wanted to underline the antithesis by juxtaposing the two prototypes in the sharpest possible key contrast, the tritone relationship of F major and B minor. Christoph Wolff has recently expressed the same idea and strengthened its case[5]. This seems to be the most plausible explanation, though we cannot entirely dismiss the possibility that Bach had no profound symbolism in mind and may have chosen the B-minor key for no more mysterious reason than that he preferred its characteristic sound for this particular work.

More intriguing than the change of key is the change of rhythm. Whenever we find notational deviations in second versions of a piece, the simplest explanation is that the second version represents a second thought — and usually the simplest explanation turns out to be the best. The sharpening of a rhythm as a second thought is not foreign to Bach. We find such specimens for instance in the aria, "Süßes Kreuz", from the *St. Matthew Passion*, where certain rhythms of the autograph score (*P 25*), given in Ex. 2a, are changed in the equally autograph gamba part (*St 110*) to those of Ex. b; or in the lute transcription (BWV 955) of the Suite for Unaccompanied Cello in C minor (BWV 1011). The autograph of the latter (in the Bibliothèque Royale de Belgique) contains, in the

[4] Erwin Bodky, *The Interpretation of Bach's Keyboard Works* (Cambridge, Mass., 1960), pp. 229—230; Rudolf Eller, "Serie und Zyklus in Bachs Instrumentalsammlungen", in *Bach-Interpretationen*, ed. Martin Geck (Göttingen, 1969), p. 131.

[5] Hermann Keller, *Die Klavierwerke Bachs* (Leipzig, 1950), p. 206; Christoph Wolff, "Ordnungsprinzipien in den Originaldrucken Bachscher Werke", *Bach-Interpretationen*, p. 149.

Ex. 2
a) BWV 244, 66 autograph Score P 25 — Gamba — m.42 — m.45 — m.48

b) autograph gamba part St 110

c) BWV 1011 — Violoncello — Allemande

d) BWV 955 — Lute

Allemande, the alterations shown in Exx. c and d, respectively, as well as in all parallel spots.

The case of the rhythmic alterations in the French Overture could rest with the simple explanation of a second thought were it not for the fact that a Bach scholar of Emery's eminence saw in the change not a conscious revision but rather a more precise notation for the same intended rhythm. (As will be presently shown, this opinion is shared by Michael Collins.) Emery feels that the pervasive rhythmic design of the C-minor version: ♩ ♫♫ was only a more convenient way of writing the sharper rhythms of the printed edition. If taken literally, the slower rhythms are "dull", he says, in response to Hans David who did believe in their literal meaning and found the early version „grander and more natural" than the "fashionable" revision. Emery, in making his claim for the sharpening of the rhythm, tacitly assumed the existence of an alleged convention. For this reason we have to take a brief look at the latter which was first formulated by Arnold Dolmetsch in 1916 and widely accepted since as authorative[6]. Its gist is that all dotted rhythms in French Overtures and Suite movements must be sharpened so decisively that they move together "jerkily" (as a wellknown modern writer put it)[7]. Thus ♩. ♪ or ♩. ♫ are to be rendered approximately ♩.. $\frac{?}{?}$♪ and ♩.. $\frac{?}{?}$♫ respectively. Because such rhythmic incisiveness or "jerkiness" became to be considered an essential element of the style, the idea was extended to other rhythmic designs that occur frequently in French

[6] A. Dolmetsch, *The Interpretation of the Music of the XVII & XVIII Centuries* (London, 1916), pp. 62—65.
[7] Thurston Dart, *The Interpretation of Music*, new ed. (New York, 1963), p. 81.

Overtures, where an upbeat figure of three or more notes is separated from its left neighbor by a rest such as ♩ 𝄾 𝅘𝅥𝅯𝅘𝅥𝅯𝅘𝅥𝅯♩ or ♩. 𝄾 𝅘𝅥𝅯𝅘𝅥𝅯𝅘𝅥𝅯♩ and, in analogy, as we have seen, even to the pattern ♩ 𝅘𝅥𝅯𝅘𝅥𝅯𝅘𝅥𝅯♩ of the C-minor version.

A few years ago I examined the whole issue of this French Overture style and found that the doctrine of its obligatory sharp "overdotting" (a term coined by Bodky) was built on defective evidence[8]. I pointed out that the alleged French convention, which is supposed to apply to Overtures and Suite movements from Lully to Rameau and to include Bach and Handel, is not supported by any French theoretical source. Instead, the doctrine is based on two German sources of the mid-18th Century, namely, passages from the treatises of J. J. Quantz (1752) and C. P. E. Bach (1753). Of these two, C. P. E. Bach has to be eliminated on two counts: 1) he makes no reference to French music — let alone to Overtures and Suites; 2) the confused and obscure passage which Dolmetsch used (but misquoted by adding two whole sentences which Bach did not write), does not say what it is alleged to say. This is made evident in a lucid passage in the second volume of the treatise. In the latter Bach says that the dot is often lengthened, but sometimes played precisely, and sometimes shortened, and that it would be a mistake to limit its rendition to one style only: "if one makes a rule of one type of execution, one loses the other ones"[9]. Speaking of *German* music and rejecting a limiting manner of execution, C. P. E. Bach can hardly be a convincing witness for obligatory sharp overdotting in the French Overture style. Quantz alone remains, and he, too, presented the overdotting first as a *general* practice which had become somewhat of a mannerism in the Germany of the *galant* era. Only in a later chapter, devoted to the duties of accompanists, does he apply the principle of overdotting to French dances[10]. I explained also why certain French musical evidence — such as the peculiarities in the notation of Gigault and Couperin who often added one or more extra flags or beams to their short notes — carried no implication for overdotting. Finally, I was able to present much musical evidence that contradicted the doctrine. (More remains to be presented on another occasion.)

[8] F. Neumann, "La Note Pointée et la soi-disant 'Manière Française'", *Revue de Musicologie*, L (1965), 66—92. Hereafter: "Note Pointée". I refer the reader to this article and devote only a few sentences here to the briefest resumé.

[9] *Versuch über die wahre Art das Clavier zu spielen . . .*, Second Part, Berlin, 1762, ch. 29, par. 15: "*Wenn man also nur eine Art vom Vortrage dieser Noten zum Grundsatz leget, so verliehrt man die übrigen Arten*". The first passage is contained in the First Part of the treatise, Berlin, 1753, ch. 3, par. 23. See also *Note Pointée*, pp. 71—75.

[10] *Versuch einer Anweisung, die Flöte traversiere zu spielen . . .*, Berlin, 1752. The general German practice is discussed in ch. 5, par. 21; the principles regarding French dances in ch. 17, sec. 7, pars. 56—58. In this latter statement Quantz may have superimposed German *galant* manneristic overdotting on the French *notes inégales*, the use of which he advocated. The significance of this passage may also be reduced by a circumstance which to my knowledge has not so far been pointed out. Quantz speaks in these latter paragraphs neither of instrumental Suites nor of opera Overtures but strictly of an orchestra accompanying dancers (the pars. 56 and 57 discuss largely problems of coordination of dancers and musicians). By speaking of such ballets being inserted within Italian operas it is also clear that he had Berlin, not Paris performances in mind. It is not a matter of course that rhythms sharpened for actual dancing, had to be integrally transferred to the stylized Overture-Suites of purely instrumental music.

As is so often the case with mistaken theories, the Dolmetsch doctrine contains kernels of truth. But it mistakes an artistic license for a strict obligation, and it has been projected far beyond its legitimate range of application.

One of the "kernels" resides in the thoroughly documented French *notes inégales* convention according to which certain evenly written notes in certain specific meters (such as eighth-notes in 2 meter) were rendered unevenly, to wit: short-long, in a lilting pulse. The degree of unevenness varied, ranging from an approximately 3:2 to a 2:1 ratio, rarely exceeding the latter. When a greater unevenness was intended, the French wrote dotted notes[11]. As a consequence of this uneven pulse, we find that in such works where the eighths are *inégales* the dotted quarter-notes will be somewhat lengthened, the companion eighths correspondingly shortened because the dot takes the place of the longer first of the uneven notes[12]:

This is what Jacques Hotteterre had in mind when he wrote in his *Méthode pour la Musette* (1738), that in movements in which the eighth-notes are *inégales*, the dot after a quarter-note is the equivalent of a dotted eighth-note (using the dotted note here as a makeshift symbol for a generally lesser inequality). As I pointed out in discussing this quotation, the usually mild lengthening of the *notes inégales* is a far cry from the extremes postulated by the doctrine[13]. Moreover, it applies to *all* French music, not only to Overture-Suites.

Being tied to the *Inégales* convention, such lengthening of the dot does *not* occur in C meter in which all eighth-notes are strictly equal. Hence in such Overtures as Lully's *Bellérophone*, or in all of Dieupart's Overture-Suites for the harpsichord, the *notes inégales* would not have affected the length of the dotted quarter-notes; even assuming against all probability that Handel had honored the French *inégales* convention, not a single one of his Overtures would be thus affected, since they are all written in C meter.

The second kernel of truth resides in the imprecision of the dot during most of the 17th and 18th centuries in *all* national styles. Though theoretically the dot stood for one half of the principal note's value, in practice it was flexible in both directions. Usually it did have its exact meaning, but it could simply stand for an undetermined increment. Often it signified exactly one fourth: for instance when Bach and many of his contemporaries and predecessors wrote ♩. ♫♫ they meant ♩ ♫♫♫ The latter is simply a more precise notation for such "underdotting". More frequently still the dot signified one third when the pair ♩. ♫ was a makeshift notation for the unavailable ♩ ♪[14]. Similar

---

[11] When one or the other French writer, like Hotteterre (presently to be quoted) illustrates the unevenness of the *inégales* by the dotted pattern ♩. ♫ they did so for lack of a milder rhythmic symbol ♩, ♪ being unknown). Loulié ingeniously indicated the milder character by the following device: ♩. ♩ ♩ ♩. ♩

[12] See "Note Pointée", pp. 85—86; also my article "External Evidence and Uneven Notes", *The Musical Quarterly*, LII (1966), p. 464.

[13] See "Note Pointée", pp. 85—86.

[14] See "External Evidence", pp. 463—464.

shortenings of the dots were practiced when the "affect" of the piece called for gentler rhythms. On the other hand, the dot could be lengthened when the textbook relationship of 3:1 was, as Leopold Mozart put it, "too sleepy". The above-mentioned *galant* mannerism of such frequent lengthening, is reflected in a number of German treatises after those of Quantz and C. Ph. E. Bach. Some authors (Löhlein, for example) advocate it as a quasi-rule; others take note of this practice but (as C. P. E. Bach did in the above quotation) qualify it strongly as only one of several manners; some condemn it outright, for instance Marpurg and G. F. Wolf, or reject it implicitly as did Hiller [15]. Moreover, what all these Germans in the second half of the 18th century wrote about overdotting (including Quantz's *first* statement) is totally unrelated to the French Overture-Suite which by mid-17th century had actually gone out of fashion.

These, then, are in briefest summary the meager facts behind the legend of "jerkiness" as an essential feature of the French Overture-Suite style: a mild lengthening of the dot whenever *notes inégales* applied, valid for *all* French music with no specific link to the Overtures and often not even applicable to the latter; secondly, the freedom of the performer to lengthen as well as shorten the dot according to the "affect", valid for *all* music of *all* nations; thirdly, a — spotty — German *galant* mannerism with no reference to any kind of French style.

Michael Collins attempted to salvage the Dolmetsch theory of obligatory intense overdotting in the French Overture-Suite (thereby revising his own earlier theory of obligatory *under*dotting in the "French style" [16]).

Here I shall deal with Collins's arguments only as far as they concern Bach's French Overture with its central rhythm pattern: ♩ ♬♬ (hereafter referred to as the "C-minor pattern") but shall discuss on another occasion his ideas regarding the simple dotted pattern of French Overtures.

Collins shows the opening measures of both versions of Bach's French Overture (see above, Ex. 1) and declares that "obviously" they have to be played in the same rhythm [17]. It is not clear why the identity of rhythm should be obvious, not even if one were to take the Dolmetsch doctrine for granted: the C-minor pattern can not be "overdotted" for the simple reason that it contains no dot. The only known theoretical

---

[15] Friedrich Wilhelm Marpurg, *Anleitung zum Clavierspielen . . .* (Berlin, 1755), p. 13, where he explains that there are two ways in which to indicate an extension of the dot beyond its regular value: a second dot: ♩.. ♪ or a tie: ♩ ♩♪ and that one has to use one or the other if such lengthening is desired. "Otherwise one has no obligation to divine the composer's intentions; and since he has two ways to clarify his intentions to the performer, namely the tie or the double dot, I do not see why one should write one way and want to have it performed another way; i.e., why one would write only one dot wanting to have it interpreted as a dot and a half". Georg Friedrich Wolf, *Unterricht im Klavierspielen*, Part 1, 3d ed. (Halle, 1789), p. 26, quotes and fully endorses the passage from Marpurg; Johann Adam Hiller, *Anweisung zum musikalisch-richtigen Gesange* (Leipzig, 1774), p. 111, stresses the precision of the dot's value.

[16] "A Reconsideration of French Over-dotting", *Music & Letters*, vol. 50 (1969), pp. 111—123; concerning the theory of underdotting: "The Performance of Triplets in the 17th and 18th Centuries", *JAMS*, XIX (1966), pp. 289—299, dealing with "The French Style".

[17] "Reconsideration", p. 113.

source that might appear to link this pattern with the alleged convention of obligatory overdotting, is a passage in Quantz (ch. 17, sec. 7, par. 58) where, speaking of the orchestra accompanying French dances, he says: "when three or more thirty-seconds follow a dot or rest they are not always played according to their proper value, especially in slow pieces, but at the extreme end of their assigned time and with the greatest of speed". Then he points to their frequent occurrence in *"Overtures, Entrées and Furies"*.

If, just for argument's sake, we assume that Quantz's (dance orchestra) rule applies to Bach — which is far from self-evident — it would apply to the B-minor version where Quantz's conditions are fulfilled since we find three or more thirty-seconds after dots. These figures would then have to be played as fast as possible. The rule would *not* apply to the C-minor pattern that has neither dots, nor rests, nor thirty-seconds: all three of Quantz's conditions are missing. In claiming that the C-minor pattern has to follow Quantz's directives, Collins overlooks the absence of dots and rests[18] but is concerned about the absence of thirty-seconds. He tries to overcome this difficulty by claiming that the notation has changed. Lully, Georg Muffat, and D'Anglebert, he says, never place three or more thirty-seconds after dots or rests in their Overtures. Instead they use the sixteenths figures: ♩ 𝄽 𝅘𝅥𝅯𝅘𝅥𝅯 On the other hand, Collins says, Gottlieb Muffat, Dieupart, J. K. F. Fischer and Rameau all use thirty-seconds: ♩. 𝅘𝅥𝅯𝅘𝅥𝅯 ¦ ♩ 𝄽 𝅘𝅥𝅯𝅘𝅥𝅯[19] Handel's practice, he continues, is especially illuminating. With only *two* exceptions those Overtures between 1705 and 1738 that have upbeat figures, have them in sixteenth-notes. After 1738 Handel "modernizes his notation" to thirty-seconds. "All this clearly shows that as the eighteenth century progressed composers turned to a somewhat more accurate representation of musical meaning. It is therefore not surprising that Quantz in 1752 speaks only of the demisemiquavers in common usage at the time he was writing". The argument which is meant to prove that Quantz's rule regarding thirty-seconds, applies to sixteenths as well, fails to convince. Even if later masters had written *only* thirty-second upbeat figures where Lully had written sixteenths, and if Handel had used exclusively sixteenths until 1738 and exclusively thirty-seconds after that date, such developments could still be more plausibly explained by a change of style than by a change of notation. However, no such simple shift from sixteenths to thirty-seconds has taken place. The later masters used the thirty-second upbeat figures not in place of, but concurrently with sixteenths, as well as with sixty-fourths and with eighth-note figures. This simply shows that after Lully's time the rhythmic scope of the Overtures expanded to cover a wider range of designs from mild and stately to sharp and agitated ones[20]. Concerning the Handel

---

[18] The rests Quantz had in mind are those that separate the fast notes from their left neighbor in analogy of the dotted patterns: ♩. 𝄽 𝅘𝅥𝅯𝅘𝅥𝅯 | ♩ or ♩ 𝄽 𝄽 𝅘𝅥𝅯𝅘𝅥𝅯𝅘𝅥𝅯 | ♩

[19] "Reconsideration", p. 112.

[20] Collins quotes (pp. 112—113) an example of mine from Lully's *Amadis* where some editorial revisions for a performance in 1720 illustrate both the stylistic evolution which now includes sharper rhythms, and the fact that "in the first half of the 18th century" (*dans la première moitié du XVIIIᵉ siècle*) no convention of rhythmic sharpening existed without exact pre-scription of the notation (*Note Pointée*, pp. 80—81). By substituting "in the time of Lully" for "first half of the 18th century" Collins changed the meaning of my argument.

evidence, there were not two, but eighteen Overtures written between 1705 and 1738 with upbeat figures of three or more thirty-second-notes after dots or rests, and three more Overtures with thirty-second-notes starting from a tie[21]. Regarding Handel's "modernized" notation after 1738, the upbeat figures in Overtures are now rare, but here, too, no new developments could be discerned. In the Overture to his last opera, *Deidamia* of 1740, Handel uses sixteenths: [♩. 𝄾 ♫♫ | ♩ 𝄾 ♫♫] side by side with thirty-seconds: [♩. 𝄾 ♫♫ | ♩] *Susanna* of 1748 has the pattern: [♩ 𝄾 ♫♫ ♫.♫] and the C minor pattern: [♩ ♫♫] and in *Theodora* of 1749 the latter pattern occurs in the following combination: [♩ ♫♫♫ ♩. ♫ |] no less than fourteen times. Clearly there was no change in Handel's notation of the upbeat figures. Thus the theory of notational development failed to restore *one* of Quantz's three conditions for use in Bach's C minor version. Since the two other conditions, the "dots or rests", were absent and overlooked, the only theoretical source for the compression of the upbeat figures has to be disqualified on all three counts.

The *notes inégales* are no help here either. They would only result in the pattern: [♩ ♫♫♫] but not in rhythmic contraction. Neither can the flexible dot be invoked, because there is no dot; on the contrary, as mentioned above, the notation [♩ ♫♫♫] was a more accurate, more "modern" spelling for [♩. ♫♫] and indeed was used as an antidote against the flexible dot, as protection against the very danger of extending its meaning for more than the intended one-fourth of the principal's note value.

But let us go one step further: let us, again for argument's sake, assume that the alleged convention did exist and did apply to the C-minor pattern, then take a look at the implications.

In the second source of this early version, the Preller MS, the upbeat figures are throughout strewn with ornaments of which Ex. 3 gives a characteristic illustration. The

Ex. 3

MS J. G. Preller

---

[21] Thirty-seconds after dots or rests in the Overtures to: *Rodrigo*, 1707; *Agrippina*, 1709; *Rinaldo*, 1711 (and again in its second version of 1731); *Pastor Fido*, 1712; *Amadigi*, 1715; *Radamisto*, 1720; *Floridante*, 1721; *Flavio*, 1723; *Rodelinda*, 1724; *Admeto*, 1727; *Riccardo*, 1727; *Ezio*, 1731; *Orlando*, 1732; *Arianna*, 1733; *Alcina*, 1735; *Alexander's Feast*, 1736; *Arminio*, 1736 (in the third part of the Overture); *Serse*, 1737—38. Thirty-seconds after a tie: *Mucio Scevola*, 1721; *Giulio Cesare*, 1724; *Partenope*, 1730.

graces would be unplayable in contracted rhythm. Whether these ornaments have any connection with Bach is impossible to establish, but Preller obviously was not aware of the alleged convention[22].

In mm. 11 and 12 (given in Ex. 4 *a* in the P 226 reading, in *b* in the B-minor version) we would have to assume that whereas Bach spelled out the sharpened rhythms for the left hand he relied on the convention to achieve the same effect for the right hand. The next measure presents a special problem with sixteenth-note upbeat figures in both hands which seem to call for synchronization. Yet to match the solution of the B-minor version, the player would have to guess that the convention applied to the right hand but not to the left. Then in mm. 17—20 (given for P 226 in Ex. *c*) we find upbeat

Ex. 4

---

[22] Emery's speculating that they may be additions by a later owner is not borne out by the fact that the handwriting for *all* ornaments is identical.

patterns for both hands written in the identical sharpened rhythm of the B-minor version. True, Bach was often inconsistent but never in a way and to a degree that would completely confuse the performer or present him with such near-insoluble puzzles as offered in m. 13.

Greater trouble still awaits the convention in the Overtures to Bach's orchestral Suites. The first two measures of the C-major Overture (BWV 1066), given in Ex. 5, already lead the convention *ad absurdum*. Many similar spots in the same work repeat the message. In Overture No. 3 in D major (BWV 1068), mm. 5, 13, and 14 in the continuo; m. 15 in oboes, violins and continuo; in Overture No. 4 in D major (BWV 1069), m. 3 in oboes and violins, offer similar evidence. So does the opening of Cantata 119 whose first movement is a French Overture that contains many thirty-second figures; its first measure has sixteenth-note upbeat figures that are not contractable.

Ex. 5
BWV 1066

These examples should prove that the sixteenth-note upbeat figures starting from a tie were meant to be played as written. Yet stronger evidence is still available. Not infrequently the upbeat figures are written in eighth-notes in which case no theory of

Ex. 6

a) Lully, Ouverture to *Proserpine* (Skeleton Score)

b) d'Anglebert's transcription
   m. 5

notational evolution could conceivably link them with Quantz's thirty-second patterns. Lully's Overture to *Proserpine* (1680) has such figures as shown in Ex. 6 *a*. D'Anglebert in his harpsichord transcription of this Overture (in his *Pièces de Clavecin* of 1689) emphasizes the slowness of these figures by adding ornaments (Ex. *b* gives a brief excerpt; the comma after the note stands for a mordent).

Dieupart uses upbeat figures in three of six Overtures, (from his *Six Suittes de Clavessin . . .* of ca. 1705) and in all three of these, they are written in eighth-notes (Exx. 7 *a—c* give their starting measures). Rameau's similar figures from his Overture to *Les Indes Galantes* are shown in Ex. *d*.

Ex. 7
Dieupart a) 2 d Suite, Ouverture

b) 5 th Suite, Ouverture

c) 6 th Suite, Ouverture

d) Rameau, *Les Indes galantes*, Ouverture

For German illustrations Exx. 8 *a* and *b* show the start of two Overtures by Mattheson, one from his Sonata op. 1 No. 2 for two flutes, the other from Sonata op. 1 No. 7 for three flutes. Both contain upbeat figures in eighth-notes which resist any attempt at contraction into sharper rhythms.

Ex. 8

Mattheson a) Sonata for two flutes op. 1 No. 2, Ouverture

b) Sonata for three flutes op. 1 No. 7, Ouverture

The sixteenth-note figures have shown, and the eighth-note figures emphatically underscored, the fact that rhythmic sharpness, let alone jerkiness was not an essential characteristic of the French Overture.

Returning to Bach's two versions, it should now be clear that the first was meant as written. Whether we agree with Emery that such a rendition is "duller", or with David that it is "grander and more natural", is purely a matter of individual taste; it has no bearing on the question of historical performance.

NORMAN RUBIN

"Fugue" as a Delimiting Concept in Bach's Choruses:
A Gloss on Werner Neumann's "J.S.Bachs Chorfuge"*

For any collection of musical compositions a list of relevant characteristics can be made — characteristics which each of the individual compositions may embody fully, partially, or not at all, and which for Bach's imitative non-chorale choruses would include the following:

The initial vocal texture may involve one, two, three, ... or all voices. The initially silent voices may enter individually with the same melodic material, or in pairs with two bits of melodic material. The same melodic material may appear in different voices at the same pitch-class level, or at different levels. If at different levels, the tonal interval (expressed, throughout this discussion, as the smallest ascending interval from the first level to the second) between successive appearances may be constant, or it may alternate between two values, or it may be irregular[1]. The interval of time between voice-exchanges similarly may be constant, may alternate between two values, or may be irregular[2]. The "same melodic material" mentioned above may be intervallically identical in all voices, or adjusted chromatically (e.g., a minor third imitated as a major third), or adjusted diatonically (e.g., a fifth imitated as a fourth). The equivalence of material among voices (whether intervallically exact, chromatically adjusted, or diatonically adjusted) may be as short as the shortest interval of time between successive voice-exchanges, or virtually as long as the entire composition. The material defined by the minimum equivalence above (the "subject" or first point of imitation) may recur after it has appeared in all voices — in which case the equivalence of material might include one or more returns to the opening material — or it may not. In fact, once each of the imitating voices or pairs of voices has had the initial material, *any* of the above characteristics of presentation — constancy, alternation, or irregularity of temporal and tonal interval between voice-exchanges; these intervals themselves; the order of the voices in imitation; and the nature of the equivalence of material; as well as the presence of the opening material itself — may continue to prevail or not.

* I am indebted to Arthur Mendel, who made many invaluable suggestions regarding an earlier draft of this paper, and who has been a constant source of encouragement and guidance. William H. Scheide's unpublished study "Bach Achieves His Goal" served as both a valuable compendium of information and a source of provocative ideas. And, of course, this paper stands in the debt of Werner Neumann, not only for his procedures and insights which revolutionized the study of Bach's choruses, but perhaps more fundamentally for his readiness to reexamine and sharpen current ideas and conceptions.

[1] If the interval is constant, the imitation is often called "canonic"; if it alternates between fourth and fifth, beginning with either, "fugal". In a less restrictive sense, any strict imitation which cannot be called "fugal" is called "canonic".

[2] If it is constant, one speaks of a "periodic" presentation.

One approach to a general awareness of the procedures of such a group of compositions would be to determine which *combinations* of characteristics tend to occur frequently, and which tend to occur rarely or not at all. The frequent combinations could be considered the nucleus of a compositional type, with individual compositions arrayed from the position of "textbook example" to that of "borderline case". More strikingly, if the specification of a single characteristic were sufficient to define a group of compositions generally similar to one another and distinct from compositions outside the group, then that characteristic could be said to have "formative influence" within the larger body of compositions — in other words, there would be evidence from the compositions themselves that the composer treated compositions with that characteristic in a special way.

In as complex a collection as Bach's choruses, whose members embody many characteristics less than completely and more than not at all, and in which the compositional significance of individual characteristics (hence of similarities and differences among compositions) is somewhat a matter of personal interpretation, there will be few characteristics or groups of characteristics whose influence will not be controversial. Nevertheless, some will be more controversial than others.

Equipped with these criteria and aware of the subtlety of the issue, we will examine the formative influence of a specific characteristic — the alternation of tonal interval of imitation between fourth and fifth — for Bach's imitative non-chorale choruses. To this end we will seek the limits of the compositional affinity among members of the group defined by that characteristic — a group which we may call the "fugal" non-chorale choruses — and the limits of the compositional disparity between members of the group and non-members.

Since Werner Neumann, in his study *J. S. Bachs Chorfuge*[3], has taken the group of "fugal" choruses as his total domain of inquiry, our findings will reflect on the advisability of his choice, and the justification of his choice may guide our findings. At the outset, he limits himself to fugues, defines "fugue" in terms of the fifth-fourth, tonic-dominant-tonic relationship resulting from the succession subject-answer-subject, and explains his choice as follows:

> Die Tatsache, daß die Fuge am Ende ihres langen Entwicklungsweges schon in den frühen Instrumentalkompositionen Bachs diese Formfestigung klar aufweist, gibt uns dazu die Berechtigung. [p. 9]

Thus, the assumption is that just as it is fruitful to consider Bach's instrumental fugues as a genre, so, by analogy, it will be fruitful to consider his fugal choral compositions as a genre. It is paradoxical that this assumption would probably never have been seriously questioned without the findings of the little book which it introduces; for nobody has shown more successfully than Neumann himself just how different Bach's fugal choruses are from his instrumental fugues, and hence how dangerous it is to base decisions in one on seemingly analogous situations in the other.

---

[3] Second ed. (Leipzig, 1950); henceforth *Chorfuge*.

The danger and the paradox have been noticed by others. Joseph Müller-Blattau writes:

> W. Neumann ... gibt eine ausgezeichnete Übersicht über die eigentlichen Chor-
> fugen und trennt von ihnen die in andere Formen selbständig oder abhängig einge-
> betteten. Wenn er zu jenen ersten auch die Imitationsformen rechnet, die von vorn-
> herein auf Permutation bzw. Kombination bestimmter, im mehrfachen Kp. er-
> fundener Themen gestellt sind, so ist damit fraglos ein wichtiges Aufbauprinzip für
> Bachs Chormusik gefunden; als Fuge im Sinne unserer Darstellung können sie je-
> doch nicht bezeichnet werden[4].

Thus Müller-Blattau thinks the group of Bach "fugal" choruses (as defined by Neumann) falls on both sides of the division between "fugue" and "non-fugue." Most strikingly, the pieces Neumann considers most central to the group—i.e., those most dependent on the permutation principle and the combination process—are placed by Müller-Blattau in the group of "non-fugues". Approaching the problem from a different direction, William H. Scheide writes:

> At the start of his study of Bach's choral fugues, Neumann stated his criterion for
> identifying fugues relevant for his purpose. He would hold firmly to "dem Prinzip
> der Quintbeantwortung als Ausdruck der mit dem Dux-Comes Verhältnis gegebe-
> nen Kadenzspannung T-D-T" (p. 9). This was before he began the consideration
> of the permutation fugue as such. But here the special characteristic seems to be not
> so much the tonic-dominant alternation ... as the strict periodicity ...[5].

Scheide is appealing for a new grouping, one that would include periodic permutation choruses whether "fugal" or "non-fugal", and seems to be suggesting that Neumann him-self might prefer the new grouping, now that he has thoroughly studied "the permutation fugue as such". At any rate, both writers have profited from Neumann's study and have suggested alternative groupings for some of the pieces involved. In fact, both want to make a division between the choruses Müller-Blattau considers true fugues and the funda-mentally different permutation choruses, although all of the former and many of the latter share the "Kadenzspannung T-D-T". In other words, both are questioning the formative influence of Neumann's "fugal" characteristic in Bach's choral music.

The central fugue in BWV 40/1, „Dazu ist erschienen", newly composed for Decem-ber 26, 1723, belongs, according to Neumann, to the very small group of thoroughly linearly constructed fugal choruses in Bach's concerted sacred music[6]. Briefly, the fugue consists of: (1) a non-periodic solo exposition with a one-measure codetta leading from

---

[4] Joseph Müller-Blattau, "Fuge", *MGG*, IV (Kassel, 1955), col. 1111.
[5] William H. Scheide, "Bach Achieves His Goal", unpublished typescript, II, 443.
[6] *Chorfuge*, 88.

the first answer to the second subject[7]; followed by (2) a tutti exposition with a new counter-subject which introduces the second phrase of text, and featuring stretti on the initial subject and on the new counter-subject; (3) a partly canonic four-voiced stretto complex leading sequentially in fourths from ii to IV/IV and ending with a half-cadence, iv^6-V; and (4) a three-entry exposition featuring the new counter-subject in parallel sixths, then in stretto again, then with the stretto imitation form (a simplified and abbreviated form of the counter-subject) in parallel thirds, and cadencing on IV, preparing for the varied repetition of the opening modulating (I—V) chorus transposed to the upper fourth (IV—I).

The basic procedure in this fugue — exploring successively the contrapuntal possibilities of a subject, of its counterpoints, and even of the counterpoints to its counterpoints — is in striking contrast to the procedure in a chorus dominated by permutation principles. For an especially obvious contrast, we will examine a fugue especially devoid of linear considerations on the compositional level — BWV 243/7, "Fecit Potentiam", newly composed for Christmas Vespers, 1723, the day before the first performance of *Dazu ist erschienen.*

Figure 1, below, is Neumann's graphic representation of "Fecit Potentiam" through m. 24, after which the piece proceeds differently[8]. Generally in Neumann's diagrams each participant has a horizontal row (orchestral parts above the dividing line, voice parts below), and each period has a vertical column. Each bit of material that undergoes voice-exchange (each *counterpoint*) has a number, usually reflecting the order of appearance, and each bit of material outside the imitation scheme has a letter. Bold-faced numerals indicate the appearance of a counterpoint in an imitating voice, and light-faced numerals indicate the appearance of a counterpoint in a doubling voice. Small numerals represent varied statements of counterpoints. In some choruses, including "Fecit", voices sometimes exchange material at smaller intervals than the prevailing periodic interval. In order to represent this occurrence, Neumann uses a vertical band of several columns to represent each period, and a single column to represent the smaller interval of voice exchange. In this chorus, the consistent imitation takes place at the level of four-measure periods, but voices also occasionally exchange material in one- and two-measure units. Thus, the first complete four-measure counterpoint is represented by "1111", while "5522" represents the appearance in one part or voice of the first half of the fifth counterpoint followed by the second half of the second counterpoint. The choice of numbers for individual counterpoints represents the order of complete appearances, beginning with "1111".

---

[7] Robert Lewis Marshall has shown in *The Compositional Process of J. S. Bach* (Princeton, 1972, I, 139) that Bach first wrote in subject and answer entries for a *periodic* exposition, then squeezed three measures of material into two measures of manuscript space to accommodate the extra measure.

[8] *Chorfuge,* 24. The figure has been emended to show "6" wherever Neumann had "5", and vice versa. I believe the present numeration much more clearly represents the events of the last two periods, described below.

FIGURE 1

NEUMANN'S DIAGRAM OF
"FECIT POTENTIAM", BWV 243/7
(EMENDED AS NOTED IN TEXT)

				66	66	1111
				66	66	aa
				66	66	aa
				66	66	
bb	bb	bb	bb	bb	1111
bb	bb	bb	bb	bb	6622
bb	bb	bb	bb	bb	6644
aa	aa	aa	aa	aa	2233
aa	aa	aa	aa	aa	4466
aa	aa	aa	aa	aa	3355

Sop. I	66	33	66	66	1111	2222
Sop. II	23	66	1111	2222	3333	4444
Alto	32	1111	2222	3333	4444	3333
Tenor	1111	2222	3333	4444	2255	6666
Bass	55	55	55	1111	5522	5555
	A	B	A	A	B	A

Each period is labelled "A" or "B" at the bottom, indicating the version of the counterpoints which moves harmonically up a fifth and the diatonically adjusted version which moves up a fourth, respectively.

Looking now at the specific procedures represented in this diagram, we find an exposition in which the "silent" voices — the voices which have not yet entered the imitation scheme with **1111, 2222**, etc. — accompany the imitation with what turns out to be the first half of all the counterpoints but the fourth; and where most of the orchestra repeats two accompaniment figures, which are actually rhythmic imitations of the cry *fecit potentiam* as it appears in the beginnings of Counterpoints "2" through "6", at the space of one (a) and two (b) quarter-notes, respectively. The exposition is completely periodic and involves six voices, the last entry taking place in the first trumpet. It has complete equivalence of material in the imitating voices except for two places: (1) in the fifth period, where bass and tenor take the first halves of each other's counterpoints, and (2) in the last period, where bass and alto take each other's counterpoints entirely[9].

The constructive principle at work seems clearly to operate in a vertical direction, and one gets the impression that equivalence of material, where it occurs, is the effect, and the nearly constant appearance of all counterpoints, the cause[10]. In this piece, the "block" conception of the composition, evident from the diagram, is also reflected in the material itself, especially in the fact that the first half of each counterpoint but the first declaims the same text to the same rhythm.

I would like to maintain that the fact that both these choruses, "Dazu ist erschienen" and "Fecit Potentiam", begin with successive imitation first at the fifth then at the fourth has not led them down similar compositional paths, but rather that this feature is itself their most striking common characteristic. I would also maintain that several other pairs of "fugal" choruses would have served the purpose approximately as well, showing many important compositional differences and few important similarities.

Turning now to the task of presenting fugues and non-fugues with strong compositional affinities, we can begin with the several expositions of BWV 245/54, "Lasset uns den nicht zerteilen", as diagrammed by Neumann (Figure 2)[11]. The seven expositions are not contiguous, although the first voice of one may enter before the last voice of the preceding has completed its material. The first three are fairly typical permutation-fugue

FIGURE 2

NEUMANN'S DIAGRAMS OF BWV 245/54, "LASSET UNS DEN NICHT ZERTEILEN"
(EMENDED AS NOTED)

1. Durchführung:

```
        1  2  3  4
     1  2  3  4
  1  2  3  4
1  2  3  4
A  B  A  B  A  A  A*
```

---

[9] Since consistent duplication (equivalence of material) was evidently the simplest and most frequent procedure in Bach's permutation-motivated choruses, it is interesting to speculate on the irregularities here. The adjustments may be traceable to the heterophonic relationship between the first half of the fifth counterpoint ("55—") and the first half of the ostinato pattern in the continuo. I suspect that a transposition of "55—" to a higher register would change an acceptable heterophony into an unacceptable octave progression. This change would be unavoidable in the last period, with "5555" in the alto, and most likely in the previous period, where the voicing (high in the tenor) would make the progression more prominent.

[10] The piece is thus a prime example of "die Zufallsbildung der Horizontalen nach Maßgabe der Zusammenfügung bestimmter vertikaler Baueinheiten". (*Chorfuge*, 104.)

[11] *Chorfuge*, 45—46. This diagram has also been very slightly emended: the A's marked with asterisks were all originally **B**'s.

2. Durchführung:

```
              1  2  3  4
           1  2  3  4
        1  2  3  4
     1  2  3  4
     A  B  A  B  A  B
```

3. Durchführung:

```
              1  2  3  4
           1  2  3  4
        1  2  3  4
                 1  2  3  4
     A  B  A  A  A  A*
```

4. und 5. Durchführung (bilden eine satztechnische Einheit):

```
  1  2  3  4  a  1  2  3  4
     1  2  3  4  a  1  2  3  4
        1  2  3  4  a  1  2  3  4
           1  2  3  4  a  1  2  3  4
  B  B  B  B  B  B  B  B  B  B  A  A*
```

6. und 7. Durchführung (Spiegelbild der 4. und 5., Aufbau von unten):

```
           1  2  3  4  a  1  2  3  4
        1  2  3  4  a  1  2  3  4
     1  2  3  4  a  1  2  3  4
  1  2  3  4  a  1  2  3  4
  B  B  B  B  B  B  B  B  B  B  A  A*
```

* Original: B.

constructions, and any one of them at the beginning of a chorus would characterize that piece as a Neumann Chorfuge and a permutation fugue. Any one of Expositions 4 through 7 at the beginning of a chorus, however, would put that piece outside the realm of the Chorfuge, although its permutation characteristics would be impeccable. With their successions of "B-blocks", i.e., counterpoints which move harmonically up a fourth, these expositions fail the fifth-fourth, T-D-T, test. The four voices in each pair of expositions (4—5 and 6—7) are in strict diatonic canon except at the end of Expositions 5 and 7, when the string of B's gives way to a few A's, adjusting the equivalence diatonically. Neumann's comments on the similarities between fugal and non-fugal expositions are close enough to the issue at hand to bear quoting:

> In den letzten Durchführungen erinnert nur noch e i n gegengerichteter Block (A) an das durch den stetigen Blockwechsel bedingte harmonische Auf und Ab der ersten Durchführungen. Wenn auch dieser wegfällt — und es ist ein winziger Schritt bis dahin —, stehen wir einer kompositionstechnischen Form gegenüber, die man als harmonisch einseitig gerichtete Permutationsfuge bezeichnen könnte, wenn damit nicht ein Widerspruch in sich selbst gegeben wäre. Tatsächlich liegt hier das

Ende der Fuge, die der T-D-Spannung als Lebenselement bedarf. Für die Erkenntnis kompositionstechnischer Probleme sind indes diese Grenzfälle besonders aufschluß-reich [84] ... [[84] Gewiß kann man sie dem Zirkelkanon zuordnen, erfaßt damit aber kaum mehr als die Sekundärerscheinung. Besonders aufschlußreich ist auch die Chorfuge "Alles, was Odem hat" aus der unvollständig erhaltenen Kantate 190, in der die 1. Permutationsdurchführung in regelmäßiger Weise Dux- und Comes-blöcke alterniert (ABAB), die zweite aber durch eine Viergliederreihe von Comes-Blöcken (BBBB) zu einem kanonisch wirkenden Quintenfall führt (fis-h-E-A), der wiederum den Ausgleich zum 4-Quinten-Aufstieg (d-a-e-h) des Zwischensatz-Themas schafft [12].]

Neumann is also finding basic similarities between members and non-members of his "fugal" group, but his conclusion is somewhat different from mine. After asserting (above) that we have reached the end of "fugue" when we have reached the end of T-D-T imitation (i. e., reasserting his original definition), he finds non-fugal "permutation fugues" ("Sind Blitze, sind Donner" from the *St. Matthew Passion* and "Christe" from the *Mass in A*) and another permutation fugue like 245/54, having both "fugal" and "non-fugal" (BBBB) expositions ("Alles, was Odem hat"). But rather than concluding that "canonic" permutation forms (including "Row, Row, Row Your Boat", "Three Blind Mice", and others) and "fugal" permutation forms are simply subdivisions of permutation forms, he seems to conclude that it is misleading to connect the canonic permutation forms with rounds, and prefers rather to look at them as harmonically monotonic or unidirectional permutation fugues — "if that weren't a contradiction in terms". I would rather use the examples of permutation fugues that become periodic canons and compositions midway between periodic canons and permutation fugues to show the basic similarity between the composer's attitudes toward these two permutation forms — one of which has been a favorite since "Sumer is icumen in", the other of which enjoyed a brief heyday beginning perhaps with BWV 71/7, "Muß täglich von neuem" — and to maintain that their appar-ently deep-seated compositional affinity is no *Sekundärerscheinung*, but a deep-seated compositional affinity.

Perhaps one more example, not mentioned by Neumann, will help to underline the compositional affinities between "fugal" and "non-fugal" imitative choruses. The example is "Sie aber vernahmen der Keines", from BWV 22, Bach's intended or actual *Probestück* for the Cantorate at Leipzig. Like the two "non-fugal" choruses named by Neumann, this piece is a permutation-motivated chorus without fifth-fourth imitation. In fact, the imitation proceeds generally at the (upper) fifth, giving rise to a succession of "A-blocks" in my diagram, presented below as Figure 3 [13]. In this diagram the light-faced figure "3" represents a paraphrase or parallel of the third counterpoint ("**3**"). The small "**3**" and "**4**" indicate simple alterations of "**3**" and "**4**" respectively. The block labels indicate

---

[12] *Chorfuge*, 46—47.
[13] Unlike 245/54 and most of the other "canonic" examples above, this chorus imitates generally at the *fifth*, moving toward the *sharp* side of the circle of fifths.

tonal motion of a fourth (A), fifth (B), seventh (X), and second (Y). (Thus "A" and "B" correspond with Neumann's, while "X" and "Y" are my own.) The second line from the bottom gives the tonal level of each block, in terms of the first note of the first counterpoint as it appears in the "A-blocks" — consistently a third below the second note of the first counterpoint in any form.

FIGURE 3

DIAGRAM OF BWV 22/1,
"SIE ABER VERNAHMEN DER KEINES"

	solo										tutti (doubled) *					
S	1	2	3	4	1	1	1	2	3		1	2	3	3	1	1
A		1	2	3	4	3	3	3	4		1	2	3	3	4	3
T			1	2	3	3	3	4		1	2	3	3	3	3	3
B				1	2	3	3		1	2	3	4	1	1	2	3

b♭ f c g d c b♭ f c g c g f e♭ b♭ c

A A A A X X A A A B A X X A Y A

* In the "tutti" exposition, the tenor is doubled by viola, the alto by second violin, and the soprano by oboe and first violin. The bass is doubled somewhat freely, by continuo only, throughout the fugue. Nonetheless, I consider it most likely that a tutti exposition is intended, beginning with the bass entry (m. 56).

In all respects but the almost total absence of "B-blocks" this piece is a fine example of a permutation chorus, as the diagram shows. It is not as faithful in maintaining its fourth counterpoint as a textbook example of a permutation fugue, but it is comparable in this respect to BWV 104/1, "Der du Joseph", which also fills in with paraphrases and parallels of its third counterpoint for an absent fourth counterpoint[14]. The other divergences from model permutation-fugue behavior in BWV 22/1 are noteworthy, as they tend to make the piece more typical of fugal procedure in general than many permutation fugues. For example, the modulatory technique of substituting sequence for imitation, used here at the "X-blocks" to modulate back towards the tonic, is found in 245/38, "Wir haben ein Gesetz", after the permutation complex ends, and in the "episodes" of many of Bach's keyboard fugues. Another striking feature is the treatment of the material after the end of the diagrammed section, when all counterpoints drop out but the first, which continues in sequence, with alto and bass *in close imitation*. To the extent that the alto entries are still within the established periodicity of the

[14] *Chorfuge*, 29.

chorus, the piece is similar to BWV 65/1, "Sie werden aus Saba", which maintains strict periodicity long after its initial counterpoints have disappeared to be replaced by a close imitation.

The imitative portion of BWV 63/7, "Höchster, schau' in Gnaden an" (mm. 13—31), represents in many ways the other side of the compositional coin; for just as I consider the absence of initial T—D—T imitation in BWV 22/1 a relatively superficial detail in a permutational and in many ways fugal composition, so the *presence* of T—D—T imitation at the outset of BWV 63/7 seems not to negate its generally canonic premises. Neumann's diagram of the imitative section, Figure 4 below[15], fails to represent adequately the features of the piece which he describes well on pages 30 and 31.

FIGURE 4

NEUMANN'S DIAGRAM OF BWV 63/7,
"HÖCHSTER, SCHAU' IN GNADEN AN"

```
                                  |1 1| 22
                                  1 1|2  44
                            11    2 2|y  yy
            11 | 22 | 11 |  xx            11
                                  1 1|2  44
                                  1 1|2  44
                            11    2 2|y  yy
                 11 | 23 | 22 | 4 4|z  33
   22|33     44                11|2  44
   11|22 Zw  33 |33|42|11      22|y  yy
   11       22 |11|23|22      44|z  33
            11 |22|11| xx           11
  A B       A B       A B    A B
```

Faced with a modulating (I—V) subject and "real" or exact imitation, Neumann chooses to apply his block labels "A" and "B" on the basis of tonal *position* rather than tonal motion. Thus a statement modulating from c to g is represented by "A", while an exact transposition modulating from g to d is labelled "B"[16]. While the resulting diagram can relate this piece to a notion of "fugue", it must paradoxically gloss over the compelling relationship this piece bears to Bach's imitative choruses — the constant use of one contrapuntal complex or model in two versions (with two different tonal directions) which usually alternate regularly, but may deviate from regular alternation in order to change tonal direction. For, although this piece has a real answer, it also makes constant use of one contrapuntal model in two versions which generally alternate.

---

[15] *Chorfuge*, 31.

[16] While this procedure masks some of the devices of this chorus, it represents no inconsistency in Neumann's terms: his block labels do not represent tonal motion per se, but simply distinguish subject block (*Dux-Block*) from answer block (*Comes-Block*); cf. *Chorfuge*, 15 and *passim*. In almost every chorus Neumann diagrams, these two criteria reduce to one; here they do not, and Neumann understandably chooses to distinguish subject from answer.

The operative "block" does not, however, extend from one voice-exchange to the next, but only *half* as far. In other words, Bach has constructed his subject (and countersubject) from two statements of a single pattern. (See Example 1[17].)

Example 1

Both versions of this block are simple elaborations of the same cadential pattern (Example 2a) and differ primarily in the tonal relationship between their first note and the last note of the preceding pattern.

Example 2

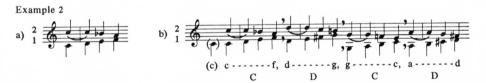

While the "1" of the C block begins "conjunctly" at the pitch-class of the preceding "1" and proceeds a fourth higher, the "1" of the D block begins "disjunctly" by dropping a third before beginning its ascent of a fourth (Example 2b). In terms of tonal motion, then, the C block raises the tonal level a fourth, while the D block raises it a second. Unlike the two blocks of a permutation fugue, these two do not close tonally by themselves. In other words, instead of octave complements, they are fifth complements. While a succession A B A B ... in a permutation fugue produces tonal stasis (I—V—I—V...), the corresponding progression in this chorus, C D C D..., produces a steady progression away from the tonic.

[17] Neumann's "**33**" parallels "**11**" at the upper third; "**44**" parallels "**22**" at the upper or lower third. I have chosen to represent them as parallel statements, in light-faced type.

Of course, Bach can alter the succession C D C D . . . in this piece to regain the tonic just as he alters the succession A B A B . . . in a permutation fugue to leave it. He does this in two fundamentally different ways: (1) by repeating the flat-tending C block, undoing the general progression in the sharp direction; and (2) by accelerating the progression (by repeating sharp-tending D blocks) and completing it (or undoing it) with a chromatically altered D block that raises the tonal level a *minor* second — in other words, by circumnavigating a *diatonic* circle of fifths. The first method is used in Bach's second and third alterations (mm. 23—24 and mm. 27—29); the second method, in the first alteration (mm. 17—18). See Figure 5, where the "altered" blocks are underscored.

FIGURE 5 *

MY DIAGRAM OF BWV 63/7, "HÖCHSTER, SCHAU' IN GNADEN AN"

												voices not doubled			voices doubled			
Orch															**1**	**1**	**2**	**2**
S	**2**	**2**	1	1	2	2	2								1	1⌉	2	2	2
A	**1**	**1**	2	2	2	1	1	1	1	2	2	⌈**1**	**1**	2	2⌋	-	-	-
T			**1**	**1**	1	2	2	⌈**1**	**1**	2	1	2	2	2	2	-	1	1
B						⌈**1**	**1**	2	2	1	1	-	-	-			1	1

c-f, d-g;

(c) c-f, d-g; g-c, a-d, b-e; c-f, d-g; g-c, a-d; d-g, g-c; c-f, d-g; g-c, a-d;   g-c, a-d.

C – D   C – D – D   D – D   C – D   C – C   C – D   C $\frac{C-D}{D}$ (C)   C – D

* Imitating voices are marked in bold type; parallel voices in light-faced type. Free material is indicated by "-". The second line from the bottom gives the rising fourth outlined by counterpoint 1. (Commas are used within each voice; semicolons between voices.) The bottom line gives the label of the block; a dash connects blocks between voice-exchanges. The three "adjustments" to the succession of blocks are underscored. Each column represents one measure.

The second alteration is the simplest. In it, the basses sing two C units (d—g, g—c) in place of the usual "C — D" (d—g, e—a). Since this second C unit is a third higher than the D unit would be, the alto line, which had been doubling 2 at the upper third, can function here as 2 itself with no change in its part.

The third alteration similarly depends on the third-relationship between C and D units. While the second alteration put a C unit in place of a D unit, the third presents a C counterpoint (trumpet) *with* the expected D unit (soprano)! The trumpet entrance —

which can be heard as another third-parallel until it is half over — asserts itself unmistakably by continuing disjunctly into a second unit. (See Example 3.)

Example 3

The first alteration, as noted above, juxtaposes second-progressions (D) rather than fourth-progressions. After the tenor part has concluded the "normal" g—c, a—d, it simply adds another D unit, b—e (with c *natural*), which prepares the way for the bass's D unit (c—f) with the compelling logic of a tonal sequence.

As we have seen, one contrapuntal model — one "block" — forms the basis of *every* *measure* of this imitative section — including the part labelled "Zwischenspiel" ("Zw") and the block left unlabelled in Figure 4. In this regard, the chorus itself exemplifies Bach's general procedures in permutation choruses much more clearly than the "fugal" Figure 4 would indicate. While this chorus can unquestionably be seen as an example of the genre "fugue", a comparison of its procedures with Bach's procedures in other choruses tends to emphasize its "permutational" features rather than its "fugal" features. The fact that Neumann considers "Höchster, schau' in Gnaden an" (and "Lasset uns den nicht zerteilen", for that matter) a fugue and "Sie aber vernahmen der Keines" a between the second and third entries in the "fugue", but waits until after the fifth entry in the "non-fugue". I cannot find anything in the body of Bach's imitative choral works to recommend this distinction as one of great moment.

I have attempted to demonstrate that the "fugal" characteristic delimits a group of Bach choruses neither unified nor distinguishable from its complement by any other important characteristic, and therefore is not itself a formative characteristic. Of course, those who judge the very presence of tonic-dominant-tonic imitation — the "fugal" characteristic itself — to be a characteristic of great inherent importance will find ample homogeneity and distinctness in the group from that characteristic alone. Such a judgment, reinforced at every turn in the case of Bach's keyboard works, searches in vain for support among the choruses.

Neumann shows some other characteristics which seem to be somewhat more influential on the mechanics of the choruses; for example, the combination of periodicity and maintenance of counterpoints is the characteristic he has used in defining his primary sub-group within the fugal group — namely, the permutation fugues. I believe this characteristic would be just as influential on the *total* group it delimits, fugal or non-fugal. Neumann's study has used this characteristic not as a simple test of admission to the group, but as a yardstick to measure each composition's proximity to the center of the group, moving outward from textbook examples to examples which seem to belong to another sphere completely. The extra subtlety gained by such a quantitative approach is evident; unfortunately the sphere was truncated before the study began.

WILLIAM H. SCHEIDE

Some Miscellaneous Chorale Forms in J. S. Bach's Vocal Works

The compositions with which this article is concerned conform to one of the following two descriptions:

A: All non-recitative movements which include both a non-chorale text and a chorale tune, or

B: Movements whose only text is a chorale stanza, while the chorale tune associated with that stanza is presented in essentially complete and unaltered form as an instrumental cantus firmus.

One of the points of interest in the movements belonging to these categories is their combination of the chorale structure with that of a concerted aria or non-chorale chorus; since such a combination is absent in the occasional recitatives which make use of chorale tunes, they have been omitted[1]. Table I lists 40 pieces of which 34 belong to category A and six to category B. The first 34 compositions entered on the list (not the same 34 belonging to category A) appear in chronological order, even though some uncertainty as to the date exists in cases such as BWV 156/2 and 159/2. No attempt has been made to arrange the last six numbers chronologically. The liturgical day, or other occasion, on which the movements were performed, is also given, wherever known, in the tabulation.

In 19 of the 34 examples belonging to type A the chorale tune is performed by vocalists — with or without doubling instruments. Since there are no chorale texts whatever in the remaining 15 pieces in category A, we may ask how the chorale tunes were chosen. In seven cases one of the chorale stanzas appears in another number of the same cantata; and in these instances the presence of a chorale text in another number may conceivably have suggested the use of the tune in a movement where the chorale text was not present. But in eight cases no stanza associated with the chorale tune appears anywhere in the work. The chorale in BWV 172/5 is closely associated with the Whitsunday liturgy, and the liturgical appropriateness of the chorales in BWV 106/5 and BWV 233/1 also seems obvious[2]. Stanza 3, line 1 of the instrumental chorale in BWV 19/5 contains the word "Engelein" which recalls "Engel" in line 1 of the aria text[3]. The precedent set in BWV 77/1 (first performed in the 13th Sunday after Trinity, 1723), in which the con-

---

[1] Cf. BWV 23/2, 70/9, 5/4, 38/4, 122/3. The modulations in these movements are often fascinating.

[2] The chorale, *Christe, du Lamm Gottes*, would be more appropriately combined with an Agnus Dei than with a Kyrie setting, but the former would not be encountered in the Lutheran liturgy.

[3] Texts of many vocally-presented chorales share important words with the non-chorale texts of the movements with which they are associated, e.g., BWV 228, 244/1 and 158/2.

TABLE I

No.	Year	Day in church year	BWV	A	B	Chorale tune Vocal	Chorale tune Only instr.	1	2	3	4	5	9	Group A No	Group A Yes
	1707	(penitential service)	131/2	x		x			x						
		(penetential service)	131/4	x		x			x						
		(funeral)	106/5	x			x				x			x	
		(funeral)	106/7	x		x			x						
5	1708	(town council inauguration)	71/2	x		x			x						
	1713	no special day	21/9	x		x					x				
	1714	3rd Sunday after Easter	12/6	x			x	x						x	
		Whitsunday	172/5	x			x		x					x	
	1715	3rd Sunday in Lent	80/2	x			x	x							x
10		Easter Sunday	31/8	x			x	x							x
		4th Sunday after Trinity	185/1	x			x		x						x
		16th Sunday after Trinity	161/1	x			x	x							x
		23rd Sunday after Trinity	163/5	x			x		x					x	
	1723	13th Sunday after Trinity	77/1	x			x				x			x	
15		14th Sunday after Trinity	25/1	x			x				x			x	
		19th Sunday after Trinity	48/1	x			x				x				x
		24th Sunday after Trinity	60/1	x		x			x						
		Christmas Vespers	243a/10		x		x			x					
	1724	Good Friday Vespers	245/40	x		x					x				
20		Good Friday Vespers	245/60	x		x						x			
		Visitation Day	10/5		x		x		x						
		5th Sunday after Trinity	93/4		x		x		x						
		10th Sunday after Trinity	101/4[4]	x			x	x							x
		Sunday after Christmas	122/4	x		x				x					
25	1725	12th Sunday after Trinity	137/4		x		x	x							
	1726	(funeral?)	228	x		x					x				
		St. Michael's Day	19/5	x			x	x						x	
		20th Sunday after Trinity	49/6	x		x			x						
	1727	Sunday after New Year	58/1	x		x			x						
30		Sunday after New Year	58/5	x		x			x						
	1729	3rd Sunday after Epiphany	156/2	x		x			x						
		Quinquagesima Sunday	159/2	x		x			x						
		Good Friday Vespers	244/1	x		x[5]							x		
	1735	4th Sunday after Epiphany	14/1		x		x				x				
35	?	Reformation Day	80/1		x		x				x				
	?	New Year's Day	143/6	x			x	x							x
	?	New Year's Day	143/7	x		x					x				
	?	Purification Day[6]	158/2	x		x			x						
	?	no special day	233(a)/1	x			x				x			x	
40	?	Good Friday Vespers?	245a	x		x			x						
TOTALS				34	6	19	21	8	17	2	11	1	1	8	7

[4] The recitative-like passage in mm. 19 f. has been left out of consideration.

[5] The chorale text is included in Picander's published libretti of 1729 and 1732, although it is omitted in the earliest musical sources.

[6] The text clearly refers to the Purification Day Gospel, but the movement has been incorporated into a cantata for Easter Tuesday.

nection between the chorale and the non-chorale text is particularly strong, may well have suggested a continuation of the practice in the cantatas performed in the following weeks: in BWV 25/1, and even BWV 48/1 (which uses the chorale tune of BWV 48/7). The stanzas associated with the instrumental chorales found in BWV 12/6 and 163/5 in each case appear to share at least one thought with the text of the respective cantata movements [7].

But the main question occasioned by the consideration of these pieces is: since there are so few of them among the many hundreds of choruses and arias, how is their particular distribution, indeed, their existence at all, to be accounted for? In the hope of uncovering relevant material bearing on this question, we will investigate, so far as possible, the contexts of the various compositions.

The first five examples in Table I belong to three cantatas, BWV 131, 106 and 71, written during the year Bach spent at Mühlhausen, that is, during the period of his first extant cantatas [8]. Along with two further cantatas generally assigned to the Mühlhausen period, BWV 196 and 150, the five early works contain a total of about thirty movements; and the chorale forms that concern us here accordingly constitute a larger proportion than they do in Bach's vocal works as a whole. In the four numbers with vocal chorales the non-chorale texts are sung exclusively by solo voices. Since in the fifth number, BWV 106/5 [9], the instrumental chorale enters only after the soprano has sung the first five measures of a long solo arioso, the chorale tune seems with respect to the formal design of the movement to be associated more closely with the soprano arioso than with the alto-tenor-bass fugato. Thus it seems fair to assert that in this earliest group of Bach's cantatas the chorales we are interested in are all associated with vocal solo music. In BWV 131, probably the earliest of the series, every solo movement has a chorale, but there is only one such movement in BWV 71; and the same is true for BWV 106, if we discount the mixed fifth movement. Table II shows a shifting of various styles in the presumed chronological order of the Mühlhausen cantatas.

---

[7] For example, "... ihr Betrüben (muß) lauter Zucker sein" from Stanza 6 of *Jesu meine Freude* may be compared with "alle Pein wird doch nur ein Kleines sein" from BWV 12/6; and "weil er sich für mich gegeben" from Stanza 1 of *Meinen Jesum laß ich nicht, weil* may be compared with " ... Gib dich mir" from BWV 163/5. But in both instances more distinctive words of the chorale texts occur in earlier arias of the respective cantatas. "Jesu", "Not", "Feind", "Kreuz", and "Schmach", characteristic of *Jesu meine Freude*, occur in BWV 12/4 and 5, and "Pflicht" occurs in both Stanza 1 of *Meinen Jesum laß ich nicht, weil* and in BWV 163/1.

[8] See William H. Scheide, "Johann Sebastian Bachs Sammlung von Kantaten seines Vetters Johann Ludwig Bach", *Bach-Jahrbuch 1959*, pp. 52 ff., where it is shown that BWV 15, considered by Philipp Spitta to have originated in 1704, was in all likelihood composed by Johann Ludwig Bach.

[9] It seems advisable to number the subsections of the opening half of the cantata independently, thus: Chorus: "Gottes Zeit"=Movement 2; Tenor solo: „Ach Herr"=Movement 3; Bass solo: "Bestelle dein Haus"=Movement 4; Chorus with Soprano solo: "Es ist der alte Bund"=Movement 5, rather than to treat them all as part of a single movement, viz., Movement 2, as is done in the *Bach-Werke-Verzeichnis*.

TABLE II

(The number in each column represents the movement number in the cantata, e.g.,
BWV 131/2, 71/5, etc.)

BWV	Ariosos	Arias with chorale	Arias with da capo	Choruses with permutation fugues
131		2, 4		
106	3, 4, 6	7		
71	5	2	4	7
196			3	2
150				6

The existence of a completely realized permutation fugue in BWV 71 marks that cantata as a work where the old ends and the new begins. Traces of permutation fugue textures occur, however, in BWV 131 and 106, and their presence in these earliest cantatas suggests that one of Bach's very first concerns as a cantata composer was to develop a special style for non-chorale choruses.

The earliest solo numbers in this group of cantatas are in general short and comparatively formless ariosi, while da capo arias at this point are little more than special combinations of ariosi such as those in BWV 106. The only freely composed solo piece of respectable length among the Mühlhausen cantatas is BWV 196/4, a duet consisting of chains of imitations between two upper voices of a trio texture. For the rest, Mühlhausen solo arias of any length are invariably associated with chorales. As Gerhard Herz has observed: "the chorale tune is the form-giving element" in all such movements [10]. In fact, I would suggest that it was the firm formal structure of a chorale tune that first enabled Bach to write a long solo cantata movement at all.

A likely enough explanation for this would be that the young composer of BWV 131/2 and 4 had already been using chorale tunes as structural elements in organ compositions, for example, the organ chorale partitas, BWV 766, 767, and 768, which may well have been composed before 1707 (BWV 768 in a lost, original form). This fact in turn recalls that Bach's Mühlhausen audition took place on Easter Sunday, 1707, and suggests that an original version of BWV 4 may have been performed at that occasion [11]. Its uniformity of key and treatment of the chorale tune are traits shared by the three organ chorale partitas just mentioned. The second movement in all three partitas contains a basso ostinato used as an interlude between the chorale lines. The chorale version in each work contains antiphonal effects in the same movement. These features are found in the

---

[10] Gerhard Herz, "BWV 131, Bach's First Cantata", in *Studies in Eighteenth-Century Music. A Tribute to Karl Geiringer on his Seventieth Birthday*, ed. H. C. Robbins Landon (London, 1970), p. 281.

[11] This possibility was mentioned by Herz, *ibid.*, p. 273. Elements of organ style in BWV 4 have been noted by various writers, for example, Alfred Dürr (cited in Herz's edition of BWV 4 [New York, 1967], p. 135).

setting of stanza 2 in BWV 4 as well. The fourth movement in each of the three partitas presents a rapid sixteenth-note version of the chorale tune in the treble; the same motion characterizes the violin obbligato of BWV 4/4. BWV 4/6 divides the chorale tune between voice and strings — a variant of the soprano-alto alternation in BWV 4/3. During the instrumental chorale presentations the voice sings short but free ariosi, very possibly the earliest examples of the "B" type settings listed in Table I.

I should like to suggest, therefore, that a 1707 version of BWV 4 is the earliest cantata of J. S. Bach of which there is any trace and that Bach had composed no cantatas before Easter, 1707 [12]. The organ chorale partitas, BWV 766, 767, and an early version of BWV 768, on the other hand, could well have been composed in Arnstadt. I therefore suggest further that Bach, desiring to perform a vocal work at his Easter Mühlhausen audition, based such a work on an Easter chorale and used his organ chorale partitas as models in fashioning a work in a new genre. In the following cantatas, too, Bach retained the chorale as a structural foundation for extended solo numbers but developed as well a new chorus style, that was independent of the chorale: the permutation fugue. After first perfecting the technique of the permutation fugue in BWV 71/7, Bach took complete leave of the chorale in the later Mühlhausen-style cantatas, BWV 196 and 150. Chorale forms are omitted also in the 1713 works, BWV 63, and, of course, the secular cantata, BWV 208.

In its present form, Cantata 21, too, probably dates from 1713; although its choruses on Bible texts (Movements 2, 6, and 11 — the last two with permutation fugues) are more like Bach's Mühlhausen than his Weimar works. They seem rather incongruous in juxtaposition to the madrigal recitatives and arias. And we are completely at sea in trying to account for the origin of the ninth movement, "Sei nun wieder zufrieden", whose two chorale stanza settings may be designated BWV 21/9a and 9b. Taken together, they form perhaps the longest chorus Bach had yet written. But were they necessarily composed at the same time? Only Movement 9b has the full Bible text as well as a greater diversity of motives and more eighth-note motion. All of this is compressed into the three lower voices which nonetheless must not overwhelm the presentation of the chorale, although the chorale is sung in a low register of the soprano. In contrast, the chorale in Movement 9a is sung by the tenor; this allows the soprano, alto and bass much greater freedom of action. Furthermore, by limiting the thematic material to a quarter-note stepwise motive and its inversion, Movement 9a achieves a textural clarity that is enhanced by, but not dependent upon, the solo character of the non-chorale voices. This suggests that BWV 21/9b, with its typical soprano chorale, was the earlier version to which Movement 9a, with its more unusual tenor chorale, was later prefixed. Thus, BWV 21/9b may be assumed to have been composed earlier than the end of 1713 and to have been associated perhaps in the earlier, orginal, version, with some other stanza of the hymn.

---

[12] The Arnstadt "reproofs", dated February 21, 1706 and November 11, 1706, certainly suggest that Bach had performed no cantatas in Arnstadt on Easter or any other day.

The next seven examples in Table I (all with instrumental chorales) date from the years 1714—15, when Bach appears to have been composing, in general, one cantata every four weeks. Each of the seven cantatas has three or more arias. Three cantatas composed at the beginning of this period — BWV 182 (for Palm Sunday), BWV 12 and 172 — have the identical form in which three aria texts occur in immediate succession. In BWV 182, the three arias are entirely free-composed, but in the third aria of each of the remaining two cantatas, i.e., BWV 12/6 and 172/5, Bach added a chorale tune[13]. The characteristic words shared by *Jesu meine Freude* and BWV 12/4 and 5 (see note 7) suggest that Bach may have selected the chorale before finally deciding in which movement he would use it. But another instance of an instrumental chorale in the third aria setting of his next cantata (the duet, BWV 172/5, four weeks later) would seem to indicate Bach's feeling that chorale tunes introduced a welcome variety in the third of three successive movements (arias) of similar character. In this way the presence of the chorale tune in BWV 12/6 might be explained even though its (unsung) texts would have no words in common with the aria text[14].

Among the other extant cantatas of 1714, Cantatas 54 and 61 each have fewer than three arias; in BWV 199 the third aria is separated from its predecessors not only by two recitatives but also by a solo chorale; and the four arias (including one duet) of BWV 21 are separated by recitatives and choruses. In none of these works is a chorale tune introduced into a setting of an aria text. The same is true of BWV 18, a setting of a text by Erdmann Neumeister performed by Bach on Sexagesima Sunday, 1715. The cantata's only aria is not combined with an instrumental chorale.

The remaining cantatas of this period are all settings from Salomo Franck's *Evangelisches Andachts-Opffer*, a set of texts covering the church year. Bach's first composition from the collection, BWV 152, was written for the Sunday after Christmas, 1714. Bach continued to draw on these texts at least through the middle of January, 1716, with the composition of BWV 155 (a cantata with two arias and no instrumental chorale). It seems altogether possible that by the end of Lent, 1715 (and perhaps earlier), musical settings of texts from the *Evangelisches Andachts-Opffer* were being regularly set and performed at the Weimar court. The collection itself, therefore, deserves our closer attention here. Since no works by Bach from this period for occasions other than the Sunday service are known, we will consider only the Sunday texts from Franck's cycle on the assumption that during this period they were set — by other Weimar composers along with Bach — for performance every Sunday, Bach having been obliged to furnish one such composition every fourth week.

The three-aria form: Aria-Recitative-Aria-Recitative-Aria-Chorale predominates so heavily in the Franck collection that we shall call it the "Standard Form" (SF). The

---

[13] The third "aria" in BWV 172 is the only duet setting in the three cantatas.

[14] The trumpet part, incidentally, which plays the chorale tune in this number, covers the diatonic scale from g' to b"♭. I know neither of any other pre-Leipzig brass part that is diatonic below c" nor of any pre-Leipzig slide horn or trumpet part.

remaining will simply be designated "Other Forms" (OF). In Table III the number of aria texts in each OF is reported (1A, 2A, etc.). Text forms for the entire period under discussion are indicated, but specific days are listed only when there is an extant Bach setting. For the intervening Sundays the list shows the totals of the text form types represented. The table also indicates the presence of instrumental chorales in Bach's settings as well as which aria texts are set as duets along with the time signatures of these

TABLE III

Settings of Salomo Franck's *Evangelisches Andachts-Opffer*, 1714—16

Year	Sundays of extant Bach works	Form	BWV	Duets	Instr. Cls.	Remarks
1714	after Christmas	OF(3A) 2SF	152	3rdA 6/4		3rdA-finale. Its rit.=instr. cl.
		1OF(2A) 4SF				J. S. B. SF lost cantata?
1715	Sexagesima	OF(1A) 3SF	18			Neumeister text
	3rd in Lent	SF 3SF	80a	3rdA 3/4	1stA	
	Easter	OF(4A) 1OF(3A)	31		4thA	1stA chorus
		6SF				J. S. B. SF lost cantata?
	Trinity	SF 3SF	165			1stA fugue
	4th after Trinity	SF 2SF	185	1stA 6/4	1stA	
	8 week mourning period assumed because of Duke Johann Ernst's death.	1OF(2A)				
	16th after Trinity	SF 3SF	161		1stA	3rdA chorus
	20th after Trinity	SF 2SF	162	3rdA 3/4		
	23rd after Trinity	SF 2SF 1OF(2A)	163	3rdA 3/4	3rdA	Cl. finale continuo only in score
	4th in Advent	SF 1OF(3A) 2SF	132			Cl. finale omitted in score
1716	2nd after Epiphany	OF(2A)	155	1stA 4/4		Form: Rec.-Aria-Rec.Aria-Cl.

duets. (The reasons for including information regarding duets will become apparent shortly; for the moment it should be noted that only the last duet in the list, BWV 155/2, is cast in common time.) It is important to note further that Bach's patron, Johann Ernst, brother of the reigning Duke, died in Frankfurt am Main on the Thursday before the seventh Sunday after Trinity, 1715. On the basis of this fact, along with the absence of any Bach cantatas for the eighth and twelfth Sundays after Trinity, I have assumed a mourning period of eight weeks from the seventh through the fourteenth Sundays during which no cantatas were performed. This break divides the period into two halves.

In the first half there are five extant Bach cantatas with at least three arias separated only by recitatives. The first is BWV 152, whose third aria and finale provides the only duet in the work. The opening ritornello in the duet, repeated at the end, is the only instrumental passage in the movement. Successive phrases of this ritornello, at intervals of from six to twelve bars, are combined with the vocal parts like the lines of an instrumental chorale[15]. But since the ritornello melody, with its incessant ♩ .♪ ♩ rhythm is more like a dance than a chorale, the real source of variety among the aria-text movements of the cantata is the dialogue character of the duet (an exchange between Jesus and the Soul).

In three cantatas from the first half of this period — BWV 80a, 31, and 185 — either the first or last aria-text setting contains an instrumental chorale. This suggests that Bach felt that such musical variety as the chorale provides was desirable even when the arias were not immediately adjacent. However, between BWV 31 and BWV 185, Bach composed BWV 165, a work containing neither duets nor instrumental chorales. Variety here was achieved by setting the opening aria in fugal style (BWV 54/3 is the only other Weimar example). Why were instrumental chorales and/or duets not included in BWV 165? Here we may note that from the second Sunday after Easter through the sixth Sunday after Trinity the *Evangelisches Andachts-Opffer* presents thirteen successive Sundays with SF texts, the longest such period of the year. Thus every Weimar composer who may have been involved in the project of supplying Sunday cantatas, and not only Bach, must have been constantly confronted with the problem of setting three arias in each cantata. Surely the easiest procedure would have been to ignore the problem altogether by composing three arias of a relatively simple type. If this had occurred in the cantatas presumably composed for the project by Bach's senior colleague, the Capellmeister Samuel Drese, it is possible that Concertmeister Bach's more varied and elaborate forms (e.g., in BWV 80a and 31) may have annoyed his superior. None of Bach's SF cantatas begins with a chorus. Considering Bach's heavy use of opening choruses at other times and the evident availability of a chorus for SF chorale finales, one cannot help wondering if comparatively complicated opening choruses were forbidden, at least on ordinary Sundays[16], perhaps on Drese's instigation. But Drese may have himself suggested

---

[15] Cf. Alfred Dürr, *Studien über die frühen Kantaten J. S. Bachs* (Leipzig, 1951), p. 149.
[16] By changing the first number of SF to a Bible text, the form most frequently found in the cantatas of Bach's first Leipzig year is obtained (BWV 136, 105, 46, 179, 69a, 77, 25, 109, 89, 104). The fact that all but BWV 89 open with choruses recalls Bach's numerous Mühlhausen choral settings of Bible texts.

that a duet with only continuo accompaniment was acceptable. However, if Bach was following Drese's advice when he composed BWV 185/1, he did not refrain from inserting an instrumental chorale[17].

Let us now consider Bach's cantatas written after the mourning period. From the sixteenth Sunday after Trinity through the second Sunday in Advent there are ten successive Sundays with SF text. BWV 161 for the sixteenth Sunday after Trinity has both an instrumental chorale and a chorus; it contains only one freely composed solo aria. Four weeks later, in BWV 162, Bach set the Franck text for two arias and a duet with continuo; there is no instrumental chorale. Bach also chose to set the third aria text of the next cantata, BWV 163, as a duet similar in style to BWV 162/5, but now including an instrumental chorale which, like the chorale in BWV 12/6, may have been originally intended for an earlier movement in the cantata — in this case perhaps BWV 163/1 (cf. BWV 161/1)[18]. However, the three aria settings of BWV 132 — an SF text following upon a two-aria OF text the preceding week — contain neither instrumental chorales, duets, or even, as in BWV 165, fugues, as means for providing variety.

The Gospel for the sixteenth Sunday after Trinity, which treats of death and re-surrection, was appropriate for Bach in expressing his feelings over the death of his friend and patron, Duke Johann Ernst. In his enthusiasm to resume composing he may not have noticed the situation of the preceding week where the text form required only two arias. This latter text may have been composed by the man who had been responsible for (and may have completely composed) the cantata for the seventh Sunday after Trinity only to be informed at the last minute that it could not be performed owing to the Duke's death. Accordingly, he may have been even more eager than Bach to get started again, and, if he was the Capellmeister, may have been irritated if his modest work for the fifteenth Sunday was overshadowed by the appearance of the instrumental chorale and chorus in Bach's cantata, BWV 161, for the following Sunday. In any event, according to this hypothesis, a reaction followed fast. And if Bach understood part of the order to be "no more chorales", the defective or omitted settings of Franck's chorale texts in the extant scores of BWV 132 and 163 may be explained[19].

This discussion suggests that in 1714—15 Bach introduced instrumentally performed chorale tunes into certain arias in order to achieve musical variety in the many cantata texts he was obliged to set at that time which contained three or more arias separated at

---

[17] Identical meters and rhythms in the two duets, BWV 185/1 and 152/6 suggests that Bach may have had the latter in mind when he composed the former.

[18] See note 7, above. The two duets, BWV 162/5 and 163/5, seem connected both in meter and vocal themes with BWV 80/7 (=80a/5). Compare BWV 80/7, mm. 17—19, 21—24, with BWV 162/5, mm. 35—37, 88—90, and BWV 163/5, mm. 9—15.

[19] BWV 163 and 132 are known only through autograph scores which show some indications of being fair copies. The former contains only the continuo part of the chorale finale; the latter omits the chorale entirely. Perhaps the chorales were included in other sources now lost. But this is not the case in the similar score of BWV 185. If Bach had meant them to be omitted, the change in treatment from BWV 161 would be considerably increased.

most by recitatives. I suspect that this feature might have been even more prominent, especially toward the end of 1715, but for the restraining hand of his superior who may not have wished that unfavorable comparisons be made with his own presumably simpler style of composition.

It may be, however, that in those years Bach employed instrumental chorales only when he had several weeks to prepare them. On December 1, 1716 (the Tuesday before the second Sunday in Advent) Capellmeister Drese died, and Bach produced cantatas for the following two Sundays, BWV 70a and 186a, apparently in the hope of being named his successor. (The position was finally given to Drese's son). Each cantata contains four successive arias, but none of the eight arias contains an instrumental chorale. Most later cantatas with three or more arias also have no instrumental chorale. Evidently Bach could change his principles when he felt that circumstances warranted doing so.

The next examples in Table I date from Bach's first year at Leipzig, 1723. Beginning with the eighth Sunday after Trinity, Bach opened every cantata with a Biblical chorus of increasing complexity. For the thirteenth Sunday his text was the commandments to love God and neighbor; and, in BWV 77/1, Bach combined the chorus with a canon in augmentation between the trumpet and continuo based on Luther's hymn on the commandments, *Dies sind die heilgen zehn Gebot*. The following Sunday he superimposed a trombone choir playing an instrumental chorale upon another complex canonic chorus[20]. Although the succession of Biblical openings was then interrupted for at least two weeks, the same style of writing returns on the nineteenth Sunday after Trinity, in BWV 48/1, with chorale canons between unison oboes and trumpet.

The voice part in the chorale of BWV 60/1, *O Ewigkeit, du Donnerwort*, is surely there to begin the "Dialogus"[21] mentioned on the title page; although the same purpose could surely have been served by a freely-composed madrigal text. This particular chorale, however, is the same that was to open the chorale-paraphrase cantatas of Bach's second *Jahrgang* begun some six months later. This "coincidence", together with the facts that 1) three weeks earlier, in October, 1723, Bach had performed BWV 109/6, an extended chorale chorus more like the chorale-paraphrase cantata openings than any other work he composed in his first Leipzig year, and 2) that examples of chorale-paraphrase texts appear in Christmas cantatas of 1723[22], suggest that the character and even some of the texts of the "Chorale Cantata *Jahrgang*", 1724—25, may have been germinating midway in the first year.

---

[20] The tune is the famous "Passion" chorale; but Bach may have been thinking of the alternate text, *Ach Herr, mich armen Sünder*, since that would suit the despairing Psalm text sung by the chorus.

[21] If two opposing statements, sharing no word other than "ich", can be called a "dialogue". That type of text occurs most clearly in the recitatives, BWV 60/2 and 4. See also BWV 66/4, from another work, which Bach labeled "Dialogus" and which was performed during the first Leipzig year.

[22] The aria texts of BWV 64/5 for the third day of Christmas, 1723, and of BWV 94/2, for the ninth Sunday after Trinity, 1724, paraphrase the same chorale stanza.

Since the instrumental chorale in BWV 243a/10 could have been used in any of the other numbers of the *Magnificat*, it is remarkable that it appears only this once. But if we look only at the 1723 *Magnificat* setting before the German interpolations were inserted, a reason for this may become apparent. In the first nine numbers, the succession chorus-aria-aria appears three times. The exclusion of chorales here is clearly part of Bach's overall design for the complete work. The last three numbers form the sequence: instrumental chorale-chorus-chorus. Thus the concluding group, while sharing the pattern "abb" with its predecessors, is of a different order and is introduced by an entirely new type of composition.

The number, "Durch dein Gefängnis, Gottes Sohn", from the *St. John Passion*, BWV 245/40, is unique in setting a non-chorale text to a chorale tune in chorale style. In the Passion it follows closely on Jesus' last saying to Pilate. The last saying of Jesus in each of the four scenes in which he speaks is followed by non-Biblical interpolations (BWV 245/9, 15, 40, 58), and three more of the fourteen sayings are similarly marked (BWV 245/7, 27, 56). Five of these are chorales, one (BWV 245/58) is an aria, and one is the hybrid form, BWV 245/40. It seems obvious that Bach preferred chorale settings to follow sayings of Jesus. Only for the last saying, „Es ist vollbracht", does he make a clear exception.

BWV 245/60, "Mein teurer Heiland", which follows directly upon the Evangelist's announcement of Jesus' death ("... und er verschied"), combines aria and chorale texts. The chorale text refers to his death as an event that has already occurred ("Jesus, der du warest tot"). One is surprised, therefore, to find the following words in the aria text addressed to Jesus:

> Du kannst vor Schmerzen zwar nichts sagen,
> Doch neigest du das Haupt
> Und sprichst stillschweigend: Ja!

These lines and the syncopated melody, shared by solo bass and continuo and illustrative perhaps of a nodding head, evidently consider Jesus to be still alive. But the aria text not only contradicts the chorale text and the Evangelist's pronouncement in the preceding recitative; it repeats Movement 58 in quoting Jesus' last saying: "Es ist vollbracht".

Perhaps there was a stage in the evolution of the *St. John Passion*, before the composition of the aria, "Es ist vollbracht"(Movement 58), when the aria text of Movement 60 existed independently of the chorale and was intended to follow the Evangelist's words "Und neigte das Haupt" now at the beginning of Movement 59 [23]. Actually several circumstances all suggest that there was a considerable confusion in the assembling of this part of the Passion. First, to repeat, instead of the usual chorale there are two aria texts — again Movements 58 and 60 — to comment on the last saying of Jesus; second,

---

[23] This is the case with the verses from which the aria text of BWV 245/60 was developed. They occur in "B. H. Brockes Der für die Sünde der Welt Gemarterte und Sterbende Jesus ... Anno 1712". We may also note that BWV 245/60 is the only example in Table I of a typical four-part vocal chorale harmonization united with a solo aria setting.

there is the internal contradiction in the two texts of Movement 60 along with the absence, in the 1724 version of the Passion, of the customary doubling instruments for the chorale voices in this movement; finally there is a problematic three-measure version of Movement 61 ("Und siehe da"), now lost but known to have existed in 1724. It seems likely, then, that Bach originally conceived the two texts of Movement 60 as separate pieces, whatever his reasons may have been for combining them in a subsequent stage.

As is well known, and already mentioned above, the main achievement of Bach's second Leipzig year was the creation of a series of chorale-paraphrase cantatas. In these works the texts of the first and last stanzas are retained unaltered and, in general, the middle stanzas are paraphrased, with varying degrees of freedom, into recitatives and arias. I say "in general" because there are eight such internal stanzas which, like the terminal stanzas, were also left unaltered. The first such example, BWV 20/7, should perhaps not be included since it serves to end Part I of the cantata with a simple four-part setting; but the next example, BWV 10/5, by a curious coincidence, involves the German version of the Latin text of BWV 243a/10 (Luke 1:54). Perhaps this relationship explains why BWV 10/5 ("Er denket der Barmherzigkeit") also contains an instrumental chorale. In both BWV 243a/10 and BWV 10/5 the voice parts are wholly independent of the chorale tune, but the latter movement is for a duet rather than a trio of voices. In the cantata for the following Sunday we find the next instance of an unaltered internal stanza, BWV 93/4. Here again, as in BWV 10/5, Bach used the texture of vocal duet plus continuo with instrumental chorale cantus firmus, but this time the voice parts are recognizably derived from the chorale tune (as they are, incidentally, in BWV 37/3, performed a few weeks earlier). The remaining five examples of unaltered internal chorale strophes are all set as vocal chorale solos[24], and they are therefore not listed in Table I.

Four of the paraphrased texts—BWV 93/3, 101/4, 113/3, and 115/4—open with an unaltered statement of the first line or two of a middle chorale stanza. BWV 93/3 is an aria in AAB form, the form of the chorale; BWV 113/3 is a homogeneous two-part aria, and BWV 115/4 is a da capo aria. But BWV 101/4, "Warum willst du so zornig sein", is hardly homogeneous. The violent changes in the music reflect the contrasts in the text—contrasts not found in the other three numbers just mentioned nor in the chorale stanza from which the text of BWV 101/4 derives—the first three lines of which stress "zornig" and "Eifers Flammen", while the last three lines pray for "väterliche Huld" and "Geduld". In the first half the solo bass sings the opening chorale line as a chorale tune, then as a vivace arioso, and finally as a quasi-recitative. The last three lines are sung mostly in an andante tempo, while behind the voice the oboe choir plays the cantata's chorale tune—which thus gives shape to the arioso in the manner of an early Mühlhausen solo.

[24] In BWV 180 a solo chorale develops out of a preceding recitative as in BWV 199 and 95. The others may be compared to solo chorales in the post-Lenten season of 1724. BWV 178/4 and 92/4 have the same scoring as BWV 86/3; the same is true of BWV 114/4 and 44/3, as well as BWV 113/2 and 166/3 (the latter two also sharing the same chorale).

The only example in this group in which the madrigal words seem intended to be a line-for-line commentary on the chorale text is the aria "O wohl uns, die an ihn glauben", BWV 122/4. There are numerous other examples of this type in the chorale paraphrase cantatas, however [25], and Bach's usual practice is to set such movements for only one voice and treat the madrigal commentary as a recitative interpolation between the chorale lines. Such a compound number might indeed connect two concerted numbers, thus functioning exactly like a normal recitative movement; it therefore should not itself be surrounded by other recitatives. But that is just the case with BWV 122/4. This seems to be the reason why Bach resorted to the very unusual form found here which dispenses with recitative passages.

Lobe den Herren, den mächtigen König, BWV 137, stands in a curious relationship to the chorale-paraphrase cantatas. It fills a gap in the 1724 series and was placed with it in the sets of parts acquired by the Thomasschule after Bach's death. But it is not itself a chorale-paraphrase cantata; it is a "through-composed" chorale with the original chorale text retained throughout. And it was not composed in 1724 with the chorale paraphrases; it was written one year later, for the twelfth Sunday after Trinity, August, 19, 1725. A similar cantata had, however, been part of the original series: BWV 107, written for the seventh Sunday after Trinity, July 23, 1724. BWV 107, then, was Bach's first through-composed chorale cantata composed in Leipzig; BWV 137 was his second. Although there are four successive arias in BWV 107, none contains an instrumental rendition of the chorale tune; the chorale tune appears only in the terminal numbers, except for a fragment at the end of the voice part in the fifth movement. But after months of preoccupation with the paraphrase cantatas, Bach used or indicated the chorale tune in all five movements of BWV 137. The second movement is a solo vocal chorale; BWV 137/3 is a duet whose vocal parts suggest the chorale tune (cf. BWV 37/3 and BWV 93/4); and BWV 137/4 contains an instrumental chorale.

The simultaneous use of a three part fugal setting of a Bible text and two stanzas of a chorale in the motet *Fürchte dich nicht,* BWV 228, is probably to be explained by the appearance of the phrase "du bist mein" at the end of the Bible text, as well as in line 2 of the first chorale stanza and in line 1 of the second chorale stanza. The Bible verse (Isaiah 43:1) was part of the text of a funeral sermon delivered in St. Nicholas Church on February 4, 1726. It has been thought that BWV 228 may have been performed at that service [26]. Bach's use of chorales in other motets (e. g., BWV 227) is enough to account for the presence of one here.

The text of the aria, "Bleibt, ihr Engel", BWV 19/5, is a stanza with the form "abbacc", a type that Bach set frequently. It is true that the word "Engel" in its first line is similar to the word "Engelein" in line 1 of the third stanza, "Ach, Herr, laß dein lieb Engelein", of the hymn *Herzlich lieb hab ich dich,* a hymn whose unusually long melody gives the aria its extended structure. But surely the opening lines of many arias share distinctive words with chorales with which Bach did not combine them. Why then did he under-

---

[25] For example, BWV 93/5, 101/3, and 101/5.
[26] See NBA III/1, *Kritischer Bericht,* p. 140.

take to do so in BWV 19/5? In previous weeks of the summer of 1726 Bach's own works had been interspersed with performances of cantatas by his cousin Johann Ludwig Bach of Meiningen. These all had essentially the same form including a New Testament text in the middle with the only chorale — always for soprano — at the end. The last such work (usually designated as JLB 16) was heard two weeks before BWV 19[27]. JLB 16 had a unique feature in that its New Testament text (as well as its finale) was set like a chorale with one of the "chorale entries" in the bass. The first two of the nine "chorale lines" are each set three times; the whole piece fills 59 measures of common time. Thus the sum of chorale lines is two-lines-times-three-settings, or six, plus the remaining seven lines, totalling thirteen. This design is clearly comparable to that of BWV 19/5 in which the first three lines of the instrumental chorale are set twice (= six), followed by single statements of the remaining seven, again for a total of thirteen lines. Both the "chorale tune" in the Ludwig Bach movement and that in BWV 19/5, furthermore, are in G major. It appears, then, that J. S. Bach was almost certainly stimulated by his cousin's unusual and curious tour de force to embark on what proved to be a rather extraordinary conception even for him.

The next five pieces in Table I are all characterized by their use of sung chorales. The first three, like BWV 60/1 discussed above, are terminal numbers of cantatas entitled "Dialogus". In BWV 49 the main "dialogue" takes place in the recitatives, Movements 3 and 5 (as in BWV 60/2 and 4 and BWV 66/4)[28]. In the final movement of BWV 49, a duet, the chorale line implores, "Komm . . . bleib nicht lange", and the madrigal text replies, "Ich komme bald". But in the music, the setting of the response is concluded before the chorale line has even entered with its invitation. It therefore seems that Bach did not care in this instance — where a chorale aria serves as the terminal number of a cantata — to emphasize the dialogue aspects of its two texts, since the dialogue idea was represented in recitative elsewhere in the same work.

But in BWV 58, composed only two months after BWV 49, the only possible dialogue texts are found in the terminal numbers. Perhaps for this reason the dialogue in Movement 1 is unusually explicit[29]. In the fifth movement the chorale text speaks of "ein schwere Reis", and the madrigal text replies "Nur getrost", adding a promise of future bliss. (That the combination of chorale text and madrigal text in this movement had nothing to do with the presence of shared words is confirmed by the fact that the only word common to both texts is "ist".)

The following cantatas, BWV 156 and 159, are not dialogues; and BWV 156/2 and 159/2 are not terminal numbers[30]. In each case the two simultaneous texts enunciate

[27] JLB 16 was for the thirteenth Sunday after Trinity. In 1726 St. Michael's Day fell on the fifteenth Sunday after Trinity.

[28] At the end of 1725 Bach composed BWV 57 as a "Concerto in Dialogo"; and exchanges between Jesus and the Soul occur in the recitatives, BWV 57/4 and 6.

[29] Compare the opening couplet, "Ach Gott, wie manches *Herze*leid begegnet mir zu dieser *Zeit*", with the first madrigal lines, "Nur Geduld, mein *Herze*, / Es ist eine böse *Zeit*", which follow in the musical setting (italics added).

[30] BWV 156/2 is the opening text number, but Bach preceded it with a sinfonia.

parallel thoughts without any trace of dialogue interchange. In 156/2 the shared words are "Gott" and "End(e)"; in BWV 159/2 they are mostly pronouns and the phrase "will ich dich". Both cantata texts were taken from Picander's 1729 series for the church year and these two chorale arias are the only such examples in the entire set [31].

In the opening chorus of the *St. Matthew Passion* it seems clear that the librettist, Picander, developed his madrigal text around words ("Lamm", "Geduld[ig]") related to the chorale stanza whose tune is incorporated in the movement. This remains true whether the chorale was performed vocally in the performance of 1729, or whether it was merely played on the organ. (In any event it was definitely sung at a later performance, since the vocal part for it exists.) Therefore, this movement, too, affords an example of the combination of chorale and madrigal texts used in a terminal number designed as a dialogue. But here the dialogue is contained only in the madrigal texts; the chorale takes no part in it. The concluding madrigal lines are "Sehet ihn aus Lieb und Huld Holz zum Kreuze selber tragen", although there is nothing about Jesus carrying his cross in the St. Matthew Gospel account. The following passage, however, appears in the Passion poem of B. H. Brockes (see note 23):

Evangelist: Und Er trug Selbst Sein Creutz.

Tochter Zion: Ach herbe Plagen!
                Ach Marter, die man nicht erwegen kan!
                Must Du mein Heiland dann
                Das Holz, das Dich bald tragen sol, Selbst tragen?
                Du trägst es ja, und niemand hört dich klagen!

Some twenty-five lines earlier one reads:

ARIA: Mit dem Chor der Gläubigen Seelen.
Tochter Zion: . . . Kommt! Chor. Wohin? Tocht. Z. Nach Golgatha.

The aria contains several such interchanges. Its similarity to the madrigal text of BWV 244/1, where Picander specifies the same characters, is evident. But the Brockes aria is also the model for the only dialogue number in the *St. John Passion*, the bass aria with chorus, "Eilt, ihr angefocht'nen Seelen", BWV 245/48.

These observations suggest the following hypothesis. We must first assume that Bach intended the first performance of the *St. Matthew Passion* to take place on Good Friday, 1729. That year was unusual in that it contained a fifth Sunday after Epiphany. In 1726,

---

[31] The chorale stanza in BWV 159/2 recurs in BWV 244/23. The penultimate madrigal line ("Und wenn du endlich *scheiden* mußt") recalls the opening of BWV 244/72 ("Wenn ich einmal soll *scheiden*"); and the last madrigal line ("*Sollst* du dein *Grab in mir* erlangen") recalls BWV 244/75 ("Ich will Jesum selbst be*graben*. Denn er *soll* nunmehr *in mir* für und für seine süße Ruhe haben"). The possibility that the fragment of BWV 244/75 preserved in the original parts for the Sanctus in D, BWV 232[III] (Berlin Staatsbibliothek, *Mus. ms. Bach St. 117*), may date from 1727 and the connection of its text with one of Picander's pre-Lenten cantatas suggest that BWV 244/75 may be a parody. See Alfred Dürr, "Zur Chronologie der Leipziger Vokalwerke J. S. Bachs", *Bach-Jahrbuch 1957*, p. 95.

the first such year during Bach's cantorate in Leipzig, Bach used a cantata by Johann Ludwig Bach. Since no cantata by J. S. Bach for the fifth Sunday after Epiphany exists, it is quite possible that he used J. L. Bach's work again in 1729. If he indeed performed some of Ludwig Bach's pre-Lenten cantatas while he was composing the Passion[32], he could also have recalled the chorale aria, "Bleibt, ihr Engel", BWV 19/5, since it is not only connected with his cousin's unusual chorale in JLB 16, as we have seen, but makes use of the chorale melody that forms the final movement of the *St. John Passion*, BWV 245/68. Since this latter is a terminal number, it could logically have stimulated Bach to think also of the terminal chorale-aria dialogues he had occasionally composed, e. g., BWV 60/1, and 58/1. Perhaps J. S. Bach envisioned a number for two choruses as the opening of the *St. Matthew*, with one singing a chorale stanza and the other a madrigal text somewhat like the chorale stetting in the motet, *Singet dem Herrn ein neues Lied*, BWV 225. But he had already composed a setting for a dialogue in a Passion: BWV 245/48, which, as we have seen, in turn depended on Brockes. If Picander then looked at the Brockes model of BWV 245/48, he would have found the "Tochter Zion", the "Chor der Gläubigen", the question-and-answer dialogue, and, a few lines further along, Christ bearing His cross (note the words "Holz" and "Selbst"). In this passage forms of the verb "tragen", which occur four times (with two rhymes), and the concluding words, "niemand hört dich klagen", suggest respectively the lines, "All Sünd hast du getragen" and "Allzeit erfunden geduldig" which are found in the chorale ultimately used in BWV 244/1, and which may have motivated its selection. Picander evidently had the idea of casting the opening movement for a solo voice (alto?), a chorus, and a chorale (probably vocal solo)[33]. But it seems clear that for Passion openings Bach preferred only choruses, and so there is a dialogue of two equal forces. Finally, we may note the key of E minor, the G-major chorale, the triple rhythm and the free da capo with return of the opening madrigal text which characterize both BWV 244/1 and BWV 19/5.

BWV 14/1, performed on January 30, 1735, consists of seven expositions of inverted canons on derivatives of the chorale lines of *Wär Gott nicht mit uns diese Zeit*. Although lines 3 and 4 are the same as lines 1 and 2, the corresponding canonic textures are different. No other vocal work makes such concentrated use of this technique, and no extant vocal work of the time shows anything similar. But its firm date may be useful in dating some of Bach's instrumental experiments of this kind. Consider the fugue in B flat minor from the Second Book of the *Well-Tempered Clavier* (BWV 891) where inverted stretti in two voices occur in mm. 80 and 89 before the four-voice version at m. 96. Three other examples occur in Part Three of the *Clavierübung*. The first is in the

---

[32] Johann Ludwig Bach's cantata for Quinquagesima Sunday contains a saying of Jesus set as a recitative with string orchestra accompaniment. The staves of the first brace of J. S. Bach's score copy read, from the top down: bass, continuo, violin 1, violin 2, viola. Apparently in 1726 Bach was not familiar with string orchestra accompaniments in recitative settings of sayings of Jesus. Since this is found in BWV 244, the suggestion may have come from the Ludwig Bach cantata and may be evidence that J. S. Bach was thinking of his cousin's music early in 1729. See Scheide, *op. cit., Bach-Jahrbuch 1962*, p. 16.

[33] Compare the opening of BWV 244, Part II, minus the chorale.

large setting of *Kyrie, Gott Vater in Ewigkeit* (BWV 669) in mm. 7 (complete) und 19 (partial). The large setting of *Kyrie, Gott heiliger Geist* (BWV 671) makes recurring use of inverted canon in the form found in the opening measures. Closest of all to BWV 14/1 is the setting for manuals of *Aus tiefer Not* (BWV 687) in which the three lower voices use chorale line derivatives in both original and inverted form.

Returning to BWV 14/1, it appears that by making the cantus firmus a fifth instrumental voice, Bach was able to present two pairs of inverted canons, and that is what in fact takes place in the movement most of the time.

For the remaining six pieces in Table I no firm dates are available. BWV 245a, although used in the 1725 performance of the *St. John Passion*, contains the chorale tune *Jesu Leiden, Pein und Tod* in a form found in the Weimar work BWV 182/7, a form different from that found in Leipzig settings such as BWV 159/5 and BWV 245/20, 56, and 60. Perhaps it bears witness, therefore, to a lost Weimar setting[34]. Every chorale line rhymes with its accompanying madrigal text. It is therefore probable that the chorale was always vocal.

Of all the genuine and fully extant vocal works of J. S. Bach few are so defective in their source tradition as BWV 143. All its sources date from the nineteenth century. Since the cantata uses the chorale *Du Friedefürst, Herr Jesu Christ*, several stanzas of which mention war and other civil disasters, Spitta dated it January 1, 1735, connecting it with a war in which Saxony was involved[35], even though Part IV of the *Christmas Oratorio* was undoubtedly performed on that date. Leonhard Wolff, however, wrote: "die Musik scheint [1735] zu widersprechen und auf eine frühe Arbeit schließen zu lassen"[36]. Four of the cantata's seven numbers set verses of Psalm 146; a fifth is a solo vocal chorale, and there are two madrigal numbers. There are also three successive arias, the third of which contains an instrumental chorale (BWV 143/6). The Biblical emphasis suggests a Mühlhausen origin for the work, while the instrumental chorale in the third successive aria suggests Weimar. Finally, the New Year's date may indicate that the cantata was written at Köthen[37]. If the work is indeed authentic, an early Köthen date, perhaps January 1, 1718, would appear most likely, a time at which Bach might have felt inclined to assemble a text combining features both of Weimar and Mühlhausen.

Whether regarded as the opening movement of the *Mass in F*, BWV 233, with an instrumental chorale, or as a separate number with vocal chorale (*Christe, du Lamm Gottes*), the Kyrie, BWV 233a, is another work known only through copies. We may never know what circumstances may have suggested this interesting composition to Bach's mind.

[34] See Arthur Mendel, "Traces of the Pre-History of Bach's St. John and St. Matthew Passions", in *Festschrift Otto Heinrich Deutsch* (Kassel, 1963), pp. 31 ff, especially pp. 37 f.

[35] Philipp Spitta, *Johann Sebastian Bach* (Leipzig, 1873, 1880), II, pp. 545 f.

[36] Leonhard Wolff, *J. Sebastian Bachs Kirchenkantaten* (Leipzig, 1913), p. 167.

[37] See Friedrich Smend, *Bach in Köthen* (Berlin, 1951), p. 18.

The use of a doubling oboe in BWV 158/2 makes it likely that the chorale was originally instrumental, in spite of the identical first lines of the two texts[38]. This would distinguish it from the vocal chorales that antedate BWV 244/1 in Table I and would create hesitation about dating it in that general period. But in fact there is no period at all which includes a Purification Day for which a Bach cantata has not already been convincingly assigned and which falls during a period when Bach is known to have been writing instrumental chorale arias and which accordingly would be a likely time for the composition of BWV 158.

BWV 80/1 is part of the Leipzig enlargement of the Lenten Weimar cantata, BWV 80a, which made it appropriate for Reformation Day. The only year when Bach is known to have enlarged pre-Leipzig cantatas was 1723—24, when BWV 70a, 186a, and 147a were enlarged, and a number of Köthen works were altered to fit the Leipzig church year. If the chorale text of BWV 80/1 (*Ein feste Burg ist unser Gott*) suggests a relationship with BWV 14/1, we may point out that the choral parts in BWV 80/1 never indulge in inverted canons. Instead, during lines 1 through 4, derivatives of lines 1 and 2 are combined in some five different ways suggestive of such double fugues and canons as appear in the choruses, BWV 69a/1 and BWV 25/1 of Bach's first Leipzig year. Now the instrumental chorale in BWV 80/1 is presented in canon between the trumpet and the continuo, and the only other example of such writing is found in BWV 77/1, a work composed for precisely the Sunday (August 22, 1723) between those on which BWV 69a/1 and BWV 25/1 (August 15, and 29, 1723, respectively) were performed. I thus incline rather strongly to believe that BWV 80/1 was written for Reformation Day, 1723. Since in that year Reformation Day coincided with the twenty-third Sunday after Trinity, it is easier to imagine Bach having performed BWV 80 on the occasion than the relatively modest work, BWV 163, although that has been suggested[39]. If BWV 80a/1 was provided with a chorale text and performed on Reformation Day in 1723 as the second movement of the new work, it could have served as a model for the vocal chorale aria BWV 60/1 performed the following Sunday.

The pre-Leipzig chorales in Table I are mainly divided between the mostly vocal chorales which provide structure for Mühlhausen solo numbers and the Weimar instrumental chorales which give variety to the three-aria cantata forms of this period. The more intensive cantata production at Leipzig leads naturally to more complex circumstances. Therefore, the contexts that may have caused Bach to revert to this type of composition are more diverse.

The instrumental chorales are occasionally suggested by chorus texts or by unpara-

---

[38] See NBA I/10, *Kritischer Bericht*, p. 167.

[39] See A. Dürr, "Zur Chronologie ...", p. 62. It is likely that the trumpet fanfares in BWV 80/1 are an addition by Wilhelm Friedemann Bach. See B. F. Richter, "Über die Schicksale der der Thomasschule zu Leipzig angehörenden Kantaten Joh. Seb. Bachs", *Bach-Jahrbuch 1906*, pp. 61 f.

phrased middle stanzas of chorale cantatas. The vocal chorales (whose model may have been BWV 80/2 after it was provided with a new chorale text) tend to become terminal numbers of dialogue cantatas. With them we associate the opening chorus of the *St. Matthew Passion.*

At other times Bach may have been moved by matters such as the problem of form in the *St. John Passion*, or by the music of his cousin, Johann Ludwig Bach, or by a desire to experiment with inverted canons when not restricted by the limitations of the keyboard. In any event, these unusual pieces seem to me to present problems which it would be certainly useful to recognize and hopefully useful also to discuss.

IV

JOHANN SEBASTIAN BACH:
STUDIES OF THE SOURCES

PAUL BRAINARD

Cantata 21 Revisited

Alongside the pioneering work of Alfred Dürr, it is to Arthur Mendel's studies, publications, and legendary Bach-seminars that we owe most of our knowledge of the complex history of *Ich hatte viel Bekümmernis* — a title that has taken on a certain autobiographical significance for those of us who have worked with the cantata from a philological point of view. Characteristically, Arthur's insights go to the heart of our "trouble" with this piece and its sole surviving original source, the part-collection *St 354* at the Berlin State Library. Equally characteristically, he has not only been generously responsive to inquiries, but has actively shared his ideas, working materials, and third-party correspondence with those whom he knew to be interested in the problem. It was such an encounter with him in 1962 that gave the first impetus to my investigations of BWV 21; and it was his intervention that led to my being assigned the task of editing it for the *Neue Bach-Ausgabe* (NBA) [1]. The following is a preliminary report of some aspects of that work, offered in homage and gratitude.

Sources

The contents of the Berlin part-set are summarized in the accompanying Table. References hereafter will be to "A" plus identifying part numbers. Source B, whose role in the present discussion (and in the NBA edition) will be negligible, is the working score [2] prepared by Wilhelm Rust directly from the part-set A for his edition of the cantata for the Bach-Gesellschaft *(BG)* [3]. At least six other distinct sources (C through H), none of them extant, can be postulated with varying degrees of certainty from internal evidence in source A.

Score C: From the transposition relationships in the oboe lines, Alfred Dürr [4] demonstrated in 1951 the existence of at least two chronological layers in the music that has come down to us as Cantata 21. The central piece of evidence is the range of the C-minor oboe part A4 in the first chorus (b♭ to b♭″), which points to an original conception of the oboe line in D-minor-*Kammerton*, with the remaining parts (possibly excepting bassoon) in C-*Chorton*, in accordance with Bach's usual practice in Weimar [5]. Yet the very existence of A4, whose paper and scribal hand can be indisputably linked to the Weimar period, virtually proves that the cantata was performed in C-*Kammerton* on or (more likely) before the date entered by Bach on the title-page *(d. 3ten post Trinit:* [June 17] *1714 musicieret worden)*. The chorus *Ich hatte viel Bekümmernis*, then, forms

---

[1] NBA I/16 (in preparation).
[2] *Mus. ms. Bach P 849* from the Staatsbibliothek holdings presently housed in Berlin-Dahlem.
[3] *Johann Sebastian Bachs Werke*, Bach-Gesellschaft edition, V, 1 (*ca.* 1855).
[4] *Studien über die frühen Kantaten J. S. Bachs* (Leipzig, 1951), pp. 19—21.
[5] Arthur Mendel, "On the Pitches in Use in Bach's Time", *The Musical Quarterly*, XLI (1955), 332—354, 466—480.

part of a work whose lost (or planned) oboe part[6] antedates part A4, and for which we can postulate the existence of an original score, referred to hereafter as "C". From additional evidence both in the oboe parts and in the cantata's text, movements 1, 3, and 6 can be assigned with considerable likelihood to the same lost score. Others, as we shall see, are probable candidates for inclusion on textual grounds alone. Only movement 11 can be categorically excluded from score C. In this, the final chorus, the notated range of the Weimar oboe part A4 is d' — d''', already a tone above the usual upper limit of Bach's oboe lines.

Score D can thus be identified as a separate earlier source, from which at least the final chorus of Cantata 21 was drawn. The ranges of both voices and strings, along with the employment of trumpets, indicate that this movement was conceived in C-*Chorton,* and hence that its original instrumentation did not include an oboe (whose notated compass in D-*Kammerton* would have had to be e' — e'''). A re-instrumentation of the movement must have preceded (or accompanied) its incorporation into the cantata as we know it. Dürr and Mendel[7] have both suggested that the oboe line might originally have been assigned to violin in a five-part string texture (with divided violas). There are, however, several indications in parts A4, 5, and 28 that the original texture may have been a four-part one whose two upper voices (Violin I — II) were redistributed to form three (Oboe, Violin I — II)[8].

Scores E and F: The existence of two lost scores of the complete cantata can be demonstrated from copyists' scoring marks[9] found in most of the Weimar parts of source A. Score E is demonstrably early. Its traces in the parts are of two kinds: (1) small dots or lightly-drawn crosses marking the end of each system in the score being copied, and (2) numbers indicating the measure-count at various points during or at the end of movements. Plate I shows both forms as they appear in part A8: crosses drawn above the staff at five-measure intervals (the first cross follows measure 40 of the sixth movement), and numbers indicating that the eleven-measure rest encompasses two systems whose beginnings lie nine and four measures, respectively, from the soprano's new entry in measure 65. Note, however, that the "9" and "4" are deleted and overlaid by an autograph *Tutti* indication[10]. This is preliminary evidence not only of the non-original character of the *solo-tutti* division of forces in the cantata, but also of the early date assignable to score E. As for score F, little can be proved beyond its erstwhile

---

[6] A28 cannot have been the part in question. Its copying almost certainly postdated that of A4 by at least a few months, and several of its readings diverge so substantially from both C-minor oboe parts as to exclude any direct source-copy relationship.

[7] "Recent Developments in Bach Chronology", *The Musical Quarterly,* XLVI (1960), 288.

[8] The strongest of these indications is the fact that the oboe part A28 uniquely includes measures 10—11 of the "Violin I" line in place of the "Oboe" reading of part A4.

[9] Concerning this form of evidence and its implications, see NBA, *Kritischer Bericht* I/2, 19—21.

[10] This judgment was arrived at only after close inspection of the Berlin MS. A reversed sequence of the entries seems all but excluded not only by the spacing, but also by what appears to be a commingling of the ink of the horizontal line of deletion with that of the downward stroke of the "T", both of which obliterate portions of the slightly different-colored "4".

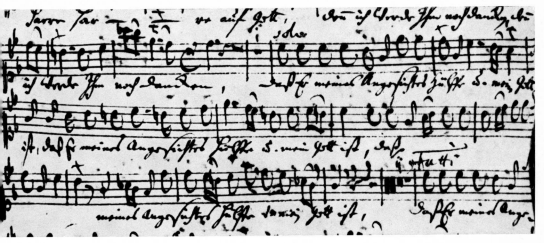

lin. Deutsche Staatsbibliothek, *Mus. ms. autogr. Bach St 354.* BWV 21, Soprano (Part A 8)

lin. *Mus. ms. autogr. Bach St 354.* BWV 21, Tenor (Part A 10)

existence. Only one of its scoring marks, consisting of short horizontal strokes across the barline, is visible in Plate I, following measure 48.

Parts G and *part-set(s) H:* "G" will designate in *NBA* those lost parts that can be presumed or conjectured as originally belonging to source A. Clearly missing are Timpani, Bassoon in c, and Trombone I; a few of the eight additional possibilities (none of which is of importance to the present discussion) are mentioned in our Table of A's contents. "H" is a collective designation for the lost parts that can be presumed to have belonged to scores C and D. Only one of them, the D-minor oboe part already mentioned as ante-dating A4, takes on more than token significance. Dubbed "H1" for *NBA* purposes, it (rather than score C itself) appears to have been the immediate source of the C-minor version A4/4a [11].

Text and Liturgical Designation

Though the composite character of Cantata 21 can be demonstrated beyond much doubt as a general proposition, the make-up of its original component works eludes precise description from the purely musical evidence at our disposal. It is thus especially regrett-able that we have not succeeded in discovering the sources of the cantata's text. True, nothing has emerged that might cast doubt on Philipp Spitta's identification of Salomon Franck as librettist [12]; but this by itself sheds little light on the larger question of BWV 21's genesis. Recently Helene Werthemann [13] drew attention to some striking parallels between the texts of movements 3—9 and the poetry of Johann Rist's *Jammer hat mich ganz umgeben* (1642), from which she deduced a direct borrowing on the part of Bach's librettist. Though this indeed appears likely, Werthemann's corollary — that *only* move-ments 3—9 formed the original nucleus of Cantata 21 — is not only indefensible on logical grounds, but also at least partially refutable by the evidence. From the longer discussion being prepared for NBA I should like to include here only a few principal points.

First, in judging what seem to be literary allusions, one must make every attempt to assess the possibility of coincidence. In movements 6 and 9 of Cantata 21, complete verses from Psalms 42 and 116, respectively, are quoted in apparent analogy to the older *Lied* of Rist, which unmistakably paraphrases the same two texts [14]. In German bibles of the period [15], however, it is fairly common to find marginal cross-references linking these same two psalm verses to each other, presumably because of their related thought-content. The Rist-Bach parallel, then, is by no means conclusive with respect

---

[11] The D-minor oboe part A28 shows fairly clear signs of transposition from a C-minor source, whereas, ironically, the reverse is true of A4/4a. From these and several other indications I have concluded that score C was notated with its oboe line at *Chorton* pitch (a common occurrence among Bach's scores of this period), and that it constitutes the putative source of A28, whereas A4/4a must have been copied from the hypothetical H1.

[12] Ph. Spitta, *J. S. Bach*, I, 527; cf. Dürr, *Studien*, 71, and Ferdinand Zander, *Die Dichter der Kantatentexte J. S. Bachs* (1967), 25—26.

[13] "Zum Text der Bach-Kantate 21", *Bach-Jahrbuch 1965*, 135—143.

[14] Werthemann, 139—140.

[15] e. g., several editions "*mit kurtzen Anmerkungen von M. Nicolao Haas*", published in Leipzig from 1707 onwards.

to this particular point. A second argument adduced by Werthemann may, however, indeed clinch the case of movement 9. It involves Bach's quotation of the Neumark chorale *Wer nur den lieben Gott lässt walten,* to which there is an apparent reference in the tenth strophe of Rist's poem. A double coincidence of this sort would hardly seem fortuitous; and in any case the assignment of the sixth and ninth movements to a common textual conception seems reasonably assured.

As for Werthemann's proposal that the second movement be excluded from the original corpus of the cantata, it is an argument based solely on the lack of any provable link between its text and that of Rist. But surely the chorus in question (unlike the final one) displays a remarkably organic textual relationship not only to the other two choruses, but also to most of the intervening movements. That relationship, moreover, is one in which the subsequent texts serve as a personalized exegesis of the psalm verse to which the first chorus is set, making the supposed later addition of the latter (either as an importation from still another pre-existing work, or as a new composition) an unlikely hypothesis indeed. We can note, in addition, a small but perhaps not insignificant change introduced into Bach's text. Orthographic variants aside, all of the 17th- and 18th-century bibles consulted for this study agree on the following reading of Ps. 94, 19:

> Ich hatte viel Bekümmernisse in meinem Hertzen,
> Aber deine Tröstungen ergötzten meine Seele.

Bach's change of verb *(erquicken* for *ergötzten)* might be quite simply explainable by the unvocal quality of the original, or (less simply) by the contemporary fondness, in quoting biblical texts, for alluding to one or more related passages [16]. Still more suggestive, however, is the change from past to present tense *(erquicken).* It establishes, in conjunction with the quasi-dramatic character of the following movements, a logical thought-connection that argues strongly for the inclusion of movement 2 as an integral part of the original conception (score C).

Finally, additional evidence can be gleaned from the works of Salomon Franck himself. A little-known cycle of cantata texts of his, published in 1711, contains numerous instances of a combination of biblical passages and "free" poetry similar to that found in Cantata 21. Of particular interest is his assemblage of biblical quotations for the Third Sunday after Trinity:

Vom verlohrnen Schaafe.
Ps. 35, v. 17. 18 / Die Angst meines Hertzens ist gross, führe mich aus meinen Nöthen; siehe an mein Jammer und Elend, und vergib mir alle meine Sünde. / Matth. 11, v. 28 / Kommet her zu mir alle, die ihr mühselig und beladen seyd, ich will euch erquicken!
Aria [4 strophes] / Chor. / Ps. 103, v. 2. / Lobe den Herren meine Seele, und vergiss nicht, was er dir gutes gethan hat [17].

[16] Among the relevant concordances, one in a Nürnberg bible edition of 1700 (*„auf Verordnung Ernsts, Hertzogen zu Sachsen"*) refers the reader of Psalm 94, 19 to Psalm 119 with its text, *dein Wort erquicket mich.* See also the Franck cantata text quoted further below.
[17] *Geist- und weltliche Poesien* (Jena, 1711), 177—179. According to L. Hoffmann-Erbrecht in *J. S. Bach in Thüringen* (1950), 125—126, the sacred poetry of the collection was written as early as 1694.

Note the striking similarities not only to movements 9 and 3 of BWV 21, but most especially to its initial chorus. No less interesting, of course, is the fact that this early Franck text is assigned to that Sunday of the liturgical calendar on which BWV 21 was performed in 1714: an indication that our score C was indeed a Third-Trinity cantata, and that the *Per ogni Tempo* designation on Bach's title-page [18] might well refer to some intended or actual performance on a different feast prior to June, 1714.

Concerning the aria movements of Cantata 21, it will be possible here only to summarize the *NBA* findings. Movement 10, the tenor aria *Erfreue dich, Seele,* may have either belonged to score D or been newly composed for inclusion along with the imported movement 11; it can be eliminated with some assurance from the assumed contents of score C. Potential doubts concerning the attribution of the duet movements 7 and 8 to score C appear to lack a cogent basis, either textual or musical [19]. All of the remaining movements appear safely attributable to our *Ur*-cantata C on either textual or musical grounds.

Performance History

The situation seen in Plate I is no isolated instance: All of the *solo* and *tutti* indications in parts A8, 10, 11, and 27 (with the possible exception of the chorale portions of movement 9 in A8 and 10) were added by Bach subsequent to the actual copying of those voice parts [20]. We can conjecture from this that at least one performance of Cantata 21 took place without the division of forces called for in its final version. Beyond the fact that they preceded the preparation of A24—26 in 1723, the entries in question cannot be dated precisely [21].

Greater certainty is attainable with respect to the varying distribution of the vocal solos between soprano and tenor, respectively, at different times in the cantata's history. A10 and 17 contain all, A8 *none* of the solo movements 3—5, 7, 8, and 10. A series

---

[18] Reproduced in Mendel, "Recent Developments", Plate I.

[19] Spitta (*Bach*, I, 531) described movement 8 as "geradezu ein wunder Punkt". Arthur Mendel ("Recent Developments", 288) inferred from a low B-flat in the continuo a downward transposition of movement 8 from an original version in F. But it was also Arthur who subsequently pointed out to me that his hypothesis would imply original voice compasses lying well above anything found elsewhere in Bach. Werthemann (p. 140) adduces at least one very persuasive argument for the inclusion of the duet on textual grounds. The credentials of the preceding accompanied recitative are somewhat weaker.

[20] Original markings are completely lacking in A9 and 17; their absence in A24 and 25 is insignificant, since these two *ripieno* parts substitute rests for all the *solo* portions of A10 and 11. This latter fact does, however, prove that the autograph *solo* and *tutti* marks in A10—11 antedate the copying of A24—25, since the two pairs of parts have a provable source-copy relationship.

[21] One is tempted to associate them with Mendel's reading of Bach's 1714 title-page inscription as „*musicieret choraliter*" ("Recent Developments", 287); but Arthur informs me he has meanwhile accepted "*musicieret worden*", a reading privately communicated to him and to Alfred Dürr by the handwriting authority Hans-Joachim Schulze. I can only concur in Schulze's opinion — somewhat reluctantly in view of the enticements presented by the above evidence, but with virtually no doubt as to the correctness of the revised reading.

of autograph revisions, consisting of two kinds of brackets and accompanying verbal directions, reflects two different stages beyond the all-tenor version represented by the original state of part A10. (See Plate II). In the first revision, corresponding to the preparation of A17 sometime after 1717, all solo movements were transferred from tenor to soprano; the inscription visible in Plate II reads, *NB. Diese Aria, folgendes Recit: und hernach kommende Aria gehören in den Diskant.* At a later date, almost certainly in connection with the Leipzig performance of 1723, a new set of brackets, together with deletions and *tacet* marks as visible in the Plate, established the distribution of solo movements adopted by the BG edition [22].

Virtually nothing, of course, is known of the performance history of the individual components of the cantata prior to their incorporation into the version we know. Even that version, however, almost certainly antedates by at least a few months the 1714 performance recorded by Bach on the title-page of *St 354*. Two main points can be adduced in support of this contention. First, the discrepancy, noted above, between the *Per ogni Tempo* title-page heading and the apparently later addition re-linking the cantata to what was almost surely its original liturgical designation. Second, the fact that the earliest preserved part-set includes an oboe in C (A4/4a) and hence must have been prepared for a performance at *Kammerton* pitch. Should this indeed correspond to the autograph date on the title-page, that would make Cantata 21 an unique exception to all that we know of Bach's practice in Weimar. Far likelier, I believe, is that A28 or a lost D-minor oboe part was employed for the 1714 performance (at C-*Chorton*), and that A4/4a represents an earlier performance, either actual or planned.

In his well-known letter of March 19, 1714, to August Becker at Halle, Bach writes of a "certain piece" which he had been "compelled" to compose and perform *(genöthiget ... zu componiren u. aufzuführen)* in connection with his candidacy to become Zachow's successor in Halle the preceding December [23]. Friedrich Chrysander [24] conjectured in 1858 that Cantata 21 was the work in question; unfortunately, he gave no reasons or supporting evidence. Since 1951, there has been a tendency to discount Chrysander's remark in favor of Dürr's detailed argument to the effect that, if BWV 21 was performed in Halle at all [25], then only in a form antedating the present one. The evidence cited above, however, would seem to remove most of the serious obstacles to a reinstatement of the Chrysander hypothesis. The principal remaining difficulty is that we

---

[22] It may in fact be closer to Bach's original conception than A10 might seem to suggest: Dialogs such as those found in movements 7—8 traditionally associated the Soul with soprano voice. In the Weimar bass part A11 one finds *tacet* directions describing movement 3 as *Soprano Solo con oboe*, but also movement 5 as *Aria soprano*, which might well describe the situation in the lost score C. Movement 10 appears to have been assigned to tenor throughout all traceable stages except that of the first revision.

[23] *Bach-Dokumente*, ed. by Werner Neumann and Hans-Joachim Schulze, I (1963), 23—24; *The Bach Reader*, ed. by Hans T. David and Arthur Mendel (1945; revised ed. 1966), 68.

[24] *G. F. Händel*, I (1858), 22.

[25] Cantata 63 seemed to Dürr a likelier candidate; cf. *Studien*, 52.

are still unable to prove the existence of a *Kammerton* organ at the Marktkirche in Halle prior to the 1716 documents reported by Serauky [26].

At any rate, the performance of June, 1714, appears to be at least the second one given the cantata in its preserved, composite form. The subsequent D-minor *(Kammerton)* performance reflected by the second part-group in A may conceivably have taken place when Bach visited Hamburg late in 1720 to apply for the vacant organist's position at the Jakobikirche [27]. The dating of the one provable Leipzig performance (others are of course likely) on June 13, 1723, is confirmed by both watermark and handwriting evidence (early handwriting stage of the principal copyist, J. A. Kuhnau, formerly known as "Hauptkopist A") [28].

The Variants and Conjectures in BG

The edition of Cantata 21 prepared for BG by Wilhelm Rust is, on the whole, a remarkably perceptive, judicious, and accurate one. Readily audible differences between it and the forthcoming NBA edition are few in number, and mostly of two basic kinds: (1) those resulting from Rust's complete reliance on the C-minor oboe version A4/4a and its copy A23, to the neglect of the D-minor readings of A28; and (2) those attributable to Rust's refusal to accept certain other readings, not contested within source A, as an accurate reflection of Bach's intentions. It will be *NBA*'s contention (1) that the D-minor oboe readings, though preserved in a slightly later source, are generally closer to those of score C and hence provide, at the very least, an indispensable corrective in those cases where A4/4a is ambiguous or defective; and (2) that at least two of the most problematic passages altered by Rust without support from source A are in fact preferable to his, or to any other philologically defensible, conjectures.

Example 1a provides one of the clearest indications that A4a reflects a downward transposition from an original conceived, and probably notated, in D minor [29]. The C-minor version, autograph at this point, avoids an unplayable low d-flat, at the same

---

[26] Walter Serauky, *Musikgeschichte der Stadt Halle*, II, 1 (1939), 487. I am grateful to Dr. Berndt Baselt for information concerning his researches in Halle.

[27] Max Seiffert, "Seb. Bachs Bewerbung um die Organistenstelle an St. Jakobi in Hamburg 1720", *AfMw* III (1921), 123—127.

[28] Alfred Dürr, "Zur Chronologie der Leipziger Vokalwerke J. S. Bachs", *Bach-Jahrbuch 1957*, 21—26.

[29] Another among several confirming indications: Movement 3 is notated in A4a with a defective signature of one flat throughout. Both of these points were first drawn to my attention by Arthur Mendel in 1962. Mention should also be made here of the rather puzzling fact that *tacet* directions occur in place of both the oboe solos, movements 1 and 3, in part A4. I believe that this resulted from a simple misunderstanding on the part of Bach's copyist. It seems quite plausible that the composer, anticipating the need for range adjustments in connection with the transposition of the *Sinfonia* (cf. Ex. 1a), instructed the copyist to omit the oboe solos for the time being in preparing part A4. Instead of allowing the necessary space, the scribe mistakenly inferred that the oboe was not to participate in the two movements at all. At the very least, the presence of the same Weimar watermark in A4a as in A4 does not contradict the assumption that the half-leaf insert A4a was prepared immediately upon discovery of the omissions in the main part.

Ex. 1

time introducing three new rhythmic subdivisions on the surrounding beats, in compensation (as it were) for the loss of motion on the first beat of measure 14. This finding, of course, in no way questions the authority of the autograph reading. It does, however, justify a closer examination of two additional places in the movement. Though it is anything but characteristic for Bach's own parts to contain transposition errors, Example 1b might well show one of the rare exceptions, explainable by the discrepancy in key signatures between A4a and the hypothetical H1 as reflected indirectly by A28. At any rate, given the A28 reading, the insertion of an editorial a-flat accidental at this point in the C-minor version has much to commend it on both musical and philological grounds [30].

---

[30] Bach's e-natural, on the other hand, is surely preferable to the A28 reading, which might itself be a transposition error in the opposite direction; cf. fn. 11.

In measure 12 of the *Sinfonia* (Example 1c), both oboe versions are rhythmically defective. Whereas the error in A28 lends itself readily to reconstruction (the scribe having mistakenly connected the topmost beam to the preceding quarter-note), Bach's intentions in A4a are less clear. He, too, has misdrawn the top beam, extending it all the way to the dotted b-natural, then noticeably blotting away the dot, as if to delete it. (The scribe of A23, copying from A4a, has faithfully reproduced the latter, but *without* the dot). The third line of the Example suggests what Bach may have intended by the deletion. Even if correct, however, this conjecture, representing as it does an attempt to "rescue" the original beaming error (which would have been considerably more difficult to undo altogether), is probably a less satisfactory reading than that of the easily reconstructible and perfectly plausible version in A28. The BG conjecture (fourth line of the Example), though acceptable in the musical context, seems to depart unnecessarily far from both original readings.

A second, equally unsuccessful, rescue attempt appears to have been made by the scribe of A15 in the fourth movement (Example 2). Copying from A6 (this is independ-

Ex. 2

BWV 21 / 4

A6

[A15]

ently demonstrable), he restored the missing fourth beat of measure 16 by the simple expedient of eliminating an eighth-note beam; Rust has adopted the "corrected" reading. It would seem, however, that the insertion of a quarter-note f' at this point in A6 provides a more satisfactory conjecture.

Example 3 illustrates another instance of the superior, or at least equal, credibility of A28 as compared to A4, which at this point is in the hand of Scribe 1. Rust's adoption of the A4 reading is debatable on two grounds. It introduces an uncharacteristic doubling of the trilled fifth of the dominant chord, and it eliminates altogether the suspension figure clearly called for by the continuo figuration, prepared by the downward leap of a fifth in the oboe, and present in *no other* line of the texture at this point.

Ex. 3

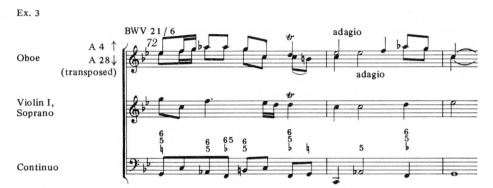

As for the f″ found in A4 on the third beat of measure 73, it would not be suspect, despite the lack of any provision for it in the continuo figures, did we not have the testimony of A28 that at least one early version existed without it.

Ex. 4

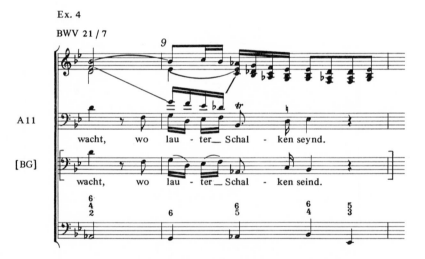

We turn now to two passages that fell victim to Rust's disbelief in what the sources clearly suggest was Bach's intention. Example 4 reproduces the contents of A11 (our sole preserved source for the vocal bass line in question) in the phrase leading up to the cadence in measure 9 of the seventh movement. Rust defends the BG reading by the none-too-plausible conjecture that either the copyist of A11 or his source mistakenly rendered the fifth and sixth notes of measure 9 a tone too high; that would not, of course, explain Rust's choice of B-flat for the final tone of the phrase. I should like to suggest that A11 is completely accurate at this point. Though I know of no exact analogy, and not even a partial one for a feature like the tonicization of the continuo A-flat on the second beat of measure 9, Cantatas 18 and 119 do offer fairly close counterparts to the voice-continuo clash [31] at that point, and to the following dominant-tonic simultaneity [32] produced by the original cadence-tone. Let it be noted, by the way, that the harshness of the trilled B-flat is considerably mitigated by proper execution of the trill. It seems impossible, in any event, to arrive at another, musically defensible, reading that would at the same time explain the version that has been preserved.

Ex. 5

BWV 21 / 11

Finally, there is a key place near the end of the final chorus (measure 65) where Rust has quietly suppressed the original, unchanged readings of all four voice parts (Example 5) in favor of a single half-note chord sustained through beats 3 and 4. One supposes that his objections were both musical and syntactical; the word *Lob* otherwise occurs only at phrase beginnings, and on strong beats of the measure, throughout the rest of this movement. On studying the local context, however, one discovers that the suppressed chord forms the second of a continuous series of quarter-note impulses, distributed antiphonally in measures 66—67 between brass, timpani, and continuo on the one hand, and oboe, strings, and bassoon on the other, and serving each time as the rhythmic "jumping-off-point" of the sixteenth-note figure in trumpet, oboe, first violin, soprano, etc. Though Rust's unease about the chorus's *Lob* is perhaps understandable, his elimination of it ought not to be perpetuated any longer as a supposed representation of Bach's intentions.

---

[31] BWV 119, fourth movement, measure 16; cf. BG XXIV, 223.
[32] BWV 18, third movement, measure 4; cf. NBA I/7, 92.

TABLE

Source A: Berlin, Deutsche Staatsbibliothek,
Mus. ms. autogr. Bach St 354 (formerly *56ᵃ*)

No.		Part	Copyists	Remarks
First part-group (Weimar watermark):				
1—3	(27—29)*	Tromba I—III	JSB	Tamburi part missing
4	(17)	Oboe (in c)	1, JSB	Mvts. 1, 3 marked *tacet* (!)
4a		Oboe (in c)	JSB, 2	Half-leaf insert; mvts. 1, 3 only
5	(10)	Violino I (in c)	JSB, 1	
6	(12)	Violino II (in c)	3	Possibly a duplicate part; if so, original lost
7	(15)	Viola (in c)	4	
8	(2)	Soprano	JSB	Contains the choruses only; other mvts. *tacet*
10	(3)	Alto	JSB	
11	(5/6)	Tenore	JSB	
	(8)	Basso	5	
12	(23)	Violoncello (in c)	1	Copied from composite original score
9				(C/D), not from A13
	(25)	Organo (in c)	1, JSB	Continuo figures (JSB) apparently not
13				added until after preparation of score E
Second part-group (Köthen watermark):				
14	(11)	Violino I (in d)	6	Source possibly score D in mvt. 11, mvt. 10 uncertain; the remainder probably copied from A5
15	(13)	Violino II (in d)	6	Copied from A6 or its original
16	(14)	Viola (in d)	6	Copied from A7
17	(1)	Soprano	JSB	Presumably copied from A8 and 10
18	(22)	Fagotto (in d)	6	C-minor original missing from Weimar group
19	(24)	Violoncello (in d)	6	Copied from A12; an additional continuo part lost?
Third part-group (Leipzig watermark):				
20—22	(19—21)	Trombone II—IV (in b-flat)	7	Probably copied from A6, 7, and the lost c-minor Fagotto, respectively; Trombone I missing
23	(18)	Oboe (in c)	7	Copied from A4/4a
24	(7)	Tenore in Ripieno	8	Copied from A10
25	(9)	Basso in Ripieno	9	Copied from A11
26	(26)	Continuo (in b-flat)	7	Copied from A13
Parts of uncertain date and grouping:				
27	(4)	Alto	10	Copied from A9, 1723 or earlier; *tutti-solo* marks autograph
28	(16)	Oboe (in d)	11	Weimar origin probable

* Parts are listed according to their planned NBA reference numbers, in score order for each chronological group. Numbers in parentheses are the pencilled modern inventory numbers of the Berlin library.

ALFRED DÜRR

De vita cum imperfectis

Die Neuausgabe alter Musik, ein wesentliches Betätigungsfeld der Musikwissenschaft, verfolgt meist einen doppelten Zweck: Sie will das geschichtliche Bewußtsein bilden und zugleich der gegenwärtigen Musizierpraxis neues Material liefern — ein Ziel, für das das vielstrapazierte Wort vom „zu Unrecht vergessenen Meister" ein ebenso beredter wie dubioser Zeuge ist.

Die herausgeberische Methode, nach der dabei verfahren wird, setzt die unbestreitbar hohe Qualität des zu edierenden Werkes als gegeben voraus; das Original, so wie es der Meister konzipiert hat, gilt als makellos. Daraus folgt: Alle Fehler, mit denen das Werk auf uns gekommen ist, gehen zu Lasten schlechter Überlieferung und sind daher in der Neuausgabe zu beseitigen; alle Zutaten, die dem Werk von fremder Hand im Laufe der Überlieferung zugefügt wurden, sind der Meisterschaft des Komponisten inadäquat und daher gleichfalls zu beseitigen. Dies führt zum Ideal der „Urtextausgabe"; und wenn dieser Begriff auch in den letzten Jahrzehnten eine recht unterschiedliche Auslegung erfahren hat, so will er doch besagen, daß sich die Neuausgabe so weit wie irgend möglich am Zeugnis des Komponisten selbst orientieren müsse und daß fremde Interpretation jeglicher Art auszuschalten sei.

Nun soll die weitgehende Gültigkeit der dargelegten Grundsätze gar nicht bestritten werden. Aber gerade wer sie befolgt, wer der Überzeugung ist, daß die Verdeutlichung des Willens eines Komponisten ein Postulat der Wahrhaftigkeit ist, ohne die unsere Wissenschaft ihren Sinn verliert, der wird sich zugleich auch der Grenzen der Methode bewußt sein müssen, ehe er sie recht zu handhaben versteht. Von diesen Grenzen soll im folgenden ein wenig die Rede sein. Gerade ein Werk wie Johann Sebastian Bachs Matthäus-Passion, an dessen Neuausgabe der Schreiber dieser Zeilen gegenwärtig (1971) arbeitet, ist geeignet, die Problematik zu verdeutlichen, weil hier Zweifel an der Qualität des Werkes und an den Fähigkeiten seines Komponisten kaum am Platze sind, der Blick sich also desto ausschließlicher auf die herausgeberischen Probleme konzentrieren kann.

Zunächst stellt sich die Frage, inwieweit das originale *Schriftbild* des Partiturautographs in der Neuausgabe zu konservieren sei. Wo immer von der Schönschriftpartitur eines Komponisten die Rede ist, wird man das Autograph in der Deutschen Staatsbibliothek Berlin *Mus. ms. Bach P 25* nicht unerwähnt lassen dürfen; und da Bachs Schriftduktus nach dem übereinstimmenden Urteil aller Forscher bereits dem Auge — und dem inneren Ohr — Wesentliches über Bachs Musik verrät, wird das Bestreben jedes Herausgebers dahin zielen, von diesem Schriftbild nicht mehr als nötig abzuweichen. Max Schneider hat diese Forderung in seiner 1935 bei Breitkopf & Härtel in Leipzig erschienenen Neuausgabe auf exemplarische Weise verwirklicht; und darum zeigt auch das Ergebnis die Problematik solchen Verfahrens besonders deutlich. So faßt Bach z. B. die zwei Continuosysteme im ersten der beiden Chorsätze „Laß ihn kreuzigen" auf Bl. 54r der Partitur viereinhalb Takte lang auf dem untersten System zusammen: Für ihre

Aufteilung in der sonst üblichen Weise wäre kein Raum mehr verfügbar gewesen. Auf
Bl. 54v dagegen reicht der Raum aus, und für die übrigen vier Takte des Satzes erhält
daher jeder Chor sein eigenes Continuosystem. Gleiches wiederholt sich beim zweiten
Chorsatz desselben Textes, der auf Bl. 56v fünfeinhalb Takte lang mit nur einem
Continuosystem notiert werden mußte, während auf Bl. 57r für den Rest des Satzes
ausreichend Platz zur Aufteilung der Continuopartien auf zwei Systeme verfügbar war.
— Max Schneider notiert beide Sätze durchgehend mit nur einem Continuosystem (als
unterstem der Akkolade), erhebt also Bachs durch Platzmangel bedingte Notlösung zum
Regelfall. Wenn aber derartiges geschieht, müßte man dann in der Neuausgabe nicht
auch den Raummangel nachbilden, damit der Benutzer den Sinn dieser Partituranordnung
einzusehen in der Lage ist? Ist nicht die Verdeutlichung dessen, was den Komponisten
veranlaßt, so und nicht anders zu verfahren, wichtiger als die sklavische Kopie des äußeren
Schriftbildes? Ist aber Raummangel des Komponisten überhaupt wert, in einer Neuausgabe konserviert zu werden? Blinder Autoritätsglaube („er wird schon gewußt haben,
warum") ist hier fehl am Platze; der Herausgeber muß selbst für seine Entscheidung
einstehen.

Ein weiteres Problem stellt die Behandlung von *Satzfehlern* dar. Bekanntlich ist Johannes Schreyer in seinen „Beiträgen zur Bachkritik" (I, II, Leipzig 1911, 1913) von der
Voraussetzung ausgegangen, daß Bach schon in seinen Erstlingswerken einen fehlerlosen
musikalischen Satz nicht nur zu schreiben imstande war, sondern auch stets geschrieben
hat (was nicht unbedingt dasselbe bedeutet), daß also Kompositionen mit eklatanten
Satzfehlern nicht von Bach stammen könnten. Bei mangelhafter Quellenüberlieferung
können aber solche Satzfehler auch als Kopierfehler eingedrungen sein, und darum pflegt
unsere Editionspraxis sie auch vielfach zu emendieren. Es wäre darum wahrscheinlich
reizvoll, zu untersuchen, inwieweit Schreyer ein Opfer unterschiedlicher Editionspraxis
gewesen ist, indem er Werke, deren Herausgeber mit Satzfehlern kritisch verfuhren,
für echt ansah, andere jedoch, deren Herausgeber einen weniger strengen Maßstab an-
legten, für unecht.

Nun hat Bach aber auch zuweilen Satzfehler stehen lassen, sei es, daß er sie übersah,
sei es, daß er sie für tragbar hielt, und das erschwert die Arbeit des Herausgebers. Hier
kann also die These von der Makellosigkeit der Konzeption des Komponisten nicht alle
Schwierigkeiten beseitigen (erinnert sei an den ersten Satz des fünften Brandenburgischen
Konzerts, Takt 11 — vgl. den Kritischen Bericht der Neuen Bach-Ausgabe, Serie VII,
Bd. 2, S. 128—129); und wiederum wird man den Herausgeber nicht von der Verant-
wortung für die eigene Entscheidung entbinden können, ob er z. B. im Chor „Sind
Blitze, sind Donner in Wolken verschwunden" Stellen wie diese ändern will oder nicht:

Notenbeispiel 1
„Sind Blitze, sind Donner", Takt 108 - 109

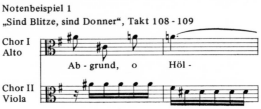

(analog auch die Takte 112—113, 116—117). Das Auflösungszeichen zum dritten Achtel des Taktes 108 ist von Bach aus einem Kreuz korrigiert worden, die Parallelstellen entsprechen unkorrigiert der neuen Lesart; und die Frage, ob Bach den vorübergehenden Zusammenklang a'—ais' für tragbar hielt oder einfach übersehen hat, wird wohl niemals mehr sicher entschieden werden können. Nur eines ist gewiß: Musiziert wurde die Stelle unter Bach so, wie sie unser Beispiel zeigt; denn so steht sie auch in den Originalstimmen.

Wollte man aber glauben, eine Lesart sei darum gesichert, weil sie in *Bachs eigenen Aufführungen* so erklungen sein muß, so würde man kaum einen brauchbaren Maßstab für die Neuausgabe gewinnen. Denn Bachs Originalstimmen sind voller Fehler, von denen der Benutzer heutiger Neuausgaben durch unsere Editionsmethode sorgsam abgeschirmt wird, die nichtsdestoweniger die Aufführungen Bachscher Kompositionen unter Leitung des Komponisten bisweilen mit recht seltsamen Klängen durchsetzt haben müssen. Geht man diesen Klängen ein wenig nach, fragt man also nicht, wie ein Werk eigentlich klingen *sollte*, sondern wie es unter Bachs Leitung notwendigerweise klingen *mußte*, so bietet sich auch hier die Matthäus-Passion als vorzügliches Beispiel an, wurde doch ihr Stimmenmaterial sorgfältiger als die meisten anderen geschrieben, so daß die Entschuldigung, die Aufführung sei eben in ungewöhnlicher Eile und darum nicht hinreichend vorbereitet worden, wegfällt. Denn:

1. Die Partiturvorlage war gegen jede Gewohnheit eine ausgezeichnet lesbare Reinschrift.
2. Die Stimmen wurden weitgehend von Bach selbst, andere von weiteren Mitgliedern der Familie Bach geschrieben.
3. Die Stimmen wurden zu mindestens zwei Aufführungen verwendet; was sich also in der ersten Aufführung als fehlerhaft erwiesen hatte, konnte zur Wiederaufführung revidiert werden.
4. Der Aufführung ging die kantatenlose Fastenzeit voran, in der nicht nur Bach, sondern auch seine Kopisten weniger als sonst beansprucht waren.

Und das Ergebnis? — Greifen wir einige ausgewählte Stellen heraus!

Natürlich erweisen sich die nichtautographen Stimmen als die ergiebigsten Fehlerquellen; Bach selbst kopiert sein Werk im allgemeinen verläßlich. Trotzdem — was soll der um eine quellengetreue *Artikulation* bemühte Bachverehrer nun für richtig halten, wenn er Bachs autographe (!) Bogensetzung vergleicht und dabei im Schlußchor auf Stellen wie diese stößt:

Notenbeispiel 2
„Wir setzen uns mit Tränen nieder", Takt 23 - 24
Chor II
Partitur
Flauto traverso I II

Da die fremdschriftlichen Stimmen der (hier mit Chor II unisono geführten) Querflöten des Chores I der Lesart aus Bachs Partitur (wie oben) folgen, müssen also die vier unisono spielenden Flöten diesen Takt in dreifach unterschiedlicher Artikulation geboten haben, deren jede unmittelbar auf Bach zurückgeht, sofern sie den Bögen, die sie in ihren Stimmen vorfanden, überhaupt einige Bedeutung beimaßen.

Daß die Unsicherheit bei Mithilfe weiterer Kopisten steigt, zeigt ein Beispiel, das wir gleichfalls dem Schlußchor entnehmen. In Takt 41 lautet der Continuopart beider Chöre gleich, und obwohl das Partiturautograph hier unbezeichnet ist, läßt doch die Parallelstelle in Takt 29 erkennen, welche Artikulation von Bach beabsichtigt war:

Notenbeispiel 3
„Wir setzen uns mit Tränen nieder", Takt 29

Chor I, II
Continuo

So schreibt Bach daher auch in der Continuostimme des Chores II, während die Kopisten der Dublette (Anna Magdalena Bach) und der Orgelstimme (Gottfried Heinrich Bach?) sich mit kurzen, flüchtig hingeworfenen Bögen begnügen. In Chor I dagegen muß Bach beim Ausschreiben der Continuostimme nach der vierten Note die Zeile wechseln und trägt keine Bedenken, den Bogen zu teilen: 2.—4., 5.—6. Note. Auch hier kopiert Anna Magdalena die Dublette; sie kann den Takt noch vollständig auf der alten Zeile unterbringen und kopiert den ersten Bogen ihres Gatten getreu, den zweiten vergißt sie. Gottfried Heinrich Bach (?), der Kopist der Orgelstimme, muß an derselben Stelle wie sein Vater die Zeile wechseln. Er aber läßt den ersten Bogen weg und setzt nur den zweiten. Nimmt man nun an, alle Aufführenden hätten die Artikulationsbezeichnung ihrer Stimmen ernst genommen, so wären die Noten zwar durchweg unisono erklungen; die Artikulation jedoch hätte folgende Unterschiede aufgewiesen:

Chor I

Continuo, 1. Pult: 2.—4., 5.—6. Note gebunden
          2. Pult: 2.—4.   Note gebunden
Organo: 5.—6. Note gebunden

Chor II

Continuo, 1. Pult: 2.   —   6. Note gebunden
          2. Pult: 3.   —   6. Note gebunden
Organo: 3.—4. (5.?) Note gebunden

Die genannten Stellen mögen beispielhaft sein; ungewöhnliche Ausnahmen sind sie nicht.

Seltsam widersprüchlich ist auch die Artikulation in der Arie „Mache dich, mein Herze, rein". Während nämlich Oboe da caccia I und die Erstkopie der Violine I die Sechzehntelmotive, dem Partiturautograph folgend, in der uns vertrauten Weise artikulieren, weicht die von Anna Magdalena Bach geschriebene Violindublette konsequent hiervon ab:

Notenbeispiel 4

„Mache dich, mein Herze, rein", Takt 4 - 5 und Parallelstellen

Ob. da c. I, Viol. I
Viol. I Dublette

Dabei steht der Punkt auch mehrfach — ganz widersinnig — über der 3. statt 4. Note.

Einzelne *falsche Noten* treten vielfach auf; doch mögen sie den Gesamtklang nicht allzu spürbar beeinflußt haben. Ähnliches gilt von stellenweise fehlerhafter Bezifferung. Unerfreulicher wird es schon, wenn eine Reihe falscher Töne aufeinanderfolgt, etwa im Chor „Sind Blitze, sind Donner", wo sich die Violinen I des I. Chors infolge einer Unaufmerksamkeit Anna Magdalenas in Takt 91 für einige Noten entzweien:

Notenbeispiel 5
„Sind Blitze, sind Donner", Takt 91

Chor I

Violino I 1. Pult
2. Pult

Ähnliches gilt für den Chor „Weissage", wo der Kopist des Tenorparts des I. Chores in Takt 31 wegen graphischer Gleichheit des Anfangs in den Altpart hineingerät, was dann folgenden „reizvollen" Zusammenklang ergibt:

Notenbeispiel 6
„Weissage", Takt 31
Chor I

Soprano, Alto
Tenore

Basso
Continuo

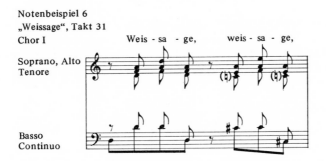

Sicherlich werden die Tenöre hier nicht ernstlich c′ gegen cis′ gesungen haben (das cis′ in Chor II schon 1 Achtel früher); aber richtig gesungen haben sie in gar keinem Fall!

Peinlich muß es auch geklungen haben, wenn die Differenzen gerade auf den Anfang eines Themas fallen, über dessen endgültige Gestalt sich Bach offenbar selbst nicht rechtzeitig klargeworden war — so im Chor „Wozu dienet dieser Unrat":

Notenbeispiel 7

„Wozu dienet dieser Unrat", Takt 12

Viola
Tenore

Un - rat? Die - ses Was - ser hät - te

Schlagartig schweigen hier nach dem 1. Taktviertel alle Stimmen bis auf die beiden in Sekundintervallen einsetzenden Thementräger!

Ähnlich unerquicklich sind Dissonanzen innerhalb eines Cantus firmus. In „O Mensch, bewein dein Sünde groß" waren Bachs Transpositionskorrekturen im Partiturautograph Anlaß für einen Lesefehler des Kopisten in Takt 41, der zu einer Entzweiung der Melodieträger führte:

Notenbeispiel 8

„O Mensch, bewein dein Sünde groß", Takt 41

Soprano in ripieno, Organo
Soprano (Chor I + II)

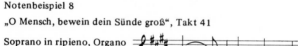

für_____   uns   er   hie   ge - - (boren ward)

Wenig später, in Takt 46, spaltete sich der Chorsopran I nochmals für 2 Töne ab, was zwar innerhalb des Soprans zu lieblichen Terzenparallelen, dafür aber mit dem Tenor zu Sekundreibungen führte:

Soprano, Organo: a'   gis'
                     fis'   e'
Tenore: e'   dis'

Auch das gleichzeitige Erklingen zweier Lesarten, deren jede für sich sinnvoll ist, kann die beabsichtigte Wirkung verfehlen. Im Rezitativ „Ach Golgatha", in dem übrigens ein Kopierfehler in Oboe da caccia I bereits zu unerfreulichen Dissonanzen der beiden letzten Noten des Taktes 6

Oboe da caccia I: as' ges'
Oboe da caccia II: ges' f'

geführt hatte, wählt Bach für den Schlußtakt in den Continuostimmen offenbar spontan im Zuge des Ausschreibens eine Sonderlesart (Ganzenote As), die er dann in der Orgelstimme eigenhändig in die Lesart der Partitur zurückkorrigiert, in den beiden übrigen Continuostimmen jedoch stehen läßt — ein Verfahren, das bei der originalen Aufführung zu folgendem Klangbild geführt haben muß:

Notenbeispiel 9
„Ach Golgatha", Takt 14 - 15

Es steht zu hoffen, daß der Organist in der rechten Hand wenigstens (klingend) des gegriffen hat, obwohl die autographe Bezifferung eigentlich d verlangt.

Überhaupt zählen *Akzidenzienfehler* zu den häufigsten, vielfach veranlaßt durch gedankenloses Weiterführen einer nicht mehr zutreffenden Vorzeichnung durch den Kopisten. Wir dürfen annehmen, daß einige derartige Fälle bei der Aufführung instinktiv richtiggestellt wurden. Selbstverständlich haben z. B. die Soprane des II. Chores im folgenden Beispiel nicht wirklich a″ und a′ statt as″ und as′ gesungen, obwohl das dritte ♭ in der Vorzeichnung fehlte. Aber ob auch die Altisten des I. Chors, die in ihren Stimmen überhaupt keine Schlüsselakzidenzien vorfanden, alle Noten korrekt gesungen haben werden, da sie doch, wie üblich, keinerlei Stichnoten oder sonstige Hinweise auf die richtige Tonart zur Verfügung hatten, das scheint schon fraglicher. Immerhin konnten sie sich wenigstens an den mitgehenden Instrumenten und den Sängern des jeweils andern Chores orientieren, deren Stimmen korrekt notiert waren.

Notenbeispiel 10
„Wahrlich, dieser ist Gottes Sohn gewesen", Takt 19 - 21

Wenig mag es auch aufgefallen sein, daß der Alt des I. Chors das Wort „Barrabam"
auf cis" statt c" sang, weil der Kopist die 2♯-Vorzeichnung des Satzanfangs beibehalten hatte.

Schlimmer wirken sich Akzidenzienfehler in den Instrumentalstimmen aus, da die
Spieler gewöhnlich auf das Treffen des geforderten Tones weniger Reflexion verwenden
als die Sänger. Im Chor „Was gehet uns das an" entzweien sich z. B. die beiden Pulte
der Violine I (Chor I), da die Duplierstimme versehentlich die A-Dur-Vorzeichnung des
voraufgehenden Chorals beibehält:

Notenbeispiel 11

„Was gehet uns das an", Takt 18 - 19

Chor I

Es reizt den Betrachter dieser Takte, sich vorzustellen, wie Bach den Violinspielern,
nachdem sie zweimal nacheinander cis" und c" zugleich erklingen ließen, wütend zu-
gerufen haben mag: „c!"; und wenn die Spieler geistesgegenwärtig genug waren, griffen
sie beim dritten Mal wirklich c". Nur leider — hier wäre allerdings cis" am Platze
gewesen! Wenn dann im folgenden Takt 20 der II. Oboer (Chor I) als 2. Note noch f'
statt fis' spielte — seine Stimme enthielt nämlich überhaupt keine Vorzeichnung! —
und der Alt (Chor I) als letzte Note a' statt g' sang, mögen alle Beteiligten mit
Genugtuung wahrgenommen haben, daß der Chorsatz im darauffolgenden Takt ohne
weitere Panne zu Ende ging.

Das letzte Mal freilich war es nicht, daß unterschiedliche Vorzeichnung zu einer Kako-
Heterophonie unisono geführter Instrumente führte. Im Chorsatz „Andern hat er geholfen" behält der Kopist der Flöte II (Chor I) die 2♯-Vorzeichnung des vorhergehen-
den Chores („Der du den Tempel Gottes zerbrichst") bei, was zu häufigen c"/cis"-
Zusammenklängen mit Flöte I führt, zuletzt in dem berühmten Unisono(?)-Schluß

Notenbeispiel 12

„Andern hat er geholfen", Takt 63

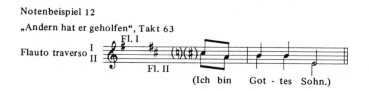

Eine sicherlich ungewollte Textinterpretation boten auch die beiden Pulte der Violine II (Chor II) in dem Rezitativ „Erbarm es Gott", in dem die Duplierstimme zu

Takt 6 zweimal ais' vorschreibt, obwohl die autographe Erstkopie deutlich a' verlangt:

Notenbeispiel 13
„Erbarm es Gott", Takt 6

Hier ist wahrhaftig Picanders Text am Platze: „Erweichet euch ... der Anblick solches Jammers nicht?"!

Am schwersten sind *ausgelassene Takte* oder Taktteile für den Spieler zu korrigieren. Hier hilft kein Instinkt; unausweichlich spielt der Spieler zunächst eine Reihe falscher Noten, bis er merkt, daß nicht nur ein Verschreibungsfehler einzelner Noten vorliegt, er muß aussetzen und warten, bis er den Anschluß wieder gefunden hat. Das mag mit Bachs Hilfe zuweilen schnell gegangen sein; aber ohne falsche Töne und nachfolgendes Aussetzen sind solche Auslassungen nicht zu bewältigen.

Wenige Takte nach der eben geschilderten Panne haben die Spieler des 2. Pults der Violine II (Chor II) schon wieder Anlaß, ganz schuldlos den Zorn Bachs auf sich zu laden, findet sich doch der Beginn der Arie „Können Tränen meiner Wangen" in ihrer Stimme in einer vom Komponisten ungewollten Kurzform, die auf Takt 4a gleich Takt 6b folgen läßt:

Notenbeispiel 14
„Können Tränen meiner Wangen", Takt 1 ff.

Nach Takt 5 etwa mögen die Spieler — hoffentlich die richtigen! — ausgesetzt haben. Aber ihr Leidensweg ist noch nicht zu Ende. Fehlten eben nur zwei Takte, so fehlen zwischen Takt 58 und 64 deren fünf, was das Hineinfinden erschwert. Etwas verwundert mögen sie die Schlußnote g (Takt 64) in den Dominantnonenakkord der übrigen Instrumente (Takt 59) hineingespielt haben, und wir wollen hoffen, daß sie rechtzeitig merkten, *woran* dieser Fehler lag. Hätten sie nämlich ihre folgenden Pausen (Takt 64—68) gewissenhaft durchgezählt, so wäre ihr Einsatz — forte! — genau mit dem Mittelteil des Altparts zusammengetroffen und hätte den Sänger alsbald hoffnungslos aus dem Konzept gebracht. Nun, da vielleicht gar nur *ein* Spieler am zweiten Pult stand, wird er sich wohl widerspruchslos der Mehrheit der übrigen drei Pulte gefügt haben! Kummer war er jedenfalls schon gewöhnt, hatte er sich doch bereits im 10. Takt des Chores „Weissage" den Kopf darüber zerbrechen müssen, wie die insgesamt vorhandenen drei Viertelnotenwerte auf den vorgeschriebenen Viervierteltakt zu verteilen sein könnten.

Von all diesen Sorgen Bachs und seiner Spieler ahnt der Benutzer heutiger Neuausgaben nur wenig; und wir sind versucht, zu fragen, was die Leipziger Thomasgemeinde wohl davon geahnt oder gehört haben mag. Vielleicht meinten manche, der Kantor Bach möge doch endlich seinem Ehrgeiz zur Aufführung derart schwieriger, gekünstelter und mühsamer Musik ein Ende setzen und lieber was Rechtes von Telemannischer oder Graunischer Komposition aufführen. Das falle besser in die Ohren und sei überdies kein onus für den Herrn Cantor. Aber leider sei der Herr Bach darin ja wohl incorrigibel. — Andere mögen sich einfach gar nichts gedacht haben.

Aber dennoch, irgendwie muß Bach seine Aufführungen zum guten Ende gebracht haben, das verlangte sein Amt in einer derart auf die Erfüllung praktischer Anforderungen gerichteten Musizierpraxis wie der der Bachzeit. Auch erfahren wir trotz allen Vorwürfen gegen Bach nirgends ein Wort, daß seine Kirchenmusik Mängel in der Ausführung aufgewiesen habe; im Gegenteil, Thomasrektor Gesner bewundert Bachs Dirigierpraxis aufs höchste.

Wir wollen daher unsere Vermutungen zu Bachs Aufführungspraxis am Schluß dieser Plauderei in einigen Thesen vortragen, die vielleicht geeignet sind, zugleich auch einige heutige Editions- und Aufführungsfragen ein wenig zu klären.

1. Die Ansprüche der Hörer waren weniger auf Perfektion ausgerichtet als heute. Man war gewöhnt, „mit imperfectis" zu leben, und die Zuhörer scheinen diesen Zustand geduldiger ertragen zu haben als Bach selbst.

2. Eine intensive Probentätigkeit im heutigen Sinne scheint Bachs Kirchenaufführungen nicht vorausgegangen zu sein. Vielleicht wurden Gesangsproben unter Leitung des Präfekten abgehalten, vielleicht wurden ferner den Instrumentisten und Gesangssolisten ihre Stimmen zum Selbststudium übergeben. Hätte jedoch eine Gesamtprobe stattgefunden, so hätten schwerlich noch ausgelassene Takte in einem zu mindestens zwei Aufführungen verwendeten Stimmenmaterial stehengeblieben sein können. Zwar ist uns für Bachs Köthener Zeit die Abhaltung wöchentlicher Proben ausdrücklich bezeugt (Ernst König in: Bach-Jahrbuch 1957, S. 166); doch geht aus eben diesem Zeugnis auch hervor, daß die Köthener Instrumentalmusiker sich weigerten, an den kirchenmusikalischen Proben des Kantors Göbel teilzunehmen. Wenn in der Leipziger Ratssitzung vom 2. 8. 1730 laut wird, Bach tue nichts und halte die Singestunden

nicht, so deutet auch dieser Vorwurf nicht auf eine ausgedehnte Probentätigkeit Bachs. Damit soll nicht eine intensive musikalische Übungstätigkeit des Thomanerchores in Frage gestellt werden, ohne die Bachs Kantaten und Passionen niemals hätten aufgeführt werden können (die Abhaltung der „Singestunden" wird Bach an seine Präfekten delegiert haben); doch scheinen diese Übungen mehr auf eine allgemeine Fertigkeit ausgerichtet gewesen zu sein als auf das sorgfältige Erarbeiten eines bestimmten Werkes und seiner speziellen Probleme.

3. An die Stelle einer perfekten Ausarbeitung trat eine Praxis, die man die „perfekte Improvisation" nennen könnte, wobei unter Improvisation nicht nur das Anbringen von Auszierungen und Ornamenten zu verstehen ist, sondern die Beherrschung jeglicher Art von Aushilfen, die nötig werden könnten, um eine Aufführung nicht scheitern zu lassen. Meister dieser Improvisationskunst war Bach selbst, und wir dürfen vermuten, daß er alle die Tätigkeiten, die Johann Matthias Gesner über Bachs Dirigierpraxis berichtet, wie Kopfnicken, Aufstampfen mit dem Fuß, Drohen mit dem Finger, Tonangeben in hoher, tiefer und mittlerer Lage, nicht nur in den Übungsstunden, sondern auch bei den kirchenmusikalischen Aufführungen selbst anzuwenden pflegte.

4. Diese Improvisationskunst umfaßte höchstwahrscheinlich auch die Anwendung bestimmter Artikulationsmodelle, die eine exakte Vortragsbezeichnung des Stimmenmaterials notfalls entbehrlich machte. Damit soll nicht bestritten werden, daß Bach, hätte er mehr Zeit darauf verwenden können, auch exaktere Artikulationsanweisungen zu geben für nötig erachtet hätte. Aber nicht nur die oben angeführten Beispiele, auch die schlechthin überall zu beobachtende Nachlässigkeit in der Kennzeichnung des Geltungsbereichs von Legatobögen zwingen zu der Annahme, daß der Spieler sich nicht so sehr am Einzelfall des geschriebenen Notenbildes orientierte als an allgemeinen Regeln, die nur die Praxis selbst lehrte. Ein flüchtig hingeworfener Bogen besagte dann nicht mehr, als daß hier die Regeln für das Legatospiel anzuwenden seien, und das genügte.

5. Aus alldem resultiert die Aporie des heutigen Herausgebers, der mit seiner Edition bestenfalls die gestellte Momentaufnahme einer einstmals lebendigen Szene geben kann. Von den unzähligen Möglichkeiten, die die „perfekte Improvisation" vorsieht, wird eine einzige herausgegriffen und kanonisiert; die übrigen werden unterdrückt. Ein Herausgeber, der sich dessen bewußt ist, wird diesen Zustand vielleicht nicht grundsätzlich ändern können; doch wird er sich wenigstens vor der Illusion hüten, seine Ausgabe sei nun die „perfekte Edition".

GERHARD HERZ

J S Bach 1733: A "new" Bach Signature

This small musical offering to America's foremost Bach scholar serves a threefold purpose: (1) It intends to authenticate a most unusual signature by Johann Sebastian Bach; (2) it will show to what manuscript or book this signature may have once belonged; and (3) it will try to evaluate the significance of this find.

The provenance of the signature is highly trustworthy. A cousin of mine, Ernst Lippmann, acquired it in Cologne from Georg Kinsky who was his close friend and curator of the Wilhelm Heyer Museum from 1909—1926. My cousin, a good dilettante violist and professionally a successful wholesale grocer, was able in the years of dire need that followed World War I, to supply Kinsky with some of the things he cherished most: scarce food, wines, but above all, his favorite Antonio cigars. Whether the Bach signature was a gift of appreciation by or purchase from Georg Kinsky, I do not know. After the death of my cousin in the mid-thirties, the signature remained in the possession of his widow who emigrated to Israel and who, during a visit to America in the late 1950's, presented it to me. When she revisited Louisville in 1970 she recalled for me the aforementioned somewhat unromantic facts of her late husband's acquisition of the Bach signature. It might be worth mentioning in this connection that my cousin also obtained from Kinsky the autograph envelope of the letter in which Mozart announced to his father the birth of his first son (June 18, 1783) [1].

I

The Bach signature in question (see Ex. 1) measures 2.7 × 7.5 cm [2]. Its ink, originally probably black, has by now faded into black-brown while the paper has from age and exposure to light (?) turned into a yellowish brown.

The signature is unusual in several respects. To those conversant with Bach's customary way of penning his name, the identity of the *"ac"* and the *"17"* is as evident as is the dissimilarity of the *"h"*, the shape of the two *"3's"* and above all, the *"JSB"* monogram. The latter recalls Bach's well-known seal. But there the letters *JSB* are more flamboyantly shaped and, instead of forming a monogram, it is a pair of them that is artfully intertwined. Aside from the seal, until 1969 only one other instance was known in which Bach had made an artistic monogram out of the initial letters of his name. What happened in that year will be related later. Suffice it to say here that it is the reason for making my signature known at this time. There is sufficient evidence now to claim authenticity also for the more unusual aspects of this signature.

---

[1] This envelope has since been auctioned off by J. A. Stargardt in Marburg, Germany.

[2] Georg Kinsky's description on a lined 3 x 5 filing card gives as measurements 2.8 by 7.4 cm. (see Ex. 2).

Bach, Johann Sebastian; 1685—1750. Autograph signature "J S Bach" (its initial letters intertwined in monogram fashion) together with date of year "1733". Clipping on small piece of paper measuring 2,8 : 7,4 cm. (Translated by the author.)

When Bach wanted to create the impression of a certain formality he seems to have tended to use the g-like *h* of our signature. For instance the title page of the Prelude and Fugue in B minor for Organ [3] shows the same g-like *h* (see Ex. 3a). Yet, on the very next page of the same manuscript Bach writes his name in the more familiar manner (Ex. 3b). It was apparently natural for him to execute two different shapes of *h*, one right after the other, reserving, however, the unusual shape for the title page. The same observation applies to the *Clavier-Büchlein vor Wilhelm Friedemann Bach,* begun in Cöthen in 1720. On its title page (see Ex. 4) the g-like *h* appears consistently four times. While many more examples could be given, these two will have to suffice. They point to the fact that the signature of 1733 might at one time also have adorned the title page of some work by Bach or, perhaps, of some book owned by him.

The number 3 written with indented, i.e. concave top that forms a small halfmoon-like crescent, is by no means a rarity among autograph Bach manuscripts, though the familiar shape with rounded top prevails. Example 5 shows Bach's Sinfonia 13, named Fantasia in its earlier version in the *Clavier-Büchlein* for Friedemann. In the *Clavier-Büchlein* as well as in the autograph of the Inventions and Sinfonias of 1723 the number 3 appears consistently in this form though not often written with such sculpted penmanship as here. Example 6, showing the number 13 in the top right-hand corner, is from the *Kyrie eleison* of the *Missa* of the later *B minor Mass,* that is from the same year as our signature: 1733.

The lower right-hand corner on the title page of one of the three copies that Bach owned of Elias Nicolaus Ammerbach's *Orgel oder Instrument Tabulatur* of 1571, shows the composer's signature in the form of a stylised monogram fashioned out of the initial letters of his name (see Ex. 7). This signature was made known by Stanley Godman in 1956 [4]. Aside from a certain stiffness not found in the signature of 1733 and the customary shape of the letter *h,* the chief difference consists in the use of *ISB* rather than *JSB* for the monogram. But I and J were, as we know, interchangeable letters in Bach's time. This copy of Ammerbach's tablature bears on the flyleaf the following inscription in Dr. Burney's hand:

> "This book which formerly belonged to Sebastian Bach was a present from my honoured friend Mr. C. P. E. Bach, Musick director at Hambro 1772. C. Burney".

Stanley Godman then traces the history of this volume from Burney to its present repository at Cambridge University Library. In 1956 he could still claim the signature "a unique example of this form with the initial monogram".

[3] Also acquired from Georg Kinsky in Cologne (by Mrs. Gisela Selden-Goth) when some of the contents of the Heyer Museum were auctioned off prior to the Museum's moving to Leipzig in 1926. See also facsimile ed. by O. E. Deutsch, *The Harrow Replicas,* No. 4 (Chiswick Press, London, 1942).

[4] "Bachs Bibliothek" in *Musica,* 1956, Heft 11, pp. 756—761 (from hereon called: Godman I). See also the same author's "Bach's Copies of Ammerbach's 'Orgel oder Instrument Tabulatur' ", in *Music and Letters,* XXXVIII (1957), 21—27 (from hereon called: Godman II). The latter is a free translation of the German article.

In contrast to the Cambridge signature the signature of 1733 derives a certain sweep-
ing rhythm from the swinging curve of the initial letter J, an élan that carries through
the remaining portions of the monogram and letters including the two horizontal dashes
that serve as periods. Except for this, the monogram of 1733 shows only one small
additional feature not found in the other monogram: a little crescent to the right of
the letter *S*. It is an ornament found frequently in Bach's handwriting, usually added to
the capital letters C (Continuo!) and G. Example 8 shows it adorning the autograph solo
part of Bach's Violin Concerto in A minor while Example 9 is from the Dresden parts of
the B minor Mass, hence again from 1733, the year of our signature. Just as the monogram
and the *g*-like *h*, so does this little crescent point to a similarly representative environment for our still unplaced signature of 1733.

Until recently, this signature with its unusual monogram, had only one distant cousin,
so to speak, in the signature of the Cambridge copy of the Ammerbach tablature. In
1969 its true family miraculously re-appeared. In that year the three folios of Bach's
Calov-Bible re-emerged. This Lutheran Bible, with vast commentary by the orthodox
Lutheran theologian Abraham Calov (1612—1686) headed the list of books left by
Bach at his death. Long believed lost like most of the books from Bach's library, it was
exhibited at the 1969 Bach Festival in Heidelberg for which Christoph Trautmann had
gathered together the six books still extant as well as copies of others that had once
been in Bach's possession.

That Bach's Calov Bible came to America in the early 19th century, was acquired by
a Herr Reichle in Philadelphia in 1847 and kept in his family in Frankenmuth, Michigan,
until 1938, is no more than one of those unpredictable occurrences that makes the study
of history so fascinating. What is incredible is that not until 1933 did Reichle Jr. realize
that the former owner of his family bible was Johann Sebastian Bach although Bach's
signature appears in the lower right-hand corner on each one of its three title pages. It
is still more incredible that after Mr. Reichle gave the three precious folios to the Library
of Concordia Seminary in St. Louis in October 1938, their identity and provenance were
not made known beyond the local level even then. Christoph Trautmann has told in
Musik und Kirche (1969) the story of his successful detective work that resulted in the
discovery of the whereabouts of the Bible, its subsequent airflight back to Germany and
its exhibition at the Heidelberg Bach Festival. The Calov Bible was returned from its
brief sojourn in Germany to St. Louis in October 1969 and I spent the 29th of December
with it at Concordia Seminary. The significance of this spectacular find is obviously the
subject for a paper of considerable length that only prolonged study of the Calov Bible
can produce.

What is of paramount interest to our present investigation is that Bach's name not only
appears on each one of its three title pages but that the monogram made out of *JSB*
is quasi-identical with that on my signature. Furthermore, the year of Bach's inscription,
1733, is also the same (see Ex. 10).

1

Bach, Johann Sebastian; 1685–1750.

Eigh. Namenszug „J S Bach" (mit monogrammartig verschlungenen Initialen) nebst der Jahreszahl „1733". Ausschnitt auf einem Blättchen in Größe 2,8 : 7,4 cm.

2

3a

3b

Clavier-Büchlein
vor
Wilhelm Friedemann Bach.
angefangen in
Cöthen Anno

4

Fantasia

5

6

7

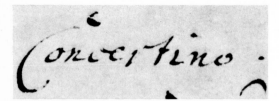

8

9

10

11

12

13a

13b

14

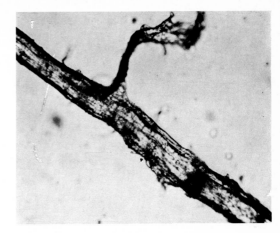

15

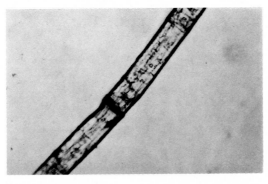

16

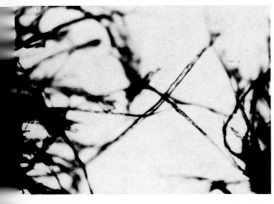

17

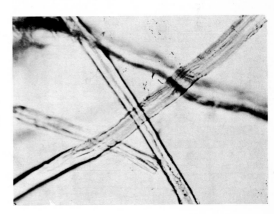

18

The re-emergence of Bach's Calov Bible with its three almost identical signatures proved to me conclusively the until-then still slightly doubtful authenticity of my signature. If Bach's signature had been cut out from one of the three title pages of the Calov Bible my search would have come to a sudden and happy end. Obviously such was not the case. The search had to continue.

II

In his article of 1956 Stanley Godman described two further copies of Ammerbach's tablature of 1571, of which one probably, the other certainly, was also owned by Bach. Both copies belonged in the 19th century to the Leipzig organist and bibliophile Carl Ferdinand Becker. He parted with the copy that is now in the British Museum presumably after he had acquired another copy that is still in Leipzig. The British Museum copy bears this inscription on its flyleaf:

constat: 1 Louisdor, in gelt (?) (goldt or gold) J. Seb. Bach Isen.

The unusual "Isen" after Bach's name, the Latin abbreviation for *Isenacensis,* that is "of Eisenach", is the cause of some doubt as to the authenticity of this inscription and its provenance from Bach's library [5].

Only two other books once owned by Bach are extant. One is the Hymn-Book by the Moravian Brethren, published in Ulm in 1538 — the only extant copy of that edition. It is preserved in the Glasgow University Library [6]. It bears no signature by Bach but an inscription by Burney that attests to Bach's original ownership and the fact that the copy was given to Burney by C. P. E. Bach in the same year 1772 in which he also received the Cambridge copy of Ammerbach's tablature. The other extant book from Bach's library, a copy of J. J. Fux's *Gradus ad Parnassum,* was bought by Friedrich Chrysander in Hamburg and is now in that city's State and University Library. It contains signature and price of the volume in Bach's handwriting; but the letters JSB are not fashioned into a monogram [7]. The letters *"ach"* seem to have been added at a later time, squeezed into what little space there remained after *"JSB"*.

Of the third and last of Ammerbach's tablatures, the Leipzig copy, Godman says:

> Whatever the exact origin of the British Museum copy, there is no doubt about the provenance of the two other copies (Cambridge and Leipzig). Did Bach present a copy to each of his sons, W. Friedemann and C. P. E., in his lifetime (which would explain why they did not appear in the "Specificatio" of his library in 1750)? Burney's copy, presented to him by C. P. E. Bach himself, may well have been the one given to that son, and in view of a tradition linking C. F. Becker's father with W. Friedemann, it is possible that the Leipzig copy came originally from that son [8].

[5] For further detail see Godman II, p. 24.
[6] In its Euing Collection. "Ein hübsch new Gesangbuch". Cf. Godman II, p. 22.
[7] Reproduced in Godman I, p. 761.
[8] Godman II, p. 25.

When Carl Ferdinand Becker (1804—1877) retired in 1856, at the early age of 52, from an active life as composer, teacher and organist, he left his large music collection, particularly rich in theoretical works, to the City Library at Leipzig. Bach's Ammerbach tablature is still among the treasures of the *Becker Stiftung* of the Stadtbibliothek. Professor Werner Neumann kindly furnished me with the following two photos. Example 11, the title page, shows the name C. F. Becker and beneath it the date: 1842. Example 12, from the blank last page of the Leipzig copy of Ammerbach's tablature, contains the following all-important note written by Alfred Dörffel, Becker's successor as custos of the Music Division at the Stadtbibliothek:

> Dieses Buch ist einst im Besitze Johann Sebastian Bach's gewesen. Bach hatte seinen Namen auf dem Vorsatzblatt des Buchbinders rechts unten in die Ecke eingeschrieben; diese Ecke hat nach 1870 Jemand ausgeschnitten, später hat Jemand das ganze Vorsatzblatt herausgerissen. Die Sachbeschädiger konnten nicht bestimmt ermittelt werden.

This then leaves no doubt that Bach had been the owner of this book and that he had inscribed his name in the lower right-hand corner of the flyleaf. This corner was cut out by someone after 1870 and later the whole flyleaf, having lost its significance once Bach's name had disappeared, was also torn out. The culprits could not be apprehended.

The obvious question is whether our signature of 1733 is perhaps the one that was cut out of the Leipzig book about a hundred years ago. As long as no other case of a Bach signature removed from its original setting can be documented — and I know of no other — an attempt at verification will have to be made.

The reverse side of the 1733 signature supplies some startling facts (Ex. 13b). Above all, there is a curious (in the original) light blue, blotting paper-like area and at right a turned over border. The latter is nothing but a stamp hinge, made of quite different paper and glued to the back of the signature, probably to allow the signature to be properly displayed. The explanation of the blue area proved to be infinitely more complex.

According to Werner Neumann, Becker used to paste his own *ex libris* label into his books, this one included. Upon request, Dr. Neumann kindly sent me a sample of such a deep blue C. F. Becker *ex libris* label which Example 13a reproduces along with the back of the signature of 1733. As the film of blue on the reverse side of the signature is extremely thin its color seems more faint. The considerably lighter color of the blue is caused, as shall be documented later, by the shining-through of the original yellow paper beneath it. However, the size of the blue area coincides in width nearly exactly with that of the Becker label. If the blue area on the back of the signature were only one millimeter wider than the Becker label, no case could be made. But since the blue area is about one half cm. shorter than the Becker label, our case gains considerably in credibility. Both the existence of such a blue area and its size seem to transcend the realm of coincidence. They lead to the assumption that Becker had pasted his *ex libris* label onto the other side of the flyleaf, perhaps led by the desire of thereby strengthening this precious and precarious corner. The culprit who later cut out Bach's signature had every reason to hide the source of his theft. He obviously tried to erase the incriminating evidence that Becker's label would have supplied. He stopped only when his efforts at removing the blue label began to threaten the paper of the signature proper.

One thing speaks, however, strongly against this theory. The rectangular darker area in the lower right-hand corner on the title page of the Leipzig copy of the Ammerbach tablature (see Ex. 11) indicates the former presence of a label in that spot. Hans Joachim Schulze verified some years ago that Becker's *ex libris* had indeed been in that corner and had been removed only rather recently because it constituted a blot on the purity of the title page that was already marred by the unerasable stamp of the "Stadtbibliothek zu Leipzig — C. F. Becker Stiftung". With this, my hypothesis that Becker's label was originally affixed to the flyleaf seemed to collapse. It seemed extremely far-fetched to assume that Becker might have placed two labels in one and the same book. When I reached this point some years ago I gave up my investigation.

The recent reappearance of the Calov Bible that proved the authenticity of my signature beyond any reasonable doubt, caused me to take up the quest again. Upon careful consideration the following occurred to me as lying at least within the realm of possibility. We know that the original thief was interested only in the Bach signature because, according to the librarian's entry on the back page, only the signature was cut out after 1870. "Later", this librarian continues, "someone tore out the whole flyleaf". The latter was obviously not done by the thief of the signature but by a second person. This leaves us with a puzzling question. Who would possibly have had an interest in the empty flyleaf? My only answer is that somebody in the library, irritated by the blemish of the cut-out corner, felt that this now worthless empty flyleaf might just as well be removed and the book's appearance thereby be improved. Also the neat and straight edge left after the removal of the flyleaf speaks for such an "inside job". This torn-out flyleaf must have shown on its reverse side the upper half of the Becker label — provided it was there to begin with — as the latter is almost twice as high as Bach's signature of 1733 (cf. 13a and b)[9]. While nobody could ever restore Bach's signature, restoring Becker's label was quite another matter. The book remained, after all, in the Becker collection of the Stadtbibliothek in Leipzig. Would it not seem rather typical of a librarian, or rather of a conscientious employee at the library, to place a Becker label on the corresponding spot of what, since the theft, had become page 1, the title page? Since Becker had already inscribed his name and the date 1842 on the title page, there was certainly

---

[9] The above documents are obviously not reproduced in proper size. While Nos. 13a and especially 7 and 10 are greatly enlarged, Nos. 4, 11 and 12 are substantially reduced. This matters, however, only in the case of 13a and 13b. Their true proportions are as follows:

     13a: 4.2 x 6 cm.
     13b: 2.7 x 7.5 cm.

no need for him to add also his *ex libris* on the same page. This was obviously done by someone else and at a later time. That such a label was readily available to an employee of the library is further proven by the fact that Werner Neumann graciously sent me such a label (Ex. 13) without any hesitation or the request to return it.

Conscious of the fact that the above assumption, though plausible, is entirely in the realm of speculation, more substantial documentation had to be produced to prove my theory. My signature can no longer be fitted into the cut-off corner since the flyleaf itself no longer exists. The corresponding flyleaf at the end of the tablature does not belong to the same gathering and is further glued to the hard cover of the book.

I have on occasion questioned those who for many years have been in constant contact with Bach's manuscripts in Germany and in America. Except for the last (7th) page of the autograph *Continuo pro Violoncello* part of Cantata 100 which I saw in West Berlin, but which for several reasons does not qualify, neither they nor I have come across a cut-off corner in a Bach manuscript. The one I suspected years ago apparently remains the only instance known to Bach scholars.

In order to advance the quest for truth, I turned to paper research. If the paper of Becker's *ex libris* label and that of the blue remnants on the reverse side of my Bach signature could be proven to be identical, documentation would take the place of speculation. In an attempt to establish the identity of the two blues I sought and was granted permission to avail myself of microscopic photography at the Department of Pathology at the Medical School of the University of Louisville.

Cost of color reproduction prevents us from illustrating here what the microscope saw on the reverse side of the Bach signature: the clearly discernible, wide separation of the blue fibres between and beneath which the yellowish orange of the signature paper proper shone through, giving the few "blue" top fibres a greenish-silvery rather than bluish color. This color slide documented the actual thinness of this layer of blue and explained the at first worrisome difference in intensity between the blue of the Becker label which glowed in rich blue pigmentation under the microscope, and that of the Bach signature.

Examples 14, 15, and 16 present in increasing magnification fibres plucked from the yellow paper of the Bach signature. No. 14 looks at first glance like seaweed. It shows the typical twisted, frizzled and fragmented appearance of these fibres as well as their conically widening ends that resemble trumpet bells. Example 15 is a close-up of a portion of the long fibre in Ex. 14. It highlights the splintered nature of the former and adds, photographed in water, a bark-like surface in almost three-dimensional relief. Example 16 presents an enlargement of a fragment of one of the rare straight and un-twisted fibres that could be found among those plucked from the Bach signature paper. Purposely much more brightly lighted to reveal its inner structure, it shows one of the fret-like crossings that could already be detected on the long fibre in Ex. 14. Greatly magnified in Ex. 16, this characteristic vertical crossing resembles the joint of a bamboo reed. The surface of the fibre is not smooth but as if broken out in a rash.

Microscopic pictures of the blue fibres present an altogether different picture. Attempting to demonstrate that the blue fibres on the back of the Bach signature were indeed identical with those of the Becker label we plucked with surgical tweezers two fibres, one each from the Becker label and from the blue area on the Bach signature. The microscope revealed that again we had plucked whole clusters of fibres. By careful manipulation we succeeded in pushing these clusters towards each other until two fibres crossed over into each other's territory, so to speak (Ex. 17). The fibre at the left stems from the blue area of the Bach signature, the one on the right from the Becker label. Greatly magnifying this x-like field in the center, example 18 shows the similarity, if not identity, of the two crossing fibres. Both fibres seem more transparent than those of the Bach signature paper. The greater brightness of the one fibre is explained by the fact that it lies on top of the other and therefore picks up more of the side light that was used. The structural similarity of the two crossing fibres as regards their general smoothness and lack of fuzziness is evident. The streaky pattern that characterizes these fibres runs like a long vein the whole length of both fibres. Unlike the fibres from the Bach signature paper these blue fibres are neither bark-like nor composed of separate joints. Since the two crossing fibres come evidently from the same kind of paper — a paper certainly different from that of the Bach signature — my hypothesis that the blue area on the back of the Bach signature consists of remnants of a Becker *ex libris* label gains substantially in credibility. It has furthermore been the experience that in the realm of Bachiana 'new' finds usually turn out to be lost documents found again. This seems to be the case here as it was with the infinitely more significant reappearance of Bach's Calov Bible. Also the fact that our signature came into Georg Kinsky's possession towards the end of World War I, i.e., 45 to 50 years after the theft, seems to speak for our theory. Within this span of time the life of the perpetrator of the theft of the early 1870's — quite likely committed by an overly enthusiastic youngster — may well have come to an end and caused the turnover of the signature.

III

The satisfaction of rediscovering a Bach signature that had disappeared a century ago, is enhanced by its unusual nature. It joins the small family of monogrammed book signatures by Bach of which four out of five are dated — all of them: 1733. This is the year after which Bach returned to his new living quarters in the rebuilt Thomas School, after having lived with his family for ten months away from home in the house of a Dr. Donndorf. The death on February 1, 1733 of Bach's sovereign, Friedrich August I, resulted in a 4$^{1}/_{2}$-month period of public mourning which gave Bach a no doubt welcome breathing spell in his many activities that at that time also included the Collegium Musicum. Beyond composing Kyrie and Gloria of the later *B minor Mass* for his new sovereign, Bach may well have used these months to re-assemble and put in order his library, penning at that time his "ex libris" into some of his favorite and oldest books. This would explain why the date 1733 alone appears among the extant books from Bach's library.

That our signature of 1733 should have been handed down to us by Carl Ferdinand Becker is no caprice of history. This native of Leipzig was himself trained as a Thomas pupil under Cantor Schicht (1753—1823). Already organist at St. Peter at the age of twenty-one, Becker moved on to the more prestigious position of organist at St. Nicolai. One of the most diligent collaborators of Schumann's *Neue Zeitschrift für Musik*, the many-sided Becker was also an indefatigable collector, a compiler of bibliographical works as well as the author of several books on old music and composer of organ and piano pieces. When the Leipzig Conservatory was founded in 1843 Mendelssohn asked Becker to head its organ department. In the same year Becker edited Bach's four-part chorales for Breitkopf & Härtel and, seven years later, founded together with Schumann, Otto Jahn and Moritz Hauptmann, the Bach-Gesellschaft. According to his book on *Hausmusik in Deutschland*[10] Becker also owned a number of unspecified compositions by Bach written in German tablature. That such a man should have acquired two copies of Ammerbach's tablature of 1571 is indicative of the early 19th century trend towards collecting and reviving the music of the past. Becker must thus not only be seen in the light of Mendelssohn and Schumann but also in the context of the first music historians: Forkel, Rochlitz and von Winterfeld.

While Becker's interest in Ammerbach is a phenomenon of his historicizing time, Bach's own apparent high regard for Ammerbach's work has to be seen rather in contrast to the trends and tendencies of his time. But it is typical of Bach's own love for the old, for what his contemporaries considered already outmoded. Bach's interest in Ammerbach, this venerable organist (1560—97) of St. Thomas Church who was Bach's senior by 155 years, is not antiquarian. It is characteristic of Bach's loyalty to the century and middle-German homeland of the Reformation. It was not just the German letter notation which attracted Bach to Ammerbach's tablature. Here was indeed a forerunner of his own *Clavier-Büchlein, Orgel-Büchlein* and *Clavierübung* ideal, namely a systematically constructed work that combined the musicianly with the didactic, the explanation of ornaments and fingering with an early form of *Gebrauchsmusik*, especially for the organist. That Gerber and Gustav Schilling speak of Ammerbach as a great contrapuntist of the 16th century[11], a compliment which the transcriptions in the tablature hardly bear out, makes one wonder whether Bach did not perhaps know music by Ammerbach which has since vanished but which was worthy of this description.

Since only seven (or possibly eight) volumes from Bach's library are presently known to be extant we can for the time being say no more than that the five monogrammed signatures appear to be a special tribute paid by Bach to the old: the Calov Bible of 1681 and Ammerbach's tablature of 1571. Was it perhaps the venerable age of these folios that caused Bach with his inborn instinct for form to try to match the beautiful printing of the books by his own stylized and ornamented signatures? While new finds might throw new light on this question, a final observation remains.

---

[10] *Die Hausmusik in Deutschland im 16., 17. und 18. Jahrhundert,* 1840. See also Godman II, p. 22.
[11] Cf. *Mendels Musikalisches Konversations-Lexikon,* vol. I, 1870, p. 504.

Bach showed by his own, though rare, use of German letter notation[12] that this space-saving mode of writing had not yet lost its meaning for him. His ownership of two, if not three, copies of Ammerbach's tablature may well indicate that Bach still taught his pupils to read tablature. Further research might prove this to be the case. Whatever its results, he two monogrammed signatures on Ammerbach's tablature (and the three on the Calov Bible) present a touching bit of new evidence of Bach's retrospective attitude, of his loving and simple understanding of music and techniques of the past that he was the last in history to preserve and to pass on.

---

[12] For instance BWV 605 (see BG, vol. 44, No. 6, plate 9) or BWV 616 — both from the *Orgel-Büchlein* — (see W. Neumann, *Auf den Lebenswegen Johann Sebastian Bachs*, Berlin, 1957, p. 103).

ERNEST MAY

J. G. Walther and the Lost Weimar Autographs
of Bach's Organ Works

With an Item for The Bach Reader *and a Conspectus of the Organ Works in the
Mempell-Preller Manuscripts*

... Jetzo habe nur noch zu berühren: daß, außer denen in Paquetgen enthaltenen
Clavier-Sachen, noch mit des Hrn. Anglebert, Begue: und von Teütschen Organisten, sonderl. mit des berühmten Buxtehudens und Bachs Arbeit, einem Liebhaber,
auf schon gemeldte Art, dienen kan, weil von beyden sehr viele, ja über 200 Stücke
zusammen ohngefehr besitze. Die erstern habe mehrentheils von dem seeligen
Herrn Werckmeister, und des Herrn Buxtehudens eigner Hand in Teütscher Tabulatur; die zweyten aber von dem Herrn Auctore selbst, als welcher 9 Jahr Hof-
Organist alhier gewesen, mein Vetter u. Gevatter ist, bekommen ...

(J. G. Walther's letter to H. Bokemeyer, dated 6 Aug. 1729)[1]

Among Bach's contemporaries, Johann Gottfried Walther[2] is one of the prominent
figures in present-day Bach research. His estimable organ chorales[3] provide an interesting
counterpoint to Bach's own output in this form, and his *Musikalisches Lexikon* (1732)[4]
continues to serve as a primary source for biographical and theoretical information.
Most notably, however, Walther's passion for copying and collecting the music of his
own and the preceding generation of German organists was prodigious, and, to a
remarkable extent, it is in his manuscript collections[5] that the organ works of the
"golden age", including the organ works of J. S. Bach, are preserved.

---

[1] From a collection of 36 "Briefe J. G. Walther" in the Deutsche Staatsbibliothek, Berlin. I am
indebted to Mr. H.-J. Schulze of the Bach-Archiv in Leipzig for first pointing out this letter to
me. Georg Schünemann's "J. G. Walther und H. Bokemeyer. Eine Musikerfreundschaft um Sebastian Bach" (*Bach-Jahrbuch 1933*, pp. 86—118; hereafter referred to as Schünemann *BJ 1933*)
is an extensive commentary on this whole collection of letters and gives this particular text
on pp. 99—100.

[2] The fundamental sources for Walther's biography are the autobiographical article in Mattheson's
Ehrenpforte (Hamburg, 1740; reprinted Berlin, 1910, and Kassel, 1969), and a long autobiographical letter to Bokemeyer dated 3. Oktober 1729 (excerpted in Schünemann *BJ 1933*, p. 88 ff.).
Otto Brodde's *Johann Gottfried Walther: Leben und Werk* (Kassel, 1937) and other summaries
of Walther's life add little to the original documents.

[3] Published by Seiffert in *Denkmäler Deutscher Tonkunst (DDT)*, 1. *Folge*, Band 26 und 27;
the re-publication (Wiesbaden, 1958) is revised by Hans Joachim Moser.

[4] Leipzig, 1732. Facsimile edition, ed. Richard Schaal, Kassel und Basel, 1953.

[5] The extant Walther autographs are described by Seiffert in the foreword to *DDT*(1), vols.
26 & 27, pp. XXV—XXVII: (a, b, c, d) Berlin, Deutsche Staatsbibliothek, Mus ms 22 541/1—4;
(e) Königsberg 15 839 (now lost); (f) Den Haag, Gemeente-Museum, Ms. 4.G.14 (formerly the
"Frankenbergersche Autograph"); (g) a Konvolut, now lost, formerly in the possession of the
Kgl. Akademische Institut für Kirchenmusik in Berlin. Other manuscripts in Walther's hand
include Berlin, Deutsche Staatsbibliothek, Mus ms 2329/5, Mus ms 30 091, Mus ms 30 210,

In addition to the rather distant family relationship [6], there is substantial evidence of a personal relationship between Bach and Walther. During Bach's employment at the Weimar court (1708—1717), Walther was organist at the Weimar town church of St. Peter and St. Paul. It is recorded that Bach was godfather to Walther's oldest son (*Bach-Dokumente II*, #54), and that Bach and Walther were both godfathers to one J. G. Trebs (*Bach-Dokumente II*, #61). Further, Walther's *Lexikon* records that Bach and Walther had a common student, *Krebs (Johann Tobias):*

> ... hat er bis an. 1717 so wohl anfänglich bey mir in der Composition und Clavier-Spielen, als in diesem bey Hrn. Joh. Sebastian Bachen ... [7]

Most significantly, musical cooperation between Bach and Walther can be documented. First, Berlin, Deutsche Staatsbibliothek, Mus ms 30091 is a copy of Joh. Baal's *Missa tota,* the Kyrie of which is in the pre-Leipzig hand of Bach, while the remainder is in the hand of Walther. Second, the principal surviving source for the Bach cantata "Widerstehe doch der Sünde" (BWV 54) is a fair copy in Walther's hand: Bruxelles, Bibliothèque Royale, Ms II. 4196 (Fétis 2444). Although the date of this manuscript cannot be fully proven, circumstances strongly suggest that it was copied from the autograph between 1714 and 1717 [8]. In summary, Walther seems to have been one of the early and important members of the Bach circle, and his authority as a scribe should be almost impeccable. He was related to Bach, he lived in the same city, by all accounts on good terms, he himself was an intelligent musician and composer, on one demonstrable occasion he shared with Bach the task of copying out a manuscript, and on another occasion he made a fair copy of one of Bach's Weimar cantatas. For these reasons, and because of the general high quality of their text, Walther's copies of Bach's organ works have traditionally carried an authority in most cases exceeded only by that of the autograph itself.

However, it is now well-known that the Weimar and pre-Weimar autographs of the Bach organ works have largely disappeared [9]. The sources which remain are either

---

Mus ms autogr J G Walther 1—7, Mus ms theor 910 and 917, Mus ms Bach P 805 and P 1074, and New Haven, Yale University, LM 4695, LM 4718, and LM 4794. Also, Walther is the initiator and a principal scribe of the so-called "Walther-Krebs manuscripts" P 801, P 802, and P 803. (Hereafter, the manuscripts listed in Kast, *Die Bach-Handschriften der Berliner Staatsbibliothek* [Trossingen, 1958], will be referred to only by the *P* and *St* numbers).

[6] Bach's mother and Walther's grandfather had the same father, Valentin Lämmerhirt, Sr. (See W. Neumann and H.-J. Schulze, *Fremdschriftliche und Gedruckte Dokumente zur Lebensgeschichte Johann Sebastian Bachs 1685—1750* [Kassel und Leipzig, 1969; hereafter referred to as *Bach-Dokumente II*], p. 193.

[7] Walther, *Lexikon*, p. 345.

[8] See NBA I/18, Krit. Ber., pp. 9—26.

[9] The extant autographs are the following: pre-Weimar, P 488 (BWV 739 and BWV 764), and the autograph entry of BWV 535a in the so-called Möllersche Handschrift; from Weimar, P 271, pp. 108—110 (BWV 660a), P 330 (BWV 596), and P 283 (*Orgelbüchlein*, BWV 599—644). For a discussion of the handwriting characteristics of these manuscripts, see Georg von Dadelsen, *Beiträge zur Chronologie der Werke Johann Sebastian Bachs* (Trossingen, 1958; hereafter referred to as Dadelsen, *Beiträge*), pp. 72—80.

Bach's own fair copies from the Leipzig period or copies made by other organists, students, or collectors. It is evident that Bach's own Leipzig copies of earlier works are completely authoritative, when such copies exist. However, since a large number of works do not appear in autograph sources at all, the accurate assessment of the various copies and copyists, and a determination of the proximity of any given copy to the hypothetical autograph, becomes important.

It is in this connection that the excerpt from Walther's letter, quoted above, assumes significance. The first part of the excerpt informs us that Walther possessed over 200 works by Buxtehude and Bach, a statement which would surprise no one familiar with the Walther manuscript collections. The second portion of the excerpt, however, tells where Walther obtained these works — in the case of Bach, from the composer himself. Two interpretations of this statement, I believe, are possible: (1) Walther figuratively obtained (= copied out) the works in question from Bach's autographs, or (2) Walther physically obtained the autographs themselves — that is, he must have received them as a gift. The two modern commentaries on this passage have tacitly adopted the second possibility. Schünemann summarizes the passage as follows:

> Von Bach spricht Walther mit ganz besonderer Hochachtung. Besitzt er doch von ihm und Buxtehude über 200 Kompositionen! Sein „Vetter und Gevatter" Bach hat ihm alle diese Stücke in Weimar geschenkt (6 August 1729) [10].

In *Bach-Dokumente II* the excerpt is entitled "263. Walther: Besitz an Bach-Handschriften" and is provided with the following note:

> ... Der Verbleib der Buxtehude-Handschriften, die Walther z. T. durch den Organisten Andreas Werckmeister erhalten hatte, und den Handschriften, die Walther von Bach bekommen haben will, ist ungeklärt ... [11]

If it can be imagined that Walther owned autographs of Bach organ works, it is not difficult to hypothesize a situation in which he could have received them. As is well-known, Bach's departure from Weimar was not made under friendly conditions, to say the least, and Bach probably departed rather hurriedly after his release from jail. In the hurry, perhaps, he presented his organ manuscripts to his friend and colleague Walther (a more logical choice would be hard to imagine); after all, Capellmeister Bach would not need organ music in Köthen anyway. Continuing this line of speculation, a plausible explanation can be offered for the fact that the Bach autographs were eventually lost. During the last twenty years of his life, Walther's economic condition sank

---

[10] Schünemann *BJ 1933*, p. 107.
[11] *Bach-Dokumente II*, p. 193.

very low, and he was forced to sell off his library [12]. If the Bach autographs were among the manuscripts sold in this way, there is little reason to expect that they would have survived.

Speculative as it is, this hypothesis has an important implication for the transmission of Bach's organ works during the first half of the eighteenth century and needs to be investigated further. If Walther did indeed own Bach autographs for a period of time beginning about 1717, then copies made from such Bach autographs would logically have to come from the Walther circle in Weimar rather than the Bach circle in Leipzig. Several important collections of manuscripts fit the chronological requirements; is it possible that one or more of them can be connected with the Walther circle in and around Weimar, thus indirectly confirming the possibility of Walther's ownership?

Möllersche Handschrift and Andreas-Bach-Buch [13]. Although the main scribe of these collections displays handwriting characteristics similar to those of J. G. Walther [14], Walther is definitely not the main scribe [15]. Judging from the handwriting of Bach's autograph entry (BWV 535a) in the Möllersche Handschrift, it seems likely that the manuscript was well under way before 1707—08 [16]. In any event, however, there is no evidence to suggest that these manuscripts indirectly reflect Walther's ownership of Bach autographs.

The Walther-Krebs Manuscripts P 801, P 802, and P 803. These extensive collections offer abundant evidence of J. G. Walther's close connections to Bach during his period in Weimar, 1708 to 1717 [17]. Apparently initiated by J. G. Walther before 1710, these

[12] Described in Schünemann *BJ 1933*, p. 101 and 115, and in *DDT* (1), vols. 26 and 27, p. XIII.

[13] Berlin, Stiftung Preußischer Kulturbesitz, Mus ms 40 644, and Leipzig, Musikbibliothek der Stadt (hereafter referred to as MB Lpz), III.8.4. A facsimile page in the hand of the main scribe is published in Krause, *Handschriften der Werke Johann Sebastian Bachs in der Musikbibliothek der Stadt Leipzig* (Leipzig, 1964; hereafter referred to as MB Lpz-Katalog), p. 17.

[14] In Wolffheim's "Die Möllersche Handschrift. Ein unbekanntes Gegenstück zum Andreas-Bach-Buche" (*Bach-Jahrbuch 1912*, pp. 42—60), it is asserted that J. G. Walther is, in fact, the main scribe.

[15] Alfred Dürr, "Neues über die Möllersche Handschrift" (*Bach-Jahrbuch 1954*, 75—79).

[16] According to Dadelsen, *Beiträge*, pp. 72—76. However, if an early date, about 1707—08, is accepted, Dürr's tentative identification of the main scribe as Johann Bernhard Bach (1700—1743) is untenable. The Möllersche Handschrift could not have been planned and largely executed by so young a musician. Although the actual identity of the main scribe remains in doubt, a certain sketch can be drawn: (1) he was probably born no later than about 1690, (2) he may have had an association with J. G. Walther, (3) he definitely did have an association with Bach about 1707—08, or earlier, and (4) he may still have been a member of the inner circle of Bach scribes in December, 1718 (see NBA I/10, Krit. Ber., p. 70 ff.), when he must have been about 29 years old, or older.

[17] In a recent study, *Quellenkritische Untersuchungen an den Bach-Handschriften P 801, P 802 und P 803 aus dem "Krebs'schen Nachlass" unter besonderer Berücksichtigung der Choralbearbeitungen des jungen J. S. Bach* (Hamburg, 1969), Hermann Zietz has analyzed the handwriting and reconstructed the history of these manuscripts. Unfortunately for those interested in the chronology of other Walther manuscripts, Zietz concludes that Walther's handwriting did not change significantly after 1712.

manuscripts were taken over by Johann Tobias Krebs [18], a student of J. G. Walther (about 1710—14) and then of Bach (about 1714—17). In the absence of the Bach autographs from the Weimar period, these collections are the most authoritative sources we possess for our knowledge of Bach's activities as an organ composer in Weimar. However, they do not inform the present discussion of Walther's letter of 6 August 1729 for two reasons: (1) it is very likely that the Bach pieces were copied into the Walther-Krebs manuscripts from Bach autographs which were still in Bach's possession [19], and (2) by 1729—31 the Walther-Krebs manuscripts seem not to have been in the possession of Walther but of Johann Ludwig Krebs, whose entries on blank pages in two of the volumes are datable in the period 1729—31 [20]. While conclusive evidence of ownership during the 1720's is lacking, the transmission appears to be simply from father to son. Thus, the history of these manuscripts, which has now been investigated in some detail by Zietz, does little to clarify the problem under consideration.

The Kellner-Circle Manuscripts: P 804. An extensive number of Bach's keyboard and organ compositions are preserved in copies by Johann Peter Kellner [21] and scribes of his circle. Most of these copies are preserved in the Konvolut P 804. Until recently, most of these copies were believed to be in the hand of Kellner himself, but it now appears that the majority are in the handwritings of his copyists and students, some of whom are now known by name — Wolfgang Nikolaus Mey [22], Johannes Ringk [23], Johann Nikolaus Mempell [24], Leonhard Frischmuth [25], and Johann Anton Gottfried

---

[18] See Karl Tittel's dissertation, *Die musikalischen Vertreter der Familie Krebs mit besonderer Berücksichtigung der Bachschüler Johann Tobias und Johann Ludwig* (Marburg, 1963), as well as his articles on J. T. and J. L. Krebs in *MGG*.

[19] For example, P 801 contains a majority of the pieces from the *Orgelbüchlein* autograph P 283, but in a different order, and with a mixture of "early" and "late" readings. „Dieses Nebeneinander von früheren und späteren Fassungen in P 801 läßt sich kaum anders erklären, als daß die Kopien noch während der Anlage des Orgelbüchleins hergestellt wurden" (Georg von Dadelsen, "Zur Entstehung des Bachschen Orgelbüchleins", *Festschrift Friedrich Blume zum 70. Geburtstag* [Kassel, 1963], hereafter referred to as Dadelsen *OB*, p.78). If the Orgelbüchlein pieces were copied into P 801 while Bach was still at work on the autograph itself, Walther's possible ownership of the autograph cannot come into question at this time.

[20] See Zietz, pp. 91 and 97.

[21] 1705—1772. Autobiography in Marpurg, *Historisch-Kritische Beyträge zur Aufnahme der Musik*, vol. I (Berlin, 1754; reprinted Hildesheim, 1970), pp. 439—445. Adlung reports that Kellner "gehört unter die stärksten Spieler…" (*Anleitung zu der musikalischen Gelahrtheit* [Erfurt, 1758; reprinted Kassel, 1953], p. 714).

[22] Mey's handwriting, although hardly distinguishable from Kellner's, is identifiable in MB Lpz Ms R 16(8) and in P 804(48).

[23] Johannes Ringk (1717—1778) is known to Bach research primarily for his copy of BWV 202 — MB Lpz Ms R 8 — which he probably copied from a source in the possession of his teacher, J. P. Kellner (see NBA I/40, Krit. Ber., pp. 10—12). Later he studied with, and copied for, Stölzel; ultimately, he became organist at the Marienkirche in Berlin.

[24] 1713—1747. Löffler, "Die Schüler Joh. Seb. Bachs" (*Bach-Jahrbuch 1953*, 5—27), #13. Mempell, who is known principally in relation to the MB Lpz manuscripts 7 and 8, appears only once as a scribe in the Kellner manuscripts (P 804[10]). However, this fascicle bears

Wechmar [26]. Nevertheless, most of the scribes are anonymous, and some resemble the hand of Kellner so closely that it is exceedingly difficult to distinguish Kellner's own hand (which may occur in several chronological phases) from that of his students. The NBA has dealt with this problem twice already, but even these findings will undoubtedly have to be improved [27].

Yet, despite these uncertainties, it can be assumed that J. P. Kellner was responsible, directly or indirectly, for the compilation of P 804 and a few other related manuscripts [28]. To my knowledge, there is no direct biographical or musical evidence connecting Kellner with J. G. Walther [29]. Plath has suggested that the "Unbekannter Schreiber IV" who appears on pp. 25—31 of P. 804 may be "(Joh. Gottfried Walther?)" [30]. However, on the basis of Zietz's description of Walther's handwriting, this suggested connection seems very unlikely. The remaining scribes in P 804 whose names are known — Mey, Ringk, Mempell, Frischmuth, and Wechmar — have no known links with J. G. Walther.

On the other hand, Kellner's circle seems to have had a direct connection with the Bach circle. Kellner's autobiography [21] indicates that Kellner himself was a student of one Johann Schmidt [31], organist in Zella, and a former associate of J. S. Bach in Arnstadt. The same source also reports that Kellner later became acquainted with Bach himself, although it does not say that Kellner was a Bach student [32]. Kellner's son reports that his father was "a good friend of S. Bach" and that he "provided himself with all his (Bach's) ... (organ and keyboard) compositions" [33]. Kellner and Bach also had at least one common student, J. P. Kirnberger [34]. Most important, either Kellner or a scribe of his circle was involved in completing a copy of BWV 548 begun by Bach him-

Kellner's signature as an indication of possession; whether there may have been any substantial connection between Kellner and Mempell remains an open question.

[25] ?—1764. The Gerber *Lexikon der Tonkünstler* (1790—92) lists a Klavierist of this name who lived (1762) in Amsterdam. The Gerber *Neues Lexikon der Tonkünstler* (1812—14) lists a publication by him.

[26] 1727—1799.

[27] See NBA VI/1, Krit. Ber., pp. 16—21, and NBA V/5, Krit. Ber., pp. 24—35. Throughout this investigation, and particularly in this instance, I am greatly indebted to Dr. Dietrich Kilian of the Bach-Institut in Göttingen for fundamental guidance. The details of Dr. Kilian's extensive research appear in NBA IV/5—6.

[28] P 274, P 286, P 287, P 288, P 891, St 125(?).

[29] Among the surviving Walther autographs, one piece by J. P. Kellner is transmitted (Den Haag 4.G.14, pp. 193—194). Taken alone, however, this one piece can hardly be regarded as proof of an association.

[30] NBA V/5, Krit. Ber., p. 27.

[31] Löffler #8.

[32] "Ich hatte sehr viel von einem grossen Meister der Musik ehemahls theils gesehen, theils gehöret. Ich fand einen ausnehmenden Gefallen an dessen Arbeit. Ich meine den nunmehro seligen Herrn Capellmeister Bach in Leipzig. Mich verlangte nach der Bekanntschaft dieses vortrefflichen Mannes. Ich wurde auch so glücklich, dieselbe zu geniesen." (Marpurg I, p. 444.)

[33] From a letter of J. C. Kellner, quoted in Kinsky, *Die Originalausgaben der Werke Johann Sebastian Bachs* (Wien, Leipzig, Zürich, 1937; reprinted 1968), pp. 111—112.

[34] See Siegfried Borris, *Kirnbergers Leben und Werk* (Kassel, 1933), pp. 6—7. Kirnberger also studied with H. N. Gerber.

self [35]. From this case it is established that someone in the Kellner circle had access to the original manuscript of a Bach organ work and was working in the closest possible connection with Bach himself. The transmission of BWV 202 through the Kellner circle [36] reinforces this conclusion.

Nevertheless, it cannot be demonstrated exactly how Kellner provided himself with Bach's keyboard and organ works, and, thus, it cannot be entirely excluded that he obtained them through J. G. Walther. However, this investigation has uncovered only the slightest hint of contact between the Kellner circle and Walther, while, to the contrary, there are a number of demonstrably strong connections between the Kellner circle and J. S. Bach. This circumstantial evidence reinforces quite strongly an attitude which has never really been questioned in discussions of the Kellner-circle manuscripts: namely, that the Kellner-circle copies in P 804 and other manuscripts were taken from autograph sources in Bach's possession.

The Heinrich Nicolaus Gerber Manuscripts [37]. H. N. Gerber's [38] close relation to Bach's original manuscripts during his period as a Bach student in Leipzig (1724—26) is established beyond question by the two sources copied out by Gerber but revised by Bach himself. This study has produced no evidence connecting H. N. Gerber with J. G. Walther.

Musikbibliothek der Stadt Leipzig Manuscripts III.8. 7, 8, 9, 10, 11, 17. That the anonymous scribe of these manuscripts must have been working in close connection with Bach is established by a 2-bar entry by Bach himself in Ms. III.8.7 [39]. These manuscripts are tentatively dated 1740—50.

The Mempell-Preller Manuscripts [40]. Although this collection is remarkable both for the quantity of material which it transmits and for the quality of the transmission, almost nothing is known about its origin, about Johann Nikolaus Mempell [41], or about Johann Gottlieb Preller [42]. It is assumed that the three principal scribes are Mempell [43], a scribe working for Mempell [44], and Preller. However, it cannot be excluded that the signatures of Mempell and Preller on these manuscripts only indicate possession. Thus,

[35] P 274 (JSB, pp. 10—14; JPK[?] from p. 15). The musical hand of JPK(?) in this example varies considerably from the authenticated examples of J. P. Kellner's hand. It may either be a later phase of Kellner's own hand or the hand of one of his students.

[36] See NBA I/40, Krit. Ber., pp. 10—12.

[37] (1) Berlin, Stiftung Preußischer Kulturbesitz, Mus ms 40 268, (2) P 1009, (3) Berlin, Deutsche Staatsbibliothek, Mus ms 455 (*with revisions by JSB*), (4) the manuscript mentioned in NBA IV/2, Krit. Ber., p. 51, now in Den Haag, (5) the manuscript of which a facsimile is given in NBA V/3, p. XI (*with revisions by JSB*).

[38] 1702—1775. Löffler #25. Further, see *MGG* and Borris, *Kirnbergers Leben*, pp. 8—9.

[39] See the facsimile of this autograph entry in the MB Lpz — Katalog, p. 18.

[40] Principally MB Lpz Mss 7, 8, and 9. Also, P 804(10), P 1082, P 1087, P 1093, P 1095, P 1098, P 1099, and Berlin Mus ms 11 544 (IX, X, XI).

[41] Löffler #13.

[42] Löffler #14.

[43] See the facsimile in the MB Lpz-Katalog, p. 38.

[44] See the facsimile in the MB Lpz-Katalog, p. 35.

it is possible that the manuscripts were in fact copied by unidentified scribes somewhat earlier than the dates of 1743 and 1749 which occur in the manuscripts. It is noteworthy that the main watermark [45] also occurs in the Kellner-circle manuscripts, but it does not help with the dating, which remains imprecise. Outside of the manuscripts themselves, there is no direct evidence of a relationship between Mempell and Preller on the one hand and the Bach circle on the other.

A most significant aspect of the Mempell-Preller collection was noted by Seiffert in 1904 [46]: namely, that as far as the organ works are concerned, the Mempell-Preller manuscripts transmit almost exclusively the "early" (Weimar and pre-Weimar) versions. Considering the quantity of material which these manuscripts transmit, it is hard to imagine a single group of sources, other than the autographs themselves, from which they could have been copied.

Summary of the Source Situation. The above-mentioned collections include virtually all the copies from before 1750 of Bach's Weimar organ works. The Möllersche Handschrift, Andreas-Bach-Buch, and Walther-Krebs manuscripts P 801, P 802, and P 803 are irrelevant to the discussion of Walther's letter of 6 August 1729 because of their date and provenance. The evidence concerning the remaining manuscripts (the Kellner-circle manuscripts, the H. N. Gerber manuscripts, and MB Lpz Mss III.8.7 — 11, 17) clearly establishes their origin within the Bach circle in Leipzig rather than the Walther circle in Weimar — with the notable exception of the Mempell-Preller collection, for which no direct evidence is available. Thus, of all the known possibilities, only the Mempell-Preller collection remains as a source for possible confirmation of Walther's hypothetical ownership of Bach autographs.

∗

In order to test the working hypothesis that the organ works in the Mempell-Preller collection may have been copied from autographs not in Leipzig but in the possession of J. G. Walther in Weimar, a table has been constructed, listing all the Bach organ works which appear in the Mempell-Preller collection and showing their principal concordances in other manuscripts from before 1750. The object of this table is to determine whether the Mempell-Preller manuscripts avoid the inclusion of works whose autographs were demonstrably in Bach's possession in Leipzig. It is being regarded as established that if a Bach organ work was copied from the autograph during the period 1723 to 1750 by a Bach-circle scribe (for example, the Kellner circle scribes, H. N. Gerber, or the anonymous scribe of MB Lpz III.8.7, whose close connections to Bach have been established above), then the location of the autograph can be regarded as being in Leipzig.

[45] (a) Kursives A (b) Monogramm JMS, in several variant forms. Papiermühle Arnstadt (Thüringen), Papiermacher Johann Michael Stoss, Inhaber 1714—1762, according to Weiss, *Papier und Wasserzeichen der Notenhandschriften von Johann Sebastian Bach* (unpublished), I 32, I 33, and I 34.

[46] Max Seiffert, "Neue Bach-Funde" (*Jahrbuch der Musikbibliothek Peters 1904*, p. 21 ff.).

BACH ORGAN WORKS IN THE MEMPELL-PRELLER COLLECTION, *

WITH CONCORDANCES FROM BEFORE 1750. **

A. Free Organ Works (BWV 525—598).

BWV:	MEMPELL-PRELLER COLLECTION:	LEIPZIG AUTOGRAPHS & BACH-CIRCLE COPIES:	LOCATION OF LOST "EARLY" AUTOGRAPH:
527a(1)	Ms 7(16) [Kopist Mempells]	P 271 [JSB, ca. 1730, BWV 527] P 1089 [anon 18] MB Lpz Ms 1 [Wechmar]	Leipzig
532(1)	Ms 7(11) [Mempell]		
(2)	P 1095 [Mempell]	P 595 [Ringk]	Leipzig
533a	Ms 7(19) [Preller]	P 804 (BWV 533,2) [Su 2 = A.C.?]	Leipzig
535	P 1098 [Preller]	Möllersche Handschrift [JSB, before 1708, BWV 535a] P 804 (BWV 535,1) [Kellner or Mey?]	Leipzig
538	P 1099 [Preller]	P 803 [JG Walther, ca. 1712]	undetermined
541	Ms 7(17) [Preller, "1749"]	MB Lpz Ms a 1 [JSB, 1735—42] P 288 [Kellner?] P 595 [Ringk]	Leipzig
548	Ms 7(18) [Kopist Mempells]	P 274/II [JSB, 1735—42, & Kellner?] MB Lpz Ms 1 [Wechmar]	Leipzig
550	Ms 7(20) [Mempell]		undetermined
551	Ms 7(13) [Mempell]	P 595 [Ringk]	Leipzig
569	Ms 7(22) [Preller]	P 801 [Walther, after 1712] P 288 [Kellner?]	Leipzig
574	P 1093 [Preller]	MB Lpz III.8.4 [anon, ca. 1720?] P 805 [Walther]	undetermined
585	Ms 7(1) [Kopist Mempells]		undetermined
586	Ms 7(2) [Kopist Mempells]		undetermined
1027a	Ms 7(3) [Kopist Mempells]		undetermined
588	Ms 7(21) [Preller]	Möllersche Hs (fragment)	undetermined
597	Ms 7(15) [Preller]		undetermined

* Musikbibliothek der Stadt Leipzig (MB Lpz) Ms 7 is the principal source for the Bach organ works of the Mempell-Preller collection. See MB Lpz-Katalog, pp. 29—36, for a more precise description of each fascicle.
** Dates for manuscripts and identifications of scribes are taken primarily from the MB Lpz-Katalog, Dadelsen, *Beiträge*, Dadelsen *OB*, and Zietz.

B. Orgelbüchlein (BWV 599—644).

BWV:	MEMPELL-PRELLER COLLECTION:	LEIPZIG AUTOGRAPHS & BACH-CIRCLE COPIES:	LOCATION OF LOST "EARLY" AUTOGRAPH:
617	Ms 7(24) [Preller]	P 801 [JTKrebs, ca. 1714] Berlin Mus ms 22541/1&2 [JGWalther]	Leipzig. "Early" autograph extant (P 283).
635	Ms 7(23) [Mempell]	P 801 [JTKrebs, ca. 1714] "Mendelssohn Autograph" [Meißner, 1727—30]	Leipzig. "Early" autograph extant (P 283).

C. 17 Chorales (BWV 651—667).

651a	Ms 7(33) [Preller]	P 802 [JTKrebs, 1710—14] Königsberg 15839 (lost) [JGWalther] P 271 [JSB, 1744—48, BWV 651]	Leipzig
652a	Ms 7(34) [Preller]	P 802 [JTKrebs, 1714—17] P 271 [JSB, 1744—48, BWV 652]	Leipzig
653b	Ms 7(31) [Preller]	P 802 [JGWalther, 1710—14) P 271 [JSB, 1744—48, BWV 653]	Leipzig
653a	Ms 7(31) [Preller]	P 802 [JGWalther, 1710—14] P 271 [JSB, 1744—48, BWV 653]	Leipzig
654a	Ms 7(39) [Preller]	P 802 [JTKrebs, 1714—17] P 271 [JSB, 1744—48, BWV 654]	Leipzig
655a	Ms 7(32) [Preller]	P 802 [JTKrebs, 1714—17] P 1009 [HNGerber, 1724—26] P 271 [JSB, 1744—48, BWV 655]	Leipzig
656a	Ms 7(38) [Preller]	P 802 [JTKrebs, 1714—17] P 271 [JSB, 1744—48, BWV 656]	Leipzig
658a	Ms 7(40) [Preller]	P 802 [JGWalther, 1710—14] Königsberg 15839 (lost) [JGWalther] P 271 [JSB, 1744—48, BWV 658]	Leipzig
659a	Ms 7(35) [Kopist Mempells]	P 802 [JTKrebs, 1714—17] P 271 [JSB, 1744—48, BWV 659]	Leipzig
660a	Ms 7(36) [Preller]	P 802 [JTKrebs, 1710—14] Berlin Mus ms 22541/1&2 [JGWalther] P 271 [JSB, 1744—48, BWV 660]	Leipzig. "Early" autograph extant (P 271, pp. 108—110).
661a	Ms 7(37) [Preller]	P 802 [JTKrebs, 1710—14] Königsberg 15839 (lost) [JGWalther] Berlin Mus ms 22541/1&2 [JGWalther] P 271 [JSB, 1744—48, BWV 661]	Leipzig

[C. 17 Chorales (BWV 651—667) cont'd]

BWV:	MEMPELL-PRELLER COLLECTION:	LEIPZIG AUTOGRAPHS & BACH-CIRCLE COPIES:	LOCATION OF LOST "EARLY" AUTOGRAPH:
662a	Ms 7(30) [Kopist Mempells]	P 802 [JTKrebs, 1710—14] Königsberg 15839 (lost) [JGWalther] P 271 [JSB, 1744—48, BWV 662]	Leipzig
664a	Ms 7(29) [Preller]	P 801 [JTKrebs, 1714—17] MB Lpz III.8.8 [Bach-circle anon, 1740—50] P 271 [JSB, 1744—48, BWV 664]	Leipzig

D. Third Part of the "Clavier-Übung" (BWV 669—689).

| 676 | Ms 7(28) [Kopist Mempells] | Original Print, 1739 | undetermined |

E. Miscellaneous Organ Chorales (BWV 714—765).

717	Ms 7(27) [Preller]	P 802 [JTKrebs, 1710—14]	undetermined
722	Ms 7(26) [Preller]	P 802 [JTKrebs, 1710—14, BWV 722a] Berlin, Mus ms 22541/1 [JGWalther]	undetermined
729	Ms 7(26) [Preller]	P 802 [JTKrebs, 1710—14, BWV 729a]	undetermined
732	Ms 7(26) [Preller]	P 802 [JTKrebs, 1710—14, BWV 732a]	undetermined
738	Ms 7(26) [Preller]	P 802 [JTKrebs, 1710—14, BWV 738a]	undetermined
743	Ms 7(8) [Mempell]		undetermined
747	Ms 7(9) [Kopist Mempells]		undetermined
751	Ms 7(7) [Preller]		undetermined
754	Ms 7(5) [Mempell]		undetermined
762	Ms 7(6) [Kopist Mempells]	P 802 [JTKrebs, 1710—14]	undetermined
765	Ms 7(4) [Preller]	P 801 [JTKrebs, ca. 1714]	undetermined

F. Partitas (BWV 766—771).

| 768 | Ms 7(25) [Preller] | Carpentras Ms 1086 [anon] P 802 [JTKrebs, 1714—17] Königsberg 15839 (lost) [JGWalther] MB Lpz III.8.17 [Bach-circle anon, 1740—50] | Leipzig |

Among the free organ works there are several unambiguous examples. BWV 532(2) appears in a copy, P 595, by Johannes Ringk, a Kellner-circle scribe whose connection to the Bach circle is well established by his copy of BWV 202 [47]; it would be very difficult to establish that Ringk was copying in Weimar, not Leipzig. BWV 541 appears in 3 significant sources outside the Mempell-Preller collection: (1) MB Lpz Ms a 1, a fair copy by Bach himself from the Leipzig period, (2) P 288, a Kellner-circle copy, and (3) P 595, a copy by Ringk. All three sources apparently depend on the Weimar autograph (now lost), and it seems impossible that this autograph could have been located in Weimar rather than Leipzig. For BWV 548 there exists a fair copy, P 274/II, made by Bach himself and a Kellner-circle scribe, dating from after 1735 (to judge from Bach's handwriting). It is most unlikely that this copy was made in Weimar. The complete list of free organ works in the Mempell-Preller collection which appear in copies by known Bach-circle scribes of the Leipzig period is as follows: BWV 527a(1), BWV 532(2), BWV 533a(2), BWV 535(1), BWV 541, BWV 548, BWV 551, and BWV 569. The fact that these pieces were copied by Bach-circle scribes, who have no known connections with Walther, establishes the location of the Weimar autographs of these works in Bach's possession in Leipzig, rather than in Walther's possession in Weimar. It therefore follows that the Mempell-Preller copies of these free organ works could not have been copied in Weimar either.

Proceeding to the organ works based on chorales (BWV 599—771), the Mempell-Preller manuscripts seem to neglect the *Orgelbüchlein* pieces (BWV 599—644). However, the possibility that the two *Orgelbüchlein* pieces which are extant in the Mempell-Preller manuscripts, Preller's copy of BWV 617 and Mempell's copy of BWV 635, were copied from Bach autographs in Walther's possession can be virtually eliminated. The autograph of the *Orgelbüchlein*, P 283, the principal surviving Weimar autograph of Bach's organ works, was begun about 1713—14 and completed about 1715—16; Bach himself added the title-page in Köthen, and he added BWV 613, as well as the fragment "O Traurigkeit..." in Leipzig after 1740 [48]. J. T. Krebs's copy in P 801 was taken from P 283 while it was still a work-in-progress, about 1714 [49], and the variant readings show that Walther's version (Berlin Mus ms 22541/1&2) was not taken from J. T. Krebs's copy, but probably from P 283 slightly later. Meißner's copy, made about 1727—30 [50], demonstrates that P 283 was located in Leipzig at that time, since Meißner was an intimate member of the Bach circle. In summary, P 283 accompanied Bach from Weimar, where it was composed, and where J. T. Krebs and Walther made copies from it, to Köthen, where Bach added the title-page, to Leipzig, where Meißner made a copy of it about 1727—30, and where Bach himself made revisions and additions after 1740.

---

[47] MB Lpz Ms R 8. See NBA I/40, Krit. Ber., pp. 10—12.
[48] Dadelsen *OB*, p. 77.
[49] See footnote 19.
[50] Dadelsen *OB*, p. 78, footnote 15. "Anonymus 1" in Dadelsen's nomenclature, elsewhere known as "Hauptkopist B" and "Schreiber des Continuo", has been identified in H.-J. Schulze, "Johann Sebastian Bach und Christian Gottlob Meißner" (*Bach-Jahrbuch 1968*, 80—88).

Thus, if Walther were to have owned an autograph of BWV 617 and BWV 635 from which Mempell and Preller copied, it could not have been P 283; it would have to have been a now lost "second" autograph. Had Walther owned such an autograph, it is highly likely that his own copies of BWV 617 would have been taken from it. However, the variant readings in Walther's copies are not reflected in Preller's copy. A study of the variants indicates that all the copies shown in the table were probably taken from P 283. Thus, there is little reason to suspect the existence of a lost "second" autograph for this piece, and it appears virtually certain that Preller's copy of BWV 617 and Mempell's copy of BWV 635 were taken from the autograph P 283 in Leipzig.

Of the 17 chorales (BWV 651—667), the Mempell-Preller manuscripts record 13 early versions. Bach's revised fair copy P 271, dated by Dadelsen as 1744—48 [51], establishes the later versions of these pieces, and its existence is evidence that the Weimar autographs, upon which P 271 was presumably based, must have been in Bach's possession at this time. Bach's possession is also confirmed by Gerber's copy of BWV 655a in P 1009 (presumably 1724—26) and by an anonymous Bach-circle scribe's copy of BWV 664a in MB Lpz III.8.8 (1740—50). Particularly notable among the 17 chorales is one example, BWV 660a, for which the Weimar autograph has been preserved [52]. As shown in the table, there are several important concordances to this valuable document: (1) J. T. Krebs's copy in P 802, (2) two copies by J. G. Walther in Berlin Mus ms 22541/1&2 (the two copies transmit virtually the same reading of the work), and (3) Preller's copy in MB Lpz Ms 7(36). A comparison of the significant variant readings (which are only 3 in number) does not suggest dependence among the copies. It would appear that each scribe copied independently from the autograph. Thus, in the three cases for which Bach's Weimar autograph is extant (BWV 617, 635, and 660a), the Mempell-Preller manuscripts seem to be taken from the autographs [53].

The exclusion of Walther as the owner of the Weimar autographs of the 17 chorales appears to be readily demonstrated by the existence of Bach's revised fair copy of them in P 271, which must have been based on Weimar autographs in Bach's possession. However, the logic of this exclusion is clouded by one of Klotz's proposals — the hypothetical existence of a second, earlier (lost) set of Weimar autographs [54]. Were this hypothesis

---

[51] Dadelsen, *Beiträge*, pp. 109—110.

[52] P 271, pp. 108—110. This fascicle is clearly a later addition to the main body of the manuscript.

[53] In his description of Ms 7 (NBA IV/2, Krit. Ber., p. 40), Klotz asserts that Ms 7 is "wahrscheinlich unmittelbar oder mittelbar nach Waltherschen Vorlagen (geschrieben)". In his "Stemma 5: Die hs. Gesamttradition der 'Siebzehn Choräle'" (NBA IV/2, Krit. Ber., p. 63), it is indicated that the Mempell-Preller manuscripts are taken from the Walther-Krebs manuscripts. This relationship seems very unlikely to the present writer. The resemblances which definitely do exist between the Walther-Krebs manuscripts and the Mempell-Preller manuscripts result from the fact that both collections were copied from the same models, rather than the fact that one was copied from the other. In the time between the copying of the two collections, some of the models were revised (see the discussion of BWV 722, 729, 732, and 738 below).

[54] Manuscript [U] in NBA IV/2, Krit. Ber., p. 55.

demonstrable, it would be possible that both Bach and Walther owned autographs of the 17 chorales. However, just as the evidence for the existence of the later set of Weimar autographs depends on the extant Weimar autograph of BWV 660a at the end of P 271, the evidence for the existence of the earlier set of Weimar autographs depends on a fragment of BWV 667b in P 801 which Klotz believed to be autograph, and which he published in facsimile as an autograph[55]. Recent research indicates, however, that this fragment is definitely not in the hand of Bach[56]. Deprived of the one "hard" fact upon which this hypothesis is based, the existence of a second set of Weimar autographs for the 17 chorales, which might also be doubted on other grounds, seems most unlikely. Thus, despite certain complications, it remains a reasonable supposition that during his lifetime, Bach appears to have been the sole possessor of the Weimar autographs of the 17 chorales.

Among the miscellaneous organ chorales (BWV 714—765), the transmission of BWV 722, 729, 732, and 738 is particularly informative. In Preller's copy, MB Lpz Ms 7(26), these four pieces are transmitted with the title *Vier/Weynachts Chorale* in the order BWV 722, 738, 729, 732. J. T. Krebs's copy in P 802 (1710—14 according to Zietz) observes the same order, but offers the early versions of the pieces, that is, BWV 722a, 738a, 729a, and 732a. It would appear that both J. T. Krebs and Preller copied from the now lost autograph, but that the autograph was revised sometime between the two copies. In any event, it is not possible that Preller's copy was taken from that of J. T. Krebs[57].

The partita *Sey gegrüßet* (BWV 768) is particularly rich in concordances from before 1750, although no autograph has survived: (1) a presumably early copy, Carpentras, Bibliothèque Inguimbert, Ms 1086[58], (2) J. T. Krebs's copy in P 802 (1714—17 according to Zietz), (3) Walther's copy in Königsberg 15839 (lost), (4) Preller's copy in MB Lpz Ms 7(25), and (5) an anonymous Bach-circle scribe's copy in MB Lpz III.8.17 (about 1740—50). The existence of this last source (5) indicates that the early autograph of BWV 768 was probably still in Bach's possession during the later years of his life, while the existence of sources (2) and (3) indicates Bach's possession of it at earlier periods. Thus, it is highly unlikely that Preller's copy (4) could have been copied from the autograph anywhere else than in Leipzig.

The evidence which has been summarized in the table is not nearly as complete as would be desirable, since relevant concordances for all the organ works in the Mempell-

---

[55] NBA IV/2, p. VI.

[56] "Aus dem Schriftduktus des Fragmentes ergibt sich jedoch einwandfrei, daß es nicht von J. S. Bach geschrieben ist . . . Die Form der Viertelpausen (Takte 11, 16, 20) sowie auch die der Achtelpausen schließen Bach als Schreiber mit Sicherheit aus." (Zietz, p. 104.)

[57] The filiation of manuscripts proposed by Klotz in NBA IV/3, Krit. Ber., ignores this fact.

[58] A facsimile page is given in Lohmann (ed.), *Joh. Seb. Bach: Sämtliche Orgelwerke*, Band 10 (Wiesbaden, 1969), p. IX. There is a certain similarity between the hand of this scribe and that of the anonymus scribe of the Plauener Orgelbuch (see Lohmann [ed.], *Joh. Seb. Bach: Sämtliche Orgelwerke*, Band 9 [Wiesbaden, 1969], p. X).

Preller manuscripts do not exist. Yet, it appears sufficient to exclude the Mempell-Preller manuscripts from the search for evidence of Bach autographs in Walther's possession. Of the 17 free organ works in the Mempell-Preller manuscripts, 8 of the Weimar autographs can be shown to have been in Leipzig rather than Weimar after 1723. The extant *Orgelbüchlein* autograph, P 283, from the Weimar period, was demonstrably in Leipzig at the time Mempell and Preller made two copies from it, as were the Weimar autographs of the 17 chorales, from which Mempell and Preller took 13 copies, and the early autograph of BWV 768, of which Preller made a copy. Thus, of the 49 Bach organ works in the Mempell-Preller manuscripts, it can be demonstrated that 24 of the autographs were in Bach's possession in Leipzig. For the remaining 25 pieces, the concordances are insufficient to establish the location of the autograph. Not one autograph can be located in Weimar. Thus, the hypothetical connection of Mempell and Preller with the Walther circle must be rejected. The evidence of the concordances seems to confirm that Mempell and Preller were members of, or connected with, the Bach circle in Leipzig.

The Mempell-Preller manuscripts can thus be added to the previously discussed list of major collections emanating from the Bach circle in Leipzig — the H. N. Gerber manuscripts, the Kellner-circle manuscripts, and the copies by the anonymous scribe of MB Lpz III.8.7. In conjunction with Bach's own fair copies from the Leipzig period, these collections represent virtually all the sources for Bach's Weimar organ works dating from the Leipzig period. Had Walther owned autographs of Bach's Weimar organ works, it could reasonably be expected that at least one copy of these works would have survived indicating Weimar, not Leipzig, as its point of origin. Indeed, it might be expected that all the copies of a given work whose autograph was in Walther's possession would point toward Weimar. In fact, not a single such "Weimar" copy has been discovered. A number of individual fascicles offer no evidence concerning geographical point of origin, but these neutral fascicles can nearly all be grouped with fascicles for which Leipzig is the demonstrable point of origin. Thus, the extant musical sources, incomplete as they may be, offer no support for the hypothesis that Walther was the possessor of the Weimar autographs of Bach's organ works.

At the outset, it was proposed that if Walther had indeed owned a large number of Bach autographs, as is implied by the letter of 6 August 1729 to Bokemeyer, it would be reasonable to suppose that one or more of the extant copies would show Weimar, rather than Leipzig, as the point of origin. A survey of the major sources for the Bach organ works, however, has failed to produce even a single "Weimar" source. Without doubting the accuracy of either the document or the evidence from the musical sources, tentative explanations for this apparent conflict might include: (1) the autographs referred to by Walther did not include organ works, (2) Walther withheld the autographs from his students, and, therefore, they could not have made copies, and/or (3) the autographs in Walther's possession were re-acquired by Bach soon after Walther wrote the letter to Bokemeyer in 1729.

The first explanation is unlikely in light of the wording of the letter itself. The excerpt is concerned with "Clavier-Sachen". Bach and Buxtehude are referred to as "Teütschen Organisten". Furthermore, "Herrn Auctore selbst, als welcher 9 Jahr Hof-Organist allhier gewesen" is surely a reference to Bach's Weimar period. Assuming that at least half of the "über 200 Stücke" mentioned in the letter were by Bach [59], that "Clavier-Sachen" are continuously being referred to in the excerpt, and that Walther received the autographs during Bach's Weimar period, it can only be concluded that the collection of autographs must have included a considerable number of organ works.

The second explanation — that Walther withheld the autographs from his students — is difficult to validate, but it brings up the question of whether Walther even had any students while he supposedly owned the autographs. In another letter to Bokemeyer, dated 12 March 1731, Walther reports that the number of his students has dwindled to three, whereas he earlier had fifteen to eighteen [60]. The later Walther-Bokemeyer letters show that during the 1730's and 1740's he suffered greatly from the lack of students. Apparently, however, during the 1720's he had quite a few, and several are known by name — Adlung, Labes, Roth, Seyfarth. For this reason, if copies of Bach autographs are to be hypothesized and searched for, such copies would most likely have been made in the 1720's, not later. This circumstance strongly favors the conclusion reached above on other grounds, namely, that the major collections of the 1730's and 1740's, such as the Mempell-Preller manuscripts, were not copied from sources in Walther's collection, but rather in the context of Bach's teaching in Leipzig. However, it remains puzzling that Walther's presumably rich collection of Bach autographs is not witnessed by at least one copy from among his students of the 1720's unless he specifically withheld the collection from them.

The third tentative explanation — that the autographs were re-acquired by Bach — does not clarify the lack of copies from the Walther circle of the 1720's, but it explains why the extant copies of the Bach organ works, which mostly date from the 1730's and 1740's, were copied in Leipzig, not in Weimar. From as early as 1726, Walther's material circumstances were deteriorating [61], and from as early as 1729 the sale of items from his library is recorded [62]. Walther sent musical items to Bokemeyer partly in return for his help on the *Lexikon*, partly in trade for items from Bokemeyer's own musical library, and partly for cash. (Indeed, the excerpt from the letter of 6 August 1729, describing Walther's holdings of Bach and Buxtehude, might well be read in this context.) Yet Bokemeyer apparently did not place an order for the Bach and Buxtehude repertoire, as there is little trace of it in the letters or in his library, which has been preserved and recently reconstructed [63]. A similar letter to Bach, however, might well have received a favorable response. Although an exchange of letters between Walther

[59] Actually, Bach's share of the 200 pieces would probably have to be greater than half, since Buxtehude's entire (extant) production for the clavier is less than 100 pieces.

[60] Schünemann *BJ 1933*, p. 115.

[61] See Brodde, p. 13.

[62] See Schünemann *BJ 1933*, p. 100.

[63] Harald Kümmerling, *Katalog der Sammlung Bokemeyer* (Kassel, 1970).

and Bach is not extant, it is to be assumed, since Bach is listed as the Leipzig agent
for Walther's *Lexikon* [64], since Bach later acted for Walther in recommending his variations on *Allein Gott* to a publisher [65], and since a Walther-Bokemeyer letter of 24 January
1738 records that Bach responded to Walther's request for a canon solution [66]. Thus,
the re-acquisition by Bach of his autographs is a possibility, although there is no real
evidence to support it.

The second and third explanations — that Walther withheld the Bach autographs
from his students and that Bach re-acquired the autographs — seem to be required
if Schünemann's interpretation — that Bach gave Walther all these pieces in Weimar as
a gift — is to be reconciled with the other "facts" of the case. It is to be acknowledged
that Schünemann's interpretation (with the resulting explanations) deserves primary
consideration, based on the evidence of Walther's letter alone. However, the complete
lack of support for it in the musical sources suggests another possibility: that "von dem
Herrn Auctore selbst ... bekommen" refers not to Bach's gift-giving but to Walther's
copying activities in Weimar. It is quite possible, perhaps even quite likely, that Walther
obtained the pieces "from the author himself" by copying them out from the autographs. The evidence of Walther's prodigious copying activities is not hypothetical — it
has been well-preserved [67], and such a reading of Walther's statement resolves the apparent conflict between Schünemann's interpretation and the evidence of the extant
musical sources [68].

Yet, if this somewhat oblique reading is accurate, it would be reasonable to expect
support for it in other sources. The extant Walther documents have been carefully
searched for references to Bach in the preparation of *Bach-Dokumente II*, and the
relevant items appear to be:
(1) Documents #369 and #410, from two Walther-Bokemeyer letters dated 3. 8. 1735
and 24. 1. 1738, concerning the canon BWV 1074. Apparently, after 3. 8. 1735 Walther
requested a resolution from Bach, who complied with the request before 24. 1. 1738, at
which date Walther included the autograph resolution in his letter to Bokemeyer.

---

[64] *Bach-Dokumente II*, p. 191.
[65] Schünemann *BJ 1933*, p. 108; Brodde, p. 10; *Bach-Dokumente II*, pp. 265, 268, 329.
[66] *Bach-Dokumente II*, #410
[67] See the Walther manuscripts listed in footnote 5. Zietz provides a thorough study of the
Walther-Krebs manuscripts P 801—3, but the remainder of Walther's library has not yet
received intensive treatment.
[68] If this reading of Walther's statement is suggested for the Bach pieces, then it probably also
applies to the pieces by Buxtehude. "Die erstern habe mehrentheils von dem seeligen Herrn
Werckmeister, und des Herrn Buxtehudens eigner Hand in Teütscher Tabulatur ... bekommen"
can be read to mean that Walther copied from Buxtehude autographs and Werckmeister copies,
not that he actually owned them. Walther's autobiography (Mattheson: *Ehrenpforte*, p. 388)
provides the following supplementary information: "(Werckmeister) stifftete ... einen ver-
gnügten Brief-Wechsel mit mir, wodurch ich manches schönes Clavier-Stück von des kunstreichen
Buxtehudens Arbeit bekommen". Further, Schünemann quotes a Walther-Bokemeyer letter
(30. 7. 1738) in which Bokemeyer's son-in-law is sent a "Buxtehudischen schön und kunstlich
gesetzten Choral" (*BJ 1933*, p. 101). However, as in the case of the Bach pieces sent to Bokemeyer, it is impossible to prove whether this piece was an autograph or a copy.

(2)   Document #322, a Walther-Bokemeyer letter dated 29. 7. 1733, concerning the transmission of a Heinichen cantata manuscript from Walther to Bokemeyer. According to Walther's letter, "Die Überschrift ... ist von des Leipziger Herrn Bachs Hand". This manuscript is preserved as Berlin, Deutsche Staatsbibliothek, Mus ms 30210, and a facsimile of the first page is given in Kümmerling's *Katalog der Sammlung Bokemeyer* (page 272). As is noted in *Bach-Dokumente II* (page 238), only the attribution "d. J: Dav: Heinichen" is in Bach's hand. The manuscript itself is in the hand of J. G. Walther. According to Zietz's handwriting criteria, it seems to fall in the transition from Walther's "early" to his "late" hand, that is, approximately 1712 [69].

(3)   Documents #361 and #377, Walther-Bokemeyer letters dated 27. 1. 1735 and 26. 1. 1736, referring to Bokemeyer's purchase of a "Bachische Kupfer-Exemplar" — presumably one of the six partitas BWV 825—830.

The first documents, concerning the canon, provide no new insights into Walther's autograph collection. The second document is more relevant, since it refers to a copy by Walther, bearing some relation to Bach in Weimar, which was eventually purchased by Bokemeyer. Were this copy a clavier work by Bach, the question of whether Walther's letter of 6 August 1729 refers to autographs or copies would be resolved in favor of copies. However, since this copy is a cantata, and by Heinichen rather than Bach, it proves nothing, suggestive as it may be. The third document, concerning the "Bachische Kupfer-Exemplar" *is* a specific example of a Bach clavier work which Walther obtained "from the author himself" and subsequently sold to Bokemeyer. The problem with this bit of evidence is that (1) it does not date from Bach's Weimar period and (2) the remaining 199 pieces mentioned by Walther could not, likewise, be original prints, since Bach and Buxtehude published so few works. Thus, the extant Walther documents are suggestive, but they provide no clear evidence either for Schünemann's interpretation, that Bach presented Walther with a large number of autographs as a gift, or for the alternative interpretation, that Walther obtained the Bach and Buxtehude clavier pieces by copying them out in the manner of the Heinichen cantata manuscript. The extant sources do not support Schünemann's interpretation, but the possibility that supporting sources may simply have disappeared, like most of the autographs themselves, cannot be excluded.

Therefore, to summarize, the extant evidence has turned out to be insufficient to answer definitely the question of whether Walther actually owned the now lost autographs of Bach's organ works or whether his letter of 6 August 1729 refers to copies instead of autographs. While the sum of the extant evidence presented above appears to favor the hypothesis of copies rather than autographs, this appearance could be illusory. The extant sources are known to be fragmentary, and the extant evidence is quite circumstantial; it cannot be considered logically conclusive. Thus, Walther's possible ownership of

---

[69] The 4/4 equivalent "C" is the large "late" form, while the black-note stems are often connected at the middle of the notehead, an "early" characteristic.

Bach autographs and, in fact, his whole relationship to Bach after the Weimar period, remain open questions [70].

Yet, it has been shown that even if Walther did own the lost autographs, his ownership was inconsequential for posterity. No doubt, Walther's personal copies of Bach organ works were taken from autograph sources, whether he owned them or not. However, the aspect of his alleged ownership which has far greater implications for Bach research is the possibility that the other extant copies of Bach's organ works were partly or totally produced in Weimar. The foregoing investigation denies this possibility. All the extant copies from before 1750 of Bach's organ works are to be associated not with Walther, but with Bach himself.

Thus, as in the case of Walther's potentially invaluable *Lexikon* (which in reality includes only a brief article on Bach and articles on only four of his students), Walther's musical library is a tantalizing, but nevertheless disappointing source of information about J. S. Bach. No doubt, the extant manuscripts are but a fraction of the original collection, and it is much to be regretted that Walther was economically compelled to scatter these holdings as early as two decades before his death. Nevertheless, indications are that Walther the musician, teacher and scholar was not nearly as concerned about clarifying Bach problems for posterity as the present-day researcher would desire. In the case of the lost Weimar autographs of Bach's organ works, Walther's testimony seems to create as many problems as it solves.

[70] The problem of Walther's relationship with Bach, especially after Bach's departure from Weimar, is discussed in Jauernig, "Johann Sebastian Bach in Weimar" (*Johann Sebastian Bach in Thüringen* [Weimar, 1950]), p. 78 ff. Jauernig seeks to explain the remarkable brevity of the Bach article in Walther's *Lexikon*, which Spitta interpreted as a sign of a cooling of the Walther-Bach friendship, as resulting from court censorship. However, despite censorship, it can still be suggested that Walther may have had somewhat mixed feelings about Bach. After all, Bach was a staunchly practical musician, while Walther was much less successful as a practical musician than as a theorist and writer about music. In fact, Bach's students, especially Vogler, received more recognition as practical musicians in Weimar than Walther. Walther's heroes were not practical musicians but theorists, and the longest articles in the *Lexikon* are about theorists — Augustinus, Boethius, Paulinus, Vanneo, Mattheson. Practical musicians in general are the subjects of shorter articles, although in comparison to Telemann, Oesterreich, and Kuhnau, the articles on Bach and Buxtehude still seem short. Finally, however, satisfactory coverage of this interesting but problematic relationship would have to be based on new evidence.

CHRISTOPH WOLFF

Johann Sebastian Bachs „Sterbechoral":
Kritische Fragen zu einem Mythos

Es diente weder der Glorifizierung von Bachs Lebenswerk, noch ging es um das Aufrichten eines Mythos, wenn dem Torso der *Kunst der Fuge* in dem bald nach Bachs Tode veröffentlichten Originaldruck ein Choralsatz beigefügt wurde. Der Grund für die Beigabe der vierstimmigen Choralbearbeitung *Wenn wir in hoechsten Noethen* (BWV 668) findet sich in einer knappen *Nachricht* des ungenannten Herausgebers auf der Rückseite des Titelblattes:

> Man hat ... die Freunde seiner Muse durch Mittheilung des am Ende beygefügten vierstimmig ausgearbeiteten Kirchenchorals, den der selige Mann in seiner Blindheit einem seiner Freunde aus dem Stegereif in die Feder dictiret hat, schadlos halten wollen.

In einer ganz ähnlichen Formulierung erscheint diese Notiz innerhalb des längeren Vorwortes, das Friedrich Wilhelm Marpurg der von ihm betreuten 2. Auflage der *Kunst der Fuge* (Leipzig 1752) mitgab:

> Man hat indessen Ursache, sich zu schmeicheln, daß der zugefügte vierstimmig ausgearbeitete Kirchenchoral, den der selige Mann in seiner Blindheit einem seiner Freunde aus dem Stegereif in die Feder dictiret hat, diesen Mangel ersetzen, und die Freunde seiner Muse schadlos halten wird.

Dies sind die ältesten literarischen Quellen, die etwas über die Umstände der Entstehung dieses Chorales anzugeben wissen. Sie machen zugleich klar, daß der Choral mit der *Kunst der Fuge* überhaupt nichts zu tun hat, sondern in pietätvoller Geste als Entschädigung für die unvollendete Schlußfuge beigegeben worden ist.

Es verwundert, daß der von Carl Philipp Emanuel Bach und Johann Friedrich Agricola verfaßte *Nekrolog*[1] als älteste authentische Biographie sich über den Choral und die denkwürdigen Umstände seiner Entstehung ausschweigt. Wußten sie nichts darüber, oder erschien ihnen die Geschichte nicht sonderlich erwähnenswert? Berichtet wird sie dann in Johann Michael Schmidts *Musico-Theologia*[2] bei einer Diskussion der späten kontrapunktischen Werke, insbesondere der *Kunst der Fuge*:

> ... oder, welches ihm noch wunderbarer vorkommen muß, den in seiner Blindheit von ihm einem andern in die Feder dictirten Choral: Wenn wir in höchsten Nöthen seyn.

---

[1] Abgedruckt in der *Musikalischen Bibliothek*, Bd. IV, hg. von L. Mizler, Leipzig 1754.
[2] Bayreuth und Hof, 1754, S. 124.

Schmidts Formulierung stützt sich deutlich auf die Notiz im Originaldruck der *Kunst der Fuge*; er läßt nur „aus dem Stegereif" fort. Dafür leitet er die Zitierung mit einer ehrfürchtig-staunenden Wertung („noch wunderbarer vorkommen") ein.

Die nächste literarische Erwähnung findet sich erst rund ein halbes Jahrhundert später bei Johann Nicolaus Forkel, und zwar nicht im biographischen Teil seines Buches, sondern im Werkkatalog. Hier heißt es im Zusammenhang mit der *Kunst der Fuge* [3]:

> Zum Ersatz des Fehlenden an der letztern Fuge ist dem Werk am Schluß der 4stimmig ausgearbeitete Choral: Wenn wir in höchsten Nöthen sind etc. beygefügt worden. Bach hat ihn in seiner Blindheit, wenige Tage vor seinem Ende, seinem Schwiegersohn Altnikol in die Feder dictirt. Von der in diesem Choral liegenden Kunst will ich nichts sagen; sie war dem Verf[asser]. desselben so geläufig geworden, daß er sie auch in der Krankheit ausüben konnte. Aber der darin liegende Ausdruck von frommer Ergebung und Andacht hat mich stets ergriffen, so oft ich ihn gespielt habe, so daß ich kaum sagen kann, was ich lieber entbehren wollte, diesen Choral, oder das Ende der letztern Fuge.

Forkel weiß offenbar mehr als der Editor der *Kunst der Fuge*, obwohl er sich im ganzen an den überlieferten Wortlaut hält, wie eine Gegenüberstellung der entscheidenden Partien verdeutlicht:

Kunst der Fuge	*Forkel*
in seiner Blindheit	in seiner Blindheit, wenige Tage vor seinem Ende
einem seiner Freunde	seinem Schwiegersohn Altnikol
aus dem Stegereif	
in die Feder dictiret	in die Feder dictirt

Forkel nennt ein genaues Datum für den Zeitpunkt des Diktats, ebenso den Namen desjenigen, der das Diktat aufnahm. Woher nimmt er diese Kenntnisse? Nach eigenen Angaben hat er wichtige Informationen biographischer Art von den beiden ältesten Bach-Söhnen erhalten. Diese lassen sich auch teilweise aus dem Text eruieren [4]. Doch an der Stelle, wo Forkel Bachs Ende beschreibt (mit falschem Sterbedatum: 30. Juli 1750), findet sich nichts über das Choraldiktat. Und hätte er hier einen authentischen Bericht bekommen, dürfte er ihn zweifellos an dieser Stelle verarbeitet haben. So aber findet sich die Geschichte innerhalb des Werkkataloges (der sich im übrigen auf keine Auskünfte der Bach-Söhne stützt), noch dazu in deutlicher Anlehnung an die Formulierung im Originaldruck der *Kunst der Fuge*. Es scheint, als habe Forkel hier die historische Überlieferung eigenmächtig ergänzt bzw. konkretisiert [5]. Er macht sich ein anschauliches Bild von Bachs Ende und verschweigt dabei nicht seine subjektiven Empfindungen.

---

[3] *Johann Sebastian Bachs Leben, Kunst und Kunstwerke*, Leipzig 1802, S. 53 f.
[4] *Bach-Urkunden*, hg. von M. Schneider, = Veröff. der NBG, 17. Jg., Leipzig 1916.
[5] Vgl. Anm. 19.

Philipp Spitta schließt sich in seinem grundlegenden biographischen Werk an Forkels Darstellung an; ja, er ergänzt sie um weitere Einzelheiten[6]:

> Um das Sterbebett stand neben der Gattin und den Töchtern der jüngste Sohn Christian, der Schwiegersohn Altnikol und der letzte Schüler Müthel. Mit Altnikol hatte Bach noch wenige Tage vor seinem Tode gearbeitet. Ein Orgelchoral aus alter Zeit schwebte vor seiner sterbensbereiten Seele, dem er die Vollendung geben wollte. Er dictirte und Altnikol schrieb. „Wenn wir in höchsten Nöthen sein" hatte er den Choral früher bezeichnet: jetzt schöpfte er die Stimmung aus einem andern Liede: er ließ es überschreiben „Vor deinen Thron tret ich hiemit".

Dieser kleine Abschnitt ist überaus bezeichnend für Spittas Arbeitsweise. Einerseits stellt er seine Vertrautheit mit den historischen Daten und Fakten zu Bachs Leben und Werk, wie sie zuvor niemand besessen hat, unter Beweis. Andererseits verknüpft er solche Einzelbausteine oft in einer der historischen Exaktheit widersprechenden Weise, daß sie sich seinem Ideal und Ziel eines geschlossenen Bildes fügen, mit dem tatsächlichen Sachverhalt jedoch nicht übereinstimmen. Aus Forkels Bericht übernimmt er z. B. den Namen des Diktatempfängers und das Datum. Dies ist jedoch nicht ausreichend für eine historische Szene, denn um eine solche geht es ihm. So zieht er weitere Personen heran, von denen er annimmt, daß sie dabeigewesen sein könnten, und versammelt sie um Bachs Sterbebett. Auf dokumentarische Belege kann er sich hierbei freilich nicht stützen. Was Forkel und offenbar auch dem Editor der *Kunst der Fuge* unbekannt war, läßt Spittas Sachkenntnis aber nun noch in die Darstellung einfließen, nämlich die Verbindung des „Sterbechorals" zu einem älteren Satz. Er meint damit die kleine Choralbearbeitung „Wenn wir in höchsten Nöten sein" (BWV 641) aus dem *Orgelbüchlein.*

Spitta wird an romanhafter Bildhaftigkeit und poetisierendem Stil von Wilhelm Rust, dem Chefeditor der alten Bach-Ausgabe für mehr als ein Vierteljahrhundert, noch weit übertroffen, wenn dieser in seinem Revisionsbericht zu den Choralbearbeitungen Bachs seiner Fantasie nunmehr freien Raum gibt[7]:

> Aber in dem umnachteten Körper lebte und webte in altem Glanze jene Gotteskraft, die ihn zum musikalischen Apostel erhoben. Noch einmal wollte sie zeugen und reden, und ging auf das Lied einer früheren Zeit zurück, das sie hier in verklärter, vollendeter Gestalt zur Erscheinung bringt. Waltete bei dieser Wahl vielleicht die Erinnerung an seine erst Frau, die er einst verreisend wohl und munter verließ, um sie, ahnungslos zurückkehrend, auf dem Friedhofe schlummernd wiederzufinden? War die Urgestalt im Orgelbüchlein eine Gedenktafel für sie, die er auf dem eigenen Sterbebette noch einmal aufschlug? Damals hatte er die geistliche Dichtung „Wenn wir in höchsten Nöthen sein" im Sinne; jetzt aber liess

---

[6] Spitta II, S. 759 f.
[7] BG 25/2 (1878), S. XX f.

er durch seinen Schwiegersohn, dem er den Choral in die Feder dictirte, die Überschrift ändern, und zwar mit der ausgesprochenen Beziehung auf das Lied: „Vor
deinen Thron tret' ich". Leider ist der Schluß von dem Dictat abhanden gekommen, das im ganzen noch 25 und einen halben Takt zählt. Aber schon bis dahin
kennzeichnet die Schrift alle die Ruhepunkte, die sich der Kranke gönnen mußte;
nicht minder aber auch die Hindernisse, die dem Schreiber seine Arbeit in dem
Zimmer des Augenleidenden erschwerten. Die versiegende Dinte ward von Tag
zu Tag wässriger. Schwer verhangene Fenster und ein mattes Dämmerlicht beein-
flussten die Deutlichkeit der Noten zu ihrem Nachtheile. Ein trübes, trauriges
Bild, das in dem Beschauenden unwillkürlich den Eindruck hervorruft, wie in der
Werkstatt des Meisters Alles dem Ende und der ewigen Ruhe zuneigte.

Der Philologe Rust erwähnt nun sogar das Diktatmanuskript und beschreibt den Ablauf
des Diktierens. Bei dem Manuskript handelt es sich um den fragmentarisch erhaltenen
Eintrag in der sog. Leipziger Originalhandschrift, auf die wir noch näher zurückkommen
müssen. Doch ist das betreffende Blatt weder von Altnikol geschrieben noch stellt es die
Diktatniederschrift dar. Rusts Bemerkung über die Ruhepunkte und die versiegende Tinte
entbehren überdies jeder Grundlage [8].

Verfolgt man nun die Entwicklungsstufen, die die anfänglich fast unscheinbare Notiz
aus dem Originaldruck der *Kunst der Fuge* bis hin zu der aufgeblähten Erzählung Rusts
durchgemacht hat, ohne daß neue Dokumente aufgetreten wären, so kommt man zwangsläufig zu dem Schluß, daß hier so etwas wie Mythenbildung vorliegt. Alle wesentlichen
Charakteristika eines echten Mythos treffen zusammen: Aus einer kleinen Keimzelle,
einer unkommentierten Tatsachennotiz, erwächst ein konkret-anschaulicher Bericht mit
stark religiöser Einfärbung. Und der Mythos des vom Ewigkeitshauch durchwehten
Sterbezimmers Bachs hat mit den letztgenannten Quellen seinen Höhepunkt noch nicht
einmal erreicht. Doch scheint es kaum notwendig, seine weitere noch heute wirksame Entwicklung über Albert Schweitzer und dann die ganze populärwissenschaftliche Bach-
Literatur hinaus zu verfolgen. Die Weichen wurden im späten 19. Jahrhundert mit den
autoritativen Arbeiten Spittas und Rusts gestellt. Der „Fünfte Evangelist" war damit
sozusagen vorprogrammiert.

Unsere kritischen Fragen entzünden sich nun nicht an der Mythenbildung als solcher
(und es wäre dies hier ja auch nicht der erste und einzige Fall in Richtung Idealisierung
oder gar Ideologisierung des Bach-Bildes), sondern an dem beglaubigten literarischen Kern
der „Erzählung", wie er im Originaldruck der *Kunst der Fuge* vorliegt, und in seinem
Verhältnis zu dem erhaltenen musikalischen Quellenmaterial. Spitta und Rust haben
auch die handschriftlichen Quellen nicht befragt, sondern sich vielmehr von ihrem Enthu-
siasmus hinreißen lassen, was man ihnen angesichts der Zeitsituation auch wohl kaum
zum Vorwurf machen kann. Es handelt sich um folgende drei Quellen:

---

[8] Vgl. G. v. Dadelsen, *Beiträge zur Chronologie der Werke Johann Sebastian Bachs,* = Tübinger
Bach-Studien, Heft 4/5, Tübingen 1958, S. 114.

1. die 9taktige Choralbearbeitung *Wenn wir in höchsten Nöten sein,* BWV 641, aus dem *Orgelbüchlein*[9a] (nachfolgend Fassung O),

2. die 45taktige Choralbearbeitung *Wenn wir in höchsten Nöten sein,* BWV 668, im Anhang der *Kunst der Fuge* (nachfolgend Fassung W),

3. das 25½taktige Fragment der Choralbearbeitung *Vor deinen Thron tret ich hiermit,* BWV 668a, am Schluß der sog. Leipziger Originalhandschrift[9b] (nachfolgend Fassung V).

Spitta und Rust haben bereits darauf hingewiesen, daß V und O miteinander zusammenhängen. V sei eine erweiterte Fassung von O. W erwähnen sie merkwürdigerweise nicht. Hans Klotz[10] hat nun ausgeführt, daß W eine ältere Gestalt von V sei, woraus sich die Chronologie von O über W zu V ergibt. Damit erledigt sich Rusts Behauptung, V sei die Diktatfassung. Nach Klotz nimmt W diese Stellung ein, während V ihm als spätere Überarbeitung gilt[11]. Zeitlich verlegt Klotz W „gegen Ende seines [Bachs] Lebens, während seines Krankenlagers" und V in die Tage „kurz vor seinem Tode".

Der Sachverhalt wäre einleuchtend, käme man nicht an den kritischen Punkt des Verhältnisses von O und W. Eine genaue Untersuchung ergibt nämlich, daß die beiden Sätze in ihrem Kernbestand identisch sind. Der vierstimmige Satz des *Orgelbüchleins* kehrt bis auf die dekolorierte Oberstimme mit dem cantus firmus und geringfügige Abweichungen in den Unterstimmen wörtlich im „Sterbechoral" wieder, wie die Synopse auf Seite 287f. verdeutlicht. Die Erweiterung der Fassungen W und V bestehen in eingeschobenen Vorimitationsabschnitten, deren motivisches Material samt kontrapunktischer Verarbeitungsweise (Gegenbewegung) dem *Orgelbüchlein*-Satz entnommen ist. Der Interpolationsvorgang stellt sich in der Taktaufgliederung folgendermaßen dar:

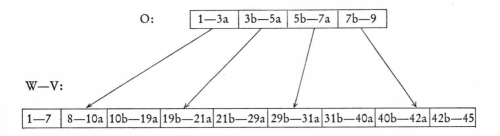

[9a] Deutsche Staatsbibliothek Berlin, *Mus. ms. autogr. Bach P 283.*
[9b] Deutsche Staatsbibliothek Berlin, *Mus. ms. autogr. Bach P 271.* Das letzte Blatt dieser Handschrift mit dem Rest des Chorals ist vermutlich bereits im 18. Jahrhundert aus dem Band herausgelöst worden und seither verschollen.
[10] Kritischer Bericht zu NBA IV/2, S. 102 ff.
[11] Beide Fassungen abgedruckt in NBA IV/2.

Wie aber soll man sich nun ein Blindendiktat vorstellen, das über weite Strecken hin exakt eine wohl mehr als dreißig Jahre ältere Komposition kopiert? Selbst im Blick auf Bachs virtuose Handwerksbeherrschung dürfte hier die Grenze zur Unwahrscheinlichkeit überschritten sein. Bachs Arbeitsweise ist uns heute so weit vertraut, daß wir wissen, wie er sich selbst im Vollbesitz seiner Kräfte selten auf sein Gedächtnis verließ und etwa beim Stimmenausschreiben gerade fertiggestellter Partituren, beim Parodieren und Transkribieren älterer Werke die jeweiligen Manuskripte als direkte Vorlage benutzte [12]. Wieviel eher wäre es denkbar, daß Bach aus dem Stegreif heraus eine völlige Neuschöpfung diktiert hätte, ohne daß er sein Gedächtnis dabei hätte strapazieren müssen!

Unsere Zweifel an dem Stegreifdiktat stellen nun freilich auch die Zuverlässigkeit des ältesten literarischen Zeugnisses in Frage. War Carl Philipp Emanuel Bach der Editor der *Kunst der Fuge,* was mit einiger Sicherheit angenommen werden muß [13], so wissen wir mit Bestimmtheit, daß er beim Tode seines Vaters oder auch unmittelbar vorher nicht in Leipzig weilte. Er konnte von dem Choral-Diktat demnach nur aus zweiter Hand informiert worden sein. Und derartige Informationen sind nicht immer unbedingt präzise, zumal man noch die allgemeinen Animositäten im Bachschen Hause im Zusammenhang mit den Erbteilungsschwierigkeiten in Betracht ziehen muß. Eine weitere Frage an den Informationsstand des Editors der *Kunst der Fuge* ist: Warum wählt er die Fassung W anstelle der jüngeren Fassung V mit dem sehr viel wirkungsvolleren Schwanengesang-Titel? Dies konnte nur geschehen, weil er V gar nicht kannte, also offensichtlich keinen Zugang zu P 271 hatte. Die sich hier ausbreitende Problematik scheint infolge der schlechten Quellenlage und der zahlreichen Unbekannten aussichtslos. Und in der Tat muß eine endgültige Beantwortung der entscheidenden Fragen offenbleiben. Das hindert jedoch nicht, hypothetische Erwägungen anzustellen, um sich wenigstens zu einer Möglichkeit der Problemlösung vorzutasten.

Der methodische Ansatz der folgenden Erwägungen besteht in einer Untersuchung der Konstellation, in welcher die drei erhaltenen musikalischen Quellen zueinander stehen. Nachfolgendes Stemma gibt eine Rekonstruktion der Filiation der Fassungen bzw. der Quellen wieder, wobei die verlorenen bzw. unbekannten Glieder durch Einklammerung als Konjekturen gekennzeichnet sind:

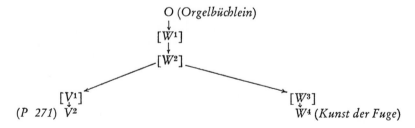

---

[12] Vgl. hierzu die Kritischen Berichte der NBA mit den entsprechenden Detailangaben zu zahlreichen Werken.

[13] Die Stichplatten und das Autograph waren in seinem Besitz. Vgl. den Revisionsbericht von W. Rust in BG 25/1.

[W^3] und W^4 sind als postume Produkte von dem engeren Bestand der Originalquellen abzutrennen: W^4 repräsentiert den mit der *Kunst der Fuge* veröffentlichten Choral, [W^3] ist die in vierstimmige Partiturnotation gebrachte Stichvorlage, die von unbekannter Hand auf Veranlassung des Editors der *Kunst der Fuge* oder von diesem selbst nach der vermutlich zweisystemigen [14] Vorlage [W^2] kopiert wurde. [W^2] muß diejenige Quelle gewesen sein, die dem Editor als jene Choralbearbeitung bekannt wurde, die „der selige Mann in seiner Blindheit einem seiner Freunde aus dem Stegereif in die Feder dictiret hat". Demnach kann es also kein von Johann Sebastian Bach geschriebenes Manuskript gewesen sein, weil ein solches im engeren Kreise Bachs gewiß identifiziert worden wäre. [W^2] gibt die erweiterte Fassung von O wieder, und zwar in genau derselben Gestalt, wie sie W^4 überliefert. Da Eingriffe des Editors ausgeschlossen werden können, müssen die Lesarten von W^4 und [W^2] übereinstimmen. Die Lesarten von W^4 und V^2, folglich auch von [W^2] und V^2, differieren jedoch in entscheidenden Partien, die weiter unten beschrieben werden. Nun ist das Fragment in *P 271*, die Fassung V^2, eine korrekturlose Reinschrift des Kopisten „Anonymus 12" [15] und muß eine unmittelbare Vorlage gehabt haben. [W^2] kann diese Vorlage nicht gewesen sein, da sie keine verbesserten Lesarten enthalten hat. Sie wären sonst zweifellos von [W^3] übernommen worden. Folglich muß als notwendiges Zwischenglied [V^1] fungiert haben, und zwar entweder als Abschrift bzw. Teilabschrift von [W^2] mit den entsprechenden Verbesserungen oder als einfache Korrekturliste mit Tabulaturbuchstaben.

Damit ist der Weg von V^2 zurück nach [W^2] in großen Zügen geklärt. Welchen Ursprung hat aber nun [W^2] als die eigentliche Schlüsselquelle? Daß die Fassung [W^2] auf das Blindendiktat zurückgehe, wurde oben bereits angezweifelt. Einleuchtender erscheint es, die Provenienz von [W^2] in Zusammenhang mit den übrigen 17 Chorälen der sog. Leipziger Originalhandschrift zu sehen. Wahrscheinlich nicht ohne Grund findet sich die Reinschrift V^2 in den Band *P 271* eingetragen, von den 17 Chorälen nur durch die autographe Niederschrift der *Canonischen Veränderungen* über *Vom Himmel hoch* getrennt [16]. Ein gemeinsames Merkmal der voranstehenden 17 großen Choralbearbeitungen ist, daß sie allesamt Überarbeitungen älterer Sätze aus der Weimarer Zeit Bachs darstellen. Der „Sterbechoral", dessen Urfassung im Weimarer *Orgelbüchlein* steht, fügt sich zwanglos dieser Reihe an. Es ist jedenfalls nicht möglich, ihn losgelöst von den übrigen 17 Chorälen zu sehen. Denn aus Bachs letztem Lebensjahrzehnt ist kein Einzelfall bekannt, in dem er sich (außer im Zusammenhang mit besagter Choralsammlung in *P 271*) mit der Überarbeitung oder Neufassung einer alten Weimarer Komposition befaßt hätte.

[14] V^2 ist auch auf 2 Systemen notiert.
[15] G. v. Dadelsen, S. 114. Anonymus 12 ist in Originalhandschriften aus den letzten Leipziger Amtsjahren Bachs vor allem als Kopist der Continuo-Stimmen zu BWV 195, 245 und 232III nachweisbar. Vermutlich war er Organist.
[16] *P 271* enthält die sechs Triosonaten für Orgel (S. 1—57), die 17 Choräle (S. 58—99), das Kanonwerk über *Vom Himmel hoch* (S. 100—106) und den Choral *Vor deinen Thron* (S. 106). Bis auf die beiden letzten der 17 Choräle und das Schlußstück sind alle Einträge von Bach selbst geschrieben.

Noch schwerer denkbar erscheint, daß sich der Erblindete plötzlich so genau an das kleine Weimarer Sätzlein erinnert hätte, um es fehlerfrei zu diktieren.

Ziehen wir die Verbindung von dem „Sterbechoral" zu den 17 Chorälen, so ist bezeichnend, daß der 16. und 17. Choral (BWV 666, 667) nicht von Bach selbst, sondern von Altnikol geschrieben sind. Bach hat sich beim Übertragen der Stücke nach den alten Handschriften oder nach neueren Konzeptmanuskripten helfen lassen. In gleicher Weise ist V^2 in diesen Band eingetragen worden, und zwar offensichtlich gleich Altnikol von einem Organisten [17]. Ein weiterer Anknüpfungspunkt besteht darin, daß der 17. Choral ebenfalls eine Erweiterung eines *Orgelbüchlein*-Satzes darstellt. Es ist dies der einzige Fall innerhalb der 17 Choräle, und es kann kaum Zufall sein, daß diese beiden Stücke sozusagen nebeneinander stehen.

Zu der Choralsammlung in der Leipziger Originalhandschrift gehörte ursprünglich ein umfangreicherer Komplex von Manuskripten in Einzelblättern oder Einzelbogen mit den älteren Fassungen und Entwürfen, die Bach dann großenteils nach Eintragung der Reinschrift vernichtet hat, oder die auf andere Weise verloren gingen. Lediglich ein solches Blatt zu BWV 660a hat sich erhalten und ist *P 271* beigeheftet [18]. [W^2] könnte ein ähnliches Blatt gewesen sein, vielleicht ebenfalls von Altnikol als dem Kopisten des anderen erweiterten *Orgelbüchlein*-Satzes geschrieben [19]. Altnikols Tätigkeit bei Bach muß sich auf seine Schülerzeit in Leipzig von 1744 bis 1747 beschränkt haben. Zu diesen Daten paßt, daß Bach selbst die *Canonischen Veränderungen* (BWV 769) im Anschluß an die letzte Eintragung Altnikols in *P 271* niedergeschrieben hat. Und der Terminus ad quem oder post quem ist Bachs im Juni 1747 vollzogener Eintritt in die Mizlersche *Societät der Musicalischen Wissenschaften*, für die er das Kanonwerk geschrieben hatte. Der Abbruch der Arbeiten an den Reinschriften der redigierten Weimarer Choräle muß demnach 1746/47 etwa gleichzeitig mit dem Weggang Altnikols stattgefunden haben. Zählen wir den „Sterbechoral" als 18. Choral zu dieser Sammlung, so dürfte das Manuskript [W^2], ganz gleich ob von Altnikol geschrieben oder nicht, in jene Zeit der Redaktion Weimarer Orgelchoräle zu datieren sein.

Da [W^2] fremdschriftliche Kopie ist, muß es auf eine Vorlage [W^1] zurückgehen, deren Beschaffenheit im Gegensatz zu [W^2] nicht genau festzulegen ist. Es spricht vieles für ein korrekturenreiches Kompositionsmanuskript oder für eine Konzeptschrift, die sich möglicherweise im wesentlichen auf die erweiternden Einschübe zu O beschränkte, da sonst die Abschrift [W^2] nicht notwendig geworden wäre. Der Schreiber von [W^1] muß Bach selbst gewesen sein. Wann aber wurde die in [W^1] erstmalig festgehaltene

---

[17] Vgl. Anm. 15.

[18] Vgl. Klotz, Kritischer Bericht zu NBA IV/2, S. 5.

[19] Es wäre möglich, daß Forkels Erwähnung von Altnikol doch auf einen entsprechenden Hinweis von C. P. E. Bach zurückgeht. Demnach hätte Emanuel den Schreiber von [W^2] (diese Quelle mußte ihm als Vorlage für [W^3] und [W^4] bekannt sein) als J. Chr. Altnikol identifiziert und infolgedessen mit der Diktataufnahme in Verbindung gebracht. Oder er hätte in den 1770er Jahren, der Zeit seines Schriftwechsels mit Forkel, den Schreiber von V^2 in *P 271* (diese Quelle gelangte später in seinen Besitz; vgl. Anm. 27) irrtümlicherweise für Altnikol gehalten, in Verbindung mit den beiden tatsächlichen Altnikol-Einträgen dieses Bandes.

Erweiterung von O vorgenommen? Bei *Komm, Gott Schöpfer* (BWV 667) steht aufgrund des erhaltenen Quellenbestandes fest, daß die Erweiterung durch Anfügen einer zweiten Choraldurchführung mit dem cantus firmus im Baß bereits in Weimar stattgefunden hat [20]. Analog müßte man dieses auch von [W¹] annehmen. Dagegen spricht, daß anders als bei BWV 667 von [W¹] keinerlei Kopien aus der Weimarer Zeit, die üblicherweise im Schüler- und Bekanntenkreis Bachs in jenen Jahren kursierten, nachzuweisen sind. Von allen 17 Chorälen gibt es derartige Kopien [21]. Bei [W¹] liegt der Schluß nahe, daß die Erweiterung des *Orgelbüchlein*-Satzes zu jener Zeit noch nicht existierte.

Genauso wäre jedoch denkbar, daß [W¹] später als der Hauptteil der Weimarer Orgel-choräle, die zumeist in die früheren Weimarer Jahre vor 1714 gehören, entstanden ist und sich auf diese Weise dem Kopistenzugriff entzogen haben mag. Auch von zahlreichen Sätzen des *Orgelbüchleins* sind keine Kopien überliefert, da sich die Eintragungen Bachs hier zum Teil auch auf die späteren Weimarer Jahre erstreckten. Und O gehört dieser späteren Schicht an [22]. Eine andere Erklärung für das Fehlen von Kopien nach [W¹] könnte darin zu finden sein, daß [W¹] als möglicherweise unvollständiges Konzept (siehe oben) nicht kopierenswert war.

Die Stilkritik kann hier zur Entscheidung der Frage kaum herangezogen werden. Das motivische Material der Erweiterungsabschnitte von W ist ganz aus der Urfassung O entwickelt, wie die Klammern in Notenbeispiel 1 andeuten. Die harmonischen Strukturen weisen nicht über die 17 Choräle und das *Orgelbüchlein* hinaus. Allerdings hebt sich die Konsequenz der Motivik und die Logik der Stimmführung von den Verhältnissen in den 17 Chorälen ab und deutet auf eine reifere Stufe. Diese ist jedoch gegenüber dem Großteil der 17 Choräle bereits im *Orgelbüchlein* mit einer bis dahin beispiellosen Konzentration des musikalischen Materials erreicht [23]. Von dorther gesehen liegt eine Entstehung der ersten Fassung von W in der Zeit kurz nach der Komposition von O im Bereich der Wahrscheinlichkeit. An den analogen Fall von BWV 667 muß hier erinnert werden. Auf der andern Seite läßt sich jedoch eine Entstehung in Bachs letztem Lebensjahrzehnt weder mit quellen- noch mit stilkritischen Argumenten völlig ausschließen. Stilistisch nehmen sich nur die rhythmische Uniformität und gewisse Unebenheiten (wie das Stocken des Bewegungsflusses in Takt 32; vgl. die Diskussion unten) in der Umgebung des Spätwerkes seltsam aus.

---

[20] Vgl. Klotz, a. a. O. S. 80 f.

[21] Vgl. Klotz, passim. Die Kopien stammen vorwiegend von Johann Gottfried Walther und Johann Tobias Krebs aus den Jahren 1710—1714; vgl. hier die im Detail weit über Klotz hinausgehenden Untersuchungen von H. Zietz, *Quellenkritische Untersuchungen an den Bach-Handschriften P 801, P 802 und P 803 aus dem „Krebs'schen Nachlaß"* unter besonderer Berücksichtigung der Choralbearbeitungen des jungen J. S. Bach, = Hamburger Beiträge zur Musikwissenschaft, Bd. 1, Hamburg 1969, S. 30, 60, 137 ff.

[22] Vgl. Dadelsen, a. a. O. S. 80; E. Arfken, *Zur Entstehungsgeschichte des Orgelbüchleins*, BJ 1967, S. 50.

[23] Für die Mehrzahl der 17 Choräle kann die Priorität gegenüber dem Orgelbüchlein als gesichert gelten. Vgl. Zietz, a. a. O. S. 137 ff. — In Textur und Deklamation kommt unserem Satz der einzeln überlieferte frühe Orgelchoral *Ach Gott und Herr, per canonem* (BWV 714) sehr nahe.

Nun besteht jedoch kein Zweifel daran, daß sich Bach in seinen letzten Lebensjahren mit *W* beschäftigt hat. Anders ist die Eintragung von *V* in *P 271* nach dem Kanonwerk BWV 769 ebenso wie die Notiz im Originaldruck der *Kunst der Fuge* nicht zu erklären. Für den entscheidenden Schritt von der älteren Fassung [*W²*] zu der Endfassung *V²* bietet sich nun folgende Hypothese an. Bach beschäftigt sich während seiner Erkrankung [24] mit seinen noch unfertigen opera und nimmt möglicherweise mit dem Ziel der Drucklegung auch die Arbeit an der Choralsammlung in *P 271* auf. Einer aus dem engsten Kreise Bachs spielt dem Erblindeten die Fassung aus [*W²*] vor. Bach hört kritisch zu und diktiert wichtige Verbesserungen, die der Gehilfe in [*V¹*] festhält. Die Korrekturen bewegen sich auf einer Ebene, wie sie für die ausgefeilte Arbeit der Spätwerke charakteristisch ist, und dienen als Grundlage für die Reinschrift *V²*.

Die erste Korrektur intensiviert im letzten Takt des 1. Einschubes (T. 7) das rhythmischmelodische Gefüge durch komplementäre Angleichung des Tenors an den Alt. Die Hinführung auf den ersten cantus firmus-Ton wird damit dichter und zwingender:

Die zweite Korrektur ist ebenfalls rhythmischer Art, indem der Baß in T. 9 nunmehr das einförmige Einmünden des Kopfmotives in eine gleichmäßige Achtelkette durch Antizipation der rhythmischen Verbindungsfloskel im cantus firmus vermeidet:

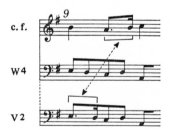

Der dritte Eingriff in T.10 beseitigt das zweimalige Kadenzieren nach G-Dur auf kleinstem Raum. *W* hatte die erste Kadenz wörtlich aus *O* übernommen und bei der

[24] Vgl. H. Zeraschi, *Bach und der Okulist Taylor*, BJ 1956, S. 52—64.

Überleitung in den 2. Einschub erneut nach G kadenziert. *V* führt statt dessen über den Halbschluß e-Moll in den Ganzschluß G-Dur und verleiht dadurch der harmonischen Struktur eine ganz andere Eleganz:

Die letzte Verbesserung findet sich in T. 26 unmittelbar vor dem Abbruch des Fragmentes in *P 271*. Erneut greift Bach in die rhythmische Gestalt ein und ändert die gleichmäßig aufsteigende Achtelkette in eine punktierte Klimax, die den in der zweiten Takthälfte erreichten melodischen Kulminationspunkt spannungsvoller ansteuert:

Der Rest der Endfassung ist leider verloren, so daß man Bachs korrigierende Eingriffe nur bis zu diesem Punkt verfolgen kann. Doch es zeigt sich auch an dem erhaltenen Bruchstück, wie die Endfassung *V* der älteren Fassung *W* an kompositorischer Qualität überlegen ist, auch wenn die Grundsubstanz des Satzes unverändert bleibt. Dies mag die Zweifel an der späten Entstehung von [*W²*] erneut unterstreichen.

Nicht zu unterschlagen ist die Abänderung des Titels in *V*. Es ist verständlich, daß Bach in seiner Krankheit, vielleicht nach den mißglückten Augenoperationen [25], von Jenseitsgedanken umgetrieben ist. Und man kann es nur mit Ernst betrachten, wenn er seinen Empfindungen durch die Wahl des stark eschatologisch ausgerichteten Chorales Ausdruck verleiht, der als Morgen-, Mittag- oder Abendgebet auf die Melodie *Wenn wir in höchsten Nöten sein* gesungen werden kann [26].

[25] Nach Zeraschi (S. 63 f.) fanden die Operationen, die schließlich zur völligen Erblindung Bachs führten, erst im April und Mai 1750 statt.

[26] Vgl. A. Fischer — W. Tümpel, *Das deutsche evangelische Kirchenlied des siebzehnten Jahrhunderts*, Bd. 2, Gütersloh 1905, S. 409: *Am Morgen, Mittag und Abend kan man singen:*
> 1. *Für deinen Thron trett ich hiemit,*
>   ... [15 Strophen]
Erstmalig in: *New Ordentlich Gesang-Buch*, Hannover 1646. Die Autorschaft Bodo von Hodenbergs (1604—1650) ist ungewiß.

Nach unseren aus einer langen Indizienkette bestehenden Überlegungen zu den sich aus der Konstellation der drei erhaltenen Quellen ergebenden Fragen stellt sich die rekonstruierte Filiation folgendermaßen dar:

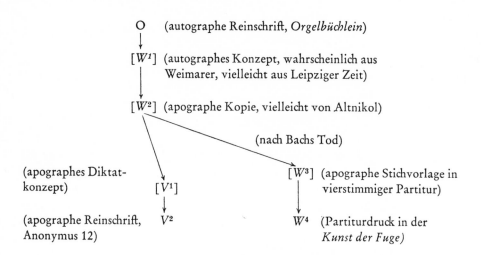

O   (autographe Reinschrift, *Orgelbüchlein*)

[W¹]   (autographes Konzept, wahrscheinlich aus
            Weimarer, vielleicht aus Leipziger Zeit)

[W²]   (apographe Kopie, vielleicht von Altnikol)

(nach Bachs Tod)

(apographes Diktat-   [W³]   (apographe Stichvorlage in
konzept)   [V¹]   vierstimmiger Partitur)

(apographe Reinschrift,   V²   W⁴   (Partiturdruck in der
Anonymus 12)   *Kunst der Fuge)*

Der Gang unserer Untersuchungen zur Aufhellung der Entstehungsgeschichte des „Sterbechorals" bestand aus einer Reihe von hypothetischen Schlüssen in logischer Abfolge. Daß diese Hypothesen zu einem Teil anfechtbar sind, versteht sich von selbst, doch bieten sie weniger Angriffspunkte als die bisherigen Interpretationen der Entstehungsgeschichte des „Sterbechorals".

Unser Hauptergebnis besteht in der begründeten Annahme, daß dieser sog. „Sterbechoral" als solcher niemals „aus dem Stegereif ... dictiret" wurde, sondern daß der erblindete Bach Verbesserungen zu einer bereits bestehenden älteren Komposition diktiert hat. Möglicherweise war dies seine letzte kompositorische Arbeit. Der Editor der *Kunst der Fuge* erfährt von dieser Arbeit, ohne jedoch die genauen Umstände zu kennen. Und das familiäre Klima nach Bachs Tod mit dem Erbprozeß und dem Streit der älteren Bach-Söhne mit Anna Magdalena Bach und ihren Kindern war gewiß nicht dazu geeignet, sich ein klares Bild von Bachs letzten Lebenswochen und -monaten zu machen, falls man daran überhaupt interessiert war. Jedenfalls steht ihm *P 271* mit der Endfassung des Chorales nicht zur Verfügung, da dieser wichtige Orgelband aller Wahrscheinlichkeit nach an den Organisten Wilhelm Friedemann Bach ging [27], wie Autograph und Stich-

[27] *P 271* war später in Emanuels Besitz (laut Ausweis seines Nachlaß-Verzeichnisses). Unmittelbar nach Bachs Tod war sie ihm nicht zugänglich, wie gezeigt wurde. Mit zahlreichen anderen Handschriften aus Friedemanns Erbteil muß er sie später erworben haben. Vgl. A. Dürr, *Zur Chronologie der Leipziger Vokalwerke J. S. Bachs,* BJ 1957, S. 9. Eine Spezialstudie über die Provenienz der Bach-Handschriften aus dem Friedemannschen Erbteil steht noch aus.

platten der *Kunst der Fuge* dem Cembalisten und theoretisch interessierten Carl Philipp Emanuel zufielen. So ließe sich erklären, warum im Originaldruck der *Kunst der Fuge* merkwürdigerweise die Veröffentlichung der älteren Choralfassung *W* erfolgte, mit der sich offenbar vage Vorstellungen von einem Diktat verbunden hatten.

Ausgangspunkt unserer kritischen Fragen war der Mythos, der sich im Laufe der Zeit um den „Sterbechoral" gebildet hatte. Der Gedanke, daß Bach auf dem Sterbelager seinen Schwanengesang diktierte, in dem weniger der Komponist selbst als vielmehr „jene Gotteskraft, die ihn zum musikalischen Apostel erhoben ... zeugen und reden" (Rust) wollte, weckt Assoziationen mit dem klassischen mythischen Bild von Papst Gregor dem Großen, der die vom Heiligen Geist in Gestalt einer Taube vermittelten Choralmelodien einem schreibenden Mönch in die Feder diktiert. Eine Entmythisierung der vertrauten frommen Legende um Bachs letzte Komposition ist unvermeidbar. Der verbleibende harte Kern ist jedoch mehr als ein blasses Faktum. Denn die Quellen bezeugen unbestreitbar Bachs künstlerisches Engagement bis zum letzten Atemzug. Die Verbesserungen, die die Endfassung *Vor deinen Thron tret ich hiermit* über die ältere Gestalt *Wenn wir in höchsten Nöten sein* hinausheben, sind ein letzter Abglanz des lebenslangen Ringens um eine *ars perfecta*.

V
HANDEL AND THE OPERA SERIA

ROBERT FREEMAN

Farinello and his Repertory

Of all the performers active during the 18th century, none was more highly praised than Carlo Broschi, the Neapolitan castrato known as Farinello; nor was any performer more widely credited than he with having influenced the evolution of contemporary musical style [1].

Born on 24 January 1705 in Andria, the young singer studied in Naples with Nicola Porpora, performing there in public for the first time at the age of 15 in *Angelica e Medoro*, a Porpora *serenata* composed to honor the birthday of the Habsburg Empress Elisabeth Christine on 28 August 1720 [2]. The youthful Farinello's name appeared last among those of the six singers listed in the printed libretto, and the three arias that comprise his role in Porpora's score are the most modest in that relatively brief two-part work. But the performance marks a milestone in operatic history, involving the debuts

---

[1] P. Metastasio, *Tutte le Opere*, ed. B. Brunelli (Milan, 1943—54), esp. III, 555, but also V, 88—89, 125, 308; G. Mancini, *Pensieri e riflessioni pratiche sopra il canto figurato* (Vienna, 1774), pp. 104—107; A. Goudar, *Le Brigandage de la musique italienne* (Paris, 1780), pp. 31—32; J. B. LaBorde, *Essai sur la musique ancienne et moderne* (Paris, 1780), III, 311—312; C. Burney, *Memoirs of the Life and Writings of the Abate Metastasio* (London, 1796) III, 284—285.

[2] Though a variety of lexicons beginning with Fétis's assign this work a first performance date of 28 August 1722, I am convinced by the rationale for a 1720 date put forward by Frank Walker ("A Chronology of the Life and Works of Nicola Porpora", *Italian Studies* VI, 36—37). Moreover, the names of the performers that appear in the *licenza* of Porpora's dated autograph score (GB-Lbm Add. 14120) are the same as those listed in the possibly unique, undated, printed libretto for the work (I-Nn 74.H.35), whose title page reads: «L'Angelica, / Serenata / da cantarsi in occasione del giorno natalizio / d'Elisabetta / Augusta / Imperatrice Regnante / In Casa del Signor / Principe della Torella / Dedicata / all'Eccellentiss. Sig. Conte / Giovanni, Guglielmo / di Sinzendorf / . . . . / La musica è del Sig. / Nicolo Porpora / Maestro di Cappella di SAS / Il Sig. Principe di Darmstadt». The dates in Porpora's autograph score seem themselves clearly autograph — at the beginning of part 1: 7 agosto 1720; at the beginning of part 2: 19 agosto 1720. Elisabeth Christine's birthday fell on 28 August, though musical works performed in Vienna to honor it often occurred a few days afterwards. (Franz Hadamowsky, *Barocktheater am Wiener Kaiserhof* [Vienna, 1955], includes a reliable calendar of secular and sacred dramatic works performed at the Habsburg court of Vienna through the death of Charles VI in 1740). Even should the first performance date ultimately turn out to have taken place later than the fall of 1720, *Angelica e Medoro* would still appear to have been Metastasio's first dramatic text set to music, a fact which would explain Metastasio's and Farinello's well-known habit of referring to one another as "caro gemello". Burney reports having been told by Farinello that ". . . Metastasio and he were twins of public favor, and entered the world at the same time, he having performed in that poet's first opera" (*The Present State of Music in France and Italy* [London, 1771], p. 212). Bruno Brunelli (Metastasio, *Tutte le Opere*) does not take account of the information in his chronology of Metastasio's work. Farinello's first biography, Giovenale Sacchi's *Vita del Cavaliere Don Carlo Broschi* (Venice, 1784) indicates Metastasio's *Angelica e Medoro* as the first work in which Farinello performed publicly, and lists his age at that time as about 15 years.

of both Farinello and Metastasio and the collaboration of Porpora and the well-known
soprano Maria Anna Benti Bulgarelli, "la Romanina", an important figure in Metastasio's early career[3]. As indicated in the calendar of Farinello's operatic career on
pp. 324—330, based on dated libretti containing printed casts and, in a few instances, on
appearances of his name in datable manuscript scores, one sees that Farinello sang in
Rome during the Carnival of 1722, appearing in _Flavio Anicio Olibrio_ and in _Sofonisba_
as second and third singer, respectively, in the all-male casts characteristic of contemporary operatic performances there[4]. In the early months of 1723, performing the
title role in Porpora's _Adelaide_[5], Farinello was already allocated as many arias as any
singer in the cast; three of the six arias he sang in _Adelaide_ were, moreover, pieces of
extended dimensions demanding the vocal resources of an accomplished virtuoso. During
1724 Farinello began the remarkable travels which in the next decade took him to
performances at the principal centers for Italian opera all over the Continent.

The first extant account of Farinello's early accomplishments survives in Quantz's
autobiographical sketch in Marpurg's _Historisch-kritische Beyträge_. There Quantz describes hearing Farinello in Naples during the carnival of 1725, first in an opera of Sarri
(in which Farinello is described as "constantly approaching his later famous perfec-
tion"), then in a private performance of a Hasse _serenata_ (which in Quantz's view
led to the commissioning of Hasse's first operatic score in Italy), and finally at several
concerts in honor of the visiting Prince of Lichtenstein, at which Quantz says he made
Farinello's personal acquaintance[6]. Quantz's subsequent Italian travels took him
through Florence to Venice, thence through Modena to Reggio and Parma, and finally
to Milan and Turin. At both Parma and Milan, during the spring of 1726, he heard
additional Farinello performances:

> The opera in Parma was called _I fratelli riconosciuti_. The music was by the at that
> time outstanding Giovanni Maria Capelli, a priest and at the same time a fiery
> and very inventive composer. The best singers were the already cited Farinelli,
> Giovanni Carestini, and Paita ... Farinelli had a penetrating, full, rich, bright
> and well-modulated soprano voice, whose range extended at that time from a

[3] Metastasio, _Tutte le Opere_, III, 101—103.
[4] F. Haböck, _Die Kastraten und ihre Gesangskunst_ (Berlin and Leipzig, 1927), pp. 223—224.
[5] Behind this production is a story still to be researched: two parallel libretti, both entitled
Adelaide, were published in Rome during 1723. One of them (US-Wc Schatz 8376) bears
a title page reading «Adelaide / Drama per Musica / da recitarsi / nel Teatro Alibert pe'l
Carnevale / dell'anno 1723. / Presentato alla Maesta / di / Clementina / Regina della Gran
Bret- / tagna ... / In Roma, nella Stamperia del Bernabò, 1723 ...», as well as a _dramatis
personae_ listing Farinello in the title role and an attribution of the music to Porpora. The
other (US-Wc ML. 50.2.A31P6), printed by «Pietro Ferri sotto la Biblioteca Casanatense»,
includes no _dramatis personae_ and no composer attribution. Two-thirds of its aria texts, including all of those from II/8 through the end of the libretto, differ from those in the
version printed by Bernabò.
[6] The works in question are identified by Sven Hansell, _Works for Solo Voice of Joh. Ad. Hasse_,
Detroit Studies in Music Bibliography XII (1968), 14—16.

through d'''. A few years afterwards it had extended lower by a few tones, but without the loss of any high notes, so that in many operas one aria (usually an adagio) was written for him in the normal tessitura of a contralto, while his other arias were of soprano range. His intonation was pure, his trill beautiful, his breath-control extraordinary, and his throat very agile — so that he performed even the widest intervals quickly and with the greatest ease and certainty. Passagework and all varieties of melismas were of no difficulty whatever for him. In the invention of free ornamentation in adagio he was very fertile. But the fire of youth, his great talent, the general applause and his ready throat brought it about that at times he proceeded in too spendthrift a fashion. His figure was advantageous for the theater, but acting was not his forte [7].

Charles Burney, who half a century later interviewed the then retired Farinello at the singer's villa in Bologna, reports Farinello performances in Vienna during 1724, 1728, and 1731, and relates an anecdote that seems to bear out Quantz's testimony concerning the singer's early tendency to overuse spectacular effects.

He told me that at Vienna . . . where he received great honors from the Emperor Charles VI, an admonition from that Prince was of more service to him than all the precepts of his masters, or examples of his competitors for fame: His Imperial Majesty condescended to tell him one day, with great mildness and affability, that in his singing he neither *moved* nor *stood still* like any other mortal; all was supernatural. 'Those gigantic strides; those never-ending notes and passages . . . only surprise, and it is now time for you to please; you are too lavish of the gifts with which nature has endowed you; if you wish to reach the heart, you must take a more plain and simple road'. These few words brought about an entire change in his manner of singing; from this time he mixed the pathetic with the spirited, the simple with the sublime, and by these means, delighted as well as astonished every hearer [8].

It is not possible to date precisely the time of Emperor Charles's criticism. But a letter from Paolo Rolli in London to the castrato Senesino in Venice, dated 21 December [1728?] by O. E. Deutsch, certainly does not suggest that the greatest Italian opera composer of the time found much to criticize in Farinello.

The Man [Handel] returned from his travels very full of Farinello [9] and extremely loud in his praises [10].

[7] F. W. Marpurg, *Historisch-kritische Beyträge zur Aufnahme der Musik* I (Berlin, 1754), 233—34.
[8] C. Burney, *The Present State of Music in France and Italy* (London, 1771), pp. 207—208.
[9] While "Farinello" is the form of the singer's stage-name which appears most often in the libretti printed for his own performances and in his last will and testament (reprinted in Ralph Kirkpatrick's *Domenico Scarlatti* [Princeton, 1953], pp. 362—363), both "Farinelli" and "Farinello" are to be found in contemporary documents.
[10] O. E. Deutsch, *Handel, a Documentary Biography* (London, 1955), p. 229.

When in fact the impresario Heidegger returned to London without having contracted the singers he had sought in Italy, Handel set out once more, as reported in another letter from Rolli to Senesino, dated 4 February 1729:

> Handel is in fact departing today, and ten days ago Haym dispatched circular letters to Italy to announce this new project and Handel's arrival to the professional singers. Farinello comes first in estimation, and all the more so as news has recently arrived from Venice ... that all throng to the theatre at which Farinello is singing, and that the theatre where you and Faustina are singing is nearly empty [11].

On February 7 Rolli wrote Senesino that he would undoubtedly see Handel before the end of the carnival, "... because, for sure, he is going directly to Venice for Farinello [12]." Handel reached Venice, but returned to London early the following summer with a new group of singers that did not include Farinello. A letter from Metastasio to the Roman impresario Cavanna, dated 21 June 1732, suggests why Farinello may have preferred Italy and near-by German courts at this point in his career. In the letter Metastasio claims to have done his best to recruit Farinello for Cavanna's Teatro Aliberti; he reports having failed in the end because "... it does not suit Farinello's obligations to agree to long-term engagements" [13].

Ultimately Farinello did travel to London in the fall of 1734 to join Porpora and Handel's other new competitors of the Opera of the Nobility, and for a three-year stay that both enriched Farinello and contributed to Handel's eventual withdrawal from the operatic scene. By the time of Farinello's arrival in London, Paolo Rolli, Handel's principal librettist during the 1720's, was adapting libretti for the Opera of the Nobility; but his letter of 9 November 1734 to Giuseppe Riva in Vienna, written just two weeks after Farinello's London debut, must be read, too, in the context of Rolli's friendship for the castrato Senesino.

> I must have you know — for it deserves to be known — that Farinelli was a revelation to me, for I realized that till I had heard him I had heard only a small part of what human song can achieve, whereas I now conceive that I have heard all there is to hear. He has, besides, the most agreeable and clever manners, hence I take the greatest pleasure in his company and acquaintance. He has made me a present which I much desired and which will help me pass many pleasant hours, directing my thoughts to our country's and our common master's fame, which perhaps we two alone have further increased in poetical honour; the present I mean is the works and verses of the Abate Metastasio, to whom, please, remember me [14].

[11] *Ibid.*, p. 237.
[12] *Ibid.*, p. 238.
[13] Metastasio, *Tutte le Opere*, III, 40.
[14] Deutsch, *op. cit.*, p. 374.

From a Rifacimento of *Artaserse* (Modena, 1750)

18

ATTO

E sogna il pescator
Le reti, e l'amo.
Sopito in dolce obblio...
~~Sogna pur~~
~~Cambia~~
Colei, che tutto il dì
Sospiro, e chiamo.
Sogna &c.

SCENA VII.

Semira.

VOi della Persia, voi
Deità protettrici, a questo Impero
Conservate Artaserse. Ah, ch'io lo perdo,
Se trionfa di Dario. Ei questa mano
Bramò Vassallo... ~~sdegnerà Sovrano.~~
perderò purche viva,

Se lo bramassi estinto, empia sarei.
Nò, del mio voto io non mi pento, o Dei.

*Lasciami in pace, e taci
fiero tiranno amore
che doppo è vio dolore
non vi vorrai pietà
lieta sarò fra pene
se fia, che il caro bene
con un soglii l'oprore
nega d'infedeltà
Lasciami &.*

PRIMO

19

SCENA VIII.

Mandane, poi Artaserse.

Mand. DOve fuggo? Ove corro? E chi da que-
Empia Regia funesta (sta
M'invola per pietà: chi mi consiglia?
Germana, amante, e figlia
Misera in un'istante
Perdo i germani, il genitor, l'amante.
Artaf. Ah Mandane.....
Mand. Artaserse,
Dario respira? ~~Commiseri anco o suoi reo?~~
Artaf. ~~Io bramava o Principessa,
Di scolparmi innocente. Il cielo, oh Dio!
Mi sigillò delle labbra
Un comando crudel, un duro oppera~~
Mand. ~~Ma dì. Per impedirlo~~ io scorro
Sollecito la Regia, e cerco in vano
D'Artabano, e di Dario.
Mand. Ecco Artabano.

SCENA IX.

Artabano, e detti.

Artab. ~~Signore.~~
Artaf. ~~Amico.~~
Artab. ~~Lasciami e cerco.~~
Artaf.
Vengo in traccia di te;
Artab. Forse paventi?

Artaf.

From a Rifacimento of *Artaserse* (Modena, 1750)

Other evidence of Farinello's enormous success in England is provided by a variety of contemporary letters and press notices assembled by O. E. Deutsch, of which two further are cited here.

From the *Old Whig: or The Consistent Protestant,* 20 March 1735:

> Farinello surpasses everything we have hitherto heard. Nor are we wanting in our acknowledgments; for, besides the numerous presents of considerable sums made him by the Nobility, Foreign Ministers, and others (which amounted to some thousand pounds), he had an audience at his benefit larger than was ever seen in the English theatre; and there was an attention that shew'd how much everyone was charm'd. In the flourishing state of this Opera, tis no wonder that the other theatres decline. Handel, whose excellent compositions have often pleased our ears and touched our hearts, has this winter sometimes performed to an almost empty pit [15].

From Prevost's *Le Pour et Contre* — Paris (May? 1735), translated by O. E. Deutsch:

> Signor Farinelli, who came to England with the highest expectations, has the satisfaction of seeing them fulfilled by generosity and favour as extraordinary as his own talents. The others were loved: this man is idolized, adored; it is a consuming passion. Indeed, it is impossible to sing better (than he does). Mr. Handel has not omitted to produce a new Oratorio, which is given on Wednesdays and Fridays, with chorus and orchestral accompaniments of great beauty. Everyone agrees that he is the Orpheus of his age and that this new work is a masterpiece. He plays the organ himself in it, with consummate skill. He is admired, but from a distance for he is often alone; a spell draws the crowd to Farinelli's. Imagine all Senesino's and Carestino's art combined, with a voice more beautiful than the two taken together . . . [16].

During the summer of 1736 Farinello took temporary leave from England to perform before new audiences in and near Paris, where he was heard by the Italian actor and historian Luigi Riccoboni. In his *Réflexions historiques et critiques sur les différens théâtres de l'Europe,* the permission for whose first edition is dated in Paris, 5 January 1738, Riccoboni sketches a recent history of Italian singing. For the past 30 years in Venice, says Riccoboni, one has paid the singers so much more than before as to bankrupt the impresarios, while during the past 20 years the great reputation which Italian music acquired among foreigners has been greatly diminished, because

> . . . it is now only bizarre; the artificial has taken the place of the beautiful and simple; and those who seek expression and truth as they found it in earlier Italian music now find there only peculiarities and difficulties. They admire, to be sure,

---

[15] *Ibid.,* p. 384.
[16] *Ibid.,* p. 390.

the astonishing ability of the singers but they are not at all moved, and they claim with justice that to force a voice to execute what a violin or an oboe can scarcely perform is to overturn nature [17].

Riccoboni praises Francesca Cuzzoni and Francesco Bernardi (Senesino) for having preserved to the present what he calls the true manner of Italian singing, but attributes the invention of a new style of singing to the "singular talents and prodigious nimbleness of Faustina Bordoni". Riccoboni speaks of Farinello last

> because he is the most recent and youngest of the Italian singers of great reputation. He sings in the style of Faustina; but, in the opinion of the greatest connoisseurs, he is infinitely better than she, having reached the last degree of perfection [18].

Not surprisingly, it was not only Riccoboni whom Farinello impressed in France. An article from Paris in London's *Daily Post* of 13 September 1736 relates that to Farinello ". . . his most Christian Majesty has lately made a present . . . of his picture in diamonds" [19]. The *Journal des Nouvelles de Paris* includes an entry dated 24 September that ". . . the great Farinelli . . . has sung before the King who presented him with a golden snuffbox", and another dated 24 November that at recent performances of *Medée et Jason* ". . . la Hambre, Chassé, and Pélicier play the principal roles, while petite Mlle. Fel sings an Italian aria in which it appears that she is animated by the taste and spirit of Farinelli" [20]. In a patent dated Paris 18 April 1737 Louis XV granted Marie Fel the exclusive privilege all over France for eight years of publishing Italian arias [21].

Farinello returned to London for another season at the Opera of the Nobility, where business had become notably less good [22]. But the 1736—37 season, while the young singer's last on any public stage, proved preliminary to an extraordinary series of events. After the cancellation of several performances during May and June of 1737 as the result of what were announced as indispositions of Farinello, he left London quietly, followed by Porpora [23].

In Madrid King Philip V had for some time been in a state of debilitating depression; Elisabeth Farnese, Philip's Italian-born Queen, had on 18 February 1737 been described by Benjamin Keene as

---

[17] L. Riccoboni, *Réflexions historiques et critiques sur les différens théâtres de l'Europe* (Amsterdam, 1740), pp. 37—38.

[18] *Ibid.*, p. 40.

[19] C. Burney, *A General History of Music,* ed. Frank Mercer (New York, 1957), II, 803.

[20] N. Dufourcq, « ‹Nouvelles de la cour et de la ville› (1734—38), extraits concernant la vie musicale», *Recherches sur la musique française classique* X (1970), 105.

[21] F-Pn VM⁷ 635(1).

[22] Deutsch, *op. cit.,* pp. 408—9.

[23] *Ibid.*, p. 437, where one finds a complete calendar of works produced by the Opera of the Nobility (between 29 December 1733 and 24 May 1737).

endeavoring to look out for the diversion of the King, who has a natural aversion to music. If she can change his temper as far as to amuse him with it, it may keep them both from thinking of more turbulent matter [24].

Burney reports an announcement of July 7 to London's operatic public that "Sig. Farinelli..., who had been at Paris for a considerable time, was setting out for Spain, where he designed to continue till the close of the year, and then return to England". Burney, who had interviewed Farinello in Bologna, then continues with the first detailed account in print of the event in whose anticipation the Queen had apparently drawn Farinello to Madrid [25].

> Upon the arrival of Farinelli... her Majesty contrived that there should be a concert in a room adjoining to the King's apartment, in which this singer performed one of his most captivating songs. Philip appeared at first surprised, then moved; and at the end of the second air, made the virtuoso enter the royal apartment, loading him with compliments and caresses; asked him how he could sufficiently reward such talents; assuring him that he could refuse him nothing. Farinelli, previously instructed, only begged that his Majesty would permit his attendants to shave and dress him, and that he would endeavour to appear in council as usual. From this time the King's disease gave way to medicine: and the singer had all the honour of the cure [26].

On September 26 the London *Daily Post* announced that Farinello was about to stay permanently in Madrid [27]. On September 28 the Modenese Ambassador to Turin reported home that the Piedmontese were impressed by the news that Farinello had joined the service of the King of Spain "... with an annual salary of 3000 *dopie* as well as free housing and maintenance, and a carriage of his own when the court is in the country" [28].

Farinello's remarkable career in Spain, in the service of both Philip V (1700—46) and Ferdinand VI (1746—59) included a great deal more than his apparently unbroken

---

[24] cited by Edward Armstrong, *Elisabeth Farnese* (London, 1892), p. 338.

[25] The chronology of early Farinello biography involves the following sequence of events: 1770, Burney interviews Farinello; 1771, publication of the first edition of Burney's *Present State of Music in France and Italy;* summer of 1782, Farinello dies in Bologna; 1 January 1784, dated dedication of Giovenale Sacchi's *Vita del Cavaliere Don Carlo Broschi* signed in Milan, where Sacchi was «professore d'eloquenza nel Collegio de'Nobili». (Internal evidence in Sacchi's *Vita* makes it appear unlikely that his work was based on any personal acquaintance with Farinello); 1789, publication of last volume of Burney's *General History of Music*, containing additional material on Farinello.

[26] Burney, *General History of Music*, II, 815. It should be noted that Burney presents the episode quoted as an anecdote, which in general he calls "below the dignity of history".

[27] *Ibid.*, p. 814.

[28] Modena, Archivio di Stato, Schedario per materia (musica), Farinello.

series of private recitals of a handful of arias for those two royal insomniacs [29]. Among a variety of other projects, he was charged with the importation of a herd of Hungarian horses, with the redirection of the course of the River Tago, with the direction of music at the Royal Chapel, and, under Ferdinand VI, with the redesign of the royal opera house and the production of a long series of sumptuously staged Italian operas, on which he corresponded at length with Metastasio [30]. Ralph Kirkpatrick's well-known work on Domenico Scarlatti, Farinello's principal musical compatriot at the Spanish

[29] Burney was unable for *The Present State of Music in France and Italy* to reconstruct exactly what Farinello had told him about the identity of the pieces he had sung so often for Philip V and Ferdinand VI; and no one has succeeded since. Burney recalls in 1771 that Farinello had spoken of four arias, three of which he identified as " 'Pallide il sole' and 'Per questo dolce amplesso', both by Hasse, and a minuet he used to vary at his pleasure". Sacchi, who must have known *The Present State* and in all probability interviewed Padre Martini and surviving relatives of Farinello after the singer's death, lists the three arias already mentioned by Burney, then adds that the fourth, which he says was never omitted from a Farinello recital, involved a simile concerning a nightingale. In his English translation of Metastasio letters published in 1796 (I, 206), Burney remembers the title of an additional aria, «Ah non lasciarmi, no», also by Hasse. Franz Haböck, in studying A-Wn 19111, a handsome manuscript dedicated to Maria Theresa by Farinello in Madrid on 30 March 1753, possibly in Farinello's hand, identifies "Quell'-usignolo", the first of the six arias it contains, as a good candidate for the last of the four arias on Burney's 1771 list. But he does not notice the relevance of Farinello's dedicatory introduction: «Sacra Reale Cesarea Maesta: Pieno di confusione, e di gloria per la benignissima ricordanza, che la Cesarea Maesta vostra si degna di conservare della mia profonda venerazione, ed incoraggito dalle sicurezze avutene da Monsignor Migazzi, ardisco presentarle in questo libro una piccola scelta di quelle ariette, che per una serie non interrotta di molti anni anno servito in bocca mia al privato sollievo di questi adorabili Sovrani miei Clementissimi Benefattori la musica di esse, cui sacrifai per passatempo i voli del mio capriccio, e particolarmente quella delle tre prime destinate alla sola mia abilità (qualunque ella siasi,) rinovando forse nella mente della Cesarea Maesta vostra la idea della estensione, e delle altre qualità della mia voce, servira talvolta a renderle meno nojosa la pena, che mi lusingo si vorra prendere di ripassarle, al quale oggetto ho creduto di doversi inserire in note di color rosso, ed in strisce volanti alcuni dei molti cambiamenti ne'passaggi, e nelle cadenze. Sara mia gran sorte, se onorandole Vostra Maesta di una benignissima Occhiata nei pochi istanti di riposo, che le permettone le vaste cure dell'Impero, si degnera di ricercare in esse qualche ristoro alle sue gloriose fatiche, e riconoscere in me la continuazione di quell'appassionate Ossequio, con cui prondamente mi umilio». Someone's memory seems to have played him false. Farinello may very well have performed in Madrid the arias identified by Burney. Hasse's «Pallade il sole» had been performed as a substitute aria in various productions of *Artaserse* in which Farinello took part (Venice, 1730 and 1734; London, 1734), but always in the role of Artabano, sung in the Venetian versions cited by Nicolo Grimaldi and by Pellegrino Tomy, in London by Francesco Bernardi (Senesino). Hasse's «Per questo dolce amplesso», a substitute aria sung by Farinello as Arbace in the 1730 Venetian production of *Artaserse,* was repeated by him later that fall in the Lucca production and in the London version of 1734, but substituted for in his performances of the role in Ferrara (1731) and Venice (1734). No one has been able to locate a textual or musical source for «Ah non lasciarmi, no», the aria mentioned by Burney in 1796. But Farinello's repertory in Madrid was not so limited as Burney has led posterity to believe. A list of the six pieces which comprise A-Wn 19111 follows; none of them is identified in the manuscript with respects to provenance:

court until Scarlatti's death in 1757, has made generally available much archival material concerning Farinello in Spain and his retirement to Italy after 1760, upon the succession of a king more interested in hunting than in music. Less familiar is a series of essentially 19th-century operas in which Farinello at the court of Madrid figures as the principal character, sometimes in a scenario concerning his initial appearance before Philip V, sometimes in the role of a supernaturally empowered court intriguer scheming against the Inquisition in behalf of Ferdinand VI:

> *Farinelli ou le Bouffe du Roi, Comédie Historique en trois actes mêlée de chant* par Jules Henri Vernoy de Saint Georges (composer of the music anonymous), first performed at the Theatre of the Palais Royal, Paris, 3 February 1835 [31].
>
> English adaptation: *Farinelli, a Serio Comic Opera in two acts by C. Z. Barnett, ...the whole of the music composed by John Barnett;* first performed at the Theatre Royal, Drury Lane, London, 8 February 1839 [32].

---

1 — fol. 5—18ᵛ — «Quell'usignolo che innamorato» — an expanded version of the aria by Giacomelli first performed by Farinello in *Merope* (Venice, 1734); suggested by Haböck as the comparison aria about the nightingale mentioned by Sacchi.

2 — fol. 19—23ᵛ — recitative: «In van ti chiamo...»
    fol. 24—37 — «Al dolor che vo sfogando», performed by Farinello in *Sabrina* (London, 1737).

3 — fol. 38—55ᵛ — «Son qual nave che agitata», apparently by Giai, performed by Farinello in *Mitridate* (Venice, 1730), *Demetrio* (Venice, 1734), and *Artaserse* (London, 1734), but with small changes in the seven-line text in both of the 1734 productions. The text found in A-Wn 19111 agrees with that of the libretto for the London production.

4 — fol. 56—65 — «Io sperai del porto insano».

5 — fol. 66—74 — «Vuoi per sempre abbandonarmi»; text identified by Haböck; from Metastasio's *Il natal di Giove* (Vienna, 1740); the same sentiment as that of the the text remembered (?) by Burney in 1796, «Ah non lasciarmi, no».

6 — fol. 76—89ᵛ — recitative: «Ogni di più molesto dunque...» «Non sperar lusingarti»; text identified by Haböck: from Metastasio's *Le Cinesi* (Vienna, 1735), possibly the aria referred to by Burney as "a minuet he used to vary at his pleasure".

Numbers 1, 2, 3, 6, and fragments of 4 and 5 appear in transcription in Haböck's anthology, *Die Gesangskunst der Kastraten*. The manuscript, as is well known, is a prime source of material on the art of improvised vocal elaboration performed by one of its most celebrated practitioners. I can offer no explanation for the fact that the "cambiamenti" Farinello mentions occur in the manuscript very often in number 1, occasionally in number 3, and not at all in numbers 2, 4, 5 and 6.

[30] Farinello's side of the correspondence has disappeared, for Metastasio was not in the habit of retaining copies of letters written *to* him. For an index and summary of Metastasio's side, see Metastasio, *Tutte le Opere*, V, 843, and L. Frati, "Metastasio e Farinello", *Rivista musicale italiana* XX (1913), 1—30.

[31] libretto: GB-Lbm 11738.h.29

[32] libretto: GB-Lbm 2304.a.17, vol. 33—34; the adaptation was written for and the title part sung by Michael Balfe.

German adaptation: *Farinelli; oder König und Sänger. Schauspiel mit Gesang in 3 Aufzügen, nach einer wahren Begebenheit, aus dem Französischen . . . von W. Friedrich* (pseud.). Berlin (?), 187? [33].

German adaptation: *Farinelli. Operette in 3 Acten mit Benutzung eines älteren Stoffes von J. Wilibald Wulff und Charles Cassmann, Musik von Hermann Zumpe*, Hamburg (1886?) [34].

La Part du Diable, Opera Comique en trois actes, paroles de M. Scribe . . . Musique de M. Auber, first performed at the Théâtre Royal of the Opéra Comique, Paris, 6 January 1843 [35].

(For a list of two dozen adaptations, 1843—1930, in a dozen languages, all over Europe and in North and South America, see A. Loewenberg, *Annals of Opera* I, col. 829—30).

Farinelli. Opera en un prólogo y tres actos; text by J. A. Cavestany, music by Tomás Bretón y Hernandez, Madrid (1901?) [36].

Farinello's reputation in the 20th century was materially furthered by Franz Haböck's posthumous publications *Die Gesangskunst der Kastraten* (Vienna, 1923) and *Die Kastraten und ihre Gesangskunst* (Berlin and Leipzig, 1927), the first of which includes a biography of Farinello and an unclassified anthology of 42 miscellaneous arias and fragments from arias sung by him between 1720 and 1737 [37]. The rationale for the present study of Farinello's repertory lies, thus, not in another review of the singer's virtuosity, but in an attempt to collect as many as possible of the arias he sang, with a view to investigating considerations affecting his use of the substitute aria. That so large a proportion of Farinello's repertory is traceable, that he appeared over a relatively brief time-span in so many different cities in so many different roles, and that both he and his brother Riccardo Broschi were themselves composers comprised contributory considerations in the choice of Farinello for such a study. The situation as it concerns Farinello will be put in improved perspective by a review of some otherwise scattered information concerning the substitute aria in Italian opera generally.

The phenomenon of reusing already existing operatic poetry and/or music in a new context may be virtually as old as Italian opera itself. Stuart Reiner has generously informed me of correspondence dated 21 January 1612 in Mantova wherein Adriana Basile sends thanks for the gift of "La lagrimosa pietà". In Mr. Reiner's view it seems likely that the correspondence relates on the one hand to a piece on an 11-line text entitled "Lagrimosa pietà", published by Paolo Quagliati together with his *Carro di fedeltà d'amore* (Rome, 1611), and on the other to an 11-line song entitled "Lagrimosa pietà che più consolami", paraphrasing the text of 1611 and added to the role of Armida in the 1616 libretto for *intramezzi* to a play called *Bradamante gelosa*.

---

[33] libretto: US-NYp NKM.p.v.154
[34] scenario: US-Wc ML 50.Z9F3 (Case); score: GB-Lbm H 657
[35] libretto: F-Pn ThB 1879
[36] vocal score: GB-Lbm F 1267.n.m
[37] The anthology seems to have been intended essentially for practical use. There is no indication of sources for the music printed; orchestral accompaniments are transcribed for keyboard.

Particularly because one is accustomed to think of the three works by Mozart and Lorenzo Da Ponte as culminating instances of originality in the history of operatic collaboration, it is surprising to discover that the textual source for Don Alfonso's opening quatrain in his trio with Guglielmo and Ferrando from the first act of *Così fan tutte* is a Metastasio aria from the second act of *Demetrio* (1731)!

Metastasio	Da Ponte — Mozart
E la fede degli amanti	E la fede delle femine
Come l'araba fenice;	Come l'araba fenice;
Che vi sia, ciascun lo dice,	Che vi sia, ciascun lo dice,
Dove sia, nessun lo sa.	Dove sia, nessun lo sa.

Both Benedetto Marcello and Josse de Villeneuve report on the prevalence in early 18th-century Italy of handy collections of already used arias maintained by intimidated, lazy, or greedy librettists, composers, impresarios, and copyists [38]. The facsimiles shown facing p. 304, from a Modenese *Artaserse* rifacimento of 1750, represent but part of a large collection of mostly Modenese libretti dating from 1660 to 1780, wherein previously printed libretti were used as the actual physical basis in the act of remodelling. The following manuscript note, addressed to the Ducal printer of the 1750 *rifacimento* and now enclosed on a separate sheet in the revised text from 1739 just cited, alludes to a dilemma that must have been reasonably frequent for contemporary impresarios:

> Because Lucca Mengoni gave me a lad who is worth nothing whatever, it is necessary to change the role of Arbace which Catena was to sing but will be done now by Taus, and to give the part of Artaserse to Catena. Wherefore, my dearest Sig. Bartolomeo Soliani is earnestly implored by Bartolomeo Giovanardi to change these two parts in the libretti [39].

The *dramatis personae*, which had already been printed with Taus in the role of Artaserse and Catena in the much more critical part of Arbace, was duly reprinted with the singers for those roles exchanged; if alterations additional to those already made in the roles were used in performance, they were not taken into account in the printed libretto of 1750.

Nor were emergencies of the kind just documented the only cause for the last-minute haste characteristic of so much operatic production of the period. Metastasio preferred

---

[38] B. Marcello, «Il teatro alla moda», trans. R. Pauly, *MQ* XXXIV (1948), 371—403, and XXXV (1949), 85—105; R. Haas, „Josse de Villeneuves Brief über den Mechanismus der italienischen Oper von 1756“, *ZfMw* VII (1924—25), 129—63; also H. Bedarida, «L'opéra italien jugé par un amateur français en 1756», *Melanges de musicologie, offerts à M. Lionel de la Laurencie* (Paris, 1933), pp. 185—200.

[39] Modena, Archivio di Stato, Spettacoli pubblici teatrali. The libretti concerned bear title pages as follows: *Artaserse / Dramma per musica / da rappresentarsi in Modena nel Teatro Molza / Il Carnovale MDCCXXXIX*; and *Artaserse, Dramma per musica / da rappresentarsi nel Teatro del Pubblico / di Sassuolo / l'autunno del MDCCL (Modena)*.

a three-month period to write a libretto, but was capable of doing so in 18 days [40].
Contemporary libretto prefaces often make a fetish of apologizing for literary sins ostensibly committed as the result of the press of time [41]. Patrons of the kind familiar from
the Hofmannsthal-Strauss *Ariadne auf Naxos,* demanding almost instant opera conforming to idiosyncracies of personal taste or local convenience seem not to have been at all
so unusual in the middle of the 18th century as the outraged reactions of Hofmannsthal's
Musiklehrer and *Komponist* might lead one to believe. The following scene from *Prima
la musica, poi le parole,* an opera in one act by G. B. Casti and Antonio Salieri, produced
at Vienna's Schönbrunn Palace in February 1786, throws light on the manufacture of
substitute arias. It concerns a poet and a composer in the employ of a count who has
given but four days for the preparation of an operatic production in which a weak
soprano admired by the poet for charms other than her singing, is to have a principal
role. The poet and the composer, having just suffered through their opportunity to learn
the lady's vocal merits, now try together to concoct an aria suitable to her.

P: Can you imagine, just four days!
C: That's what was said. Then the first thing for you to do is to find words for the
   aria [just sung by the soprano].
P: That will be difficult.
C: What use are difficulties? We are not known here; eight or ten years ago at Forli I
   composed an aria on the text «Se possono tanto due luci vezzose». I think that
   would work here beautifully. The music is superb and ought to produce results.
   You'll see that everyone here will take it for the latest thing.
P: Your aria uses six-syllable lines. Let's see now (taking something from his pocket):
   I just happen to have here a tragic libretto entitled *I vespri siciliani.*
C: What an actor!
P: I wrote 15 of the aria texts, but 10 of them are tiresome. Let's see if we can't find
   one suitable to our purpose. Ah, here's one, a beauty! "Ferma oh Dio! non son
   francese". It has two extra syllables.

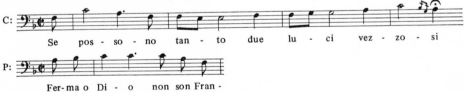

C: Se   pos - so - no   tan - to   due   lu - ci   vez - zo - si

P: Fer - ma o Di - o   non son Fran -

[40] Metastasio. *Tutte le Opere,* III, 133—34.
[41] My own favorite occurs in the notice to the reader for the libretto by G. N. Giannini for
Onorio in Roma (Venice, 1692): «E stata ideata in momenti: sceneggiata in ore: verseggiata in
meno di un giorno: Reso armoniosa dal Signor Carlo [Francesco] Polaroli in poco più d'una
settimana. Non dico favole: Lo creda chi vuole; ma e così in verità». Libretto: US-Wc Schatz
8305. Marcello suggests that insecure librettists might cloak their inadequacies in such language:
"It will be most useful to the modern poet to protest to the reader that he composed the opera
in his most tender years; and if he can add that he did this in a few days (even if he has worked
upon it for more than a few years), that will be a particularly good modern touch".

C: It doesn't work. Look further.
P: Here's another: «A che proposito vuoi tu ammazarmi?»
C: Let's not bother with that.
P: Oh, this one will go beautifully.
C: Let's hear it.
P: «Se questo mio pianto,
    Se questo mio canto,
    Ancor non espugna
    Quel barbaro sen;
    Via sfodera ma pugna
    Quel ferro spietato
    E questo costato
    Trafiggimi almen».

    This will be problematic. Instead perhaps we might . . .
C: No, I'd like here . . .
P: «Se questo . . . mio pianto . . . non mi . . . non ti . . .»
    It won't work.
C: Courage, keep going!
P: «Il cor . . .» Ah, here it is: «Il cor non ti tocca»!
C: Marvelous! «Non ti tocca».
P: Now we have to find a rhyme for «occa». I don't have my rhyming dictionary
    here but I'll do what I can. «Rocca . . . sciocca . . .»
C: Good, keep it up!
P: «Trabocca . . . bocca . . . questo canto di bocca».
C: Yes, that's fine!
P: «Se questo mio canto
    Che m'esca di bocca . . .»
C: (writing): «di bocca». That's amazing; what an eccentric! Give me your scrap pad
    for a moment, and let's chat further about this. If your Count insists, I see that
    we won't be able to avoid making a part for this soprano [42].

The libretti and scores from 1720—37 catalogued in the Appendix on pp. 324—30,
including 350 aria texts used by Farinello and 250 musical settings of those texts, undoubtedly
do not comprise the entire repertory used during Farinello's career. But the calendar of the
productions in which he participated is sufficiently dense for us to assume an adequate
statistical sample for the discussion of the singer's repertory which follows.

A goodly number of contemporary critics of early 18th-century Italian opera have
commented on the wholly inadequate attention given by many Italian singers of the
time to the dramatic character of the roles they represented [43]; and it will be remember-

---

[42] Libretto: I-Vc Salieri; score: A-Wn 17184.
[43] See, for example, B. Marcello, «Il teatro alla moda», trans. R. Pauly, *MQ* XXXIV (1948),
     389—403, and R. Haas, *op. cit.*, p. 139.

ed in that context that Quantz had been specifically critical of Farinello's weakness as
an actor. Thus, it is not surprising that, after the first few years of his career, Farinello
was normally allotted roles which, like that of Don Ottavio in Mozart's *Don Giovanni*,
offer more by way of vocal than dramatic opportunity. The great majority of the roles
sung by Farinello after 1723, moreover, involve a repetition of the same stereotyped
dramatic figure: the long-suffering young hero who, though abused and reviled, in the
end triumphs over the forces of evil, attaining the princess, the kingdom, or both. But
if the figure portrayed by so many Farinello roles was relatively flat and unchanging,
almost from the beginning there is normally a good deal of demonstrable musical variety
within individual roles. The arias and duets sung by Farinello in the operatic productions
he took part in range in number from three in *Angelica e Medoro* (1720) and in *La ninfa
riconosciuta* (1730) to eight in *Artaserse* (1734), Farinello's English debut; but from 1722
he was never given fewer arias than any colleague in the cast. Very often, especially
after 1730, his role included arias in what appear to have been special places of honor:
the ends of the first and/or second acts, and in the third act, just before the concluding
chorus [44]. Among Farinello's several arias within a given role, one can expect to find
variety with respect to mode, key, tempo, meter, length, orchestral accompaniment, and
degree of vocal elaboration — though elaborately virtuoso, binary meter, allegro arias
in major keys of few accidentals always preponderate. Like many of his contemporaries,
Farinello sang a great many arias in which the violins simply double the vocal part [45],
but much of the time in the scores he performs in it is Farinello who sings the majority
of the characteristically limited number of arias involving obbligato instrumental parts.
But though there is musical variety, there is no apparent effort in any of his roles to
balance the shares of the five aria types — *patetica, bravura, parlante, mezzo carattere,*
and *brillante* — into which, according to the Milanese Count Prata quoted in the Italian
version of Goldoni's memoirs, a principal role of the period was inevitably divided [46].

[44] These are clearly moments of special emphasis, for always in the first two and often in the
last of the three situations cited the performer singing the aria is alone on stage, a fact which
also lightens the burden of his dramatic responsibility.

[45] It seems true, as Marcello and others suggest, that a great many Italian opera composers of the
time knew little about counterpoint and realized it: one finds innumerable arias, sung by
Farinello among others, wherein four or five staves of score are unnecessarily devoted over
long stretches of music to a texture comprising two or three real parts. It may be that the
doubling of the voice by other instruments was often intended as a support for singers insecure
of intonation. But the frequent use of the device in Farinello's repertory indicates that part of
the rationale for the custom comes from an aesthetic preference for this characteristically Italian
texture. Charles de Brosses, accustomed to a more contrapuntal style, writes in admiration of
the Italian propensity for doubling the soprano with the first violins (*Lettres familières sur
l'Italie*), ed Y. Bezard (Paris, 1931, I, 357). But not all of the French were equally enthusiastic
(see, for example, Goudar, *op. cit.*, 108—13).

[46] It is classification schemes like this which suggest the possibility that the substitution of one
aria may, in order that balance of the kind outlined by Count Prata be retained, have neces-
sitated the substitution of still other arias. One reads of *arie cantabile* and *di bravura* in the
contemporary letters and treatises of writers close enough to the real world of Italian opera
for their testimony to be taken seriously; and Tosi bemoans at length the disappearance of what
he calls the *aria patetica*. But Goldoni's memoirs do not let us know what he thought of Count

Given Pier Jacopo Martello's complaint about contemporary singers and their transfer of arias from one opera to another, given the pressure that Farinello's enormous popularity must have enabled him to assert over impresarios, and given the ease with which the great majority of the arias he sang might in fact be transferred, one would expect that his collected repertory would in the end contain a considerable number of substitute arias. That this is not at all the case comes as a surprise. There are a few traceable cases wherein two distinctly different settings of exactly the same aria text survive, both unambiguously relatable to Farinello. But since neither member of such a pair is ever locatable as a contrafact, it does not appear that the second member of the pair was prepared as a way to save time. Quite the contrary, as in the incipits cited below from two Hasse settings of a Metastasio text from *La Clemenza di Tito,* one often has the impression that for some composers at least it must have been easier to try to dash off an aria, anew or from memory, than to go to the trouble of sorting through the myriad musical materials in one's trunk. The two almost equal-length Hasse settings of «Deh

Prata's judgment on aria classification: the context of the Count's remarks is advice to the youthful Goldoni concerning the lack of interest shown towards Goldoni's first libretto by a group of hardened professional singers.
The five-fold design of John Brown — *arie cantabile, di portamento, di mezzo carattere, parlante,* and *di bravura* — often cited in the literature, deserves less attention than it has had. A Scotch painter who studied in Italy during the 1770's before his death at age 35, Brown left behind a series of letters to a patron interested in Italian music, published in 1789 with the hope of providing financial help to his widow and child. The passage below, which follows Brown's outline for an aria classification scheme, is not generally enough known: "I shall now say something of each class, and, in doing so, I hope to give your Lordship some idea of the great extent as well as precision of the Italian music, and to show, that, though the names of these classes be evidently taken from circumstances of practice, yet these circumstances, if properly attended to, will be found to be strictly connected with, and indeed, to originate from distinctions of a higher kind, which must have been previously made with respect to the nature of the passions, and their effect on utterance and expression. Whether the Italian composers, in observing these distinctions have been guided by some system, or have been merely influenced by feeling, I cannot take upon me to say. I am rather, however, inclined to think that the latter is the case; in the first place, because I never heard of any such system existing among them, and, because I have been personally acquainted with several of their finest composers now living, that had no idea of it; and, again, because I think that, to the want of such a system can be alone attributed the gross deviations (which even in the works of their greatest masters are sometimes to be met with), from its most obvious and essential principles". (John Brown, *Letters upon the Poetry and Music of the Italian Opera* [Edinburgh, 1789], pp. 41—42).
I have yet to find any piece of music from the period bearing any contemporary label of the kind at issue here.

se piacer mi vuoi», for sopranos of almost identical range and vocal facility, and for exactly the same orchestral accompaniment, differ principally with respect to apparent tempo designation.

More numerous but still surprisingly few are the cases tabulated below in which an aria text used by Farinello in one role then migrates to another role. Those instances in which music for the aria survives as well as the text are preceded in the tabulation by asterisks.

Table 1

Cervo in bosco, se lo impiaga	*Medo (Parma, 1728) Vinci	L'abbandono di Armida (Venice, 1729) A. Pollaroli	*Catone (Venice, 1729) Leo
Chi non sente al mio dolore	*Merope (Turin, 1732)	Merope (Lucca, 1733) R. Broschi	Artaserse (Venice, 1734) Hasse
Giusti cieli eterni Dei	Artaserse (Ferrara, 1731)	Merope (Lucca, 1733)	
La sorte mia tiranna	*Siroe (Bologna, 1733) Hasse	Artaserse (Venice, 1734) Hasse	
Mi lusinga il dolce affetto	L'isola d'Alcina (Rome, 1728) R. Broschi	*Catone (Venice, 1729) Leo	Catone (Turin, 1732) R. Broschi
Navigante che non spera	*Medo (Parma, 1728) Vinci	Demetrio (Vicenza, 1734) Araja	
Pastorel che trova al fine	*Idaspe (Venice, 1730) R. Broschi	La ninfa riconosciuta (Lucca, 1730)	
Quel vapor che in valle impuro	L'abbandono di Armida (Venice, 1729) A. Pollaroli	*Semiramida riconosciuta (Venice, 1729) Porpora	La ninfa riconosciuta (Lucca, 1730)
Questo core amato bene	Berenice (Venice, 1734) Araja	Demetrio (Vicenza, 1734) Araja	
Scherzo dell'onda	*Medo (Parma, 1728) Vinci	*Catone (Venice, 1729) Leo	
Serbarmi o cara	Ezio (Turin, 1731) R. Broschi	Merope (London, 1737) R. Broschi	
So che pietà non hai	L'abbandono di Armida (Venice, 1729) A. Pollaroli)	*Catone (Venice, 1729) Leo	Catone (Turin, 1732) Hasse
Son qual nave che agitata	*Mitridate (Venice, 1730) Giai	Artaserse (Lucca, 1730) Hasse	Demetrio (Vicenza, 1734) Araja
Son qual nave in ria procella	*Zenobia (Naples, 1725) Leo	Il Cid (Rome, 1727) Leo	

In none of the cases listed is there any notable violence to dramatic context because of the substituted aria text. In the Venetian *rifacimento* of Metastasio's *Catone in Utica*, for example, Arbace's unhappiness at being rejected by his adored Marzia seems equally well expressed through an aria sung by Farinello the previous year in Vinci's *Medo*.

Text original to II/16 of Metastasio's *Catone* (Rome, 1728)

Text sung by Farinello in *Medo* (Parma, 1728) then substituted for his use in II/16 of *Catone* (Venice, 1729)

Che sia la gelosia	
Un gelo in mezzo al foco,	Cervo in bosco, se lo impiaga
E ver; ma questo è poco.	Dardo rapido, e mortale
E il più crudel tormento	Varca il colle, cerca il fonte
D'un cor che s'innamora;	Dalla valle al prato va.
E questo è poco ancora.	Trova al fin, mentre divaga,
Io nel mio cor nel sento,	Erba, onor d'aprico monte
Ma non lo so spiegar.	Che gustata l'empio strale
Se non portasse amore	Dal suo fiano cader fa.
Affanno si tiranno,	
Qual è quel rozzo core	
Che non vorrebbe amar?	

Nor does it make any obvious dramatic incongruence when, in a son's departure from a father who, having murdered his king then knowingly helps attribute that crime to his own son, Farinello performs an aria he had sung the year before in another opera.

Text original to I/11 of Metastasio's *Artaserse* (Rome, 1730)

Text original to I/13 of Metastasio's *Siroe* (Venice, 1726), performed in that position by Farinello (Bologna, 1733), then substituted for his use in a *rifacimento* of Metastasio's *Artaserse* (Venice, 1734)

Per quel paterno amplesso	La sorte mia tiranna
Per questo estremo addio	Farmi di più non puo:
Conservami te stesso,	M'accusa e mi condanna
Placami l'idol mio	Un'empia ed un germano,
Difendimi il mio re!	L'amico e il genitor.
Vado a morir beato,	Ogni soccorso è vano,
Se della Persia il fato	Che più sperar non so.
Tutto si sfoga in me.	So che fedel son io,
	E che la fede, oh Dio!
	In me diventa error.

Of note in the tabulation of Farinello's traceable substitute arias is the singer's apparent fondness for arias from Vinci's *Medo* and the fact that the substitute arias occur so regularly in connection with productions from which there is no surviving score, a phenomenon suggesting that it was as often the convenience of the impresario as that of the singer which was served by the substitute arias. Equally striking is the markedly brief life-span of the migrating arias. Farinello, for example, repeated the role of Epitide in *Merope* in Venice during 1734 and in London during 1737, but without repeating «Chi non sente al mio dolore» or «Giusti cieli eterni dei», for which still other arias had been substituted. This bears out Josse de Villeneuve's remark that, while the French were fond of older music, Italians of the time wanted to hear nothing but new music, sung if possible by new singers [47]. An anecdote told by Carlo Goldoni about his own early Venetian career as a refurbisher of old libretti makes a similar point. The time is March 1740, the occasion the Venetian visit of Prince Ferdinand Christian of Saxony; Pietro Foscarini, one of the procurators of St. Mark and a governor of the conservatory called Ospitale della Pietà, had been anxious to impress the Prince with the performance of the young ladies resident there, but there was no time for the composition and rehearsal of any new works.

> I had previously written three chamber cantatas at the Cavaliere's request and for the young ladies' use: one for two voices, entitled *La ninfa saggia,* one for three, entitled *Gli amanti felici,* and one for four, entitled *Le quattro staggioni,* all three set to music by Sig. Gennaro d'Alessandro, Master of the Chapel and composer at that Ospitale. His Excellency the Sig. Procurator did me the honor of consulting me on this occasion and of asking me whether in those cantatas (which had been successful) it might not be possible to engraft something bearing on the Prince. I asked for time to ponder my answer; the next day I informed him of my intentions; they pleased him; this is what I did.
>
> Nine of those choristers, the main ones, had performed in those three cantatas. I wrote a new composition, entitled *Le nuove muse,* and without changing a note, either in the arias or in the recitatives, caused the music of the three cantatas to do duty for the words of the new composition; and since I made the muses speak according to the attributes ascribed them by the poets, I found ample occasion to speak of the Prince who was to be in attendance. Nobody noticed my artifice, and everybody could have sworn that all, both words and music, was new. The Master of the Chapel himself was stunned when he saw his own music transferred to a new subject, without having had to take the trouble of altering the least thing; not only did he find the measure preserved, but the longs and the shorts, the accents and the breaths — in short, everything was in its place.
>
> I had done similar pieces of work before, to mask old arias for the sake of some singer or composer; but I had never done this with recitatives, which are even more difficult to transfer. In the end it turned out to everyone's satisfaction; the entertainment was thought new; the Prince was pleased with it; the public

---

[47] See, for example, François Raguenet, «Parallèle des Italiens et des Français», trans. O. Strunk, *Source Readings in Music History* (New York, 1950), p. 481; O. E. Deutsch, *op. cit.,* p. 409; De Brosses, *op. cit.,* p. 237; C. Burney, *The Present State of Music in France and Italy,* pp. 189—90; A. Goudar, *op. cit.,* p. 137.

admired it; and I became more confirmed than ever in the opinion that with ingenuity and patience a man can accomplish anything he pleases [48].

Table 2, indicating the number of occasions in which, upon repeating a role he had sung earlier, Farinello introduced arias on texts he had not apparently performed before, is relevant in the same connection.

Table 2

Title	Place	Year	Composer attribution in libretto	# arias sung by F	# apparently new arias sung by F
I fratelli riconosciuti	Parma	1726	Capello	5	
Nicomede	Munich	1728	Torri	7	7
Catone in Utica	Venice	1729	Leo	6	
Catone in Utica	Turin	1732	Hasse	5	2
Artaserse	Venice	1730	Hasse	6	
Artaserse	Lucca	1730	Hasse	5	1
Artaserse	Ferrara	1731	Vinci	5	4
Artaserse	Venice	1734	Hasse	6	4
Artaserse	London	1734		7	3
Merope	Turin	1732	R. Broschi	5	
Merope	Lucca	1733	R. Broschi	5	3
Merope	Venice	1734	Giacomelli	5	3
Merope	London	1737		6	4
Adriano	Venice	1733	Giacomelli	5	
Adriano	London	1735	Veracini	7	3
Siroe	Bologna	1733	Hasse	5	
Siroe	London	1736		5	3

Of the seven arias sung by Farinello in the *rifacimento* of Handel's *Ottone* performed at London's Haymarket Theater in the fall of 1734, not one is on a text used in any previous *Ottone* production by Handel or in any previous role by Farinello. Table 3, summarizing the situation regarding the exchange of aria texts in the five productions of *Artaserse* for which Farinello sang the role of Arbace, is tantalizing, for it indicates how much will remain unknown about 18th-century Italian opera until we are able to make more than single-handed efforts to solve its formidable bibliographic problems.

Table 3

Venice, 1730 (Hasse)		Ferrara, 1731 (Vinci)	
I/2	Fra cento affani e cento	I/2	— Venice, 1730
I/14	Se al labbro mio non credi	I/14	— Aprimi o cara il petto
II/2	Lascia cadermi in volto	II/2	— Rome, 1730 (Mi scacci sdegnato)
II/11	Per questo dolce amplesso	II/11	— Per placarti, o Padre amato
III/1	Perche tarda è mai la morte	III/1	— Giusti cieli eterni Dei
III/2	Parto qual pastorello		

[48] Quoted from the translation of Piero Ernesto Weiss in that author's Columbia University dissertation, "Carlo Goldoni, Librettist: the Early Years" (1970), pp. 53—54.

Lucca, 1730 (Hasse)
    I/2 — Venice, 1730
    I/14 — Venice, 1730
    II/11 — Venice, 1730
    III/1 — Venice, 1730
    III/2 — Son qual nave che agitata

Venice, 1734 (Hasse)
    I/2 — Se penso al tuo periglio
    I/15 — Chi non sente al mio dolore
    II/2 — Venice, 1730
    II/11 — La sorte mia tiranna
    III/1 — Venice, 1730
    III/8 — Quell'ardor che il sen m'accende

London, 1734 [48a] (Hasse)
    I/1 — Un altro volta o Febo
    I/2 — In sen mi tace
    I/6 — Venice, 1730   I/14
    II/2 — Venice, 1730   II/2
    II/5 — Venice, 1730   II/11
    III/1 — Lucca, 1730 III/2
    III/6 — Or la nube procellosa

Our study of Farinello's repertory shows that he sang moderate numbers of new aria texts. But it suggests, too, especially because of the essentially complete absence of traceable contrafacts [49], that, unlike many of the singers who were his contemporaries, he preferred singing new music to old. That is a situation which contrasts strikingly with that outlined by Goldoni for the *rifacimento* of Zeno's *Griselda*, produced in Venice during 1735 with music by Vivaldi.

> The prima donna's part that year was to be played by Signora Annina Giro, or Giraud ... who, being Vivaldi's pupil, was commonly known as Annina del Prete Rosso. Her voice was not beautiful, but she was graceful and handsome; she acted well (a rare thing in those days) and had protectors, which is all that is needed to deserve the rank of prima donna. Vivaldi was hard pressed for a poet who should adjust or patch up the drama to his taste, and put in it, for

[48a] Walsh's undated publication of *The Favourite Songs in the Opera Call'd Artaxerxes* includes two Farinello arias not contained in the London libretto of 1734: «Quanto affanno bell' aurora» and «Fortunate passate mie pene». I can find no libretto for any of Farinello's subsequent London performances of *Artaserse* mentioned by Burney.

[49] That introductory ritornelli can be added or dropped, that vocal incipits can be altered as the result of accommodation to a new text, that arias which begin alike do not necessarily continue so, that keys, orchestral accompaniments, and even tempi vary in multiple versions of what is clearly the same aria naturally makes one hesitant, in dealing with several hundred incipit cards, to assert the almost complete absence of contrafacts in Farinello's repertory. But I can find only two pairs of *bona fide* examples:

    «Colei, che t'invaghi»   «Se mi togliete quella»
      Farnace (Rome, 1724)   *Mitridate* (Venice, 1730)
      music by Vinci   music attributed to Giai
    «Parto quel pastorello»   «Parto seguendo amore»
      Artaserse (Venice, 1730) *Orfeo* (London, 1736)
      music by Hasse   libretto identifies no composer;
                        Burney labels the work a pasticcio.

better or for worse, the arias his pupil had sung before; and I, having been ap-
pointed to perform that task, presented myself to the composer, by order of my
patron the Cavaliere. He received me very coolly. He took me for a novice,
and he was not mistaken; and finding me uninformed in the science of the
drama-manglers, he appeared most anxious to send me away.

'If only, sir, you were acquainted with the rules', said he ... 'Enough, you
cannot know them. See here, for example: after this tender scene there is an
aria cantabile; but Signora Annina is not ... not ... not fond of this sort of
arias'. (That is, she could not sing them.) 'She wants an *aria d'azione* here ...
that will disclose the sentiment without being pathetic, without being *cantabile*'.

After further discussion Goldoni sits down in Vivaldi's workroom.

I peruse the scene attentively; I gather the sentiment of the *aria cantabile*,
and I make it into an *aria d'azione, di passione, di movimento*. I take it over
to him, let him see it. He reads it softly, holding his Breviary in his right hand,
my paper in his left; and when he had finished, he flings the Breviary aside, rises
to his feet, runs to the door, calls Signora Annina. Signora Annina comes in,
Signora Paolina her sister comes in, too; he reads them the arietta, loudly exclaim-
ing, 'He wrote it here, here he wrote it, he wrote it here', and embraces me
anew, cries 'bravo'; and now I was his dear friend, his poet, his confidant, and
he never forsook me thereafter. I later butchered Zeno's libretto entirely to his
satisfaction [50].

The situation contrasts equally with what Josse de Villeneuve wrote about the prepara-
tions normal for a contemporary opera production:

The composer arrives with 40 or 50 arias prefabricated during hours of inspiration.
He adjusts these as soon as possible to the words of the opera to be performed.
If these words just cannot be fitted to the music determined for them, he has
others made which work better — or less badly. Whether or not the new words
have any relationship to the action is a matter of no importance. The composer's
only concern is that the arias suit the taste and the voice of the singer who is
to perform them. The underlaying of the text gives him no trouble whatever.
People who understand such matters know with what ease one can stretch or
compress, and that with a text of two lines one can easily provide words for a
whole sonata.

It happens rather often that the virtuosi — the principal male and the principal
female singer — who determine the fashion of their colleagues, present the
composer, the impresario, and the public with arias which they have sung with

[50] P. E. Weiss, *op. cit.*, pp. 32—33.

success in other operas; they compel the composer to adjust these at once to their present roles, in order, as they say, to assure the opera's success. One must subordinate oneself to their directions, for there is no court of higher authority than these people, of whom the maxim says, 'Impertinent as a singer' [51].

Vivaldi has admitted with some embarrassment in the case of Annina Giro that the lady was less than adept in performing arias in the *stile cantabile*. The soprano in Metastasio's *L'Impresario delle Canarie* dislikes the agitated scene she is to play while representing Cleopatra in chains, because she fears anger may be prejudicial to her voice [52]. The singers who are to perform in the parodistic *La critica teatrale* (Venice, 1775) vie with one another over the relative merits and lengths of their individual roles [53]. Metastasio himself wrote of the prevailing sense of uncertainty regarding the causes for an aria's or an opera's public success [54]. But the principal cause for singers' insecurity and, thus, for the tenacity with which they insisted on new texts for old arias, may well have lain in their markedly low levels of verbal and musical literacy. The principal castrato in *La critica teatrale* is so defensive about his learning capacity that he insists on garbling an aria text simply because he has learned it that way [55]. Ange Goudar, admittedly no friend of Italian opera, maintained that of the 300—400 female singers of the Italian repertory active during the 1770's, very few could read Italian and only five or six could read music [56]. Clearly, once an aria had been learned, particularly were it a difficult one, many a singer saw himself constrained to use it again, especially on those frequent occasions when the time for preparation of a new production was very limited.

Many of the singers who were Farinello's contemporaries were insecure people of narrow outlook. But Farinello, in addition to being the possessor of unrivalled vocal equipment, must have been endowed with an exceptionally broad education for an Italian musician of his time. Able to write both music and poetry, he was proficient as a performer on the harpsichord and the viola d'amore, and interested himself in experiments concerning harpsichord design. Among his incidental benefactions to musical history are a unique manuscript preserving a fascinating variety of the elaborate divisions

---

[51] R. Haas, *op. cit.*, p. 144

[52] Metastasio, *Tutte le Opere*, I, 63

[53] libretto: I-Vc Astaritta

[54] Metastasio, *Tutte le Opere*, III, 122

[55] Singer (who several scenes earlier has misread «Sicilia» for «Scilla»):
   «Quel nocchier che scioglie aventi
   Troppe vele in mar turbato:
   In Cariddi evita il fatto
   Va in Sicilia a naufragar».
 Poet: What sort of obstinacy is this? Why can't you understand that the words are «. . . va in Scilla»?
 Singer: For me and for the music «va in Sicilia» is better.
   Print it as you wish; but I've made up my mind on this point, and I shall listen to no one.

[56] Goudar, *op. cit.*, pp. 60—61.

for which he was so famous [57], his negotiations for the acceptance of the dedication of Padre Martini's *Storia della musica,* vol. I [58], a continuous correspondence with Metastasio between 1747 and the poet's death in April 1782 [59], and, through Charles Burney, the survival of almost all of the presently extant biographical information on Domenico Scarlatti, whose manuscript and instrument collection he inherited and did his best to preserve intact [60]. Probably the wealthiest musician of the 18th century, in his retirement he counted Pope Benedict XIV and the Duke of Parma among his patrons; Gluck, Burney, Casanova, the Electress of Saxony, and Emperor Joseph II among his visitors; the Cardinal Legate of Bologna, Senators Spada, Zambecari, Ratta, Tanara, and Padre Martini among his friends [61].

An understanding of the mechanisms controlling the manufacture of substitute arias is vital to a history of Italian opera in the 18th century especially. But to secure it we shall need to turn, I think, to the repertories of other singers — to secondary figures or to a principal perhaps such as the castrato Gaetano Majorano detto Caffarelli. Burney wrote of Farinello that "... it seems as if the involuntary loss of the most gross and common of all animal faculties had been the only degrading circumstance of his existence« [62]. But Caffarelli was known to his contempories as «il babbo degl'impertinenti» [63].

---

[57] A-Wn 19111, for a discussion of which see note 29, above. Excerpts from the music it contains are printed in Haböck, *Die Gesangskunst der Kastraten.*

[58] Sacchi, *op. cit.,* p. 40. An autograph letter of Farinello to Martini, dated «Villa Viziosa 4 Giugno 1759», explaining the arrangements for the acceptance of the dedication of volume 1 and the impolitic aspects of further negotiations regarding subsequent volumes of the *Storia,* exists in the manuscript collection of the Austrian National Library.

[59] For an index to 172 extant Metastasio letters addressed to Farinello, see Metastasio, *Tutte le Opere,* V, 922—23.

[60] Kirkpatrick, *op. cit.,* pp. 177 ff., 362—63.

[61] Metastasio, *Tutte le Opere,* many letters subsequent to Farinello's return to Italy, the first of which is dated in Vienna on 31 July 1760; Burney, *The Present State of Music in France and Italy* (London, 1773), pp. 222—23; Sacchi, *op. cit.,* pp. 38—39.

[62] C. Burney, *Memoirs of the Life and Writings of the Abate Metastasio* (London, 1796), III, 287—88.

[63] R. Haas, *op. cit.,* p. 144.

Calendar for the career of Carlo Broschi detto Farinello
1720—37[64]

Abbreviations:

L: libretto
S: complete score
–S: score containing only some of the arias in the libretto
FS: Walsh publication of the "favorite songs"

Title	Date & Place of first performance	Role	Composer(s)	Source(s) for information
Angelica e Medoro	1720, Naples, home of "il Sig. Principe della Torella"	Tirsi	Porpora	L: I-Nn 74.H.35 S: GB-Lbm Add 14120 A-Wn 17050
Sofonisba	1722, carn. Rome, Teatro Aliberti	Sofonisba	Predieri	L: I-Bc 4432 –S: F-Pc X1257
Flavio Anicio Olibrio	1722, carn. Rome, Teatro Aliberti	Placida	Porpora	L: I-Bc 4317 S: F-Pc D12721 –S: B-Bc 4658-75
Cosroe	1723, carn. Rome, Teatro Aliberti	Palmira	A. Pollaroli	L: I-Bc 4308 –S: F-Pc D12707 –S: D-Müs 174

Adelaide	1723, carn. Rome, Teatro Aliberti	Adelaide	Porpora	L: US-Wc S 8376
				S: D-SW M A/460
				–S: F-Pc D12719
				  F-Pn VM⁷ 7694
				  GB-Lbm Add 31504

Imeneo	1723, Naples, wedding of Leonardo Tocco and Camilla Cantelini	Tirinto	Porpora	L: I-Nn Sala 6, Misc. 12 & 38 S: I-MC 126A22
La Tigrane	1724, Jan. Rome, home of Portuguese ambassador	Titiro	F. Gasparini	L: I-Bc 7219 S: ?
Farnace	1724, carn. Rome, Teatro Aliberti	Berenice	Vinci	L: I-Vgc Vinci S: D-Müs 4243 –S: F-Pc D14259
Scipione	1724, carn. Rome, Teatro Aliberti	Salonice	Predieri	L: I-Bc 4434 S: F-Pc D12740 –S: I-Rc 2222
Semiramide, regina dell'Asseria	1724, spring Naples, Teatro San Bartolomeo	Nino	Porpora	L: I-Bc 4319 –S: GB-Lcm 629 –S: I-Nc 22–2–1 (anonymous)

---

[64] For a good deal of information contained in the Calendar I am indebted to the generosity of Claudio Sartori (Milan) and Reinhart Strohm (Munich). I am grateful, too, for the graciousness of Gerald Coke, who permitted a microfilm to be made for my use of his unique libretto for the 1734 London production of *Ottone*.

Turno Aricino	1724 Naples, Teatro San Bartolomeo	Geminio	Leo, Vinci	L: S: ?
Eraclea	1724, fall Naples, Teatro San Bartolomeo	Damiro	Vinci	–L: I-Bc 5507 S: I-MC 126E24–26
Unknown work	1724 Vienna			Burney
Il Florindo	1725, winter Naples, Teatro San Bartolomeo	Florindo	Sarro	L: I-Vgc Sarro –S: D-Müs 4262
Antonio e Cleopatra	1725, winter Naples	Cleopatra	Hasse	L: ? S: A-Wn SA 68B33[65]
Astianatte	1725, winter Naples, Teatro San Bartolomeo	Oreste	Vinci	L: I-Bc 5311 S: I-Nc 33.6.2
Tito Sempronio Gracco	1725, carn. Naples, Teatro San Bartolomeo	Rosanno	Sarro	L: I-Bc 21955 S: ?
Zenobia in Palmira	1725, spring Naples, Teatro San Bartolomeo	Decio	Leo	L: I-Nc U.1.102 S: I-Nc 28.4.24
Amore e fortuna	1725, 1 Oct. Naples, Teatro San Bartolomeo	Aristeo	G. Porta	L: I-Nc 5.11.28/9 S: ?
La Lucinda fedele	1726, carn. Naples, Teatro San Bartolomeo	Ernando	G. Porta	L: I-Nc 5.3.7 S: ?
I fratelli riconosciuti	1726, spring Parma	Nicomede	G. M. Capello	L: US-Wc S 1590 S: B-Bc 2050 GB-CDp
a serenade	1726, May Milan			Quantz
Il Ciro	1726, 28 Aug. Milan, Teatro Ducale	Idaspe	F. Ciampi	L: I-Mb 6038/6 S: ?
Il Cid	1727 Rome, Teatro Capranica	Rodrigo	Leo	L: I-Vc Leo –S: I-Rvat Chigi QVIII.201.N42
Antigona (La fedeltà coronata)	1727, summer Bologna, Teatro Malvezzi	Ceraste	Orlandini	L: US-Wc ML 50.2.A71801 S: GB-Lbm Add. 16066
L'amor generoso	1727, carn. Rome, Teatro Capranica	Aldano	Costanzi	L: I-Mb 3710 S: ?
L'isola d'Alcina	1728, carn. Rome, Teatro Capranica	Ruggiero	R. Broschi	L: I-Bc 682 –S: I-Rc 2768, 2771

[65] Sven H. Hansell, *op. cit.*, 14—16.

Cesare in Egitto	1728, carn. Rome, Teatro Capranica	Tolomeo	Predieri	L: B-Bc 19632 S: ?
Medo	1728, spring Parma, Teatro Ducale	Giasone	Vinci	L: I-Bc 5518 S: F-Pc D 11899 B-Bc 2196 D-Müs 4262
Unknown work	1728, Vienna			Burney
Nicomede	1728, Oct. Munich, court theater	Nicomede	P. Torri	L: I-Mb 2193 S: D-Mbs 214 S: I-MOe E340[66]
L'abbandono di Armida	1729, carn. Venice, Teatro San Giov. Gris.	Rinaldo	pasticcio	L: I-Bc 5692 S: ?[67]
Catone in Utica	1729, carn. Venice, Teatro San Giov. Gris.	Arbace	Leo[68]	L: US-Wc S 5557 S: B-Bc 2194 S: GB-Lam 75
Semiramida riconosciuta	1729, carn. Venice, Teatro San Giov. Gris.	Mirteo	Porpora	L: US-Wc S 8361 S: GB-Lam 81 −S: GB-Lcm 510
Lucio Papirio	1729, spring Parma, Teatro Ducale	Quinto Fabio	Giacomelli	L: I-Vgc Giacomelli S: GB-Lam 71 −S: F-Pc D 4629
Edippo	1729, Oct. Munich	Edippo	Torri	L: I-Mb 3346 −S: D-Mbs 156
Artaserse	1730, carn. Venice, Teatro San Giov. Gris.	Arbace	Hasse	L: US-Wc S 4576 S: I-Vnm lxxxiv.c.6 S: GB-Cfm 23F2
Idaspe	1730, carn. Venice, Teatro San Giov. Gris.	Dario	R. Broschi	L: US-Wc S 1339 S: A-Wn 18281
Mitridate	1730, carn. Venice, Teatro San Giov. Gris.	Farnace	Giai	L: US-Wc S 3815 S: GB-Lcm 209

[66] The score now in Modena is undated and anonymous, but the participating singers listed at the beginning of its first volume and the incipits of its successive arias match apposite materials in I-Mb 2193 and D-Mbs 214. To facilitate the identification of such anonymous scores was but one of the goals of the computer-implemented catalogue for Italian arias in development a few years ago at MIT.

[67] From the dedication of the short two-part libretto "all Eccellentissime Dame Veneziane" (a sign that no more remunerating a dedicatee could be found): «... tutto il resto del breve giro di questa picciola composizione serve solamente a connettere con qualche scenica armonia, e regolata ragione quell'Arie, che in altri tempi, luochi, e circostanze diverse si sono concepite ed eseguite, e che ora sono nuovamente introdotte a solo fine di rinnovare il piacere ...» There is no locatable score for the production, but all of the aria texts sung by Farinello stem from previous Farinello roles for which musical sources are extant.

[68] Though the Venetian libretto names Leo as the composer of the music, Farinello's role contained two arias by Leonardo Vinci: «Mi lusinga il cor d'affetto» (so marked by the scribe of GB-Lam 75) and «Cervo in bosco, se lo impiega» (apparently by Leo in both GB-Lam 75 and in B-Bc 2194, but occurring earlier in all the scores for the 1728 production of Vinci's *Medo*).

Scipione in Cartagine nuova	1730, spring Piacenza, Nuovo Ducal Teatro	P. C. Scipione	Giacomelli	L: I-Pc 65200 S: D-Mbs 159
Artaserse	1730, autumn Lucca	Arbace	Hasse	L: I-Vgc Hasse S: ?[69]
La ninfa riconosciuta	1730, autumn Lucca	Silvio		L: I-Vgc vari autori N-O S: ?[70]
Ezio	1731, carn. Turin, Regio Teatro	Ezio	R. Broschi	L: I-Rsc G139/4 −S: F-Pn VM⁷204
Poro	1731, carn. Turin, Regio Teatro	Poro	Porpora	L: L-Rsc G139/5 −S: −
Farnace	1731, spring Bologna, Teatro Malvezzi	Merione	G. Porta	L: I-Bc 4359 S: ?
Arianna e Teseo	1731, August Milan, Regio Ducal Teatro	Teseo	R. Broschi	L: I-Bc 685 S: ?
Artaserse	1731, autumn Ferrara, Teatro Bonacossi	Arbace	Vinci	L: I-MOe lxx.1.32 S: GB-Lcm 629[71]
Catone in Utica	1732, carn. Turin, Regio Teatro	Arbace	Hasse	L: I-Rsc G139/6 −S: I-Mc Q.8.81 −S: D-Mbs 141 −S: F-Pc D 247 −S: GB-Lbm Add. 31592, Add. 31603
Merope	1732, carn. Turin, Regio Teatro	Epitide	R. Broschi	L: I-Rsc G139/7 S: A-Wgm 1222

[69] The Lucca libretto lists Hasse as composer. Farinello's role includes a number of texts apparently set by Hasse for the Venetian production of *Artaserse* in which Farinello had sung several months earlier. And an introductory "protesta" of the Lucca libretto copies materials from a prefatory note in the 1730 Venetian libretto for *Artaserse*: «Sie avverte, che siccome per accommodarsi alle circostanze del teatro fu di bisogno abbreviare tutto quello, che con virgole segnato si vede; così d'aliena penna è tutto cio ch'è con questa* stelletta contrasegnato.» But «Son qual nave che agitata», the only Farinello aria in the Lucca libretto marked with an asterisk, appears to have been taken from the 1730 Venetian production of *Mitridate*, for which music had been written by Giovanni Antonio Giai. Thus, the attribution of this aria by Burney and others to Riccardo Broschi is probably in error.

[70] The evidence of footnote 69, together with the fact that two of the three arias sung by Farinello in *La ninfa riconosciuta* (a comparatively brief work for but five singers) can be traced to earlier productions in which Farinello had taken part (see table 1), suggests that, if the Lucca impresario of 1730 went to the expense of employing a composer, that *maestro* went to very little effort.

[71] GB-Lcm 629, which names Leonardo Vinci as its composer, comes very close to matching the libretto for the 1731 Ferrara production of *Artaserse*, but is not quite congruent. In O. G. Sonneck's view (*Library of Congress, Catalogue of Opera Librettos Printed before 1800* I, 168), Vinci's original setting of the *Artaserse* libretto was first performed in Rome on 4 February 1730, not long before the composer's death on 28 May 1730.

Sedecia	1732, Lent Vienna	Sedecia	Caldara	S: A-Wn 17069[72]
La morte d'Abel	1732, Lent Vienna	Abel	Caldara	S: A-Wn 18146
Nitocri	1733, carn. Venice, Teatro San Giov. Gris.	Mirteo	G. Selliti	L: US-Wc S 9827 –S: A-Wn 17566 [73]
Adriano	1733, carn. Venice, Teatro San Giov. Gris.	Farnaspe	Giacomelli	L: US-Wc S 3805 –S: A-Wn 17566
Siroe	1733, spring Bologna, Teatro Malvezzi	Siroe	Hasse	L: I-Vgc Hasse S: GB-Lbm RM 22.e.18 S: F-Pc D 5485–87 S: A-Wn 17256 S: I-Vnm 9855–57
Merope	1733, autumn Lucca	Epitide	R. Broschi	L: I-Bc 686 S: ?
Merope	1734, carn. Venice, Teatro San Giov. Gris.	Epitide	Giacomelli	L: I-Vnm Dram. 1246.5 S: A-Wg 1404 S: B-Bc 2110
Berenice	1734, carn. Venice, Teatro San Giov. Gris.	Demetrio	Araja	L: I-Vnm Dram. 1246.6 S: ?
Artaserse	1734, carn. Venice, Teatro San Giov. Gris.	Arbace	Hasse	L: I-Vnm Dram. 1246.7 S: ?
Il Demetrio	1734, May Vicenza, Nuovo Teatro delle Grazie	Alceste	Araja and others	L: I-Mb 2232 S: ?
Unknown work	1734 Florence		Hasse, R. Broschi and others	Burney
Artaserse	1734, 29 Oct. London, Haymarket Theater	Arbace	Hasse & R. Broschi	L: GB-Lbm 11714.aa.21(12) FS: GB-Lbm G173.a FS: B-Bc 5421[74]

[72] A search through scores in A-Wn listed in Franz Hadamowsky's calendar (see footnote 2) for the periods during which Burney records Farinello's presence at the Habsburg Court in Vienna, reveals the singer's name among the performing soloists only in the two Caldara oratorios listed from Lent of 1732.

[73] A-Wn 17566, containing 19 miscellaneous arias from two Venetian productions of 1733, Sellitti's *Nitocri* and Giacomelli's *Adriano,* includes 10 arias sung in those operas by Farinello. This phenomenon, indicating special contemporary interest in arias sung by Farinello, is by no means an isolated one among apposite scores containing only some of the arias from one or more productions of a local *stagione*. But B-Bc 5498, «Chants pour Farinelli, 1734—36», is the only manuscript I know of from the period before 1737 devoted only to Farinello's repertory.

[74] GB-Lbm 173.a and B-Bc 5421 (which lacks a title page and is presently unbound), contain the same arias but in different orders. That the two prints make use of diverging but apparently original systems of pagination suggests that, as the result of the sensation created by Farinello's London debut, Walsh undertook more than one printing of *The Favourite Songs in the Opera Call'd Artaxerxes*. Seven of the eight arias contained in each print were sung by Farinello.

Ottone	1734, 10 Dec. London, Haymarket Theater	Adelberto	Handel?	L: GB-collection of Gerald Coke
Polifemo	1735, 1 Feb. London, Haymarket Theater	Aci	Porpora	L: GB-Lbm 163.g.20 S: GB-Lbm RM 23a7–9 –S: GB-Lbm Add. 14115 FS: GB-Lbm G 193/3 FS: B-Bc 5477
Issipile	1735, 8 Apr. London, Haymarket Theater	Giasone	P. Sandoni	L: GB-Lbm 163.g.47 –S: B-Bc 5498
Adriano	1735, 25 Nov. London, Haymarket Theater	Farnaspe	F. Veracini	L: GB-Lbm 11714.aa.23(3) S: GB-Lbm Add. 32460 FS: GB-Lbm G.206.c(5)
Mitridate	1736[75], 24 Jan. London, Haymarket Theater	Siface	Porpora	L: GB-Lbm 162.e.54 S: ?
Orfeo	1736, 2 Mar. London, Haymarket Theater	Orfeo	Hasse, Vinci, Araja, Porpora[76]	L: GB-Lbm 163.g.19 S: GB-Lbm RM 22.i.11–13 –S: B-Bc 5498 FS: B-Bc 5471
Onorio	1736[77], 13 Apr. London, Haymarket Theater	Eucherio	?	L: GB-Lbm 11714.aa.22(1) S: ?
Festa d'Imeneo	1736, 4 May London, Haymarket Theater	Imeneo	Porpora	L: GB-Lbm 163.g.13 S: GB-Lbm RM 23.a.10–12 –S: GB-Lbm Add. 14122
Siroe	1736, 23 Nov. London, Haymarket Theater	Siroe	Hasse	L: GB-Lbm 907.i.2(7) FS: GB-Lbm G.173b
Merope	1737, 8 Jan. London, Haymarket Theater	Epitide	?	L: GB-Lbm 907.1.2(6) S: ?

[75] This at any rate is the date of first performance given by Burney, who adds that "...no composer is mentioned in the bills of the time". The title page of GB-Lbm 162.e.54, which differs in several particulars from the information provided by Burney, is unusual for what is implied concerning the origin of the libretto: «Mitridate / dramma per musica / da rappresentarsi / nel / Regio Teatro / dell' / Hay-Market / tradotto in lingua / Italiana / dall / Inglese / composto da / Nicolo Porpora / Londra / per Carlo Bennet. MDCCXXXV ...» (The normal process involved a revision of some Italian original in which the recitatives were abbreviated, the arias multiplied, and the Italian complemented by facing pages of English translation).

[76] The printed libretto lists no composer(s); GB-Lbm RM 22.i.11 (the surviving manuscript score) attributes the music to «diversi autori»; and B-Bc 5471 (Walsh's publication of the favorite songs) assigns some of the arias it contains to Araja, Vinci, and Porpora. It appears to be Charles Burney who first applies the term «pasticcio» to the work. Reinhart Strohm suggests that the absence of that word — though not the phenomenon! — in contemporary Italian sources is to be explained by that country's nonchalance concerning operatic theory and nomenclature.

[77] Here, too, there is disagreement about the date of the first performance. Burney indicates 13 April 1736, but the facing title pages of GB-Lbm 11714.aa.22 both print MDCCXXXIV.

Demetrio	1737, 12 Feb. London, Haymarket Theater	Alceste	G. B. Pescetti	L: GB-Lbm 907.i.3(4) FS: GB-Lbm G193/2
La Clemenza di Tito[78]	1737, 12 Apr. London, Haymarket Theater	Sesto	F. Veracini	L: F-Pn Res VS 710 S: ?
Sabrina	1737, 26 Apr. London, Haymarket Theater	Brunalto	?	L: GB-Lbm 11714.aa.23 FS: B-Bc 5480
Demofoonte	1737, 24 May London, Haymarket Theater	?	?	Burney

[78] The libretto is based on Metastasio's text and was undoubtedly performed as usual in Italian, but the only traceable copies of the libretto bear only title pages in English.

J. MERRILL KNAPP

The Autograph of Handel's "Riccardo Primo" [1]

In recent years musicology has become increasingly interested in the preliminary stages of a composer's work. What are the different steps that lead to the final product? Can these be traced with any certainty from sketches, revisions, discards? Is there a logical progression, or is it largely a matter of guesswork? Aesthetically, are first thoughts better than second or third? When very little or no material exists, obviously these questions cannot even be asked. But with a man like Beethoven a speculative industry has come into being which sheds considerable light on this progression. The creative process will always be to a great extent mysterious no matter how searching the analysis, in that the mind cannot reveal its innermost twists and turnings. But when the end product is the artistic achievement of a major composer, then investigation into how it arose will always have fascination.

If a composer's first thoughts do survive, their original shape will obviously be largely determined by the nature of the medium — symphony, song, chamber work. Music with words adapts itself to the human voice which will guide (at least true of the past) its flow and structure. Yet this need not hinder the composer's search for musical ideas as long as the text is an integral part of his thinking. In an opera, he must embrace a large time span because continuity and unity is spread out over several acts. If there is a librettist, the creative process becomes dual unless the composer writes his own text. Changes in the words change the music, and the composer's thoughts take a different form. This restatement of the obvious becomes necessary when a very confusing holograph of a particular opera is examined. The piecing together of fragments which on the surface have no connection generally achieves some logical goal if the thread through the labyrinth can be found. Like the last chapter in the mystery story, the bits can fall into place with pleasing relevance if the motivation becomes clear. Reasons for action then shine forth like one of those "beacons" 18th century librettists are always steering their metaphorical ships by.

It is common knowledge that Handel took great pains to preserve his "Musick books", as he called his autograph scores in his will. Although they may not have been the direct source for performance, they were the repository of his original musical ideas. This magnificent collection, handsomely bound and carefully preserved over the centuries in one of the great treasures of the Royal Music Collection in the British Museum. As has been said, "It is by far the largest one of the autographs of any of the great musicians of the past now preserved in a single institution anywhere in the world" [2].

---

[1] I am warmly indebted to Mr. Dennis Libby for preliminary work on the sorting out of this autograph.

[2] A. Hyatt King, *Handel and His Autographs* (London, 1967), p. 17. The remainder of the autographs are in the Fitzwilliam Museum, Cambridge (15 vols.) and miscellaneous bits in various other libraries, including the Department of Manuscripts, British Museum.

It is also common knowledge that when Friedrich Chrysander was preparing his German Handel edition in the 19th century, he placed most reliance on the so-called John Christopher Smith performing scores (purchased by the city of Hamburg) rather than the autographs to which he had access in London. Although criticized later for this action [3], there was a certain rough logic in his decision. He was strongly pressed for time if he was to complete the edition, since he was doing most of the work himself; the Hamburg scores were at his disposal at home; he was more concerned with a practical score than he was with historical completeness; he felt that the latest version of a work was the composer's best effort (which is, of course, not necessarily true). Unfortunately, he compounded our difficulties by never explaining what he was doing and why. He also had a penchant for flaying others with his critical scalpel but never admitting his own work could stand some radical surgery.

A comparison between the autograph of Handel's opera, *Riccardo Primo* (1727), and its Hamburg score is an example of what occurred. It is a particularly interesting case. A look at the Hamburg score (No. 232) shows that it conforms very closely, except for the beginning of Act III, with the Händel-Gesellschaft *(HG)* printed edition. The autograph, on the other hand, is quite different in form and content, although it does contain much of the printed music scattered throughout. Chrysander says nothing about this and, without explanation, prints only one of the many additional arias from the autograph in the HG Appendix.

What is immediately striking about the autograph is the amount of extra music in it — both recitative and aria. Most of this music is found nowhere else, but some of it is preserved in one odd manuscript copy (Royal Music 18.c.11). Even Barclay Squire, when he was making his summary list of contents of the Handel manuscripts [4], merely had to label folio after folio of music in *Riccardo Primo* "not in HG" and let it go at that. There is almost enough unpublished music in the score to put together another opera on the same subject. This bonanza puzzled observers even in the 18th century. On the first folio is written (in the hand of Burney or Nicolay?) "This Opera is very imperfect". The search for a plan of this autograph and an answer to the question of why there is so much extra music in it has proved to be a challenging adventure in musical scholarship.

Riccardo Primo is one of the Royal Academy operas from the late 1720's that was never revived after its initial season of 1727—1728. Handel finished the autograph of the work on May 16, 1727 (date on last folio), but the first performance did not take place until the following autumn (November 11) when there was a total of eleven performances through December (perhaps more in January and February, 1728, but London newspapers are missing for these months). A six-month period between Handel's completion of the score and its first stage performance helps to explain many of the

---

[3] Winton Dean, *Handel's Dramatic Oratorios and Masques* (London, 1959), pp. 93—95 among others.

[4] *British Museum, Catalogue of the King's Music Library: Part I, The Handel Manuscripts* (London, 1927), pp. 63—66.

discrepancies in the autograph. Handel generally worked on an opera almost up to the last minute (i.e. a week or two before opening night) and produced it "at white heat". This method of production was made possible by J. C. Smith, Handel's amanuensis, who was given one act or less at a time to copy as the work progressed. (Handel wrote his music on loose folio sheets that were not bound or held together in any permanent fashion and so could be separated at will). Smith's factory of copyists then manufactured vocal and instrumental parts (and other copies of the score) from the parent copy, so that the singers could learn their roles gradually and not have to wait until the work was completed to get the music. (Much of this procedural explanation is hypothesis, but the evidence accords with it).

The circumstances were evidently somewhat different with *Riccardo Primo*. The opera had probably been intended for production in the spring of 1727 but was put off. Events of those months help to explain the delay. The three stars of the company were Cuzzoni, Faustina, and Senesino. Rivalry between the two ladies was being built up to a fever pitch by their aristocratic adherents, who used the two "warblers"for both musical and political ends. (See the various accounts in Deutsch [5] about who was supporting whom). Handel's *Admeto,* performed in February and March, 1727, had left the three chief singers reasonably happy about the amount of music they had to sing and their relative importance in the company. But the operatic enterprise itself was floundering because of the classic difficulty of too little audience and too much expense for singers and stage settings. *Riccardo Primo,* which has important roles for a high soprano, a mezzo soprano, and a castrato mezzo may have been planned for middle or late May but for some reason was postponed. Instead, Bononcini's *Astianatte* was presented to fill out the season. At its first performance [6] with some of the royal family present (May 6, 1727), there were cries and catcalls in the theater from the opposing factions supporting Faustina or Cuzzoni, but the performance finished without serious incident. Tension was rising, however, and on June 6th with *Astianatte* came the notorious hairpulling scene on the stage between the two ladies that scandalized fashionable London and brought the season to a close. On June 11th, George I, who had seemed in reasonably good health, although 68, was seized with a stroke while travelling in Germany (Osnabrück) and never recovered consciousness. George II, his son, was proclaimed king on June 15th. All these events had some bearing on *Riccardo Primo*.

Several Handel biographers have stated over the years that *Riccardo Primo* was chosen by Paolo Rolli, the librettist, and Handel, the composer, because the subject, taken from

---

[5] Otto Erich Deutsch, *Handel, A Documentary Biography* (London, 1955), pp. 207—213 passim. Among the ladies, the Countess of Pembroke supported Cuzzoni; the Countess of Burlington, Faustina. This support was satirized in the oftquoted stanza, attributed to Henry Carey, and published in the *British Journal,* March 25, 1727:

> At *Leicester Fields* I give my Vote
> For the fine-piped *Cuzzoni;*
> At Burlington's I change my Note,
> *Faustina* for my Money.

[6] Deutsch, pp. 207—208.

British history (it concerned one of the adventures of Richard-the-Lion-Hearted on the Third Crusade in the 12th century), could be used to honor the new British monarch. They forgot that the opera came into being in the spring of the year and that the libretto was chosen two or three months before George I died when there was no sign of his demise. The link to George II was therefore a later fortuitous event and not one planned at the outset. When the opera was performed in November, Rolli did write a dedicatory Italian sonnet to George II in the printed libretto, but that was just after his coronation in October when the London world was eager to honor him. These same writers neglected to remember also that Richard the First was not a native Englishman and that he became king largely by dynastic accident. Therefore we find "an Italian and an ex-German compare another ex-German to a Norman who spoke no English as the *ne plus ultra* of British valour and justice" [7].

The principal reason for the choice of this libretto back in early 1727, then, probably had nothing to do with British history and the monarchy but with the equal musical opportunity it accorded the three stars: Faustina as Pulcheria; Cuzzoni as Costanza; and Senesino as Riccardo Primo. Handel may have had some desire to pay tribute to his new status as a British citizen (February, 1727), but it was probably Rolli who chose the libretto, while Handel acquiesced in the choice. The two collaborators were primarily men of the theater first and not politicians.

But where did this libretto come from? Was it written *de novo* or was it modelled on some earlier Italian libretto that Rolli happened to have in his baggage? If Nicolo Haym had been Handel's collaborator, some earlier Italian libretto adapted to the London stage would have been a near certainty. But the author was Paolo Rolli, a man of some reputation as a poet, who, while admitting that part of the source came from elsewhere, claimed that «quasi tutto» of the text was his own [8]. This statement, as we shall see, was only partially truthful and in any case could only have been applied to the version of the opera performed in November and not the one Rolli originally devised.

A search for models or duplicates among Italian 18th-century librettos is usually a guessing game. Even in that non-copyright age when one libretto freely borrowed either story or text from another, librettists tried to cover their tracks by giving their "revised edition" a new title bearing no resemblance to the old one or one that was vague enough («La Forza del Virtù»; «Il Trionfo d'Onore») to mean anything. Thus the location of an original source becomes a little like finding treasure under a rock after numerous other rocks have been overturned with no result. But the frustrating hunt becomes worth the effort if the treasure is found; for it often contains a key that unlocks doors which before had refused to open.

In the case of *Riccardo Primo,* the extra music of the autograph — written to texts not found in the printed London libretto — and Rolli's only partial claim to authorship seem to imply a previous model. But over the years none has been found, and the matter has rested without further investigation.

[7] Winton Dean, "Handel's 'Riccardo Primo' ", *Musical Times*, vol. 105 (July, 1964), 498.
[8] Original London libretto: *Riccardo I / Re d'Inghilterra / Melodrama . . .* M.DCC.XXVII.

Since a perusal of libretto titles, chance as it may be, will often establish connections, library lists of major libretto collections are required reading for 18th-century opera historians. A glance through Sonneck [9] one day suddenly revealed a title that established a possible connection with *Riccardo Primo*. The name of the libretto was *Isacio tiranno* (1710) by Francesco Briani. Isacio or Isaac is one of the characters in *Riccardo Primo*, and the gentleman was certainly a tyrant. Examination of this source from the Library of Congress quickly revealed that here was the treasure sought. Rolli had not appropriated anything wholesale from Briani, but he certainly borrowed the story and many of the recitative and aria texts. His method was to cut liberally, take a few lines here and there, and intersperse them with lines of his own. There are two distinct versions of the opera in the autograph as far as the text is concerned. The first relates more directly to Briani than the second. Act I shows the least difference between the two versions; Acts II and III the most. Almost all the extra music in the autograph can be accounted for by reference to the Briani libretto. The texts which do not fit anywhere are Rolli's own invention. Apparently Rolli prepared his first version for the earlier planned *Riccardo Primo* of the 1726—1727 season. When the opera was postponed until the autumn of 1727, Rolli rewrote a good deal of the libretto and Handel followed suit by rearranging and composing new music where necessary.

This extra effort and work would probably not have taken place if Rolli had been a different person. As a poet he was largely concerned with the sound and quality of his verse rather than with its dramatic force for music. His fame, which was not inconsiderable in Italy, rested on his *Rime* and *Liriche*. Although libretto writing was regarded as an inferior occupation undertaken merely to make money [10], it still demanded mellifluous lines. Briani was not in Rolli's class as a poet, and since Rolli had taken over many of Briani's aria texts for his first version, it behooved him to compose something better when he had a second chance. His newer verses are certainly more elegant, but they lose dramatic vigor by lapsing into more typically Metastasian similes and metaphors. The recitatives were also cut a little further and plot motivation became weaker accordingly. On the other hand, there was gain for the music. For the most part, Handel strengthened what he had already written and composed new music that gave more variety and interest to the whole. The third act was the chief recipient of his creative impulse, and it had much fine music added to it.

[9] Library of Congress, *Catalogue of Opera Librettos Printed before 1800* (Washington, 1914).
[10] In a letter of October 11, 1749, that Rolli, in his retirement in Todi, Italy, wrote to his friend, Abate Frugoni, he confessed that libretto writing and the proceeds from their sale in London enabled him to retire.
«A ciò si aggiunsero le frequenti occasioni di scrivere quelli accennati dramatici scheletri che mi venian pagati dugento scudi ciascuno, oltre la vendita de'libretti a mio profitto, e che mi produssero bastante lucro ad assistere altri, ch'io doveva, e stabilirmi in questo agiato Ritiro. Se avessi voluto far più lungo soggiorno in quella Corte, sariami continuato l'impiego presso nuova sorgente e numerosa famiglia; ma per la totale ruina della Opera Italiane, effetto dell'incorsa guerra, e per le consecutive, economie, mi risolsi alla partenza nell'Autunno dell 44». As quoted by Sesto Fassini, *Il Melodramma Italiano a Londra Nella Prima Metà del Settecento* (Torino, 1914), p. 176.

Isacio tiranno, presented at Venice in the autumn of 1710 with music by Antonio Lotti, was dedicated to John Churchill, Duke of Marlborough. What that great soldier was doing in Venice at the time is unknown, perhaps relaxing between his European campaigns[11]. The dedication was signed by N.N.[12]. The *Argomento* (presumably by Briani) told of Isacio Comneno (Isacus Comnenus), a prince sent by the Eastern emperor to govern the island of Cyprus. Isaac ended by becoming ruler and dictator over the land. His success having made him a tyrant, he took into custody a group of English vessels on their way to the Holy Land in a Crusade but stranded on his shores. One of them carried Berengaria, the Princess of Navarre, to whom Richard-Cœur-de-Lion was betrothed. Richard's vessel had been separated from the others by a storm. He eventually reached Cyprus and demanded satisfaction from Isaac for the treatment of his ladies. Isaac was haughty and Richard, attacking him with his army, managed to free Berengaria and her women after defeating Isaac's forces. The ruler, cornered, sent his daughter out to beg for mercy. Richard spared their lives, married Berengaria in Limisso[13], the capital of Cyprus, and eventually pushed on to relieve the siege of Acre.

Briani said he took his story from the history of the Crusades as told by Louis Maimbourg[14] in the 17th century and from Ozenora and Biondi for the history of England. The plot had an historical basis, but, as usual, embroiderment was necessary to create the inevitable complications and counterplots.

Historically, Richard in Sicily had made peace with his rival, Philip of France, and with Tancred, king of Sicily in the spring of the year, 1191. (Sicily was a Norman kingdom then, and all three monarchs were Normans). This left him free to marry Berengaria, daughter of the King of Navarre, who was brought to Sicily by Eleanor of Aquitaine, Richard's mother. A fleet was assembled in Sicily to carry Richard and his followers to the East on the Third Crusade. They set forth on April 19th, the Wednesday before Easter, with forty to fifty galleys and added transport vessels carrying horses and other equipment. A severe storm on Good Friday, April 12th, separated the fleet. The forward vessels (three) containing Joan, Richard's sister, and Berengaria, put in at Limisso on Cyprus for protection. Two of the three vessels were dashed against the rocks, but the third, containing the ladies, managed to remain afloat just off the harbour. The men who survived the shipwreck were imprisoned on shore. Richard, in the meantime, had arrived in Crete April 17th, hoping to hear news of the missing vessels and to get a lead there on Cyprus and its tyrant, Isaac Comnenos, who was now allied with the Saracens and denied food and supplies to the Crusaders. When Richard arrived in Cyprus, he attacked Isaac and managed to subdue him in about fifteen days. The incident involving Isaac's daughter did take place, but the girl was a child at the time. Richard was married to Berengaria on May 12, 1191.

Briani introduced Berardo as Berengaria's (now called Costanza) cousin and tutor; Corrado, a Prince of Bohemia, as Riccardo's confederate; Oronte, a Prince of Syria, as Isacio's confederate; and Pulcheria[15] as Isacio's daughter. Oronte is betrothed to Pulcheria. Riccardo has never seen his fiancé, Costanza. Costanza and Berardo, when cast ashore in Cyprus by the storm, meet

[11] There is no record of the Duke of Marlborough being in Italy during 1710. He spent most of these months in The Hague, London, or various campaigns in Flanders.

[12] Emilie Dahnk-Baroffio, in „Zur Quelle von Händels Riccardo Primo", *Programm Göttinger Händel-Festspiele* (1970, p. 87) said this dedication was by Matteo Noris. But the initials in the Library of Congress copy are N.N., not M.N.

[13] With Briani, Rolli, and Handel, this place name gets different spellings: Limisso, Larisso, Lamisso, Limissol, etc.

[14] *Histoires des croisades pour la délivrance de la Terre Sainte,* par le P. Louis Maimbourg de la Compagnie de Jesus. (Paris: Sebastian Mabre-Cramoisy, 1682), 4 vols.

[15] The part was sung in 1710 by Handel's old confederate, Margherita Durastanti, who had performed in Handel's operas in both Italy and England.

Isacio, Pulcheria, Oronte, and company and pretend to be Doride and Narsete, followers of Riccardo. Isacio falls in love with Doride-Costanza and determines to keep her for himself. Riccardo and Corrado plan an attack on Isacio once they land and hear that Costanza and Berardo have fallen into the tyrant's hands. Pulcheria befriends Costanza in the palace. Oronte finds Costanza's beauty so overwhelming that he bestows florid compliments on her which are overheard by Pulcheria and cause immediate jealousy. Isacio makes improper advances toward Costanza. The situation is saved by Oronte, who breaks in to tell Isacio that Riccardo is approaching with a large armed force. Corrado is sent by Riccardo to have an audience with Isacio and to ask for Costanza's return. Through this meeting, Isacio learns who Doride really is and decides he will stall in order to hold her with him.

In Act II, Costanza dispatches Berardo to eavesdrop in the palace and learn if there is some way out of their predicament. Isacio confronts Costanza to tell her that he knows who she is. She begs to be released and Isacio surprisingly assents, informing Corrado he may return to Riccardo with the good news. Meanwhile, Isacio tells Pulcheria (who has been brooding over Oronte's waywardness) that she is to go to Riccardo as Costanza, since Riccardo has never seen his intended bride. Riccardo will be overwhelmed by Pulcheria's attractions and Isacio's ambitions will be furthered by a link to the throne of England. Berardo overhears this plan and tells both Costanza and Oronte about it. They both swear vengeance on the perfidious Isacio. Riccardo, with his army in battle array, receives Isacio and Pulcheria. The deception is carried off successfully after mutual greetings between the two kings. Pulcheria tells Riccardo that Berardo has perished. As Pulcheria and Riccardo are about to retire, Oronte bursts in and discloses Pulcheria's true identity. After the consternation subsides, Pulcheria, struck by Riccardo's magnanimity, offers to remain in chains as a hostage for Costanza. Oronte and Pulcheria upbraid each other as Oronte, now an ally of Riccardo, sets forth to take revenge on Isacio.

Act III shows Costanza in despair. Isacio once more pleads his suit and is repulsed. He threatens Costanza. Corrado appears with a letter from Pulcheria telling Isacio that Oronte has revealed the deception and taken up arms against Isacio. She, Pulcheria, will be killed unless Costanza is returned to Riccardo. Isacio, hesitating only a moment, tears up the letter, says he cares not for his daughter's fate and will fight both Riccardo and Oronte. Corrado returns to Riccardo with the news of Isacio's action. Pulcheria, sick at heart, tries to get Oronte to stab her. He naturally refuses. Riccardo and his troops are at the foot of the Rock of Limisso. As they are about to scale the walls, Isacio appears, holding Costanza by the hand. Riccardo offers to withdraw his soldiers immediately if Isacio will hand over Costanza. Isacio refuses again. Riccardo threatens to kill Pulcheria. Pulcheria appears and pleads with her father to no avail. Battle is declared. Riccardo's forces are victorious; the walls fall; and somehow Oronte manages to free Costanza and capture Isacio. In front of the assembled company, Costanza says Isacio deserves to die. She is given a sword. As she raises it, Pulcheria falls at Costanza's feet and pleads for her father's life. Costanza, overcome by Pulcheria's plea, grants her request. Pardon is given. Oronte and Pulcheria are reunited and Riccardo takes Costanza as his true bride.

When the autograph (Royal Music 20.c.2) is collated with both Briani's *Isacio tiranno* libretto and J. C. Smith's Hamburg score of *Riccardo Primo*, the explanation for most of its puzzling features becomes apparent. Yet arranging the autograph in proper order is not an easy task. There are still uncertainties. The manuscript must have been in a state of considerable confusion when it was finally bound in the late 18th century. Folios often do not follow each other in any kind of progression. In Act II, several scenes can only be pieced together by reference to autograph fragments in the Fitzwilliam Museum, Cambridge, which were somehow separated from the others. Moreover, the autograph sheets must have lain around for years in a pile where folio corners were subject to damp and fading. Many of these areas are blackened beyond repair and can only be read with great difficulty. Handel's gathering numbers help to some extent, and once the main pattern is grasped, a great deal falls into place. In the description that follows, the HG printed edition will be used as a source instead of Smith's Hamburg score for ease in comparison. It is to be understood that reference to a first and second version of the opera applies both to text and music unless stated otherwise. A table will be supplied at the end to show in more succinct form the differences between Briani's original libretto and Rolli's two versions of it.

At the beginning of the autograph, the overture and the instrumental opening of Act I depicting the storm are the same for both versions up to the vocal entrance of Costanza and Berardo (ff. 1—7r). Noteworthy are Handel's directions for the timpani in English ("soft, very soft, loud") and the vivid instrumental depiction of the wind and sea which has shipwrecked Riccardo's fleet. Briani's scene description is more vivid than Rolli's: «Lido di Limisso seminato di cadaveri e arnesi di Navigli laceri, gettati dal naufragio. Alla parte gran dirupi, quali conducono alla Città». When Costanza and Berardo sing, their accompanied recitative is much longer and fuller in the first version (ff. 7;11—12) than the second. Rolli took directly from Briani I,1, cutting and adding a few lines of his own. Both versions end the scene with Costanza's aria, «Se perì l'amato bene» (ff. 13—14), the words of which are Briani's, modified. Rolli's general technique in this and other instances can be seen by comparing the two texts:

Briani	Rolli
Se perì l'amato bene	Se perì l'amato bene
Fra l'angoscie, in su l'arene	Fra gli affanni e tra le pene
Anch'io l'alma spirerò.	Anch'io l'alma spirerò.
Se ben non visto,	Non lo vidi, e pur l'adoro
E'l mio tesoro,	E si grave è il mio martoro
L'amo, l'adoro;	Che s'è morto io non vivrò.
Di lui se priva non viverò.	

(Handel or Rolli further changed Rolli's second line in the music after it was originally written in, so the HG version is slightly different). Handel at first had the second version recitative (ff. 8—9) stop at meas. 35 (HG 9, «Lido») (f. 97). Then he added the remaining measures (f. 9v). Folios 11—12, which contain the first accompanied recitative, tell much more about what has happened — Costanza's betrothal to Riccardo, the storm, the shipwreck. In despair over her plight and Riccardo's probable death, Costanza makes a half-hearted attempt to take her own life which Berardo prevents. Handel's music for this is largely an elaboration of mm.27—28 and mm.32—34 (HG 8, 9). At the end of Costanza's aria (1st version), Costanza and Berardo (dialogue) hear some people coming and decide to hide (f. 10r, top).

Scene 2 has two different texts for the recitative (ff. 10 and 15), but they are essentially the same in meaning. Costanza and Berardo meet Isacio, Pulcheria, and Oronte and pretend to be Doride and Narsete (they have heard of Isacio's reputation and want cover). Isacio is struck by Doride's beauty. The first version is fuller in explanation and leads a little less abruptly into Isacio's telling Pulcheria to retire to the royal palace with the two strangers to prepare for her wedding with Oronte. Rolli cut an extra Costanza aria from Briani which merely speaks of her change in fortune in meeting Isacio and his daughter. Handel's new recitative for Rolli's second text (f. 15) is striking, because the words are in J. C. Smith's hand and the notes are in Handel's hand. This evidence of intimate collaboration is fairly common in the Hamburg scores but rare in a Handel autograph. It shows how the second version had to be put together, with shortcuts evidently necessary. There are several instances of this later on. Pulcheria's aria (HG 13—15) was modified by Rolli from Briani («Ad'ubbidirti volo» etc. to «Vado per obidirti» etc.). In this case the changes are greater. There are two musical versions of it, the first (f. 17v) having a slightly different B part from the second (f. 18r). Rolli's paraphrased text from Briani was at first a description of how Pulcheria's hair would be adorned for her wedding. He then made it more directly her address to Oronte. Handel's second B part divides his musical ideas between voice and strings in a more interesting fashion. At the end of the first version, directions read: «[Pulcheria] prende per mano Costanza e partono seguite ad Berardo, ma Oronte vien trattenuto da Isacio». The following recitative between Isacio and Oronte has two versions, the first (f. 19r) taken directly from Briani with changes, the second (f. 18v) a paraphrase by Rolli. Both end with the same music for Oronte, but there are two texts: a Briani text slightly altered, and the second, new words («V'adoro, oh luci belle», HG 15—17), which are placed over the others in the music. The first text is: «Per due begl'occhi avvampo / Nacque da duo facelle / L'incendio ch'ho nel sen. / D'un Elena novella / Ne i roli da Poppea / Stella gemino col suo lampo / È de miei di'l seren». The music (ff. 19—20), scored for two recorders, violins, and bass, has an ostinato underpinning in the bass that, placed against the violin and voice line (the recorders double the strings an octave higher), gives the aria energetic counterpoint which demonstrates the force of Oronte's affection for Pulcheria.

Rolli's first version of Scene 3 shows Riccardo and Corrado (ff. 20v—21r). Corrado tells Riccardo that Costanza is safe in Isacio's court, but that Isacio has the reputation of being a tyrant. Riccardo is determined to go to Isacio as an unknown emissary («Io stesso andrò non conosciuto in corte d'Isacio e a lui domanderò la sposa»). In the meantime, Corrado will gather Riccardo's forces together and prepare for battle or any other eventuality. This is different from Briani who merely has Riccardo hint that Corrado will be sent to Isacio. In the final version (HG and f. 23r), Corrado as an extra character had to be eliminated by Rolli, so Riccardo learns of Costanza's being alive in Isacio's court through a letter (a feeble device). At the end of the first recitative, there is an aria (Rolli) for Corrado («Fra poco spero / Che tornerai / Felice amante / Col tuo bel sole / Quivi a goder. / T'accerti intanto / Che qui m'avrai / Fido e costante / Col brando inpugno / Al tuo voler».). Handel's music for this (ff. 21—22v) is also found in Act II, 6, HG 57—59) as «O vendicarmi» for Riccardo with some differences. Riccardo, left alone by Corrado's exit (several scenes from Briani are telescoped here), then sings an aria in which he anticipates the joy that will be his when he beholds Costanza. Rolli at first wrote a new, more compact text (Briani's was too flowery and effusive) but still including the standard metaphors. «Calmate le tempeste / Risorge il mio contento / Che desiando va / L'oggetto amato. / Pur che in dico amore / Prepara gioie al core / Felice orror sarà / Sara beato». For some reason, this did not satisfy, and the final version, «Cessata è la procelle», was substituted, although the music is exactly the same (ff. 24—25 = HG 18—21). (The change in text must have been a last minute one because when Cluer printed *Songs from Riccardo Primo* in February, 1728 he used the «Calmate le tempeste» text).

Rolli then skipped Briani's next scene (Scene 6) which showed Costanza and Berardo in the palace with Pulcheria, and the two young ladies becoming warm friends. His Scene 4 (Briani, Scene 7) takes a quasi-comic turn. Costanza and Berardo are discussing their predicament when Oronte comes in and addresses florid compliments to Costanza about her beauty. Pulcheria somehow manages to get onstage (the directions are not clear) and interpose herself between Oronte and Costanza, repeating Oronte's words to Costanza in either a flirtatious or caustic manner (f. 26). Oronte is confounded, and Pulcheria sings her aria, «Bella, teco non ho», to both of them. The A part addressed to Costanza says she finds no fault in her; the second, to Oronte, accuses him of philandering (ff. 26v—28v). Rolli took the text directly from Briani, and Handel brings on the music without ritornello. The mock seriousness of the moment is reflected in the orchestral echoes of the voice and its lilting rhythm. Even Pulcheria's peremptory «Falso» to Oronte which opens the B part cannot be taken too earnestly because Handel continues with the music of the A part.

In Scene 5, Isacio comes in, dismisses Oronte, and proceeds to make advances to Costanza. Just as he is about to embrace her, Oronte returns and announces that an ambassador from the British king has arrived. Oronte tells Isacio he must pay attention because the English forces are considerable. Rolli took over Briani's awkward stage business here. Fortunately, the autograph directions make the action a little clearer (none of them are in the London libretto). (A puzzling direction for Isacio on his words «Che vuol da noi» at Oronte's entrance are «ridendo col Oronte». What this means is difficult to tell. Costanza, on her knees before Isacio, had expected to be attacked — hardly a laughing matter). The two versions of the recitative in these two scenes consist of substituted and crossed-over words, the originals being Briani's and the changes, Rolli's (f. 29). The text to Costanza's aria, «Lascia la pace all'alma» (ff. 30—33r), comes directly from Briani with a few odd changes. Handel started to write the B part of the aria with Briani's original words (f. 30v); then he crossed out four measures and put the whole section, conforming to HG 26, on the next folio (f. 31r). This procedure presumes one of the initial stages of composition when Rolli was still following Briani closely and not yet altering the text. There are a number of musical differences between the autograph aria and the printed one — extra measures, notes in the vocal line, scoring.

The last scene of the act clearly demonstrates how a second version was inserted in front of the first version. Ff. 31v—32 are the final recitative (HG 27) with Smith's words and Handel's notes. Smith merely wrote the word «Agitato» (Riccardo's aria) on the last sheet to indicate it followed and was already written. F. 33r shows the end of the original B version of Costanza's «Lascia la pace all'alma», mentioned above. Then follows the original Riccardo-Isacio recitative, here indicated as Scene 8, which is mostly from Briani, Scenes 10 and 11, with some lines being taken from Briani, Act II,5 plus added Rolli (ff. 33—34r). Isacio learns from the ambassador (Riccardo) that Doride is Costanza and that the king has never seen her. In Briani, Riccardo leaves and Isacio ends the act with an aria, describing how, in spite of this information, he will somehow keep Costanza. Rolli, however, could not have the baritone villain (generally a minor character) conclude the act, so Riccardo was given a typical mariner-tossed-by-storms aria with his star now leading him to safety and security. The sentiment, however hackneyed, gave Handel an opportunity to bring out all his "engines" and end with a splendid flourish. There are two versions of this «Agitato da fiere tempeste», the first being incomplete (ff. 34—35r — about half the A part) and the second as HG 28—32 (ff. 35—38r). There are considerable differences. The first «Agitato» is more like a sketch: only one inner instrumental part (viola) and not two (violin II and viola) as later; a less interesting bass line; more square-cut harmonic progression. In the last few measures, the parts thin out, and it is obvious the piece was only partially completed.

Act II is much more difficult to put together. Folios were bound out of order and Rolli decided not to rely as closely on his Briani model. The first two scenes are in particular disarray. None of the first scene exists in a first version. F. 39r, which begins the act, is an inserted recitative for Berardo and Costanza (HG 34). Both Costanza's arioso, «Se m'è contrario il cielo» (HG 33), and Berardo's aria, «Dell'empia frode» (HG 34—36), are not in the autograph and were presumably taken by Chrysander from the Hamburg score. Scene 2 recitative (HG 36—37), where Isacio tells Costanza he knows who she is and he will return her to Riccardo, is found among the Fitzwilliam Museum Handel autographs (#257, Fuller-Maitland Catalogue pp. 59—60). Costanza's following aria, «Di notte il pellegrino» (HG 37—39), is not in the autograph. Isacio's few lines before Pulcheria enters as Scene 3, and all the recitative in this scene, are not in the autograph. However, a Scene 4 (Atrio Regio. Isacio e poi Pulcheria e Berardo a parte, ff. 44v—45v) first version, derived from Briani, has Isacio proposing to Pulcheria that she go to Riccardo pretending to be Costanza. This corresponds generally to Act II,3, HG 39—40. Following this in the autograph (ff. 45v—46r) are Pulcheria's accompanied recitative (HG 45, ff. 45v—46v) and her aria, «Quel gelsomino» (HG 46—47, ff. 46v—48v).

Before this, Scenes 2 and 3 of the first version differ from HG. Isacio's aria (HG 40—43) is among the Fitzwilliam autographs with a different text. The text reads: «Perch'io goda il bel d'un viso / Stratagemma consiglio / Ingegnoso il Dio d'amor. / Con sue squadre il Dio più fiero / Lunge andrà trofeo guerriero / Ingannato da un crin d'or». For some time, this extraordinary G minor aria with double fugato based partly on the *Aus tiefer Not* melody was considered to be part of an *Olibrio* fragment [16]. But

---

[16] Emilie Dahnk-Baroffio, „Die Völkerwanderungsoper und Händels *Olibrio*", *Programm Göttinger Händel-Festspiele 1969*, 37.

the presence of an added text («Ti vedrò regnar sul trono») proved the link to *Riccardo Primo*. Moreover, the very end of the aria, leading to a Scene 3, is on f. 40r of the autograph. So the original arrangement of Scene 2 seemed to be that after Isacio and Costanza had their confrontation about identity, Isacio's G minor aria followed. Scene 3, which begins on f. 40r and goes through f. 44r, is an invention of Rolli's and has no relation to Briani. Corrado is trying to tell Riccardo he should not trust Isacio and ought to reveal himself. Riccardo feels Isacio will keep his word and return Costanza. Then comes a Riccardo aria, «Nube, che il sole adombra» (ff. 40v—41v; 44), which was later used in Act II,8 (HG 65—68) and has one of those vague simile texts which could be fitted in at will. It compares the cloud that passes and reveals a brilliant sun to the grief which vanishes when the longing soul looks upon its idol. There is a sinfonia from Act II of *Semele* which suddenly appears in the middle of this aria (ff. 42—43r) and seems to have no bearing on anything preceding or following. Why it was included here is a mystery. The bouncy beginning of Pulcheria's «Quel gelsomino» (f. 46v) gave Handel a little trouble throughout until he hit on the idea of transposing it a third downward, and then it seemed to fit like a glove.

Act II, 5 has two versions of the recitative. Both deal with Berardo's telling Costanza and Oronte he has overheard Isacio planning to send Pulcheria to Riccardo as the pretended Costanza. Costanza and Oronte are outraged and vow revenge on the perfidious Isacio. Costanza tells Oronte she is Costanza, not Doride, and they decide to join forces. The first recitative (ff. 48v; 50) is interrupted by the second (f. 49) with Smith's words and Handel's notes. At the end of the scene (1st version) there is an unpublished aria for Oronte (ff. 50v—51v) with text by Rolli, not derived from Briani: «Bella già il cor s'accende / Di sdegno e di furor / Contra un tradito amor / Già s'arma il petto. / Se'il ciel non mi contende / L'usato mio valor / Vedrò nel tuo bel cor / Pago ogni affetto». (See Example 1). While the aria is not a major one, it is good vintage Handel and deserves to see the light of day.

Ex. 1

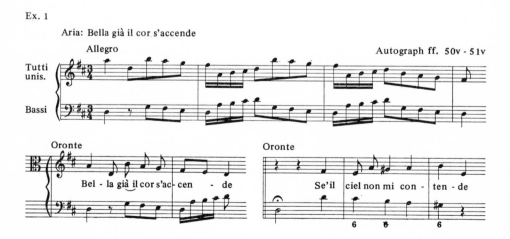

Aria: Bella già il cor s'accende

The autograph now continues for about ten folios with a first version that only partially relates to the second version order and HG. Scene 6 is for Costanza and Berardo (part Rolli and part Briani), the recitative of which (ff. 51v; 60r) has some relation to the bottom of HG 48 and is split between several folios far apart. Costanza tells Berardo that every hour brings new pain, but that she will persevere and hope that her beloved will come to her. Costanza's aria (HG 49—50) has two versions: «Caro, torna a me» (ff. 60; 62; 63r) and «Caro, vieni a me» (ff. 60r; 61). The text for the first is: «Caro, torna a me / Vieni presto non tardare / Questo cor a confortare / Che già tutto amor per te: / Osserva la mia fé. / Io saro costante ognor / Ne altro spera un tanto amor / Sol che a lui tu sia mercé». Musically, the two coincide for the first 25 measures. After that they differ considerably, although based on the same material. The B parts are quite dissimilar, Handel utilizing only continuo for the first version, and strings and continuo for the second. Both versions of the aria have their charms.

Scene 7 (crossed out and marked 5) is the equivalent of Scene 6, HG. Chrysander in HG, p. 51 forgot to eliminate Corrado from the directions he took from the autograph (f. 63v), and so the gentleman is on hand as a ghostly presence but is not found elsewhere in the second version and the HG score. Riccardo's arioso, «Quanto tardo», originally had the words: «Quando vieni o mio consorto / Questo seno a consolar». It is divided between two widely separated folios in the autograph (ff. 63v; 52r), necessitating a backtrack. The first version recitative (f. 52r), derived from Briani, Scene 12, has essentially the same action as the second: Pulcheria approaches with her train of ladies and Riccardo accepts her as Costanza. However, there is no second Riccardo arioso («Si, già vedo il mio bel sole», HG 52). When Oronte bursts in to tell Riccardo that Costanza is Pulcheria; that he is Oronte, Pulcheria's fiancé, betrayed by Isacio; and that he will join forces with Riccardo, there is a separate Scene 8 (ff. 52v; 54), derived from Briani, Scene 13. (Both the autograph and the two librettos have a new scene here. Chrysander did not indicate it because he was following the Hamburg score which has none). In the middle of this scene there is a folio (f. 53) which is completely out of order and belongs at the beginning of Act III. Pulcheria offers to remain in chains until Costanza is released. Riccardo ends the scene with an aria, «Io più soffrir non sò» (f. 55—56v), which is distantly related to Oronte's «Per mia vendetta» of Act III,1 (HG 79—81) but is really a different piece. The text is: «Io più soffrir non sò / E adesso impiegherò / La forza ed il valor / Contra d'un traditor / Contra d'un empio. / Se offese la mia fé / Non merita mercé / E fia quel empio cor / Donato dal rigor / Altrui d'esempio». (See Example 2). The aria is energetic, exciting music, well-fitted to Senesino's peculiar abilities — a limited range but great agility in his middle register. Handel uses a little imitation to fine effect (m.1); and the emphatic leap of the strings to an accented third beat (m.4) well portrays Riccardo's determination to secure the real Costanza.

Scene 9 (ff. 56v—57) shows Pulcheria and Oronte upbraiding each other for treachery and bad faith and is based on Briani, Scene 14, the last scene of Act II in *Isacio tiranno*. Briani's ends with an aria for Oronte which Rolli, under the conventions of his time, could not allow. Instead, he wrote one for Pulcheria, «L'aquilo altero» (ff. 57v—59v;

Ex. 2.

80r) (HG 69—71), the last folio of which is widely separated from the rest of the music and appears at the very end of the act (f. 80r) proving that Rolli and Handel originally meant to conclude their first version with it. Rolli's simile text about an eagle's sons who are ready for any peril and fit to triumph over other birds can be used almost anywhere, although what bearing it has here for Pulcheria is a question. Even Briani's lyric for Oronte deals with jealousy and has some relation to his confrontation with Pulcheria. Handel, however, was not deterred and wrote a splendid, rich-sounding aria with four independent melodic lines (violins, viola, voice, and bass) that press forward with powerful drive and verve.

Steps must now be retraced to see how the second version is managed. It was left at Scene 6 (HG 51), just after Riccardo's arioso, «Quanto tarda». F. 64r picks up Riccardo's few lines on this page, and, including his «Si, già vedo», continues on through HG 52—53, where Oronte tells Riccardo Pulcheria is not Costanza (ff. 64v—65r). Then comes Pulcheria's aria «Ai guardi tuoi» (ff. 65v—67v), which is exactly like HG 53—56. F. 67v carries the Oronte-Riccardo recitative (HG 57) down to the 4th brace, «intanto», and then cuts off. Ff. 68 and 69 are Act I, Scene 3 in Smith's hand with text insertions by Handel. The recitative corresponds to ff. 20v—21 of Act I in Handel's own hand. The aria, originally «Fra poco spero» for Corrado, is marked Vivace by Handel, and the new text «O vendicarmi» is written by him above the old one. This was put in here for the second version and meant for Riccardo (HG 57—59), the old recitative being included because it was on the recto side of the folio in a copy already made. F. 70 picks up the recitative interrupted on HG 57 and finishes it, Handel writing at the end: «Segue l'Aria di Riccardo. O vendicarmi». The bottom of this folio continues Oronte's recitative (HG 59) where he, now alone, is impressed by Riccardo's valor and decides to assist him. Ff. 70v—72r contains Oronte's aria «Dell'onor», which, although superfluous as drama and dragged in to give Oronte an aria in this act, is splendid music. Two F horns join the strings and winds to create a stirring victory song (victory in love as well as arms) which is Oronte's high moment. The autograph and HG differ on the aria, the autograph having a shorter ritornello by omitting mm.13—22.

Scenes 7 and 8 (HG 63—65) are included in ff. 72v—73v. They show Riccardo before Isacio still posing as an ambassador and demanding Costanza's return in the name of his king. Isacio counters by saying if Riccardo holds Pulcheria, he will hold Costanza, and there will be war. Riccardo brings in Pulcheria (Scene 8), who tells her father she could not carry out her mission because Oronte disclosed her identity. She says Riccardo has been generous in his treatment of her and begs Isacio to release Costanza. Suddenly and unaccountably Isacio relents, saying he will do so. He and Pulcheria leave the stage and Riccardo sings «Nube che il sole adombra». The dramaturgy is weak here because Rolli is merely stretching out the action (practically bringing it to a standstill) to get in more music. Handel indicates «Nube, che il sole» only by word cue at the bottom of f. 73v since it was already written out earlier in the act on ff. 40v—41v; 44.

Scene 9 begins (f. 74r) with Costanza's fragmentary recall of her first arioso in the act, «Si m'e contrario il cielo» — an important and effective musical device. Pulcheria then enters to tell Costanza Riccardo is coming to her and her troubles are over. Riccardo enters and is overcome by Costanza's charms; she, in turn, by his noble demeanour. By rights, they should go directly into their final love duet. But Pulcheria has to be removed from the stage, and so she is given the aria «L'aquila altera«. Although merely holding up the action, Handel probably could not relinquish it as music, and so it was included. Then the lovers conclude the act with their duet. Ff. 74—75r contain Costanza's arioso and following recitative for this scene (HG 67—69). After «tuo bel core» on HG 69 (f. 75r), Handel writes in a cue for Pulcheria's aria. The rest of the folio is the recitative on HG 72 with the notation, »Duetto», at the bottom. The duet, «T'amo, si», is on ff. 76—79r. On f. 79r, Handel wrote «Fine dell Atto 2». F. 79v is blank, and on f.80r is the end of «L'aquila altera«, as previously mentioned, with also «Fine dell Atto 2» in large writing on it.

The first scene of Act III in Briani shows Costanza still in despair because she has not seen Riccardo and has no idea what will happen to her. Isacio enters and starts to force his affections upon her again (Scene 2). Costanza says she will die if he comes near her. Isacio bridles but is interrupted by the arrival of Corrado who bears a letter from Pulcheria. Pulcheria writes Isacio that unless he releases Costanza she will be put to death by Riccardo. Isacio, as the good tyrant, is not going to be threatened, so he vows battle with both Riccardo and Oronte, and having little regard for the safety of his daughter, tears up her letter.

For his first version, Rolli was still sticking fairly closely to Briani. But there is continued confusion about the order and sequence of the autograph. Scene 1 (ff. 80v; 53; 117r), which is scattered all over, is taken from Scenes 1 and 2 of Briani with liberal cuts[17]. Musically, the act begins with the instrumental opening on HG 77 down to Riccardo's entrance. Instead of Riccardo, Costanza sings «Numi soccorso, ohimè» because Isacio has just come onstage. The recitative continues in dialogue between the two (f. 53), and then Corrado enters as described. F. 53v cuts off just as Isacio is about to put Costanza in chains. It picks up on f. 117r and ends the scene with Isacio's aria «Del coelo nell'abisso» (ff. 117—119r). Musically, the aria is the same as Isacio's «Nel mondo nell'abisso» (HG 95—97, III,4) with a few words changed in the A part («Nel mondo» for «Del coelo» and «l'orror» for «il furor») and a new text for the B part. The original words for the B section were: «Non son sua Padre, nò, or me contento / Udir la menti a quai / E più fieromi fa l'altrui penare».

F. 119r continues with Scene 2, Costanza and Berardo, modelled on Briani, Scene 2. Costanza bids a touching farewell to Berardo and asks him to find Riccardo and say her end is near. This is somewhat similar to HG 98—100, for the scene concludes with Costanza's «Bacia per me la mano», and the music for the aria (ff. 119v—120; 93r) is the same as HG. Again there are two texts for the B part, the original being: «Di che si'a mia penai / È il non vederlo: oh Dio / E sol la pena sua il cor tormenta». (Most of this is a Rolli paraphrase of some of Briani). The autograph breaks off at f. 120v (3rd m., 1st brace, HG 100) and finishes on f. 93r.

F. 93r continues with Scene 3 — a wood near the walls of Limisso. Riccardo is alone. The recitative, Rolli's invention, is neither Briani nor HG. It gives Riccardo a soliloquy on how he waits impatiently for Costanza, his heart badly torn. The scene ends with Riccardo's aria, «Son qual colombo amante» (ff. 93v—97r), related to Costanza's «Il volo così fido» (HG 110—114). Investigation shows, however, that they are really two different pieces, proof of which is that Handel bothered to write out Costanza's aria completely later on. Both arias derive from the same musical material, and both utilize a sopranino recorder with strings, but there the similarities end. The biggest difference lies in the vocal line. «Son qual colombo amante» was for Senesino and therefore had a restricted mezzo-soprano range (b to d″) with many long melismas.

---

[17] Act III, Scenes 1 and 2 are the only sections of the Hamburg score that do not agree with the second version of the opera. They show Smith copying the first version and then going back and altering it to conform to the second version.

«Il volo così fido» was for Cuzzoni, a high soprano, who could reach g″ and a″ without any trouble. The text for Riccardo was: «Son qual colombo amante / Che attorno alla sua cara / Par che a lei dica impara / Da me qual devi amor. / Se i pesci aman nell'onda / Amar ancor le piante / Ma in tutti amor confonde / La gioia e il sospirar». The bird image (thus the high recorder) is present in both arias, but in the first one Rolli also had recourse to Nature below the waves.

Ex. 3

Scene 4 is on ff. 97—98r. On one side are the walls of Limisso and on the other, Riccardo's camp, from which Pulcheria and Oronte emerge. Corrado comes to meet them. He has returned from his meeting with Isacio. Pulcheria asks him for her father's reaction to her letter. Corrado tells her. Pulcheria is so wildly upset that she begs Oronte to stab her. Oronte naturally refuses and leaves to go to Riccardo with Corrado.

In Scene 5 (f. 98), Pulcheria, alone and in chains, gives vent to her misery. At first Handel continued the secco recitative. He then decided the moment needed accompanied recitative, so four lines were taken from Briani: «A chi? misera: dove / Ricorro supplicante / Se incatenata ancora / Fieri nemici hò un Padre, ed un amante»? Pulcheria, on the horns of a dilemma, has for enemies both a father and a lover. (See Ex. 4). Following this is her aria, «Nubiloso fra tempeste» (ff. 98v—102r) from Briani, Scene 3, as sung by Costanza. «Nubiloso fra tempeste / Cangia in furie le sue stelle; / E col Mar, e con la Terra, / Mi fà guerra/ Il Cielo e amor, / Implacabile Fortuna, / Fato rio, che strali adduna, / Con disastri, con procelle, / Son flagelli del mio cor». The music at first seems to be a transposed E-major version of Riccardo's «All'orror delle procelle» (HG 83—87). But in reality it is different music (vocal line, scoring, melodic direction) with certain similarities.

Ex. 4

Scene 6 (f. 102v) takes place in front of the walls of Limisso, Soldiers appear on top of the battlements ready to defend the fortress. Riccardo's army is spread out below. Riccardo disposes of his forces and prepares to take the castle by assault. Oronte will come by one side; Corrado by another; Riccardo, by the center position. At the sound of the trumpets, they will attack simultaneously.

Scene 7. Isacio suddenly appears on the battlements holding the enchained Costanza by the hand. Riccardo tells Isacio he will call off the assault if Isacio will only return Costanza. Isacio refuses. Riccardo threatens to kill Pulcheria. Isacio disowns his daughter. The opposing forces are about to fall on each other when (Scene 8, f. 103) Pulcheria breathlessly appears, throws herself down in front of Isacio, and weeping, begs her father to relent. When he gives no sign, she snatches a sword from a soldier and is about to fall on it. Isacio then pulls out his own sword and holds it over Costanza, while stepping back from the battlements. This is too much for Riccardo's army, who fall upon the walls, make a breach in them, and pour into the city to the sound of a warlike sinfonia (ff. 128v, 131r, 130v, 129r). It is not clear how Handel meant to fit in f. 130r.

Scene 9 (f. 129v) shows Berardo and Costanza, her chains at her feet, within the city. Berardo asks how she managed to escape Isacio. Costanza said Oronte rescued her. This brings forth an aria: «Or mi perdo di speranza / Or la speme torna in vita. / Cosi un'onda mi sommerge. / Così un altra al ciel mi porta / Una stella è fidea scorta, / E da un'altra son tradita». (Text is Briani). The music starts on f. 129v and reverts to ff. 104—105 for the remainder. The aria can be found with modifications and a somewhat different text in *Siroe* 37 and *Olibrio* fragments.

In Scene 10, Rolli diverges from Briani. Instead of having Oronte fight Isacio in open combat and disarm him, Riccardo performs this act. A short sinfonia, not in HG, opens the scene (f. 105v). A few lines come from Briani; the rest is Rolli (ff. 105v—106r). Riccardo is about to kill Isacio. Pulcheria pleads for his life, saying she carried out the fraud; she is as guilty as he; that if he dies, she must also. The aria that follows: «Di me non ti lagnar» (ff. 106v—108v) (for Riccardo though not indicated) is an earlier version of «Volgete ogni desir» (HG 119—121). The ritornellos are the same, but the vocal sections differ considerably. The text is: «Di me non ti lagnar / Ei fu che fu spietato / E provocato ha il fato / A far gli guerra. / Or chiede il suo penar / Il mio tradito amor / L'ingiuste suo rigor / Il ciel la terra». As indicated by the words, Riccardo is not inclined to give in after all he and Costanza have gone through. When he leaves, Pulcheria is once more left to despair (a condition that seems continual with her in Acts II and III) (f. 109r). Somehow she must move Riccardo to pity. This sense of pity and forgiveness had to rule for either magnanimous kings or tyrannical villains and was a situation in baroque opera that never seemed to pall on the spectators. Pulcheria's aria (ff. 109—111r) is «Quando non vedo», reprinted in the HG Appendix 125—127. Chrysander probably decided to publish this aria because Handel had scored it for two clarinets (chalumeaux) as well as strings — a rare occurrence. Comparison of this aria with «Quel innocente» (HG 89) will show the differences. Rolli's first text reaches a new low in dramatic fitness. The matching of Isacio with a little lamb who has strayed from his mother, with Pulcheria the kindly shepherd who will bring him back into the fold, is preposterous for the situation at hand. Handel, however, wrote an ingenious aria which must have called forth all of Faustina's abilities in articulation and decoration.

The last scene is incomplete, and it is difficult to tell what Rolli planned. In Briani, Riccardo, not wishing to dispatch Isacio himself, turns him over to Costanza for whatever disposal she intends to make of him. After fulminating at length about what a monster he has been, Costanza seems ready to kill him. Pulcheria falls at Costanza's feet for the last time and begs for his life. Costanza relents because of Pulcheria's friendship and generosity to her. The pair of lovers are united, and all ends happily.

In the score, a little recitative (f. 111v) at the beginning of the scene largely reflects Riccardo's and Costanza's joy at finally being together. Then comes an earlier version of the Costanza and Riccardo duet from the end of Act II («T'amo, si») (ff. 112—114). The text is: «Quanto goda l'alma mia / Lo rivali il nostro amor. / Tutto il duol da noi s'oblia / Se la gioia torna al cor». Musically, there are differences. The duet here is in G major. It jumps right into the ritornello without the initial Adagio. Costanza begins the vocal line, not Riccardo, and the musical layout follows a different pattern.

F. 115r contains an unfinished recitative, words only, in Handel's hand. It seems to be an earlier portion where Riccardo greets Constanza and hands both Isacio and Pulcheria over to her. After a blank page, there is a sheet (f. 116r) of what appears to be musical sketches for an aria not in *Riccardo Primo*. The rarity of finding Handel in initial stages of composition gives this page considerable value, although the musical material itself is not very exciting. Ex. 5 shows Handel starting with one of ritornello (a). Then, not satisfied, he writes another line and puts a bass to it(b). Finally, he goes on to the second part of the aria(c), using the same musical idea, and tries to make a cadence. The verso of the sheet (f. 116v) indicates why it was saved. It is further *Riccardo Primo*

Ex. 5

recitative but this time in Smith's hand, words only, leading to the direction, «Segue il Coro». The text is inconclusive (Pulcheria will go with Riccardo and Costanza and peace will reign).

At this point Handel and Rolli evidently broke off. A return to earlier folios is necessary to follow the second and final version. Ff. 81 and 82r pick up Riccardo's accompanied recitative of Act III, Scene 1 (HG 77) where the first instrumental music stopped. It continues with HG 78—79 and concludes with Oronte's aria, «Per mia vendetta ancor» (ff. 82v—84, HG 79—81). Then comes Riccardo's accompanied recitative, «Oh voi, che meco» (ff. 84v—85v, HG 81—82). His aria, «All'orror delle procelle» (ff. 85v—88v, HG 83—87) follows. Scene 2 is like HG 88—93 except that Handel started a slightly different «Morte vieni» for Costanza and then returned and wrote out what is published. Pulcheria's F major, «Quell'innocente afflitto core» is the B version of the aria. Costanza's «Alto immenso poter» is on f. 121r. Scenes 3 and 4 (ff. 121v—122) follow HG except that the two arias, Isacio's «Nell mondo e nell'abisso» and Costanza's «Bacia per me la mano» are cued in by Handel from the first version since they were already written out (f. 122). Scene 5 and Riccardo's aria, «Atterrato il muro cado» (ff. 123—127r) are as HG, except there is some doubt about the ritornello of the aria. Since it is one part only, it is difficult to tell whether Handel meant a shortened ritornello at the end or at the beginning. Chrysander's extra measures on p. 104 do not make the excision clear.

The scene numbers go awry here, but there are no musical differences between the autograph (ff. 127—128r) and the recitative on HG 105—106. Scene directions for HG, Scene 8, 106 should read: «Oronte co' suoi soldati, che arresta il colpo e disarmo Isacio». Handel labels his principals on the chorus parts (f. 128v, HG 106) (i. e. the names of the singers in the London, November, 1727, production), being careful not to include Boschi, who sang Isacio and was offstage while the others hailed victory over him. In Scene 9, Costanza's «Il volo così fido» is written out in full as mentioned previously. Just after it, there is an old folio sheet (f. 136), on one side of which are some measures (mm. 22—33) of «Se perì l'amato bene», Act I, 1, which are slightly different from the published version. The verso and f. 137r contain the D-major Marche of HG 118. At first glance, it would appear the Marche should have come in the score at the beginning of Scene 10 (HG 115) and not before the last scene, since it precedes the recitative of HG 115 and Pulcheria's aria, «Tutti brillanti rai» (ff. 138v—140). But Handel's later direction for the last scene indicates it came there. Pulcheria's line of recitative (bottom of HG 118 and top of 119) was somehow omitted from this recitative and appears later on f. 144v. Riccardo's aria, «Volgete ogni desir», is written out by Handel in full. The Coro for both versions (ff. 145—146) has two texts, the first beginning «Spiri grata l'aura e il vento» and crossed out in the lowest line with «La memoria dei tormenti» written over it. Handel indicates his singers again in this «coro» but only by initial. F. and C. (Faustina and Cuzzoni) have the first soprano; S. (Senesino), the second soprano; B. (Baldi, who sang Oronte) and a mysterious A., the alto part; B. (Boschi) and P. (Palmerini), the bass part. On the bottom of the last folio, there is written: «Fine dell'Opera. G/FH. May 16, 1727».

A table is appended with the Briani and the two Handel-Rolli versions laid out in abbreviated fashion for the convenience of the reader.

Briani (scene descriptions and arias only)	Rolli–Handel (1st version)	Rolli–Handel (2nd version)
	Act I	
① Lido di Limisso seminato di cadaveri e arnesi di Navigli laceri, gettati dal naufragio. Alla parte gran dirupi, quali conducono alla Città.	① Lido di Limisso con veduta di mare, e navi naufragate, e Scogli.	① Lido presso a Limisso, Mar tempestosa con Navi rotte fra Scogli.
Costanza e Berardo Accomp. recit. Cost. Se peri l'amato bene	Costanza e Berardo ff.7;11—12 Accomp. recit. (1st) ff.13—14 Se peri l'amato bene	Costanza e Berardo ff.7r;8—9 Accomp. Recit. (2nd) ff.13—14 Se peri l'amato bene
② Isacio, Pulcheria, Oronte, Costanza e Berardo in disparte Cost. Cangia per me Fortuna Pulch. Ad ubbidirti volo	② Isacio, Pulcheria, Oronte, e Popoli. Cost. e Berardo. f.10 Recit (a) Pulcheria, Isac. Berardo, Cost, Oronte ff.16—17 Pulch. Vado per obedirti (diff. B part) f.18v Recit (a) Isacio, Oronte	② Isacio, Pulcheria, Oronte e Guardie, e poi Cost. e Berar. f.15 Recit. (b) Pulcheria, Isac. Berardo, Cost, Oronte ff.16—17r;18r Pulch. Vado per obedirti f.19 Recit (b) Isacio, Oronte
③ Oronte Oron. Per due begl'occhi	ff.19—20 Oron. Per due begl'occhi (V'adoro music)	ff.19—20 Oron. V'adoro, oh luci belli
④* Padiglione su la Riviera di Limisso. Riccardo e Corrado Corrado. Al tuo cenno suonerà	③* Riccardo e Corrado Padiglione vicino alle Rive di Limisso ff.20v—21r Recit. Riccardo, Corrado (a) ff.21—22v Corrado. Fra poco spero f.22v Recit. Riccardo	③* Padiglione non lontano dalle Rive di Limisso. Riccardo e suoi Capitani ff.23r Recit. Riccardo (b) No aria f.23v Blank
⑤ Riccardo solo Ricc. Fa, ch'io vegga il Ciel	ff.24—25 Ricc. Calmate le tempeste (Cessata music)	ff.24—25 Ricc. Cessata è la procella
⑥* Pulcheria, Costanza, Berardo. Appartamenti nel Serraglio (not in Rolli)	④* Appartamento con tavolino. Cost. e Berardo e poi Oronte e Pulch. ch'entrano da diversi parti f.26 Recit. Cost, Berar, Oron, Pulcheria	④* Appartamento con tavolino. Cost. e Berardo e poi Oronte e Pulcheria ch'entrano da diversi parti f.26 Recit. Cost, Berar., Oron., Pulcheria
⑦ Costanza, Berardo Poi Oron. e Pulcheria Pulch. Bella, teco no hò	ff.26v—28v Pulch. Bella, tecca non hò	ff.26v—28v Pulch. Bella, teco non hò
Circled numbers are scenes		

* = Change of scene

Briani	Rolli-Handel (1st)	Rolli-Handel (2nd)
	Act I (cont.)	
⑧ Improvisamente viene *Isacio e detti* No aria	⑤ *Isacio e detti* f.29r Recit. Isacio, Oron. Costanza, Berardo No aria	⑤ Viene improvisamente *Isacio e detti* f.29r Recit. Isacio, Oronte, Costanza, Berardo. No aria
⑨ Viene Oronte, frettoloso nell mentre, che Isacio vuol levar Costanza a suoi piedi genuflessa *Cost. Lascia la pace a l'alma*	⑥ *Oronte e detti* f.29v Recit. Oronte, Isacio, Costanza ff.30—31r;33r *Cost. Lascia la pace all'alma* (B part)	⑥ *Oronte vien frettoloso e detti* f.29v Recit. Oronte, Isacio, Cost. ff.30—31r *Cost. Lascia la pace all'alma*
⑩ Corrado va da *Isacio,* che grave e superbo stà appoggiato ad un tavolino No aria	⑦ No scene ⑧ *Riccardo come Ambasciadore con seguito, vada Isacio* che grave e superbo etc. ff.33—34r Recit. (a) Riccardo, Isacio	⑦ *Riccardo come Ambasciadore ed Isacio* che grave e superbo etc. ff.31v—32 Recit. (b) Riccardo, Isacio
		f.38v Blank
⑪ *Isacio solo* Isacio. Quanto è più nobile	ff.34—35r *Riccardo.* Agitato da fiere tempeste (Incomplete)	ff.35—38r *Riccardo.* Agitato da fiere tempeste
Act II	**Act II**	
①* Appartamenti Regi di Pulcheria. *Berado, Costanza* Cost. Berardo: io sento languida *Berardo.* Sara un Argo oggi mia fé	① No folios	①* Appartamento. *Costanza e poi Berardo* Cost. Arioso. Se m'e contrario *(Not in Auto.)* f.39r Recit. Berardo, Costanza f.39v Blank *Berar. Dell'empia frode (Not in Autograph)*
② *Costanza* Cost. Torna il riso sul mesto labbro	*Cost. ed Isacio.* che sopra viene Fitz. Mus. #257 Recit. Cost. Isacio Fitz. Mus. #258 Isacio. Perch'io goda il bel d'un viso (Music: Ti vedrò)	② *Costanza, ed Isacio* che sopra viene Fitz. Mus. #257 Recit. Costanza, Isacio *Costanza.* Di notte il pellegrino *(Not in Autograph)* Recit. Isacio *(Not in Autograph)*
③ *Isacio solo* Isacio. Perch'io goda il bel d'un viso		
④ Colonnati vicini al real Giardino. *Pulcheria solo* (Not in Rolli)		

Briani	Rolli-Handel (1st)	Roll-Handel (2nd)
	Act II (cont.)	
⑤ *Isacio e Corrado* Corrado. Biondo ciglio in bianca fronte ⑥ Isacio *solo. poi Costanza* Cost. Torna il riso sul mesto labbro	③* Campo di Riccardo con l'essercito accampato. *Corrado e Riccardo* f.40 Recit. Corrado, Riccardo ff.40v—41v;44 *Riccardo.* Nube, che il sole adombra ff.42—43r *Semele* sinfonia f.43v Blank	③ *Pulcheria e detto* Recit.Pulch., Isacio (*Noi in Autograph*) Fitz. Mus. #258 *Isacio.* Ti vedrò regnar su'l trono
	④* Atrio Regio. *Isacio e poi Pulcheria e Berar.* a parte ff.44v—45v Recit. Isacio, Pulch, Berardo ff.45v—46v Acc. Recit. *Pulch.* Ah padre! ah Cielo ff.46v—48v *Pulch.* Quel gelsomino	④ *Pulcheria sola* ff.45v—46v Acc. Recit. *Pulcheria* Ah padre! ah, Cielo ff.46v—48v *Pulcheria.* Quel gelsomino
⑦ Esce Berardo, da dove si era nascoso ad ascoltare. *Costanza, Oronte* Oronte. Per vendicarmi Aletto	⑤ *Costanza ed Oronte* e poi *Berardo* che esce dove s'era nasconde ff.48v;50 Recit. (a) Costanza, Oronte, Berardo ff.50v—51v *Oronte.* Bella già il cor	⑤ *Costanza, Oronte, e poi Berardo* f.49 Recit. (b) Costanza, Oronte, Berardo ff.60r;61 *Costanza.* Caro, vieni a me
⑧ *Costanza e Berardo* Cost. Cessa di bersagliarmi	⑥ *Costanza e Berardo* ff.51v;60r Recit. Costanza, Berar. ff.60;62;63r *Cost.* Caro, torna a me	
⑨* Lido di Limisso ingombrato da Navi. Reggio Padiglione, e Ponte. Seggio d'oro da un lato. *Riccardo* viene accompagnato dal suo essercito e *Corrado.* *Riccardo.* Pellegrmo, or ch'è il mio sol	⑦—⑤* Lido di Lamisso, con Regio Padiglione, e seggio d'Oro da un lato. *Riccardo* accompagnato dal suo essercito, e poi *Corrado e Pulcheria* con seguito di Damigelli ff.63v;52r *Riccardo.* Quando vieni f.52r Recit. Corrado, Ricc. Pulcheria	⑥* Same directions as 1st vers. f.63v *Riccardo.* Quanto tarda f.64r *Riccardo.* Recit. and arioso Si già vedo il mio be sole Recit. Riccardo, Pulcheria

Briani	Rolli-Handel (1st)	Rolli-Handel (2nd)
	Act II (cont.)	
⑩ Comparisce *Isacio* vestita alla Greca con *Pulcheria* alla Reale, le va incontre *Riccardo.* No aria ⑪ Torna *Oronte,* e va da *Riccardo e detti* ⑫ *Riccardo, Pulcheria* *Riccardo.* Porgimi	⑧ *Oronte* con spada nuda in mano *e detti* ff.52v;54 Recit. Oronte, Corrado Riccardo, Pulcheria ff.55—56v *Riccardo.* Io più soffrir non sò	⑦⑧ *Oronte e detti* ff.64r—65r Recit. Oronte, Pulcheria, Riccardo ff.65v—67v *Pulcheria.* Ai guardi tuoi ff.67v;70r Recit. Oronte, Riccardo ff.68—69 *Riccardo.* O vendicarmi (copyist) f.70r Recit. Oronte ff.70v—72r *Oronte* dell'onor
⑬ *Oronte* nell'uscire vista *Pulcheria,* dice tra se *e detti* *Riccardo.* Saro implacabile	⑨ *Pulcheria ed Oronte* con guardie ff.56v—57r Recit. Pulcheria, Oronte ff.57v—59v;80r *Pulcheria.* L'acquilo altera	
⑭ *Pulcheria, Oronte* Soldati incatenano Pulcheria *Oronte.* Sei Tiranna de l'alma o Gelosia		⑦ Atrio. *Isacio* poi *Berardo,* e poi *Riccardo* f.72v Recit. Isacio, Berardo, Riccardo ⑧ *Pulcheria e detti* f.73v Recit. Pulcheria, Riccardo, Isacio f.73v Cue for *Riccardo.* Nube, che il sole ⑨ Cabinetto. *Costanza* sedendo appoggiata ad un tavolino, e poi *Pulcheria e Riccardo* f.74r Cost. Sì m'è contrario il Cielo ff.74—75r Recit. Pulcheria, Cost. Riccardo f.75r Cue for *Pulcheria.* L'aquilo altera f.75v Blank ff.76—79r Duet. *Costanza, Riccardo* T'amo, si f.79v Blank

Briani	Rolli-Handel (1st)	Rolli-Handel (2nd)
	Act III	
①* Stanza nella Rocca di Limisso. Costanza Cost. Dammi o Ciel ② Isacio vista Costanza nell'uscire dice fra sui (?) No aria	①* Stanza nella Rocca di Limisso. Costanza fuggendo ed Isacio e la segue, e poi Corrado ff.80v;53;117r Recit. Costanza, Isacio, Corrado ff.117–119 Isacio. Del coelo nell'abisso	①* Fuor di citta Limisso. Riccardo con spada alla mano, seguito da sold. d'Oronte, ed Oronte che viene con l'esercito Inglese al soccorso di Riccardo f.81r Riccardo. Acc. Recit. Perfido Isacio
③ Costanza, Berardo Costanza. Nubiloso fra tempeste	② Costanza, Berardo f.119 Recit. Costanza, Berar. ff.119v–120;93r Costanza. Bacia per me la mano	ff.81–82r Recit. Oronte, Riccardo ff.82v–84r Oronte. Per mia vendetta ancor ff.84v–85v Riccardo Acc. Recit. Oh voi, che meco del Tamigi in riva ff.85v–88v Riccardo. All'orror delle pro- celle
	③* Bosco vicino alle mura di Limisso. Riccardo solo f.93r Recit. Riccardo ff.93v–97r Riccardo. Son qual colombo	②* Atrio. Costanza poi Pulcheria f.89 Costanza. Morte, vieni f.90r Recit. Pulcheria, Costanza ff.90–92v Pulcheria. Quell'innocente af- flitto f.121 Costanza. Acc. Recit. Alto immenso poter
④* Muro di Limisso da una parte, dal- l'altra il Padiglione di Riccardo da qual esce Pulcheria Pulch. Ancor tu mi lusinghi	④* S'apre il Proscenico e si discopre le mure di Limisso d'una parte e dall'altra il Padiglione di Riccardo del qual esce Pulcheria ed Oronte e Corrado che vien loro incontro ff.97–98r Recit. Pulch, Oron, Corrado	③ Isacio e detti f.121v Recit. Isacio, Costanza ④ Berardo e detti f.122r Recit. Berardo, Isacio Cue for Isacio. Nell mondo nell'abisso f.122v Recit. Berardo, Costanza
⑤ Pulcheria sola in catene. Pulcheria. Dove mai rivolgo il pie?	⑤ Pulcheria sola incatenata con guardie f.98r Pulch. Acc. Recit. A chi? misera ff.98v–102r Pulcheria. Nubiloso fra tempeste	⑤* Il muro di Limisso assalito che cadrà a colpi d'ariete. Bellicose sinfonia mentre s'avanza l'esercito. Riccardo. Atterrato il muro cada, Il muro cade, e vedesi per la breccia Isacio alla testa de'suoi soldati, che con la spada nella destra tiene Costanza con la sinistra f.127v Recit. Isacio, Riccardo
⑥ Compariscono Soldati su i Muri della Rocca di Limisso per la difesa. Eser- cito accampato di Riccardo. Miei Cam- pioni	⑥ Compariscono Soldati su i Muri della Rocca di Limisso per la difesa. Eser- cito etc. Oronte, Corrado f.102v Recit. Riccardo, Oronte	

Briani	Rolli-Handel (1st)	Rolli-Handel (2nd)
	Act III (cont.)	
⑦ Comparisce su i merli della Rocca *Isacio* tiene per mano *Costanza* incatenata e dice a *Riccardo*. No aria	⑦ Comparisce su i merli della Rocca *Isacio* tiene per mano *Costanza* incatenata e dice a *Riccardo* ff.102v—103r Recit. Riccardo, Corrado, Isacio. No aria	⑥—⑦ *Pulcheria e detti* ff.127v—128 Recit. Pulcheria, Isacio, Riccardo, Costanza ⑦—⑧ *Oronte* co'suoi soldati, che arresta il colpo e disarmo *Isacio, e detti* f.128r Recit. Oronte, Isacio, Riccardo, Pulcheria ff.128v—129r;130r—131r *Coro.* Alla vittoria
⑧ Frettoloso, e anelante viene *Pulcheria,* e si pone in ginocchio in faccia d'*Isacio,* e detti. No aria	⑧ Frettoloso e anelante viene *Pulcheria* e si pone in ginocchio in faccia d'*Isacio,* e detti f.103 Recit. Isacio, Pulcheria, Riccardo ff.130,131,129r *Sinfonia*	⑧—⑨ Scena ultima changed to Sc. 8 Sala. *Berardo, Costanza e poi Pulcheria.* ff.131v—132r Recit. Costanza, Berardo, Pulcheria ff.132v—135v *Costanza.* Il volo così fido (f.136r — Sketch for part of Se peri l'amato bene, Act I, 1) ff.136v—137r *Marche.* Allegro f.137v Blank f.138r Recit. Pulcheria ⑨ *Oronte e detti* f.138r Recit. Oronte, Pulcheria ff.138v—140v *Pulch.* Tutta brillanti rai
⑨* Strada in Limisso *Costanza.* Or mi perdo di speranza	⑨* Atrio. *Berardo* con le catene di *Costanza* in mano seguita di Costanza f.129v Recit. Berardo, Cost. ff.129v;104—105 *Costanza.* Or mi perdo di speranza	
⑩ Escono con l'armi combattendo *Isacio* con *Oronte,* qual lo abbate, egli va sopra con il ferro *Oronte.* A te'l chiedo *Costanza.* Già vendicato ⑪ *Riccardo, Pulcheria Corrado,* Popoli e Soldati. No aria	⑩ I soldati di Riccardo rispingono quelli d'Isacio; ed intanto entrano combattendo *Riccardo* ed *Isacio,* il quale resta vinto e abbatuto; e poi *Pulcheria* incatenata che si distacca dalle guardie che la custodiscano f.105v *Sinfonia* ff.105v—106r Recit. Isacio, Ricc. Pulcheria ff.106v—108v *Riccardo* Di me non ti lagnar f.109r Recit. Pulcheria ff.109—111r *Pulcheria.* Quando non vedo la cara	
⑫ Scena ultima. Esce *Costanza* da un lato della Scena accompagnato da *Oronte* e da *Berardo* con *Isacio* in catena custodito da soldati, e spogliate delle militari insegne e corre incontro a *Riccardo.*	⑪ Scena ultima. Sala regia *Riccardo* con guardie. *Corrado* e poi *Costanza* ad una parte (Berardo seguite di Damigelle etc.)	⑩* Scena ultima. Colonnato. f.141r Recit. Ricc., Pulch., Cost. ff.141v—143v *Riccardo* Volgete ogni desir f.144r— Blank f.144v— Pulcheria's cued in recit. lines (Missing from f.141r)

Briani	Rolli-Handel (1st)	Rolli-Handel (2nd)
	Act III (cont.)	
	f.111v Recit. Riccardo, Costanza, Oronte	Recit. Oronte (Not in Auto.)
Coro. Or che ride pace amica	ff.112—114v Costanza e Riccardo Duet. Quanto goda l'alma mia Entra Isacio incatenato fra guardie e Pulcheria che sostiene le sue catene, la quale poi s'inginocchio a piedi di Riccardo.	ff.145—146 Coro. La memoria dei tormenti
	f.115r Unfinished recit. Words only	
	f.115v Blank	
	f.116r Page of sketches for aria in E major	
	f.116v Unfinished recit. in copyist's hand. Words only. Ends with «Segue il Coro.»	
	ff.145—146 Coro. Spiri grata l'aure e il vento	

ALFRED MANN

Bass Problems in "Messiah"

Among memories of preparing performances under Arthur Mendel's direction, one holds a special place: rehearsing a recitative from Schütz's *Christmas Story* (for the Cantata Singers' concert at the Metropolitan Museum in December, 1948). In the phrase preceding the last Intermedium,

> Auf dem Gebirge hat man ein Geschrei gehöret,
> Viel Klagens, Weinens und Heulens,
> Rahel beweinete ihre Kinder,
> Und wollte sich nicht trösten lassen,

the sparse organ continuo, supported by cello and bass, begins to unfold in a sublime sequential, seemingly endless, descending scale [1]. Playing the bass, I found myself involved in an argument of intonation, unlike any other experienced before or after, with that magnificent and militant artist, Eva Heinitz. Each two-note progression was singled out, tested, analyzed, studied and re-studied until the ensemble had indeed approached the agony of Rachel.

It was a problem of performance practice that had occurred to none of us. How did a continuo team deal with the octave coupling of such vulnerable legato chromaticism? The solution at which we arrived was in typical duet fashion: we did away with separate stands and parts, watching eventually nothing but every move of each others fingers.

The experience helped years later in sorting out the *Messiah* performance parts prepared by Handel's copyists, in accordance with his Last Will and Testament, for the Foundlings Hospital. This material, a list of which was published by Friedrich Chrysander [2] and reprinted in Schering's Peters edition of the *Messiah* score [3] contains two part books each for cello and bassoon but none for the double bass. Chrysander suggested that one of the bassoon parts, wrongly inscribed, might have been intended for the bass player "since the use of two pairs of bassoons is scarcely conceivable", and Schering comments on this as follows:

> "The existence of two bassoon parts however is no absolute proof either of the use of four bassoons or of the correctness of the assumption that the second part is entitled Bassoon through an error, being actually meant for the double bass. The two bassoon players could presumably then as now have played from two

---

[1] See Heinrich Schütz, *The Christmas Story*, vocal score ed. Arthur Mendel (New York, 1949), pp. 72 f.
[2] Friedrich Chrysander, „Die Originalstimmen zu Händels Messias", *Jahrbuch der Musikbibliothek Peters für 1895* (Leipzig, 1896), 11—19.
[3] G. F. Händel, *Der Messias*, ed. Arnold Schering and Kurt Soldan (Frankfurt, 1939).

parts, and it seems absolutely out of the question that the double bass played only the bassoon part, for in that case long stretches of the bass, particularly in the arias, in which the bassoon is mostly silent, would have to be played by the violoncello alone.

The absence of a special double bass part and the fact that only at two [*recte*: six] points does Handel expressly require violoncello alone have given rise to certain doubts as to whether the double bass was used at all. Thus Chrysander considers also the possibility 'that for a small number of performers in a small hall a sufficiently strong bass would be supplied by violoncello, bassoon, theorbo (bass lute), clavier and organ'"[4].

Neither Chrysander nor Schering took into consideration the budgets for *Messiah* performances from 1754, 1758, and 1759 also in the possession of the Foundling Hospital (and since published in Otto Erich Deutsch's *Documentary Biography*)[5]. These show that in addition to three cellos, Handel did use four bassoons as well as two double basses. Since the orchestra parts have been preserved in perfect condition for more than 200 years within the same institution — the institution in which *Messiah* performances took place annually under Handel's direction — it is unlikely that the set is incomplete: the double bass players must have shared music and music stands with the cellists.

It is interesting that Handel used two double basses. Considering the fact that a solo-tutti division of the orchestra is recognizable from the amounts contained in the budgets, the conclusion seems plausible that one of the bass players belonged to the concertino group and read from the stand of the solo cellist, whereas the other read from that of the two ripieno players.

We are used to thinking in terms of a later orchestral arrangement in which only players of like instruments are "standmates". But the arrangement which we can gather from the evidence relating to the Foundling Hospital performances was actually retained for a considerable amount of time. It is delightfully documented in the accounts of the Three Choirs Festival from the 1830's and 1840's in which "the veterans" Robert Lindley and Domenico Dragonetti — having shared the first cello-bass stand for more than fifty years — served in effect as leaders of the orchestra.

H. Watkins Shaw, in his history of the Three Choir Festival quotes contemporaneous press comments[6]. The *Hereford Journal* singled out the two "pillars of the orchestra" and the continuo accompaniment they performed "in their masterly manner ... of the recitatives in 'Messiah' beginning 'There were shepherds', sung by Madame Clara Novello" (September 13, 1843). But this report is surpassed by that of the *Worcester Journal*:

"... before the bow had kissed the string there was a momentary pause. During this short interval our whole attention was fixed on the orchestra, and we per-

---

[4] *Ibid.*, Foreword, p. (iv).
[5] See Otto Erich Deutsch, *Handel, A Documentary Biography* (London, 1955), pp. 750 ff., 800 f., 825 f.
[6] H. Watkins Shaw, *The Three Choirs Festivals* (Worcester and London, 1954), p. 42.

ceived the two champions, Lindley and Dragonetti, interchanging civilities like high-bred courtiers, and taking a friendly pinch of snuff together. Then, and not till then, the first chord was struck". (September 29, 1836).

The bass problems in the *Messiah* sources are not limited to the instrumental parts. In his superb investigation of the changing versions of the work throughout the seventeen years of Handel's own performances, Jens Peter Larsen has shown that the most extensive changes to which the composer subjected the work were concerned with the vocal bass part [7].

These changes originated evidently with the inadequacy of the vocal forces at Dublin. "I have form'd an other Tenor Voice which gives great Satisfaction, the Basses and Counter Tenors are very good, and the rest of the Chorus Singers (by my Direction) do exceeding well" wrote Handel in the high spirited account he sent to Charles Jennens, the compiler of the *Messiah* text, a month after his arrival in Dublin. As he got down to work on *Messiah* rehearsals, it became clear that he had overestimated the ability of his potential bass soloists.

Handel had taken with him to Ireland only the women soloists: two sopranos, Sga. Avoglio and Mrs. McLaine, and an alto, the celebrated Mrs. Cibber. For male soloists he relied on the local churches from which his choir was drawn. The tenor Handel mentions in his letter was James Bailey to whom either all or the major share of the tenor solo part in *Messiah* was allotted in Dublin. The bass solo assignment was divided between two singers, John Mason and John Hill, neither of whom apparently measured up to Bailey's calibre.

The modern dichotomy of professional solo and amateur choral singers did not, of course, exist in Handel's day. All soloists were expected to sing with the chorus — as we can again gather from the *Messiah* part books in the Foundling Hospital. Thus, for the arias and recitatives various soloists were singled out from the sections, taking turns according to a plan that was adjusted from performance to performance. That a solo role was taken by a single soloist throughout the work was by no means the rule.

Handel may have tried both Mason and Hill on the different bass solos. In the end Mason sang them all, except for the aria "Why do the nations so furiously rage", which was given to Hill; but the tasks for both soloists were drastically reduced, the two most sensitive arias ("But who may abide" and "Thou art gone up on high") being entirely replaced by simple recitatives.

When Handel presented *Messiah* to the London audience in later years, he was no longer restricted in the choice of his soloists and therefore free to restore the solo numbers to their original form. He retained some of the Dublin changes, however, apparently for purely artistic reasons.

From the outset, we can discern definite criteria that guided Handel both in assignments and changes — criteria formed not only by technical demands but by stylistic considerations. For instance, the narrative portions with which the soprano role begins

[7] Jens Peter Larsen, *Handel's Messiah: Origins, Composition, Sources* (London, 1957).

were given to Mrs. McLaine, saving the solo appearance of Sga. Avoglio for the great bel canto aria "Rejoice". The alto solos leading into full chorus sections in the verse anthem manner of English Cathedral music were given to countertenors, whereas the aria "He was despised" became the alto assignment through which Mrs. Cibber rose to immortal fame. But in Dublin Handel had Mrs. Cibber also sing two soprano arias in transposed versions ("He shall feed His flock" and "If God be for us"), because in these cases he apparently preferred the performance of the English actress to that of the Italian singer.

A certain stylistic division is recognizable also in the original distribution of bass solos. The only "rage aria" in the work had been reserved for Hill, presumably the stronger of the two voices. But a distinction between different portions of the bass role becomes much more obvious in the record of the London performances. Handel's favored bass soloist, Thomas Reinhold, must have been essentially a singer of dramatic qualities, for while he sang every London performance of the work until his death in 1751, Handel never entrusted him with the two arias for which he had substituted recitatives in the Dublin performances. These two arias underwent a changing fate from season to season until Handel eventually rewrote them for the famous castrato Gaetano Guadagni who later was to sing the title role of Gluck's *Orfeo*. The re-written versions remained alto arias in most of Handel's later performances — on occasion they were even transposed for soprano — but they never returned to the share of the bass.

The deliberate reduction of the bass role in *Messiah* points out a division of dramatic and lyric roles of which Handel evidently became more and more conscious. It was this consideration that had also prompted one major change in the tenor assignment for the Dublin presentations. On the whole the tenor portions called for a light voice, approaching especially in the second part of the work the typical role of the evangelist, and this role was doubtless well suited to Bailey's voice. Only the aria "Thou shalt break them", preceding the Hallelujah chorus, demanded a forceful tone. Having only one good tenor soloist at his disposal, Handel reset the text as a brief recitative, but in his London performances he returned to the original aria. John Beard, Handel's principal tenor soloist, who had been trained in the oratorio performances from as early as 1732 (he participated as a choirboy singing in *Esther*) clearly possessed all qualities required for the entire tenor part.

In the bass part the dual demand was more pronounced and led to a permanent division of roles. In fact, the earlier, "neutral" lyricism associated with the bass range — such as the impersonation of the Rose of Sharon in Buxtehude's solo cantata — seems to have generally disappeared from the bass aria repertoire after the *Messiah* era. Singers confronted with the problem of combining the masculine character of "Quoniam tu solus sanctus" with the ethereal quality of "Et in spiritum sanctum" in the B Minor Mass may draw comfort from the consideration that Bach, too, might not have been averse to using different voices. Handel's stand on this problem, however, is clear beyond doubt: he did not wish to demand such heterogeneous tasks from a single soloist.

PIERLUIGI PETROBELLI

Un cantante fischiato e le appoggiature di mezza battuta: Cronaca teatrale e prassi esecutiva alla metà del '700

La familiarità che il proseguire degli studi ci fa gradualmente acquistare con il mondo settecentesco può soltanto confermare la convinzione che a Padre Martini spetti un posto di assoluta preminenza nella cultura musicale di quel secolo. Anche prescindendo dall'attività compositiva e da quella di insegnante, alla figura del francescano bolognese spetta una posizione del tutto originale per la smisurata varietà degli interessi professionali verso i quali di continuo la sua mente era rivolta; essi vanno dalla più astratta speculazione sui principi fisico-acustici del fenomeno musicale [1] alla ricerca di particolari biografici su musicisti del passato a lui più remoto [2], all'interesse per le forme più antiche della notazione musicale [3]; dallo studio più approfondito e vasto del patrimonio polifonico cinquecentesco, base e spina dorsale del monumentale *Esemplare o sia Saggio fondamentale pratico di contrappunto* [4], alla raccolta dei ritratii di musicisti del suo

---

[1] Basta a questo proposito scorrere le ventisei lettere di Tartini a lui indirizzate tra il 12 marzo 1751 ed il 1 dicembre 1752, relative all'esonne del *Trattato di musica* del compositore di Pirano; esse si trovano, come tutte le altre di questa corrispondenza, a Bologna, Biblioteca Musicale «G. B. Martini», Epistolario martiniano, I. 17. 26—51.

[2] Si veda la lettera di Tartini dell'11 dicembre 1761, nella quale il violinista, residente a Padova, risponde alla richiesta di particolari biografici su Johannes Ciconia; si veda anche S. Clercx, *Johannes Ciconia — Un musicien liégeois et son temps (Vers 1335—1411)*, Bruxelles 1960, T. I, p. V, nota 2. L'interesse di Padre Martini per queste notizie è probabilmente connesso con lo studio che egli stava compiendo del manoscritto forse oggi più famoso della sua biblioteca, quello ora segnato Q 15; si veda infatti la frase della lettera di lui, citata da S. Clercx, loc. cit.: «Da un codice di pergamena che ho presso di me et che dal carattere si conosce esser del XV. secolo, vi sono molte composizioni in contrappunto di varij autori fra i quali di Gio. Ciconia [...]».

[3] Cfr. le lettere di Tartini, sempre a Padre Martini, ancora dell'11 dicembre 1761: «Le aggiungo bensì che lo stesso Signor Abate Brunazzi mi ha imposto di farle sapere ch'egli ha in mano un antichissimo monumento musicale (è un antifonario) ed è del principio del 1100. Se esso può giovare a Vostra Riverenza, lo fa padrone», e del 14 maggio 1762: «Da molte settimane io ho in mia mano il libro consaputo: anticaglia famosa veramente; ma con prescrizione di doverlo mandare costì a Vostra Riverenza in quel tal modo, che non apporti pericolo alcuno al libro né di smarrimento, né di nocumento; e con la indispensabile condizione della restituzione dopo che Vostra Riverenza se ne abbia valuto. Non occorre sperare di poterlo avere a qualunque prezzo benché esorbitante, e di ciò non serve far parola».

[4] Due voll., pubblicati a Bologna da Della Volpe, rispettivamente nel 1774 e nel 1775. Inutile sottolineare il fatto che tutti gli esempi citati in quest'opera (che si può ancora considerare la più ricca antologia della polifonia classica) vennero tratti dal materiale che Padre Martini aveva a disposizione nella propria biblioteca.

tempo, e del tempo passato [5]. D'altronde, la vastità degli interessi di Padre Martini è testimoniata, più validamente che ogni qualsiasi affermazione o documento, dalla mole e dalla consistenza della sua biblioteca [6].

A questo interesse per gli aspetti più varii della musica, e per la sua storia, si accompagnava non meno viva l'attenzione alla musica del presente, in ogni sua manifestazione. Per essere al corrente di quel che succedeva negli ambienti professionali del tempo, Padre Martini adoperava un sistema sicuro ed efficace insieme, che gli permetteva di valutare in proprio la notizia o il giudizio che gli veniva comunicato. Una volta usciti dalla sua scuola, gli allievi di lui non interrompevano i rapporti con il maestro; anzi, lo tenevano informato della loro attività, dell'ambiente in cui vivevano e in cui di volta in volta lavoravano, dell'attività dei loro colleghi, sia compositori che cantanti. Dalla lettura anche soltanto parziale della corrispondenza martiniana il quadro della vita musicale settecentesca (e non soltanto di quella italiana) acquista una vivacità di colorito ed un'animazione di figure che non potremmo in alcun modo ottenere altrimenti; e poiché la corrispondenza si svolge tra professionisti, noi possiamo conoscere «dall'interno» lo svolgersi dell'attività musicale; proprio perché non provenienti da dilettanti e da osservatori occasionali (come possono essere ad esempio quelle dei varii autori di Diarii, *Lettres de l'Italie*, etc.), le affermazioni acquistano un significato ed un valore nettamente definito (e sia pure mettendo nel bilancio le inevitabili parzialità, gelosie e invidie di mestiere); in particolare, la nostra conoscenza della prassi esecutiva si potrà arricchire con precisione e pertinenza se sapremo dare all'informazione un'interpretazione corretta.

Fra gli allievi di Padre Martini che frequentarono la sua scuola alla metà del secolo Giuseppe Luigi Tibaldi ebbe forse la carriera più brillante, sebbene non come compositore [7]. Dopo aver compiuto tra il 1748 ed il 1751 un corso completo di «contrappunto» con il maestro bolognese [8], Tibaldi preferì dedicarsi alla carriera di cantante d'opera, nella quale aveva mosso già i primi passi nel 1750 cantando a Pavia. Divenuto uno dei più quotati tenori del tempo, sostenne fra l'altro per la prima volta la parte di Admeto

---

[5] I ritratti si trovano oggi, non tutti in buona conservazione sebbene si stia procedendo da tempo al loro generale restauro, presso il Conservatorio «G. B. Martini» di Bologna. Sulla figura umana e sugli interessi più ampiamente musicali di Padre Martini, come pure sull'ambiente in cui egli visse, rimane ancor oggi fondamentale, per ampiezza e precisione di documentazione, il volume di L. Busi, *Il Padre G. B. Martini, musicista-letterato del secolo XVIII*, Bologna 1891 (anche ristampa anastatica Bologna 1968).

[6] Essa costituisce ancor oggi il nucleo centrale, e la maggior parte della Biblioteca Musicale «G. B. Martini» (oggi denominata anche Civico Museo Bibliografico Musicale) di Bologna.

[7] Per Tibaldi si veda la voce, a cura dello scrivente, in MGG XIII (1966), coll. 383—384.

[8] Il manoscritto KK 200 della Biblioteca Musicale «G. B. Martini» contiene la serie completa degli appunti e degli esercizi tenuti da Tibaldi durante il corso completo di studi con Padre Martini. L'importanza di questo documento non ha bisogno di essere sottolineata: esso ci permette di seguire passo per passo l'*iter* della scuola martiniana. Per la storia della didattica musicale settecentesca un utile confronto potrebbe essere costituito con gli *Attwood Sketches*, di recente pubblicati nella *Neue Mozart-Ausgabe (Thomas Attwoods Theorie- und Kompositionsstudien bei Mozart*, vorgelegt von E. Hertzmann und C. B. Oldman, fertiggestellt von D. Heartz und A. Mann, Kassel 1965 [*W. A. Mozart. Neue Ausgabe sämtlicher Werke*. Serie X: Supplement. Werkgruppe 30, Band 1]).

nell'*Alceste* di Gluck, e Calzabigi contò molto sulla sua presenza e sulla sua collaborazione non solo per la parte musicale ma anche per la realizzazione scenica di quest'opera a Bologna nel 1778 [9]. Del resto, pochi anni prima della ripresa bolognese dell'*Alceste*, Tibaldi aveva assistito di persona alla nascita dell'*Ascanio in Alba* del quattordicenne Wolfgang Amadeus Mozart, ed aveva preso parte alla prima esecuzione della «Festa Teatrale» cantando la parte del Sacerdote Aceste [10]; che egli stesso avesse potuto rendersi conto dei quotidiani progressi della partitura, lo afferma Leopold in una lettera al conte Gian Luca Pallavicini, di cui la famiglia Mozart era stata ospite nel precedente soggiorno bolognese:

> Il mio Figlio la fece [= la Serenata, cioè *Ascanio in Alba*] in Milano in 15 Giorni, non poteva comminciar prima trovandosi la Poesia per l'approbazione a Vienna d'onde fu rimandata al ultimo punto. Il Sig.ʳ Tibaldi, chi fece l'onore al mio figlio di venire tutte le mattine à vederlo scrivere, potrà dare a V.S. un racconto authentico [11].

La lettera di Tibaldi a Padre Martini che ha fornito lo spunto per queste osservazioni risale al periodo iniziale della carriera del cantante. Nel gennaio 1753 egli si trova in Roma, dove canta al Teatro Argentina per la stagione di carnevale; scopo della lettera è quello di informare subito il maestro dei propri successi, commisurati soprattutto attraverso un fiasco abbastanza clamoroso dell'opera che si rappresenta nel teatro rivale. Indubbiamente il messaggio assolve la sua funzione, ma diviene nelle nostre mani e ai nostri occhi fonte di informazioni che vanno ben oltre la semplice cronaca ed il pettegolezzo fra le quinte:

> Molto Rev(eren)do P(ad)re   Roma li 10 Genaro 1753
> L'Incomodo di questa mia in fretta p(er)chè non hò tempo partendo subbito la posta, le dirò che siamo andati in Scena con la nostr'Opera quale à un incontro spaventoso, particolarmente Elisi quale m'impone riverirlo distintamente, la prima donna Belardi scolaro di Mazzoni anche lei incontra molto, pure il second'Omo Mazzanti si porta molto bene, ed è vero cantante. Io in mezzo a questo confronto mi sentano [sic] volentieri, et hò il mio applauso, abenche non abbi arie che fermano [?]. La musica molto buona del Maestro Auresichio Napolitano, fatta in Venti giorni, per causa del maestro Pampani licenziato alla prima prova, non pia-piacendo la Musica del Medemo fuori della prim'Aria di Giovanino di Mazzoni, e una di Mazzanti che sono restate, in somma è andata alle stelle la seconda sera doppo aver sentita l'Opera d'Aliberti quale e andata in terra a fatto,

---

[9] Cfr. le lettere di Calzabigi a Montefani per questa esecuzione, pubblicate in C. Ricci, *I Teatri di Bologna nei secoli XVII e XVIII*, Bologna 1888, ristampa anastatica Forni 1965, pp. 625, 628, 630, 632 («Per ciò che mira al dettaglio il Sig. Tipaldi che recitò la parte d'Admeto originalmente con tanta sua gloria mi conforta e mi consola»), 641, 656.

[10] Cfr. O. E. Deutsch, *Mozart — A Documentary Biography*, Stanford 1966², pp. 136—137.

[11] La lettera è datata Milano, 17 ottobre 1771, ed è stata pubblicata in A. Ostoja, *Mozart e l'Italia — Contributo biografico nel bicentenario della nascita*, Bologna 1955, pp. 30—32 in fac-simile, e pp. 43—44 in trascrizione.

Musica di Jomelli, e ci è qualche aria buona, massime le Seconde parti da Maestro;
Il Sig.ʳ Ventura Rochetti li è convenuto andar dentro alla metà del Aria del
Terz'Atto patettica, se nò poco meno li facevano li urli, essendo il medemo cantante antico, pieno di trilli, mordenti, acceccature, et appoggiature di mezza
batuta che qui non piacciono niente, e creddo che forsi non piaceranno più in
nisun luogo. L'unico che piacia e il Second'Omo quale a buona voce, ma niente
cantante, in somma il povero Jomelli è andato in terra abenche sia un Maestro
di tutta stima.

Della relazione delle musiche di Roma mi riserbo in un altra mia non avendo
tempo, e restando con tutta stima
di V(ostra) P(aternità) M(olto) R(everenda)

Um(ilissi)mo Servitore, e Scolaro immeritevole
Giuseppe Tibaldi [12].

L'opera che si rappresenta al Teatro Argentina e nella quale canta Tibaldi è l'*Andromaca*; lo possiamo ricavare dalla rispondenza perfetta fra i nomi degli interpreti indicati
nella lettera e quelli riportati dal libretto a stampa per la rappresentazione [13]; non
vi è dubbio invece che l'indicazione degli autori della musica, quale compare nell'appo-
sita sezione del libretto, non ci consente in alcun modo di conoscere la situazione reale,
che ci è svelata nella luce più cruda dalla lettera di uno degli interpreti vocali dello spettacolo. Il libretto dice infatti: «La musica è del Sig. Antonio Aurisicchio napoletano
maestro di cappella della Regia Chiesa di S. Giacomo de' Spagnoli in Roma; toltine i
recitativi senza istrumenti e le arie contrassegnate coll'asterisco ✳, che sono des sig.
Antonio Gaetano Pampani veneziano Accademico Filarmonico e maestro di coro delle
Figlie del Pio Ospitale de' SS. Giovanni e Paolo di Venezia« [14]. Quella che dall'indicazione del libretto sembra essere poco più di una semplice alternanza di compiti, spiega-
bile a prima vista con la pratica del tutto corrente di trasferire una o più arie da un'opera
all'altra (generalmente allo scopo di accontentare i «virtuosi» e le «virtuose»), è

---

[12] Bologna, Biblioteca Musicale «G. B. Martini», Epistolario martiniano, I. 19. 1. 74.

[13] *ANDROMACA, Dramma per musica da rappresentarsi nel nobil Teatro a Torre Argentina
il Carnevale dell'anno 1753*, Roma (1753), Amidei. Copie di questo libretto si trovano a
Bologna, Biblioteca «G. B. Martini», nelle Biblioteche Comunali di Macerata e di Palermo,
a Firenze, Biblioteca Marucelliana, e a Venezia, Raccolta Rolandi dell'Istituto di Lettere
Musica e Teatro della Fondazione «G. Cini».
Ecco i nomi degli interpreti, con l'indicazione delle rispettive parti: Filippo Elisi: *Pirro;*
Giovanni Belardi: *Andromaca;* Giovanni Marchetti: *Ermione;* Ferdinando Mazzanti: *Oreste;*
Giuseppe Tibaldi: *Pilade;* Antonio Costantini: *Ulearte.*
Il testo del libretto è attribuito ad A. Zeno e A. Salvi da R. G(iazotto) nella voce *Aurisicchio*
in «Enciclopedia dello Spettacolo» I (1954), coll. 1147—1148.

[14] *Andromaca*, libretto cit., p. 8. Quest'indicazione viene riportata anche da U. Sesini, *Catalogo
della Biblioteca del Liceo Musicale di Bologna. Vol. V — Libretti d'Opera in Musica*, Bologna
1943, p. 32, che considera appunto la partitura come frutto della collaborazione fra i due
musicisti.

in realtà, come ci testimonia la lettera di Tibaldi (e calcolando pure le esagerazioni tipiche dell'ambiente teatrale di tutti i tempi), una sostituzione in piena regola del compositore Pampani per inefficienza. Certamente, il problema in sé non è rilevante; ma il caso ci fornisce un'ennesima lezione sul valore da attribuire ai dati offerti dalle prove documentarie; e sulla imperiosa necessità di aver coscienza che l'informazione di cui ci serviamo può essere sempre per lo meno incompleta (se non proprio erronea) [15].

Il fatto che Elisi invii per mezzo di Tibaldi il suo saluto a Padre Martini ci prova che questo cantante aveva già incontrato il musicista francescano; ma non è stato finora rinvenuto un documento che ci testimoni la presenza di Elisi come esecutore in un teatro di Bologna, e non possiamo quindi stabilire quando l'incontro sia avvenuto [16]; ma tutta la compagnia di canto che si esibiva nell'*Andromeda* al Teatro Argentina era in un modo o nell'altro connessa con l'ambiente bolognese; ed anche Antonio Maria Mazzoni, l'insegnante di Giovannino Belardi, apparteneva alla cerchia di musicisti attiva attorno a Padre Martini; la lettera di Tibaldi ci prova per la prima volta che questo compositore svolgeva anche attività di insegnante di canto [17].

Se Belardi (definito da Tibaldi — notiamolo *en passant* — come «prima donna»: l'indicazione, alla metà del '700, si riferiva ancora al ruolo più che all'interprete) è figura pittosto irrilevante [18] nella storia dei cantanti settecenteschi (una storia ancora tutta da scrivere, e che farebbe certamente luce su settori ben più vasti ed interessanti che non la semplice carriera dei singoli esecutori), gli altri due interpreti ricordati da Tibaldi meritano un breve cenno a parte.

Filippo Elisi viene anzitutto ricordato da Mancini fra i «musici di primo rango, e di merito superiore» [19]; nel 1753 la sua carriera è all'apice: iniziatasi a Venezia nel

---

[15] Si veda, per una lucida e precisa impostazione di questo fondamentale problema dell'attività musicologica, A. Mendel, "Evidence and Explanation", in *Report of the Eighth Congress of the International Musicological Society. New York 1961, Volume II — Reports*, ed. J. LaRue, Kassel, 1962, pp. 3—18, specialmente alla p. 17.

[16] Quando non sia altrimenti specificato, tutti i dati relativi alla carriera dei cantanti sono tratti dalle indicazioni contenute nei libretti a stampa per le rappresentazioni. Queste indicazioni a loro volta sono state nella stragrande maggioranza ricavate dalla schedatura dei libretti stessi effettuata dall'Ufficio di ricerca e schedatura dei Fondi Musicali Italiani, diretto da Claudio Sartori, verso di cui viene qui volentieri riconosciuto questo debito di riconoscenza.

[17] Per Antonio Maria Mazzoni si vedano le voci, entrambe redatte da L. F. Tagliavini in «Enciclopedia dello Spettacolo» VII (1960), coll. 345—346 e MGG VIII (1960), coll. 1867—1868.

[18] All'epoca dell'*Andromeda* era poco più che agli inizi della carriera; tanto che Tibaldi lo nomina a Padre Martini ricordando anche il suo insegnante. Il nome di Belardi compare per la prima volta in libretti risalenti al 1751 per spettacoli dati a Roma ed a Spoleto; fatta eccezione per il *Catone in Utica* rappresentato a Monaco nel 1753 e per *La Nitteti*, rappresentata a Reggio nel 1757, le opere in cui Belardi canta sono tutte rappresentate su teatri romani tra il 1751 ed il 1759, e poi nel 1768 e 1769.

[19] G. B. Mancini, *Riflessioni pratiche sul canto figurato*, Vienna 1777 [3], riprodotto in A. Della Corte, *Canto e bel canto*, Torino — Milano — Firenze... 1933, pp. 97—228: p. 114 e 115. Filippo Elisi è detto da Mancini nativo di Fossombrone.

1739 [20], essa fiorisce attorno al 1746 quando, ancora a Venezia, egli incomincia ad interpretare ruoli principali, cantando accanto a Caterina Aschieri [21]; da quell'anno essa si svolge con ritmo assai intenso nei principali centri italiani (in particolare Roma, Milano e Napoli), presentando aspetti di notevole interesse per la storia dell'opera, come ad esempio quando Elisi prende parte alle rappresentazioni dell'*Ippolito ed Aricia* di Traetta (su libretto di C. I. Frugoni) a Parma nel 1759, cantando con Caterina Gabrielli [22]. Notizie non semplicemente cronologiche su di lui ci vengono fornite da Burney, il quale ha modo di giudicare il cantante italiano quando giunge a Londra nel 1760. Questa la descrizione che Burney ci dà del talento di Elisi, e che ci spiega fra l'altro come questi venne scelto per le rappresentazioni parmensi dell'anno precedente:

> [...] though a great singer, [Elisi] was still a greater actor: his figure was majestic, and he had a great compass of voice. He was fond of distant intervals, of fourteen or fifteen notes, and took them well. Several airs of Jommelli, which he introduced in different operas, were calculated to shew the dexterity and accuracy with which he could form these remote intervals [23].

Ritornato in Italia alla fine del 1762, Elisi compare di nuovo sulle scene londinesi nel 1765 e 1766, ma la sua voce, sebbene ottenga ancora successo, "was upon the decline" [24]; tuttavia sappiamo che egli canta ancora per lo meno sino al 1772 [25]. Un particolare curioso: nel 1753 Elisi conosceva già, per lo meno sul piano professionale, il principale cantante del teatro rivale, il sopranista Ventura Rocchetti; ricaviamo questa notizia da una fonte sinora poco sfruttata, che può tuttavia fornire preziose informazioni sulla storia dell'opera di questo periodo, e cioè i disegni-caricature di Pier Leone Ghezzi; i disegni sono spesso accompagnati da didascalìe ricche di abbondanti particolari non solo sui personaggi rappresentati ma anche sull'attività operistica romana della prima metà del '700. Quella accanto al ritratto di Jommelli dice:

[20] Nella *Creusa*, rappresentata al Teatro di S. Samuele con musica di P. Leone Cardena; Elisi sostiene la parte di Eurimale, l'ultima del *cast;* cfr. anche T. Wiel, *I teatri musicali veneziani nel '700*, Venezia 1897, p. 131.

[21] Al Teatro di S. Giovanni Grisostomo nella *Sofonisba* di Jommelli e nell'*Artaserse* di Abos; cfr. anche T. Wiel, *op. cit.*, pp. 157—158.

[22] Per questo spettacolo si veda soprattutto D. Heartz, "Operatic reform at Parma — Ippolito e Aricia", in *Atti del convegno sul Settecento parmense*, Parma 1968 (*Fonti e studi [della Deputazione di storia patria per le provincie parmensi]* Serie Seconda — V), pp. 271—300.

[23] Ch. Burney, *A General History of Music*, ed. F. Mercer, New York 1935, II, p. 860.

[24] Ch. Burney, *op. cit.*, p. 870.

[25] Nell'*Antigono* e nell'*Alessandro nell'Indie*, rappresentati a Roma al Teatro di Torre Argentina. Il nome di Elisi compare in non meno di trentotto libretti settecenteschi; ma è certo che questa cifra riflette una parte soltanto dell'intensissima attività di questo cantante (non abbiamo, ad esempio, libretti per gli spettacoli cui partecipò a Londra, e di cui ci parla Burney).

Niccolò Jommelli Napo(leta)no [...] Il d(ett)o S(igno)r Jumella venne in Roma p(er) comporvi la Seconda opera intitolata L'Astianatte Nel Teatro Argentina l'anno 1741 il quale fece una musica singolarissima Che ne riportò l'applauso di tutta Roma e recitorno il S(igno)r Ventura Rocchetti venuto da Polonia, e gli fù dato scudi Mille; Il S(igno)r Filippo Elissi che fece d'Andromaca assai bene, et era di Fossombruno protetto dall'E(minetissim)o Card(ina)l Passionei. et il S(igno)r Gaetano Basteris, fece la parte di Pillade, et Gavea una agilità grandissima di Voce di tenore che regolava la sua voce come un soprano, et il suo Padre suonava nell'Orchestra il Boè che in Roma non si è inteso l'uguale [...] [26].

Figura ancora più interessante è quella di Ferdinando Mazzanti. Toscano di origine ed allievo di Bartolomeo Nucci da Pescia [27], la sua carriera di cantante non è così splendida come quella di Elisi: iniziatasi a Venezia nel 1744 si estende, con un ritmo di presenze assai più pacato, fino al 1772; del resto la voce di Mazzanti, "thin, but extreme-ly flexible" [28], si imponeva soprattutto grazie alla personalità del musicista ed alla maestrìa tecnica ottenuta attraverso lungo e paziente studio [29]. Al contrario di Tibaldi Mazzanti, divenuto famoso come cantante, viene ricordato dai contemporanei con pari rispetto ed ammirazione come compositore e come cultore di cose musicali; sotto questa luce ce lo presenta Burney nella descrizione del suo soggiorno romano:

I visited several times, while I was at Rome, Signor Mazzanti, who not only sings with exquisite taste, but is likewise an excellent musician. He is both a reader and a writer on the subject of music, as well as a considerable collector of books and manuscripts. The richness of his taste, in singing, makes ample amend of the want of force in his voice, which is now but a thread. He has a great collection of Palestrini's [sic] compositions, and furnished me with several of them, which I could not get elsewhere. [...]

He has composed many things himself, such as operas and motets for voices, and trios, quartets, quintets, and other pieces for violin. He plays pretty well on the violin, and is in possession of the most beautiful and perfect *Steiner* I ever saw.

---

[26] L'originale del disegno si trova a Roma, Biblioteca Apostolica Vaticana, Cod. Ottobon. Lat. 3118, c. 153. Il disegno è riprodotto con la relativa didascalia trascritta poco fedelmente, in E. Celani, *Musica e Musicisti in Roma (1750—1850)*, in «Rivista Musicale Italiana» XVIII (1911), pp. 1—63: 10.

[27] Cfr. G. B. Mancini, *op. cit.*, ed. cit., pp. 115 e 119.

[28] Ch. Burney, *Dr. Burney's Musical Tours in Europe*, ed. P. A. Scholes, London 1959, I, p. 208.

[29] Lo afferma Mancini quando, lamentandosi dello scarso scrupolo professionale degli insegnanti di canto a lui contemporanei, afferma che «espongono maturi i loro scolari nella debole età de' loro primi anni, e per colmo di loro disgrazia li obligano a cantare le arie di Caffarelli, Egiziello, Ferdinando Mazzanti, professori ben noti per il loro raro merito, acquistato me-diante un assiduo studio diretto da profondo sapere, giudizio, arte ed esperienza di tanti anni» (G. B. Mancini, *op. cit.*, ed. cit., p. 157); e Tibaldi dice a Padre Martini che Mazzanti «si porta molto bene, ed è vero cantante».

He has advanced very far in the theory of music; has made, by way of study,
an abridgment of the modulation of Palestrini, which is well selected and digested;
and he shewed me a considerable part of a musical treatise, in manuscript, written
by himself [30].

Con particolare interesse Burney ricorda l'esecuzione, da parte di Mazzanti, dell'«aria
del Tasso»:

Signor Mazzanti is famous for singing the poem of Tasso to the same melody
as the Gondoliers of Venice. This he does with infinite taste, accompanying himself on the violin, with the harmony of which he produces curious and pleasing
effects. I prevailed on him to write me down the original melody, in order to
compare it with one that I took down at Venice, while it was singing on the great
canal [31].

Alla fine della carriera Mazzanti, che era già noto in Germania per aver cantanto nel
1755 a Monaco in due oratorii [32], e a Stoccarda nel 1759 et 1760, durante il periodo
di più intensa attività di Jommelli come compositore di corte del duca del Württem-
berg [33], ritorna presso questa corte insegnante di musica a assume anche, seppure per
breve tempo, il ruolo di Kapellmeister, prendendo il posto di A. Boroni [34].

La compagnia nella quale Tibaldi compie il suo debutto romano è formata quindi di
musicisti la cui personalità si manifesta non esclusivamente nel campo della vocalità
operistica; la varietà degli interessi e degli atteggiamenti di questi esecutori, che avranno

---

[30] Ch. Burney, *Dr. Burney's Musical Tours . . .*, ed. cit., I, p. 234.

[31] Ch. Burney, *Dr. Burney's Musical Tours . . .*, ed. cit., ibid. Per l'«aria del Tasso» nella storia
della musica, e particolarmente nel '700, si vedano P. Nettl, *Bemerkungen zu den Tasso-
Melodien des 18. Jahrhunderts*, in „Die Musikforschung" X (1957), pp. 265—271 e Pl. Petrobelli ("Tartini and folk-music"), in *"Report of the Tenth Congress of the International Musicological Society"*, Ljubljana 1967, pp. 176—181: pp. 177—179; traduzione italiana in «Chigiana»
XXVI—XXVII (= N.S. 6—7) (1971), pp. 443—450.

[32] Sono gli oratori *Isacco figura del Redentore* e *Betulia liberata*, entrambi su libretto di Metastasio, il secondo su musica di Andrea Bernasconi, mentre del primo non si conosce il nome
del compositore.

[33] Cfr. J. Sittard, *Zur Geschichte der Musik und des Theaters am Württembergischen Hofe*, II
(1733—1793), Stuttgart 1891, pp. 73—74 e H. Abert, *Jommelli als Opernkomponist*, Halle
1908, pp. 76—77.

[34] Cfr. R. Eitner, *Biographisch-bibliographisches Quellen-Lexikon . . .*, VI, Leipzig 1902, p. 408
e J. Sittard, *op. cit.*, pp. 135—136. All'elenco delle musiche di Mazzanti fornito da Eitner si
devono avgiungere le seguenti composizioni:
l'aria «Del cor gli affetti», ms. Firenze, Bibl. Cons. D.1619;
l'aria «Nell'ardir che il sen t'accende», ms. Genova, Bibl. Cons.;
una raccolta di solfeggi per soprano in Modena, Bibl. Estense, raccolta Campori, App. II, 2663.
Forse attribuibile a Mazzanti è anche l'aria «Fiumicel che s'ode appena», ms. Napoli, Bibl.
Cons. S. Pietro a Majella, 34. 4. 3.
Un manoscritto, appartenuto a Mazzanti, di arie d'opera a lui contemporanee è brevemente
descritto in S. Orlinick, *A Canzonetta Fiorentina in Don Giovanni?*, in "Mozart Jahrbuch"
1967, pp. 312—313.

in un modo o nell'altro un posto di rilievo nell'attività musicale della seconda metà del secolo, ci permette di ricavare un quadro della situazione più ricco, più mosso; soprattutto si può conoscere con maggiore chiarezza in quale direzione questi interessi si orientassero, e quindi distinguere e verificare possibili rapporti ed influenze. Tutto questo può aiutarci molto sul piano della concreta realtà musicale nel momento in cui si affrontano, ad esempio, problemi di prassi esecutiva. Ed è proprio su questo settore che ci illumina la seconda parte della lettera di Tibaldi.

L'opera che, contemporaneamente all'*Andromeda* al Teatro Argentina, si rappresenta al Teatro Alibert o delle Dame [35] nella stagione di carnevale del 1753 è l'*Attilio Regolo* [36]; per la seconda volta questo testo, forse il libretto di Metastasio drammaticamente più riuscito, viene messo in musica, e da Jommelli [37]. Gli autori che si sono occupati della produzione operistica di questo compositore non sono d'accordo sulla data della prima rappresentazione, e di conseguenza sull'anno di stesura della partitura. A quanto mi risulta, nessun tentativo è stato fino ad oggi compiuto per verificare se, fra le numerose partiture manoscritte pervenuteci [38], esistano varianti tali per cui si debba pensare a differenti versioni. Abert, correggendo Vernon Lee che indicava il 1750, sostiene che l'anno di composizione è il 1752, aggiungendo che «In dieser Datierung stimmen alle Quellen miteinander überein» [39]; a dire il vero, Abert stesso aveva in precedenza segnalato presso la Biblioteca del Conservatorio di Napoli l'esistenza di una partitura recante la data 1751 [40]. Senza cercare di risolvere in maniera definitiva la questione, facciamo osservare che, mentre non sono stati finora trovati libretti per la rappresentazione dell'opera anteriori a quello per l'esecuzione al Teatro Alibert nel carnevale 1753, l'indicazione sul frontespizio del manoscritto napoletano dice: «Attilio Regolo. / Musica del Sig.r D: Nicola Jomelli / Napolitano. / Rappresentata la p(ri)ma volta in Roma l'anno 1751 indi replicata in Napoli nel 1752»; questa indicazione ha tutta l'aria di essere opera di un copista (napoletano?), che eseguì il proprio lavoro in un'epoca

---

[35] Per la storia di questo teatro romano ed un elenco cronologico delle esecuzioni si veda A. de Angelis, *Il teatro Alibert o delle Dame (1717—1863)*, Tivoli 1951.

[36] *ATTILIO REGOLO, Dramma per musica da rappresentarsi in Roma nel Teatro delle Dame nel corrente carnevale dell'anno MDCCLIII. Dedicato alla generosa Nobiltà Romana*. Roma (1753). M. Silvestri.

Copie di questo libretto si trovano a Washington, Library of Congress; Firenze, Biblioteca Marucelliana; Milano, Biblioteca Nazionale Braidense; Roma, Biblioteca del Conservatorio di Musica «S. Cecilia»; Venezia, raccolta Rolandi dell' Istituto di Lettere Musica e Teatro della Fondazione Cini.

Il *cast* completo degli interpreti è riportato da A. de Angelis, *op. cit.*, p. 176. E' probabile che l'accenno al «Second'Omo quale a buona voce, ma niente cantante» si riferisca a Litterio Ferrari, l'interprete della parte di Manlio.

[37] Il testo metastasiano era stato messo in musica per la prima volta da Hasse nel 1740, ma rappresentato soltanto dieci anni dopo, all'Hoftheater di Dresda nel gennaio 1750; cfr. We. B(ollert) sub voce *Hasse*, in «Enciclopedia dello Spettacolo» VI, 195; cfr. anche sub voce *Metastasio*, id., VII, 504.

[38] Se ne veda l'elenco in H. Abert, *op. cit.*, p. 3.

[39] Ibid., p. 54, nota 7.

[40] Ibid., p. 3.

decisamente posteriore alle date indicate, citandole quindi senza alcuna accuratezza [41]; l'indicazione dev'essere pertanto presa con molta cautela, considerando d'altro canto la precisione e la contemporaneità agli avvenimenti del libretto a stampa.

L'«Aria del Terz'Atto patettica» è cantata da Ventura Rocchetti; poiché questo cantante, secondo le indicazioni del libretto, veste i panni del protagonista, dobbiamo riconoscere nell'aria «Io son padre, e nol sarei» il brano che tanto dispiacque agli

[41] Una rappresentazione dell'*Attilio Regolo* di Jommelli al Teatro di S. Carlo di Napoli avvenne certamente nel marzo 1761 (cfr. U. Sesini, *Catalogo* ... cit., p. 252); si può quindi ipotizzare anche una confusione di date. Devo alla cortesia di Renato Di Benedetto un'informazione, giuntami quando questo testo era già stato consegnato per la pubblicazione; essa conferma esattamente la mia ipotesi. Infatti, nel titolo del manoscritto napoletano (la cui segnatura era precedentemente 28. 6. 26—27 ed è ora Rari 7. 7. 3—4), le cifre indicanti gli anni delle rappresentazioni non sono della mano del copista che redasse il manoscritto; questi infatti lasciò in bianco (proprio per l'incertezza) gli spazi corrispondenti, e le date «1751» e «1752» vennero aggiunte dalla stessa mano che indicò più tardi l'appartenenza del manoscritto: «Giuseppe Sigismondo P(adro)ne»; il manoscritto fa parte cioè della collezione del bibliotecario del Conservatorio della Pietà dei Turchini (1730—1826).

mie - i___, a' fi - gli mie - i   un e - sem - pio di vil - tà___

. Un e - sem - - - pio di vil - tà.

spettatori romani. Come fonte è stato utilizzato un manoscritto della Biblioteca Civica «Angelo Mai» di Bergamo; dell'aria riportiamo soltanto la linea melodica, dato che è questa che ci interessa principalmente [42].

Se analizziamo questa linea melodica tenendo presenti le osservazioni contenute nella lettera di Tibaldi coglieremo subito le ragioni che suscitarono nel pubblico romano una reazione così apertamente negativa: la melodia si svolge secondo un ritmo estremamente frastagliato, nel quale proprio quegli abbellimenti, che costituivano parte integrante del virtuosismo vocale di Rocchetti (nel 1753, come vedremo, il cantante è alla fine della sua carriera), servono a specificare l'«affetto» dell'aria «patetica» e costituiscono in pratica un'assunzione diretta, da parte di Jommelli, di tutti gli stilemi belcantistici affidati fino a poco tempo prima all'improvvisazione dell'interprete [43]. Del resto Tibaldi stesso attribuisce la causa del fiasco in misura eguale ad esecutori e al compositore («in somma il povero Jommelli è andato in terra abenché sia un Maestro di tutta stima»). L'importanza della lettera del cantante bolognese che pubblichiamo qui per la prima volta mi sembra stia proprio in questo: essa ci testimonia puntualmente un mutamento deciso nel gusto del pubblico settecentesco, al cui rifiuto del virtuosismo vocale — inteso come doviziosa e continua applicazione degli abbellimenti — corrisponderà, nei decenni successivi, un generale mutamento nel concetto stesso di «opera seria».

[42] Il manoscritto, della seconda metà del Settecento, ha la collocazione Sala 32. E. 1. 22. 1—3; l'aria si trova a cc. 36r—38r del terzo volume. L'accompagnamento è affidato agli archi, che si muovono costantemente con il ritmo e l'andamento delle prime due misure.

[43] Lo stile di quest'aria non è certo un esempio isolato nell'arte di Jommelli. Il motivo iniziale può essere accostato, ad esempio, a quello dell'aria di Demetrio «Piango, è ver» nel II atto dell'*Antigono* (cfr. H. Abert, *op. cit.*, p. 264); ma le affinità non sono soltanto genericamente stilistiche: metro e tonalità corrispondono, ed assai simile è anche la figurazione dell'accompagnamento, come pure affine è la disposizione prosodica e accentuativa dei due testi poetici.

Ancora trent'anni prima la situazione era agli antipodi: quel tipo di canto ora rifiutato era considerato il non plus ultra del buon gusto musicale. Ne *La cantatrice e l'impresario* (noto anche come *L'impresario delle Canarie*), intermezzo attribuito a Metastasio per la *Didone abbandonata,* ed eseguito per la prima volta a Napoli nel 1724, la cantante Dorina sta scegliendo un pezzo che le convenga, ed espone in modo autoritario a Nibbio i suoi commenti:

> Questa [cantata] è troppo difficile:
> Questa è d'autore antico,
> Senza tremuli, trilli e appoggiature,
> Troppo contraria alla moderna scuola
> Che adorna di passaggi ogni parola [44].

L'anno prima Pierfrancesco Tosi aveva pubblicato le *Opinioni de' cantori antichi e moderni,* nelle quali l'autore, pur con i suoi atteggiamenti di passatista isterico, tesseva le lodi dell'appoggiatura in questa maniera:

> Fra tutti gli abbellimenti del Canto non v'è istruzione più facile per il Maestro ad insegnarsi, nè meno difficile per lo Scolaro ad impararsi, che quella della Appoggiatura; Questa oltre alla propria sua vaghezza ha degnamente ottenuto dall'Arte l'unico privilegio di farsi udir sovente, e di non istufar mai, purchè non esca da que' limiti, che dal buon gusto de' Professori gli sono stati prescritti [45].

Quello che il pubblico romano, attento soltanto al virtuosismo dell'interprete e insensibile ai valori più autentici della partitura, non era riuscito a cogliere nell'*Attilio Regolo* era il progressivo arricchimento di atteggiamenti drammatici nel linguaggio musicale di Jommelli, specialmente nelle scene conclusive dell'opera, dove l'impiego degli strumenti raggiunge zone espressive fino ad allora inesplorate (un fatto tanto più notevole in quanto il compositore procedeva su di una linea diametralmente opposta a quella indicata dal librettista, con il quale era pur in stretto contatto epistolare) [46].

Il cantante che impersonava Attilio Regolo era, d'altronde, un esponente tipico della scuola belcantistica italiana della prima metà del secolo: la sua carriera, iniziatasi a Venezia nel 1732 cantando la parte di Learco nell'*Issipile* di Giovanni Porta al Teatro di S. Giovanni Grisostomo, si svolse quasi costantemente presso la corte di Dresda; tant'è vero che il nome di Rocchetti compare già nel 1732 accompagnato dal titolo di «virtuoso del Re di Polonia»: il ciclo maggiore di presenze sulle scene italiane (veneziane e romane) e presso la corte sassone di estende dal 1738 al 1753; il cantante prende parte, fra l'altro, alla prima rappresentazione dell'*Attilio Regolo* di Hasse, cantando tuttavia la parte di Amilcare. Dopo il 1753, il suo nome scompare quasi completamente dai libretti per le rappresentazioni; una delle ultime notizie su di lui ci viene tuttavia

---

[44] P. Metastasio, *La cantatrice e l'impresario*, intermezzo I, vv. 10—14. (P. Metastasio, *Opere,* Trieste 1857, p. 50).

[45] P. F. Tosi, *Opinione de' cantori antichi e moderni...*, Bologna 1723, p. 19.

[46] Cfr. H. Abert, *op. cit.*, pp. 248—249.

da una lettera di Tartini, ancora una volta diretta a Padre Martini, nella quale il violinista chiede notizie di Rocchetti, rivelandoci in questo modo di aver tenuto contatti non effimeri con lui:

> [...] L'altra si è la niuna notizia dello stato del Sig.ʳ Ventura Rochetti virtuoso di S. M. Rè di Polonia; che venne costì per passar a Roma, ma costì trattenuto dal male, non so poi che ne sia seguito dopo aver secolui carteggiato per qualche mese [...] [47].

Non è certamente questo il solo dato dell'epistolario tartiniano che ci rivela rapporti e sentimenti d'amicizia e di altissima stima professionale del «Maestro delle Nazioni» verso cantanti, anche famosissimi, del suo tempo (Farinelli, Raaff); ciò che interessa però qui sottolineare è la coincidenza perfetta tra la funzione stilistica degli abbellimenti quale viene praticata da Rocchetti nell'aria dell'*Attilio Regolo* di Jommelli, e quale viene descritta e codificata da Tartini nel suo scritto sugli abbellimenti [48]. Questo scritto, sulla cui data di redazione (per lo meno della prima redazione) sembra si possa oggi concordare, e cioè intorno al 1740 [49], e la cui destinazione, si ricordi bene, non riguarda soltanto gli strumentisti ma anche i cantanti, è in realtà il primo scritto che tenti di dare una sistemazione razionalmente organica alla materia, applicando alla pratica strumentale quei principi di ornamentazione che vigevano allora nel campo della musica vocale, in particolare nella produzione operistica. Solo che, mentre nel campo vocale già alla metà del secolo il gusto iniziava a subire drastici mutamenti (e la lettera di Tibaldi ci permette, a questo proposito, di stabilire un punto fermo), nel campo della musica strumentale o, diciamo con maggiore precisione, nel campo della musica violinistica l'insegnamento tartiniano, riflettente questa pratica vocale, fiorisce e vale fino alla fine del secolo stesso; non solo attraverso la vasta e capillare diffusione della scuola tartiniana in Italia e in tutta Europa, scuola nella quale i principi stilistici avevano pari e forse maggiore importanza che non la tecnica strumentale intesa nel senso più ristretto del termine, ma anche attraverso l'adozione integrale, da parte dell'autore del più importante trattato di tecnica violinistica del tempo, del sistema di abbellimenti del compositore di Pirano. Credo di aver già dimostrato infatti [50] che tutta la sezione riguardante quest'argomento della *Gründliche Violinschule* di Leopold Mozart sia ricavata di peso dallo scritto tartiniano sugli abbellimenti. Ora, quando pensiamo che la quarta edizione dell'opera di Mozart è del 1800, ci possiamo render conto immediatamente di

[47] Lettera di Tartini a Padre Martini del 17 agosto 1759.
[48] Basterà citare un solo esempio, e cioè la definizione data da Tartini del modo di realizzare l'appoggiatura semplice discendente: «Regola generale si è, che si adatti alle Note lunghe del valore di mezza battuta, o di un quarto in tempo ordinario, a proporzione in Tripola alla Nota, che vale due quarti [...]» (da *Regole ... per arrivare ... a ben suonare ...*, ms. 323 alla Bibl. del Conservatorio di Venezia, riprodotto in fac-simile in G. Tartini, *Traité des agréments de la musique*, ed. E. R. Jacobi, Celle — New York 1960, p. 5 del fac-simile.)
[49] Cfr. Pl. Petrobelli, *Giuseppe Tartini — Le fonti biografiche*, Wien 1968, pp. 113—114.
[50] Pl. Petrobelli, *La scuola di Tartini in Germania e la sua influenza*, in «Analecta Musicologica» V (1969), pp. 1—17: 14—16.

quale fosse lo sfasamento cronologico della pratica violinistica in questo particolare settore rispetto alla contemporanea prassi vocale. Ancora nel 1791 Francesco Galeazzi si
lamenta in questo modo:

> Non ha guari, che del Trillo, e del Mordente faceasi un'insoffribile abuso; eravi
> appena nella scuola Tartiniana nota, che carica non fosse di alcuni di questi due
> ornamenti, di modo tale che in vece di ornare, opprimevano la melodia di trilli,
> e mordenti imitando così il canto degli uccelli, piuttosto che la voce umana;
> conviene però non abusarne, e farli al dovuto sito, distribuendoli con gusto e
> maniera, ed allora produrranno il dovuto ottimo effetto [51].

Il problema degli abbellimenti nella musica del '700, così strettamente legato, anzi
indissolubilmente connesso alla tecnica specifica dello strumento (sia esso la voce umana
o uno strumento musicale vero e proprio) non può essere in alcun modo risolto se si
prescinde dal momento storico in cui il fenomeno si realizza, e dalla nazionalità (o dalla
formazione) del compositore o dell'esecutore. Il mezzo tecnico (voce o strumento), il
luogo e il periodo di tempo sono gli elementi dai quali è impossibile prescindere se si
vuol formulare un giudizio od un'affermazione che abbiano una qualche pretesa di
validità. Ogni ricerca che non tenga nella dovuta considerazione questi parametri è
destinata a contenere generalizzazioni avulse dalla concreta realtà dei fenomeni accaduti.
E' questa la ragione per cui molte opere, anche pubblicate di recente, rivelano la loro
fondamentale debolezza se poste a confronto con un ben preciso e definito problema che
sorge dalla ricerca [52]: nel campo della musica vocale si procede troppo spesso per
«scuole», avendo chiaramente a disposizione una quantità di materiale storico-docu-
mentario del tutto insufficiente, oppure ci si basa quasi esclusivamente sulle affermazioni
dei teorici o degli scrittori; mentre nel campo della musica strumentale si danno, ad
esempio, come generalmente valide per ogni tipo di strumento le regole d'ornamentazione della scuola tedesca per strumenti a tastiera della seconda metà del secolo (C. Ph.
E. Bach).

La realtà storica è molto più variegata, ricca di sfumature, complessa; i rapporti e le
influenze reciproche tra le varie esperienze musicali, anche nel campo dell'ornamentazione, hanno un peso, un'importanza cui mi sembra non si sia fino ad oggi guardato
con sufficienza. Ancora una volta è bene tener presente che "The more general, the
more significant the explanation we advance, the less stubbornly we should cling to it,
for the more surely it will be incomplete, the greater will be the proportion of its
fictive content, the more surely it will be at best the outline of an explanation — a
program for further research" [53].

---

[51] F. Galeazzi, *Elementi teorico-pratici di musica con un saggio sopra l'arte di suonare il violino
. . .*, I, Roma 1791, p. 195, nota a.

[52] Elenco qui di seguito le opere che ho consultato a questo proposito: J. Arger, *Les agréments
et le rhythme*, Paris, s.a.; H. P. Schmitz, *Die Kunst der Verzierung im 18. Jahrhundert . . .*,
Kassel 1955; R. Donington, *The interpretation of early music*, London 1963; K. Wichmann,
Der Ziergesang und die Ausführung der Appoggiatura — Ein Beitrag zur Gesangpädagogik,
Leipzig 1966.

[53] A. Mendel, art. cit., p. 18.

VI
BIBLIOGRAPHY OF THE WRITINGS
OF ARTHUR MENDEL

I. Books and Articles

"Spengler's Quarrel with the Methods of Music History". In: *The Musical Quarterly* XX (1934), 131—171.

"The Early Twentieth Century". In: Waldo Selden Pratt, *The History of Music. A Handbook and Guide for Students*, Chapter XLI. Revised and enlarged edition. New York: G. Schirmer 1935, 695—713.

"The Changing Audience of the Composer". In: *Volume of Proceedings of the Music Teachers National Association, 32nd Series . . . 1937*, 21—30.

"Thoughts on the Translation of Vocal Texts". In: *A Birthday Offering to Carl Engel*, compiled and edited by Gustave Reese. New York: G. Schirmer 1943, 166—178.

The Bach Reader. A Life of Johann Sebastian Bach in Letters and Documents, edited by Hans T. David and Arthur Mendel. New York: W. W. Norton 1945, 432 pp. Revised with a Supplement: W. W. Norton 1966, vi + 474 + iv.

"Pitch in the 16th and Early 17th Centuries". In: *The Musical Quarterly* XXXIV (1948), 28—45, 199—221, 336—357, 575—593.

"Devices for Transposition in the Organ Before 1600". In: *Acta Musicologica* XXI (1949), 24—40.

"On the Keyboard Accompaniments to Bach's Leipzig Church Music". In: *The Musical Quarterly* XXXVI (1950), 339—362.

"More for *The Bach Reader*". In: *The Musical Quarterly* XXXVI (1950), 485—510.

"On the Pitches in Use in Bach's Time". In: *The Musical Quarterly* XLI (1955), 332—354, 466—480.

"The Services of Musicology to the Practical Musician". In: *Some Aspects of Musicology*, edited by Edward N. Waters. New York: Liberal Arts Press [c. 1957], 1—18.

"A Note on Proportional Relationships in Bach Tempi". In: *The Musical Times* C (1959), 683—685.

"A Brief Note on Triple Proportion in Schuetz". In: *The Musical Quarterly* XLVI (1960), 67—70.

"Bach Tempi: A Rebuttal". In: *The Musical Times* CI (1960), 251.

"Recent Developments in Bach Chronology". In: *The Musical Quarterly* XLVI (1960), 283—300.

"Evidence and Explanation". In: *International Musicological Society. Report of the Eighth Congress New York 1961*, edited by Jan LaRue. *Vol. 2 — Reports*. Kassel: Bärenreiter 1962, 3—18.

"The Doctorate in Composition". In: *College Music Symposium* III (1963), 53—59.

"Traces of the Pre-History of Bach's St. John and St. Matthew Passions". In: *Festschrift Otto Erich Deutsch zum 80. Geburtstag am 5. September 1963*, edited by Walter Gerstenberg, Jan LaRue, and Wolfgang Rehm. Kassel: Bärenreiter 1963, 31—48.

"More on the Weimar Origin of Bach's *O Mensch, bewein* (BWV 244/35)". In: *Journal of the American Musicological Society* XVII (1964), 203—206.

"Documentary Evidence Concerning the Aria, ‚Ich folge dir gleichfalls' from Bach's St. John Passion". In: *College Music Symposium* V (1965), 64—67.

"Wasserzeichen in den Originalstimmen der Johannes-Passion Johann Sebastian Bachs". In: *Die Musikforschung* XIX (1966), 291—294.

"Myra and her Audience". In: *Myra Hess by her Friends,* edited by Denise Lassimone and Howard Ferguson. London: Hamish Hamilton 1966, 38—43.

"Some Ambiguities of the Mensural System". In: *Studies in Music History. Essays for Oliver Strunk,* edited by Harold Powers. Princeton: Princeton University Press 1968, 137—160.

Studies in the History of Musical Pitch. Monographs by Alexander J. Ellis and Arthur Mendel. Amsterdam: Frits Knuf 1968. 238 pp. Contains reprints of articles for *The Musical Quarterly* XXXIV (1948) and XLI (1955) and for *Acta Musicologica* XXI (1949), listed above, with an introduction, annotations, corrections, and additions by Arthur Mendel.

"Some Preliminary Attempts at Computer-Assisted Style-Analysis in Music". In: *Computers and the Humanities* IV (1969), 41—52.

"Meliora ac Melioranda in the Two Versions of BWV 245/1". In: *Werner Neumann zum 65. Geburtstag,* edited by Rudolf Eller.

"Towards Objective Criteria for Establishing Chronology and Authenticity: What Help Can the Computer Give"? In: *Proceedings of the International Josquin Festival-Conference New York 1971,* edited by Edward E. Lowinsky.

II. Musical Editions

Heinrich Schütz: *The Christmas Story. Historia von der Geburt Jesu Christi.* For Soprano, Tenor, and Bass Soli, Full Chorus of Mixed Voices, Organ, and Ensemble of Instruments. Edited [with introductory "Remarks on the Performance"] by Arthur Mendel. *(G. Schirmer's Editions of Oratorios and Cantatas, No. 1930),* New York: G. Schirmer 1949, xviii + 90.

J. S. Bach: *The Passion According to St. John.* Vocal Score edited and with an Introduction by Arthur Mendel. New York: G. Schirmer 1951, xlvi + 242.

W. A. Mozart: *Missa Brevis in F Major* (1774 — K. 192). For Four Solo Voices, Four-Part Chorus of Mixed Voices, Two Violins and Continuo. Edited [with a "Program Note" and "A Note on Performance"] by Arthur Mendel. *(G. Schirmer Edition No. 2183),* New York: G. Schirmer 1955, viii + 80.

Heinrich Schütz: *A German Requiem. (Musicalische Exequien).* For Solo Voices, Mixed Chorus, Organ and Bass Viol. Edited in an attempt to clarify the composer's rhythmic intentions and with an introduction by Arthur Mendel. *(G. Schirmer Editions of Masses and Vespers, No. 2270),* New York: G. Schirmer 1957, xx + 106.

Johann Sebastian Bach. *Ich liebe den Höchsten von ganzem Gemüthe,* BWV 174. *(Johann Sebastian Bach. Neue Ausgabe sämtlicher Werke,* Serie I/Band 14: *Kantaten zum 2. und 3. Pfingsttag),* Kassel: Bärenreiter 1962, 63—118. *Kritischer Bericht,* Kassel: Bärenreiter 1963, 67—139.

Johann Sebastian Bach: *Johannes-Passion,* BWV 245. *(Johann Sebastian Bach. Neue Ausgabe sämtlicher Werke,* Serie II/Band 4), Kassel: Bärenreiter 1973. *Kritischer Bericht,* Kassel: Bärenreiter 1974.

III. Translations

Paul Bekker, *The Changing Opera. (Wandlungen der Oper).* New York: W. W. Norton
1935, xvi + 319.

Paul Bekker, "The Opera Walks New Paths". In: *The Musical Quarterly* XXI (1935),
266—278.

Alfred Einstein, "Dante, on the Way to the Madrigal". In: *The Musical Quarterly*
XXV (1939), 142—155.

Leo Kestenberg, "Music Education Goes its Own Way". In: *The Musical Quarterly*
XXV (1939), 442—454.

Georges de Saint-Foix, "A Musical Traveler: Giacomo Gotifredo Ferrari (1759—1842)".
In: *The Musical Quarterly* XXI (1939), 455—465.

Rudolf Felber, "Robert Schumann's Place in German Song". In: *The Musical Quarterly*
XXVI (1940), 340—354.

Max Graf, "The Death of a Music City: Vienna: 1600—1938". In: *The Musical
Quarterly* XXVI (1940), 8—18.

Hans F. Redlich, "Egon Wellesz". In: *The Musical Quarterly* XXVI (1940) 65—75.

Hermann Scherchen, "Johann Sebastian Bach's Last Composition". In: *The Musical
Quarterly* XXVI (1940), 467—482.

Margit Varró, "Imponderable Elements of Musicality". In: *The Musical Quarterly*
XXVI (1940), 446—455.

Alfred Einstein, "Mozart's Choice of Keys". In: *The Musical Quarterly* XXVII (1941),
415—421.

Richard Engländer, "The Sketches for 'The Magic Flute' at Upsala". In: *The Musical
Quarterly* XXVII (1941), 343—355.

Paul Nettl, "Mozart and the Czechs". In: *The Musical Quarterly* XXVII (1941),
329—342.

Karl August Rosenthal, "Mozart's Sacramental Litanies and their Forerunners". In:
The Musical Quarterly XXVII (1941), 433—455.

Artur Holde, "Four Unknown Letters of Richard Wagner. Presented with Comment". In: *The Musical Quarterly* XXVII (1941), 220—234. The letters translated
by Arthur Mendel.

Paul Bekker, "Franz Liszt Reconsidered". In: *The Musical Quarterly* XXVIII (1942),
186—189.

Paul Hindemith, *The Craft of Musical Composition. Theoretical Part.* New York:
Associated Music Publishers 1942.

Paul Nettl, "An English Musician at the Court of Charles VI in Vienna". In: *The
Musical Quarterly* XXVIII (1942), 318—328.

Fritz Callomon, "Some Unpublished Brahms Correspondence". In: *The Musical
Quarterly* XXIX (1943), 32—44.

Rudolf Kolisch, "Tempo and Character in Beethoven's Music". In: *The Musical
Quarterly* XXIX (1943), 169—187, 291—312.

Paul Hindemith, "Methods of Music Theory". In: *The Musical Quarterly* XXX (1944), 20—28.

Alfred Einstein, *Mozart, His Character, His Work*. Translated by Arthur Mendel and Nathan Broder. New York: Oxford University Press 1945. xiv + 492.

IV. Reviews

John Tasker Howard, *Our American Music*, New York 1931. In: *Modern Music* IX (1931), 35—38.

Richard Eichenauer, *Musik und Rasse*, München 1932. In: *The Nation* CXXXVI (April 19, 1933), 454.

Henry Cowell (ed.), *American Composers on American Music*, Stanford University, California 1933. In: *The Nation* CXXXVII (October 4, 1933), 389 f.

Sacheverell Sitwell, *Liszt*, Boston 1934. *In: The Saturday Review of Literature* XI (September 29, 1934), 139.

Paul Rosenfeld, *Discoveries of a Music Critic*, New York 1936; Vaughan Williams, *National Music*, New York 1935; Constant Lambert, *Music Ho! A Study of Music in Decline*, New York 1935; Bernard Van Dieren, *Down Among the Dead Men, and Other Essays*, New York, 1936. In: *The Saturday Review of Literature* XIV (May 2, 1936), 10.

Hendrik Willem Van Loon, *The Arts*, New York 1937. In: *The Saturday Review of Literature* XVI (October 2, 1937), 6. [On the book as it deals with music.]

Hugo Leichtentritt, *Music, History, and Ideas*, Cambridge, Mass. 1938. In: *The Saturday Review of Literature* XVIII (September 3, 1938), 20.

Oscar Thompson (ed.), *The International Cyclopedia of Music and Musicians*, New York 1938. In: *The Saturday Review of Literature* XIX (December 31, 1938), 18.

Wallace Brockway and Herbert Weinstock, *Men of Music*, New York 1939. In: *The Saturday Review of Literature* XXI (November 25, 1939), 12.

Roy Harris, Quintet. In: *The Victor Record Review* April, 1940. Roy Harris, Third Symphony. In: *The Victor Record Review* April, 1940.

Donald Francis Tovey, *Essays in Musical Analysis: Chamber Music*, edited by Hubert J. Foss, London 1944. In: *The Musical Quarterly* XXXI (1945), 383—387.

Donald Francis Tovey, *Musical Articles from the Encyclopaedia Britannica*, edited by Hubert J. Foss, London 1944. In: *The Musical Quarterly* XXXI (1945), 383—387.

Carl Philipp Emanuel Bach, *Essay on the True Art of Playing Keyboard Instruments*, translated by William J. Mitchell, New York 1949. In: *The Musical Quarterly* XXXV (1949), 323—329.

Wolfgang Schmieder, *Thematisch-systematisches Verzeichnis der musikalischen Werke von Johann Sebastian Bach. Bach-Werke-Verzeichnis*, Leipzig 1950. In: *Notes* VIII (1950), 156—159.

Werner Neumann, *Handbook of Joh. Seb. Bach's Cantatas*, Leipzig 1947. In: *Notes* VIII (1950), 156—159.

Michel Richard de la Lande, Motet, «Quare fremuerunt» (Psaume II), pour Soli, Chœurs, et Orchestre, Paris 1949. In: *Notes* VII (1950), 429—430.

Michel Richard de la Lande, Motet, «De Profundis» (Psaume CXXX), pour Soli, Chœurs, et Orchestre, Paris 1944. In: *Notes* VII (1950), 429—430.

Putnam Aldrich, *Ornamentation in J. S. Bach's Organ Works,* New York 1950. In: *The Musical Quarterly* XXXVII (1951), 290—294.

Josquin Des Prez, Miscellaneous Vocal and Instrumental Works, performed by Pro Musica Antiqua. EMS LP 213;

"Pre-Baroque Sacred Music", performed by the Harvard University Choir and the Radcliffe Choral Society. Festival LP 70-202;

Haydn, St. Cecilia Mass, performed by the Akademie Chorus of Vienna and the Vienna Symphony. Haydn Society LP set 2028;

Palestrina, Pope Marcellus Mass, performed by the Robert Wagner Chorale of Los Angeles. Capitol LP 8126;

Palestrina, Pope Marcellus Mass, performed by the Choir of St. Eustache in Paris. Vox LP 6790;

Palestrina, "Laudate Dominum" (Selected Gregorian Chants), performed by the Trappist Monks of the Abbey of Gesthsemani, Kentucky. Columbia LP 54394. In: *The Saturday Review of Literature, XXXIV* (June 30, 1951), 44.

Alfred Dürr, *Studien über die frühen Kantaten J. S. Bachs,* Leipzig 1951. In: *Journal of the American Musicological Society* V (1952), 252—257.

Heinrich Besseler and Günther Kraft (eds.), *Johann Sebastian Bach in Thüringen,* Weimar 1950. In: *Journal of the American Musicological Society* V (1952), 252—257.

Hedwig and E. H. Müller von Asow (eds.), *Johann Sebastian Bach: Briefe, Gesamtausgabe,* Regensburg 1950. In: *Journal of the American Musicological Society* V (1952), 252—257.

Heinrich Schütz, *The Resurrection Story,* performed by the Munich Viol Quintet and Chamber Choir with soloists, Karl Schleiffer, conductor. LP Mercury MG 10073;

J. S. Bach, Cantatas 140 and 32, performed by the Orchestra of the Vienna State Opera, the Akademiechor, and soloists, Hermann Scherchen, conductor. LP Westminster WL 5122;

J. S. Bach, Cantatas 6 and 19, performed by the Stuttgart Choral Society, with soloists and orchestra, Hans Grischkat, conductor. LP Renaissance X 34;

J. S. Bach, Cantatas 9 and 137, performed by the Stuttgart Choral Society, with soloists and orchestra, Hans Grischkat, conductor. LP Renaissance X 37;

J. S. Bach, Cantatas 140 and 4, performed by the choir and orchestra of the Bach Guild with soloists, Felix Prohaska, conductor. LP Bach Guild BG 511;

J. S. Bach, Cantata 4, performed by the Göttingen Bach Festival Orchestra, the Chorus of the State School of Music Frankfurt, with soloists, Fritz Lehmann, conductor. LP Decca DL 7523. In: *The Musical Quarterly* XXXVIII (1952), 673—679.

Fritz Rothschild, *The Lost Tradition in Music: Rhythm and Tempo in the Time of J. S. Bach,* New York 1953. In: *The Musical Quarterly* XXXIX (1953), 617—630.

Jacobus Obrecht, *Missa sub tuum presidium. Opera omnia: Missae, VI*, edited by M. van Crevel, Amsterdam 1959. In: *Notes* XIX (1962), 330—333.

Karl Geiringer, *Johann Sebastian Bach, The Culmination of an Era*, New York 1966. In: *Journal of the American Musicological Society* XXI (1968), 396—400.

Heinrich Schütz, *Die sieben Worte Jesu Christi am Kreuz* and *Lukas-Passion*, performed by the Monteverdi-Chor, Hamburg and the Leonhardt-Consort, with soloists, Jürgen Jürgens, conductor. LP Das alte Werk (Telefunken) SAWT 9467-A. In: *The Musical Quarterly* LVI (1970), 133—142.

V. Recordings

Heinrich Schütz, *Weihnachts-Historie (The Christmas Story)*. The Cantata Singers and Orchestra Conducted by Arthur Mendel. Soprano: Charlotte Bloecher; Tenor: William Hess; Bass: Paul Matthen. Obbligato Instruments: — Violettas: Howard Boatwright, Rubin Decker; Soprano Recorders: Alfred Mann, Carolyn Mann; Violins: Dorothy De Lay, C. Richard Adams; Trombones: Gordon M. Pulis, Clifford J. Heather; Trumpets: Theodore M. Weis, James H. Hustis; Continuo: Nellis De Lay, Alfred Mann, J. Laurence Slater, Harlan Laufman.
Recorded in New York City, January 1950. Program Notes by Arthur Mendel. LP R. E. B. Editions 3. Rowayton, Connecticut, 1950.

Heinrich Schütz, *Musicalische Exequien (German Requiem)*. The Cantata Singers Conducted by Arthur Mendel. Soprano I: Joan Brainerd; Soprano II: Charlotte Bloecher; Alto: Pauline Pierce; Tenor I: Arthur Squires; Tenor II: William Hess; Bass I: Paul Matthen; Bass II: Lee Cass; Organ: John Beaven; Bass Viol: Alfred Mann.
Recorded in St. Paul's Chapel, Columbia University, New York City, in February 1951. Program Notes by Arthur Mendel. LP R. E. B. Editions 9. Rowayton, Connecticut 1951.

Heinrich Schütz, *Little Sacred Concerts (Kleine geistliche Concerte)*. Selected, edited, and the organ parts written from the original figured basses by Arthur Mendel and sung under his direction by William Hess, Tenor and Paul Matthen, Bass-Baritone with John Beaven, Organist. Includes: *Eile mich, Gott, zu erretten; Was hast du verwirket; O Jesu, nomen dulce; Ich danke dem Herrn; O süsser, o freundlicher; Ich liege und schlafe; O misericordissime Jesu; Die Furcht des Herrn.*
Recorded in St. Paul's Chapel, Columbia University, New York City, February 1953. LP R. E. B. Editions 10. Rowayton, Connecticut 1953.

VI. Journalism

Short articles, mainly biweekly concert reviews. In: *The Nation*, from December 17, 1930 to October 4, 1933.

Occasional reports on Music in America to: *The Musical Times* from September, 1929 to January, 1942.

"First Fruits of the Season". In: *Modern Music* VI (1929), 30—32. [On concerts of contemporary music; including Hindemith, *Die Junge Magd;* Gershwin, *An American in Paris.*]

"Orchestral Version of Harris' Chorale". In: *Modern Music* XII (1934), 47f. [On Werner Janssen's orchestration of the second movement of Roy Harris' String Sextet.]

"The Quintet of Roy Harris". In: *Modern Music* XVII (1939), 25—28.

"Recollections of Paul Hindemith", by (Henry W. Kaufmann, Benhard Heiden, Kurt Stone, and) Arthur Mendel. In: *American Choral Review* Vol. VI, No. 3 (April, 1964), 6—7.

VII. Miscellaneous

Our Contemporary Composers. American Music in the Twentieth Century, by John Tasker Howard with the assistance of Arthur Mendel. New York: Thomas Y. Crowell, 1941. xvi + 447.

"Problems in the Performance of Bach's Choral Music". Abstract published in *Bulletin of the American Musicological Society* No. 7 (October 1943), 2 f.

Music. Preview Issue of a Postwar Monthly, November 1944. Arthur Mendel, editor. Copyright 1944 by Kalmbach Publishing Co. Business Office: Milwaukee, Wisconsin; Editorial Office: New York, 52 pp. Includes an unsigned article by Arthur Mendel: "The Handicraft of Music Engraving", 19—25, and a record review of J. S. Bach, *Sonata in E minor* for violin and continuo, performed by Adolph Busch, violin, and Artur Balsam, piano. Columbia 71582D, signed by "A. M.", 50.

"Papers Read at the International Congress of Musicology Held at New York 1939". In: *The Musical Quarterly* XXXI (1945), 263—267. A report submitted by Arthur Mendel and Gilbert Chase.

"Problems of Intonation in the Performance of Contemporary Music", a symposium held at Isham Memorial Library. Published in *Instrumental Music. A Conference at Isham Memorial Library, May 4, 1957,* edited by David G. Hughes. Cambridge: Harvard University Press 1959. Discussion, 79—86.

"Performance Practice in the 17th and 18th Centuries", a symposium held at the Eighth Congress of the International Musicological Society, New York, 5 September 1961. Discussion published in *International Musicological Society. Report of the Eighth Congress New York 1961,* edited by Jan LaRue. *Vol. 2 — Reports.* Kassel: Bärenreiter 1962, 122—126.

"Problems of Editing and Publishing Old Music", a round table discussion at the Eighth Congress of the International Musicological Society, New York, 6 September 1961. Discussion published in ... *Vol. 2 — Reports,* 101—104.

"Bach Problems", a symposium at the Eighth Congress ..., Arthur Mendel, chairman, 9 September 1961 at Princeton. Discussion published in ... *Vol. 2—Reports,* 127—131.

"Bach versus the Bible: a Letter from Professor Arthur Mendel". In: *The Musical Times* CII (1961), 423 f. A response to "Bach versus the Bible", by Walter Emery. In: *The Musical Times* CII (1961), 221—225.

"Musicology and the Computer I", a symposium sponsored by the New York Chapter of the American Musicological Society, New York, 10 April 1965. Discussion published in *Musicology and the Computer. Musicology 1966—2000: A Practical Program. Three Symposia*, edited by Barry S. Brook. New York: The City University of New York Press 1970, 38—41.

"Musicology 1966—2000: A Practical Program", a symposium of the New York Chapter of the American Musicological Society held in New York, 21 May 1966. Discussion published in *Musicology and the Computer . . .*, 225—227.

INDEX OF NAMES AND SUBJECTS

Aaron, Pietro 33 f.
Abert, Hermann 370n, 371, 373n
Adlung, Jakob 163, 268n, 279
Agricola, Alexander 21n
Agricola, Johann Friedrich 283
Alberto da Canossa 20
Albinoni, Tomaso 156, 158, 163
alternatim 29, 72
Altnikol, Johann Christoph 284 f., 292
Ammerbach, Elias Nicolaus 255—263 *passim*
d'Anglebert, Jean-Henri 189, 192 f., 264
Antwerp 16, 18, 21—23
Anvers 16n
Apel, Willi 71n, 83n, 90f., 121f.
Araja, Francesco 316, 328 f.
Aristotle 33
Arlotti, Ridolfo 50, 52, 68
Armstrong, Edward 307n
Arnold, Denis 47n
Arnstadt 160, 164, 213
Artusi, Giovanni Maria 47, 67 f.
Attwood, Thomas 324n
d'Avalos, Don Cesare 58

Baal, Johann 265
Bach, Anna Magdalena 183, 246 f., 296
Bach, Carl Philipp Emanuel 57, 171n, 186, 188, 255, 257, 283, 290, 292n, 297, 376
Bach, Gottfried Heinrich 246
Bach, Johann Bernhard 267n
Bach, Johann Ludwig 211n, 222, 227
Bach, Johann Sebastian 9 f., 25, 139—297 *passim*
Individual Works according to BWV Number:
BWV *4:* 156, 161, 212, 213; *5:* 209; *10:* 210, 220; *12:* 170n, 210 f., 214, 217; *14:* 210, 224—226; *15:* 211n; *18:* 161, 214 f., 240;

19: 209 f., 221 f., 224; *20:* 220; *21:* 161, 210, 213 f., 231—242; *22:* 202 f., 207; *23:* 209; *24:* 170n; *25:* 210 f., 216n, 226; *31:* 210, 215 f.; *37:* 220 f.; *38:* 209; *40:* 197 f., 199; *44:* 220n; *46:* 216n; *48:* 210 f., 218; *49:* 210, 222; *54:* 214, 265; *57:* 222n; *58:* 210, 222, 224; *60:* 210, 218, 222, 224, 226; *61:* 161, 214; *62:* 161; *63:* 161, 204—207, 213, 236; *64:* 218n; *65:* 204; *66:* 184, 218n, 222; *69a:* 216n, 226; *70:* 209; *70a:* 218, 226; *71:* 156, 161, 170n, 202, 210 f., 213; *77:* 209 f., 216n, 218, 226; *80:* 210, 217, 226 f.; *80a:* 215 —217, 226; *89:* 216n; *92:* 220n; *93:* 210, 220 f.; *94:* 218n; *95:* 220n; *100:* 260; *101:* 210, 220 f.; *104:* 203, 216n; *105:* 165—182, 216n; *106:* 156, 161, 209 —211; *107:* 221; *109:* 216n, 218; *113:* 220; *114:* 220n; *115:* 171n, 220; *119:* 192, 220n, 240; *122:* 209, 210, 221; *131:* 156 f., 161, 170n, 210—212; *132:* 215, 217; *136:* 216n; *137:* 210, 221; *143:* 210, 225; *147a:* 226; *150:* 156 f., 161, 211, 213, 225; *152,* 214—217; *155:* 214—216; *156:* 209 f., 222 f.; *158:* 209 f., 226; *159:* 209 f.; 222 f.; *161:* 210, 215, 217; *162:* 215, 217; *163:* 210 f., 215, 217; *165:* 215—217; *166:* 220n; *172:* 209 f., 214; *173a:* 170n; *174:* 10; *178:* 220n; *179:* 216n; *180:* 220n; *182:* 214, 225; *185:* 210, 215—217; *186a:* 218, 226; *195:* 291n; *196:* 156, 161, 211, 213; *199:*

19: 156 f., 170n, 214; *202:* 268n, 270, 275; *208:* 161, 213; *211:* 170n; *215:* 139; *227:* 221; *228:* 209 f., 221; *232* (Mass in B minor): 145, 170n, 223n, 255, 261, 291n, 362; *233:* 209, 225; *233a:* 210; *234:* 202; *243* (Magnificat): 184, 198— 200; *243a:* 210, 219 f.; *244* (Saint Matthew Passion): 184 f., 202, 223 f., 226 f., 243—253; *245* (Saint John Passion): 9 f., 171n, 200—203, 210, 219 f., 223—225, 227, 291n; *245a:* 210, 225; *248* (Christmas Oratorio): 139 —148, 225; *525—530:* 291n; *527a:* 272, 275; *532:* 156, 272, 275; *533:* 158, 162; *533a:* 272, 275; *535:* 272, 275; *535a:* 156 f., 161, 265n, 267; *538:* 272; *541:* 272, 275; *543:* 159, 164; *544:* 255; *548:* 269, 272, 275; *550:* 272; *551:* 156, 272, 275; *552:* 156 f.; *562:* 160; *564:* 156; *569:* 156, 272, 275; *570:* 156; *574:* 157, 163, 272; *574a:* 157n; *579:* 156, 158, 163; *582:* 159, 164; *585:* 272; *586:* 272; *588:* 156, 158, 162 f., 272; *596:* 265n; *597:* 272; *599-644* (Orgelbüchlein): 263, 265n, 275, 278, 285 —297 *passim*; *605:* 263; *613:* 275; *616:* 263; *617:* 273, 275 f.; *635:* 273, 275 f.; *641:* 285, 287—289, 291—293; *651—668* (Leipziger Originalhand-schrift): 276, 286—297 *passim*; *651a:* 273; *652a:* 273; *653:* 160; *653a:* 160, 273; *653b:* 160, 273; *654a:* 273; *655a:* 273, 276; *656a:* 273; *658a:* 265n,

659a: 273; *660a:* 265n,

273, 276 f., 292; *661a:* 273;
662a: 274; *664a:* 274, 276;
666: 292; *667:* 292 f.; *667b:*
277; *668:* 283—297;
668a: 287, 290—292, 294
—297; *669:* 225; *671:*
225; *676:* 274; *687:* 225;
690: 156; *699:* 156; *714—
765:* 277; *714:* 283n; *717:*
274; *722:* 274, 276n; *720:*
159, 162 f.; *722:* 277;
722a: 277; *729:* 274,
276n, 277; *729a:* 277;
732: 274, 276n, 277;
732a: 277; *738:* 274, 276n,
277; *738a:* 277; *739:*
265n; *743:* 274; *747:* 274;
751: 274; *754:* 274; *764:*
265n; *765:* 274; *766:*
212 f.; *767:* 212 f.; *768:*
212 f., 274, 277 f.; *769:*
291 f., 294; *772—801:*
255; *799:* 255; *803:*
150 f.; *820:* 156; *825—
830:* 281; *831:* 183—194;
891: 224; *895:* 156; *906:*
149—155; *951:* 158,
163 f.; *951a:* 158; *955:*
184; *971:* 183; *990:* 161;
992: 156; *993:* 156; *996:*
157; *997:* 149—151; *998:*
149—151; *1011:* 184;
1027a: 272; *1041:* 256;
1050: 150 f., 244; *1066:*
192; *1068:* 192; *1069:*
192; *1074:* 280; *1080*
(Kunst der Fuge): 283,
285—287, 290 f., 294,
296 f.
Bailey, James 361
Baldini, Vittorio 52
Banchieri, Adriano 35, 36, 38
Bannister, Henry 79n
Bardi, Giovanni 56
Bartlett, M. E. C. 82n
Bartolomeo de' Cavalieri
19—24
Bartolomeo de Fiandra 16—22
Baselt, Berndt 237n
Basile, Adriana 310

Barnett, John 309
Baur, Johannes 108, 114
Beard, John 362
Becker, August 236
Becker, Carl Ferdinand
257—260, 262
Becking, Gustav 119n
Beethoven, Ludwig van 166
Bente, Martin 26n, 75
Bernardi, Francesco (*see*
Senesino)
Bernasconi, Andrea 370n
Besseler, Heinrich 119 f.
Bezecny, Emil 26, 71n
Birtner, Herbert 71 f.
Bischoff, Hans 149, 164n, 184
Blankenburg, Walter 139—148
Blume, Clemens 79n, 93n
Blume, Friedrich 18
Boccaccio, Giovanni 61n
Bodky, Erwin 184, 186
Boethius 282n
Böhm, Georg 156
Bokemeyer, Heinrich 264,
278—281
Bononcini, Giovanni 333
Bordoni, Faustina 306, 333 f.,
351
Borris, Siegfried 269n
Boyleau 86n
Brabant 15
Brainard, Paul 109n,
231—242
Brancaccio, Count Giulio
Cesare 53
Breton y Hernandez, Tomas
310
Briani, Francesco 335—358
passim
Brockes, Barthold Heinrich
219n, 223 f.
Brodde, Otto 264n, 279n, 280n
Broschi, Carlo (*see* Farinello)
Broschi, Ruggiero 316, 319,
325—327
Brosses, Charles de 314n, 318n
Brown, Howard 16n
Brown, John 315n
Bruges 17
Bruhns, Nicolaus 156, 161
Bulgarelli, Maria Anna 302
Burmeister, Joachim 38

Burney, Charles 255, 257,
301n, 303, 306n, 307, 308n,
318n, 320n, 323, 327n, 329n,
330, 332, 368—370
Buttstedt, Johann Heinrich
145
Buxtehude, Dietrich 156, 161,
264, 266, 279, 280n, 281,
282n

cadence 156—164
Caldara, Antonio 328
Calov, Abraham 256 f., 259,
261—263
Calzabigi, Ranieri di 365
Cambrai 23
canon 195
Cantata Singers 9, 359
cantus firmus technique
25—30
Capelli, Giovanni Maria 302,
319, 325
Casanova, Giovanni Jacopo
323
Cassola, Don Bassano 60
Casti, G. B. 312
Cattaneo, Valeriano 49, 59
Caussin, Ernoul 23
Cavicchi, Adriano 48n
Celani, E. 369n
Charles V, Emperor of Spain
16n
"Choralis Constantinus"
(Isaac) 25 f., 71—107
chorale forms 209—227
Chrysander, Friedrich 236, 257,
332, 341, 343, 349, 350,
359 f.
Ciampi, F. 325
Cipriano (*see* de Rore)
Clercx, Suzanne 17n, 18, 363
Clibano, Jerome de 17n
"Coglia" (= Girolamo de
Sestola) 19
Coke, Gerald 324n, 329
Collins, Michael 185, 188 f.
Cone, Edward T. 149—155
Cordier, Jean 17
Corelli, Arcangelo 156, 158,
163
Corsi, Jacopo 56n
Costanzi 325

Couperin, François 131, 186
Croce, Benedetto 165
Cuyler, Louise 26n, 71n, 77, 79, 81n, 83, 88, 91, 94
Cuzzoni, Francesca 306, 333 f., 347, 351

Dadelsen, Georg von 157, 170n, 265n, 267n, 268n, 272, 275n, 276, 286n, 291n, 293n
Dahlhaus, Carl 39, 43, 45, 109n, 117—123
Dahnk-Baroffio, Emilie 336n, 341n
Da Ponte, Lorenzo 311
Dart, Thurston 185n
David, Hans T. 9, 184 f., 194, 236n
Dean, Winton 332n, 334
Descartes, René 108
Desprez, Josquin 15—24, 165
Deutsch, Otto Erich 255n, 303 —305, 318n, 333, 360, 365n
Dieupart, Charles 187, 189, 193
Divitis, Antonius 17n
dissonance treatment 47—68
Dolmetsch, Arnold 185—188
Donington, Robert 376n
Doorslaer, George van 21n
Dörffel, Alfred 258
Dragonetti, Domenico 360
Drese, Samuel 216—218
Dreves, Guido Maria 81n
Dufourcq, Norbert 306
Dürr, Alfred 139n, 140, 167n, 170n, 212, 216, 223n, 226, 231 f., 235n, 236, 243 —253, 267n, 296n

Einstein, Alfred 48n, 182
Eitner, Robert 122, 370n
Elisi, Filippo 365, 367—369
Eller, Rudolf 184
Emery, Walter 156—164, 183, 185, 191, 194
Essenga, Salvatore 52
Este, court of Ferrara
  Alessandro d'Este 50, 56
  Alfonso d'Este 22, 50—54, 58, 60 f.
  Don Cesare d'Este 52
  Ercole I d'Este 15, 18—24

Lucrezia d'Este (= Duchess of Urbino) 59 f.
Luigi d'Este 50, 55
Fano, Fabio 73—75
Farinello (= Carlo Broschi) 301—330
Fassini, Sesto 335n
Faulhaber, Johann 108—116
Faustina (*see* Bordoni)
Ferrara 15, 16n, 18, 21—23, 47—58 *passim* (*see also* Este)
Fétis, François-Joseph 301n
Fischer, J. F. K. 189
Flanders 19—21
Fontanelli, Alfonso 47—68 *passim*
Forkel, Johann Nikolaus 149, 150n, 262, 284, 292n
Formschneider, Hieronymus 71, 77 ff. *passim*
Fortune, Nigel 47n
Franck, Salomo 214 f., 233
Freeman, Robert 301—330
Frescobaldi, Girolamo 163
Fridel, Balthasar 114
Frischmuth, Leonhard 269
Fuller Maitland, John 341
Furtenbach, Joseph 108
Fux, Johann Joseph 257

Gaetano Majorano (= Caffarelli) 323
Gaffurius, Franchinus 73, 75, 92
Galeazzi, Francesco 376
Gasparini, Francesco 324
Gastoldi, Giovanni 120
Gerber, Heinrich Nikolaus 269n, 271, 276, 278
Gerstenberg, Walter 25—30
Gesner, Johann Matthias 253
Gesualdo, Don Carlo 48—50, 55 f., 61, 68
Giacomelli, Geminiano 319, 326—328
Giai, Giovanni 316, 320, 326, 327n
Giannini, G. N. 312n
Gigault, Nicolas 186
Glareanus, Henricus 25 f., 36,

38n, 43, 71n, 78, 79n
Gluck, Christoph Willibald 323, 365
Göbel, Johann Jeremias 252
Godman, Stanley 255, 257
de Goede, N. 79n
George I, King of England 333 f.
George II, King of England 333 f.
Goldoni, Carlo 314, 318—321
Gombert, Nicolas 119
Gonzaga, Vincenzo 49, 54, 59
Gonzaga, Scipione 54
Gossett, Philip 71—107
"Messer Gossino" 15—24
"Gosswin de Catulle" 23
Goudar, Ange 301n, 318n, 322
Pope Gregory XIV 61n
Grimaldi, Nicolo 308n
Guadagni, Gaetano 362
Guarini, Giambattista 50

Haar, James 39n
Haas, Robert 311, 322n, 323n
Haberl, Franz Xaver 32
Habök, Franz 302n, 308n, 309 f., 323n
Hadamowsky, Franz 328n
Halle 236
Hamburg 237
Handel, George Frideric 186, 189 f., 303 f., 319, 329, *Messiah* 359—362, *Riccardo Primo* 331—358
Hansell, Sven 302n, 325n
Harman, Alec 32n
Hasse, Johann Adolph 302, 308n, 315 f., 319 f., 325— 329, 371, 374
Hauptmann, Moritz 262
Haym, Nicolo 334
Heartz, Daniel 364n, 368n
Heckmann, Hans 120n
Hedar, Josef 161n
Heidegger, John Jacob 304
Heinichen, Johann David 281
Hellinck, Lupus 17
Henrici, Christian Friedrich (= Picander) 148, 210n, 223 f., 251
Henri de Therouanne 16n

Hering, S. 171n
Hermelink, Siegfried 31 f., 34, 37 f., 45
Hertzmann, Erich 364n
Herz, Gerhard 212, 254—263
Heyden, Sebald 71n, 78, 79n, 84n
Heyns, Cornelius 17n
Hill, John 361
Hiller, Johann Adam 188
Hiekel, Hans Otto 109n
Hoffmann-Erbrecht, Lothar 234
Hotteterre, Jacques 187
Husmann, Heinrich 108—116

d'Indy, Vincent 122
Ingegneri, Marco Antonio 48
Inglese, Guillelmo 16—18
Isaac, Heinrich 25 f., 29, 71—107 *passim*

Jacobi, Erwin 375
Jahn, Otto 262
Jannes 17
Jauernig, Reinhold 282n
Johann Ernst, Duke of Weimar 216 f.
Jommelli, Nicolò 366, 368—375

Kast, Paul 265n
Keller, Hermann 161n, 162, 184
Kellner, Johann Peter 268—272, 278
Kilian, Dietrich 164, 269n
King, A. Hyatt 331n
Kinsky, Georg 254 f., 261
Kirkpatrick, Ralph 303, 308, 323n
Kirnberger, Johann Philipp 269
Kirsch, Winfried 95
Klotz, Hans 276 f., 287, 292n, 293n
Koch, Heinrich Christoph 120, 127
König, Ernst 252
Köthen 225, 252
Knapp, J. Merrill 331—358
Kneller, Andreas 156

Krause, Peter 267n
Krebs, Johann Ludwig 268
Krebs, Johann Tobias 159, 268, 273—275, 277, 293n
Kruse, Georg Richard 108n
Kuhnau, Johann 156, 161, 282n
Kuhnau, Johann Andreas 237
Kümmerling, Harald 279n, 281

La Borde, Jean Benjamin 301n
Lämmerhirt, Valentin 265n
Larsen, Jens Peter 361
Lee, Vernon 371
Legrenzi, Giovanni 157, 163
Leichtentritt, Hugo 122
Leo, Leonardo 316, 319, 325 f.
Lerner, Edward 71
Leyding, Georg Dietrich 156
Libby, Dennis 331n
Lindley, Robert 360 f.
Lippman, Ernst 254
Lipstorp, Daniel 108
Lockwood, Lewis 15—24
Loewenberg, Alfred 310
Löffler 268n, 269n
Löhlein, Georg Simon 188
Löschenbrand, Augustin 108, 111, 113, 114n, 116
Lotti, Antonio 336
Louis XII, King of France 21n
Lowinsky, Edward 79n, 86n, 89n
Lübeck, Vincent 156, 161
Lully, Jean-Baptiste 186 f., 189, 192 f.
Luther, Martin 143, 218
Luzzaschi, Luzzasco 47, 50, 53, 56 f., 59 f., 61n
Lyons 20 f.

Machatius, Franz-Jochen 120, 121n, 123n
MacClintock, Carol 48 f., 60n
Madrid 306—309
Mahrenholz, Christhard 163n
Maimbourg, P. Louis 336
Malipiero, Gian Francesco 47n
Mancini, Giovanni Battista 301n, 367n, 369n
Mann, Alfred 359—362, 364n

Mantua 22, 48 f., 59
Marcello, Benedetto 311, 312n, 313n, 314n
Marenzio, Luca 48, 50
Marpurg, Friedrich Wilhelm 188, 268n, 283, 302, 303n
Marshall, Robert 165—182, 198n
Martello, Pier Jacopo 315
Martini, Giambattista (Padre) 323, 363—365, 367, 375
Martini, Johannes 18
Marx, Adolf Bernhard 173n
Mason, John 361
Mattheson, Johann 194, 264n, 280n, 282n
Mattingly, Garrett 20n
Maximilian I, Emperor 25
May, Ernest D. 183n, 264—282
Mazzanti, Ferdinando 369
Mazzoni, Antonio Maria 367
Meier, Bernhard 31, 43
Meißner, Christian Gottlob 273, 275
Meistersinger 108—116
Mempell, Johann Nikolaus 268—278 *passim*
Mendel, Arthur 9—11, 71, 72n, 76n, 150n, 165, 167n, 171n, 195n, 225, 231 f., 235, 236n, 237n, 359, 367n, 376n
Mendelssohn, Felix 262
mensural notation 108—116
mensural system 71—107
Metastasio, Pietro 301n, 302n, 304, 308 f., 311, 312n, 315, 317, 322 f., 330n, 371, 374
meter 117—123
Mey, Wolfgang Nikolaus 268
Metzger, Ambrosius 109
Miller, Clement 71, 72n, 79n
Milan 18, 23
Mizler, Lorenz 283n, 292
modality 31—46
Modena 52, 311
Monteverdi, Claudio 47—50, 55 f., 60, 61n, 67 f., 119, 121 f.
Monteverdi, Giulio Cesare 47, 49

Morinensis, Henricus 16n
Morley, Thomas 31, 32n
Mozart, Leopold 188, 375
Mozart, Wolfgang Amadeus
254, 311, 364n, 365, 375
Muffat, Georg 189
Muffat, Gottlieb 189
Mühlhausen 160, 162—164,
211—213, 216n, 225 f.
Müller-Blattau, Joseph 197
Münzer, Georg 112n
musical form 149—155

Nanino, Giovanni Maria 48n
Naples 301—330 *passim*,
363—376 *passim*
national styles 123—135
Naumann, Ernst 164n
Niedt, Friedrich Ehrhardt
171n, 179n
Nettl, Paul 370n
Neumann, Frederick
183—194
Neumann, Werner 195—208,
236n, 258, 260, 265n
Neumark, Georg 234
Newcomb, Anthony 47—68
Nicola Fiorentino 18
notes inégales 187n, 190
Nürnberg 109—115 *passim*

Obrecht, Jacob 17n
Oldman, Cecil 364n
Orff, Carl 122
Orlandini 325
Orlinick, S. 370n
Osthoff, Helmuth 15, 18, 24n
Ott, Johann 25
"Ottuso" 47, 67 f.
overdotting 186, 188, 189

Pachelbel, Johann 156, 161
Padua 56
Palestrina, Giovanni Pierluigi
31—46 *passim*, 119
Palisca, Claude 47n, 67
Pampani, Antonio Gaetano
366 f.
Päminger, Sophonias 27
Pannechin, Piero (Pannethin)
16
parody technique 139—148

Pastor, Ludwig 61n
Pätzig, Gerhard-Rudolf 26n,
27n, 71n, 75, 76n, 79
Pavia 20 f.
Pelicelli, N. 23n
Penna, Lorenzo 117—121
performance practice 108—
116, 123—135, 179n, 183—
194, 363—376
Pergolesi, Giovanni Battista
134
Perkins, Leeman 79
permutation fugue 195—208
Pescetti, G. B. 330
Petrarca, Francesco 40, 45
Petrobelli, Pierluigi 363—376
Petrucci, Ottaviano 73—75,
80, 92
Philip the Fair, Duke of
Burgundy 21
Philip V, King of Spain 306
Picander (*see* Henrici,
Christian Friedrich)
Picardo, Gillet 18
Picardo, Piero 18
Picardy 15—17, 21
Pidoux, Pierre 163n
Pierre de la Rue 21n
Piovesana, Francesco
117—121
Pirrotta, Nino 61n
Polaroli, Carlo Francesco
312n
Pollaroli, Antonio 316, 324
Porpora, Nicola 301 f., 304,
306, 316, 324, 326 f., 329
Porta, G. 325, 327
Powers, Harold S. 31—46,
172n
Praetorius, Michael 109n
Prautzsch, Ludwig 141 f., 146
Predieri, Antonio 324, 326
Preller, Johann Gottlieb 183,
264—278 *passim*
Purcell, Henry 156
Puschmann, Adam 112 f.

Quagliati, Paolo 310
Quantz, Johann Joachim 186,
188—190, 193, 302 f., 314

Raaff, Anton 375
Rabl, Walter 26n, 71n
Raguenet, François 318
Rameau, Jean-Philippe 156,
186, 189, 193
Raphael, Günther 173n
Reese, Gustave 17n
Reiner, Stuart 310
Reinhold, Thomas 362
Reinken, Jan Adams 156
Rembold, Mattheus 108
rhythm 10, 117—123, 183—
194
Ricci, C. 365n
Riccoboni, Luigi 305 f.
Richter, Bernhard Friedrich
226n
Ringk, Johannes 268 f., 272,
275
Rinuccini, Ottavio 56n
Rist, Johann 233 f.
Riva, Giuseppe 304
Rochetti, Ventura 366, 368 f.,
372—375
Rochlitz, Johann Friedrich
262
Roediger, Karl Erich 76n
Rolli, Paolo 303 f., 333—358
passim
Rore, Cipriano de 31, 40, 43n,
61
Rousseau, Jean-Jacques
124—135
Rubin, Norman 195—208
Rudall, Nicholas 82n
Rust, Wilhelm 164, 169n, 231,
237, 239 f., 285—287, 290n,
297

Sacchi, Giovenale 301n, 307n,
308n, 323n
Sachs, Hans 112—115
Salieri, Antonio 312
Sandoni, Pietro 329
Santi, Venceslao 50n
Sarri, Domenico (Sarro) 302,
325
Sartori, Claudio 324n, 367n
Scarlatti, Domenico 309, 323
Schaal, Richard 264n
Scheifele, Michael 108
Schering, Arnold 171n, 359 f.

Schicht, Johann Gottfried 262
Schilling, Gustav 262
Schmidt, Johann 269
Schmidt, Johann Michael
  283 f.
Schmitz, Hans-Peter 376n
Scheide, William H. 195n,
  197, 209—227
Schneider, Max 243 f., 284
Schreyer, Johannes 149 f., 244
Schulze, Hans-Joachim 235n,
  236n, 259, 264n, 265n, 275n
Schumann, Eva 108
Schumann, Robert 262
Schünemann, Georg 117, 264n,
  266, 267n, 280 f.
Schütz, Heinrich 9 f., 143, 359
Schweitzer, Albert 149, 171n,
  286
Scribe, Eugène 310
Scotto, Ottaviano 15
seconda prattica 47—68
Seiffert, Max 161n, 237n,
  264n, 271
Selden-Goth, Gisela 255n
Selliti, Giuseppe 328
Senesino, Francesco (Bernardi)
  303—306, 308n, 333 f.
Senfl, Ludwig 25—30, 80n
Serauky, Walter 237
Sestola, Girolamo da 19
Shaw, H. Watkins 360
Siegele, Ulrich 124—135
Simrock (Publisher) 173n
Smend, Friedrich 171n, 225
Smith, John Christopher
  332 f., 337—340, 342, 345 f.,
  350
Solerti, Angelo 53
Sonneck, Oscar 327n, 335
Spengler, Oswald 10
Spitta, Philipp 141, 149, 158,
  171n, 184, 211n, 225, 233,
  235, 282n, 285—287
Staehelin, Martin 71n, 72

Staiger, Rober 108, 110, 116
Steiger, Renate 141
Stölzel, Gottfried Heinrich
  268n
Strohm, Reinhart 324n, 329n
Strunk, Oliver 33, 47n, 318n
Svaghere, Cornelio 16

tactus 117—123
Tagliavini, Luigi 367n
Tartini, Giuseppe 363, 375
Tasso, Torquato 50, 61n, 370
Telemann, Georg Philipp
  282n
tempo designations 123—135
Therouanne 16 f., 22
Tibaldi, Giuseppe Luigi
  364—367, 369—371, 373,
  375
Tinctoris, Johannes 26 f.
Tiraboschi, Girolamo 50n, 61n
Tittel, Karl 268n
Tommaso de Parixe 18
Tomy, Pellegrino 308n
Torri, Pietro 319, 326
Tosi, Pierfrancesco 374
Traetta, Tommaso 368
Trautmann, Christoph 256
Trebs, J. G. 265
Tunder, Franz 161
Tura, Cosima 23

Ulm 108, 111, 113, 116

Van den Borren, Charles 17n
Van der Straeten, Edmond
  15, 16n, 17 f.
Vecchi, Orazio 52, 55
Veracini, Francesco 319,
  329 f.
"Verdelotto" 15
Villeneuve, Josse de 311, 318,
  321
Villichin (Willechin) 16 f.
Vinci, Leonardo 316 f., 319,
  320n, 324—327, 329

Vivaldi, Antonio 320—322
Vogel, Emil 48n, 51n, 52, 58,
  61n
Vogel, Hans 115
Voigt, Valentin 114 f.

Wagenseil, Johann Christoph
  109, 112
Walker, Frank 301n
Walsh, John 320n, 324, 328n
Walther, Johann Gottfried
  156, 161, 264—282, 293n
Watt, Benedict von 108
Webern, Anton von 26n, 83,
  85n, 90
Wechmar, Johann Anton
  Gottfried 269, 272
Weckmann, Matthias 156
Weerbecke, Gaspar 18
Weimar 160, 163 f., 213 f., 216,
  225 f., 231, 265, 267, 271
Weiss, Piero Ernesto 319, 321n
Werckmeister, Andreas 264,
  280n
Wert, Giaches 48 f., 61
Werthemann, Helene
  233—235
Weyermann, Albrecht 108
Winterfeld, Carl von 262
Wolf, Georg Friedrich 188
Wolff, Christoph 184,
  283—297
Wolff, Leonhard 225
Wolffheim, Werner 267n

Zacconi, Lodovico 35 f., 38,
  43, 45
Zachow, Friedrich Wilhelm
  156, 236
Zander, Ferdinand 233n
Zarlino, Gioseffo 26, 31, 33 f.,
  36, 38n
Zeno, Apostolo 320, 366n
Zeraschi, Helmut 294n, 295n
Zietz, Hermann 267n, 268n,
  269, 272, 280n, 293n